SEVENTH EDITION

Research Methods in Social Relations

Rick H. Hoyle
University of Kentucky

Monica J. Harris
University of Kentucky

Charles M. Judd
University of Colorado

WADSWORTH
CENGAGE Learning™

Australia • Brazil • Japan • Korea • Mexico • Singapore • Spain • United Kingdom • United States

WADSWORTH
CENGAGE Learning™

Research Methods in Social Relations 7e
Rich H. Hoyle, Monica J. Harris,
Charles M. Judd

Editor: **Vicki Knight**

Marketing Manager: **Kathleen Morgan**

Project Manager, Editorial Production:
Elaine Hellmund

Print/Media Buyer: **Lisa Kelley**

Production Service:
UG/GGS Information Services

Compositor:
UG/GGS Information Services Inc.

ISBN-13: 978-0-15-506139-2

ISBN-10: 0-15-506139-9

Wadsworth
10 Davis Drive
Belmont Drive, CA 94002-3098
USA

Cengage Learning is a leading provider of customized learning solutions with office locations around the globe, including Singapore, the United Kingdom, Australia, Mexico, Brazil, and Japan. Locate your local office at:
international.cengage.com/region

Cengage Learning products are represented in Canada by Nelson Education, Ltd.

For your course and learning solutions, visit **academic.cengage.com**

Purchase any of our products at your local college store or at our preferred online store **www.ichapters.com**

Printed in the United States of America
9 10 11 12 13 14   11 10 09 08

PREFACE

To what factors can the escalation of violence in schools be attributed? Why, in the midst of an AIDS epidemic, do people engage in risky sexual behavior? Can ethnic prejudice be reduced? Why do some social programs succeed and others fail? How do people respond to an expanding array of environmental stressors? This is the sort of question addressed by social scientists, and the array of strategies social scientists use to address such questions is the topic of this book.

Research Methods in Social Relations is intended for graduate students and advanced undergraduates in psychology, sociology, education, social work, communications, and other social science disciplines in which there is an interest in empirical research on normal human social behavior. A distinctive feature of the book is its "applied" bent. Although all the major research methods used by social scientists are covered in the book, special attention is devoted to methods that are well suited to the study of real-world problems of a social nature. Moreover, most of the examples drawn from the published literature or developed specifically for the book concern a social problem for which social science research is relevant or a social policy that such research might inform.

The text is organized in four parts designed to move the reader from abstract matters, such as the philosophical underpinnings of social science research, to concrete matters, such as how to sample research participants, gather data from them, analyze those data, draw inferences from the results, and communicate the findings in a research report. A broad organizing theme that runs throughout the book is a tripartite notion of validity. Each measurement strategy, sampling procedure, and research design is evaluated in terms of its construct, internal, and external validity. Implicit in this evaluation is the assumption that no research method is perfect; hence, researchers must choose from an array of imperfect tools whose strengths and weaknesses must be considered with reference to the research question, the population to whom the findings are intended to apply, and the audience toward which the research report will be directed.

A secondary theme is that the inherent shortcomings of any particular research method can be overcome by coupling it with a second or third method with complementary strengths. Throughout the book, we strongly advocate multiple operational definitions (e.g., self-report, observation) of important constructs within a given study as a means of addressing the limited construct validity of any single operational definition. And we argue (and illustrate) that the seemingly incompatible goals of inferring cause and effect (internal validity) and generalizing findings beyond the specific people, operational definitions, and research setting in a particular study (external validity) can be reconciled by using multiple research methods (e.g., survey, laboratory experiment) that vary in their strengths and weaknesses for addressing a specific research question. Doubts about findings generated using a particular method are substantially weakened when the same findings emerge from a different study using different methods and measures.

Enduring Features

There are many textbooks on research methods written for graduate students and advanced undergraduates in the social science disciplines. Yet *Research Methods in Social Relations*, as it has for more than 50 years, offers a unique and compelling perspective on the methods by which social scientists generate new knowledge. According to this perspective, reflective of the values embraced by the book's sponsoring organization, the Society for the Psychological Study of Social Issues, the social sciences can lead the way in addressing seemingly intractable social problems, such as ethnic prejudice, interpersonal violence, and overconsumption of limited resources. Flowing from this problem-focused perspective is an acknowledgment of the role of values in social science research. The influence of personal and cultural values on which questions are asked, how they are asked, and how they are addressed is discussed in the opening chapter and resurfaces in discussions and illustrations of specific methods throughout the book. This focus on the importance of conscience and conviction in research on social behavior is a unique and enduring feature of *Research Methods in Social Relations* that is preserved in the Seventh Edition.

In addition to these foundational features are more specific features carried forward from previous editions. The book features in-depth coverage of sampling and measurement, practical aspects of research that take on additional importance, and meet with additional complications, in problem-focused research. The heart of the book is detailed coverage of a broad array of research methods, ranging from tightly controlled laboratory experimentation to nonintrusive observation of people in their natural environment. The book includes basic coverage of descriptive and inferential statistics, including examples that illustrate the link between research design and data analysis. Two areas of content introduced in the Sixth Edition of the book—the laboratory setting and meta-analysis—are retained in this new edition. Such material is not often covered in methods books written at this level but is essential for equipping students to understand and evaluate published research in the social sciences. Like its predecessors, the Seventh Edition offers thorough and detailed coverage of social science research methods and procedures.

New in the Seventh Edition

This edition features a new organization that presents topics in an order typical of research methods courses. The chapter on ethical principles has been moved from the end of the book to the end of the introductory section. Covering general ethical issues and principles before methods of research allowed us to address in a more complete matter ethical concerns associated with specific research methods as they were presented. We abandoned the separation of logical and practical issues regarding measurement and sampling procedures, returning to a more traditional structure that integrates this material in sections devoted exclusively to the two topics. And chapters devoted to specific research strategies are now gathered in a single section that begins with the randomized experiment and moves systematically to less tightly controlled and more naturalistic methods. The chapters on data analysis and writing appear together in the final section, a juxtaposition of seemingly disparate material that works because of our focus in the data analysis chapters on communicating statistical results and our expanded coverage of narrative reviews in the chapter previously devoted exclusively to meta-analysis.

Four chapters either have been rewritten or are new to this edition. The chapter on ethical principles was completely rewritten. It is shorter than the corresponding chapter in previous editions, and it includes more material on the procedures by which ethical approval for a social science study is obtained. The chapter on meta-analysis has been replaced with a new chapter that covers the activity of building on published research reports in social science research. The chapter begins with advice on how to critically review individual research reports, moves to a discussion of narrative reviews of research literatures, and concludes with a relatively nontechnical presentation of meta-analysis. A short section of a chapter in the previous edition on strategies for questionnaires and interviews has been expanded into a new chapter on modes of measurements. The chapter moves beyond traditional modes of measurement, such as paper-and pencil questionnaires and face-to-face interviews, to cover new and emerging methods, such as Web-based measurement, physiological monitoring, and strategies for tapping implicit processes. Finally, owing to the increasing popularity and sophistication of research that captures people's thoughts, feelings, and behaviors *in situ*, this edition features a new chapter on experience sampling methods.

Several other chapters are substantially revised in the Seventh Edition. The material on questionnaire construction has been reorganized into two chapters, one devoted to single-item measures characteristic of surveys and the other focused on scales and inventories typical of smaller-scale studies. Additional sampling methods are covered in the chapter on fundamentals of sampling, and the chapter on probability sampling is now centered around the use of computer-based random number generators as a means of building a probability sample from a population. The chapters on more naturalistic methods of research now include detailed coverage of focus groups and written narratives. The chapter on data management and exploration begins by introducing readers to the central role of statistical software in data analysis, and both data analysis chapters are replete with screen shots from SAS and SPSS. The second data analysis chapter integrates material on partial associations, covered in a separate chapter in the previous edition, into a single chapter on estimating and testing associations. In both data analysis chapters, the presentation of statistical formulas is held to a minimum, and the focus is more on how to interpret and present statistics rather than how to compute them. Finally, Daryl Bem's classic chapter on writing research reports has been revised to reflect changes in style and expression since publication of the previous edition.

Beyond these revisions and updates to the content of the book, we added material designed to make the book more useful to students and instructors. Each chapter now concludes with three new features designed to help students interact more effectively with the material. Key terms are listed alphabetically at the end of each chapter. These terms are set in bold typeface in the text, where they are defined and illustrated. A second feature, which we call "On the Web," lists the addresses for and briefly describes a number of sites on the World Wide Web at which students can learn more about the material covered in the chapter. (Updates and additions to this list of sites will be posted at http://psychology.wadsworth.com.) A third feature is a list of references to readily accessible books and professional journal articles that provide deeper coverage of material presented in the chapter.

Less recognizable are more diffuse updates to the book. We carefully edited the text for outdated language and language that was acceptable in scientific writing a decade ago but would now be offensive to some readers or contrary to contemporary style. The computer, which had just begun to influence social science research when the previous edition was published, is now used in virtually every aspect of research. In the Seventh Edition, we prominently feature computer software, electronic mail, and the World Wide Web in our discussions of how research is done. Finally, we updated most examples from the published literature with a goal of drawing from publication outlets to which students interested in reading further would have ready access.

Acknowledgments

Although we thoroughly reorganized, revised, and updated the book, a fair amount of the material in this edition was written by authors commissioned by the Society for the Psychological Study of Social Issues to produce earlier editions. We are particularly grateful to Louise Kidder and Eliot Smith, who worked with Charles Judd to produce the previous edition. The fundamental strengths of that edition provided a strong foundation from which to produce this new edition.

We benefited from thorough reviews of the Sixth Edition and recommendations for revisions and updates by Tracy L. Brown (Department of Psychology, University of North Carolina at Asheville), Gloria Cowan (Department of Psychology, California State University, San Bernardino), Jacque E. Gibbons (Department of Sociology, Anthropology, and Social Work, Kansas State University), Robert A. Hoff (Department of Psychology, Mercyhurst College), and Christopher J. Recklitis (Dana-Farber Cancer Institute, Harvard University). We are grateful to Louis Penner, Blair Johnson, and other members of the Publications Committee of the Society for the Psychological Study of Social Issues for their support at every stage of preparing the book. Lou was particularly generous with his time and expertise.

A number of colleagues graciously granted permission to reprint or adapt their work for inclusion in the book. We thank Geoff Urbaniak and Scott Plous for permission to include screen shots illustrating their Web-based Research Randomizer program. Our coverage of handheld computer strategies for experience sampling was enhanced by graphics provided by Lisa Feldman Barrett from her Experience Sampling Program. And we were able to include a number of example tables and figures in the chapter on narrative and quantitative reviews thanks to Jeanne Brooks-Gunn, Bernadette Gray-Little, Adam Hafdahl, Judith Langlois, Tama Leventhal, Eric Turkheimer, and Mary Waldron.

We were privileged to work with outstanding publishing professionals from start to finish. In the early going, we received advice and encouragement from Brad Pothoff and Sarah Zedler at Harcourt College Publishers. Evelyn Podsiadlo at UG/GGS Production Services did an expert job of shepherding the manuscript through the production process, allowing us ample opportunity to fine tune the text to the very last minute. Elaine Hellmund kept production on track during the transition from Harcourt to Wadsworth Publishing. And Vicki Knight at Wadsworth expertly ushered the manuscript through the final stages of production.

Thanks to contributions by Julie Mellon and Tammy Herring in the Department of Psychology at the University of Kentucky we were able to focus on writing while progress was made on other important fronts. Julie was instrumental in securing permissions for reprinted and adapted material, and Tammy helped prepare the indexes.

No doubt, you would not be holding this book now were it not for the patience and support of the authors' families during its preparation. Monica Harris thanks her husband, Jonathan, for his good cheer, patience, and understanding when work on this book intruded on family time. And Rick Hoyle owes a debt of gratitude to his wife, Lydia, and their children Matthew, Michael, and Jessie for their unwavering support.

Rick H. Hoyle (Lexington, Kentucky)
Monica J. Harris (Lexington, Kentucky)
Charles M. Judd (Boulder, Colorado)
September 2001

FOREWORD

As Co-Chairs of the Publications Committee of the Society for the Psychological Study of Social Issues (SPSSI), we are extremely pleased to write this foreword to the Seventh Edition of *Research Methods in Social Relations*. This book will be published 50 years after the publication of the First Edition, written by Marie Jahoda, Morton Deutsch, and Stuart W. Cook. Thus, with the publication of this edition, we celebrate the unofficial golden anniversary of this important book on research methods.

Before we wrote this foreword, we read the preface to the First Edition of *Research Methods*. It tells the story of how SPSSI came to sponsor a research methods book. SPSSI is an international organization of social scientists that seeks to better understand the nature and causes of social problems, with the goal of reducing or eliminating these problems through both basic and action research, and the dissemination of the findings from such research. Thus, it is not surprising to learn that the initial impetus for the First Edition was a desire to systematically address a social problem, namely prejudice. In 1948, Gordon W. Allport proposed that SPSSI produce a book on the measurement of prejudice. After substantial discussion (and probably some considerable debate), SPSSI council concluded that measurement must be "placed in the broader context of the entire research process," and that therefore the scope of the book should address *all* the measures and methods of "social relations," not just prejudice. Thus was born a methods book that over the years has played an invaluable part of the educational experiences of literally tens of thousands of undergraduates and graduates interested in social relations. It is our hope—make that our belief—that this edition will continue to educate and inform the social scientists of the future.

It is also important for you to know that the current edition of this book continues the tradition of being largely a "labor of love" by its authors. Despite the enormous amount of time and effort required to create an edition of *Research Methods*, its authors receive only a modest initial stipend; the royalties from sales go to SPSSI to further its educational and scientific activities. Thus, we must thank Rick H. Hoyle, Monica J. Harris, and Charles M. Judd for their willingness to undertake this task for the Seventh Edition. SPSSI is truly fortunate to have found authors with their extraordinary skills and expertise. Moreover, because of their admirable dedication and efficiency, this edition was completed in a remarkably short period of time, even while upholding the book's time-honored quality. We also are grateful to SPSSI council for enthusiastically supporting our recommendation that the organization sponsor a new edition of *Research Methods in Social Relations*. This action is indicative of SPSSI's strong commitment to the educational part of its mission.

The Seventh Edition contains an organizational scheme that is slightly different from the Sixth Edition; users of the previous edition will find some old chapters in new places. These chapters, of course, have been updated and, when necessary, expanded. Additionally, the authors have written what are essentially new chapters on the three topics of ethics; sampling of thoughts, feelings, and actions; and reviewing research literatures. Embedded in all the chapters is material that reflects the changes and advances in methodologies that have occurred since the last edition, published in 1990. The result is a highly readable, thoughtfully organized, up-to-date, and accurate guide to contemporary research methods in social relations. It is with pride that SPSSI presents this volume to the students who will use it. It is our hope that they will find this book useful and be persuaded of the value and the excitement of research on social problems.

In closing, we invite students and their instructors who are not already SPSSI members to learn more about the organization. Our 3,000 members come from all over the world, and in addition to sponsoring books such as this one, we also publish print and electronic journals; support national and international conferences; and provide grants and awards for research related to social issues. More information about joining SPSSI can be found on the Web at http://www.spssi.org.

Louis A. Penner (Tampa, Florida, USA)
Blair T. Johnson (Fontainebleau, France)
Co-Chairs, SPSSI Publications Committee
June 2001

CONTENTS

Chapter 3

PART TWO

Chapter 4

Chapter 9

Chapter 10

Chapter 12

Chapter 13

Chapter 19

Chapter 20

PART

I

Introduction

I

CHAPTER

1

Ways of Knowing

Gazing down at people from a tall building or a window of a low-flying airplane gives us a different view of humanity from that to which we are accustomed. A crowded park or congested freeway feels different when we look at the crowds from afar. Somehow the distance gives us a sense of objectivity: We can observe without feeling the congestion ourselves. At the same time, much would be missed if we always observed from afar. We would miss the feelings, the excitement, and the crush and enthusiasm of the crowd if we never entered into it ourselves. Social scientists observe people from various distances because different vantage points give different information about people—how they feel, act, and interact. Confining ourselves as social scientists to a single method or procedure limits what we can know. No one procedure or method can provide a complete description. Some research methods allow the observer to be a participant in the group that is being observed. Other methods enable the observer to remain hidden or anonymous and to see from a distance. In this book, we describe these different methods in detail.

In this opening chapter, we describe how social science is similar to and different from two other ways of knowing with which readers already are familiar: the physical sciences and casual observation. The social sciences (e.g., anthropology, psychology, sociology) are similar to the physical sciences (e.g., physics, chemistry, biology) in the logic of inquiry but different in the degree to which the objects (or participants) under observation play an active role in the inquiry, thereby raising questions about social values. The social sciences are similar to casual observation in the quest to understand how people behave and relate to each other, but they are different in their systematic methods of inquiry.

We pursue two major themes in this chapter. The first concerns the place of values in social science research. Social scientists can borrow the logic of the physical sciences but must make use of different methods because the "things" we study are not inert objects but rather sentient beings engaged in complex social behavior.

When we study social behavior involving individuals or groups of people, we encounter their reactions to us as observers and we raise value-laden questions. The physical sciences also are not value free, as Einstein pointed out when he discovered the formula for nuclear energy, but the place of values is more immediately apparent in the social sciences. Also, the reactions of the observed to the observer must be taken into account.

The second major theme in this chapter concerns the comparison between the social sciences and casual observation as ways of knowing about social behavior. Examining social behavior scientifically sometimes appears to be "common sense" because most people observe and try to understand social behavior daily in the process of casual observation. In this chapter we show how the social sciences differ from casual observation in their deliberate search for sources of bias or invalidity.

The Place of Values in Social Science Research

This might seem to be an odd topic to introduce at the outset because research, any research, strives to be objective, which means "not biased by someone's point of view." **Values,** however, represent a point of view, a judgment that "this is good and that is bad," which someone else might dispute. Arguments about values cannot be settled by scientific evidence because the disputing parties would like to believe that the evidence is on their side. Where does this assertion leave the social sciences?

The inextricable connection between values and social science research requires researchers to be aware of the implications their research can have for human welfare. They cannot extricate themselves from value questions, but they can be aware of what the implications are for the welfare of various parties. This tension between objectivity and values is apparent in the case study of a controversial social science study presented in Table 1.1. Using procedures described in Chapter 19 of this book, Rind, Tromovitch, and Bauserman (1998) concluded that victims of childhood sexual abuse do not suffer long-term harm, a conclusion that stands in stark contrast to values held strongly by many members of the public. As detailed in Table 1.1, the published research report received considerable negative attention in the popular press and ultimately was unanimously condemned by both houses of Congress.

In looking for a silver lining in an otherwise entirely regrettable incident, we suppose it is remarkable that any social science research report is capable of attracting so much attention. On the whole, though, it is frightening to think that the major professional organization of a discipline would agree to consider public reaction in its determination of whether a research report should be published. That path leads only to censorship and suppression of free scientific inquiry. It is particularly distressing that public pressure was able to exert such influence, even though it is clear that the

TABLE 1.1

Case Study of When Science Clashes with Values: The Rind et al. (1998) Meta-Analysis

In 1998, *Psychological Bulletin*, the premier review journal in the field of psychology, published a meta-analysis of the long-term psychological outcomes of having been sexually abused as a child (Rind, Tromovitch, & Bauserman, 1998). A meta-analysis is a quantitative synthesis or literature review that summarizes a group of studies all bearing on the same topic (see Chapter 19). In their meta-analysis, Rind et al. summarized 59 studies examining the association between psychopathology and childhood sexual abuse history in college students. Somewhat counterintuitively, they discovered that having been abused as a child was only weakly associated with later maladjustment. Moreover, the association between abuse and later psychopathology was even smaller when the abuse was deemed consensual by the victim. Perhaps their most controversial finding was that nonnegligible proportions of the samples (11% of women and 37% of men) reported retroactively that their immediate response to the abuse had been positive.

Rind and his colleagues were very careful in their report to state, repeatedly, that the lack of demonstrated long-term negative outcomes for childhood sexual abuse did not mean that sexual abuse was acceptable or not immoral; however, despite their careful caveats, their paper provoked an intensely negative reaction from the public, who interpreted the findings to mean that the authors were endorsing pedophilia and other forms of childhood sexual abuse. Criticisms of the research findings circulating on the Web eventually found their way to Dr. Laura Schlessinger, a media personality whose talk show attracts millions of listeners. After Schlessinger criticized the Rind et al. paper as "junk science" on her show for two consecutive days, and thus generated countless irate phone calls and letters, Congress became involved. Several members of Congress held a press conference demanding that the American Psychological Association (APA; the organization that publishes *Psychological Bulletin*) denounce the Rind meta-analysis and calling for a congressional resolution condemning the study.

Two months of intense public pressure ensued, and ultimately the president of APA wrote a letter to the House representative who was leading the condemnation campaign. This letter stated that (1) findings reported by Rind et al. were inconsistent with the APA's stated and deeply held positions; (2) the editors should have evaluated the Rind et al. research report based on its potential for affecting public policy and would take such implications into account when reviewing future research reports; and (3) the APA would seek an independent review of the article by a panel of outside experts.

Even these concessions were not enough for Congress, and in July, the House of Representatives voted 355 to 0 (with 13 abstentions) to condemn the Rind et al. meta-analysis. This resolution was passed unanimously two weeks later by the Senate.

---

vast majority of the people who were writing the irate letters and making the irate phone calls had never even seen the Rind et al. (1998) research report but rather were reacting to how it was being portrayed—which was in a distorted manner—in the public media.

Given the potential for misunderstanding surrounding politically sensitive topics such as this, we wish to be clear about what our message here is. We are not saying that sex abuse is good. It is not. From any human values perspective, the sexual abuse of children who are vulnerable and incapable of providing consent in either a legal or psychological sense is one of the most heinous crimes a society can visit on its own people. But it also would be tragic for scientific results to be suppressed simply because they convey findings that people find personally repugnant. The reactions of the general public and Congress to the Rind et al. (1998) meta-analysis had a "kill the messenger" flavor that undermines the spirit of free scientific enterprise. In short, values are an inevitable part of science, in that they affect the questions we ask and the way we react to what we find. But they should not be used as a justification for preventing a given question from being asked.

In sharp contrast to the Rind et al. (1998) research on the effects of childhood sexual abuse, the values in some areas of research are so uncomplicated or noncontroversial that they almost cease to exist. For instance, a large body of research exists in the field of cognitive psychology on the concept of "natural categories," showing that people use preferred or basic levels of categorization in perceiving objects; that is, people will first categorize an object they sit in as a "chair," rather than a more specific ("desk chair") or global ("furniture") category (Rosch, 1988). The research seems quite uncontestable and noncontroversial: People use natural categories in how they approach and structure their worlds. Indeed, these categories are regarded as being helpful ways of navigating the overwhelming mass of stimuli that confronts them in everyday life; however, research on a particular type of category, racial categories, has produced observations that evoke open value judgments. Nobody seems to mind if people use categories to make inferences about pieces of furniture, but there is a negative reaction when racial categories (stereotypes) are used to make inferences about individual members of those categories. Indeed, the impact of values is evident even in the title of a research report on racial categories, which begins with the clause: "Just Say No (to Stereotyping) . . ." (Kawakami, Dovidio, Moll, Hermsen, & Russin, 2000). In short, stereotyping is viewed as acceptable and even helpful when the stereotypes are categories referring to physical objects; when people are stereotyped, however, it is viewed as unacceptable. What makes this research more controversial than the research on using natural categories to classify furniture is the interpretation of the findings. The observations or "facts" are quite straightforward; it is the interpretation that introduces social and political beliefs and values.

The act of framing a question about social behavior also encompasses values, beliefs, and differing perspectives. For instance, there are many studies that ask, "What are the effects of maternal employment on child development?," but fewer that concern the effects of paternal employment. Is this asymmetry neutral or does it reflect cultural beliefs and values? Consider another example: In the past there were many studies designed to investigate the causes of homosexuality. There were few investigating the causes of heterosexuality. The act of asking a question and framing it, with both an implied answer and an implicit set of values about social behavior, is rarely neutral.

Thus, values can directly influence the type of social science research that is and is not done. Sometimes this influence is positive, as when scientists struggle intensely to discover a vaccine for HIV/AIDS, prevent birth defects, or develop interventions to increase the academic success of at-risk youths. Unfortunately, sometimes values can have a chilling effect on science. Morton Hunt (1999) observed that in the past 15 years there has been a dramatic increase in the public's efforts to impose limits on the freedom of social scientists to investigate potentially controversial questions. For example, in 1991 an $18 million grant that had already been awarded to researchers to examine sexual behavior in adolescents that placed them at risk for HIV infection was abruptly canceled mere weeks before the project was to begin because of public and congressional pressure on the grounds that it was inappropriate to ask teenagers sensitive questions about sexual practices. Unfortunately, the consequence of this action is that we now know less than we could have known about practices that teenagers engage in that endanger their lives; thus, we are less equipped to intervene and decrease the incidence of a fatal disease.

Contestability in Social and Physical Sciences

Readers who have taken a laboratory course in the physical sciences probably remember white laboratory coats and physical equipment that convey the message, "This is serious; this is science." The dissection tools, microscopes, titration jars, and other uncommon instruments make it clear that this is no ordinary way of apprehending the world. This is science, and it promises to reveal information available only to science. Casual observation cannot compete.

Compare this experience with the typical first exposure to the social sciences. Usually there are no lab coats or uncommon instruments. And the sense of mystery and importance engendered by these objects often is lacking. For example, imagine that someone read that day care centers in the United States or communal child care in Israel create self-reliant and sociable children. If that person was not opposed to the idea that mothers of young children can work and their children can thrive, he or she might have believed the results were true; however, if the person believed that mothers of young children should stay home, it would be relatively easy to find apparent fault with the research and conclude that the results were erroneous. The results of social science research appear to be more **contestable** than the results of research in the physical sciences.

We do not want to suggest that there is no ambiguity in the physical sciences. The debate over the existence of cold fusion shows that physical scientists are just as capable as social scientists of debating the mere existence of a phenomenon. Electron microscopes and other sophisticated methods of observation have a significant share of ambiguity and error. We intend only to say that "in most people's eyes" the results of social science research often appear to be more contestable than the results of physical science research.

What makes social science research seem more contestable? Few people would say, "Amoebas do not reproduce by dividing in half! They reproduce just like dogs and cats; I don't care what you say with your fancy microscopes!" In contrast, a fair number of people might say, "Children of working mothers do not develop as well as children whose mothers stay home! I don't care what you say with your fancy surveys!"

We do not oppose argumentation and debate; they are essential for a science to grow and test itself. Instead, we are impressed by the difference between the public acceptance of observations made by physical scientists on the one hand and those made by social scientists on the other.

Two features of social science research leave it particularly open to debate. One is the seemingly ordinary quality of most methods of observation. Instead of using dissection kits or electron microscopes, social scientists often use their unadorned eyes and ears to make observations. They ask people questions, listen to their answers, and observe their behaviors. In the following chapters we show that the methods used by social scientists differ in significant ways from casual observation; the requirements imposed on measuring techniques are stringent and far from casual. For now, however, we wish to point out that to the public, the methods commonly used by social scientists sometimes look informal and unimpressive, and therefore the conclusions seem contestable.

The second feature that makes the results of social science research seem more contestable is the fact that they often address issues about which there are serious, deeply felt, politically identifiable differences of opinion. It is, therefore, difficult for researchers to persuade someone that they have observed "the facts" when those facts contradict the person's beliefs, values, or political interpretations. For instance, someone who believes mothers should stay home with young children might not be dissuaded by social science research. The prior belief is deeply rooted in the person's beliefs about men and women, about family, about power, and perhaps about religion. The case study of the Rind et al. (1998) meta-analysis is an excellent example of what happens when conclusions from social science research contradict people's very strongly held beliefs.

Social science research can never (or hardly ever) be value free because it is an investigation of relations between people instead of between objects. We qualify this statement to say "hardly ever" and allow the possibility that some social research might be value free. We leave the reader to find examples and to argue with classmates about whether a particular example is value free. Readers, in reaching their own conclusions, probably will create some very convincing cases that also show how much values come into play in social science research.

We do not want to leave the impression that physical sciences are "really" scientific and social science is not. Rather, we want to evoke an appreciation for the features of social science research that make it particularly challenging. Research in the social sciences has many similarities with other forms of research. This book contains language that is technical and teaches methods that are not simple. If sheer difficulty and complexity were qualifications for being considered "scientific," the social sciences would be high on the scientific ladder; however, they sometimes look like casual observation, and they are usually embedded in a set of social and political values.

Casual Observation

The study of social behavior is the study of how people behave with and toward others. Defined broadly in this way, we are all social scientists. To see this, imagine a party on a weekend evening. We all have expectations about how people at a party are likely to behave, although these expectations vary across individuals. A party attended by a 20-year-old will be different than a party attended by a 40-year-old. We can also easily think of behaviors that we are unlikely to see at the party. Reading *War and Peace*, for instance, is not a typical party activity. Not only do we have expectations about people's behavior at the party, but also we are likely to have explanations for at least some of this behavior. Suppose we saw someone at the party spill a drink on someone else. At least implicitly, we would look around to figure out why the drink was spilled and what the consequences were. Was the accident not an accident at all but rather intended? Did it occur because the drinker already had one too many drinks? Was the party too crowded, with the inevitable jostling when too many people are jammed into a small room?

Consider another example: A family is sitting in their apartment when they hear someone shout in a loud voice, "I'm going to kill you!" from the next apartment. Because this is not expected behavior, more or less automatically the family tries to figure out what is going on. That is, they try to find explanations for the behavior they are observing. Is this a serious argument? Is someone in genuine risk of being injured? Or is it merely the kind of joking threat family members are prone to make to one another? Should the family call the police or mind their own business? The family might try to gather more information to arrive at a conclusion, for example, by pressing their ears against the wall to try to hear other parts of the conversation that would clarify the nature of the threatening remark.

As both these examples illustrate, we are all naive observers or students of social behavior, regardless of what our actual professions are. That is, we are all engaged daily in the ordinary pursuit of understanding social behavior because we have expectations, hunches, and hypotheses about how people are likely to behave in given situations and why they behave as they do. For instance, we expect certain behaviors at a party and not others. When someone spills a drink, we try to figure out what caused that behavior. The expectations, hunches, or hypotheses of **casual observation** are ultimately utilitarian. If we have ideas about how others are likely to behave with and toward us in different situations and in response to our own behavior, ultimately we can act in ways that elicit desired behaviors from others. Casual observation of social behavior is useful for planning our own behaviors to reach our goals, objectives, or desired outcomes.

This discussion does not imply that our ordinary hunches and hypotheses about others' behaviors are necessarily right. We certainly have expectations about behavior that are violated routinely. For instance, we might think it inappropriate to have too much to drink at a party. Nevertheless, someone might do just that. Likewise, when driving a car we expect others to look for oncoming cars before making a left turn. Nevertheless, people sometimes turn left in front of approaching traffic.

Thus, our expectations about how others are likely to behave can be wrong. In addition, our explanations for why they behave as they do can also be wrong. For instance, after seeing someone at a party spill a drink, we might surmise that the accident was caused by mere clumsiness. This explanation might well be in error; perhaps the spill was intentional and in retaliation against someone who had been insulting. Without seeing that prior insult, our explanation for the behavior would certainly be wrong. Similarly, if we hear a threatening shout from a neighboring apartment, we might conclude that it is just a minor argument, and as a result we might not realize a serious crime is about to be committed.

Because our ordinary hunches, hypotheses, and explanations ultimately are constructed to help us achieve our own goals, and because we must inevitably realize that our hunches are not always correct, part of casual observation involves trying to figure out when our hunches, hypotheses, and explanations are right and when they are wrong. Therefore, two characteristics distinguish our casual observation of social behavior. First, we have hunches and hypotheses about others' behavior. Second, we continue to examine, at least somewhat critically, those hunches and hypotheses. We are motivated both to explain others' behaviors and to figure out whether our explanations are correct. We do both routinely and spontaneously, hardly ever bothering to reflect on the fact that we are in fact studying social behavior.

These two tasks also characterize scientific studies of social behavior, regardless of whether the studies are conducted by psychologists, sociologists, political scientists, educators, or others. They all share the goals of constructing theories of human social behavior and critically examining those theories to improve their accuracy.

The goal of this book is to provide an introduction to the methods commonly used by social scientists to study human social behavior. That is, what are the methods used to construct scientific theories of social behavior? To answer this question, we first examine how we operate as casual observers of social behavior—methods we routinely use in constructing and critically examining our hunches and hypotheses about human social behavior. Then we compare and contrast these methods with those that characterize a scientific approach to the same phenomena.

First, what form do our ordinary hunches, hypotheses, and theories about human social behavior take? That is, what constitutes a "naive" social science hypothesis or theory? Second, what methods are ordinarily used in critically examining these hypotheses? What are the sources of support routinely used to figure out if a hypothesis is right or wrong, firmly grounded or not?

Naive Hypotheses and Theories of Social Behavior

Most aphorisms or clichés about human social behavior are **naive hypotheses:**

> Birds of a feather flock together.
>
> Absence makes the heart grow fonder.
>
> The early bird gets the worm.

Each of these naive hypotheses has a characteristic form that is seen most clearly if we reduce it to its basic meaning:

> Similarity results in increased contact.
>
> Absence results in increased affection.
>
> Acting on opportunities early results in success.

Each of these naive hypotheses argues that one phenomenon or behavior—the subject in the sentence—causes or is associated with another phenomenon or behavior—the object. These phenomena, both subject and object, are called constructs. A **construct** is an abstract concept that we would like to measure. Love, intelligence, aggression, self-esteem, and success are all constructs. Although these things are real and affect our lives in many different ways, they do not exist as physical objects. We cannot go down to our local supermarket and pick up a six-pack of love, as much as we might like to. Instead, we can only measure constructs indirectly and imperfectly through an operational definition. The **operational definition** of a construct is the set of procedures we use to measure or manipulate it. For example, one operational definition of intelligence is a person's score on a standardized IQ test. The operational definition of aggression might be the number of electric shocks a participant chooses to deliver to another person. Chapter 4 is devoted to the complex issues of operationally defining a construct and how we determine whether our operational definitions of a construct are correct, or valid.

A social science **hypothesis,** naive or not, is a falsifiable statement of the association between two or more constructs that have to do with human social behavior. These hypothesized associations can be causal or not. They can state that one construct causes another, or they might simply state that one construct tends to be found with another. There are two notions that require elaboration: the notion of constructs and the notion of what is a causal association.

As stated, constructs are the phenomena of which a hypothesis speaks. When a hypothesis concerns **causal associations,** some constructs are identified as causes and others as effects. If we believe that the three naive hypotheses presented earlier are causal, the causal constructs are similarity, absence, and early action. The three affected constructs—the effects—are contact, affection, and success. Notice that all these constructs, whether involved in a hypothesized causal association or not, concern general phenomena having to do with social behavior, and they all require further definition or elaboration. What, for instance, is similarity or success? Different people might define these in different ways. Success for one person might mean having good friends, whereas for someone else it means having money or status. Thus, constructs need further definitions to be tied to actual observable behavior. We do not directly see success, for success is a construct and does not exist physically. Success can mean different things to different people. Instead, we observe various ways of defining or measuring success (e.g., someone's stated quality of friendships or someone's average yearly income).

Our naive hypotheses frequently concern causal associations among constructs because most of us believe that behaviors have causes. We believe, for instance, that success is not entirely the result of luck or good fortune or random events. Rather, we accept the notion that it is partly affected by activities or constructs like early action. Likewise, in arguing that similarity results in contact between people, we implicitly acknowledge that our choice of friends is not random; rather, some phenomena or constructs cause us to like or dislike others. Naive hypotheses by their very nature imply that human behavior is partially determined or caused. For although we implicitly believe that human behavior is to some extent caused or determined, we also believe that human behavior occurs as a result of random events, luck, and individual whims.

Hypotheses vary not only in whether they describe a causal association but also in the complexity of the association they describe. Some hypotheses can be linked with other hypotheses to make up a theory. A **theory** is a set of interrelated hypotheses that is used to explain a phenomenon (e.g., attraction, success) and make predictions about associations among constructs relevant to the phenomenon. For instance, the following set of hypotheses forms a small theory. Like many such sets, it takes the form of a syllogism:

> Being unemployed frequently leads to personal depression.
>
> Depression is often a cause of divorce.
>
> Therefore, increased unemployment in society often is associated with higher divorce rates.

This syllogism consists of three hypotheses, the third being logically inferred from the other two. Some theories of social behavior can be as simple as this, linking a few hypotheses. Others are exceedingly complex, linking many more hypotheses. For instance, some of the founding documents of this country, such as the Declaration of Independence, set forth relatively complex theories about the conditions under which people will be happy and will prosper.

Hypotheses vary in complexity not only by being linked with others in theories but also by bringing in qualifying conditions or constructs that must be met for the hypotheses to be applicable. For instance, someone might hypothesize that "absence makes the heart grow fonder" holds true only when the absent target is of the opposite sex. This qualifying condition makes the hypothesis more complex than the original one. Now, instead of maintaining simply that one construct leads to another, the hypothesis states that construct A results in construct B only under condition C.

There is one very common form of qualifying condition that we often add to hypotheses: We frequently specify a group or kind of person for which a hypothesized causal effect should hold. For instance, we might say, "Among men over 50, unemployment increases the probability of personal depression." We have then added a qualifying condition that specifies the group or population for whom the hypothesis is expected to be true. Adding such a condition suggests by implication that the hypothesis might not hold for other groups or populations. Because people having different backgrounds and experiences do in fact behave differently, it is generally a good idea to increase the complexity of a hypothesis by adding a condition that specifies the population for which the hypothesis should hold.

Hypotheses thus vary both in whether they describe a causal association and in their complexity. In addition, there are differences in the confidence with which they are held or maintained. We might, for instance, firmly believe that being unemployed can cause a person to be depressed. We might feel less strongly, however, about whether personal depression is a cause of divorce. Because theories are made up of sets of hypotheses, often in syllogistic form, and because these hypotheses differ in the confidence with which they are held, the syllogistic conclusion of the theory as a whole ought to be held with no more confidence than the least confident premise. Whether this is in fact how we operate in our casual observation of social behavior, however, is open to question.

So far we have discussed the nature of hypotheses, that is, what form they take and ways in which they vary. Once we realize that they can vary in the confidence with which they are held, we must raise the second question that was posed earlier about our casual observation of social behavior. Why are some hypotheses held with more confidence than others? To answer this question, we must know how people ordinarily gather evidence to test hypotheses.

Sources of Support for Naive Hypotheses

There are at least five sources of support routinely used to develop and modify naive hypotheses and theories, that is, hypotheses and theories rooted in casual observation: (1) logical analysis, (2) authority, (3) consensus, (4) observation, and (5) past experience. Each of these sources suffers from at least some weaknesses that make its reliability suspect.

Logical Analysis We often derive hypotheses and decide whether they are accurate by examining whether they are logically consistent with other hypotheses that we hold. An example of such **logical analysis** is contained in the syllogism presented previously. If we take it to be true that unemployment frequently leads to personal depression, and if we take it to be true that personal depression can often lead to marital discord and divorce, then it necessarily follows that unemployment increases the chance of divorce. This final hypothesis is deduced, or logically inferred, from the combination of the two earlier ones. Schematically, we can represent the syllogism this way:

Being unemployed → depression → divorce

As this illustration makes clear, the influence of unemployment on the probability of divorce follows from the intervening role played by depression in the process.

Syllogistic reasoning is frequently used to derive and modify hypotheses based on their consistency with other hypotheses. Generating support for hypotheses by such reasoning, however, is not without its pitfalls. Alan Cromer (1993) argued in his book, *Uncommon Sense: The Heretical Nature of Science*, that the human brain is not wired for the type of logical thought required for science and that instead people hold the mistaken belief that they have intuitive knowledge about the way the world works. The problem is that our "intuition" and logical processes are often incorrect. Cromer gives the well-known physics example: If one were to fire a bullet from a gun straight across a field, while simultaneously dropping a bullet from the same height, which bullet would hit the ground first? Most people would say that the bullet being dropped would hit first, but the answer is that both bullets would hit the ground at the same time. Downward velocity is independent of horizontal velocity. This is elementary physics, but our intuitive reasoning would lead us to the wrong answer every time. Cromer argued that in order to think scientifically, we need to think in formal logical terms, and this is not something that comes naturally but rather must be taught.

In the social sciences, especially, what we ordinarily regard as a logical conclusion can be influenced not only by pure logic but also by our wishes or desires (Gilovich, 1991). We might invent seemingly logical justifications for hypotheses that we hold simply because we wish these hypotheses to be true. Although we strive for logical consistency in many of our beliefs, we also have a remarkable ability to ignore inconsistencies in other beliefs. For instance, it was not unusual in the 1950s to encounter White Americans who believed both that "anyone in this country can achieve whatever he or she wants" and that "Blacks should not be allowed to attend the same schools as Whites." When we want to ignore contradictions in our thinking, we have a remarkable capacity to do so.

Authority We are likely to turn to various authorities or experts to determine what hypotheses make sense in our casual observation of social behavior. To figure out how to cope with a difficult child, a parent might consult an **authority**—a pediatrician, a counselor, or a teacher. To decide how to behave in a foreign country we have not visited before, we might consult someone who knows the country well. To understand why riots occur sometimes in some large cities in the summer, we might consult a sociologist or a specialist in race relations. As long as we have faith in the expert we consult, we might regard the expert's opinion as sufficient justification for a hypothesis.

Using experts to decide which are good hypotheses and which are not is efficient as long as they are indeed expert in the area under consideration. All too often, however, we presume someone to be an expert when he or she only has the trappings of expertise without the actual knowledge to back it up. We rely on the symbols of authority without making sure that the authority is truly knowledgeable (Cialdini, 2001).

In addition, we are inclined to let our beliefs and values define whom we identify as an expert, which occurs when we seek so-called experts merely to provide a confirmation for our hypotheses rather than a critical assessment. For instance, some might regard an astrologer as an expert on how to choose a spouse. Someone who defines the astrologer as an expert in this area is already convinced of the wisdom of astrological advice on such matters.

A final problem with reliance on authorities is that authorities can have their own interests at heart. Because authorities presumably like their status, they might provide advice that perpetuates or justifies the status quo rather than suggest novel social arrangements. If we wanted to arrive at a solution for our energy problems, the answers we probably would receive from diverse authorities would be likely to differ simply as a result of the positions these authorities occupy. For instance, if we were to ask the chief executive officer of a major oil company, it is unlikely that this person would argue for the infusion of federal funds and tax breaks for funding research on renewable fuel sources.

In sum, in our casual observation of social behavior, we seek input from authorities to help us evaluate our hypotheses and theories. Just as relying on logical analysis is not without pitfalls, so, too, relying on the wisdom of authorities can lead to biased conclusions.

Consensus Instead of appealing to the wisdom of authorities, we might appeal to the wisdom of our peers seeking **consensus** regarding our hypotheses. We decide what are good or bad beliefs or hypotheses by finding out whether our friends agree with us. How might a mother decide when to wean a child? She might appeal to a physician as an authority. It is equally likely, however, that she will ask her friends when they weaned their infants. If a client of our business makes an unreasonable request, we might ask our coworkers why the client acted that way and how we should respond. If we want to evaluate our opinions regarding why high schools do not seem to be doing as good a job as they used to, we might discuss it with our neighbors. All these examples illustrate the validation of our hypotheses or theories by consensus with peers.

This source of support for hypotheses is not a great deal different from the use of authorities. In both cases, others are the referent who helps us decide what we should and should not believe. As a result, consensus is subject to the same kinds of biases and distortions as is consultation with authorities. With whom of our peers will we discuss our ideas on schools? Most probably the discussion will be with people like us who are quite likely to agree with us on such things.

In addition, groups of people can be notoriously poor as independent judges. Groups frequently are pushed toward unanimity so that dissenting voices are not heard (Janis, 1997). Also, the group might give the listener what he or she wants to hear, especially if the listener is highly regarded. As a result, group consensus is often inadequate for validating hypotheses. In our casual observation of social behavior, however, we sometimes rely on it heavily.

Observation To determine whether our naive hypotheses are correct, we routinely compare them to the behaviors of ourselves and others through **observation**. When our hypotheses are not consistent with what we observe, we might modify or abandon them. Suppose we believe that women are able to "read" nonverbal messages more clearly than men (Hall, Carter, & Horgan, 2000). That is, we think that women are more sensitive in understanding nonverbal signals that are sent to them, intentionally or not. To determine whether this hypothesis is accurate, we might watch members of both sexes in a number of different settings. If we are serious enough about examining our hypothesis, we might even do an informal experiment. For instance, we might try to communicate nonverbally with some female and some male acquaintances and then see who figures out our signals more clearly.

Let us take another example. Suppose we believe that prejudice toward other ethnic groups is caused by a lack of personal acquaintance with members of those groups. To learn whether this hypothesis is accurate, we might conduct some informal interviews with various acquaintances, asking about their friendships with members of various ethnic groups. We might then see if our estimates of each person's degree of prejudice toward each group seems to be related to the number of friendships he or she has.

Such observational procedures are as full of pitfalls as the other procedures we use to support our naive hypotheses. There are four major problems in using observation to validate hypotheses. We can use the example in the preceding paragraph to illustrate. First, as we argued in defining hypotheses and theories, the constructs mentioned in a hypothesis (e.g., prejudice or personal acquaintance) can mean different things to different people. One person's impression of someone's prejudice might not be the same as someone else's because different observers might look for different things. Similarly, what one person means by personal friendships with members of different ethnic groups might be different from what another person means. Hence, in deciding what behaviors to observe, we might observe behaviors that do not represent or capture the constructs with which our hypothesis is concerned. For instance, instead of measuring people's actual friendships, we might, when we interview them, measure how much they desire such friendships.

Second, inferring that one construct causes another can be very difficult. Suppose in our example we indeed found that people who seemed more prejudiced reported fewer friendships. Such a finding does not necessarily mean that differences in contact with members of various ethnic groups cause differences in prejudice. It is at least as plausible that the causal effect is the other way around: that prejudice causes differences in friendship patterns. Using observation to support hypotheses can be misleading because causal direction can be very hard to establish.

Third, we might make our observations on a very select group of people, a group of people, perhaps, for which the hypothesis might be especially true but one that is not representative of the world at large. For instance, although it might be true that prejudice and contact with members of ethnic groups are associated in our select sample of friends, they might not be associated in general or in other samples. Thus, we might engage in biased sampling in such a way that we have more or less confidence in our hypothesis than we should.

Fourth, we probably are biased in deciding which observations are relevant. Trope and Ferguson (2000), for instance, have written that when testing hypotheses about individuals, people look for instances that confirm those hypotheses and tend to ignore instances not consistent with them. Thus, the very process of collecting observational data can be biased. Just as we might choose authorities who tend to confirm our hypotheses, so, too, we might judge observations as relevant or not depending in part on whether they support our hypotheses.

Past Experience Probably we most frequently generate support for our hypotheses as casual observers of social behavior by reflecting on or remembering **past experiences.** We think back to instances or events that confirm the hypothesis, and then we attempt to make modifications to take into account disconfirming instances.

Although the use of past experience is, we suspect, very frequent, it is susceptible to all the dangers inherent in the use of observation, plus others. Memory is inherently reconstructive. We do not passively store information about past experiences; rather, we store and organize events selectively. Theories and hypotheses are tools that we use in organizing our memories. It has been repeatedly shown that information that is consistent with a theory or expectation is more easily remembered than information that is irrelevant (Hirt, 1990). Hence, it is perhaps unlikely that hypotheses will be disconfirmed by recollected experiences.

Toward a Science of Social Behavior

Try as we might to obtain an accurate understanding of social behavior, we encounter innumerable difficulties in constructing and validating hypotheses and theories in everyday life. Acquiring accurate knowledge about how people behave and why people behave as they do is not easy. Yet we all persist at it. So, too, do the scientists of social behavior, whether they are a psychologist, sociologist, political scientist, or educator. Although the scientists' path toward acquiring knowledge about social behavior is in many ways just as hazardous and difficult as the path of the casual observer, there are differences in how they proceed. In the remainder of this chapter we identify some of these differences, most of which are differences of degree rather than of kind. That is, scientists differ from casual observers not so much in *what* they do but in *how* it is done. The scientific study of social behavior and the casual observation of social behavior are not qualitatively different from each other; the differences are subtle and, at times, hard to identify. They are nonetheless present.

The most important difference concerns the extent to which scientific studies are on the alert for biased conclusions. Scientists ideally operate as if their hypotheses and conclusions about human behavior might be in error. Social scientists look for biases and pitfalls in the processes used to support and validate hypotheses. Scientists are aware of the research on such biases and submit their conclusions to the scrutiny of other scientists, who attempt to find biases that were overlooked. The casual observer often gathers evidence in support of hypotheses without being aware of or worried about the biases inherent in the process. This difference is one of degree, however. Although scientists are on the lookout for biases, they are not aware of them all. Likewise, casual observers might strive to be as accurate as possible in reaching their conclusions. The difference is this: The scientist systematically studies how to avoid biases in examining hypotheses, and there is an established set of methods for avoiding many such biases.

Unlike the casual observer, scientists rely mainly on observation to evaluate a hypothesis critically. They engage in empirical research to try to determine whether hypotheses are accurate and how they need to be modified to make them more accurate. **Empirical research** is observation that is systematic in attempting to avoid biases. Although scientists might also use logical analysis, authorities, consensus, and past experience in evaluating hypotheses, unlike the casual observer, they must and do ultimately engage in empirical research. Scientists ultimately put confidence in a hypothesis or a theory if it has been able to withstand empirical attempts to falsify it.

Because of this reliance on empirical research, social scientists tend to be more concerned about the problem of linking up theoretical constructs with observables than are casual observers. A good scientific hypothesis contains not only statements about associations between constructs of interest but also statements about what observable indicators go with each construct. In other words, scientists who rely on empirical research are necessarily concerned with how to measure theoretical constructs. An ordinary observer using observation to support hypotheses is perhaps unlikely to spend much time thinking about what observable qualities indicate constructs of interest. Scientists are very concerned with that question.

To rely ultimately on empirical research to validate hypotheses means that social scientists assume that all constructs of interest can indeed be measured or observed. This is the assumption of **operationism.** For each construct of interest in the study of social behavior there must be observable features we can measure that represent the construct. This is not to say, of course, that scientists assume anything can be perfectly measured. In fact, they assume quite the contrary—that all constructs are measured with error. Nevertheless, the scientific assumption of operationism means that all constructs of interest can be measured, albeit imperfectly.

Earlier we argued that one of the characteristics of a scientific inquiry is that the scientist is constantly wary of biases in attempting to validate hypotheses. Ultimately this means that scientists can never actually accept a hypothesis as correct or accurate, for the observations that support it might have been biased or in error in unknown ways. Strange as it might seem, scientists never can actually prove a hypothesis based on empirical research because that research could conceivably have been biased. The best scientists can do is to gather a large quantity of empirical evidence consistent with the hypothesis, while acknowledging that the hypothesis remains unproven in a formal sense because the evidence is, to an unknown degree, faulty. Although scientists of social behavior, like casual observers, are invested in their hypotheses and ultimately wish to support them, to function scientifically means that, regardless of the outcomes of empirical research, we can never accept hypotheses as absolutely true.

Let us examine more closely the logic underlying that last statement. When a researcher designs a study, he or she is implicitly using the logical argument: "If Theory X is true, then Association Y should be observed." However, the converse does not hold: We cannot say, with confidence, that "Association Y was observed; therefore, Theory X is true." The logical snag is that there could be other reasons besides Theory X—say, Theory Z—for observing Association Y. If Association Y were *not* observed, that is clear evidence against Theory X and we can safely reject the theory. (In reality, scientists do not reject their theories so easily but instead would search for other reasons—inadequate measures or methodological flaws—for why Association Y was not observed.) In short, scientists talk of rejecting hypotheses and theories but not of proving them. We say that the results are "consistent with" or "support" a hypothesis but not that the hypothesis has been accepted. At best, hypotheses can withstand attempts to show that they are incorrect. There almost always are other explanations for a set of findings that seem to support a hypothesis, so a truly scientific stance is always a skeptical one.

What makes a scientific hypothesis a good one, then? A hypothesis gains gradual acceptance if it is repeatedly supported, survives numerous attempts to falsify it, and seems to account for observations conducted by different scientists in different settings. Because any particular observation in support of a hypothesis can be biased or in error, science requires **replication.** That is, empirical research must repeatedly reveal the same conclusions when conducted independently by different researchers. Only in this way can the biases of any one investigator or procedure be overcome.

Likewise scientists submit their interpretations of their research to the critical review of fellow scientists. Before most research reports are published, a journal editor solicits the opinion of several reviewers, experts on the topic of the research. They read the research report thoroughly and critically, looking for biases or alternative explanations of the findings that the authors might have missed. The reviewers then provide detailed feedback aimed at improving the research report or the research study on which it is based. In many cases the report is deemed not suitable for publication; indeed, rejection rates at the most prestigious scientific journals easily exceed 80%. The publishing process in the social sciences is long and grueling, but the system is an effective one and ensures that research is scrutinized closely and is as accurate as possible before being communicated to policy makers, practitioners, and other researchers.

All this sounds very laudable, and in theory it is. Yet in fact, scientists are rarely as noble as this idealized picture paints them. Scientists, like everyone else, are personally invested in what they do. They want to be right. They might even on occasion be a little more vain than most. And the "publish or perish" mentality at many academic institutions might pressure researchers to publish their work prematurely. The social sciences do, however, provide a structure that necessitates the critical review of hypotheses and research. Although individual scientists might invest a great deal in trying to "prove" a hypothesis or in trying to demonstrate that all competing hypotheses are in error, the scientific community, by requiring that research be critically reviewed before being published, sees to it that hypotheses are usually critically evaluated, and they are only cautiously accepted by the scientific community as a whole.

A science of social behavior consists of the interchange between theories and empirical research. We do research in an attempt to examine the validity of our theories. Hence, systematic observation always starts with a question or hypothesis that motivates it. Research, in turn, leads to modification of hypotheses and theories. Ideally the path of science, circling between theory and observation, is always guided by a skeptical and self-critical stance.

Summary

The social sciences differ from the physical sciences in a number of ways. First, the social sciences concern people rather than inert objects, and as a result, questions of value arise more frequently. These questions concern both how the results of social science research are to be interpreted and what questions are asked in the first place. Second, social science methods and conclusions often seem to be little more than common sense because—as casual observers—we routinely think about or try to explain people's behaviors.

As casual observers, all of us routinely put together explanations about our own and others' behaviors so that we can plan our lives and pursue our goals. These explanations take the form of hypotheses and theories about the causes of observed behavior. They are similar to aphorisms or clichés that are commonplace in everyday language. Not only do we put together such explanations, but we also attempt to figure out whether they are valid and appropriate. We rely on five kinds of evidence to help us determine the appropriateness of our explanations: logical analysis, advice of authorities or experts, consensus of our peers, further observations that we make, and reflections about past events and behaviors. Each of these sources of evidence necessarily involves some bias in the appraisal of our explanations.

The social sciences differ from casual observation in at least two ways, although the ultimate goal of both is to arrive at valid explanations for people's behavior. First, social scientists ultimately rely on systematic empirical observation in order to have confidence in a hypothesis. Second, scientists study the biases that are inherent in attempting to determine which explanations are good and which are poor, and they deliberately design their studies to minimize these biases. As such, the scientific stance is always a skeptical one. A good scientist never accepts a hypothesis as true. The best that can be done is to gather empirical data that are consistent with the hypothesis. Ultimately, however, the scientist realizes that the hypothesis can never be proven.

Key Concepts

authority
casual observation
causal association
consensus
construct
contestability
empirical research
hypothesis
logical analysis
naive hypothesis
observation
operational definition
operationism
past experience
replication
theory
values

On the Web

http://home.xnet.com/~blatura/skep_1.html Good description of the scientific method from a Web site devoted to skeptics, with an emphasis on the need to hold paranormal phenomena to rigorous scientific standards.

http://www.project2061.org/tools/sfaaol/sfaatoc.htm This Web site contains a textbook, published by Science for All Americans Online, on the scientific enterprise. Especially relevant is Chapter 1, "The Nature of Science."

http://www.scientificmethod.com/b_body.html Description of the 11 major stages of the scientific method.

http://www.dharma-haven.org/science/myth-of-scientific-method.htm A site entitled "The Myth of the Magical Scientific Method," written by Terry Halwes. Halwes argues that scientists deviate in important ways from the logical hypothesis-testing view taught by most science textbooks.

http://www.ems.psu.edu/~fraser/BadScience.html An amusing Web site that provides numerous examples of researchers making bad mistakes in talking about scientific findings.

Further Reading

Brannigan, G. G., & Merrens, M. R. (Eds.). (1993). *The undaunted psychologist: Adventures in research*. New York: McGraw-Hill.
Cohen, J. (1994). The earth is round ($p < .05$). *American Psychologist, 49*, 997–1003.

Cromer, A. H. (1993). *Uncommon sense: The heretical nature of science.* New York: Oxford University Press.

Gilovich, T. (1991). *How we know what isn't so: The fallibility of human reason in everyday life.* New York: Free Press.

Hunt, M. (1999). *The new Know-Nothings: The political foes of the scientific study of human nature.* New Brunswick, NJ: Transaction Publishers.

CHAPTER

2

Evaluating Social Science Theories and Research

There are two purposes to this chapter. First, we want to explore the nature and rationale for the scientific study of social behavior. What is empirical research and why is it done? To answer this question, we will need to be more precise about the nature of scientific theories and hypotheses. We can then examine the various ways in which research can be used to support, criticize, and construct theories. Our second goal is to discuss the ways in which any particular piece of empirical research on social behavior can be sound or unsound, valid or invalid, useful or useless. In other words, we introduce criteria that can be used to judge the quality of scientific research. These criteria are the building blocks for sound social science research. In subsequent chapters we explore each of these topics in depth, but we offer an overview in this early chapter as context for understanding specific issues and strategies covered in the remainder of the book.

The Purposes of Research in the Social Sciences

We said in the first chapter that social scientists conduct empirical research, or systematic observation, to support and modify theories and hypotheses about social behavior. To be more precise about the purposes of empirical research, we need to review the specific features of theories and hypotheses about social behavior.

The Nature of Social Science Theories

In Chapter 1, we defined a **theory** as a set of interrelated hypotheses that is used to explain a phenomenon and make predictions about associations among constructs relevant to the phenomenon. Thus, a theory about social behavior has three features. First, it contains constructs that are of theoretical interest and that it attempts to explicate or account for in some way. Second, it describes associations among these constructs. These associations are frequently causal, specifying which constructs exert effects on which others under varying conditions. These hypothesized associations are the heart of a theory. Finally, a theory incorporates hypothesized links between the theoretical constructs and observable variables that can be used to measure the constructs. These links specify the behaviors or other indicators used to conduct empirical research. Nonscientific or naive theories of social behavior also consist of constructs and causal relations among them, but because the scientific study of social behavior relies on empirical research to support and modify theories, a scientific theory also specifies the observable indicators that define the constructs of theoretical interest.

A few examples will clarify what constitutes a theory. In political science there is a theory of political information processing (Lavine, Borgida, & Sullivan, 2000). This theory holds that when people have higher levels of attitude involvement (i.e., they care more about the issue under discussion), they are more likely to engage in biased information-gathering strategies. This in turn leads to more extreme and unidirectional attitudes. Lastly, such extreme attitudes should result in lower degrees of decision conflict and thus be more readily accessed in memory. Notice that this example consists of a complex chain of hypothesized causal associations among several constructs: Attitude involvement leads to biased information gathering, which leads to extreme attitudes, which leads to greater attitude accessibility. A good theory of political information processing also specifies how the constructs of interest could be measured, observed, or manipulated. For instance, the theory might state that attitude accessibility is best indicated by reaction time in responding to items on an attitude scale.

Sociobiologists have developed an elaborate theory to account for human mating patterns. Sexual strategies theory (Buss & Schmitt, 1993) argues that human courtship patterns have evolved through natural selection. Women are limited in the number of offspring they can produce. They also invest more resources in offspring due to the biological requirements of pregnancy and lactation. Sexual strategies theory therefore predicts that women should be more discriminating than men in their choices of mates, basing their choices to a greater extent on the resources that a potential mate can provide her and her family. Men, on the other hand, are not limited in their reproductive capability, as they can theoretically reproduce every time they have sex. Thus, men have less to lose on a "bad" mating; sexual strategies theory therefore predicts that men should be less discriminating than women with respect to their choices of mates, and they should be more likely than women to base their choices on cues that signal fertility. As with the previous example, sexual strategies theory encompasses a complex set of assumptions and hypotheses that are interrelated. It is also an interesting example because the constructs that are at the heart of the theory, reproductive fitness and natural selection, are not directly observable but take place over hundreds or thousands of generations. Nonetheless, as we discuss later in this chapter, one of the crucial hallmarks of a theory is that it must generate testable hypotheses. Although we cannot capture natural selection in the time frame available to scientific study, sexual strategies theory does suggest certain associations that should hold if natural selection is occurring. The theory has in fact been supported by many empirical studies in many different countries, showing, for example, that men desire more lifetime sexual partners, tend to marry women younger than themselves, and place a higher emphasis on traits related to fertility such as youth and physical appearance. Women, on the other hand, desire fewer sexual partners and place a higher emphasis on a man's resources and fidelity (Buss & Schmitt, 1993).

Both of these examples show the basic structure of a theory. A theory is comprised of **hypotheses,** which in turn are comprised of statements about associations among constructs (e.g., attitude involvement leads to biased information gathering) and associations between constructs and observable indicators (e.g., biased information gathering is indicated by selective attention to attitude-consistent information). The observable indicators are known as variables. A **variable** is any attribute that changes values across people or things being studied. Thus, hair color, IQ test scores, height, introversion, gender, and blood pressure are all variables, and variables are used to represent the constructs addressed by a theory. In sum, any theory is made up of hypotheses, which are of two types: (1) hypothesized associations among constructs and (2) hypothesized associations between constructs and observable indicators, or variables. Both types of hypotheses have characteristic forms. The first, concerning associations among constructs, typically takes the form:

Construct A causes construct B for population X under condition Y.

Each of the examples of theories we discussed earlier contains hypotheses that conform to this model, although the word "causes" might be replaced with "leads to," "produces," or "is associated with." Note, however, that in any given hypothesis, much can remain implicit. For instance, the populations or conditions for which the causal association between construct A and construct B holds might not be explicitly mentioned.

A few further examples illustrate hypotheses about associations among constructs:

Contact with members of other ethnic groups decreases prejudice when in equal status settings.

Crowded classrooms in inner-city schools adversely affect educational achievement.

The social class of one's parents has a strong effect on one's aspirations in our society.

Deinstitutionalization of the mentally ill enhances community acceptance.

The second type of hypothesis concerns associations between constructs and observable indicators. They usually are of this form:

Behavior X or response Y is a valid indicator of construct A.

Examples include the following:

Delinquency can be defined as being arrested more than once prior to age 18.

The SAT or ACT is a valid measure of scholastic achievement.

Ideologues are those who explicitly refer to underlying ideologies in discussing political issues.

What Makes a Theory Productive?

It seems that some theories in the social sciences attract a great deal of attention and are extremely productive of research, whereas others attract very little attention and, therefore, produce very little research. An important question, then, concerns not only the definition of theories and hypotheses but also the characteristics of productive or important social science theories. Table 2.1 lists the criteria of a productive theory; our discussion here expands and explains these criteria.

The first prerequisite of a good theory is that it must be falsifiable. When we say a hypothesis or theory is **falsifiable,** we mean that we could conceive of a pattern of

TABLE 2.1 CRITERIA OF A PRODUCTIVE THEORY

A productive social science theory

- is falsifiable;
- states hypotheses as specifically as possible;
- is as parsimonious as possible;
- addresses an important social phenomenon;
- is internally consistent; i.e., the hypotheses do not contradict one another;
- is coherent and comprehensible;
- specifies its relevant constructs and how they are measured;
- agrees with what is already known about the topic;
- explains data better than existing theories on the same topic;
- agrees with existing theories about related topics;
- generates new insights about the topic.

findings that would contradict the theory. In other words, a falsifiable hypothesis is one in which a researcher can set up an empirical test in such a manner that if the findings turned out in a given way, the researcher would agree that the hypothesis had been disproven. The falsifiability criterion of a theory is often difficult for students to understand abstractly, so we borrow an analogy from Meehl's (1978) classic article to illustrate it. We could predict that the high temperature tomorrow will fall between -100° and +200° Fahrenheit. This is not a useful hypothesis because it is not falsifiable; no matter what happens tomorrow, it will support the hypothesis. A hypothesis that allows for every possible outcome actually explains nothing. On the other hand, a hypothesis predicting that tomorrow the high temperature will fall between 70° and 74° Fahrenheit is both eminently falsifiable and—if supported—potentially very useful.

This example makes two points: First, falsifiability is a necessary and minimum requirement for a theory. Second, the more specific a hypothesis is, the more useful the theory becomes. Meehl (1978) argued that science progresses to the extent that theories have been subjected to and passed risky (i.e., specific) tests and that the more such risky tests a theory has survived, the better corroborated it is. In Meehl's words, "a theory that makes precise predictions and correctly picks out *narrow intervals* or *point intervals* out of the range of experimental possibilities is a pretty strong theory" (p. 818; emphasis in original).

Obviously, the ultimate criterion by which we need to evaluate theories is whether they provide compelling explanations and interpretations for the world around us. There are actually two components to this criterion. First, a productive or useful theory is one that addresses some important or significant phenomenon or social behavior that needs explication (e.g., violence in the classroom). Second, the theory must provide a plausible and empirically defensible explanation for that phenomenon.

An implication of this criterion is, first, that a theory can be particularly important or productive at one particular time but not at others. Phenomena that seem to demand attention change with time. During the late 1980s, environmental hazards were of major public concern. Early in the new millennium, violence in schools seems to be a major social phenomenon that captures our attention. So theories are used and are productive in part if they address phenomena that are socially significant at a particular historical moment.

The second component to this criterion is that a useful theory provides a plausible and empirically defensible explanation for the phenomenon. Again, this component can be broken down further. A plausible explanation means that the theory must be internally consistent, coherent, and comprehensible. It must be accessible to those who use it, that is, who conduct the research in support of it, and it must not run entirely counter to common sense or ordinary explanations. It should be more parsimonious and/or do a better job of explaining research findings than existing theories on the topic. In addition, to be productive of research and to be empirically defensible, the theory must be relatively specific about its constructs and how they are to be measured. This means that a productive theory necessarily includes hypotheses about the links between variables and constructs.

There are other criteria for defining a useful or productive theory. One is that the theory must be consistent with both existing research findings and existing theories for related phenomena. The need to be consistent with known research findings is obvious; there is little utility in proposing a theory that has already been disproven. The need to be consistent with related theories is less obvious but also important. For instance, a theory about human memory must be relatively consistent with existing theories about reading comprehension, judgment, and perception. Memory does not exist independently of these other cognitive phenomena and neither can an adequate theory of memory. Similarly, a theory about the origins and effects of poverty cannot afford to ignore current theoretical approaches to relations between ethnicity and crime. The phenomena are linked, and so, too, must be the theories.

Finally, a productive theory is one that opens up new insights or offers the possibility of unforeseen implications. That is, good theories grow and prosper as individual researchers examine their implications and build them up logically. Useful theories offer the possibility of growth, allowing researchers to think about connections that they would not have thought about otherwise. This aspect of theory development is exemplified in computer simulations for theory development. When a theory identifies a complex set of interrelated phenomena and is specific about the forms of the associations among them, a computer can often examine the dynamic implications of the theory. Such simulations often provide new and empirically testable hypotheses that derive from the theory's basic postulates and that might not have been seen otherwise, for example, Latané's (1990) theory about individuals' behavior in groups, Hastie's (1988) theory about memory for people, and Nowak, Vallacher, Tesser, and Borkowski's (2000) dynamic model of self-regulation.

The Functions of Research in Constructing Theories

In general, the purpose of conducting empirical research is to test hypotheses derived from theories. Typically, empirical research is conducted to examine hypotheses about the associations among the constructs specified in the theory. In doing this sort of research, we usually make assumptions about the second sort of hypotheses, that is, those linking the constructs with variables, observable indicators of the unobservable constructs. For instance, we might conduct research designed to demonstrate that interracial contact decreases prejudice. In the process, we make assumptions about how both constructs, interracial contact and prejudice, are to be measured.

Although research that examines hypotheses of the first sort, causal associations among constructs, is perhaps more typical, research on hypotheses of the second sort is also a major occupation of social scientists. Research designed to examine whether a given variable accurately or validly measures a given construct is called measurement research. **Measurement research,** sometimes referred to as psychometric or sociometric research, usually is conducted by examining whether two or more ways of measuring the same construct give the same results. As will become apparent in later portions of this chapter and Chapter 4, such research is vitally important to the success of research examining hypothesized causal associations among constructs. Only if we can successfully manipulate, observe, or measure the constructs of interest can we empirically examine hypotheses about the causal associations among them.

We have said that the purpose of conducting empirical research is to examine hypotheses. At this point we need to be more specific about what this means. There are four different functions or purposes of empirical research that, in total, constitute the process of examining social science hypotheses: (1) discovery, (2) demonstration, (3) refutation, and (4) replication.

Discovery Researchers frequently gather information to attempt to discover what might be responsible for some phenomenon or behavior. For instance, in studying depressed clients, we might interview and observe the clients' families to see if there are any patterns of interaction that might be responsible for the depression. In doing such systematic observation, we do not as yet have a well-defined hypothesis about the causes of depression. Rather, we are attempting to **discover** what might be plausible causes of constructs. Thus, research as discovery is used primarily to develop or generate hypotheses. When conducting research for this purpose, the researcher is operating in what is called an **inductive** manner, attempting to move from observation to the development of hypotheses, rather than the other way around, which is known as working deductively. Of course, research never serves solely as a discovery function. In other words, the researcher never exclusively operates inductively. There is always some ill-defined or implicit theoretical orientation that guides the research, even when the researchers have no explicit hypotheses they are examining. For instance, in the depression example, a researcher who interviews family members implicitly assumes that causes of the depression might lie in the family and their interactions with the client. A researcher who believes that depression is a result of a genetic or neurochemical malfunction would never look for causes in patterns of family interaction. In other words, without some kind of underlying or implicit theory, a researcher would not know where to begin looking for the causes of a given phenomenon or behavior. It is simply not possible to conduct research as pure discovery or to proceed purely inductively. Even when research is used primarily to generate hypotheses, the researcher inevitably makes theoretical assumptions in deciding what to observe or where a potential cause might lie.

Demonstration If researchers have a hypothesis about the associations among constructs of interest, they are quite likely to gather data in an attempt to **demonstrate** or support it. Suppose, for instance, that researchers believe that living in an integrated neighborhood reduces prejudice. They might then try to generate information or make observations to demonstrate the validity of this hypothesis. For instance, they might interview residents of both integrated and segregated neighborhoods about their attitudes toward various ethnic groups. If the interviews showed that those who lived in integrated neighborhoods had more favorable attitudes, the findings from the research would be consistent with the hypothesis. Such consistency of observation with hypothesis is the best that research as demonstration can accomplish.

Research findings can only be consistent with or demonstrate a hypothesis. They can never prove the hypothesis. This point was made in the first chapter but bears repeating here. Just because residents of integrated neighborhoods express less hostility toward other ethnic groups than residents of segregated neighborhoods, it does not mean that the hypothesis, which states that integration causes a reduction in prejudice, is correct. There are always alternative explanations equally consistent with the research results. For instance, residents of integrated neighborhoods might express less hostility because they were initially less prejudiced before they moved into the neighborhood. Hence, although the research findings are consistent with the hypothesis or demonstrate that it might be correct, there always remain alternatives that might be equally consistent with the research results.

Research designed to demonstrate a hypothesis is **deductive** rather than inductive. Whereas in discovery the research is used to generate a hypothesis, here the hypothesis generates the research. Scientists, when acting deductively, start with the hypothesis, which they then seek to support or demonstrate using the information generated by empirical research.

Once again, however, the researcher's activity is never pure deduction or pure demonstration. Although it could turn out that the research results are nearly perfectly consistent with the hypothesis that motivates the research, inevitably there are some inconsistencies or results that cannot be entirely explained by the hypothesis. The researcher then proceeds inductively, examining the findings and hypothesis to determine how the hypothesis might be modified to account more perfectly for the research findings. In this way, research never exclusively serves a discovery or a demonstration function, just as the researcher never reasons exclusively deductively or inductively.

Refutation Although researchers can never conclusively prove a hypothesis, it is possible, if they proceed with care, to **refute** competing hypotheses. For instance, suppose we conduct research on the "integration reduces prejudice" hypothesis that we have been discussing. Suppose we find that residents of integrated neighborhoods express less hostility than residents of segregated neighborhoods. We might then want to refute the competing or alternative hypothesis that residents of the two neighborhoods differed in prejudice initially, before they moved into the segregated or integrated neighborhoods. To do so we would have to conduct further research, interviewing people when they first move into integrated neighborhoods and then following them over time. If we found that initially they expressed hostility equal to that of segregated residents but that over time they developed more positive attitudes, we would have generated evidence to refute the competing hypothesis.

The process of supporting a hypothesis, and ultimately a theory that is made up of numerous hypotheses, is one of demonstration and repeated refutation of alternative hypotheses. Although in a formal sense there are always alternatives as yet unrefuted, the remaining alternatives become more and more far-fetched, and gradually we develop confidence in a hypothesis through repeated demonstration and repeated refutations of alternatives to it. This brings us to the fourth purpose of research.

Replication In the first chapter we argued that the researcher's biases inevitably affect how observations are gathered and interpreted. The only way to overcome these biases is to replicate the research. **Replication** means that other researchers in other settings with different samples attempt to reproduce the research. If the results of the replication are consistent with the original research, we have increased confidence in the hypothesis that the original study supported.

These then are the ways research is used to develop, examine, support, and modify hypotheses. The functions or purposes of empirical research in examining hypotheses are not mutually exclusive. Any given study is likely to serve a number of functions simultaneously. Research to demonstrate a hypothesis usually ends up as discovery as well. Likewise, replication inevitably involves discovery and refutation, as the conditions of replication change and hypotheses must be modified to account for those changes.

The purpose of empirical research is to inform hypotheses, to enable us to build better and more accurate hypotheses about how human beings behave. Of course, not all research is equally informative or useful in constructing and modifying hypotheses. It is to this issue that we now turn: What makes empirical research useful or not in helping us to discover, demonstrate, revise, and ultimately support hypotheses?

Criteria for Evaluating Social Science Research

To discuss these criteria we will use one of the example hypotheses presented earlier:

> Crowded classrooms in inner-city schools adversely affect educational achievement.

Let us suppose that we want to examine whether this is a reasonable hypothesis. To do so, we want to gather information in such a way that our observations will be most informative about the merits of the hypothesis.

Construct Validity

To conduct research that will help determine whether this is a good or bad hypothesis and whether it should be modified in some way, we first need to measure successfully the theoretical constructs of interest. Clearly, if the researcher never examined a variable that was intended to represent educational achievement, the research would not be very useful in figuring out whether the hypothesis needs modification. In this hypothesis two constructs are involved: Degree of crowdedness in classrooms is the first, and it is the causal one. Educational achievement is the second, and it is hypothesized to be an effect. Both of these must be measured successfully for the research to be useful in informing the hypothesis that motivates it. The variable used to measure the causal construct, crowdedness of classrooms, is called the **independent variable.** The variable used to assess the affected construct, educational achievement, is the **dependent variable.** These labels refer to the fact that the affected variable is presumed by the hypothesis to be dependent on the causal variables. The degree to which both the independent and dependent variables accurately reflect or measure the constructs of interest is known as the **construct validity** of the research. If a study has high construct validity, all the constructs in the hypothesis that motivated the research have been successfully measured or captured by the specific variables on which the researcher has gathered data.

Internal Validity

Assume we had met the first criterion for useful research, and we had good measures of both the degree of crowdedness in classrooms and students' achievement. Suppose we then gathered information on a number of classrooms and found, indeed, that in more crowded classrooms students in fact did less well. Certainly this result is consistent with the hypothesis. What we do not know, however, is whether our research supports the notion that crowdedness *causes* a decrease in achievement. The second criterion for useful or informative research, known as **internal validity,** concerns the extent to which conclusions can be drawn about the causal effects of one variable on another. In research with high internal validity, we are relatively more able to argue that associations are causal ones, whereas in studies with low internal validity, causality cannot be inferred as confidently. Later in this chapter, we describe how studies can be designed to maximize internal validity.

External Validity

A final criterion for useful research concerns the extent to which one can generalize the results of the research to the populations and settings of interest in the hypothesis. This is known as the research study's **external validity.** In the example we are considering, suppose the constructs were well measured (high construct validity). Suppose further that we found an association between crowdedness and achievement and could reasonably claim that association to be a causal one (high internal validity). We then would want to know further whether that causal association held in only the relatively few classrooms we observed in our research or whether we could generalize the causal associations to other classrooms that we did not observe. The hypothesis states that the effect appears in all inner-city classrooms. Clearly it would not be possible to observe them all. But we might select a few to observe so that we would have confidence in generalizing the results of our research to other classrooms. Such a study has relatively high external validity. A study from which generalization is difficult has relatively low external validity.

Although all three of these validities, summarized in Table 2.2, are important in evaluating research, their relative importance depends on the purposes the research is designed to serve. For instance, in the early stages of a research program, it might be sufficient initially to measure constructs that are associated with the behavior of interest, without worrying too much for the time being about whether the association is a causal one. In other words, in discovery research, construct validity might be relatively more important than internal validity. Or consider research whose primary purpose is

TABLE 2.2 Definitions of Research Validities

Construct validity:	To what extent are the constructs of theoretical interest successfully operationalized in the research?
Internal validity:	To what extent does the research design permit us to reach causal conclusions about the effect of the independent variable on the dependent variable?
External validity:	To what extent can we generalize from the research sample and setting to the populations and settings specified in the research hypothesis?

replication. It might be argued that such research is especially concerned with external validity because in replication we are concerned with whether a previously obtained result continues to be found in a new setting at a different time. Because the conditions of the original research and the replication are never exactly identical, we are always examining issues of generalizability in conducting replication research.

The remainder of this chapter concerns the factors that determine whether a study has high or low construct, internal, and external validity; however, our discussion here serves only as an introduction to the subject of how valid and informative empirical research is designed and conducted. The major portion of this book is devoted to this topic as well. Hence, the remaining pages in this chapter serve as an introduction to many of the later chapters, in which the same issues are considered in greater detail.

Maximizing Construct Validity

In Chapter 4 we extensively examine the issue of construct validity—how we measure what we want to measure. Our discussion here provides a preliminary idea about how we decide whether given variables measure the constructs of interest.

Suppose we wanted to measure the school achievement of children in different classrooms to test our hypothesis about the deleterious effects of crowded classrooms. There are a number of ways to measure achievement. We could give the students achievement tests, we could look at students' grades, we could ask teachers to evaluate their students verbally, and so forth. Each of these measures of achievement is called a variable. Earlier we defined a variable as any attribute that varies across the people or things that we are measuring. Another way to look at variables is to consider them simply as rules or ways of classifying people into different categories so that those who are in the same category are more similar in some way of interest than those who are in different categories. For instance, scores on an achievement test constitute a variable that is thought to measure achievement. If we line up students according to their scores on the achievement test, we believe that students close together in that rank order are more similar on achievement than students farther apart.

Actually, however, variables never measure only the construct of interest. They measure other irrelevant characteristics as well. Think about an achievement test. To some extent it does measure that which we call achievement; however, it also probably measures test-taking anxiety, motivation to do well on the day the test was administered, ability to read English, and so forth. Each of these other factors, over and above pure achievement, influences to some extent whether the student gets a relatively high or low score on the achievement test. Thus, to some extent, the achievement test is a measure of each of these other factors as well as of pure achievement. In sum, variables measure not only the construct of interest but also what we might call **constructs of disinterest**—things we would rather not measure. Finally, any variable is likely to contain within it random errors of measurement. We might, for instance, suspect that the scores of some students are affected by coding or grading errors or whether they were not feeling well that day.

As shown in Figure 2.1, any variable is therefore most likely made up of three different components: (1) the construct of interest, (2) other things that we do not want to measure—constructs of disinterest, and (3) random errors. Thus, if we lined students up in order of their scores on the test, that order would not be identical to the ordering that would result if somehow we could line them up according to their true achievement. Motivation, test-taking anxiety, and random errors are also responsible in part for the ordering of students based on their achievement test performance.

A variable that has a great deal of construct validity is one that mostly measures the construct of interest, with minimal contributions from constructs of disinterest and random error. Given this, how do we know the degree to which any given variable has construct validity? Because we cannot measure true achievement directly, we cannot

FIGURE 2.1 THREE COMPONENTS OF A VARIABLE

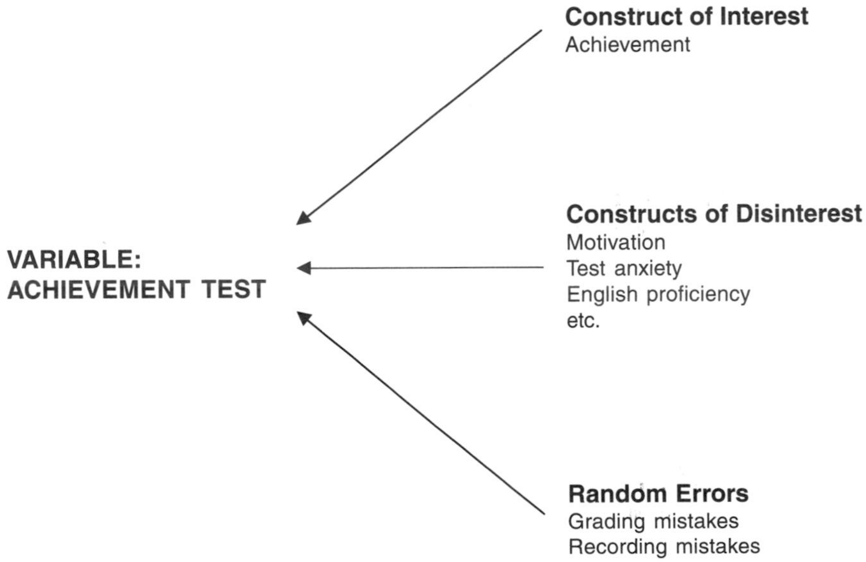

know whether the rank ordering of students on the test is similar to the rank ordering of students on true achievement. The only solution is to measure other variables that we think are also measures of achievement. For instance, we could look at school grades. School grades probably measure achievement, that is, the construct of interest, but they probably measure other things as well, like teachers' biases and preferences, students' extraversion, and so forth. We therefore compare the ordering of students on what we think are our two measures of achievement, test scores and grades. If the two orderings are similar, and if we believe that the only thing these two variables measure in common is achievement, the similarity of their orderings is evidence for their construct validity.

Let us review the general point. Because all variables measure not only the construct of interest but other things as well, and because we cannot positively know the order of people on the true construct, the best we can do is measure another variable that we think also assesses the construct of interest and then compare orders on the two variables. If two variables that we think measure the same construct give us similar orderings of people, we have increased confidence that, in fact, each of them is measuring, among other things, that construct that we think they have in common. Most fundamentally, to assure ourselves that our research has construct validity, we need to measure each construct in more than one way. Only if the different ways of measuring constructs give similar results can we have confidence that our variables in fact capture the constructs of interest. Construct validity is best examined by employing *multiple operational definitions*, or multiple ways of measuring, and then comparing them to see whether they seem to be measuring the same things.

The need for multiple operational definitions, and how, more specifically, we examine the quality of our variables are discussed in much greater detail in Chapter 4. Here we wish to stress the importance of construct validity to research. If empirical research is to be useful or informative in examining hypotheses, it must measure the constructs to which the hypotheses refer. If the observed variables do not have construct validity, there is no way the research can inform our theory. Even worse, poor construct validity can actually mislead researchers by yielding seemingly positive results that in actuality do not reflect the constructs of interest. Contributing to this problem is the fact that detecting poor construct validity is harder than detecting problems with other types of validity. For example, there is a set of widely known and accepted procedures for documenting adequate internal validity, and if the criteria for establishing internal validity are not present in a given study, it is obvious to other researchers. As we will see in Chapter 4, though, establishing construct validity is more challenging, and unless the authors of a research report are careful in describing their measures and validation procedures, it might not be clear to readers that a given construct is or is not valid.

Maximizing Internal Validity

In Chapters 11 and 13, we discuss different research designs. Differences among designs affect the internal validity of a study—the extent to which we can infer causal connections from an association between two variables. Our discussion of internal validity here is intended to provide an intuitive understanding of how to maximize our ability to argue for causal connections in the research we do.

In the crowded classrooms example, suppose we went into 100 classrooms and measured their degree of crowdedness and the average student's achievement. Suppose further that our research had perfect construct validity: Our measures of both crowdedness and achievement measured those constructs and nothing else. Finally, suppose we found that the average student's achievement score was 10 points lower in classrooms that were classified as crowded than in classrooms that were not crowded. In other words, we found that the two variables, crowdedness and achievement, were related in the predicted way. Could we argue from this association that we have evidence for a causal effect of crowdedness on lowered achievement? We could not.

A simple empirical association, or **correlation,** between two variables is not enough to infer that one causes the other. Simply showing that people or classrooms that have high scores on one variable (i.e., degree of crowdedness) have low scores on a second (i.e., achievement) does not necessarily mean that one variable causes the other. To argue for causality, there must be an association, but by itself an association between two variables is not sufficient. Inappropriately inferring causality from a simple association between two variables is called the **correlational fallacy.** This is a simple yet utterly important concept. We often tell our students that if there is only one thing they remember from this text 10 years from now, we hope that it will be that "correlation does not imply causality."

Consider a few classic examples in which associations exist between two variables yet clearly there is no causal effect of one on the other. Among elementary schoolchildren it is certainly the case that those children having larger feet are better readers. The two variables of shoe size and reading ability are clearly related to each other. Does that mean that size of feet affects reading ability? Certainly not. Age affects both, and that is why foot size and reading ability are related. Older children tend both to have larger feet and to be better readers. Another example: In England in the last century it was noticed that more babies were born where more storks were roosting. Does that mean that the presence of storks assures many births? No. What accounts for the association is population density. Where there are lots of people, there are lots of chimneys, where storks are fond of roosting. Likewise, where there are lots of people, there are lots of babies. Hence, storks and babies are found together.

In sum, whenever two variables are associated with each other, there are four possible explanations for why they are associated: (1) variable X can cause variable Y; (2) variable Y can cause variable X; (3) variables X and Y can cause each other; or (4) some third variable, Z, can cause both X and Y. This latter possibility is often called the "hidden third variable" problem, hidden because the researcher might have only measured X and Y but not Z. Figure 2.2 illustrates these four possibilities with a research question of social importance: What is the nature of the association between media violence and aggression in children? The research findings are very clear on the existence of an association: As the amount of media violence watched by children

FIGURE 2.2

Possible Causal Pathways to Explain The Association Between Exposure to Media Violence and Aggression

Nature of Association	Example
$X \rightarrow Y$	Watching media violence (X) causes children to become more aggressive (Y)
$X \leftarrow Y$	Aggression in children causes them to seek out and watch more violence in the media
$X \leftrightarrows Y$	Watching media violence causes aggression, and aggression causes children to watch more violence in the media
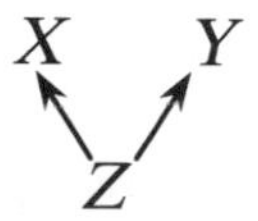	Lack of parental attention and supervision (Z) causes children to become more aggressive as well as to watch more violence in the media

increases, so does their aggression (although this association is generally weaker than most people assume). What is not so clear is whether this association is causal and, if so, which construct is the cause and which is the effect. As Figure 2.2. shows, there are four possible explanations for the association between exposure to media violence and aggression. Perhaps watching violence on television does in fact make children more aggressive—the interpretation preferred by the public and lawmakers. But it is also possible the causal path runs in the opposite direction and that aggressive children deliberately seek out and watch more violent television programming; indeed, there are research findings to support this contention. To make things even more complicated, it is possible that both of these hypotheses are true and that media violence and aggression cause each other in a complicated pattern over time called **reciprocal causation.** Lastly, it is also possible there is a third variable that causes both aggression and the watching of violent television programming; inadequate parental attention and supervision, for example, is one such plausible third variable.

Readers might be tempted to ask if it matters which of the causal pathways is the true one. Is it not more important to show that two variables are associated and less necessary to show how? The answer is that it matters a great deal. Scientists are in the business not only of describing and predicting events but also of controlling events. In the social sciences, especially, we wish ultimately to put our findings to the use and benefit of humankind; however, in order to design an effective intervention for some social problem, we must be able to identify the precise cause of a targeted behavior. Returning to the media violence example, if watching media violence causes aggression, then a campaign that encourages or requires the entertainment industry to decrease the amount of gratuitous violence in television shows and movies would be an effective way of reducing aggression; however, if the cause of aggression is actually inadequate parenting, legislation to require reductions in media violence will accomplish no good and serve only as unnecessary censorship and abridgment of First Amendment rights. Instead, a better intervention would be geared toward improving parenting skills. Identifying the correct causal direction, if the two constructs are causally related, is crucial.

We stress this point because this is an area in which the public is occasionally misled by the news media or other information outlets such as the Internet. Frequently, findings of research studies are presented in a distorted manner because reporters or news anchors draw an inappropriate causal conclusion from a correlational finding. This is done even if the researchers who conducted the study were very careful when reporting their findings to draw appropriate conclusions. For example, a newspaper headline might state "Exercise Makes Pregnancy Easier" and the accompanying article claim that pregnant women who exercise regularly have shorter and less painful deliveries and healthier babies. The causal claim is explicit: Readers are told that it is exercise that elicits these beneficial effects. But a careful reading reveals that the scientists had available only correlational data; that is, pregnant women were asked how often they exercised, and frequency of exercise was then related to pregnancy outcomes.

We are not trying to argue here that exercise is not good for pregnant women. In all likelihood, exercise does in fact cause better deliveries and healthier babies. Our point is merely that we are unable to draw that conclusion on the basis of the research finding presented in the hypothetical newspaper article. Other explanations exist for the association between exercise and pregnancy outcomes. Women who are concerned with their health in general probably engage in a variety of activities in addition to exercising that are good for their unborn babies. For instance, they might avoid drinking alcohol or smoking during pregnancy; their diets might be healthier; they might take prenatal vitamins; or they might obtain better prenatal care overall. And it could be one or more of these other factors, not exercise, that account for the positive outcomes. As detailed in Chapter 11, the only way we can conclude that exercise was the causal factor is to conduct a randomized experiment.

These kinds of misrepresentations of scientific research abound. And because the misrepresentations usually sound plausible, readers too often fall into the trap of agreeing with the causal claim. Our hope for readers of this book is that, if we cannot convince you to become a practicing social scientist, at least we would like you to become an educated consumer of findings from empirical research on social behavior. We invite readers to scrutinize newspapers, magazines, and reports on the Web with a critical eye, looking for inappropriately drawn causal inferences. Their frequency will be both surprising and disheartening. Do not be drawn in by them.

To illustrate other threats to internal validity, we return to our example of crowded classrooms and achievement. Let us assume that those classrooms classified as crowded were found to have lower average achievement than those classified as uncrowded. We cannot argue for causality in this case because it is possible that students in the crowded classrooms were less able initially than students in the less crowded classrooms. In other words, the differences in achievement might predate the students' experiences in one classroom or another. Perhaps crowded classrooms are more common in poorer school districts, and so students in crowded classrooms are of substantially lower socioeconomic status than students in less crowded classrooms. Alternatively, students might be selectively placed in crowded or uncrowded classrooms according to their initial ability. Such selective placement could be intentional or not, but in either case it is clearly a reason for refraining from inferring causality. Selective placement is known, therefore, as the **selection threat** to internal validity.

How might we get around this selection threat? One way might be for us as researchers to place students in either crowded or uncrowded classrooms in such a way that we knew there were no initial differences in achievement. If we could do so, we might have confidence that any differences in achievement later on were not due to initial achievement differences. To do this we might find a group of children and measure their achievement initially. Suppose we then match boys and girls on their achievement scores, putting all the matched boys in the crowded classrooms and all the girls in the uncrowded ones. For every boy who initially had a score of 10 on the achievement test, we would find a girl with an identical score. We would then place the matched children in the crowded and uncrowded classrooms, boys in the former and girls in the latter. Such matching would mean that initially the two groups of students would not differ in achievement.

If after such matching to equate the groups initially we later found differences between classrooms, with those in crowded classrooms doing less well, we might be tempted to argue for a causal effect of crowdedness; however, we might still be in error. Although the boys in the crowded classrooms might initially have the same achievement scores as the girls in the uncrowded classrooms, they might be changing on their own at a different rate. That is, even if crowdedness of classroom made absolutely no difference to achievement, we might still observe differences between boys and girls at the end of a few months, even though they were initially the same, simply because they were changing or learning on their own at different rates. The problem is not that the boys and girls differ initially; that problem has been eliminated by matching. The problem is that the two groups could be growing or changing at different speeds. Hence, if we find a difference in achievement at a later time, we cannot infer confidently that the difference is caused by the difference in classroom crowdedness. The problem that we have just discussed—that is, the difficulty of reaching causal conclusions because the individuals in the two kinds of classrooms might be growing or maturing at different rates even though they were the same initially—is known as the **selection by maturation threat** to internal validity.

What we need is some way to equate the children in the two types of classrooms not only now but also in the future. We need to assign them to classrooms in such a way that if crowdedness had no effect on achievement, we would find no achievement difference between the two groups of children at a later time. Unfortunately, there is no such characteristic of the children, such as their gender, that we can use. Any characteristic might be related to achievement later, even if it is not now, and hence we would find differences between the two types of classrooms later even if crowdedness had no effect on achievement.

There really is only one type of variable that we could use to assign children to type of classroom to accomplish our goal. Suppose for each child we flipped a coin. Is there any reason to expect that heads or tails is related to a child's achievement now or in the future? Certainly not; just as we would not expect the result of the coin toss to be related to hair color or height. By definition, a variable whose values are randomly determined, like the flip of a coin or the throw of a die, is unrelated on average to all other variables now and in the future. Hence, if we decided who was to be in the crowded classroom and who in the uncrowded by a flip of a coin, we would expect no differences in achievement later if crowdedness made no difference.

Instead of achievement, think about hair color for a minute. Suppose we put students in crowded or uncrowded classrooms according to whether they got heads or tails on a coin toss. We certainly would not expect that as a result of our coin toss, all the brunettes would wind up in one type of class and all the blondes in the other. Rather, we would expect both types of classes to have a mixture of brunettes and blondes. Because, presumably, the type of class has no effect on hair color, we would expect the same mixture of brunettes and blondes in each type of class both now and in the future. Similarly, if achievement were unaffected by crowdedness, and if we randomly decided who was in which type of classroom, we would expect to find no difference between classrooms in achievement at a later time. If we did find a difference, we would believe that it must have been caused by crowdedness.

The moral of this example is that we can confidently infer causality from the association between two variables only if people have been randomly assigned to the levels of the independent variables. Degree of crowdedness is the independent variable in our example and it has two levels: crowded and uncrowded. If it is related to achievement later and if children were assigned to its levels (or type of classroom) on a random basis, we can argue that it had a causal effect on achievement, the dependent variable. Causal inference is possible only when students or other participants have been randomly assigned to levels of the independent variable. (Remember that the independent variable is the one that represents the causal construct in the hypothesis.) Research studies carried out in this manner, with random assignment to the independent variable, are called **randomized experiments.** They are discussed in considerable detail in Chapter 11.

Although randomized experiments are the best choice if causal conclusions are important in research, they require the researcher to have a great deal of control. The researcher must be able to determine who is in which sort of classroom, for example. Frequently, such control over the independent variable is impossible. It would be quite unusual if a school system and parents allowed a researcher to decide which students were assigned to which type of classroom. When such control is not possible, some type of **quasi-experimental research** design is used instead of a randomized experimental design. These research designs are discussed in Chapter 13. Briefly, quasi-experiments are those in which research participants are not, and perhaps could not be, randomly assigned to levels of all independent variables implicated in the hypothesis. Although they do not permit causal inferences with the same degree of confidence as randomized experiments do, they are essential tools for the social scientist. In the social sciences, there are frequently practical and ethical considerations that force the researcher to use some design other than a randomized experimental one. Although some internal validity is sacrificed, quasi-experiments can still yield exceedingly rich and useful information. Randomized experiments are nice, but they are not the only tools in the researcher's bag.

Maximizing External Validity

In Chapters 8, 9, and 10 we look at procedures designed to increase the external validity of research—procedures to increase our ability to generalize the research results to the populations and settings of theoretical interest. As we did with the other validities, our purpose in this section is to introduce the material covered in detail in later chapters.

Returning to our example once again, suppose we had measured both constructs, crowdedness and achievement, well and had done what we could to ensure internal validity; how would we ensure that our research results were generalizable to the extent we desired? First, it is necessary to specify before the research is conducted the limits of desired generalization. Rather than remaining implicit in the hypothesis, the population and setting to which generalization is sought should be made explicit. We need to define precisely the group of people and the settings for which we think our hypothesis holds. For instance, we might say that crowded classrooms adversely affect achievement in fourth through sixth grades in schools located in cities having more than 500,000 residents. In this example we wish to generalize to a population of classrooms in schools. The more precise we can be about which classrooms we are concerned with, the easier the generalization becomes.

Ideally, if cost and time did not matter, we might gather data from all classrooms in the population of classrooms. That is, we might see if crowdedness and student achievement are related across all fourth through sixth grade classrooms in all large cities in the country. If we gather data from the entire population and find support for our hypothesis, generalization to the desired population is not a problem.

However, it is not efficient (nor is it necessary) to measure every classroom or every person in the population and settings of interest. Rather, we can only afford to gather data from a sample taken from that population. To enhance generalization, we want to select a sample so that it is as similar as possible to the population as a whole. What we want is a sample that is representative of the population. How do we obtain it? Suppose we selected only fourth grade classrooms. Are they representative of all fourth through sixth grade classrooms? Probably not. Suppose we selected for our sample all fourth through sixth grade classrooms in one particular city. Would they be representative? Probably not. The only way we can be confident about generalizing from a sample to a population of interest is to draw a **random sample.** That means that instead of using any characteristic of the classroom (e.g., fourth grade only or one city only) to decide which ones are in the sample, we use a variable whose values are randomly determined. We do something like flipping a coin to determine the classrooms from which we gather data.

It is important to be clear that flipping a coin to select a sample from a population, random sampling, is not the same thing as flipping a coin to decide which children are assigned to which type of classroom, random assignment. Using a random process to select a sample from a population is done to enhance our ability to generalize, that is, external validity. Using a random process to decide who is in which type of classroom is done to increase internal validity, that is, our ability to reach causal conclusions about the effects of classroom crowdedness.

Frequently in the social sciences it is not practical to draw a random sample. We might wish to generalize to classrooms across the country, but we simply cannot afford to travel across the country to measure crowdedness and achievement in our randomly drawn sample. Generalization must then be done on a theoretical basis. We must speculate about how classrooms that we have not observed might differ from those we have, and then we must decide if those differences should influence whether crowdedness affects achievement. Such speculation ultimately gives rise to further research to increase our confidence in its conclusion. Hence, replicating research in other settings and with other samples is an important part of maximizing external validity.

Summary

There are two major foci of this chapter. In the first, the purposes of empirical research for the scientific study of social behavior were examined. We argued that research is used fundamentally to examine hypotheses. As such, research can be used for discovery, demonstration, refutation, and replication.

Discovery is the inductive process of gathering data to formulate hypotheses. Demonstration is predominantly a deductive process, gathering data that we hope are consistent with a hypothesis. Although such demonstrations can be used to support a hypothesis, the hypothesis can never in fact be proven because there always remain alternative ways to account for a research finding. Research as refutation involves the attempt to refute competing hypotheses, that is, to show that alternative explanations for previous results are not in fact valid. Finally, research as replication involves repeating research with different samples or in different settings to gain increased confidence in a previous demonstration. In all four cases, discovery, demonstration, refutation, and replication, the ultimate reason for gathering empirical data is to support, evaluate, and refine our hypotheses so that they do a better job of describing social behavior.

In the second half of the chapter we defined three criteria that determine the extent to which research is useful in examining hypotheses: construct validity, internal validity, and external validity. Research has high construct validity if the variables that are in fact measured correspond closely to the constructs that the hypotheses implicate. Research that is internally valid permits us to reach causal conclusions about the association between the independent and dependent variables. Finally, in research that is high in external validity, we can generalize the results from the sample studied to the population and settings of interest. In addition to defining these validities, we also discussed on an intuitive level the necessary conditions for achieving each one. This discussion serves to introduce the more complete presentations in the next chapters.

Key Concepts

construct validity
constructs of disinterest
correlation
correlational fallacy
deductive research
demonstration
dependent variable
discovery
external validity
falsifiability
hypothesis
independent variable
inductive research
internal validity
measurement research
quasi-experimental research
random sample
randomized experiment
reciprocal causation
refutation
replication
selection by maturation threat
selection threat
theory
variable

On the Web

http://www.burns.com/wcbspurcorl.htm Very clearly written discussion of the correlational fallacy, with lots of examples and quotes from relevant readings.

http://faculty.washington.edu/chudler/stat3.html Great Web page entitled "how to lie and cheat with statistics." Reviews how graphs and charts can be misleadingly created and reported in the media. Nicely done and interactive.

http://www.cogs.susx.ac.uk/users/martinl/ITAI/paper.pdf A pdf version of a paper by Martin Langham, "Psychologists at Work: Hazardous Conclusions Possible." Although written for accident investigators, it is a good overview of how science is done and the possible flaws in reasoning that occur.

http://chem.tufts.edu/science/FrankSteiger/theory.htm Good discussion of the distinction between facts and theory, in the context of the evolutionary debate.

Further Reading

Cross, C. (1996). *The tainted truth: The manipulation of facts in America.* New York: Simon & Schuster.

Huff, D. (1993). *How to lie with statistics.* New York: Norton.

Meehl, P. E. (1978). Theoretical risks and tabular asterisks: Sir Karl, Sir Ronald, and the slow progress of soft psychology. *Journal of Consulting and Clinical Psychology, 46,* 806–834.

Paulos, J. A. (1995). *A mathematician reads the newspaper.* New York: Anchor Books.

CHAPTER

3

Ethical Principles

The Tuskegee Syphilis Study

In 1932, a 40-year longitudinal study was begun by the U.S. Public Health Service to determine what the natural course of syphilis would be if left untreated. Four hundred African-American men in Tuskegee, Alabama, who had syphilis were compared with 200 uninfected men. Participants were recruited with promises of "special free treatment" for "bad blood." The researchers never explicitly told the participants that they had syphilis. This "special treatment" was actually spinal taps (performed without anesthesia, by the way) administered to detect the neurological effects of syphilis. Even though it was known as early as the 1940s that penicillin was an effective treatment for syphilis, the 400 infected men were never informed of that fact, nor were they ever treated with penicillin. In 1972, public outcry arising from the first media accounts of the study caused the government to halt the study. By that time, only 74 of the original 400 test participants were alive. Of those who had died, at least 28—but possibly more than 100—had died as a direct result of complications of syphilis.

What is right to do to people in the name of science? Is it ethically justified to withhold treatment from people in order to learn more about a disease and therefore, hopefully, help many more people in the future? Is it ethically justified to study people without their knowing that they are part of a study? Is it ethically justified to lie to people about the procedures they are undergoing as part of the study? In the example of the Tuskegee study, the research procedures that were followed were clearly ethically wrong. But it would be equally wrong to conclude that control (i.e., untreated) groups should *never* be used or that experimenters should *never* deceive their experimental participants. In this chapter, we describe first the history of concerns regarding ethical issues surrounding social science research with human participants; outline the three broad ethical principles that underlie the formal regulations that have been created to deal with these issues; describe examples of specific ethical issues relevant in

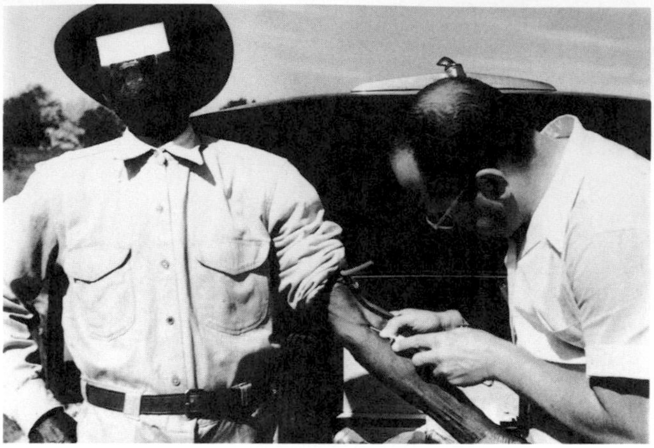

A physician, working from the trunk of a car, draws blood from a participant in the Tuskegee Syphilis Study. (Photograph from Records of the Centers for Disease Control and Prevention, maintained by the National Archives.)

dealing with experimental, quasi-experimental, and nonexperimental research; and we close with a case study illustrating the ethical review process.

Why Did Ethical Concerns Arise?

What makes the social sciences unique from the physical sciences is that the subject matter of the social sciences is people—living, sentient beings with feelings and thoughts of their own. Geologists who study rocks do not first ask the rocks' permission to study them, nor do the geologists have any qualms about smashing the rocks to pieces to study them. Because the objects studied by social scientists are humans, we have a special obligation as researchers to safeguard their rights and dignity.

Most students are aware, if vaguely, of the fact that almost all research with human participants in the United States is regulated by mysterious bodies called **Institutional Review Boards,** or **IRBs.** As we will describe in detail later, before a particular study is allowed to be carried out, the investigator must have the procedures approved in advance by an IRB. What students might not be aware of is that IRBs are a fairly recent institution, dating back to 1974. A federal investigation of the Tuskegee study concluded that the study was unethical and that the men should have been provided with penicillin. The outcome of this investigation led to the passing of the National Research Act in 1974, requiring that all federally funded research with human participants be approved in advance by an IRB. Prior to that time, there was no federal or institutional oversight of human research, and investigators were able to do whatever they wanted with their human participants.

It is important for readers to keep in mind that the vast majority of research carried out before the creation of IRBs was harmless, but a few studies attracted considerable public attention and dismay because participants were physically harmed, seriously deceived, or placed under substantial stress. The most notorious examples of ethical abuses were seen in medical studies, with perhaps the most flagrantly immoral of these being the experiments conducted by Nazi researchers on concentration camp inmates. The Nazis were interested in developing techniques to save aviators who had fallen into frigid seas from hypothermia. To this end, they submerged concentration camp inmates in freezing water and then tried various means of reviving them. Many, however, died.

Many other infamous examples of ethically questionable studies exist. The Milgram experiments of obedience, in which participants were led to believe they were administering severe and painful shocks to an unwilling victim, created considerable controversy among both scholars and the lay public. Although Milgram took great pains to debrief his participants and follow them up to ensure they had not incurred any lasting harm, some scholars argued that the stress and unwelcome self-knowledge experienced by the participants (e.g., "I am the sort of individual who would hurt an innocent person") was so severe the study should never have been done (Baumrind, 1964).

In addition to these prominent examples, many other studies were conducted in the social sciences that involved ethically questionable procedures. It was not unusual to deceive participants through **false feedback** about their personality and intelligence. Such studies were generally designed to induce low self-esteem in participants or to investigate the reactions of individuals to threatening feedback. For example, a participant might be told that a supposed intelligence test he or she had taken earlier had been scored and revealed that the participant had subnormal intelligence. Alternatively, the participant might be told that personality tests revealed that he or she was a latent depressive. As we discuss in more detail later, these kinds of studies pose two special risks: first, that participants will be (justifiably) angry when they learn of the **deception,** and second (and more serious), that participants might not completely believe the debriefing but still cling somewhat to the original deception ("I've always been afraid I might have some depressive tendencies . . .").

In many other instances, data were collected from individuals who had not given consent for the data collection to take place or indeed were unaware that a study was taking place. In some instances, these studies involved considerable invasion of privacy. For example, in the infamous "tearoom study" (Humphreys, 1970), the experimenter posed as a "lookout" in a men's room and would watch for people entering the rest room while homosexual encounters occurred within. The experimenter would follow the homosexual men out of the rest room, surreptitiously record the license plate numbers on their cars, and determine their names and addresses through the Department of Motor Vehicles. Weeks later, he would call the men and ask to interview them, without disclosing how they were chosen for study.

The Belmont Report

The negative publicity surrounding these and other studies from that time period eventually prompted enough public concern that the federal government decided that a formal set of regulations and procedures for evaluating the ethics of studies with human participants was needed. As a direct consequence of the Tuskegee study, the U.S. Department of Health, Education, and Welfare (as it was known at the time) appointed an investigatory panel in 1972. Their findings led in 1974 to the passage of the National Research Act, which mandated that all federally funded research with human participants must first be approved by an Institutional Review Board and led to the establishment of a special commission given the charge of generating a basic set of ethical guidelines in conducting research.

The final product of this commission was the **Belmont Report.** This report lays out three overarching ethical principles—respect for persons, beneficence, and justice—and the implications of these three principles for conducting research with human participants. In this section, we discuss at length each of these ethical principles and how they are translated into research procedures.

Respect for Persons

As described in the Belmont Report, "**Respect for persons** incorporates at least two ethical convictions: first, that individuals should be treated as autonomous agents, and second, that persons with diminished autonomy are entitled to protection." The concept of autonomy, obviously an important part of this principle, means simply that human beings have the right to decide what research experiences, if any, they will be exposed to. And in those cases in which individuals have diminished autonomy—for example, because of incapacity, illness, or young age—researchers are particularly obligated to safeguard their rights. Respect for persons thus serves as the basis for the most fundamental ethical principle underlying research with human participants, which is the idea that researchers should obtain **informed consent** from people who are freely and voluntarily choosing to participate in the research.

What does it mean to obtain informed consent? In most research, it means that the participant is given a form that describes in full detail the purpose of the study, the procedures to occur during the study, risks and benefits of the research, and alternatives to participating. The participant signs the form, indicating that he or she has read the form and agrees to be in the study. Although the process of obtaining informed consent sounds straightforward, in reality it is not as easy as it appears. For many years, consent forms contained a fair amount of obtuse legalese because they were designed to conform to federal regulations. It became apparent that participants were not bothering to read or were unable to comprehend the forms they were signing, which undermines the whole point of obtaining informed consent. This was especially problematic when dealing with less-educated populations, yet it is generally those populations who are most vulnerable and who need the greatest protection of their rights. In recent years, IRBs have been working hard to create templates for consent forms that would contain all the necessary information yet be written in a user-friendly, easy-to-understand manner. The case study at the end of the chapter includes a sample of such a user-friendly consent form.

There is also a certain tension between providing adequate detail about the study versus providing so much detail that biases are introduced into it. If participants are told too much about the study ahead of time, they might be able to guess accurately the study's hypotheses, and that can influence them to behave in the way they feel they are expected to behave by the experimenter. Or, if they are feeling particularly cranky that day, they might deliberately act in a way *opposite to* what they think the experimenter expects. A good consent form describes the procedures the participant will undergo, and the risks accompanying those procedures, in enough detail that the participant can reasonably judge whether he or she wants to participate but not so much that the hypotheses are revealed.

The flip side of informed consent, and consequently respect for persons, is **coercion.** Forcing somebody to be in a research study is clearly unethical, with the Nazi medical experiments on concentration camp inmates the most egregious example. Outside of horror movies of alien abductions, this kind of coercion occurs only rarely now, if ever. However, coercion lies on a continuum, with the Nazi medical experiments and alien abductions on one end and truly free and informed choice on the other end, and it is the cases that fall in the middle that present special ethical concern.

Such cases are more common than one might think. Take, for example, a study looking at the associations among personality, drug use, and crime among a sample of prisoners. Is this coercive? If the study is presented by prison administrators, it might be perceived as coercive by the prisoners, who would feel pressure to "volunteer" for the experiment in order to gain good behavior credit or to avoid being perceived as uncooperative. Does this mean that no research on prisoners should be allowed? Not necessarily. The principle of respect for persons would imply that prisoners are human beings, too, and that it is not fair to deprive them of the opportunity to volunteer for research, especially if the research involves some sort of benefit or financial remuneration. But it does mean that, in general, a good ethical rule to follow is that the person soliciting participants for a research study should not be in a position of authority or power over the potential participants, due to the very real potential for dual role conflict or perceived coercion. For example, it would generally not be a good idea for professors to ask students in their classes to participate in their own studies because the students might not feel comfortable risking displeasing their instructor, who directly controls their grade, by saying no.

The issue of payment to participants raises other ethical concerns of coercion. What would seem like a small sum might seem very large to prisoners who do not have access to other sources of money; so large, in fact, that they feel pressured to participate even if they have misgivings about the experimental procedures. Incentives including payment to participants can be coercive to other populations besides prisoners. Children or people with low incomes might feel especially pressured to participate if payment is involved. To an eight-year-old child, $50 is a fortune, and he or she might be willing to do anything to get $50. A desperately poor family might agree to participate in a medical study because it would provide free checkups and other medical care, despite grave concerns and reluctance about the discomforts of the procedures (blood draws and so forth) involved. A delicate balancing act therefore exists between appropriately compensating people for the inconveniences involved in being part of the research versus presenting such a large inducement that people do not feel they can afford to decline, even if they wanted to. Ironically, an IRB can ultimately decide that a researcher is proposing to offer *too much* money to participants, with the likely result being that their consent is no longer freely given but coerced by the magnitude of the inducements.

A special, and ethically troublesome, case of coercion is one familiar to most students: the widespread practice of **subject pools** at research universities. At most colleges where social science research is conducted, students in introductory psychology, communications, or other courses are asked to participate in a certain number of experiments (usually between 2 and 10) as part of their course requirements. The rationale given to students for this requirement is that it is educational to view the research experience from the perspective of a participant, but it is well understood by all that the subject pool exists primarily for the convenience of the researchers. Although there is certainly some educational benefit involved in seeing how research is implemented in the laboratory, one could argue that this benefit is fully attained after participation in one or two studies and that there is little more to be gained by participating in several more studies.

To remove or reduce the coercive element involved in subject pools, most universities offer some sort of alternative to experimental participation; for example, rather than participating in an experiment, the student might be asked to read a research article and answer a few questions about it. These alternatives, however, do not present a cure to the problem of coercion. They are often deliberately designed to be perceived as more unpleasant than experimental participation (how many students would gladly write a report about a research article?), because, after all, every alternative activity engaged in means one fewer participant hour available to the pool. The empirical fact that very few students choose to perform the alternative activity constitutes prima facie evidence that some degree of coercion is occurring. If the alternative were truly perceived as desirable as experimental participation—which is what we would want if our goal is to ensure that no coercion is occurring—we would expect about a 50–50 split between the two, which clearly does not happen.

So what can one conclude about the ethicality of subject pools? A pessimistic answer would be to say that subject pools very well might not survive close ethical scrutiny. Certainly, most introductory psychology undergraduates do not perceive a whole lot of free choice regarding their participation. A more optimistic conclusion would be to state that even if some coercion is present, the alternatives *do* exist should students feel strong objections to participating in experiments, and the fact that students do not opt to do the alternative means only that participating in experiments is ever so much more fun. And even though they do not feel much choice over the matter, neither do most undergraduates dislike their participation experiences, and in fact, many find the experiments quite interesting.

One could also make a practical argument that subject pools are a necessary evil. A review of the social psychological literature, for example, indicated that fully 74% of the research reported in the top scientific journals used college undergraduates as participants (Sears, 1986). Banning the use of subject pools would shut down a large portion of social-psychological research, and one could argue from a cost-benefit perspective that the costs of a subject pool are so slight weighed against the benefits obtained that the coercive element is ethically justified. This is a tempting conclusion to reach in light of the consideration that there are no easy alternatives to a subject pool. One of the authors of this text attended graduate school at one of the few research universities that had decided, for ethical reasons, not to have a subject pool. Instead, participants were paid, often out-of-pocket, for their time ($8 per hour during the 2000–2001 academic year). This presented a significant hardship for graduate students and faculty members who did not have research grants to pay for their research expenses, and it probably resulted in smaller-than-optimal sample sizes. Purists would argue that the research got done anyway, without the ethical cloud of coercing unwilling undergraduates. Perhaps the only safe and sure conclusion to draw about subject pools is that they illustrate just how slippery the slope is in debating ethical issues and how it can sometimes be hard to say with exactitude what the right thing to do is.

The ethical principle of respect for persons has important implications for the practice of deception in social science research. Deception raises two major ethical concerns. The first is the broader moral question that if lying to one's friends, relatives, and acquaintances is wrong, then is it not also wrong to lie to one's participants? When we lie to someone, we are not showing respect for him or her. Can it be ethically permissible to do something—that is, lie—for the sake of science when it is not acceptable to do so in the course of daily life? The second concern is more narrow in scope and involves the fact that participants cannot provide true informed consent to participate in a research study if they are being deceived about important aspects of the procedure.

Deception remains perhaps the most problematic ethical issue in social science research, and considerable attention has been devoted to untangling the thorny issues involved. Because deception arises primarily in experimental research, we will postpone our discussion of these issues to a section later in the chapter devoted specifically to ethical issues in experimental research and move now instead to the second broad ethical principle delineated in the Belmont Report, that of beneficence.

Beneficence

The word **beneficence** means being kind or a charitable act or gift. In a research context, the ethical principle of beneficence means that one should not harm one's participants and that benefits to participants should be maximized while possible harms are minimized. The principle of beneficence has greater ramifications for medical research, in which experimental treatments and procedures are assessed, than it does for social science research, as little of the research done in the social sciences has the potential of actually physically harming research participants. That does not mean that social scientists can safely ignore the principle of beneficence, however; as described earlier, there are examples of studies in the social sciences in which participants were greatly distressed by the research procedures. The primary ethical objection to the Milgram studies of obedience to authority, remember, was not the considerable deception involved but rather the severe stress and anxiety experienced by the participants.

The primary ethical issue of the principle of beneficence involves the possibility of direct harm caused by the treatment or experimental procedures. Most readers are familiar with the famous edict of the Hippocratic oath taken by physicians since ancient times: "*First, do no harm.*" This edict embodies the spirit of the beneficence principle. In carrying out research, our quest for knowledge should not come at the price of harm to our participants. Even if the Nazis uncovered useful information about the treatment of hypothermia (and this is a debatable point), they did not have the right to endanger and even end the lives of their research participants to discover this information. However, it is important to acknowledge that the edict of "do no harm" is easier to follow in a routine clinical practice, in which treatment validity and dangers have been long well-established, than it is in the context of research, which by definition involves procedures and treatments whose benefits and risks are not yet fully understood.

This poses a considerable dilemma for researchers. On the one hand, they believe they have identified a promising treatment that they *think* can be helpful, but they have no way of knowing for sure that this is the case nor can they guarantee that no harmful side effects will occur. They might think there will be few or no adverse effects, but until it is actually tried out on humans, there is no way to tell for sure. Animal models and computer simulations can help in gauging the risks and harm likely to occur from a given treatment, but they cannot substitute completely for human trials.

The problem is that most, if not all, experimental treatments and procedures (in the medical area, at least) pose some degree of risk or harm; however, the researchers obviously also believe these treatments hold the potential to help, if not the research participant directly, large numbers of people in the future. The key to resolving this ethical dilemma—and indeed, all ethical dilemmas in research—is a careful weighing of the risks versus the benefits of the research. If the risk of harm to participants is low, then there is little ethical concern in conducting the study. This does not mean that research is automatically unethical if it involves risk or harm to participants, however. A treatment or procedure can involve substantial discomfort or risk of serious side effects. But if the potential benefits of the treatment are large (e.g., alleviating a serious disorder suffered by the patient), both the researchers and the participant might decide that the benefits outweigh the risk and that the research should continue. Thus, the ethical task faced by researchers and IRBs is a **risk-benefit analysis:** the careful determination of the magnitude of the potential harm to participants and whether that risk is outweighed by the potential benefit of the treatment.

Most of the ethical controversies currently gripping the community of science involve experiments in which the calculation of risks and benefits went awry. For example, gene therapy received a lot of early enthusiasm as a technique holding great promise as a cure for many serious diseases; however, in 1999, an 18-year-old man named Jesse Gelsinger died suddenly after receiving experimental gene therapy. This death was clearly tragic and unexpected, and as a result IRBs all over the country have halted ongoing gene therapy clinical trials until researchers have a better understanding of what went wrong in this trial and the likelihood of it happening again. (A moving description of the Gelsinger case, written by Jesse's father, can be found on the World Wide Web using the address listed at the end of the chapter.)

In other instances, the risks and harm are clearly known before the experiment starts, and the ethical question is whether the potential benefits of the research are large enough in view of the documented risks or perceived costs. A good example would be the intense controversy that is occurring over the use of embryonic stem cells in biological research. Stem cells are those undifferentiated cells that are present early in the growth of a human embryo. What makes stem cells unique and valuable is that they can be cultivated to grow into different types of human tissues (unlike differentiated human cells, which can be used for one function only; e.g., skin cells can only divide into other skin cells). Biomedical researchers believe they can use stem cells to grow replacement tissues or organs, as well as for treatments for Alzheimer's disease, cancer, or spinal cord injuries.

The problem with stem cells is that they must be taken from human embryos, and the process of extracting the cells destroys the embryo. Most researchers using stem cells have obtained them from aborted fetuses or leftover frozen embryos from in vitro fertilization procedures, embryos that will not be implanted. This raises clear ethical concerns, and there are people who vehemently object to research using stem cells. Archbishops from the Roman Catholic Church, for example, have called stem cell research "evil" and argued that the use of cells from embryos—which in their opinion should be treated as human beings—can never be ethically justified, no matter how many lives might be saved from the research. Medical researchers, on the other hand, have argued that embryos only have the potential to develop into human beings; moreover, the embryos that would be used in this research do not have any such potential, as they would be obtained only from embryos that have either been aborted or would never be implanted.

Fortunately, in most social science research, the ethical ramifications of the beneficence principle are rarely this thorny. The risks inherent in social science research are several orders of magnitude lower than in biomedical research; however, this does not mean we can safely ignore the risk-benefit calculations, as one can argue that the benefits of social science research are also several orders of magnitude lower. The knowledge we obtain in a social science study almost never has any direct benefit for the participants involved, and at best we can usually only argue that the benefit to society in general is intangible and delayed. Yes, we are finding out more about prejudice, or overconsumption of resources, or any other social problem, and this knowledge could lead to improvements in these problems someday, but social scientists are often hard-pressed to point to actual concrete results of their research. The ethical question thus becomes whether we have the right to subject our participants to the inconvenience and time investment of participating in our research when we can assure them of no tangible benefit.

Ethical considerations also demand that researchers monitor the well-being of their participants continuously throughout the experiment and halt the experiment when circumstances demand it. For example, a large-scale study looking at the efficacy of a daily aspirin in preventing heart attacks was ended prematurely when it was discovered that the aspirin was significantly effective. The researchers felt that the efficacy of aspirin had been demonstrated beyond a doubt and that therefore it was unethical to continue administering the placebo to the control group. Studies might also be halted prematurely if ill consequences occur to some participants, as was the case in a recent clinical trial of a blood pressure reducing medication. Several unexplained deaths occurred in the experimental group, and although the deaths did not appear to be related to the experimental drug, the researchers felt they had no choice but to discontinue the experiment.

In social science research, negative consequences are typically not as severe, but researchers nonetheless are obligated to track their data collection efforts and ensure that participants are not experiencing unanticipated negative reactions or distress. Part of the federal regulations of the IRB process, in fact, requires researchers to report each and every "adverse event" that occurs during the course of a study.

In sum, the principle of beneficence is translated practically into the assessment of the risks and benefits involved in participating in the research. Only when the benefits outweigh the risks can the proposed study be deemed ethical. The investigator's responsibility is to minimize the risks to the participant whenever possible, and the IRB's responsibility is to make the informed judgment that the risks are appropriate in light of the presumed benefits.

Justice

The **justice** principle is relevant to the investigator's choice of participants. Researchers should seek representative samples and avoid choosing certain groups of participants (e.g., the economically disadvantaged, the very sick, or the institutionalized) simply because they are more accessible. In short, the Belmont Report cautioned against adding the "burdens" of participating in research to members of populations already burdened. In particular, it is not fair to utilize a disadvantaged population as research participants for interventions that primarily would benefit more advantaged populations. For example, this concern has been raised about AIDS research currently under way in Africa. Africa has the highest incidence of AIDS cases of any country, making it an attractive locale for obtaining research participants, but many of the drug treatments currently under investigation are extremely expensive and would be out of the reach of most of the local population. Is it fair to try out a new drug—one that might not work and could have harmful side effects—on people who would not have access to it once it was deemed effective? Again, this is not an issue with an easy ethical resolution. Proponents of such research argue that the clinical trials might be the only way such impoverished populations can gain access to the latest and best medical treatments. Opponents raise the point that if it is true that participating in these trials is the only way to gain the best medical care, this constitutes a possibly significant source of coercion, raising yet another set of ethical concerns.

In addition to selecting the sample for a research study, the justice principle has implications for how individuals within a given study are treated. The main concern here is the ethicality of control groups. Is it fair to give a potentially helpful treatment or intervention to one group of participants but withhold it from another? As we discuss in detail in Chapter 11, the only way to conclude with certainty that a given treatment or manipulation is effective involves, in part, comparing a group that receives it to one that does not. In much research, the control group does not "miss out" on anything significant. But in medical research, in which the treatment might be a cure to a deadly disease, or in social policy research, where the treatment might be an educational intervention that could lead to a lifetime of accomplishment, those participants relegated to the control group could be missing out, literally, on their lives.

This ethical dilemma is poignantly highlighted in the classic book, *Arrowsmith*, by Sinclair Lewis (1925). In the story, Arrowsmith is a young and brilliant scientist who has invented what he hopes will be a cure for a deadly tropical disease. As a good scientist, he knows that the only way to be assured of its effectiveness is to conduct a randomized trial, and he is in the process of conducting such a trial when an epidemic of the disease strikes. The local citizens plead with Arrowsmith to make his drug available to all, and he must deal with the conflict between the emotional impulse to do all he can to help this town—people are dying all around him, after all—and the more scientific need to adhere to the randomized trial that will enable him to decide whether the medicine even works in the first place. We will not spoil the book for readers by revealing what he ultimately decides, though we will pique readers' interest further by saying that Arrowsmith's dilemma becomes agonizingly acute when his own wife contracts the disease.

Those who are not well acquainted with experimental methodology might suggest that researchers should ask for volunteers to be placed in the control group, thus obviating the ethical problem of withholding treatment from individuals who believe they are receiving it. However, this is not a satisfactory solution, as individuals who know they are in the control group will have different expectations and perceptions than those who are receiving a treatment, and these differential demand characteristics can render the results of the study uninterpretable.

In most studies, the potentially different expectations of control group members are controlled for through the use of placebos. In medical experiments, **placebos** are treatments of the same size and format as the experimental treatment (e.g., pills of similar size, color, and even sometimes yielding similar side effects) but which are medically inert. In clinical psychology research, the control group might receive what is called an "attention placebo" therapy, in which clients meet regularly with a therapist for the same amount of time they would in the experimental therapy, but standard therapeutic techniques are not incorporated. In experimental psychology, the control group generally receives materials that are matched in terms of length, intensity, format, etc., except for the critical dimension(s) being manipulated.

The ethical problem is that in order for a control group to be effective, the participants in the control group cannot realize they are in fact the control group. Yet in many cases, participants volunteer for the experiment mainly because they hope to receive the experimental treatment. This problem is especially acute in clinical trials of experimental treatments for fatal diseases; people with advanced cancer or HIV/AIDS, for example, are often desperate to be accepted into a clinical trial that might offer some hope, however slim, of curing their disease. Fewer would be willing to do so if they knew they would be in a control group that receives no treatment.

Fortunately, there is a solution to this ethical dilemma that is fairly easy to implement. If the research involves a treatment or intervention deemed to be highly desired by the participants, the first and most important consideration is to make full disclosure to participants in the consent process: Tell them of the necessity both of including control groups in the experiment and of keeping participants and researchers unaware of the experimental condition of the participants. Second, make it explicit to participants what their chances are of being assigned to the control condition. Third, assure participants that at the conclusion of the experiment, if the intervention is shown to be effective, it will be offered to all control participants at no expense. If participants come into the experiment ahead of time knowing that they might not receive the actual treatment until the conclusion of the study and are still willing to participate, ethical concerns of justice are allayed.

Focus on Ethical Issues in Experimental Research: Deception

Earlier, we noted that deception is perhaps the trickiest ethical issue facing social scientists. Deception tends to be especially prevalent in experimental research, as most experimental manipulations involve some element of deception. There are two major forms of deception in experimental research: deception by omission and active deception. In **deception by omission,** participants are not told any outright untruths; rather, detail is left out about relevant experimental details. For example, a study looking at whether participants would cheat on a test if given the opportunity might be described to participants as a "study of mental and behavioral processes." Strictly speaking, this is not actively deceptive (cheating is a behavioral process), but it is misleading in that participants are not told that cheating is the behavior of primary interest in the study.

When deception is defined this way, most experiments contain an element of deception, as few researchers divulge the precise behaviors or hypotheses being studied—for the obvious reason of wishing to avoid demand characteristics or expectancy effects (Chapter 12). In most cases, these instances of deception by omission are not cause for ethical alarm, as participants are still given adequate information about the nature of the experiment and what they will be experiencing so that they can give meaningful informed consent. Deception by omission becomes an ethical problem primarily when the detail omitted is something that might have affected people's willingness to participate in the study had they known the true purpose of the study in advance. For example, it is possible that some people would not have volunteered for the cheating study described above had they known that it was about cheating, and these participants would become offended and distressed once debriefed about the real purpose of the study. An implication of this is that deception is not necessarily bad in and of itself but primarily in those cases when it would lead the participants to behave in ways that they would regret doing. For example, Sieber (1992) notes that the well-known Isen and Levin (1972) study looking at the effects of cookies on helping behavior does not pose an ethical problem, despite the lack of informed consent and deception involved, because the behavior elicited by the manipulation was socially desirable. In dealing with deception, then, the primary challenge for IRBs is to review the consent form and the experimenter's cover story and then judge whether a "reasonable person" would react too negatively to the deception involved in the study.

Active deception is obviously a more serious ethical problem. In these cases, participants are actively misled about aspects of the experiment. Milgram's (1974) studies of obedience are a famous example of this type of deception, as participants were lied to about the identity of the confederate, the purpose of the study, and the supposed shocks they were administering to the confederate. Although active deception of any kind is problematic, the form that is most problematic involves studies that deliver false feedback to participants; that is, people are given information about themselves that has no basis in fact but rather was assigned randomly. As described earlier, it is not uncommon in social science research for experimenters to manipulate mood or self-esteem of participants by giving them either positive or negative feedback about their alleged performance on ability or personality tests. Also as noted earlier, this kind of deception creates two problems: the anger felt by participants when they realize they've been lied to and the possibility of **perseverance effects,** that is, that participants will continue to believe the false feedback even after having been told about the deception. Research shows that such perseverance effects do occur, but they can be ameliorated by a "process debriefing" that addresses not only the fact of the deception but also the existence of perseverance effects themselves (Ross, Lepper, & Hubbard, 1975). In other words, once participants are told that there is this tendency for people to cling to the originally deceptive feedback, they are much less likely to do so.

Another particularly problematic form of deception in experimental research is called **double deception** or **second-order deception** and refers to the once-standard practice of experimenters telling participants that "the experiment is over" but then going on to collect additional data. A famous example of such double deception is the classic Festinger and Carlsmith (1959) study of cognitive dissonance, in which the entire dissonance manipulation and measurement of the dependent variables did not take place until after the participants were told the experiment was over. The problem here is that when participants are told a second time that the experiment is now "really" over, they will be angry or unconvinced. More problematic, such deception can seriously undermine the individual's general trust in science. Kelman (1968) thus holds, and most IRBs concur, that double deception is ethically unacceptable and that no further data collection should take place after telling participants the study has been concluded.

Using Deception in an Ethical Manner

Is deception in social science research necessary? Some ethicists have argued that it is not, that valid data can be obtained through deception-free procedures. Kelman, in his influential chapter, "The Human Use of Human Subjects" (1968), argued that deception is wrong on moral grounds and almost never warranted on practical grounds, and he advocated instead relying on role-playing in collecting data. For example, if we wanted to see how threats to self-esteem affect later behavior, rather than administering false feedback, we could ask participants to go through the experimental procedures while pretending they have received negative personal feedback. Kelman offers data to suggest that role-playing participants provide results that are comparable to those yielded by participants who are deceived in the traditional manner. However, the obvious hitch to this recommendation is that one can never be sure that role-playing will yield realistic data, especially when the focus of study is sensitive or socially undesirable behavior. For example, it seems highly unlikely that the same high percentage of participants asked to role-play Milgram's procedure would shock to the limit as was actually observed. Because of this fear, role-playing has not caught on as a viable alternative to deception.

What, then, can researchers do to ameliorate the ethical problems raised by deception yet still obtain high-quality data? As it turns out, there are a number of creative approaches to the problem, most involving participants giving **consent to conceal** (Sieber, 1992). First, researchers can explicitly obtain participants' permission to be deceived. In this approach, participants are told in the consent process that there may be misleading aspects of the cover story that will not be revealed until the end of the experiment. Although this is probably the most ethically "pure" solution to the deception dilemma, it is not a perfect solution, as tipping off participants that they will be deceived undoubtedly leads to atypical behavior as they try to figure out what they are being deceived about throughout the experiment. An alternative approach is to ask participants to waive the right to be fully informed; that is, they are told that the researchers are unable to give full detail about the study beforehand but that they will be debriefed following the experiment. Unlike the former approach, this approach does not explicitly warn participants that they will be deceived. This has the obvious benefits of preventing suspiciousness on the part of the participants, but it also has the disadvantage that participants might still feel upset upon learning of the deception.

Unlike these approaches, which vary what participants are told about the study in the consent process, the next method of dealing with deception involves the **debriefing** stage. This method involves divulging thoroughly to participants all aspects of the deception and then giving them the opportunity to withdraw their data from the study (with no penalty or loss of benefits). The ethical reasoning behind this approach is clear: If deception, as we have argued, subverts the informed consent process, then participants have the right to say, after debriefing, that they would not have participated in the study had they known the full details of what was going on. It is impossible to turn back time and erase the fact that the participants did in fact participate, but a compromise is for the participants to refuse to let their data be used. In sum, an increasing number of IRBs require that researchers who use deception in their studies obtain a signed **consent to use data** form during debriefing; the form details the nature of the deception and why it was necessary and then explicitly offers the participant the option of withholding his or her data.

Focus on Ethical Issues in Quasi-Experimental Research: Confidentiality and Anonymity

As we discuss in Chapter 13, nonrandomized, or quasi-experimental, studies are generally done when random assignment is impossible but researchers would like to draw as firm of a causal inference as they can. Much quasi-experimental research takes place in the field and involves survey administration, program evaluation, and the like. Thus, one of the major ethical issues that arises in quasi-experimental research involves the confidentiality and anonymity of the data. In a typical laboratory experiment, most participants would not necessarily care whether others saw the responses they gave. But in a workplace setting, for example, when asked to give their impressions of certain managerial practices, participants may feel very strongly that they do not wish their individual responses to be divulged.

Fortunately, the ethical issues of confidentiality and anonymity are the easiest to address. The key is to be aware of the distinction between confidentiality and anonymity and to be sure not to promise anonymity to participants unless anonymity can be assured. **Anonymity** means that absolutely no identifying characteristics are recorded on the data and that it would be impossible for the researcher to figure out who contributed a given piece of data. **Confidentiality** means that although the researcher can figure out whose data are whose, within certain legal limits (described later), the researcher promises never to share that information. In the workplace survey example given above, a confidential survey would be one in which identifying data are collected but the researcher promises not to share individual results with the managers. In contrast, an anonymous survey would be one in which completed surveys are deposited in a central location with no identifying data being collected.

As noted earlier, the crucial ethical prescription for researchers is not to promise anonymity unless the conditions under which the data are gathered truly are anonymous. In many survey situations, that is not the case. Often, identifiers are placed on the surveys so that individuals can be contacted later to remind them to complete the survey, for follow-up data collection purposes, or so that their responses can be related to other existing data about the participant from other sources. Furthermore, even if the researchers originally intended for a survey to be anonymous, the survey might contain a combination of questions that could actually serve to identify the respondent, especially if the sample were small. For example, it is not uncommon for faculty members to be administered questionnaires asking for their impressions of the college administration—a situation in which many faculty members would wish to remain anonymous. But if the questionnaire asks for the respondent's department, rank, and gender (as such questionnaires typically do), that can be tantamount to identifying the individual if, say, she happened to be the only tenured female in that particular department. Another example of how anonymity can be unintentionally undermined is if the raw data (which lack any identifiers) are placed in file folders along with the signed consent forms (which contain the participants' names). The simple solution to that problem, obviously, is that consent forms should be stored separately—under lock and key—from the raw data.

Confidentiality should always be assured to the fullest extent possible. What this means is that nobody else besides individuals on the research team should have access to or see the raw data. There are, however, a few circumstances in which researchers are legally obligated to violate confidentiality. For example, if a participant admits to thinking about or planning to commit suicide or murder, or if the study uncovers any evidence of child abuse, most states have **duty to warn** laws that require the researcher to report the individual to the proper agency. Such circumstances are not as rare as one would think; for example, the Beck Depression Inventory (one of the most commonly used measures of depression) has an item that asks specifically about whether the respondent is considering suicide. Legally, the researcher is obligated to refer to authorities any respondent who indicates that he or she would commit suicide, even if confidentiality had been promised in the consent form. The easiest solution to this ethical dilemma is to design one's study in such a manner that participants remain anonymous; if there is no possible way of tracking down who indicated that they would kill themselves if they had a chance, there is no longer any obligation to report. If anonymity is not possible, then participants should probably be warned of the limits to confidentiality in the consent form.

This issue also arises in research done with children and adolescents, especially when the research involves sensitive or illegal behaviors like sexual behavior or substance use. Obviously, researchers want participants to feel that their responses would be kept private (otherwise, they would be unlikely to respond honestly), but the bottom line is that if a parent were to insist on viewing his or her child's questionnaire, the researcher would be legally and ethically forced to comply unless the researcher had explicitly told parents in the consent process that they would not have access to their child's data. Again, the best solution in such a case would be to include such a statement in the parental consent form or to design the study in such a way that participants' responses were truly anonymous, so that the parents could be honestly told that there is no way to retrieve their child's individual responses.

Focus on Ethical Issues in Nonexperimental Research: Participant Observation

The method of participant observation has a long and honorable history in sociology. More recently, it has enjoyed a resurgence of popularity in social science research, as qualitative methods have become increasingly in vogue. As we describe in Chapter 15, in participant observation, the researcher joins a naturally occurring social group and observes its proceedings, keeping detailed field notes about what goes on. The other group members are often not aware that the researcher is observing them for scientific purposes, sometimes not even at the conclusion of data collection. Later, a description of the group is published, with identifying features deleted or changed.

The ethical concerns with participant observation studies are rather obvious: There is a great deal of deception going on, as researchers might not inform the participants that research is being conducted nor may they identify themselves as researchers. The consequence of this deception is that informed consent is usually not obtained. Invasion of privacy is another, related ethical concern. Because participants are often unaware there is a study going on, they might say and do things that they would not normally or intentionally disclose to a researcher. (There is irony here that researchers are bound by ethical constraints that other professionals, e.g., journalists, are not. Reporters can and do infiltrate groups all the time to gather material for their articles or broadcasts without divulging what they are doing.)

Lastly, confidentiality and anonymity are of concern in participant observation. Although most researchers follow basic ethical guidelines of keeping identifying information strictly confidential and locked in a secure location, as well as changing identifiers in publications, the possibility remains that people (particularly those familiar with the group) could figure out who is being talked about, especially if the group is of a highly specialized nature. For example, in the mid-1950s, there were not many cults predicting the destruction of the world and subsequent salvation by alien beings, so readers of Festinger, Riecken, and Schachter's (1956) classic participant observation work, *When Prophecy Fails*, could have determined the identity of the individuals involved with only a modest amount of effort.

How might these ethical concerns be resolved? Some researchers avoid the deception problem by informing group members ahead of time about the study and requesting their permission to be observed. This clearly satisfies most ethical objections (although confidentiality and identifiability concerns still remain), but it does so at the rather heavy cost of introducing substantial reactivity into the data collection. How reasonable is it to think that people would behave normally if a researcher were sitting there taking notes or tape-recording the proceedings? However, as advocates of this solution and years of "reality TV" can attest, people eventually do become largely accustomed to the presence of observers and video cameras, and they might very well start to behave naturally even when they know they are being studied.

The Ethics of Not Doing a Study

As you have seen, the major theme underlying our discussion of research ethics is that determining whether and how a given study should be done ultimately rests on a consideration of the costs and benefits of doing the research. Rosenthal and Rosnow (1984; Rosenthal, 1994) suggest, however, that a thorough ethical review also requires a consideration of the costs and benefits associated with *not* doing the study. In some cases, the long-term social costs of not discovering a cure for a disease or an intervention for an acute social problem such as poverty or prejudice might be so high that one could argue that researchers have an ethical obligation to undertake such research, even if the risks and costs associated with such research are heavy.

Taking such a perspective can help to resolve some of the ethical controversies currently raging in the biomedical sciences, such as the debate over using fetal stem cells mentioned earlier. The perennial debate over the use of animals in research provides another good opportunity to consider the ethics of not performing research. There are those who would ban completely the use of animals in biomedical or behavioral research. Their arguments are often emotionally compelling: What right do we have to hurt or kill an innocent little puppy? We would argue, though, that the question instead should focus not only on the relative costs and benefits of doing the research but also the costs of not doing the research. Suppose, for example, a treatment is under investigation for cerebral palsy, a disorder that affects about three of every thousand babies born. If this hypothetical treatment were effective, it could restore mental and physical capabilities to children who might otherwise be doomed to a lifetime of mental retardation and wheelchairs. Is not the prospect of such a cure that would help thousands of children this year, and the same number the next year, and for each year after that unto perpetuity, worth the lives of a hundred puppies or so, no matter how cute and furry?

Some bioethicists argue that not only is such research ethical, but also it would be unethical to refuse to do the study. The potential risks of a study can be entirely eliminated simply by not doing the study; however, in making that decision, we should consider not only the risks that have been avoided but also the benefits that would be forgone. In some cases, the potential benefits that are doomed never to be fulfilled if the research is not done are tremendous indeed. As Kaplan (1988) once eloquently asked, "Who speaks for the sick, for those in pain, and for the future?"

This is not meant to suggest that there are no ethical problems at all in using animals in research. As researchers we have an obligation to protect all living organisms from unnecessary pain and to use animals only when no feasible alternative exists. In some cases, it might be possible to rely on computer simulations instead of experimenting on animals. In other cases, though, computer simulations are not adequate, and sooner or later the treatment must be tried out on a living organism. In such cases, assuming the proposed benefits of the research in question are great enough, research on animals is ethically justified, even if it means their ultimate death. As Dr. Benjamin Trump of the University of Maryland Medical School once said in an interview, later quoted widely by Ann Landers, "We in the medical profession find it painful to accept a dead child over a dead mouse."

Case Study of the Ethical Review Process

We would like to end this chapter by providing an illustration of how the ethical review process operates. Our example comes from social psychology, but the process and principles would work the same way in other social sciences. The case study is an experiment on personality variables related to interpersonal expectancy effects, or self-fulfilling prophecies. The study itself involves bringing in two naive participants, having them complete personality measures, and then giving one participant (the perceiver) a manipulated expectancy about the problem-solving abilities of another participant (the target) that is either positive or negative in nature. The two participants then work together on a problem-solving task, and the dependent variables include self-reports from the target and perceiver, performance on the task, and ratings of the participants' behavior done on the videotapes of the interactions.

The ethical review process begins in the planning stages of a study. Researchers should and do consider ethical issues when planning the design of a study and choosing the procedures and measures to be administered. More formally, the researcher must obtain IRB approval prior to the collection of any data. The IRB process is generally lengthy. The first step is to prepare the IRB proposal. This involves filling out forms with basic information about the researcher and all other research personnel who will be involved in data collection, indicating the number and type of participants to be enrolled in the study, and providing a full description of the proposed research project. The project description includes several critical sections:

1. A background and introduction section, which summarizes relevant past research. This section provides a historical and research context for IRB members, most of whom are not from the researcher's discipline, to understand the basis for the research and why this particular study is important. In our case study, several paragraphs would be provided describing the long history of research on expectancy effects.
2. A section listing the specific objectives of the proposed research, which helps IRB members to gauge the adequacy of the proposed methods. In our example, a paragraph would be written describing the primary goal of the study, which is to identify aspects of personality that are related to expectancy effects.
3. A description of the study population (number, age range, ethnic background, and health status). This is necessary to allow a determination as to whether any vulnerable populations will be included. Special IRB regulations exist governing the protection of vulnerable populations, such as children or pregnant women. In the case of prisoners, a specially designated "prisoner advocate" on the IRB participates in the protocol review. For our example, the study population is 240 undergraduate psychology students.
4. A description of how participants will be recruited. IRBs play close attention to recruitment, as they want to ensure that no coercion is involved. If the researcher is planning to recruit via advertisements or flyers, the IRB will want to see a copy of the recruitment ad prior to approving the study. If the researcher is gaining access to participants through some other channel (e.g., school system, medical clinic, etc.), the IRB will need to be assured that the researcher has the legal right to view names and contact information for

potential participants. In many school systems, for example, it is illegal for a principal to provide a list of names and addresses of students to researchers. In our example, the participants will be undergraduates recruited through the traditional introductory psychology subject pool.

5. A short section describing the study design. The IRB will want to know how many experimental conditions there are and if randomization will occur. In our example, the expectancy manipulation consists of two levels (positive/negative) to which perceivers will be randomly assigned.

6. A longer section describing the research procedures to be carried out. This section is analogous to the method section in a journal article, and it should describe everything that happens to the participants. Copies of all research instruments to be administered should be included. In many ways, this section is the most important part of the IRB proposal, for it is difficult to gauge the extent and magnitude of risks experienced by the participants without knowing exactly what they will be doing. In our example, we would describe thoroughly the procedures undertaken by the participants, explaining the expectancy manipulation and the interaction the perceiver and target would have, and we would include copies of all the measurement instruments.

7. A description of all the potential risks—physical, psychological, social, legal, and other—faced by the participants. Here the researcher states more explicitly the risks that are inherent in the procedures described in the preceding section. In our example, the primary risk involves the deception of the expectancy manipulation, and we would explain that participants might become upset upon discovering they have been deceived.

8. The researchers need also to describe the safety precautions they will take for protecting against or minimizing potential risks. When procedures are particularly stressful, a common safeguard is for researchers to have available for participants referrals to counselors or mental health agencies. In our example, the primary safeguard will be to conduct a lengthy, sensitive debriefing in which the deception is carefully and gently explained, including the need for deception. We probably would include a word-for-word script of our deception debriefing in our IRB proposal.

9. The next step is to provide an explicit risk-benefit analysis, explaining why the risks to participants are reasonable in relation to the anticipated benefits. In our example, we would explain that the risk due to the deception in our study is fairly minor. We could also point out that there is considerable research in psychology indicating that not only are participants generally not angered by deception in an experiment, but also that they find deception experiments on the whole more interesting and enjoyable to participate in

than other types of studies (Christensen, 1988; Epley & Huff, 1998; Smith & Richardson, 1983).

10. A summary of relevant incentives and research-related costs. In order to assess the possibility of coercion, IRBs want to know what kinds of incentives are being offered to participants. The IRB also wants to make sure that all incentives and research-related costs (including such things as transportation to the study, time involved to participate, etc.) are clearly spelled out in the consent form. In our case study, the main incentive is course credit for participating in research.

11. A listing of any available alternatives to the study. This section is relevant primarily in the medical field, in which it is important to provide potential participants with the knowledge of any comparable treatments that might exist besides participating in the study. In our case study, we would describe the alternative method of earning research credit (e.g., the student writing a summary of a research article).

12. A description of how and where research materials will be stored and a discussion of confidentiality. The IRB wants to know what kinds of data are being obtained from participants, where it will be stored, and how participants' confidentiality will be preserved. In our example, we would explain that the sources of data include the measures completed by the participants and videotapes of their interaction. We would explain that all data will be kept strictly confidential and that all identifying information (e.g., names on consent forms) would be stored separately from the data under lock and key.

13. Lastly, the IRB proposal must include a copy of the informed consent form to be used in the study. As we discussed earlier, these forms should be written in everyday, easy-to-understand language. Some studies require multiple consent forms; for example, if the study is a longitudinal one with measurements widely separated in time, a separate consent form for each phase of the study might be called for. Studies that address disparate populations might need a different consent form for each class of participant. For example, a qualitative study looking at communication between health care providers and Latino patients probably would need two sets of consent forms, one for the health care providers and one for the patients (not to mention a Spanish translation for the patient version). When the participants are minors, obtaining consent is more complicated. Legally, the consent form must be directed to and signed by the parent(s) of the participant; however, the children themselves should also be consulted and fully informed as to the nature of the research, and their wishes regarding participation should be honored whenever possible. Some IRBs require written assent from any minor participant between the ages of 12 and 17.

TABLE 3.1 **Sample Consent Form for a Case Study of Interpersonal Expectancy Effects**

Consent to Participate in a Research Study

Personality and Social Interactions

Why am I being invited to take part in this research?
You are being invited to take part in a research study about the personality factors that are related to how people interact with other people. You are being invited to participate in this research study because you are enrolled in Psychology 101. If you take part in this study, you will be 1 of about 240 undergraduates to do so.

Who is doing the study?
The person in charge of this study is Dr. Jane Doe of the Psychology Department at the University of Social Science. There may be other people on the research team assisting at different times during the study.

What is the purpose of the study?
By doing this study, we hope to learn more about the relations between personality and people's social interactions.

Where is the study going to take place and how long will it last?
The research procedures will be conducted in Research Hall at the University of Social Science. The session should last no longer than 50 minutes.

What will I be asked to do?
First, we will ask you to complete a number of questionnaires. These questionnaires are designed to measure aspects of your personality, such as extraversion, friendliness, dominance, and anxiety. We will then ask you to work on a problem-solving task with another undergraduate. This interaction will be videotaped. Following the interaction, we will separate you and your partner and ask you to complete some questionnaires asking for your impression of the interaction and your partner.

What are the possible risks and discomforts?
To the best of our knowledge, the things you will be doing have no more risk of harm than you would experience in everyday life. There is a slight possibility that you may feel self-conscious or uncomfortable about being videotaped. You can discontinue being in the study at any time, and you can have the videotape erased at any time.

Do I have to take part in this study?
If you decide to take part in the study, it should be because you really want to volunteer and participate. You will not lose any benefits or rights you would normally have if you choose not to volunteer. You can stop at any time during the study, and you will still keep the benefits and rights you had before volunteering.

What will it cost me to participate?
There are no costs associated with taking part in this study.

Will I receive any payment or rewards for taking part in the study?
You will receive one hour of experimental credit toward your Psychology 101 grade for participating in this study.

Who will see the information I give?
Your information will be combined with information from other students taking part in the study. When we write up the study to share it with other researchers, we will write about this

(Continued)

TABLE 3.1 **SAMPLE CONSENT FORM FOR A CASE STUDY OF INTERPERSONAL EXPECTANCY EFFECTS (CONTINUED)**

combined information. You will not be identified in these written materials. We will make every effort to prevent anyone who is not on the research team from knowing that you gave us information or what that information is. For example, your name will be kept separate from the information you give us, and these two things will be stored in different places under lock and key. Only members of our research team will see the videotape we made of your interaction.

Can my part in the study end early?
If you decide to take part in the study, you still have the right to decide at any time that you no longer want to continue. You will not be treated differently if you stop taking part in the study.

What if I have questions?
Before you decide whether to accept this invitation to take part in the study, please ask any questions that might come to mind. You can contact the investigator at 000-555-1234 if you have any questions following your participation. If you have any questions about your rights as a research volunteer, contact the staff in the Office of Research Integrity at the University of Social Science at 000-555-5678. You may keep this copy of the consent form.

What else do I need to know?
You will be told if any new information is learned that may influence your willingness to continue participating in this study.

____ ________________
Signature of person agreeing to participate in study Date

____
Printed name of person

____
Name of person providing information to participant

> Table 3.1 shows an example of a consent form that could be used for our case study. Note the question-and-answer format and straightforward language contained in the form. Note also that the consent form stresses repeatedly that the participant can discontinue the study at any time. But also note that the consent form is an example of deception by omission; the expectancy manipulation is not mentioned nor does the form identify expectancy effects as being the major topic of the study.

Once completed, the proposal is sent to the IRB for review. Although the makeup of IRBs varies widely across institutions, federal regulations require that IRBs contain at least five members (most contain far more than that), representing both genders, varied professions, and scientists as well as nonscientists. At least one member of the IRB must be a layperson who is not otherwise affiliated with the institution. Upon receiving the proposal, an IRB staff person determines whether the protocol needs to undergo an expedited or full review. An **expedited review** (meaning that it can be done by only one IRB member and thus can be handled more quickly than a full review) is restricted to those studies that involve no more than minimal risk and otherwise fall into one of several specified categories, such as survey research on nonsensitive topics. **Minimal risk** is defined in the federal regulations as the "probability and magnitude of harm or discomfort anticipated in the research are not greater in and of themselves from those ordinarily encountered in daily life or during the performance of routine physical or psychological examination or tests." Because our case study involves deception, it must undergo full review.

In a **full review,** all members of the IRB receive the protocol and read it carefully before meeting to discuss it and the other studies on the agenda. IRB members first raise among themselves the concerns they had upon reading the proposal. Then the researchers are invited in to answer specific questions from the IRB members. These questions can address any and all aspects of the research procedures, down to details as minute as the wording of a given item on a questionnaire. In our case study, the major concern obviously would be the deception involved in the expectancy manipulation. An IRB member would probably ask if deception were necessary. We would need to justify deceiving our participants, explaining how the need for random assignment of the expectancy manipulation necessarily entails deception. The IRB also probably would be concerned about the videotaping and how we would ensure confidentiality of the tapes. We would stress that all participants would be well aware of the videotaping before starting the study, as covert videotaping (i.e., without the participant's knowledge) is no longer deemed ethical by the American Psychological Association. (This is a good opportunity to point out that different disciplines are governed by different sets of ethical principles. IRBs, however, are obligated only to follow and enforce the federal regulations. Most of the time the federal regulations are in close agreement with the disciplinary guidelines, but there can be discrepancies. There is nothing in the federal regulations to prohibit covert videotaping, for example.)

After the researchers have answered any questions and left the room, the IRB will vote on the protocol, almost always voting to withhold approval until certain changes are made by the researchers in the protocol. (Although it is possible in principle to approve a protocol with no changes, that rarely happens.) For our case study, let us imagine that the IRB asked us to include an explicit "consent to use data" form in our debriefing of the participants regarding the deception. Table 3.2 shows what such a consent to use data form would look like. After the researchers have made the necessary changes and resubmitted the revised protocol, IRB approval is granted, and the IRB provides a version of the consent form that bears an official IRB approval stamp. Only such stamped consent forms can be used in collecting data. IRB approval can be granted for only one year at a time, and approval applies only to the protocol as described in the most recent revision. *Any* subsequent changes that the researchers wish to make to the research procedures must be submitted to the IRB for approval

TABLE 3.2 CONSENT TO USE DATA FORM FOR CASE STUDY OF INTERPERSONAL EXPECTANCY EFFECTS

Personality and Social Interactions

Consent to Use Data

I understand that I was not originally told of some aspects of the experimental procedure. Specifically, I was led to believe that my interaction partner had scored either very high or very low on a test of problem-solving ability. I have been told that this information was randomly determined and that the experimenter actually has no knowledge of my partner's problem-solving ability. I understand that the purpose of this deception was to see how my expectations regarding my partner's ability affected our subsequent interaction. The purpose of this deception has been thoroughly explained to me, and I understand that it was necessary for the validity of the experiment.

However, because I was misled about this aspect of the experiment, I understand that I now have the right to have my data withheld from the experiment if I so wish. If I decide to withhold my data, I understand that my questionnaires will be destroyed immediately and the videotape of my interaction will be immediately erased. I understand that I will still receive full credit for my participation and that no penalties will be applied if I decide to withhold my data.

__________ I hereby give permission for the experimenters to use my data in their study.

__________ I *do not* give permission for the experimenters to use my data in their study; instead, I wish for my data and videotape to be destroyed immediately.

I have read and understood the above.

______________________________ ______________

Participant's signature Date

____

Experimenter's signature

before implementing them. This includes changes as minor as adding another question or two to the dependent measure. In short, the IRB must have full documentation of the entire research procedures at all times. At the end of the year, researchers must submit a continuation review form, in which they describe how many participants have been enrolled in the study, where the data and consent forms are being stored, and whether any adverse reactions have occurred during data collection. (Such adverse reactions are supposed to be reported immediately after their occurrence, as well.)

We have gone to such detail in our case study for two purposes. The first is to provide a concrete example of some of the important terms we have discussed, such as informed consent and deception. The second purpose is to try to convey just how seriously researchers and institutions take the issue of protection of human participants. Literally thousands of hours are devoted every year at research institutions to the oversight of research involving human participants. The time and paperwork demands may seem grueling at times to researchers, but the ultimate payoff—the protection of human participants—is worth the cost.

Closing Thoughts

This chapter began with the question, "What is right to do to people in the name of science?" Our discussion of ethical principles in the social sciences has hopefully clarified the important issues that must be taken into account when answering that question. Although specific guidelines are hard to outline without knowing the precise procedures involved in a study, in general, participants' rights are protected as long as researchers adhere to the three principles of respect, beneficence, and justice and as long as the benefits of the research outweigh the costs.

It can be easy or tempting to get so swept up in the excitement of doing research and analyzing data that we almost forget the source of our data: other human beings just like us, human beings with feelings and who can be hurt. There is perhaps no better way to close this chapter than to quote a moving plea from the Web account written by Paul Gelsinger (2000), the father of the young man, Jesse, who died as a result of a gene therapy experiment gone awry:

> Please remember Jesse's intent when you review studies or when you make policy. You are professionals and you know the issues. I ask, and life itself demands, that you take the time and energy to review each protocol as if you were going to enroll your own child. Please use Jesse's experience to give you the strength to say no or the courage to ask more questions. If researchers, industry, and those in government apply Jesse's intent—not for recognition nor for money, but only to help—then they will get all they want and more . . . they'll get it right.

Summary

When conducting research with human participants, it is essential that their rights, safety, and dignity are protected. Prior to the 1970s, there were no regulations governing research with human participants, and studies were sometimes conducted that involved clearly unethical practices. Following the adverse publicity surrounding one such unethical study, the Tuskegee Syphilis Study, the U.S. government established Institutional Review Boards, whose sole function is to approve the procedures involved in human research studies. The ethical principles underlying the federal regulations were first described in the Belmont Report and consist of respect for persons, beneficence, and justice. Respect for persons means that anybody who participates in a study should be a true volunteer and fully informed regarding the nature of the research. The principle of beneficence means we should do no harm to our participants, and it requires a careful risk-benefit analysis of the proposed research. Justice means that we should not take advantage of overburdened populations in recruiting participants and that participants are fully informed regarding the odds that they may be placed in a control group and not receive treatment.

When conducting experimental research, deception is of particular ethical concern. Deception is sometimes necessary, but it is ethically problematic because by definition the participant is unable to provide full informed consent. Several solutions to the ethical dilemma of deception exist, with perhaps the most practical being to obtain participants' consent to use their data after a thorough debriefing and disclosure of the deception. In survey research, issues of confidentiality and anonymity are central. Every effort must be made to keep participants' data confidential, and anonymity must not be promised unless it can be ensured. In participant observation research, both deception and confidentiality are issues to be resolved.

Obtaining IRB approval for a study is a time-consuming process that involves a thorough description of the methodology of the proposed study. The IRB members perform a detailed risk-benefit analysis, in which they determine whether the risks involved in the procedures are greater or lesser than the benefits to be gained from doing the study. Lastly, one needs to consider not only the risks and costs involved in conducting the study but also the potential social costs if the study is not done.

Key Concepts

active deception
anonymity
Belmont Report
beneficence
coercion
confidentiality
consent to conceal
consent to use data
debriefing
deception
deception by omission
double deception, or second-order deception
duty to warn
expedited review
false feedback
full review
informed consent
Institutional Review Boards (IRBs)
justice
minimal risk
perseverance effects
placebo
respect for persons
risk-benefit analysis
subject pool

On the Web

http://ohrp.osophs.dhhs.gov/irb/irb_guidebook.htm The IRB Guidebook—very detailed and informative, but easy to read—issued by the Office for Human Research Protection under the U.S. Department of Health and Human Services.

http://www.primr.org/jessesintent.html A moving description of the Jesse Gelsinger case, the young man who died suddenly after participating in a gene therapy study, written by his father.

http://www.apa.org/ethics/ The ethics section of the American Psychological Association Web site. It contains a draft of the latest version of the Ethical Principles for Psychologists.

http://www.nlm.nih.gov/pubs/cbm/hum_exp.html A bibliography compiled by the National Library of Medicine listing books and journal articles on ethical issues in research involving human participants. The bibliography covers 1989–1998 and includes 4,650 citations.

http://www.cnn.com/HEALTH/bioethics/archive.index.html A biweekly online column written by Dr. Jeffrey P. Kahn, entitled "Ethics Matters," sponsored jointly by the University of Minnesota Center for Bioethics and CNN Interactive.

http://www.nih.gov/sigs/bioethics/outsidenih.html A Web bibliography compiled by the National Institutes of Health (NIH) providing links to other bioethics Internet resources.

Further Reading

Beach, D. (1996). *The responsible conduct of research.* New York: VCH.

Kelman, H. C. (1968). *A time to speak: On human values and social research.* San Francisco: Jossey-Bass.

Kimmel, A. J. (1988). *Ethics and values in applied social research.* Thousand Oaks, CA: Sage Publications.

Nagy, T. F. (1999). *Ethics in plain English: An illustrative casebook for psychologists.* Washington, DC: American Psychological Association.

Rosenthal, R. (1994). Science and ethics in conducting, analyzing, and reporting psychological research. *Psychological Science,* 5, 127–134.

Sales, B. D., & Folkman, S. (2000). *Ethics in research with human participants.* Washington, DC: American Psychological Association.

Sieber, J. (1992). *Planning ethically responsible research: A guide for students and internal review boards.* Thousand Oaks, CA: Sage Publications.

U.S. National Commission for the Protection of Human Subjects of Biomedical and Behavioral Research. (1979). *The Belmont Report.* Bethesda, MD: Author. [Reprinted on numerous Web sites.]

PART

II

Measurement

CHAPTER

4

Fundamentals of Measurement

To do any research we must be able to measure the concepts we wish to study. For instance, if we want to study social power, we need an instrument to measure it. It is often difficult to develop measures or scales for such abstract ideas because the fabric of social life is not flat, firm, one-dimensional, or tangible. Therefore, we can never be sure we really are measuring what we mean when we say we are studying social power or any of the hundreds of abstract terms that refer to social behavior. A social scientist trying to capture the shape or size of abstract concepts is like a seamstress trying to measure an invisible, intangible piece of cloth.

From Abstract Concepts to Concrete Representations

Social scientists do not spend much time groping in thin air hoping to find the shape of social power. Instead, they devise concrete representations, which they can measure more directly. The abstract concepts are called constructs; the concrete representations are called variables; and the procedures for measuring variables are called operational definitions.

Constructs

Constructs are the abstractions that social scientists discuss in their theories. They are the rich theoretical concepts that make the science interesting, terms such as social status, power, intelligence, and gender roles. Because we cannot literally put a finger on any of these concepts to measure them, we must find some concrete representations that approximate what we mean when we speak of such concepts.

Any one construct can be measured in many different ways because there are a variety of concrete representations of any abstract idea. Each of these will give us an approximate representation of the construct. For instance, social power could be represented by the amount of influence a person has at work, at home, in the neighborhood, or in the mass media. Each of these concrete representations gives some indication of a person's power; no one alone contains the whole truth. Each of these representations is a different variable, but they are all related to the construct. Taken together they are what we mean when we speak of social power.

Variables

Variables are representations of constructs. They cannot be synonymous with a construct because any single construct has many different variables. Therefore, variables are partial, fallible representations of constructs, and we work with them because they are measurable. They suggest ways in which we can decide whether someone has more or less of the construct. For instance, if we select influence at work as the variable to represent social power, we can begin to devise ways to determine whether one person has more or less influence at work than another person. Being more concrete than the construct, the variable suggests some steps we can take to measure it. These steps are called operational definitions.

Operational Definitions

An **operational definition** specifies how to measure a variable so that we can assign someone a score such as high, medium, or low social power. For example, we might refer to an organizational chart to count how many subordinates an individual has. Operational definitions are the means by which we obtain the numbers or categories for variables. That is, an operational definition is the sequence of steps or procedures a researcher follows to obtain a measurement. The variable might have only two possible scores such as "present" and "absent" or "high" and "low," or it might have 100 or more possible scores, as with IQ tests. Provided there are at least two possible scores, it is a variable and the operational definition is potentially useful.

Operational Definitions Are Necessary but Rarely Sufficient

Operational definitions are never completely adequate. They are necessary but rarely seem sufficient to capture the rich and complex ideas contained in a construct. The beauty of an operational definition is that it specifies precisely how to measure a variable in such a concrete and specific manner that anyone else could repeat the steps and obtain the same measurements. Its very specificity and concreteness, however, limit the breadth and depth of what we are able to measure.

For instance, suppose someone claimed to have found a way to measure people's physical health by "sensing the auras" that surround them. The practitioner claimed the technique worked, but it was so mystical and complex that no one else could use it and obtain the same readings; this would be an unacceptable operational definition.

A thermometer reading of someone's temperature, in contrast, is an acceptable operational definition because it is a straightforward procedure that can be easily repeated. But what is a thermometer reading actually an operational definition of? Is it a measure of physical health?

Technically, a thermometer reading is a measure of how high the mercury has risen in a tube, which in turn is a measure of how warm the mercury is, which is a measure of how warm the inside of the person's mouth is. Is that a measure of physical health? We usually accept it as a measure of whether or not a person has a fever, but even that is debatable. We all have different thermometer readings at different times of day; at what point do we call a temperature a "fever"? At 99°F? Or 100°F? The connection between temperature and fever is not entirely clear. The thermometer reading, therefore, is an imperfect measure of whether someone has a fever. It is a less-than-adequate measure of health because the connection between temperature and physical health is more uncertain than the connection between temperature and fever. A person could have a normal temperature but suffer from high blood pressure or diabetes or arthritis and, therefore, not be in perfect health.

Physical health is a very complex abstract construct with many components: Blood pressure, blood sugar levels, white blood cell count, red blood cell count, degree of obesity, cholesterol level, history of cancer, and many other details constitute a person's state of health. A temperature reading, therefore, measures only one component of physical health. To obtain an adequate assessment of someone's state of physical health, we must take many readings and ask many questions, as a physician does during a general medical checkup. Any single measurement, such as a red blood cell count, is an operational definition of a component of physical health, such as degree of anemia. And each such operational definition is more acceptable as a scientific measurement of physical health than is an "aura" reading because auras are not publicly accessible. Almost anyone can learn to measure blood pressure or count red blood cells, and two people can agree in their measurements—not exactly, but to a reasonable extent. Not so with reading auras. Scientific measurement is accomplished with operational definitions that can be used and repeated by any number of people. This factor is what makes operational definitions objective.

The emphasis on objectivity in operational definitions should not be misconstrued. It does not mean that all measurement or all observations must be quantified. Good observations and measurement can also consist of words rather than numbers. Moreover, it does not mean that a number like 100 on a thermometer or achievement test *is* that person's temperature or level of achievement. If the same person were retested with another instrument or at another moment, the number might be different. Each measurement gives an approximation to a person's true standing on the construct—and each also contains some error. The emphasis on objectivity does not guarantee truth or accuracy, but it does permit social scientists to communicate with each other and with the public. It also permits anyone to challenge and check a piece of research because the operational definitions are instructions for replicating an observation or measurement.

Definitional Operationism

An ever-present danger in the transition from construct to variable to operational definition is **definitional operationism,** the assumption that the operational definition *is* the construct (e.g., "intelligence is what an intelligence test measures"). Such an assumption ignores the fact that every observation or measurement is affected by a variety of factors that bear no relation to the construct of interest. For instance, in an interview situation, answers to questions might be influenced by characteristics of the interviewer (e.g., gender, appearance), the quality of the interaction between the interviewer and the respondent, and the respondent's comfort with strangers. Similarly, paper-and-pencil measures are vulnerable to extraneous influences such as confusion created by complex response formats or use of terms unfamiliar to some respondents (Campbell, 1969a).

Any single operational definition cannot provide the one and only true measure, therefore, because it also taps irrelevant features and fails to tap all the relevant features of the theoretical construct. In the absence of other operational definitions of the same construct, we do not know how much of the measurement reflects these irrelevant features and how much reflects what we intended to measure.

A second reason for not accepting single operations as definitive measures of constructs is that doing so would logically preclude our efforts to improve measurement in the social sciences (Adler, 1947). As will become apparent after reading the sections on reliability and validity later in this chapter, there are many ways in which individual measures fall short as concrete representations of a construct. Definitional operationism, by viewing operational definitions as synonymous with the constructs they represent, fails to acknowledge the inherent and demonstrable fallibility of specific measures.

In spite of these potential problems, however, we do not advocate abandoning operational definitions. Instead, we advocate the use of *multiple* operational definitions. If we agree that each measure is an imperfect indicator of a complex abstract concept such as intelligence or social status, we can use multiple measures without violating any claims that one operational definition is supreme. In addition, by acknowledging the imperfection of all our current measures, we leave room for improvement, without which there would be little hope for scientific advance. At the practical level, researchers should realize that any single operational definition is imperfect and that it is therefore wiser to choose two or more. Each fallible operational definition provides a check on the other, and each has a different set of errors or biases.

Measurement Presupposes a Clearly Defined Construct

We have stated that the construct is the starting point for all measurement. In a way, the basic problem with definitional operationism is that it reverses the order by defining the construct in terms of an operational definition. As we have argued, this approach is doomed to failure because concrete measures always fall short of conveying the full richness of the intended construct. The approach we advocate is the alternative of defining constructs in abstract terms. A social scientist would begin by defining, say, power, social status, or intelligence in terms of other, theoretically related constructs. This definition constitutes what is called the construct's **nomological net:** the theoretical network of construct-to-construct associations derived from relevant theory and stated at an abstract level. Thus, a particular theory might define social power as the ability to influence other people's actions.

The construct's nomological net, then, becomes the starting point for decisions about operational definitions. With this definition, it might be reasonable to investigate whether the individual can give commands that others must follow, whether the individual generally wins others over to his or her viewpoint in arguments or discussions, and so on. On the other hand, it probably would not be reasonable to look at the individual's income as a measure of social power. Although income might be associated with power, it is not closely associated in terms of the theory with which we are working. In summary, measurement always presupposes a prior clearly defined construct, and the researcher should be guided by that definition in choosing candidates for operational definitions and measurement procedures.

Not only formal theory but also commonsense knowledge about constructs has a place in choosing operational definitions and measurement strategies. For example, it is intuitively clear that income is one component of social status. But how can we decide what form the association between income and status takes?

First, we use what we already know about both income and social status to determine what the association is between the two. We have an intuitive theory about the association between dollars and status. This is not a theory based on social science research—it is based on common sense and personal observations. For instance, most of us know by the time we are 18 that the social status difference between two families with annual incomes of $140,000 and $120,000 is not the same as the social status difference between two families with incomes of $40,000 and $20,000. The first difference is negligible; the second is sizable, even though in both instances the difference is $20,000. Recognizing this commonly accepted fact is one step in deciding what the association is between income and status. It is not a direct linear association such as that shown in the graph on the left in Figure 4.1. Intuition and common sense inform us that equivalent increases in income do not produce equivalent increases in social status across the range of income.

What should we assume about the association between status and our numerical indicators? In the case of income, it is probably reasonable to assume that dollars and social status are associated in a curvilinear rather than linear fashion. The graph on the right in Figure 4.1 illustrates a curvilinear pattern of association. This pattern means that, as we move higher and higher along the income scale, a particular difference in income means less and less (Carter, 1971). We cannot prove that social status is associated with income in a curvilinear fashion because we have no direct measure of social status. We will probably make fewer errors, however, and reach more insightful conclusions if we assume an association like that depicted on the right instead of the one on the left in Figure 4.1.

The association between social status and another relevant variable, education, is probably neither linear nor curvilinear, given what we know about the meaning of education. We know that completing the 16th year of school means being a college graduate, and that makes a bigger difference than any of the preceding years of schooling. Employers act as though the difference between 15 and 16 years of schooling is bigger than the difference between 14 and 15 years. Education as a measure of social status

FIGURE 4.1

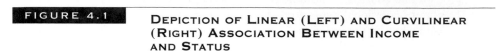

Depiction of Linear (Left) and Curvilinear (Right) Association Between Income and Status

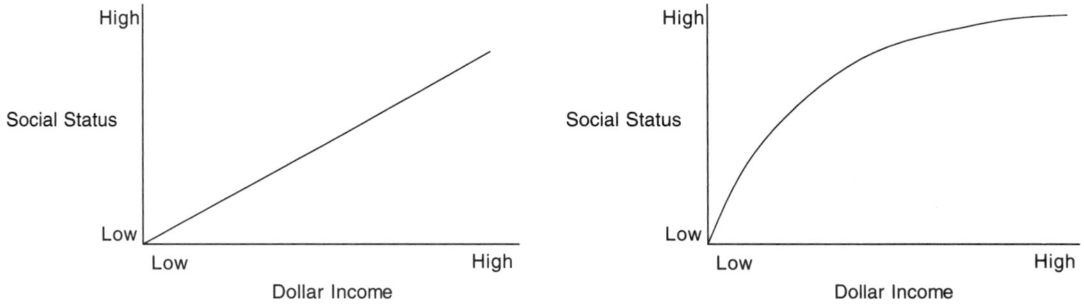

FIGURE 4.2

Association Between Number of Years of Education and Social Status

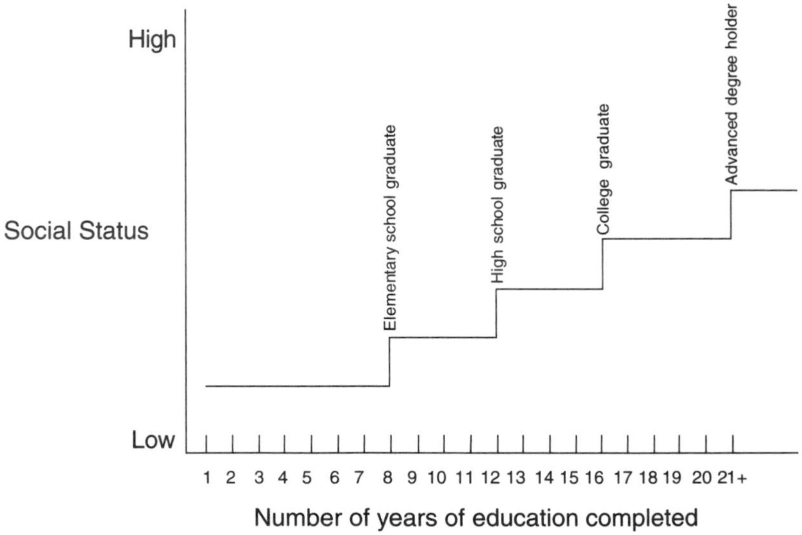

has plateaus, and college graduation is one of them. Therefore, we should assume neither a linear nor a curvilinear association between education and status like those illustrated in Figure 4.1. Instead, we can best approximate the association between education and status by using plateaus and assigning status increments to each plateau rather than each year of schooling. Each graduation signals an increase in status: elementary school graduate, high school graduate, and college graduate. Figure 4.2 illustrates this association between number of years of education and social status.

Fitting quantitative variables to abstract constructs is a bit like using a luminous ruler to measure an elephant on a moonless night. We can obtain clear numbers, but we know that the numbers do not perfectly capture the dimensions of the beast. The ruler does not bend where the elephant bends; it slips when the elephant stamps its feet; and as we grope in the dark, it is hard to tell what portions of the elephant we have measured and which parts remain untouched. When we transfer our numbers onto paper and try to sketch the elephant from the measured inches, part of our sketch must be based on what we already know about elephants—our intuition and commonsense knowledge about their shape and size.

Components of an Observed Score

Modern approaches to measurement begin with the fundamental assumption that all scores on a measure contain some components in addition to the desired construct. Expressed in a simple equation:

observed score = true score + systematic error + random error

Here the **true score** is a function of the construct we are attempting to measure; **systematic error** reflects influences from other constructs besides the desired one; and **random error** reflects nonsystematic, ever-changing influences on the score.

Two examples might clarify the nature of these components.[1] Consider first a math achievement test, in which pupils solve a number of arithmetic problems. The desired construct, or true score, is the pupil's true math ability. But other constructs also influence the observed score. For example, motivation is important; if a particular student does not believe math is important and has no wish to do well, he or she might doodle in the margins of the test instead of working to solve the problems, ending up with a score that is lower than his or her true ability. "Test-wiseness" might also be important. Some pupils will be better than others at understanding the test instructions, properly filling in the answers on the score sheet, guessing intelligently when they do not know the answer for sure, and so on, leading to scores above what one would expect from their true math ability. Finally, random error could

[1]Examples in this chapter generally involve measurements of individual persons, probably the most common situation in social science research; however, the logic illustrated by the examples applies equally well to situations in which constructs are measured in other types of units, such as cities, colleges, preliterate tribes, etc.

include such things as lucky or unlucky guesses on questions the pupil cannot solve; random slips of the pencil in filling in answers; occasional lapses of attention and simple mental mistakes in solving the problems; inability to concentrate because a student lacks sleep or is not feeling well; and the like. The total score on the test, which we would like to use as a pure measure of each pupil's math ability, will be influenced by these sources of systematic and random error as well.

Another example is a scale intended to measure a personality trait such as conscientiousness by asking respondents about their past behaviors. For example, the scale might include a question about whether the person is always, usually, sometimes, or never on time for appointments. Clearly, a series of well-chosen questions of this type could provide an indication of the person's actual level of conscientiousness, the desired true score. But the test score would also be subject to other influences. One systematic influence would be **social desirability response bias,** the general tendency to overreport one's desirable behaviors and other characteristics and to underreport one's less admirable qualities. Someone who is high on this response bias might report always being on time for appointments even if that is not altogether true, leading to an overestimate of his or her level of conscientiousness. Random errors might include the person's specific, recent experiences. If you are almost never on time, but quite by chance last Tuesday happened to get to your dentist's office five minutes early for an appointment, you might remember that specific incident when you complete the scale and respond that you are "usually" on time. Given the same scale at another time, you might have responded differently because the memory for that particular incident would not be so fresh in your mind.

Because of the effects of both systematic and random error, observed scores cannot be assumed to reflect the desired construct only. Observed scores always include undesired components. The key question becomes how to separate the various contributions to the score. We might want to do this for two reasons: (1) To improve the measuring instrument, we need to know how small or large are the contributions of systematic and random error to the scores. This knowledge might suggest the need to consider alternative measures. (2) Of course, to classify or rank people on the desired construct, we would like ways to purify observed scores and minimize the effects of measurement error.

Fortunately, there is a way to achieve both of these goals. The underlying logic involves assessing the contribution of different components to the observed score by comparing observations made under circumstances in which particular components are expected to vary. For example, we could compare two sets of scores in which the true score and systematic error components are expected to remain constant, and only random error is expected to vary. Then the degree of similarity between the two sets of scores would reveal the amount of random error in each. A high degree of similarity implies that random error is not having a great deal of influence, whereas great differences between the two sets of scores implies that random error is very important.

In this chapter, we deal only intuitively with the notion of comparing sets of scores, which in actual research practice relies on correlation coefficients. A **correlation coefficient** is a statistical index of the strength of association between two variables, and a more technical definition is provided in Chapter 18. For our purposes here, it is sufficient for you to think of a correlation coefficient simply as a measure of the strength of an association, an answer to the question, "To what extent do two variables measure the same thing?"

Reliability

The **reliability** of a measure is defined as the extent to which it is free from random error. In turn, **validity** is the extent to which a measure reflects only the desired construct without contamination from other systematically varying constructs. Note that validity requires reliability as a prerequisite. A perfectly unreliable score cannot have any validity. We might imagine a group of students taking a test in an unknown foreign language and guessing wildly at every answer. Any differences in their scores would be attributable to chance rather than an identifiable construct. A measure, though, can be perfectly reliable and yet completely invalid, as would be a poorly constructed test that only measured "test-wiseness" and not the students' actual knowledge of the subject matter. Only when a measure is both reliable and valid can we confidently use its scores in research. In a sense, then, reliability is a question that must be addressed prior to validity, and, as we shall see, it is also the easier question to answer.

Test–Retest Reliability

The source of random error that is the focus of concerns about reliability is expected to vary, rather than remain constant, from one occasion to another. Specific mental mistakes, slips of the pen, and the like would not recur if the test were repeated after some time delay. Therefore, the correlation between scores on the same measure administered on two separate occasions—a **test–retest correlation**—provides an estimate of the measure's reliability. The two occasions should be far enough apart so that respondents cannot remember specific responses from the test to the retest but close enough together so that change in the true score is expected to be minimal. A completely unreliable measure, in which all the variation in scores stems from random errors, would show a complete lack of correlation between test and retest. On the other hand, a perfectly reliable measure, in which no random error whatever affected the score, would produce scores that correlate perfectly over a short period of time.

Internal Consistency Reliability

Test–retest reliability estimates are conceptually easy to understand and are widely used. But they can be difficult to obtain; it is cumbersome to assemble a group of people twice to repeat the measurement, and issues of memory for responses and of change in the true construct being measured can make an appropriate time period difficult to select. An alternative estimate, called **internal consistency reliability,** is not subject to these concerns and, therefore, more widely used.

This estimate rests on the idea that random error varies not only over time but also from one question or test item to another within the same measure. That is, making a mistake, misunderstanding a word in a test question, or other sources of random error would be expected to influence some specific items on the measure but not others. If we can make the crucial assumption that all the questions or items on the measure are measuring the same construct, lack of correlation among specific items can serve as the basis for an estimate of the influence of random errors. If random error has a strong effect, it would make scores on some individual items high and others low, reducing the item-to-item correlation. On the other hand, a weak effect of random error would mean that each item measures the same underlying characteristic of the person, so a high score on one item would go together with a high score on another; the items would be highly correlated.

This basic insight has been used in different ways to develop methods of estimating the reliability of a measure without the need to assess people on two separate occasions. One method that has been widely used is the **split-half reliability.** The set of items in the measure is split into two halves. The split is usually done by separating the full set of items into odd-numbered and even-numbered sets; a strategy that ensures an equivalent number of items from early and late in the measure appear in the two sets. The correlation between the two half-tests provides the basis for an estimate of reliability.

Split-half reliability estimates, however, have this problem: The exact estimate depends on how the split of the items was achieved (odd versus even, first half versus last half, or some other way). This factor introduces an unwanted degree of arbitrariness into the reliability estimation process. For this reason, the preferred measure of internal consistency reliability is now **coefficient alpha** (Cronbach, 1951). This estimate is derived from the correlations of each item with each other item and so does not rest on any arbitrary choice of ways to divide the items into two halves. In fact, coefficient alpha can be shown to be numerically equal to the average of all possible split-half reliabilities. Like all other reliability estimates, coefficient alpha ranges from 0 to 1, with 0 meaning complete unreliability and 1 meaning perfect reliability.

Inter-Rater Reliability

In some studies, the operational definition of a construct requires the direct observation of behavior. For instance, the operational definition of toddlers' activity level might be the amount of movement about a room by toddlers during a 10-minute period of free play. As a means of quantifying movement, the room could be divided into a grid made up of equal-size cells and observers could count the number of times a toddler crosses from one cell to another. Or the quality of communication between romantic partners could be measured by observing or listening to conversations about what each likes least and most about their partner and rating them on a 5-point scale anchored by "destructive" and "constructive." In either case, any particular observer's rating of behavior is, like an item on a questionnaire, subject to error. For instance, while counting toddlers' movement from cell to cell in the grid, an observer might lose concentration and fail to record all instances of crossing from one cell to the next. Or perhaps certain children move about the room in such a way that it is not always clear whether they moved from one cell to another. Similarly, different observers might take a different view of the quality of a conversation between romantic partners as a result of the current status of communication in their own romantic relationship.

In much the same way that random errors in responses to items on a paper-and-pencil questionnaire reduce the reliability of scores, random errors in ratings by observers reduce the reliability of behavioral ratings. Our strategy for addressing this problem is to enlist multiple observers. An added benefit to this strategy is that we can use the logic of internal consistency reliability to estimate inter-rater reliability. For instance, if the observers are rating behavior on a continuum (e.g., the quality of conversation between romantic partners), then their ratings can be treated like items on a questionnaire and reliability estimated using coefficient alpha. If the task given observers is to rate whether a research participant did or did not enact a behavior, then a measure of agreement such as **kappa** (Cohen, 1960) can be used to estimate inter-rater reliability.

Influences on Reliability

Specific procedures and guidelines for constructing high-quality measures are provided in Chapters 6 and 7; however, it is worth listing a few influences on reliability now for reference. Longer measures are more reliable than shorter ones, other things being equal. A larger range of variation on the measured construct among the individuals being tested also leads to higher reliability. It is easier to make reliable distinctions among individuals when they vary a lot than when they are all very close together on the target characteristic. Finally, freedom from distractions, misunderstandings, and the like, which can be provided by clear instructions and an optimal testing situation, decrease people's tendencies to make random errors and simple mistakes, which create unreliability.

Validity

Even if a measure is highly reliable, it might not be high in validity because it measures the wrong construct. A measure intended to tap people's levels of conscientiousness might instead reflect only the extent to which they are biased in the direction of reporting good things about themselves. Or for instance, if we wished to measure intelligence and we gave a standard IQ test in English to a group of French high school students, we might find a high test–retest reliability but have an invalid measure of those students' intelligence. Instead, we would have a measure of their knowledge of English. For French students, an English IQ test is a measure of English language proficiency rather than a measure of intelligence. That test would be an inappropriate and, therefore, invalid test of intelligence for that group of respondents.

Using an English language IQ test to measure the intelligence of French students is an obvious case of measuring a construct other than the one intended. Most measures in the social sciences do not contain such gross errors, but all measures share this problem to some extent. Operational definitions inevitably include constructs that are not supposed to be included and exclude portions of the underlying construct that should be measured. Because the underlying construct cannot be tapped directly, but only indirectly through operational definitions, we can never be sure what portion of the construct the operational definition taps and what portions are unmeasured. This principle of measurement is illustrated in Figure 4.3. Notice that, although a substantial majority of each circle representing an operational definition overlaps with the rectangle representing the underlying construct, the circles themselves do not overlap completely, a portion of each circle does not overlap with the rectangle at all, and a portion of the rectangle is not covered by any of the circles. It is especially noteworthy that, as illustrated in the figure, coverage of the underlying construct is significantly improved through the use of multiple operational definitions.

In the preceding sections, estimating reliability was based on the key idea of comparing scores that should be differentially influenced by random errors but otherwise should be the same. Test–retest and internal consistency reliability estimates use this basic approach in different ways. In fact, this idea can be extended to give information about the validity of a measure as well as its reliability. The key concept is again the comparison of scores that are expected to have different blends of components.

FIGURE 4.3 **OPERATIONAL DEFINITIONS INCLUDE IRRELEVANT COMPONENTS AND FAIL TO INCLUDE ALL RELEVANT PORTIONS OF THE UNDERLYING CONSTRUCT**

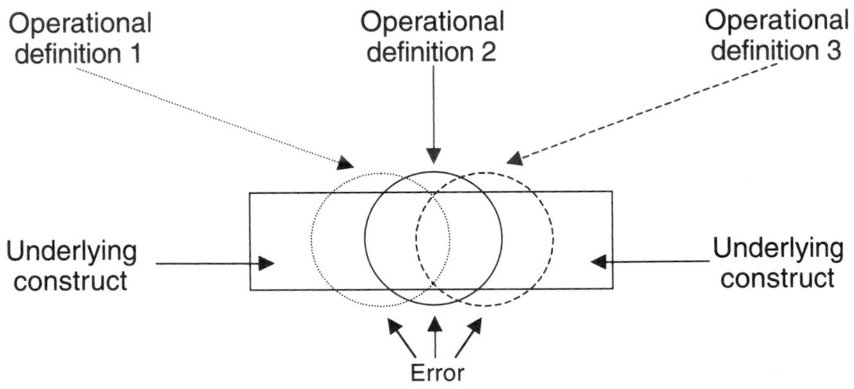

For example, if two measures are expected to measure the same target characteristic (e.g., two of the circles in Figure 4.3) but have different sources of systematic error, the extent to which they correlate is an indication of the extent to which they measure the target construct, that is, their validity. If both measures are completely pure and valid measures of the construct, they will correlate perfectly. On the other hand, if the measures are useless as assessments of the target construct, showing only systematic biases, they will correlate zero because we are assuming that the sources of systematic error in each measure are different. Before describing variations on this fundamental idea and the ways it can be used to assess validity, we describe a more informal approach to validity assessment.

Face Validity

Face validity is evaluated by a group of judges, sometimes experts, who read or look at a measuring technique and decide whether in their opinion it measures what its name suggests. For instance, professional speech therapists could look at a test designed to measure degrees of speech impairment and decide whether, in their opinion, the test measures what the testers claim. Evaluating face validity is a subjective process, but we could calculate a validity figure by computing the amount of agreement among judges using an index such as kappa. Most instruments must pass the face validity test, at least informally; however, at times indirect, or subtle, measures that lack face validity are used when it is important to disguise the purpose of the measure from the people whose characteristics are being measured. An example would be a hypothetical measure of prejudice based on asking people about their color preferences.

Convergent Validity

We now discuss ways of comparing scores from different measures to arrive at a picture of the relative contributions of the desired construct and other, undesired constructs, to the observed scores. The tests a measure must pass are twofold: assessments of convergent and discriminant validity.

Convergent validity refers to the overlap between alternative measures that are intended to tap the same construct but that have different sources of systematic error. For example, suppose we wish to measure the intelligence of French students. We could use an English language intelligence test as operational definition 1, a French IQ test as definition 2, and a face-to-face interview conducted by a panel of French educators as definition 3. Table 4.1 shows a hypothetical rank ordering of students' intelligence scores obtained from the three measures.

By counting the number of agreements in the rank ordering between any two tests, we get a rough picture of the correlation between them. The greater the number of agreements, the higher the correlation. Here, the amount of agreement between definitions 2 and 3 is quite high; two students reverse position and seven remain the same. The amount of agreement between definition 1 and the other two

TABLE 4.1 **RANK ORDERING OF NINE HIGH SCHOOL STUDENTS' INTELLIGENCE SCORES OBTAINED ACCORDING TO THREE HYPOTHETICAL OPERATIONAL DEFINITIONS OF INTELLIGENCE**

Operational Definition 1: English IQ Test	**Operational Definition 2: French Translation of English Test**	**Operational Definition 3: French Interviews**
Jacques	Pierre	Pierre
Carole	Marie	Marie
Marie	Jeanne	Jeanne
Marianne	Jacques	Jacques
Lisa	Lisa	Lisa
Charles	Charles	Charles
Pierre	Carole	Carole
Jeanne	Robert	Marianne
Robert	Marianne	Robert

is much less; five or six students reverse positions in each case. The amount of agreement between any two measures tells us the extent to which they are measuring the same thing. It is represented conceptually as the overlapping portions of the circles in Figure 4.3 and is numerically equal to the square of the correlation coefficient (see Chapter 18).

Here, measures based on operational definitions 2 and 3 show good levels of agreement, pointing to the convergent validity of the two measures. That is, both are intended to assess intelligence, and they tend to rank-order respondents in the same way. To what can this correspondence be attributed? Obviously, to the extent that both measures effectively tap intelligence, they will correlate highly. But biases and systematic errors should not lead to a high correlation because the biases and errors in these three measures would be expected to be different. Systematic errors in the three measures include knowledge of English for definition 1 (the English language intelligence test) and conversational skills and poise for the interview, definition 3. Indeed, here the English language assessment does not correlate highly with the other two, showing that it does not have good convergent validity. Most of the variability in responses to this measure appears to be due to knowledge of English rather than intelligence, for if this were not the case, it should correlate with the other two measures of intelligence.

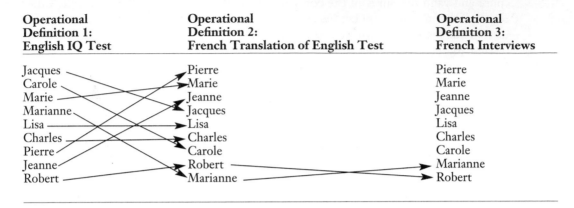

These biasing factors are not part of what we mean by intelligence, for an intelligent French student might be unable to answer any questions on the English test because he or she has never studied English. Similarly, a student might do well on written tests but become anxious during an interview. Knowledge of English and the tendency to become anxious are irrelevant constructs that could enter as biases into these measures of intelligence. But comparing the three measures allows us to assess the amount of overlap between them, learning the extent to which the measures tap what we intend and to what extent they tap other factors. Convergent validity indicates that the correlated measures are picking up the common intended construct.

Discriminant Validity

A valid measure has to show good convergence with other measures of the same thing, as already noted. It should also fail to correlate with measures that are supposed to tap basically different constructs; this is the definition of **discriminant validity.** Consider a self-report measure of conscientiousness as an example. We might be concerned that the test only picks up a tendency to give socially desirable responses. We could assess this suspicion by a convergent validity strategy, looking for correlations between the measure and other measures of conscientiousness that do not rely on self-reports. We also could use a discriminant validity strategy. If another measure that is known to reflect socially desirable responding is available (as it is: Paulhus, 1991), it can be administered to people along with the conscientiousness measure. To the extent that the measure is valid, it should not correlate highly with the social desirability score, for there is no reason to think that conscientiousness and the tendency to give socially desirable responses are actually associated constructs. On the other hand, a high correlation supports the suspicion that social desirability bias is a strong contributor to the conscientiousness scores obtained from our measure.

In short, a measure should correlate with alternative measures of the same construct that vary in potential sources of invalidity. In addition, a measure should fail to correlate with other measures that do not tap the target construct but that pick up expected sources of systematic error. These dual types of evidence are the strongest empirical support of a measure's validity.

Validity and the Nomological Net

Both convergent and discriminant validity can be put into a common framework by considering the nomological net of the target construct. As defined earlier, this is the theoretically derived set of associations with other constructs that serves to define the target construct. With this definition, the assessment of validity can be summed up in a single sentence: Validity is demonstrated when the associations observed with a measure match the theoretically postulated nomological net of the construct. In effect, the measure correlates with what it is supposed to correlate with and does not correlate with what it is not supposed to correlate with. This is a somewhat more general statement than that made previously under the heading of convergent validity. There we stated that a measure should converge with alternative ways of assessing the same construct. Now we are pointing out that theory might tell us that other constructs, although not identical, should be correlated; such constructs could also furnish evidence of a measure's validity. Thus, if we have a measure of a person's resources (money, status, knowledge) and a theory that says such resources contribute

FIGURE 4.4 **Schematic Depiction of Desired Correspondence Between the Construct's Nomological Net and the Measure's Empirical Pattern of Associations**

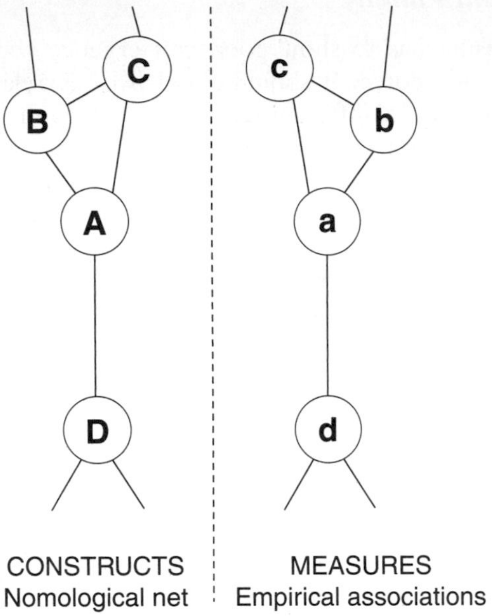

to a person's social power, a correlation between the measure of resources and a proposed measure of social power would help support its validity. This is a form of convergent validity, even though we are not comparing the proposed measure against other measures of the same construct but rather against other measures with which it is theoretically expected to correlate. Figure 4.4 shows this notion schematically. Note how the pattern of associations among the measures, indicated by circles labeled with lowercase letters, mirrors the theoretical pattern of associations among the constructs.

The Multitrait–Multimethod Matrix

Validity, then, is based on an assessment of how much one method of measuring a construct agrees with other measures of the same or theoretically similar constructs and disagrees with measures of theoretically dissimilar constructs. The **multitrait–multimethod (MTMM) matrix** is a table of correlation coefficients that enables us to simultaneously evaluate the convergent and discriminant validity of a construct (Campbell & Fiske, 1959). As an example, suppose we are interested in the theoretical

TABLE 4.2 **MULTITRAIT–MULTIMETHOD MATRIX OF CORRELATIONS BETWEEN ATTITUDES TOWARD WOMEN AND ATTITUDES TOWARD MEN**

	Paper-and-Pencil Questionnaire		Observations of Behavior	
	Attitudes Toward Women (ATW)	Attitudes Toward Men (ATM)	Attitudes Toward Women (ATW)	Attitudes Toward Men (ATM)
Questionnaire				
ATW	(.90)			
ATM	.30	(.90)		
Behavior				
ATW	.70	.10	(.90)	
ATM	.10	.70	.30	(.90)

Note: The coefficients in parentheses are reliability estimates.

construct called "attitudes toward women" and we design an instrument to measure it. In order to demonstrate the validity of our measure, we would need to show not only that it converges with other measures of the same attitude but also that attitudes toward women are distinct from other attitudes such as political liberalism or attitudes toward men. To demonstrate validity in these ways, we would have to measure those other attitudes, too, and find lower correlations between our measure and measures of political liberalism, attitudes toward men, and the like than we find among multiple measures of attitudes toward women.

To construct an MTMM matrix, we must have at least two constructs measured with at least two methods. An example of a matrix for evaluating the validity of our hypothetical measure of attitudes toward women is shown in Table 4.2.

The matrix is based on the principle that the more features two measurements have in common, the higher their correlation will be. Measurements can share two types of features: traits and methods. **Traits** are the underlying construct the measurement is supposed to tap—attitudes toward women in our example. **Methods** are the mode of measurement. We describe and illustrate different modes of measurement in the next chapter. For our example, we select two modes that vary considerably in terms of potential threats to validity: paper-and-pencil questionnaire and observations of behavior. Referring to Table 4.2, you can see that our selection of two traits and two methods yields a matrix of correlations arrayed in four columns and four rows. The first two columns and rows include correlations involving attitudes toward women and attitudes toward men measured using a paper-and-pencil questionnaire. The remaining columns and rows include correlations involving the two types of attitudes measured using behavioral observation. Only the lower portion of the matrix is printed because a correlation matrix is symmetric about its diagonal.

The values on the diagonal are reliability coefficients, which could be estimated using either a test–retest or internal consistency strategy.

Ideally, scores should reflect only the intended construct and not be influenced by the mode of measurement. In reality, the mode of measurement also affects the score, and some of the variation in observed scores is a product of the method used to obtain the scores. For instance, look at coefficients in the first two columns of Table 4.2. The correlation between attitudes toward women and attitudes toward men is .30 when both are measured using a paper-and-pencil questionnaire; however, the correlation between them is only .10 when they are measured using different methods. In light of this pattern, we conclude that scores on our hypothetical measure of attitudes toward women are, to some degree, influenced by the way they are measured. To the extent that the two correlations we just highlighted were the same, we could conclude that mode of measurement is not a threat to the validity of our measure.

The MTMM matrix lets a researcher assess the extent to which scores on a measure reflect the trait (i.e., construct) the measure was designed to tap as opposed to the method (i.e., mode of measurement) by which scores were assigned. Because every score is made up of two systematic elements—a trait and a method—the correlation between two sets of scores depends on how much they share both the trait and the method. By comparing coefficients representing different combinations of trait and method in the MTMM matrix, a researcher can learn a great deal about the validity of a measure. Correlations between scores that reflect the same trait and the same method are **reliability coefficients.** Although these coefficients are not themselves indicative of validity, as we noted at the beginning of the chapter, they indicate the limit to the validity of our measure. Correlations between scores that reflect the same trait measured by different methods are **convergent validity coefficients.** The reliability coefficients of an instrument should logically be higher than its validity coefficients because the former are based on more shared elements. The MTMM matrix includes two additional correlation coefficients to assess the validity of an instrument. These are both correlations between different traits. One is a **discriminant validity coefficient** that indicates the correlation between different traits measured by the same method, and the other is a **nonsense coefficient** that reflects the correlation between different traits measured by different methods.

The reliability and convergent validity coefficients should be high, whereas the discriminant validity and nonsense coefficients should be low. If the latter two coefficients are as high as the convergent validity coefficients, it means the two traits are not different but are the same or highly similar. For instance, our hypothetical measures of attitudes toward women and attitudes toward men should not be too highly correlated if they tap truly separate attitudes. If the intercorrelations between these measures were like those shown in Table 4.2, we would be satisfied that they measured two distinct traits or attitudes. The convergent validity coefficients (.70) are higher than the discriminant validity coefficients (.30) and the nonsense coefficients (.10). This is justification for saying the measures tap two different traits. If, however, the matrix looked like the one in Table 4.3, the measures would be invalidated, not because the correlations were too low but because some of the correlations were too high.

TABLE 4.3

MULTITRAIT–MULTIMETHOD MATRIX OF CORRELATIONS BETWEEN ATTITUDES TOWARD WOMEN AND ATTITUDES TOWARD MEN SHOWING LACK OF CONVERGENT AND DISCRIMINANT VALIDITY

	Paper-and-Pencil Questionnaire		Observations of Behavior	
	Attitudes Toward Women (ATW)	**Attitudes Toward Men (ATM)**	**Attitudes Toward Women (ATW)**	**Attitudes Toward Men (ATM)**
Questionnaire				
ATW	(.90)			
ATM	.80	(.90)		
Behavior				
ATW	.40	.30	(.90)	
ATM	.30	.40	.80	(.90)

Note: The coefficients in parentheses are reliability estimates.

The correlations in Table 4.3 show that the two attitudes are very similar because they are highly correlated with one another. The correlation between two different traits measured by the same method (.80) is higher than the correlation between the same trait measured by different methods (.40). The measures of these two attitudes have no discriminant validity because they produce scores that are highly intercorrelated. If the two measures truly tap different attitudes, the correlation between them should not be higher than the convergent validity correlations of the same trait measured by different methods (.40).

Particularly if a researcher is trying to develop a measure of a newly conceptualized construct, it is important to assess its discriminant validity to demonstrate that it is indeed new and different. Such measures can be invalidated not only because of low correlations but also correlations with other measures that are too high to justify the claim that they measure different constructs. If we observed the pattern of correlations shown in Table 4.3, we would conclude that the two measures tap the same attitude; and rather than talk of attitudes toward women and attitudes toward men, we might combine the measures and reconceptualize the construct as attitudes about gender roles.

To summarize, the validity of a measure, like its reliability, can be assessed by comparing scores obtained under conditions in which different components of the observed score are assumed to vary. The three components of any observed score are the true or desired construct itself, systematic errors, and random errors. Logically, examination of the validity of a measure always involves assessing the match between the empirical associations demonstrated by the measure and the theoretically expected set of associations: the construct's nomological net.

Summary

We began this chapter by saying that operational definitions are always essential. Without them there would be no scientific measurement. They provide a public process for reproducing and replicating measurements and manipulations so that we can assess their reliability and validity.

Operational definitions are necessary but also inevitably inadequate. They contain errors by including irrelevant components and omitting other relevant portions of the underlying construct that we want to tap. For this reason, no single operational definition completely defines the construct. Each is only an approximation. Because no single measure is 100% reliable or 100% valid, we advocate using multiple operational definitions of any construct.

With multiple measures of multiple constructs, a researcher can construct a matrix of reliability and validity correlations known as the multitrait–multimethod matrix. This provides a very thorough assessment of construct validity by allowing the researcher to examine both the convergent and discriminant validity of the methods and the traits being measured.

Key Concepts

coefficient alpha
construct
convergent validity
convergent validity coefficients
correlation coefficient
definitional operationism
discriminant validity
discriminant validity coefficients
face validity
internal consistency reliability
kappa
methods
multitrait–multimethod matrix
nomological net
nonsense coefficients
operational definition
random error
reliability
reliability coefficients
social desirability response bias
split-half reliability
systematic error
test–retest correlation
traits
true score
validity
variable

On the Web

http://paradigm.soci.brocku.ca/~lward/pubs/MEAD_006.HTML This brief piece by George Herbert Mead gives a sense of how the earliest social scientists thought about measurement.

http://ericae.net/ft/tamu/Valid.htm Complete text of an essay entitled, "Controversies Regarding the Nature of Score Validity: Still Crazy After All These Years."

http://www.unl.edu/buros/ Home page of the Buros Institute of Mental Measurements. Provides links to thousands of tests of potential interest to social scientists.

http://wwwcsteep.bc.edu/ctest Home page of the Consortium for Equity in Standards and Testing, a group committed to responsible use of test results.

http://www.testpublishers.org/question.htm An informative page about uses and abuses of tests in a variety of settings. Sponsored by the Association of Test Publishers.

Further Reading

Hogan, R., & Nicholson, R. A. (1988). The meaning of personality test scores. *American Psychologist*, 43, 621–626.

Traub, R. E. (1994). *Reliability for the social sciences: Theory and application.* Thousand Oaks, CA: Sage.

CHAPTER

5

Modes of Measurement

As detailed in Chapter 2, a fundamental concern for social scientists is construct validity, that is, the extent to which the constructs implicated in the hypothesis under examination are adequately represented by the variables chosen to define them. Recall that we identified two general classes of variables: independent variables, which represent the causal constructs in our hypothesis, and dependent variables, which represent constructs that are effects or outcomes of the causal constructs. All dependent variables require some form of measurement. By **measurement** we mean rules for assigning symbols, usually numbers, to objects, usually people (Nunnally & Bernstein, 1994). In randomized experiments, independent variables are manipulated (i.e., imposed on participants by the researcher); however, in nonrandomized experiments, one or more independent variables are measured as well. Meaningful hypothesis tests require adequate measurement.

A critical decision for researchers in the social sciences is how to measure variables and, thereby, operationally define constructs. For instance, a researcher interested in whether test anxiety influences students' test scores must decide how to measure test anxiety. One option would be to simply ask students how anxious they feel just before copies of the test are distributed. Alternatively, observers might rate individual students on variables related to anxiety such as fidgetiness, distraction, wringing of hands, and so forth. Yet another approach would be to continuously monitor heart rate before, during, and after completion of the test. These alternative measurement approaches to operationally defining a construct are different **modes of measurement.** In this example, the modes of measurement we considered are paper-and-pencil questionnaire, observation, and physiological monitoring. These are three of a growing number of ways to operationally define constructs through measurement. In this chapter, we review modes of measurement commonly used in research on social behavior.

A basic principle of sound scientific research is that constructs are best defined using multiple operations or measures. In this chapter we elaborate a refined version of this principle: The strongest test of hypotheses are those that involve multiple measures representing multiple modes of measurement. In other words, although two paper-and-pencil measures of a construct are better than one, a paper-and-pencil measure coupled with an observational measure would be better still. This reasoning follows from a basic principle elaborated in Chapter 4: All measures are fallible. To extend this principle, we suggest here that, to some degree, the fallibility of a measure is tied to the mode of measurement. For instance, all paper-and-pencil measures, regardless of the construct they were designed to measure, are subject to similar systematic and random errors. As such, the use of two or more measures of the same mode does little to overcome the fallibility of each. By using multiple measures acquired by different modes, researchers can be more confident that overlap between the measures represents the construct of interest rather than overlapping errors of measurement.

This chapter includes two major sections. In the first and longer of the two sections, we discuss the advantages and disadvantages of different modes of measurement that involve direct questioning of research participants. Specifically, we cover paper-and-pencil questionnaires, face-to-face interviews, telephone interviews, questionnaires administered via the Internet, and experience sampling. In the second section we discuss less frequently used approaches to measurement that do not involve direct questioning of research participants regarding the constructs of interest. We devote specific attention to collateral reports, observation, and physiological monitoring.

Modes of Direct Questioning

Whether casual observer of social behavior or social scientist, when we want to know something about another person's beliefs, attitudes, behaviors, feelings, perceptions, motivations, or plans, our first recourse is often simply to ask them a question. Responses to direct questions—whether a highly constrained choice from a small set of alternative answers or a lengthy, open-ended description of the respondent's thinking—are the most widely used source of information in the social sciences. The most obvious reason is the flexibility of verbal communication. Human language is a powerful and precise medium for phrasing and answering questions about attitudes, behaviors, experiences, or virtually any other topic, real or imagined, past, present, or future.

Once a researcher has decided to measure using direct questioning, he or she must consider whether information is best acquired by paper-and-pencil questionnaires, face-to-face interviews, telephone interviews, the Internet, or by asking respondents to answer questions when prompted by an electronic device (e.g., programmed wristwatch) during a set period of time. The advantages and disadvantages associated with these modes of direct questioning are discussed in the remainder of this section of the chapter. The next two chapters extend the material covered in this section by addressing issues that apply to all modes of direct questioning: how questions are written and responses to them acquired.

Paper-and-Pencil Questionnaires

It seems highly unlikely that any reader of this text would not have completed at least one paper-and-pencil questionnaire during his or her lifetime. Indeed, paper-and-pencil questionnaires are the workhorse mode of measurement in the social sciences as well as schools, places of employment, and other arenas in which personal or public opinion is sought. Before we take up the advantages and disadvantages of paper-and-pencil questionnaires, consider these examples from published social science research: Arriaga (2001) examined the association between dating couples' relationship satisfaction and their likelihood of breaking up during a 10-week period. Both relationship satisfaction and dating status at the end of 10 weeks were measured using paper-and-pencil questionnaires. Satisfaction was measured by a series of statements to which participants expressed their level of agreement. An example statement is, "I feel satisfied with our relationship at the moment." Dating status was measured by a single item simply asking participants whether they were still dating the person they were dating at the beginning of the study. Schmader, Major, and Gramzow (2001) used paper-and-pencil measures to investigate the association between African-American students' beliefs about ethnic injustice and the value they assign to academic success. Students' beliefs about ethnic injustice were measured by asking them to state the extent of their agreement or disagreement with statements such as, "Differences in status between ethnic groups are the result of injustice." The degree to which students valued academic success was measured by responses to items such as, "Being good at academics is an important part of who I am." As these examples illustrate, paper-and-pencil questionnaires can be used to define a wide array of constructs in a relatively straightforward manner.

As is true for all modes of measurement, there are advantages and disadvantages to the use of paper-and-pencil questionnaires in social science research. The advantages are sufficiently compelling to explain the widespread use of this mode of measurement; however, the disadvantages are sufficiently worrisome to argue against the conclusion that a hypothesis has been subjected to a definitive test when the only approach to operationally defining the constructs is paper-and-pencil questionnaires.

Advantages Low cost is the primary advantage of paper-and-pencil questionnaires, whether they are mailed, administered to small groups of respondents in a designated room, or distributed in other ways. It might appear that printing and postage or other costs of distributing and collecting the questionnaires are all that need to be taken into account, suggesting a very low cost. However, as discussed in Chapter 6, this is certainly an underestimate if the steps needed to obtain high-quality data are included in the costs. Still, paper-and-pencil questionnaires are the least expensive means of data gathering, and cost is not a trivial consideration. Cost often determines whether research can be done at all, and low cost might mean that responses can be obtained from more people, increasing the sample size.

A second advantage of paper-and-pencil questionnaires is the avoidance of potential interviewer bias. Research has shown that the way an interviewer asks questions and even the interviewer's general appearance or vocal qualities can influence respondents' answers. Although these biases can be minimized in interviews, they can be completely eliminated only with a self-administered questionnaire.

A third advantage is that when paper-and-pencil questionnaires are distributed by mail, or by some other means (e.g., the Web) given to respondents to complete as time allows, there is less pressure for an immediate response. This factor might be important, for example, when the participant has to look in personal records for the information to answer a question. Responses to attitude questions might also benefit if the participant takes ample time to consider each question carefully rather than giving the response that springs immediately to mind. The latter is more likely under the social pressure of long silences in a face-to-face or telephone interview or the appearance of other respondents in a small-group session completing the questionnaire. However, participants queried under these conditions must also be motivated to give such extensive, careful consideration to their responses, and interviewers and test proctors can generally motivate participants more than can written instructions.

Paper-and-pencil questionnaires are sometimes credited with another advantage—giving respondents a greater feeling of anonymity and therefore encouraging open responses to sensitive questions; however, the merits of this claim are uncertain, given recent research and the development of new techniques for handling sensitive questions in interviews (e.g., Palmgreen, Donohew, Lorch, Hoyle, & Stephenson, 2001). At present, there is no evidence of large differences between the quality of responses to sensitive questions in paper-and-pencil questionnaires versus carefully constructed interview situations.

Disadvantages The paper-and-pencil questionnaire also has important disadvantages, particularly in the quality of data that can be obtained. At least two considerations are involved. The first is the **response rate,** defined as the percentage of respondents in the initial sample from whom complete responses are obtained. Response rate is the chief index of data quality in a survey because it defines the extent of possible bias from nonresponse. Nonrespondents might differ in important ways from respondents, so that if only 25% or 50% of the sample actually responds, there is no way of knowing if their characteristics can be generalized to describe the whole sample let alone the population the sample is intended to represent. Therefore, particularly when the research is concerned with estimating prevalence of behavior or otherwise describing a population, a low response rate calls into question any conclusions based on the data. A response rate of 80% or 90%, on the other hand, means that even if the nonrespondents differ substantially from those who respond, the overall estimates will not be badly biased.

It is important to remember, though, to ask the question "90% of what?" That is, even a high response rate is meaningless unless the sample design itself is strong. We might hand out questionnaires to 20 of our friends and acquaintances and achieve a near-perfect response rate, but the results would not be meaningful because they do not constitute a representative sample of any larger population (see Chapters 8 and 9 on sampling people). Therefore, response rate is not the only consideration in evaluating the quality of data from a survey; it is meaningful only when the initial sample is properly drawn and the research questions demand good estimates of the prevalence of a behavior or the strength of an opinion in a specified population.

Mail surveys generally have the lowest response rate of the various approaches to direct questioning using paper-and-pencil questionnaires, usually less than 50% when the target population is the general public. This fact alone limits the usefulness of mail samples because the unknown bias from extensive nonresponse makes the sample estimates quite untrustworthy. On the other hand, when specialized populations are sampled (such as members of a particular profession or alumni of a particular college) response rates from mail surveys can reach respectable levels.

Data quality has another aspect besides response rate—the accuracy and completeness of responses to questions. Here the key issue is the motivation of the respondent, and there are problems in creating and maintaining motivation when direct questions are posed using a paper-and-pencil questionnaire. A face-to-face or telephone interview makes it easier to build rapport between interviewer and respondent, motivating the respondent to give full and accurate answers. On this dimension of data quality as well as on response rate, paper-and-pencil questionnaires generally fall short.

Other, less serious disadvantages also characterize studies in which paper-and-pencil questionnaires are mailed to respondents. One is the requirement to use a short questionnaire. Dillman (1978) found that questionnaires up to about 12 pages or 125 individual responses produce response rates that do not depend on length. But for questionnaires exceeding that length, which represents a relatively short questionnaire, increasing length is associated with decreasing response rate.

Another problem when paper-and-pencil questionnaires are mailed to participants is a lack of control over question order. It is often important that the respondent answer one question before seeing another. For example, a questionnaire might start by asking what the respondents see as the most important problem facing their community and then go on to ask numerous questions about the availability of parks and recreation facilities. It is safe to assume that if the respondents were aware of this focus of the questionnaire, it would bias their response to the initial open-ended question. With a self-administered paper-and-pencil questionnaire, the respondents are likely to glance through the entire questionnaire before starting to answer, so there is no way to control question order.

Another problem with paper-and-pencil questionnaires completed apart from supervision by a member of the research team is the inability to control the context of question answering and, specifically, the presence of other people. Respondents to a mailed survey might ask friends or family members to examine the questionnaire or comment on their answers, causing bias if the respondent's own private opinions are desired.

A certain number of potential respondents, particularly the least educated, will also be unable to respond to paper-and-pencil questionnaires because of illiteracy or other difficulties in reading or writing (e.g., poor vision). Complex questions or instructions for some respondents to skip certain questions can lead to confusion, errors, or complete nonresponse. For everybody, not just the uneducated, writing long responses to open-ended questions is more work than giving the same responses orally to an interviewer, and this factor can reduce response rates.

Finally, paper-and-pencil questionnaires do not allow an interviewer or member of the research team to correct misunderstandings or answer questions that the respondent might have. The respondent might answer incorrectly or not at all out of confusion or frustration, often without the researcher being able to tell that a question has been misinterpreted.

If the researcher accepts these secondary disadvantages, which are intrinsically part of mail surveys, steps can be taken to reduce the primary disadvantage of low response rate and hence low data quality. Dillman (2000) and others have developed techniques for carefully following up mail surveys with multiple waves of letters, postcards, and the like to attain as high a response rate as possible, sometimes reaching 70% or higher in samples of the general public with a short questionnaire. However, these techniques increase cost and can substantially reduce the cost advantage of a mail survey over a telephone interview, the next most costly alternative.

Face-to-Face Interviews

An alternative to the paper-and-pencil questionnaire as a means of direct questioning is the face-to-face interview. Face-to-face interviews often are used when there is reason to believe that prospective research participants either would not be motivated to complete a paper-and-pencil questionnaire or would encounter difficulty reading the questionnaire or understanding how to indicate responses. Perhaps due to the relatively high costs associated with face-to-face interviews, they are perhaps the least used of the modes of direct questioning. Nonetheless, as these examples illustrate, they can be used to great profit for certain types of hypothesis tests. Palmgreen et al. (2001) were interested in the degree to which a televised antidrug campaign affected marijuana use by seventh-to-twelfth graders. Because research on this topic and this population conducted in a school setting using paper-and-pencil questionnaires often meets with disapproval from school administrators and results in unacceptably low response rates from students, Palmgreen and colleagues elected to dispatch interviewers to students' homes. Interviewers posed questions to students and their parents and recorded responses using a notebook computer and computer-assisted personal interviewing software. A key feature of this strategy is the ability to allow the students to input their responses to questions of a sensitive nature (e.g., "Have you used marijuana anytime during the last 30 days?") directly into the computer without divulging responses to the interviewer. In a study of the association between stress and emotions in older adults, Zautra and colleagues (2000) interviewed adults between the ages of 60 and 80 who had either recently experienced the death of a spouse, had recently experienced declining health, or were healthy and had not recently experienced the death of a spouse. Interviewers queried participants regarding their personality, health, and emotions. In both of these examples, the researchers deemed it important that members of the research team work directly with respondents in acquiring responses to direct questions.

As with paper-and-pencil questionnaires, there are trade-offs involved with the use of face-to-face interviews for direct questioning.

Advantages Face-to-face interviews are the most costly form of data collection in general, but they also offer important advantages, some of which are shared by telephone interviews. The ability of the interviewer to notice and correct the respondents' misunderstandings, to probe inadequate or vague responses, and to answer questions and allay concerns is important in obtaining complete and meaningful responses. The interviewer can control the order in which the respondent receives the questions, which is not possible with self-administered paper-and-pencil questionnaires. And in general the interviewer can control the context of the interview, including the possible biasing presence of other people.

Other advantages are specific to the face-to-face interview. Visual aids (photographs, maps, or cards with possible responses printed on them) are useful in a number of contexts; for example, in surveys of prescription drug use it is helpful to show illustrations of different types of pills and capsules to aid the respondents' memory for medications they might have used but whose names they have forgotten.

The most important advantage, though, is in quality of information. Face-to-face interviews can attain the highest response rate of any survey technique, sometimes over 80%. Their advantage is particularly marked with special populations, such as low-income minority populations, who might not have telephones or respond to mail surveys. Moreover, a face-to-face interviewer can best establish rapport and motivate the respondent to answer fully and accurately, again improving the quality of data. Face-to-face interviews also allow the greatest length in interview schedules. An hour or so is typical, and interviews two to three hours long with samples of the general public are not unknown. The additional length permits extensive in-depth questioning about complex or multifaceted issues.

Disadvantages Related to the potential rapport between interviewer and respondent is the possibility of large **interviewer effects.** The interviewer's expectations or personal characteristics (such as ethnicity or sex) can influence responses (Frey & Oishi, 1995). Consistent with the idea that face-to-face situations create the strongest rapport—and hence the strongest tendency for respondents to give invalid, socially desirable answers to suit the interviewer's expectations or desires—studies have found larger interviewer effects in face-to-face than in telephone interviews (e.g., Schuman, Bobo, & Steeh, 1985).

The primary disadvantage of personal interviews is their high cost, which depends heavily on the geographic coverage required by the study. For a city or other limited area, costs for face-to-face interviews might not greatly exceed those for telephone interviews; however, for larger geographic areas, travel and subsistence costs for interviewers in the field are large, and face-to-face interviews typically cost two to three times as much as telephone interviews of equivalent length (Groves & Kahn, 1979).

Telephone Interviews

The use of telephone interviews in social science research expanded rapidly as telephones in homes became more commonplace in the 1960s and 1970s. Now, just as it seems unlikely that readers of this text have not completed a paper-and-pencil questionnaire, it is hard to imagine that readers have not at least been asked to submit to a telephone interview. The use of the telephone interview as a mode of direct questioning is illustrated in these published research studies: In the study of relationship satisfaction and breakups used earlier to illustrate the use of paper-and-pencil questionnaires, Arriaga (2001) used telephone interviews to determine whether couples were still intact four months after the conclusion of the paper-and-pencil portion of the study. The interview was brief and had been agreed to by participants during the first portion of the study. Participants were asked whether they still were dating the individual they were dating at the beginning of the study and, if not, who was responsible for the breakup. In a more typical use of telephone interviews for direct questioning, Spoth, Redmond, and Shin (2000) conducted interviews of more than 1,200 parents of sixth-grade children in rural Iowa. Eligible parents were sent letters alerting them that they would be called for an interview and describing the goals of the study. About one week after parents received the letter, they received a call from an interviewer. When the initial call did not reach an eligible parent, additional attempts—up to 30—were made to reach the parent. When an eligible parent was reached, the interview was conducted using computer-assisted telephone-interviewing software. The researchers reported an impressive 84% response rate. As these examples illustrate, the telephone interview is an effective mode of direct questioning when very little information is needed from research participants and when the population of interest is scattered across a wide geographic area.

Advantages As exemplified in the Spoth et al. (2000) study, telephone interviews often yield a high response rate, on the average just 5 percentage points lower than personal interviews (Groves & Kahn, 1979). Other studies even find that higher response rates are attainable by telephone than by face-to-face interviews in special situations such as urban-area samples (Bradburn & Sudman, 1979). Telephone response rates average 10 to 15 percentage points higher than even the best conducted mail surveys, with a much larger advantage over more typical mail response rates (Dillman, 1978).

Telephone interviews do not impose strict limits on interview length, although they generally do not extend much over an hour, as do some face-to-face interviews. It was once believed that five minutes or so was an upper limit to the length of telephone interviews, but this belief has been thoroughly discredited (Quinn, Gutek, & Walsh, 1980). For example, Dillman (1978) reported that in one survey of the general public, with telephone interviews averaging over 30 minutes, only 4% of the respondents broke off after the interview started. Another large-scale study was successful in using interviews that averaged nearly an hour in length, covering such topics as beliefs about opportunity for racial minorities (Kluegel & Smith, 1982) and women (Smith & Kluegel, 1984). Special populations (e.g., cancer survivors) might allow even longer interviews without major problems.

All the other advantages of face-to-face interviews, except the ability to use visual aids, are also available in telephone interviews. These include the interviewer's ability to correct misunderstandings, motivate the respondent, and probe for more detail when answers are vague. Although the ability to motivate the respondent might not be as great with telephone interviews as in person, this is compensated for by the somewhat smaller interviewer bias and tendency toward socially desirable responses in telephone interviews (Bradburn & Sudman, 1979). Carefully designed studies comparing face-to-face and telephone interviews using the same questions have found few if any differences in overall data quality (e.g., Quinn et al., 1980).

Telephone interviews, then, seem to offer response rates and data quality comparable to face-to-face interviews. They also have several advantages over face-to-face interviews, besides the obvious one of substantially lower cost. The cost advantage, as mentioned, is generally a factor of two to three, depending mainly on the geographic coverage needed. Larger areas give greater cost advantages to the telephone because long-distance toll charges actually depend little on distance (or depend not at all if special WATS phone lines are used). One advantage that is sometimes overlooked is the supervision of interviewers. Because interviewers can all work from a single room equipped with a bank of telephones and computers loaded with computer-assisted telephone-interviewing software, their supervisors can be constantly available to answer questions, resolve problems, or even talk to difficult respondents. The problem of a dishonest interviewer faking data, which occasionally occurs with face-to-face interviews in distant geographic areas, is virtually ruled out by this type of arrangement for telephone interviewing. This arrangement also allows errors in the questionnaire or interviewing procedures to be corrected immediately upon discovery, which is usually impossible with face-to-face interviewing. All these factors contribute significantly to higher data quality as well as lower cost.

Another advantage of telephone interviews is speed. A questionnaire can be put together quickly and hundreds of interviews conducted almost overnight to assess public responses to a disaster, assassination, television program, or some other event. Mail or face-to-face interviews would reach respondents only many days after the event, greatly reducing the likelihood of valid immediate responses.

Finally, as noted, contemporary telephone interviews typically make use of computer-assisted telephone-interviewing software. The interviewer sits with the telephone in front of a computer display and keyboard, reads questions displayed one at a time on the screen, and types in codes for the respondent's answer. The computer can check for valid data and signal the interviewer to recheck implausible responses, eliminating most coding and data-entry errors. Furthermore, the computer controls the sequence of questions, preventing interviewer errors in sequencing questions or in asking questions of the wrong subgroup of respondents (e.g., asking unmarried respondents about their spouses' occupation). Finally, biases deriving from question order can be reduced or eliminated by having a set of questions asked in a different, randomly selected order for each respondent; this would be difficult if not impossible for interviewers to do manually. Owing to the power and widespread availability of notebook computers, the same sort of computer assistance is now available and increasingly widely used in face-to-face interviews.

Disadvantages Sampling can be a significant issue in telephone interviewing. Since the notorious 1936 *Literary Digest* survey, which wrongly predicted the presidential election of that year by using a mail survey of names and addresses largely drawn from telephone directories, researchers have been wary of directories as sources for samples. It is argued, first, that not all households have telephones, and second, that not all those who have phones have listings in the directory (because they are new arrivals in an area or because they choose to be unlisted). The first point is often exaggerated. Nationally, over 92% of households can be reached by phone (estimates range from 87% of households in New Mexico to 98% of households in Minnesota). Face-to-face interviews cannot reach 100% of the national population either; small percentages of the population do not have fixed addresses or other characteristics that allow interviewers to locate them. All types of surveys tend to underrepresent the poor, socially isolated, transient, younger, and male members of society (Groves, 1987). Thus, although the accessibility concern should not be taken lightly, it is no greater an obstacle to telephone interviewing than face-to-face interviewing and mail administration of paper-and-pencil questionnaires.

To overcome the second concern, that telephone directories yield inadequate samples of phone subscribers, researchers now routinely use random-digit-dialing techniques. These techniques are discussed in detail in Chapter 9 as an example of a probability sampling strategy. Here it will suffice to note that **random digit dialing** is a means of including in a telephone sample the significant number of homes for which the telephone number is unlisted. The most rudimentary application of random digit dialing involves using a computer to randomly generate four-digit suffixes to the three-digit prefixes known to identify telephones in a geographic area of interest. This strategy can be improved upon by taking advantage of rules by which telephone companies assign telephone numbers and only generating numbers that satisfy these rules.

Telephone interviews do have a few more serious disadvantages. Interviewer effects are possible, although they usually are smaller than with face-to-face interviews. The inability to use drawings, maps, or other visual aids means that some types of questions must be reworded for telephone use. Some questions are difficult to ask on the phone because of their complexity; if the respondent misses even a single word the entire question might become unintelligible. The interviewer does not have visual cues (a puzzled look, a shake of the head) that a misunderstanding has occurred. As a result, more attention probably needs to be paid to question wording with telephone interviews than with other techniques. Finally, there are technical problems in the computation of response rates in random-digit-dialed telephone surveys because calls that are never answered on repeated calls are of uncertain status. If they are nonworking numbers, they should not be counted in the response rate calculations, but if they represent households at which nobody was home at the time of any of the calls, they should be counted as nonrespondents.

Direct Questioning via the Internet

During the 1980s and 1990s there was a dramatic increase in the number of homes with computers in the United States. Toward the end of this period, entry-level home computers had evolved from relatively modest units primarily used for word processing to powerful and compact units capable of processing rich audiovisual material. The explosion in home access to formidable computing power was followed in the late 1990s by a dramatic increase in the number of home computers with access to the Internet. As home users grow more comfortable and capable using electronic mail and working in the World Wide Web environment accessed via the Internet, researchers are increasingly turning to the Internet as a mode of direct questioning.

A particular appeal of the Web as a means of gathering information is that it potentially provides access to a worldwide sample. Moreover, through the creative use of "chat rooms" and news groups, it is possible to target populations that would otherwise be difficult or impossible to access. This feature of Web surveys is nicely illustrated in a study by McKenna and Bargh (1998). These researchers were interested in the degree to which involvement in an Internet news group by individuals with a stigmatized identity results in higher self-esteem, greater self-acceptance, and reduced feelings of social isolation. They surveyed participants in three news groups dealing with marginalized sexual identities. In addition to posting the 19-item survey to the news groups, they sent a copy via e-mail to all individuals who posted a message during a three-week period. Of the 160 people in the latter group, 103 (64%) responded. An additional 49 "lurkers" (individuals who read but do not post to the news group) responded to the survey. The worldwide reach of the Internet is apparent in an on-line experiment conducted by Williams, Cheung, and Choi (2000). Williams et al. developed a Web site that was accessible to any Web user for a period of 15 months. Of the 1,720 individuals who accessed their site during this period, 1,486 completed the experiment. Respondents hailed from 62 different countries and ranged in age from 13 to 55 years. The typical respondent had been using the Internet from two to three years for two to four hours per day.

Although the use of the Internet for research is increasing rapidly (Birnbaum, 2000), at present the body of published research in which the Internet is the primary mode of data gathering is small. As such, the full array of strengths and weaknesses is not yet clear. Nonetheless, there are several obvious advantages and disadvantages.

Advantages A unique advantage of the Internet is exemplified in the Williams et al. (2000) study: The Internet is a global phenomenon, making it possible to reach large and diverse populations at relatively low cost. In order to fully realize this advantage, surveys would need to be available in the different languages represented in the population likely to access the survey. On a more technical note, an appreciation for the diversity of Web browsers, Internet service providers, and computers in use throughout the world is important if a survey is to capitalize fully on the global reach of the Internet.

A second advantage of the Internet as a mode of direct questioning is apparent in the McKenna and Bargh (1998) study. The existence of "Internet communities" consisting of like-minded individuals makes it possible to target very specific and otherwise hard-to-reach populations. News groups, chat rooms, and Web rings provide access to potential respondents who have declared a particular interest, concern, or set of values.

Similar to mail surveys, Internet-based research permits participants to provide information at the time and place of their choosing. An appealing feature of Internet-based research not shared with mail surveys is the degree of anonymity afforded the respondent. Although many Web sites require respondents to "log in" by providing an e-mail address or other identifier, many respondents, aware of the virtues of anonymity in cyberspace, have taken on virtual identities that effectively render their true identity undetectable. This sense of anonymity is particularly important in research on sensitive topics in marginalized populations (e.g., McKenna & Bargh, 1998).

Disadvantages A key concern with research on the Internet is response rate. Not only are response rates often poor, it is often impossible to precisely calculate a response rate in the usual sense because it is not clear how many individuals could have responded but did not. When surveys are posted on a Web page, response rates typically are calculated as the proportion of individuals who completed the survey among those who accessed the page. As noted earlier, Williams et al. (2000) reported that 1,486 of 1,720 individuals (86%) who accessed their pages went on to complete their study. In a second Internet-based study, these same researchers achieved a response rate of only 46%. McKenna and Bargh (1998) reached 64% of individuals who posted to the news groups they targeted; however, it is not possible to calculate the proportion of lurkers who responded. In a formal study of this issue, Dillman et al. (2001) compared response rates to a questionnaire administered either by telephone, mail, or the Internet. Only after repeated telephone prods were they able to secure a response rate near 50% for the Internet. In comparison, response rates for telephone and mail surveys were 80% or greater. Given these findings, the Internet is not yet a viable means of gathering information for purposes of estimating prevalence or opinions for particular populations.

Other drawbacks to the Internet as a means of direct questioning are similar to those for mail surveys. There is no way to be certain that participants who respond to an on-line survey are the person they claim to be. Perhaps unique to the Internet is the possibility that some individuals have multiple virtual identities, creating the possibility that they could respond more than once to a survey without being detected. Finally, it is never clear under what conditions respondents complete an Internet-based survey. The alternatives are many, including at home, at school, in a private office, or at a public access terminal at a library or Internet café. As the use of the Internet for research on social behavior becomes more prevalent—particularly as results using this mode of measurement are compared with results using more traditional modes, the impact of these factors will be determined and ways to overcome them will be developed.

Experience Sampling

All of the modes of direct questioning described to this point typically query respondents about immutable personal qualities (e.g., ethnicity, birth order), past behavior (e.g., marijuana use the last 30 days), or personal beliefs or opinions (e.g., "Do you favor capital punishment?"). Although there is much to be learned about social behavior from such questions, there are rather severe limits on the type of hypothesis information generated by such questions can address. For instance, it would not be possible to investigate the time course of a change in attitude or identify recurring temporal cycles of emotional experience using those modes. Moreover, the validity of measures of past behavior can always be questioned on the grounds that respondents cannot accurately reconstruct even the recent past. To some degree, these limitations are overcome by a set of procedures called experience sampling.

Experience sampling strategies, sometimes referred to as "diary methods," require participants to provide an account of what they are experiencing on repeated occasions over a short period of time. What constitutes an "occasion" is dictated by the focus of the research. If, for instance, a researcher wishes to know what portion of the time people have certain experiences, then occasions might be determined randomly throughout the waking hours during which the participant is providing information. Participants are signaled by some electronic device—a programmed wristwatch, a pager, or, with increasing frequency, a handheld computer—at random intervals to complete a brief questionnaire. Copies of the questionnaire might be contained in a pocket-sized booklet or on the same handheld computer that signaled the occasion. Alternatively, the researcher might focus on the impact of particular kinds of experiences, in which case participants might be instructed to complete a questionnaire each time they experience a particular event, circumventing the need for a signaling device and sampling schedule.

Because a key concern in experience sampling research is the rules by which experiences are sampled, we defer detailed coverage of these methods until the section of the book on sampling (Chapter 10, to be specific). At this juncture, our main concern is the means by which direct questioning is undertaken in experience sampling studies. Two examples from the published literature give a sense of how experience sampling strategies are used in social science research. For a period of 30 days, Mohr et al. (2001) asked adult men and women to carry a handheld computer. The particular computer used by these researchers is battery operated and weighs less than 9 ounces. Because these researchers were interested in a specific type of behavior, alcohol consumption, they sampled experiences using an event contingent strategy. That is, each time participants anticipated engaging in a period of alcohol consumption, they responded to a series of questions administered by the computer. Using this strategy, the researchers were able to address in compelling fashion the contexts in which people consumed alcohol (e.g., alone or with other people) and the emotions that accompanied their alcohol consumption. In a study of the accuracy with which people recall emotions, Thomas and Diener (1990) randomly sampled the emotional experiences of college students four times a day for three weeks. Participants carried brief paper-and-pencil forms, which they completed each time they were signaled by a wristwatch alarm. As is clear from these examples, experience sampling research explicitly incorporates the element of time and generates detailed information regarding the experiences of individual research participants.

As with the other modes of direct questioning, there are advantages and disadvantages to experience sampling.

Advantages An obvious advantage to experience sampling is that it generates detailed information about the experiences of respondents. For instance, in their sample of 100 adults who provided data for 30 days, Mohr et al. (2001) acquired information on approximately 15,000 interpersonal exchanges. Thomas and Diener (1990) acquired information about 40 college students' emotional experience on 84 occasions over the course of three weeks. For research questions that concern patterns of thoughts, feelings, and behaviors over time, experience sampling offers a significant advantage over typical, static approaches to direct questioning.

Another advantage to experience sampling is the relatively short lapse in time between the event of interest and participants' responses to it. Again, it is useful to compare experience sampling to traditional approaches to direct questioning in this regard. Traditional approaches require respondents to remember or reconstruct events and experiences that perhaps took place years before the information is provided. Some findings from the research by Thomas and Diener (1980) illustrate the issue. As noted, these researchers asked students to describe their emotions on four randomly chosen occasions during each day for three weeks. At the end of three weeks, participants were asked to indicate the intensity and frequency of emotions they experienced during the previous three weeks. By comparing the randomly sampled ratings of emotion with the summary ratings, Thomas and Diener found that students tended to overestimate the intensity of their positive and negative emotions and to underestimate the frequency of positive emotions. These findings suggest that, after as little as three weeks, the degree to which people can accurately recount their emotional experiences is suspect. Experience sampling enjoys a clear advantage over traditional modes of direct questioning for the study of such phenomena.

A third advantage to experience sampling methods, one that might not be apparent to most readers, is that considerably fewer participants are required in order to meet the sample size demands of the statistical methods used to formally test hypotheses. Whereas the sample size needs for research that uses traditional modes of questioning can exceed 1,000, samples in experience sampling research rarely exceed 100 participants. The large number of observations of each participant affords ample statistical power for hypothesis tests, which tend to be within—rather than between—participants as in traditional direct questioning methods.

Disadvantages Along with the unique variety of information generated by experience sampling methods come unique problems. Handheld computers typically used for data gathering in experience sampling research are expensive and fragile. Equipment loss or failure is not uncommon and must be anticipated. For instance, Mohr et al. (2001) provided participants with paper copies of the questionnaires in the event their handheld computer failed.

Another concern in experience sampling research is the extreme reliance on the participant to generate the data according to the sometimes strict rules of sampling required to test the hypothesis of interest. The immediacy advantage afforded by experience sampling is compromised if participants do not respond to questions when they are signaled or when the events about which they are to provide information take place. When participants describe their experiences using paper-and-pencil questionnaires, it is difficult to track the extent to which they responded to questions immediately upon being signaled or experiencing the events of interest. Handheld computers automatically track compliance when respondents are signaled because they can be programmed to store the time of the signal and the time at which responses were recorded. When responses are event contingent, handheld computers cannot monitor when an event occurs or the amount of time that passes between the occurrence of the event and participants' recording of their responses to it. Research on this issue suggests that, if participants are scheduled to check in with members of the research team on a regular basis, they tend to respond promptly to more than 90% of events that occur (Wheeler & Nezlek, 1977).

Modes of Direct Questioning: Summary

The only completely defensible answer to the question "What is the best way to gather information that involves direct questioning of participants?" is, of course, "It depends." Table 5.1 presents a schematic summary of the strengths and weaknesses of the different modes that were presented in more detail, so readers can weigh specific considerations as they choose. Nevertheless, to give a general guideline, for surveys of the general population that cover more than a local geographic area, telephone interviews and, increasingly, the Internet, are the methods of choice.

Exceptions to this generalization include a number of specific situations. Mailed paper-and-pencil surveys should be considered (1) for homogeneous groups—such as alumni of a specific college or members of an organization—if they are widely scattered geographically; (2) if mailing lists are available, to minimize sampling costs; or (3) if cost constraints are maximal and low data quality is acceptable for the specific research purpose. With mail surveys, the techniques of Dillman (2000) should be used to improve response rate at some additional cost. If, for a homogeneous group, one has access to a list of e-mail addresses, then the Internet is a fast, low-cost method. Also, if the target population is likely to have a strong virtual presence in the form of news groups, chat rooms, or Web rings, then the combination of e-mail and a well-designed Web site is a viable option.

Face-to-face interviews should probably be chosen (1) if maximal data quality is required and cost is no object; (2) if the study calls for special populations difficult to reach in other ways (e.g., low-income rural residents who might not have phones and might be too uneducated to respond well to mail questionnaires); or (3) if the population to be studied is geographically concentrated, making face-to-face interview costs comparable to telephone costs or only somewhat higher.

Experience sampling is unrivaled by the other modes of direct questioning for research that requires rich, detailed information from individual respondents in natural settings. Unlike the other modes of direct questioning, the sampling of members of a population is less of a concern than the sampling of the experience of individuals recruited for the study. Although with a carefully selected sample of individuals experience sampling could be used to estimate the prevalence of specific experiences, the

TABLE 5.1 **SUMMARY COMPARISON OF DIFFERENT MODES OF DIRECT QUESTIONING**

Dimension of Comparison	Paper-and Pencil-Questionnaire	Face-to-Face Interview	Telephone Interview	Internet	Experience Sampling
Cost	Low	High	Moderate	Low	High
Data quality					
Response rate	Low	High	Moderate to high	Low	High
Respondent motivation	Low	High	High	Moderate to high	High
Interviewer bias	None	Moderate	Low	None	None
Sample quality	Low, unless high response rate	High	Moderate to high, if directory; high, if random digit dialing	Low	Not typically a concern
Possible length	Short, if by mail; long, if in small groups	Very long	Long	Very long	Short
Ability to clarify and probe	None, if by mail; some, if in small groups	High	High	None	Moderate
Ability to use visual aids	Some (e.g., maps)	High	None	High	Moderate
Speed of implementation	Low	Low	High	High	Low
Interviewer supervision	—	Low	High	—	—
Anonymity	High	Low	Low	High	Low
Ability to use computer assistance	None	High	High	High	High
Dependence on respondent's reading and writing ability	High	None	None	High	High
Control of context and question order	None	High	High	None	None

more appropriate use is for focused hypothesis tests that involve the element of time or concern phenomena regarding which memory cannot be trusted.

Other Modes of Measurement

In a classic article on the pitfalls of direct questioning, Nisbett and Wilson (1977) persuasively argued that people are not able to accurately describe many aspects of their own experience. They demonstrated in compelling fashion that people appear to be unable to accurately describe or recount higher-order cognitive processes such as cause and effect involving their own behavior. In light of their findings, direct questioning would not appear to be a viable means of measuring an entire class of constructs. Their concern is a critical one that might not be apparent to all readers. We illustrate with an example. Kernis and colleagues were interested in not just whether self-esteem in the traditional sense affects behavior; they were interested in the effects of *fluctuations* in self-esteem on behavior (e.g., Kernis, Granneman, & Barclay, 1989). They refer to this construct as stability of self-esteem. To measure stability, they asked participants to complete a measure of self-esteem on repeated occasions for several days. Then, for each participant, they computed a statistic that reflects the degree of fluctuation apparent in their set of scores. Note that this procedure does not require participants to directly report the stability of their self-esteem. Consistent with the reasoning of Nisbett and Wilson, stability scores obtained in this way were not associated with scores obtained using a direct measure of self-esteem stability (e.g., "Do you find that on one day you have one opinion of yourself and on another day you have a different opinion?") but were associated with other measures according to predictions.

There are other reasons that social scientists cannot rely completely on direct questioning of participants to determine their standing on all constructs. When the research concerns children, then it might not be possible to phrase questions about certain constructs in such a way that participants can understand them. When the research involves constructs that reflect socially undesirable qualities, then respondents cannot be counted on to accurately describe themselves, particularly when they do not feel as if they are responding anonymously. And, as we emphasized in Chapters 2 and 4, causal inferences always are stronger when multiple, methodologically distinct operational definitions of constructs are used. In other words, if a finding holds regardless of whether the key constructs were measured by direct questioning or through some indirect mode of measurement, then causal inferences are strengthened. In short, indirect modes of measurement are indispensable in some research domains and an asset in domains that generally rely on direct questioning.

In the remainder of this section, we discuss the advantages of three classes of indirect measures: collateral reports, observation, and physiological monitoring. Beyond these three broad classes of strategies, we touch on other promising but less frequently used strategies.

Collateral Reports

Collateral reports are third-party responses to a questionnaire or interview. By "third party" we mean someone other than the participant provides information about the participant. We refer to such reports as collateral because they are gathered in addition to rather than instead of information provided by the participants. Moreover, the information provided by the informant is in response to the same questions posed to the participant. By gathering the same information from multiple sources, it is possible to detect biases that might contaminate self-reports.

Collateral reports are commonplace in research on children. Typically, the informants are parents and teachers. For instance, Michaels, Roosa, and Gensheimer (1992) investigated the factors that affect whether middle-school students participate in a school-based prevention program for children of alcoholics. Characteristics of children were measured both by directly questioning children and by questioning parents' about their children. Chassin, Pitts, and DeLucia (1999) studied the influence of alcohol and drug use by adolescents on their adjustment as young adults. During adolescence, measures of key constructs were obtained both from participants and informants. It is worth noting that at least some of the constructs involved in these studies concerned illegal behavior of the sort that participants might either under- or overreport. By obtaining collateral reports, which should not be subject to the self-serving biases that influence self-reports of such behaviors, the researchers were able to probe for biases and, in the end, increase confidence in the validity of participants' reports.

Advantages The primary advantage of collateral reports is the potential to overcome biases inherent in self-reports of constructs of interest to social scientists. Through the strategic selection of informants, it is possible to use collateral reports to evaluate the veracity of self-reports as well as pinpoint sources of potential bias in self-reports. In this regard, obtaining collateral reports is a good example of the use of multiple operational definitions. Although the items on the survey do not vary, the sources of the information used to respond to them do. And it is this variability in source that permits the use of statistical techniques such as factor analysis to tease apart the construct of interest from constructs of disinterest, which should vary from one source to the next.

Disadvantages An unfortunate drawback to obtaining collateral reports is the dilemma that must be resolved when the reports are not in agreement either with each other or with the participants' self-reports. For instance, Chassin et al. (1999) found stronger support for their hypothesis using collateral reports as opposed to adolescents' own reports of their drinking behavior and adjustment. Indeed, such departures in findings between collateral reports is well documented in research with younger children, in which parents' and teachers' ratings not only depart from students' self-ratings, they depart from each other. It is easy to see how this could be true. Parents, teachers, and the children themselves witness the child's behavior from different perspectives, in different contexts, and with reference to different comparison groups. Although this diversity is an asset, it can create a conundrum for researchers. What is the correct inference if the results are consistent with the hypothesis when the children's own ratings are used but inconsistent with it when parents' or teachers' ratings are used? Resolution to this inferential dilemma often requires additional research that focuses on the peculiarities of the different perspectives represented by the different sources.

Another set of drawbacks to the use of collateral reports stems from the need to gather data from both participants *and* informants in order to complete a study. There are a number of specific complications introduced by this necessity. First, it potentially doubles (or triples) the cost of the study without adding to the size of the sample. Of course, if the quality of the information about participants is significantly improved, or if collateral reports are the only way to measure certain constructs given the target population, then the cost is justified. Second, it potentially requires different recruitment strategies for informants than those used to enlist participants. This is not a concern if, for instance, the informants are parents; the parents of minors typically would need to be contacted for permission to recruit their children anyway. If the informants are peers or coworkers, then it is unlikely that the recruitment strategy used to enlist participants will work for informants. Moreover, the kind of recruitment that often is required might result in informants that are not comparable from one participant to the next. For instance, if high school students are asked to recruit their best friend to provide information about them, there is no guarantee that every participant interprets "best friend" in the same way, that every participant's best friend is accessible, and so forth. Moreover, it can be difficult to ensure that participants do not work with informants to provide information about themselves, thereby defeating the purpose of obtaining information from a perspective other than the participants' own. Despite the appeal of acquiring information about participants from multiple sources, the costs and potential problems associated with obtaining collateral reports mean that researchers rarely obtain them unless the research question or characteristics of the population they are studying requires them.

Observation

Although collateral reports move outside respondents in order to gather information not directly influenced by them, they often are combined with responses obtained by questioning the respondent directly. As such, they only partially extricate the process of measurement from the biases and shortcomings inherent in participants' self-reports. Observation is an approach to measurement that does not rely at all on participants to report their preferences, opinions, or behaviors. Instead, judges are trained by the researcher to detect and record observable indicators of the construct of interest.

In Chapter 15 we provide detailed coverage of observational techniques. For our purposes here, we only need to give readers a feel for the ways in which observation can be used to measure constructs. In a study of the effects of family influences on relationship quality, Conger, Cui, Bryant, and Elder (2000) visited families in their home for a two-hour session. During the session, family members were videotaped while they took part in four structured interactions. Five years later, adolescent family members who were in a romantic relationship were videotaped interacting with their partner while engaged in tasks designed to generate discussion or create conflict. Videotaped interactions were rated by multiple judges on characteristics such as supportiveness and hostility. In another longitudinal study, Caspi et al. (1997) were interested in the degree to which temperament at age 3 predicted personality at age 18 and health-risk behaviors at age 21. Of course, 3-year-olds do not have the facility with language necessary to provide responses to direct questions about their personality. Instead, these researchers used observational methods to classify the children at age 3 as either undercontrolled, inhibited, reserved, or well adjusted. As illustrated by these examples, observational methods are useful when participants might not be willing or able to accurately report their standing on a construct.

Advantages An obvious advantage to observation is the relative objectivity of ratings. Presumably, judges are unbiased observers trained by researchers to document what they see or hear without interpretation. As such, their ratings of participants should not be contaminated by sources of bias that threaten the validity of participants' self-ratings. Moreover, observers can take note of subtle, nonverbal cues to participants' motives and emotions, constructs that might not be apparent to the participants themselves.

Another advantage of observation is that it is occasionally the good fortune of a researcher to find audio- or videotaped recordings relevant to a hypothesis that were gathered for other purposes (e.g., surveillance video in a food market). In such cases, the costs of measurement are minimal and the observation itself is in no way affected by the goals of the research. The latter feature adds an additional layer of objectivity and distance between the hypotheses of the study and the means by which the information used to test the hypotheses was gathered.

A third advantage to observation is that it can often be accomplished while participants are in a natural setting. For instance, the Conger et al. (2000) study involved observing families interacting in their home. In this study, the families knew they were being observed, and the observations were of interactions manufactured by the research team. A purer form of naturalistic observation is unobtrusive observation, in which research participants are not aware they are being observed. For instance, we might obtain information about the radio station preferences of people in a city by recording the station to which radios are tuned in cars that are being serviced. A limitation on such studies, discussed in Chapter 15, is the invasion of privacy without participants' consent. Such concerns aside, unobtrusive observation in naturalistic settings can generate information that is high in external validity relative to information gathered in artificial or contrived settings in which researchers are present.

Disadvantages Perhaps the greatest disadvantage to observational measurement is that many constructs are not amenable to observation. Most overt behaviors are readily observed, and independent judges often are in near-unanimous agreement in their ratings of whether participants did or did not engage in a behavior. Other constructs are not so readily observed. For instance, emotions are not always manifested outwardly. People do not always communicate their motives, desires, or preferences in their actions. For constructs such as these, observation is not particularly useful.

Another disadvantage concerns the use of observational information to test causal propositions. Typically, observational measurement involves neither manipulation of putative causes nor random assignment of participants to levels of the causal variable. As such, even when certain behaviors regularly co-occur with certain features of the setting, it is not possible to draw firm causal inferences. So, with observational research in natural settings, there is a trade-off between external validity and internal validity. For this reason, observational research often is an adjunct to research in which the researcher exerts more control over the setting and the critical constructs.

Physiological Monitoring

Whereas observational methods are used to measure overt characteristics, physiological monitoring targets covert characteristics such as emotions, evaluations, and preferences. **Psychophysiology** is the study of the interplay of physiological systems and people's thoughts, feelings, and behaviors. By "physiological systems" we mean bodily systems that might typically be viewed as serving a purely physical function, for instance, the cardiovascular system and the immune system. It is now apparent that these systems influence and are influenced by people's experience of themselves and the world around them (Blascovich, 2000). Moreover, it is possible to identify particular patterns of physiological activation that indicate constructs of interest to social scientists. We illustrate with two examples.

Blascovich, Mendes, Hunter, Lickel, and Kowai-Bell (2001) proposed that individuals interacting with a stigmatized person would feel threatened, although they might not report as much when asked directly. They tested this stigma-threat hypothesis by creating laboratory interactions between participants and stigmatized confederates (accomplices of the researchers posing as participants). Threat was operationally defined as a pattern of cardiovascular activity indicative of decreased blood volume and flow. The results were consistent with their hypothesis. Confirming the researchers' suspicion that the threatening nature of the interaction would not be apparent using more traditional measures of threat, they found no support for their hypothesis using paper-and-pencil measures or observational measures provided by confederates.

Another example of physiological monitoring in research on social behavior is a study by Harmon-Jones and Sigelman (2001) on the effects of an insult on anger and aggression. Of relevance to our discussion here is their operational definition of anger. Harmon-Jones and Sigelman recorded electroencephalographic (EEG) activity in order to test their hypothesis that anger is indicated by increased left-prefrontal activity in the brain. Results confirmed their expectation: Participants who were insulted evinced greater activity in the left-prefrontal cortex, and their level of activity was associated with their self-reports of anger and their engagement in aggressive behavior.

Advantages There are two primary advantages of physiological monitoring relative to other modes of measurement. First, despite the fact that participants know they are being assessed, they cannot control the outcome of the assessment. Thus, unlike direct questioning in all its forms and intrusive observational methods, there is little or no concern that participants' biases are reflected in their scores. A second advantage is that measurement is continuous in real time. In this regard, physiological monitoring shares a strength of experience sampling—it permits the introduction of time into hypotheses and research design. Thus, we can go beyond the relatively simple question of *whether* a stimulus has an influence to the more refined question of *when* it exerts an influence relative to the onset of a stimulus or event.

Disadvantages This latter advantage carries with it a disadvantage: Because signals are read at $\frac{1}{2}$-second intervals or less, the sheer amount of information produced by physiological monitoring can be overwhelming. For instance, if a researcher monitors participants during a 15-minute period at $\frac{1}{2}$-second intervals, the result would be 1,800 pieces of information for each participant. Extracting signals from noise in such large amounts of information requires considerable expertise and sophistication.

Indeed, it is the "noise" factor that often proves the most challenging for researchers interested in measuring social constructs using physiological monitoring. For, while the cardiovascular system is responding to a stimulus presented by the researcher, it is also responding to other factors such as room temperature, physical health, novelty of the laboratory setting, events that took place just prior to entering the laboratory, and so forth. For this reason, many research studies in which key constructs are operationally defined using physiological monitoring include numerous **control factors** aimed at determining the degree to which the physiological signal is influenced by factors not relevant to the hypothesis.

Three additional concerns limit the use of physiological monitoring. First, as must be apparent by now, a considerable amount of expertise is required both to understand the functioning of the physiological systems to be monitored and run the monitoring equipment. Second, the equipment used for monitoring is expensive and fragile. As such, equipment is often shared by multiple research groups whose members are well trained in use and maintenance of the equipment. Finally, the extreme sensitivity of most physiological monitoring equipment requires that participants are seated and relatively still throughout measurement. This constraint is severe, as many behaviors of interest to social scientists are best studied in engaging social contexts.

Other Indirect Modes

Social scientists regularly develop new and creative ways to buttress research findings that are suspect because they are based solely on direct questioning. To give readers a flavor of these approaches, we describe three.

An approach to measurement that focuses on constructs that can *only* be measured indirectly is the implicit association method (Greenwald, McGhee, & Schwartz, 1998). The **implicit association method** makes use of the computer-administered Implicit Association Test (IAT) to measure automatic evaluative judgments. The term "automatic" is used here to refer to thoughts and feelings that are not under the conscious control of the individual. Such *implicit* thoughts and feelings about an object (e.g., another person, a group of people, oneself) can be contrasted with *explicit* thoughts and feelings, of which an individual is aware and able to control. The latter typically are measured using one of the direct questioning modes described in the first section of this chapter. The logic of the IAT is as follows: Participants are seated at a keyboard facing a computer screen. They are instructed to indicate as quickly as possible by pressing designated computer keys the correspondence between evaluative attributes (e.g., pleasant, ugly) and concepts (e.g., young–old, Black–White, self–other). The computer records the amount of time that lapses between the presentation of the stimuli and key press for the different pairings of evaluative attributes and concepts. (The best way to understand how the IAT works is to experience it firsthand. Try one of the demonstration tests at http://buster.cs.yale.edu/implicit/measure3.html.) Implicit attitude is computed using an algorithm that takes into account the differences in speed of responses to the different attribute–concept pairings. Faster responses to pairings of negative attributes and a given concept compared to positive attributes and the same concept indicate a negative implicit evaluation. The implicit association method has been used to study implicit attitudes toward a variety of groups, products, and activities. A particularly appealing application of the method is the assessment of implicit attitudes toward the self, or implicit self-esteem, which is only weakly associated with traditional direct measures of explicit self-esteem (Greenwald & Farnham, 2000).

Another indirect means of gathering information from people is the card sort. In the **card sort,** research participants are given a stack of cards, each containing a single adjective or descriptive phrase. Participants are asked to sort the cards into piles that in their opinion belong together when describing a person, group of people, or themselves. Linville (1987) has used the card sort effectively to measure self-complexity, the number of different ways people view themselves and the degree of overlap among their self-views. She finds that self-complexity is not a quality that people can effectively report about themselves in response to direct questions, but it is nonetheless consequential in their emotional reactions to stress.

A novel approach to gathering information about participants is autophotography. In **autophotographic research,** participants carry disposable cameras with them for a short period of time and photograph aspects of their experience as directed by the researchers. For instance, Dollinger and colleagues (1996) asked college students over the course of a semester to create a photo-essay by taking 20 photographs that "describe how you see yourself and tell something about who you are" (p. 1270). The photographs were then coded by trained judges for various features relevant to the research questions. The findings both corroborated and extended similar research using paper-and-pencil measures.

Other Modes of Measurement: Summary

Although direct questioning continues to be the measurement mode of choice among social scientists, not every construct of interest to social scientists can be measured by direct questioning. Moreover, findings from research studies that relied solely on direct questioning are strengthened when they are replicated using a mode of measurement that does not rely on participants' self-reports of the key constructs.

We reviewed three categories of measurement that do not rely on participants' self-reports and, as with the various approaches to direct questioning, each has strengths and weaknesses. When the research questions concern populations that cannot be counted on to provide valid self-reports, collateral reports are an effective means of bolstering confidence in the veracity of information about participants. Another approach is to circumvent self-reports altogether and gather information about participants by observing their behavior either in strategically created environments or in natural settings. And for a select category of hypotheses, physiological monitoring is a compelling means of operationally defining constructs of which self-reports are suspect. Each of these measurement approaches is a necessary and appealing adjunct to the questionnaires and interviews that dominate research in the social sciences.

Summary

Some fundamental methodological issues must be addressed when research is planned and conducted. First is the appropriateness of the mode of measurement to the study topic: Are participants theoretically capable of giving the desired information, or should some indirect method of measurement be used instead? Second, individuals' self-reports of facts, beliefs, attitudes, or behaviors can be elicited in many different ways. In deciding whether to use a paper-and-pencil questionnaire, face-to-face interviews, telephone interviews, or the Internet, researchers should consider the advantages and disadvantages of each mode as they relate to the purposes of the study. The nature of the target population and the sampling design chosen for the study also have implications for the mode of data collection. Finally, either to buttress findings from research in which constructs are operationally defined using direct questioning or to study phenomena for which direct questioning is not feasible, a number of measurement strategies are available. As with direct questioning methods, the choice between collateral reports, observation, physiological monitoring, or some other indirect method of measurement requires careful consideration of the population under study and the constructs implicated in the hypotheses to be tested. The strongest hypothesis tests are those in which key constructs are operationally defined using multiple methods that offset the strengths and weaknesses of each.

Key Concepts

autophotographic research
card sort
collateral reports
control factors
experience sampling
implicit association method
interviewer effects
measurement
modes of measurement
psychophysiology
random digit dialing
response rate

On the Web

http://www.psych.upenn.edu/~baron/qs.html An example of a Web-based research program. The author requires that respondents register and, for many questionnaires, offers payment for completed questionnaires.

http://www.zoomerang.com/ Create your own on-line survey and administer it via e-mail and the Web using this innovative site.

http://www2.bc.edu/~barretli/esp/ Download the Experience Sampling Program from this site and turn your handheld computer into a tool for gathering data.

http://www.gsu.edu/%7Epsyejv/psyphy.html The Psychophysiology WWW Directory, an international directory of psychophysiology-related Web sites.

http://buster.cs.yale.edu/implicit/index.html A Web site that provides detailed information about the IAT, including demonstrations and descriptions of research using the IAT.

Further Reading

Birnbaum, M. H. (Ed.). (2000). *Psychological experiments on the Internet.* New York: Academic Press.

Blascovich, J. (2000). Using physiological indexes of psychological processes in social psychological research. In Harry T. Reis & C. M. Judd (Eds.), *Handbook of research methods in social and personality psychology* (pp. 117–137). New York: Cambridge University Press.

Dillman, D. A. (2000). *Mail and Internet surveys: The tailored design method* (2nd ed.). New York: Wiley.

Patten, M. L. (2000). *Questionnaire research: A practical guide* (2nd ed.). Los Angeles: Pyrzcak Publishing.

Ziller, R. C. (1990). *Photographing the self: Methods for observing personal orientations.* Thousand Oaks, CA: Sage Publications.

CHAPTER

6

Single-Item Measures in Questionnaires

As noted in the previous chapter, although social scientists use many modes of measurement, direct questioning is the predominant approach to measurement. Whether the questions directed at participants are conveyed on paper, face-to-face, over the phone, or via the Internet, the key concern in direct questioning as with all modes of measurement is that responses are high in construct validity. To obtain reliable and valid responses, question content, wording, and sequence must all work together to convey to the respondents what information is desired and motivate them to provide it.

In this chapter and the next, we discuss the many issues involved in developing questions and questionnaires that are reliable and valid. In this chapter, our focus is on writing individual items to operationally define constructs. By **items** we mean the questions or statements to which participants provide a response. **Responses** typically are numeric (e.g., "On a 1 to 10 scale . . . ."); however, they can involve simple binary choices (e.g., true–false) or verbal reports (e.g., "Describe in your own words how you felt . . . ."). The next chapter is devoted to strategies for eliciting responses to direct questions with a particular emphasis on the use of groups of items, or **scales,** to operationally define constructs. In the latter part of this chapter, we take up issues that are specific to the use of interviewing—face-to-face or telephone—as a means of gathering information using direct questioning. The chapter begins with a sketch of the full set of procedures involved in conducting questionnaire research using any of the various modes described in the previous chapter.

Outline of Procedures in Questionnaire Research

A step-by-step guide for planning and carrying out questionnaire research will help organize the decisions and issues that the researcher must consider, which are discussed in this chapter and the next. This outline begins after the investigator has weighed possible alternative modes of measurement and decided that some form of direct questioning is the most appropriate method to obtain all or part of the desired information.

1. The most basic choice is among modes of direct questioning: paper-and-pencil questionnaire, face-to-face interview, telephone interview, questionnaire posted on the Web, or experience sampling. Advantages and disadvantages of each were presented in Chapter 5; however, this decision also overlaps with issues surrounding sampling (Chapters 8 and 9) and with the nature of the population that is to be investigated. For example, the existence of a list of names, postal addresses, and e-mail addresses of members of the relevant population makes mail or Internet surveys and face-to-face interviews more feasible and random digit dialing unnecessary; the geographic area covered by the population affects the relative costs of face-to-face versus telephone interviews, and so on.
2. The next decisions involve the specific content areas to be covered by the questionnaire. Obviously, the purpose of the study dictates certain central areas. For example, if the study is to determine attitudes toward the location of a toxic waste disposal site near a particular city, questions on that specific issue would be included. However, related topics might also be important, perhaps including the respondents' perceptions of risks from toxic waste; beliefs about the causes of cancer and other diseases; general optimism or pessimism; attitudes of trust or distrust toward the authorities who will make the decision about the site; and attitudes about the chemical industry in general. The investigator might consult other social scientists as well as experts in areas specifically related to the topic of the study to decide what related issues should be included in the questionnaire.
3. Given a list of specific content areas to be covered, several other decisions need to be made before questions can actually be written. On some topics, existing questions or scales can be used, saving the work of writing new questions and preserving some comparability with earlier research. In addition, it should be decided what content areas are central to the research and warrant coverage with a scale, including follow-up questions or open-ended probes (questions allowing the respondent to answer in his or her own words) and what topics are less important and only require a question or two.
4. Finally, the process of writing questions starts. Wording decisions must be made on a host of detailed issues. At this point, a number of questions might be written in open-ended form, to be converted to closed-ended questions (those with a fixed set of alternative responses) after pretesting.
5. The questions are put together into a complete draft of the questionnaire. A number of guidelines on question sequence and transition should be observed

and a balance of open-ended and closed-ended questions maintained. There might be more open-ended questions at this stage than in the final questionnaire.

6. At this stage the draft questionnaire should be circulated to experts and consultants for comments and suggestions, and revised accordingly to eliminate obvious problems even before the pretest stage. As much as possible, the experts should represent different theoretical approaches or social orientations to maximize the chance of identifying biases and blind spots due to the researcher's personal values as well as simple technical defects.

7. The questionnaire is now pretested. This stage is absolutely essential in questionnaire research and should not be confused with the informal examination of the questionnaire by experts. A proper pretest involves respondents from the same population as the actual study, not just a sample of students, secretaries, researcher's friends, or whoever happens to be conveniently accessible. If the mode of measurement is face-to-face or telephone interview, the interviewers should also be those who will be conducting interviews in the main study. Even if the main study is to involve a paper-and-pencil or Web-based questionnaire, it is wise to do some face-to-face interviews as part of the pretest so that respondents' immediate verbal reactions or expressions of difficulty with some questions can be noted.

    The interviewers in the pretest should be aware of the overall purposes of the study and the aim of every individual question, so they can note whether the question is understood and answered as intended. The comments and reactions of the respondents should be recorded as clues to questions that might be misunderstood or cause difficulties in other ways. After the interview is complete, the interviewer should go back over the questionnaire topic by topic and ask the respondents for their overall reactions: what difficulties they had, how the questions were interpreted, what further topic-related ideas were not tapped by the questions, and what the respondents' thoughts were when they responded "don't know." The interviewers as well as the pretest respondents should critique the questionnaire, pointing out difficulties they had in following the sequence, explaining particular questions, holding the respondents' interest, or maintaining rapport.

    The pretest serves a number of purposes. It can identify unforeseen problems in question wording, question sequence, or questionnaire administration so that they can be eliminated before the actual study. No researcher, no matter how experienced, avoids such unforeseen problems. It might indicate the need for additional questions on some topics or the elimination of others. It can provide data for item analysis for any scales included in the questionnaire. The amount of time required to complete the questionnaire (and possibly, the necessity for shortening it) can be determined. Open-ended responses can be collected to permit the phrasing of closed-ended response alternatives for the final questionnaire. Finally, the pretest can serve as part of the interviewers' training if the study involves face-to-face or telephone interviewing.

8. The pretest results are analyzed and any necessary changes made in the questionnaire. If the changes are major, further pretesting should be done. Few experiences in research are more common or more frustrating than changing a questionnaire to correct a problem revealed by a pretest and then taking it immediately into the field for the final study, only to discover that the change introduced a new problem that was worse than the first. Because problems with wording or respondents' comprehension can vitiate the worth of the entire study, pretesting is low-cost insurance against such potential disasters.
9. With the final version of the questionnaire, final training of personnel (e.g., interviewers, proctors) can proceed. More pretesting can be done in conjunction with training, or training can begin in conjunction with the pretest of step 7. The content and form of the questionnaire and associated instructions (e.g., for interviewers to skip certain questions for certain respondents or for proctors to seat participants in a particular way) should be reviewed for clarity and completeness.
10. Finally, the actual administration of the questionnaire begins. If either face-to-face or telephone interviewing is the mode of measurement, supervision of interviewers and continuous monitoring of completed interviews as they come in are essential to detect problems as soon as they appear and institute corrections if possible. The administration of the survey must include standard procedures for tracking down members of the sample who cannot easily be reached, screening out ineligible respondents, sending out repeated reminders (in a mail or Internet survey), or making several callbacks (in face-to-face or telephone interview studies) to maximize the response rate, and so on.
11. The resultant data are coded and analyzed, and (if all is well up to this point) conclusions are drawn about the issues that were the focus of the research. All the preceding steps are justified by their contribution to the validity of these conclusions.

Question Content

With this set of procedures as context, we now take up the topic of developing single-item measures of constructs. Constructs of interest to social scientists might concern what research participants know (facts); what they think, expect, feel, or prefer (beliefs and attitudes); or what they have done (behaviors). A questionnaire generally includes questions referring to more than one of these categories, and at times a single question has aspects of more than one category; however, these distinctions are convenient for discussing the issues involved in selecting content.

Questions Aimed at Facts

Often the simplest and most economical way of ascertaining facts is to approach people who know them and ask. We expect people to know a variety of facts about themselves and their situation, and a significant proportion of many questionnaires is devoted to obtaining factual information, such as the respondent's age, education, religion, income, marital status, and occupation. Questions about events, circumstances, or conditions known to the respondent, such as details of recent illness or medical treatment, also are common.

The possibility of error in reported facts must always be taken into account. Errors can arise from memory problems or from response biases of various forms. For example, when questions are posed by an interviewer, respondents might overstate their incomes in an effort to impress the interviewer with their prestige, or they might understate them if they fear that the interviewer is connected with the taxing authorities. In one study of potential bias in reporting factual information, comparisons of respondents' answers with official records showed that approximately 40% of the respondents inaccurately reported on whether they had contributed to the United Fund, 25% erred concerning whether they had registered and voted in a recent election, and 17% misstated their age (Parry & Crossley, 1950). These inaccuracies could be due either to a motive to give socially desirable responses or to lapses of memory.

Memory failures are more likely for events that are farther in the past or that are more trivial and routine. The structure of the questionnaire itself can ease the respondents' task of remembering the desired facts; for example, fertility, occupational, or medical history data are often collected in a chronological format. Remembering temporally related events can aid recall of more of the desired details. Reassessments also increase the probability of recall. Cannell, Fisher, and Bakker (1965) found that in a first interview, respondents failed to report about 30% of hospitalizations that had occurred a year earlier. In a second interview, after the interviewer urged the person to remember, a higher proportion was reported. **Memory telescoping** also can be a problem in people's reports about past events (Thompson, Skowronski, & Lee, 1988). This is the tendency to recall events as more recent than their actual dates. For example, an episode of illness that was actually 16 months ago might be reported in response to a question about illnesses in the past 12 months, perhaps leading the researcher to overestimate the frequency of illness.

In reporting their ages, people tend to round off (to 30, 40, 50, and so on) rather than reporting exactly; we also could expect some older people to understate their ages. To avoid both of these problems, survey researchers have learned to ask for the year of the respondents' birth rather than their current age.

Specificity is important in factual questions, to give precise information about what response is desired and to avoid interpretation of questions in terms of respondents' own frame of reference. For instance, Mauldin and Marks (1950) asked farmers whether they had any fruit or nut trees. A large proportion answered no, but when more specific follow-up questions were used (e.g., whether they had even one or two trees or any that were not producing fruit), over half the farmers who originally said no now said yes. The researchers concluded that the farmers were not intentionally deceptive but were simply answering in terms of a frame of reference in which one or two trees, particularly if they were not producing, were not worth mentioning in response to the initial question. The more specific questions successfully elicited the desired information.

On the whole, specific facts from the recent past that are nontrivial and therefore memorable should be reported relatively well—if they are nonthreatening to respondents. This is particularly true if question wording, questionnaire forms, and administration procedures are properly designed. But even such major events as hospitalizations can be substantially underreported just a year later; memory cannot be completely trusted.

Questions Aimed at Beliefs or Attitudes

A frequent focus of questionnaire research is relatively subjective judgments, such as the respondent's belief that the president is managing the economy well or poorly, attitude toward one's job, or feelings about abortion. For convenience, in this section we refer to all such judgments as attitudes except where finer distinctions are necessary.

Questions about attitudes are probably the most difficult type to write, for a number of reasons. First, there is always the possibility that respondents do not have an attitude because they never thought about the issue until the interviewer asked about it. Researchers cannot count on the respondent saying "I don't know" in this situation; many people simply respond with an opinion that is reached on the spot and therefore not well considered. Research, however, has shown that, when responses are gathered by computer, people who have formed an attitude toward an object can be distinguished from those who have not by the shorter time they take to answer an attitude question (Fazio, Powell, & Herr, 1983). The amount of time between a question and response could be unobtrusively measured in telephone interviews (or less unobtrusively in face-to-face interviews), possibly helping to overcome the problem of respondents expressing an opinion they do not hold with any certainty. Indeed, Fazio and Williams (1986) used this technique in face-to-face interviews, and their results illustrate its potential usefulness. They found, as predicted, that the quicker respondents reported their attitudes toward presidential candidates, the better those attitudes predicted their actual presidential vote several months later.

Second, attitudes often are complex and multidimensional, a concern we address in the next chapter. A person might not have a single overall attitude toward abortion but might favor it in some circumstances and reject it in others or favor it on medical grounds but disapprove of it on moral grounds. Third, attitudes have a dimension of intensity. People who have the same attitude (e.g., opposing legal abortion) can differ widely in the intensity of the attitude, with some viewing the issue as relatively trivial and others feeling very strongly, actively writing letters, attending demonstrations, and so on.

The result of all these factors is that expressed attitudes are dependent on details of question wording, question sequence, and interviewer effects to a greater extent than are responses involving facts, for instance. There are numerous examples of this phenomenon. Two questions used by the Gallup and Harris polls just three or four months apart in 1969 produced estimates of support for President Nixon's Vietnam War policy of 29% and 49%, undoubtedly because of differences in wording rather than because popular opinion actually changed that much in such a brief period (Schuman & Duncan, 1974).

Besides the necessity to word attitude questions carefully, a number of other considerations are worth noting. It might be important to measure the attitude's intensity. The respondent could be asked to rate directly the intensity of the attitude with a question such as, "How strongly do you feel about this issue?" Alternatively, an attitude question could be followed up with questions about related behaviors: After asking, "How well did you like the book?" the interviewer could ask whether the respondent has recommended it to other people or sought out other books by the same author. Still another approach is to point out difficulties or costs implicit in the respondent's position and ask if he or she stands by it. For example, those who favor improved protection of the environment could be asked whether they would be willing to pay $5, $50, or $500 more in taxes per year to attain that goal. Whatever approach is taken, the measurement of attitude intensity is an important adjunct to the measurement of attitude position.

The level of specificity of questions about attitudes is as important as it is for questions about facts or behaviors. General and specific questions often do not elicit the same responses, as when a person expresses a negative attitude toward a particular ethnic group in general but a positive attitude toward individual members of the same group. Usually, specific questions obtain more valid responses than general ones. For instance, simply asking people whether they favor more educational television programs would not reveal whether they wanted them for themselves or simply thought they would be generally good for other people. It would be preferable to ask whether they would watch more educational programs if they were available. On the other hand, answers to seemingly specific questions can sometimes reflect general attitudes, making the answers subject to misinterpretation by the researcher. For example, people might be asked, "Do qualified Black teachers have just as good a chance as qualified White teachers to be hired in the schools in this city?" Unless the respondents have some specific knowledge about practices in the school system, it is very likely that the question will be answered on the basis of a general opinion that Blacks are (or are not) treated fairly. The answer will not actually refer to the specific issue, although it might seem to. It is always important to frame questions at an appropriate level of specificity, avoiding both questions that are so general as to be meaningless and questions that are too specific to be answered meaningfully.

Attitudes can best be measured by using multiple related questions and constructing an attitude scale according to principles outlined in the next chapter. A properly constructed scale virtually always has better reliability and validity than a single item.

Sociometric Questions One specific category of judgments of interest to some social scientists is people's attitudes toward other people in a group or social network to which they belong. Sociometric studies focus on positive and negative attitudes or actual interactions among all members of a defined group. A **sociometric questionnaire** asks each member of a group to indicate which other members he or she would like to have as a partner in some interaction (e.g., "eat lunch with") and which group members he or she would not like to have as a partner. Respondents might be allowed to name as many others as they wish or might be restricted to naming three or some other specific number. It is often assumed that preferences will be stated more honestly if the respondent believes they will really determine subsequent social arrangements (e.g., that seating arrangements or work partnerships actually will be assigned on the basis of their responses). Therefore, sociometric questionnaires are sometimes given with the statement that the investigator will arrange circumstances to fulfill the participant's preferences if possible. Of course, ethical problems arise if any statement of this sort is made without the promise being fulfilled.

Sociometric data can provide information about individuals' position in the group, the social subgroups or "cliques" within the group, the relations among subgroups, the group's cohesiveness, the leadership structure, and other matters. Sociometric measures of this type have been used in studies of various social phenomena including leadership, peer relations in racially mixed schools, effects of experimental treatments on group structure, and so on.

Questions Aimed at Behavior

People are in a uniquely favorable position to observe their own behavior, so questions often concern the respondents' present or past behaviors. The most important guideline for asking about behaviors is that the question should be specific. For example, "What brand or brands of coffee do you have in the house today? Do you usually buy that brand?" is preferable to a more general question such as "What brand of coffee do you usually use?" A telephone survey on television viewing should ask, "Is your television on right now? What program is it tuned to?" rather than "What television programs do you usually watch?" Similarly, it would be preferable to ask, "For whom did you vote in the last mayoral election? What made you vote for this person? Did you know the religion of any of the candidates? Were you influenced for or against any candidate by knowledge of that person's religion?" rather than "Do you usually tend to consider a candidate's religion in deciding for whom to vote?" In each case the first question offers better cues for recall by anchoring the respondent to the concrete instance.

As with questions about facts, the length of time elapsed since the behavior in question influences the accuracy of responses. The shorter the interval, the better. Because of the problems of memory, studies of behavior often use techniques such as diaries, in which respondents log their behavior as it occurs rather than relying on recall after the event (e.g., LoSciuto, 1971).

Question Content: General Issues

A number of considerations apply to questions regardless of their specific content category. One crucial decision is the number of questions to devote to a topic. It is important to avoid unnecessary questions and unnecessary levels of detail. For example, instead of asking the age of each child in a family, it might be sufficient for the research purposes to know the number of children under age 16.

On the other hand, particularly for the central topics of a study, enough questions should be included to permit full understanding of the responses. Often this principle implies using multiple-item scales for high reliability and validity in the measurement of key attitudes, but it has other implications as well. For example, asking for the respondents' opinions of a particular ethnic group should be done in the context of parallel questions about other groups. Otherwise, we would not know whether a negative opinion was specific to this group or reflected a negative view of all ethnic out-groups or even of all people in general. It is also valuable to ascertain how important the respondents consider a particular issue or condition. Some respondents might say that they favor the provision of more parkland in the community but might perceive the issue as relatively unimportant in the context of other pressing problems. People can be asked directly to rate the importance of different issues or can be asked an open-ended question such as, "What two or three problems do you consider to be the most important ones facing our community today?" (Such a question should be asked before any mention of specific issues, to avoid biasing the responses.)

Often, question content needs to differ for different subsets of respondents, and such situations should be anticipated. Those who watch a television program "regularly," for example, can be asked about their attitudes toward the program, whereas those who watch "occasionally" or "never" might be asked instead about what other programs they watch, what they know about this program, and so on.

Finally, the sensitivity or level of threat posed by the question content needs to be carefully considered. If the response might be viewed as private or personal by respondents, special precautions in wording and presentation can be applied to maximize the chance of obtaining valid answers instead of misinformation or refusals to answer. Techniques for measuring opinions on sensitive topics are discussed later in this chapter.

Question Wording

The wording of questions is perhaps the most difficult and important task in developing questionnaire items. Improperly worded questions can only result in biased or otherwise meaningless responses, and as noted, attitudes are particularly subject to biases caused by wording. An essential prerequisite for developing properly worded questions is to have a clear conceptual idea of just what content is to be measured. It is then important to pretest the questions to revise and improve them, as was outlined at the beginning of this chapter.

Prior decisions about question content dictate some aspects of wording. The specification of the desired content must be detailed enough to provide guidance. For example, a researcher might want to measure respondents' "income." This is too vague, for it could mean the respondents' earnings from their occupation, the respondents' total income (including interest or other payments besides earnings), or the respondents' total family or household income; it could mean before-tax or after-tax income; and so on. The question would have to be worded differently in each case. As another example, consider these questions: "Are working conditions satisfactory or unsatisfactory in the plant where you work?" and "Are you personally satisfied or dissatisfied with working conditions in the plant where you work?" The general thrust of the questions is similar, but the second probably will elicit a more individual expression of feelings and the first a judgment more tempered by what the respondents suppose other people think, what comparable workplaces are like, and so on. Conceptual clarity is therefore the essential starting point of wording adequate questions.

At times, wording decisions can be bypassed. The overall research purpose might involve the replication of a question or an entire study that was conducted earlier. This eases decisions about question wording because wordings should be repeated exactly when this goal is important. Even seemingly minor wording changes—such as the use of the term "forbid" instead of "not allow"—can result in large differences in responses, so they should be avoided. A similar situation arises when information derived from the questionnaire is to be compared to other sources of information (e.g., U.S. Census data, personnel records, or directory listings); again, the question and the response categories should follow those used in the other source. Often, the goals of the research involve both the exploration of new areas and the partial replication of an existing study, creating a conflict between the desire to replicate questions that were used before and the desire to improve them. An attempt to compromise and maintain both goals is often unsatisfactory because wording improvements can interfere with comparability. If it is important to replicate a previous study, then it will be necessary to faithfully repeat the errors of the original study as well as capitalize on its strengths.

Even when replication is not a primary purpose of the research, the ability to compare results from a study with those of earlier research often greatly increases the meaningfulness of the results by placing them in context. It is therefore common for researchers to search out earlier questions on the topic of their interest and repeat them exactly in a new study. This also allows them to avoid spending time and effort developing a usable measure of a construct that other researchers have measured in the past. Survey archives, discussed in Chapter 15, and compilations of questions and scales (e.g., Robinson, Shaver, & Wrightsman, 1991) are useful sources in which to locate previously used questions.

This section on question wording is divided into discussions of a number of specific issues, including the choices of individual words to identify concepts in questions; question structure; the proper expression of alternatives in questions; the avoidance of unwarranted assumptions; the choice of response categories; and the assessment of "no opinion" or "don't know" responses. A final section discusses differences among the modes of direct questioning that influence decisions on wording.

Terminology

The choice of specific terms to convey the question's concepts is often the most difficult part of question wording. As noted, the use of terms such as "earnings" versus "income" can completely change the meaning of a question. The first guideline, therefore, is that terms should be exact, reflecting just what the question content is intended to mean. A second guideline, of equal importance but often conflicting with the first, is that terms must be simple—comprehensible even to the least-educated respondents. Many commonly used terms are frequently misunderstood, including personal characteristics such "nationality," "marital status," or "unemployed" and attitude objects such as "gene therapy," "guaranteed wage," or "mass media." Such terms should be avoided and simpler equivalents substituted, or else they should be spelled out and clarified in detail. For example, instead of asking, "What is your marital status?" which might elicit reports of marital problems, plans for the future, opinions about marriage, or feelings about personal fitness for marriage, it is best to ask, "Are you currently married, widowed, divorced, or separated or have you never been married?" This recommendation cannot be followed in all cases, however, because the substitution of simple words for difficult ones often turns simple sentences into difficult ones. Dillman (1978) gives an example: "Should the state sales tax on prescription drugs be reduced from 5% to 1%?" (difficult words) could be rewritten as "Should the state sales tax on those medicines that can only be bought under a doctor's order be lowered so that people would pay 1 cent tax instead of 5 cents tax for every dollar spent on such medicine?" (difficult sentence).

Ambiguous or vague words are frequent sources of trouble. Even familiar, simple words can give rise to ambiguity: In "What kind of headache remedy do you usually use?" the word "kind" might be understood by some respondents to refer to a "brand" and by others to mean "pills versus powder." Quantifying words (e.g., "frequently," "often," "sometimes," "almost never," "usually") are intrinsically vague and should be avoided in favor of numerical ranges when possible. In "Do you attend religious services regularly?" one respondent might take "regularly" to mean weekly, whereas for another it might mean once a month.

Finally, biased words in questions can produce biased responses. Terms that produce powerful emotional responses, such as "freedom," "equality," "justice," "loss," "bureaucrat," or "big business," should be avoided if possible. Two people holding opposite viewpoints might word questions about wage and price controls in two different ways: "Do you think that government bureaucrats should be involved in regulating workers' wages and the prices charged by businesses?" versus "Do you think that big business and powerful union leaders should be able to set prices and wages at whatever levels they choose, or should the government step in to protect consumers from increases in the cost of living?" The second version is likely to elicit more pro-control responses. These examples of biased questions, although extreme, are not fanciful; newsletters sent by congressional representatives to their constituents often contain "surveys" that use equally biased questions. One suspects that the purpose of such questions is as much to persuade voters of the wisdom of the representative's position as to determine the voters' true opinions, a strategy that can backfire if respondents feel as if they are being manipulated (Schuman & Presser, 1996).

Question Structure

Complex and lengthy sentences are particularly likely to be misunderstood by respondents, so questions should be short and simple. As previously noted, however, the need to use simple words often results in lengthy sentences, and compromises sometimes must be struck. One guideline is that the key idea in the question should come last to avoid a premature formulation of an answer. Qualifications and conditional clauses should come first. For example, researchers ask, "If your party nominated a woman for president, would you vote for her if she were qualified for the job?" instead of, "Would you vote for a woman for president if . . . ." Even the standard wording might be improved by moving the phrase about qualification for the job to the beginning.

Finally, questions should simplify the respondents' task as much as possible. For example, instead of asking what percentage of income the respondents spend on rent, it is preferable to ask for both the respondents' monthly income and monthly rent payments. Instead of asking about the average length of recent vacation trips, ask for the length of the three most recent trips. The researcher can calculate the desired percentage or average from the respondents' answers.

Expressing All Alternatives

Questions should make the alternatives clear unless they are totally unambiguous (e.g., favoring versus opposing some policy proposal). Even when the implied alternative is reasonably clear, stating it explicitly can make it more vivid and salient and hence place the two possible answers on a more equal footing. Payne (1951) gives a striking example of the effect of failing to state alternatives explicitly. To the question "Do you think most manufacturing companies that lay off workers during slack periods could arrange things to avoid layoffs and give steady work right through the year?" 63% said companies could avoid layoffs, and 22% said they could not (the rest had no opinion). An equivalent sample of respondents was asked the question with the alternative made explicit: The phrase "or do you think layoffs are unavoidable?" was simply added at the end. To this question, only 35% said companies could avoid layoffs and 41% said they could not.

Omitting some alternatives or not treating them equally in the question actually constitutes a form of bias. The question "In the mayoral election, do you plan to vote for Mayor Jones or the challenger?" is blatantly biased; the names of both candidates should be given, and perhaps the fact that one is the incumbent should be omitted ("... do you plan to vote for Jones or Brown?").

Finally, one fairly common practice is to describe a policy by introducing it with "Some people say we should . . ." to lead in to a question about "Do you agree or disagree?" or "What do you think?" The result can be a biased question unless care is taken to treat the opposing position equally, as in, "Some people say that women should have an equal role with men in running business, industry, and government. Others say that women's place is in the home. What do you think?" Without the second sentence the question might be biased. An alternative strategy is to avoid questions that present a statement with which respondents agree or disagree, in favor of a **forced-choice format.** For example, instead of "Some people say that individuals are more to blame than social conditions for crime and lawlessness in this country" followed by an agree or disagree response scale, we might ask, "Which in your opinion is more to blame for crime and lawlessness in this country—individuals or social conditions?" (Schuman & Presser, 1996). Under certain conditions, this forced-choice wording elicits more valid responses than the agree or disagree wording, perhaps because the latter is more susceptible to response biases, such as a general tendency to agree with statements regardless of their content (Petty, Rennier, & Cacioppo, 1987).

Avoiding Unwarranted Assumptions

The question "What is your occupation?" assumes that all respondents have an occupation. "For whom did you vote in the last presidential election?" assumes that all respondents voted. Such examples of the "Have you stopped beating your wife?" type annoy respondents and are likely to produce invalid data. The general solution to this problem is to ask a preliminary question about whether the respondent is working, did vote, or whatever is appropriate, and then ask the question of interest for only those respondents who fall into the relevant category. Other respondents are instructed to skip the irrelevant question.

Another way unwarranted assumptions can be introduced into questionnaires is by **double-barreled questions,** which inappropriately combine two separate ideas and require a single response. Asking about the attitude of respondents' "parents" is inappropriate, for the father's and mother's attitudes might be different. Other examples are "Do you think that the government's policy on inflation is effective and fair?" and "Do you think that taxes on corporations should be increased and taxes on individuals lowered?" However, the last example might be appropriate if a specific policy proposal combining those two elements is currently being considered; a question about the respondents' attitude on the policy would necessarily be double-barreled in form.

Response Categories: Open-Ended Versus Closed-Ended Questions

The primary decision about the form of the respondents' choices is between open-ended, or free-response, versus closed-ended, or fixed-alternative, questions. **Open-ended questions** allow the respondents to answer in a relatively unconstrained way, either writing or typing a response or telling it to the interviewer, who is instructed to record the response verbatim. Later, the researcher can enlist judges to code the responses in terms of a system of categories. **Closed-ended questions,** on the other hand, present two or more alternatives, and the respondents select the choice closest to their own position.

Open-ended and closed-ended questions have complementary strengths and weaknesses. Open-ended questions allow respondents to convey the fine shades of their attitude to their own satisfaction instead of forcing them to choose one of several statements that might all seem more or less unsatisfactory. For this reason, open-ended questions can be more motivating to respondents. Also, they can be used even when the researcher does not know the full range of attitude positions in the population under study, whereas construction of a closed-ended question requires such knowledge in advance.

Open-ended questions also have disadvantages, however. The most important are the cost and difficulty of adequately coding the responses. Open-ended responses are frequently self-contradictory, incomprehensible, or irrelevant, and a significant portion of them will usually defy all efforts at meaningful categorization. They are functions of the respondents' attitude position but also of their intensity, knowledge about the issue, involvement, education, general verbal fluency, communicative style, and other factors. To code such responses meaningfully requires a major effort and is sometimes simply impossible. Closed-ended questions are easily scored to produce meaningful results for analysis.

Another advantage of closed-ended questions is that the provision of response categories can help clarify the intent of the question for the respondents or help their memory. For instance, respondents might be unable to recall the name of their preferred political candidate before a primary election but might be able to pick the name out of the list of candidates if it is provided. Or people might not be able to remember all the state parks they have visited in the past year without the aid of a list of their names and locations. At times, though, providing a list of possible responses is unnecessary, and an open-ended format will suffice, as when the respondent is asked "In which state were you born?" Often, open-ended questions are asked about the respondents' reasons or explanations for a response. The follow-up might be worded, "Just how do you mean?" "Why do you feel that way?" or "Would you tell me a little more about your thinking on that?" Full information often requires more than one question, however. For example, the question "Why do you feel the way you do about abortion?" might elicit answers involving personal or educational experiences, beliefs about legal restrictions, political attitudes, moral or religious values, or beliefs about when human life begins. (This variety of possible frames of reference for responses illustrates the difficulties of coding open-ended responses in ways that permit comparisons across respondents.) The goals of the research might be best served by using a series of questions to ask each respondent about each of these different aspects of the issue.

Researchers often seek to obtain the benefits of both open-ended and closed-ended questions. One approach is to give a set of fixed response alternatives and also an open-ended "other" category, allowing people who are not comfortable with any of the given alternatives to fill in their own; however, this type of question rarely obtains enough "other" responses to warrant analysis. Most respondents choose one of the offered response categories rather than create their own, perhaps because the former involves less effort. This type of question remains useful in identifying situations in which important response alternatives are not included among the fixed set: A relatively large number of "other" responses indicates that the set of responses is incomplete and should be revised.

Perhaps the best way to combine the advantages of open- and closed-ended questions is during the early stages of questionnaire development. Initially, open-ended questions are asked with a relatively small pretest sample of the population that is to be studied. On the basis of their responses, closed-ended questions can be constructed that represent the most common response categories found in the pretest sample. This approach saves work (for only the open-ended responses from the pretest, not from the whole study sample, need to be coded), while ensuring that the closed-ended question that is finally used adequately represents the range of opinions on the issue. The approach avoids both the danger of using a large number of open-ended questions in a survey and the danger of writing closed-ended questions that fail to reflect the diversity of opinion that exists in the population. Closed-ended questions constructed in this way generally have equal or superior validity to the open-ended questions from which they were constructed (Schuman & Presser, 1996). Most researchers today use mainly closed-ended questions in attitude measurement but with a sprinkling of open-ended questions to obtain reasons for or illustrations of attitudes on key issues. The open-ended responses can help in the formulation of new hypotheses and often are quoted to lend interest and concreteness to research reports.

Response Categories: Other Issues

If closed-ended questions are used, there are additional decisions to be made. The question might call for a response scale along a single dimension, for example, "How frequently do you attend religious services: never, a few times a year, about once a month, about two to three times a month, about once a week, or more often than once a week?" A common response scale involves the dimension of agreement versus disagreement, sometimes using just those two categories, other times using qualified categories like "strongly agree," "agree," "disagree," and "strongly disagree." Questions using response scales are appropriate when the dimension of the desired response is known and the respondents are to classify themselves along it, a procedure discussed in the next chapter. These are usually among the easiest types of questions for respondents to answer because the response dimension is so clearly identified.

Closed-ended questions can also involve unordered response choices that do not fall along a single dimension, for example, "If the election were being held today, which presidential candidate would you vote for: George W. Bush or Al Gore?" "Which of these things will influence you most when it comes to choosing your next car: appearance, gas mileage, comfort, pickup, dependability, safety, ease of driving, smoothness, cost, or speed?" or "Would you say the group most responsible for causing inflation is business, labor unions, government, or some other group?" As the last example illustrates, a residual "other" category can be included in a set of responses. One danger with lists of unordered response categories is that they might fail to include the preferred choice of some respondents, a possibility that can be reduced by pretesting. Another problem is that generally each of the given response alternatives must be individually considered by the respondents, and this makes the question difficult to answer. When such questions are posed in face-to-face interviews, a lengthy set of response choices can be printed on a card, which is handed to the respondents to reduce the memory burden of retaining all the options. A final problem is that the categories might not be mutually exclusive, forcing respondents to choose between equally true alternatives, for example, "How did you first hear about the proposed freeway: from a friend or relative, at a meeting of an organization to which I belong, at work, from my spouse, over television or radio, or from a newspaper?" (Dillman, 1978). What if some respondents heard about it from a friend at work? Poorly constructed sets of response categories are among the most common faults in questionnaires.

Response categories must strike the appropriate balance between vagueness and overprecision. Most respondents would find it hard to answer such a question as "How many meals did you eat at restaurants last month: _____ meals," for too much precision is implied by the request for a specific number. On the other hand, "very many, quite a lot, not too many, just a few, none" would be too vague. Ranges of numbers are usually the best solution in such cases. An example is "none, 1–2 meals, 3–5 meals, 5–10 meals, 11–20 meals, more than 20 meals." Income is generally measured using numerical categories because respondents often are more comfortable placing their income in a category like $15,000–$19,999 than giving an exact figure. As with any set of response categories, the ranges should be mutually exclusive and exhaustive. Income categories, for instance, should not be given as $15,000–$20,000, $20,000–$30,000, and so on. This point might seem minor (not many respondents will have an income of exactly $20,000), but the manner in which such details are treated in a questionnaire creates an overall impression of sloppiness or care in question construction and therefore indirectly influences the respondents' motivation to take the task seriously.

Finally, response categories should be properly balanced. Consider this example: "Do you think that judges should sentence criminals to prison terms that are much longer than at present, longer than at present, about the same as at present, or shorter than at present?" With more response categories on the "longer" side than on the "shorter" side, the set of categories is implicitly biased rather than balanced.

Filters and the Assessment of No Opinion

People responding to surveys have an unfortunate tendency to answer questions such as "Do you agree or disagree with the governor's policy on layoffs for state employees?" or "Do you favor or oppose the extension of the Agricultural Trade Act?" even if they do not know what the governor's policy or the act in question is. Unless the purpose of the research includes the measurement of such off-the-cuff, uninformed reactions, the assessment of "no opinion" or "don't know" responses should be allowed for in question construction.

The most common approach is to list "don't know" as one response alternative. In the interview context, this option is usually not mentioned in the question read to the respondents, but the interviewer is instructed to check "don't know" on the questionnaire if a respondent gives that answer. Sometimes the "don't know" response is explicitly mentioned in the question, as in, "Do you favor or oppose . . . or haven't you thought much about it?" A variant of this approach is to include a neutral point in a response scale, for example, "strongly agree," "agree," "no opinion," "disagree," or "strongly disagree." Of course, more "don't know" responses are obtained when the possibility is explicitly mentioned than when it is not. Sometimes the substantive opinion question is preceded by a separate **filter question** intended solely to screen out respondents who do not have any knowledge or opinion on the issue: "The governor has recently taken a position on the issue of layoffs for state employees. Have you heard or read enough about this to have an opinion on the matter?" Respondents who answer affirmatively might even be asked to state what the governor's position is, to verify that their understanding is correct. Finally, they would be asked about their opinion. Respondents who claim not to have an opinion are never asked the opinion question; their interview simply proceeds from the filter to the subsequent question. The use of filter questions produces an increase in "don't know" responses of as much as 25 percentage points over the standard (unfiltered) version of the same question (Schuman & Presser, 1979).

If different approaches to assessing "don't know" responses merely changed the proportion of respondents who choose that response, the issue would not be very important. But in fact, research shows that different approaches to assessing "don't know" responses (using filtered versus unfiltered questions) can change the distribution of substantive responses—that is, the relative balance of agreement versus disagreement on an issue. For example, in a 1978 survey, one question concerned cutting federal taxes even if it meant that some public employees would lose their jobs. Although 48% of the respondents who gave an opinion favored the tax cut with the standard (unfiltered) form of the question, 58% had a favorable opinion when a separate filter question was used—a substantial difference in support (Bishop, Oldendick, & Tuchfarber, 1983).

The research seems to show that there is a substantial number of people, perhaps as many as 25% of the population, who will give a "don't know" response when a filter question invites it but will give a substantive opinion to an unfiltered question. Such respondents are called **floaters** (Schuman & Presser, 1996). Using unfiltered questions and therefore including the floaters' responses can seriously affect conclusions drawn from attitude surveys. An overall recommendation is to use filters to screen out uninformed respondents if the measurement of only informed opinion on the issue is the goal but to use standard (unfiltered) questions if basic values, ideologies, or general attitudes are desired.

Special Considerations for Different Modes

Paper-and-pencil questionnaires, face-to-face interviews, telephone interviews, Internet-based surveys, and experience sampling studies have somewhat different requirements for question wording, telephone interviews being perhaps the most distinct. One obvious consideration is that the use of visual aids and printed materials (such as lists of response categories) is impossible over the telephone. Photographs, line drawings, or maps can greatly clarify certain types of questions. Particularly when children or people of limited literacy are being studied, visual techniques are valuable, for they reduce the demands placed on verbal comprehension; however, even with general populations, pictures, diagrams, or maps can help communicate some types of situations or concepts. As previously noted, in face-to-face interviews printed lists of response categories also are useful when the lists are long and would pose a burden on the respondents' memory. The inability to use visual aids of either the pictorial or the list type frequently makes it necessary to reword questions that perform well when administered on paper, by computer, or in face-to-face interviews for telephone interviews.

These questions need to be carefully constructed, especially for brevity and clarity. Respondents to a written questionnaire, presented either on paper, via the Internet, or on a handheld computer, have the question in front of them and can reread it if necessary; in a face-to-face interview the interviewer can detect nonverbal signs of incomprehension or confusion. But the telephone interviewer faces special problems because question content that is often complex and abstract must be communicated completely by voice, without the respondents having much chance to control the pace of the interview. The maxim "keep it short and simple" applies with even more force to questions that will be asked over the telephone. If questions are necessarily complex (e.g., summarizing a complex program), they should include considerable redundancy, and the key elements should be summarized at the end so that respondents can check their comprehension (Dillman, 1978). Sometimes complex questions can be divided into two or more parts, each of which is conceptually simpler.

Sets of response categories must also be kept simple for telephone use. Obviously, large numbers of unordered categories, for which printed lists would be provided in the other modes of direct questioning, cannot be used. Neither can questions that ask respondents to rank-order a number of choices; these should be replaced with a separate evaluation of each individual choice (Krosnick & Alwin, 1988). Even response scales should probably be kept to no more than five or so categories. It is tempting to request numerical responses (e.g., "on a scale from 1 to 10, where 1 means strongly disagree and 10 means strongly agree") to avoid giving respondents a list of possible responses, but this technique produces mixed results (Dillman, 1978). Some people understand the technique quickly and are comfortable using it, but others never seem to get the idea.

A number of special considerations for paper-and-pencil and computer-administered questionnaires involve page layout and typography to clarify and simplify the respondents' task; Dillman (2000) presents a detailed set of recommendations. One significant point is that paper-and-pencil questionnaires cannot use skips and filter questions as freely as questionnaires administered by computer or trained interviewers; respondents frequently have trouble comprehending written instructions to skip over one or more questions depending on their response to a previous question.

Question Sequence

The sequence of the questions in a questionnaire has two major implications. First, an appropriate sequence can ease the respondents' task in answering, which is particularly important at the very beginning in order to capture the respondents' interest and motivate completion. Second, the sequence of questions can either create or avoid biases that influence responses to the later questions. **Context effects,** the effects of preceding questions on the response to later questions, pose the same sorts of issues as effects of question wording, although they seem to be less powerful. The following guidelines should be followed to produce questionnaires that are as free from bias as possible and seem natural to respondents.

Overall Sequence

Respondents often begin a questionnaire or interview with some doubts about whether they can provide meaningful information. After all, they are not experts on the topic or (perhaps) even highly educated. Will they simply embarrass themselves by not knowing the answers to all the questions? To overcome these doubts, every questionnaire should begin with a few easy and unchallenging questions (probably closed-ended questions offering only two or three response categories). At the same time, the initial questions should be interesting to the respondent, having clear social importance and clear relevance to the stated study purpose (Dillman, 1978). Therefore, one common practice, beginning the questionnaire with easy-to-answer background items like age, marital status, or education, is unwise. Examples of reasonable opening questions (assuming that the stated study topic involves household financial matters) are, "There's been a lot of talk about inflation. How much would you say you and your family have been hurt by inflation recently: a great deal, somewhat, not too much, or not at all?" or "We are interested in how people are getting along financially these days. During the last few years, has the financial situation of you and your household been getting better, staying about the same, or getting worse?" Questions like these should be both interesting for respondents and easy to answer, increasing their confidence that they can successfully complete the questionnaire or interview.

Following a few initial questions of this sort, the main questions follow; they might be concerned with the respondents' beliefs, behaviors, attitudes, or whatever is entailed by the purpose of the study. Questions about the respondents' social and demographic background should be put at the end. At that time the respondents are ordinarily more willing to give such personal information, and in case they are not, at least the replies to the belief and attitude questions will not be affected by the suspicion or resentment that personal questions occasionally arouse.

A final consideration is to keep topically related questions together. Respondents are frequently confused and angered if questions skip around from topic to topic, as when one question asks about tax policy, the next about the number of children respondents have, and the next about their satisfaction with their job. Both the respondents' comprehension and ability to answer the questions are facilitated by keeping topically related questions together. Moreover, each topic in turn should be linked in the respondents' mind to the overall purpose of the study. Questions with no evident connection to the topic are bound to arouse suspicion and resentment, for example, if a questionnaire about "how people feel about the Social Security system" suddenly turned to a series of questions on drinking and drug use. Even background questions, such as those regarding income and education, often will be resisted by respondents if their purpose is not understood. This is another reason for putting such items at the end of the questionnaire; the implicit or explicit message is then that they will be used to compare the beliefs or opinions of people with different characteristics. Thus, the respondent can see their relevance.

Clear and meaningful transitions between topics that point out the relevance of the new topic to the study purpose are essential. At a minimum, transitional statements signal that one topic has been completed and a new one is coming up. These statements might be as simple as "The next few questions are about the upcoming election" or "We've been talking so far about your general feelings about your neighborhood. Now I'd like to ask a few questions about your family." Beyond this level, transitions can explain—although not with great technical detail—the rationale for the succeeding questions in terms of the study purpose or their association with the preceding topic. An example is "An important part of understanding people's attitudes toward Social Security has to do with their feelings about retirement from work. So next we would like to ask some questions about your plans and thoughts about retirement" or, to introduce the personal background items at the end of the questionnaire, "Finally, we would like to ask some questions about yourself, to help interpret the results." Well-written transitions are indispensable for smoothing the flow of a questionnaire, thereby easing the respondents' task and motivating them to continue by showing the inquiry to be meaningful and relevant. Sensitive questions demand particular attention to transitions, to ensure that respondents understand the relevance of the questions to the research purpose.

Sequence Within a Topic Area

Within a specific topic area, two general guidelines relate to question sequence. The first is the **funnel principle:** General questions should come first, followed by increasingly specific and detailed questions, with the sequence "funneling down" to the most detailed questions at the end. This sequence has several points in its favor. The more general questions (e.g., satisfaction or dissatisfaction with one's work in general) are most easily justified in terms of their relevance to the study purpose. They then serve as a natural lead-in to more specific questions about, for example, the activities involved in the job, working conditions, feelings about coworkers, wages, and so on. In addition, the general-to-specific sequence should produce less bias than the reverse. For example, if a series of specific questions about satisfaction with wages preceded the general question about satisfaction with the job as a whole, the focus of the respondents' attention on wages would undoubtedly lead to wages being overweighted in their overall judgment. Such biases are probably less frequent when general questions precede specific ones.

The second general principle is to avoid context or question sequence effects by looking out for possible associations among questions that might produce bias if two or more questions are close together in the questionnaire. For example, we would not want to ask a series of questions about strikes and labor troubles before a question about attitudes toward unions.

Schuman and Presser (1996) summarize their extensive research on question order effects by noting that they can be large (as much as 15 percentage points in some cases). For example, a 1979 survey used a general question on abortion: "Do you think it should be possible for a pregnant woman to obtain a *legal* abortion if she is married and does not want any more children?" When this question was asked before any other abortion-related questions, 60.7% of the respondents said yes; however, when it was asked of an equivalent subsample of respondents after a separate, more specific question about abortion in the case of a defect in the unborn child (to which 84% said yes), the general question obtained only 48.1% yes responses, a decrease of 13 percentage points. A second survey used the same questions and obtained a slightly larger decrease, 17% in yes responses. In neither case did responses to the specific question differ much depending on whether it was asked first or second.

Question sequence effects are more likely to occur with general or summary questions than with others (Tourangeau & Rasinski, 1988); however, there are instances of order effects influencing specific attitude questions and even factual responses. In a crime victimization survey, respondents reported that they had been the victims of more crimes if a series of crime-related attitude items preceded the factual questions, perhaps because the attitude questions aided recall (Schuman & Presser, 1996). Our ability to predict what questions are susceptible to order effects is not complete, but common sense must be applied in questionnaire construction to avoid obvious problems. One possibility available when questionnaires are administered by computer is to ask a series of questions in a different random order for each respondent, thereby avoiding any systematic order effects.

Perhaps the most serious implication of order effects involves the replication of questions between different surveys to assess changes over time. Although researchers have long known that even seemingly minor wording changes can greatly influence responses, confounding intended replications, it now appears that the context of a question, and particularly the few preceding questions, can have similar effects. As such, the most persuasive replications carry over a whole sequence of questions, rather than just a single question, for maximum interpretability.

Researchers have used split-ballot experiments within surveys to determine the effects of differences in question wording and sequence; some of their results have already been cited. In a **split-ballot experiment,** two (or more) versions of a questionnaire, with different wordings or sequences, are used for different, randomly chosen subsets of respondents. Because the random choice means that the respondents receiving the different forms are equivalent, any differences in response can be attributed to the wording or sequence variation. Not only are split-ballot experiments useful for methodological investigations like those previously cited, they also can be valuable in any questionnaire study in which the researcher wishes to rule out question wording effects as a major influence on the results. For example, we could use two different wordings of a crucial question in a split-ballot experiment. If the results were identical or similar in the two halves of the sample, we would conclude that question wording effects probably did not play a major role in the results. This approach can be an important tool in showing that survey results are not specific to one particular wording or question order, and it deserves to be more widely used.

Special Techniques for Sensitive Content

When the content of interest might prove embarrassing or threatening to the respondents or is viewed as private or personal, direct questioning can elicit deceptive responses or refusals to answer. Questions about illegal behaviors, sexual practices, and attitudes toward out-groups pose obvious problems, and even questions about income and political affiliation are viewed as threatening by some respondents. A number of techniques have been developed in an effort to maximize the proportion of truthful answers on such topics. The basis on which valid responses to all sensitive questions depend is, however, the respondents' belief that measures are in place to ensure that the information they provide is not disclosed in such a way that their identity can be ascertained. It is also important that sensitive topics be fully introduced by transition statements in the questionnaire and their association with the study topic made clear. Respondents are more willing to respond if they understand the need for the information than if the questions seem gratuitous or unnecessary.

Standard Precautions

For topics of only marginal sensitivity, certain precautions in wording are typical. As mentioned, it is wise to ask for the year of the respondents' birth rather than their age and to ask how many years of school they completed rather than whether or not they graduated from high school. Income is typically requested using a set of broad categories rather than an exact figure.

When one possible response is marginally socially undesirable, the wording can "explain away" the behavior and make respondents more comfortable in giving that reply. Examples are "Did you vote in the presidential election last November, or didn't you find the time to vote?" and "Do you favor or oppose the program of . . . or haven't you happened to hear much about this?" Not having voted or not knowing enough to have an opinion are implicitly excused in the wording to encourage respondents to answer truthfully.

Other practices also seem effective in encouraging reporting of threatening behavioral items. Wording variations have little effect on yes or no responses to simple "Have you done it?" questions about various socially undesirable behaviors but have major effects on quantitative responses to questions about how much or how often (Bradburn & Sudman, 1979). The most valid results seem to arise from long questions instead of short ones and open-ended rather than closed-ended formats. There is some indication that another practice also helps: the use of the respondents' own preferred word for the behavior, ascertained in a prior question, rather than some standard term. A recommended strategy is to embed a threatening behavioral question in a connected sequence of questions (Dillman, 1978). That is, respondents should be asked about how frequently they think other people perform the behavior, how much they approve or disapprove of it, whether anyone they know personally has done it, and so on, before asking whether they have done it.

One special issue of sensitivity that arises in the many questionnaire studies is the assessment of ethnic identification. Some respondents object to terms such as "African American," whereas others object equally strenuously to alternatives like "Black." The term "Native American," if used without further clarification, is selected by many White people as well as by American Indians (whom it is intended to denote). The best solution is the liberal use of alternatives in each response category: Black—not of Hispanic origin (African American); Hispanic (Latino, Chicano); American Indian (Native American); White—not of Hispanic origin (Caucasian); Multiracial (Black and White); Multiracial (Other); Other (specify:__________).

Because of the direct contact between the respondents and another person, the face-to-face interview gives rise to additional concerns about response biases on sensitive questions. During such interviews, a self-administered paper-and-pencil questionnaire on a few topics can be given to the respondent, who can return it by mail or sealed in an envelope that is handed back to the interviewer. If the interview is facilitated by notebook computer, the interviewer can hand the computer over to the respondents to self-administer sections of the questionnaire that concern sensitive topics. Telephone rather than face-to-face interviews can generally help increase respondents' feelings of anonymity and hence encourage accurate reporting on sensitive topics. Comparisons of information obtained by face-to-face and telephone interviews indicate the former to be slightly better with low-threat topics, but telephone interviews obtain fewer response distortions with highly threatening questions, particularly reducing overstatements of desirable acts (Bradburn & Sudman, 1979).

Randomized Response Techniques

To obtain information on sensitive topics when direct questioning is not a viable option, **randomized response techniques** can be employed (Warner, 1965). There are a number of variations of the technique, but they have similar characteristics, which can be illustrated by an example. In a face-to-face interview, interviewers hand respondents a small box that contains 70 red beads and 30 blue beads and is constructed so that when it is tipped, one bead appears in a small window on the box. The respondent also is given a card with two yes or no questions on it. Opposite a red dot is a question on a sensitive topic, for example, "I have been arrested and charged with drunken driving." Opposite a blue dot is an innocuous question, such as, "My birthday is in the last half of the year, from July to December." The respondents are told to tip the box and answer the first question if a red bead appears and the second question if a blue bead appears, saying only yes or no in either case. They are assured that the interviewer cannot tell which question is being answered and is only recording the yes or no response.

The key characteristic of any randomized response technique is that the interviewer does not know whether the answer pertains to the sensitive or innocuous question, so the respondents' privacy is protected in some measure. A randomizing device—the throw of a die, flip of a coin, or a special device as in the preceding example—is used to tell the respondent privately whether to answer the sensitive or the innocuous question. Because the properties of the randomizing device are known (e.g., 70% of the time a red bead will appear), the results can be statistically analyzed to reveal meaningful variations in responses to the sensitive question, such as differences among population subgroups.

A particularly simple version of the technique, suitable even in telephone interviews, was developed by Dawes and Moore (1979). Respondents are asked to flip a coin and either answer the yes or no question if it is heads or simply respond yes if it is tails. (It is assumed that the undesirable or unflattering answer to the question on a sensitive topic is yes.) The calculation of the true response probabilities is also simple in this case. If a particular subgroup (say, female respondents) gives 60% yes responses, it is known that 50% of the subgroup (on the average) responded yes due to the coin falling tails. The 50% of the subgroup who answered the question because the coin fell heads includes the 10% of the subgroup who must have said yes. Therefore, 20% of all females (10% divided by 50%) are estimated to have the characteristic in question. Subgroups can also be compared: If 70% of males say yes, it is clear that a larger proportion of males than females have the characteristic.

Other randomized response techniques (Himmelfarb & Edgell, 1980) are suitable when numerical responses are required (e.g., for questions about how many times a behavior was performed). In general, these techniques are most useful for questions that concern highly sensitive topics (e.g., arrests for a crime), offering no real advantage over direct questioning for questions on mildly sensitive topics (e.g., voting in a primary election). In short, although carefully worded and administered direct questions produce valid responses to most questions on sensitive topics, randomized response techniques are a viable option when the topic is sufficiently sensitive that the validity of responses to direct questions is suspect.

Interviewing

Any questionnaire study has the dual goals of motivating the respondent to give full and precise replies while avoiding biases stemming from social desirability, conformity, or other constructs of disinterest. When the questionnaire is administered by face-to-face or telephone interview, it is the interviewer who must attempt to fulfill these goals in interaction with each individual respondent. The ability of the interviewer to elicit valid responses depends first on adherence to the procedures for questionnaire design outlined at the beginning of this chapter. But given a well-designed questionnaire, proper training and proper interviewer behavior can help greatly in achieving the goals.

As an overall framework for thinking about interviewing, it is useful to examine the processes needed to generate complete and valid responses in the interview. These processes include the respondents' comprehension of the questions and response alternatives and the accessibility in memory of the information that is requested, as well as the respondents' motivation to make the necessary effort. Comprehension and accessibility largely depend on the design of the questionnaire; the task of the interviewer centers on motivation, including both creating and maintaining motivation to answer fully and correctly and avoiding the creation of motives to give socially desirable, confirming, or other biased responses. The specific tasks of the interviewer that contribute to these overall goals involve creating a positive atmosphere, asking the questions properly, obtaining adequate responses, recording the responses, and avoiding biases.

Creating a Positive Atmosphere

The first few moments of contact between the interviewer and respondents are crucial. Even the interviewer's voice qualities (e.g., high pitch, variation of pitch, or fast rate of speaking), measured in the first 30 seconds of telephone contact, can influence respondents' decisions to cooperate in an interview (Oksenberg, Coleman, & Cannell, 1986). Motivational forces that encourage the respondents to participate in the study must be mobilized and negative forces counteracted. The positive forces available to the interviewer are the respondents' liking for the interviewer, any prestige or positive feelings attached to the research sponsor, the respondents' self-image as a dutiful citizen, and perhaps curiosity or loneliness. The negative forces include the press of competing activities and demands for time, worries about appearing ignorant or becoming embarrassed, dislike for the interview content, and perhaps fear of the consequences of participating.

To take advantage of the positive forces and suppress the negative ones, the interviewer's introduction should be brief and positive. The goal is for interviewers to introduce themselves, identify the sponsoring agency, and give the general topic of the study in an interesting way, for example,

> I'm from the Survey Research Center of the University of Michigan. We're doing a survey at this time, as we have for a number of years now, on how people feel things are going financially these days. The study is done throughout the country, and the results are used by government and industry. The addresses at which we interview were chosen entirely by chance, and the interview will take only about a half hour. All information is entirely confidential, of course.

For many respondents, an introduction of this sort will suffice; many people are flattered and interested at the prospect of being singled out for an interview. Once the actual questions begin, a properly designed questionnaire quickly removes respondents' lingering doubts, for example, about their ability to answer the questions. Other respondents might have questions to which the interviewer will need to respond or might want to receive a fuller account of the research and its value or the tasks and topics involved in the interview. In face-to-face interviews, the interviewer should be prepared to show credentials (a card or letter on official stationery identifying the interviewer by name), and in both face-to-face and telephone interviews the interviewer should have a phone number that respondents could call to verify the sponsor's identity.

The task of responding to a questionnaire is sufficiently unfamiliar to many respondents that explicit instructions, stressing completeness and accuracy of response, are helpful. The beginning of the interview, therefore, might include a paragraph like this: "In order for your answers to be most helpful to us, it is important that you try to be as accurate as you can. Because we need complete and accurate information from this research, we hope you will think hard to provide the information we need."

Once the interview begins, the interviewer's manner should be friendly, courteous, conversational, and unbiased. The idea is to put respondents at ease so that they will talk freely and fully. The opportunity to talk to a good listener and to have their ideas taken seriously and recorded is the chief positive outcome of the interview for most respondents, and a major part of the interviewer's task is to use this reward to maintain cooperation. For interviewers, maintaining a conversational tone depends on a thorough mastery of the questionnaire. They must be familiar enough with the questions to ask them conversationally rather than reading them stiffly, and they should know what questions are coming next so that awkward pauses do not occur.

The interviewer's job is fundamentally that of a reporter, not an apologist, a curiosity seeker, or a debater. Interviewers should take all opinions in stride and never show surprise or disapproval of a respondent's answer. They should assume an interested manner toward the respondents' opinions and never divulge their own. If the interviewers should be asked for personal views, they should deflect the request with the remark that the job at the moment is to get opinions, not to have them.

Interviewers must keep the direction of the interview in hand, discouraging irrelevant conversation and endeavoring to keep the respondents on the point. Fortunately, interviewers usually find that the rambling, talkative respondents are the very ones who least resent a firm insistence on attention to the actual business of the interview.

Asking the Questions

Interviewers must be impressed with the importance of asking each question exactly as it is worded. Each question has been carefully pretested to express the precise meaning desired in as simple a manner as possible. Interviewers must understand that even a slight rewording of the question can so change the stimulus as to provoke answers in a different frame of reference or bias the response.

Any impromptu explanation of questions is similarly taboo. Such an explanation again can change the frame of reference or bias the response, and it is easy to see that if each interviewer were permitted to vary the questions, the researcher would have no assurance at all that responses were in comparable terms. If any respondents give evidence of failing to understand a particular question, the interviewer can only repeat it slowly and with proper emphasis, offering only such explanations as are specifically authorized in his or her instructions and, if understanding is still lacking, noting this fact.

For similar reasons, the questions must be asked in the same order as they appear on the questionnaire. Each question sets up a frame of reference for succeeding questions, and it is assumed that each respondent will be exposed to the same stimulus.

The interviewer, finally, must ask every question, unless the directions on the questionnaire specifically direct skipping certain ones. It might sometimes seem that respondents have already, in answering a prior question, given their opinion on a subsequent one, but the interviewer must nevertheless ask the later question to be sure, perhaps prefacing the inquiry with some such phrase as, "Now you may already have touched on this, but . . . ." Similarly, even if the question seems foolish or inapplicable, the interviewer must never omit asking it or take the answer for granted. Again, the inquiry can be prefaced with some such remark as, "Now I have to ask . . . ."

Obtaining the Responses

It might seem to be a simple matter to ask respondents the required questions and to record their replies, but interviewers often find that obtaining specific, complete responses is perhaps the most difficult part of their job. People often qualify or hedge their opinions; they answer, "Don't know" to avoid thinking about the question; they misinterpret the meaning of the question; they launch off on another discussion; they contradict themselves—and in all these cases, the interviewer usually has to probe.

Alertness to incomplete or nonspecific answers is perhaps the critical test of a good interviewer, and as no one can foresee all the possible replies that might call for probes, each interviewer must understand fully the overall objective of each question, the precise thing it is trying to measure. Both the written instructions and the oral training should emphasize the purpose of the question and should give examples of inadequate replies that were commonly encountered during the pretest. When asking open-ended questions, interviewers should form the habit of asking themselves, after each reply, "Does that completely answer the question I just asked?"

When the first reply is inadequate, a simple repetition of the question, with proper emphasis, usually will suffice to elicit a satisfactory response. This is particularly effective when respondents seemingly misunderstand the question or answer it irrelevantly or respond to only a portion of it. If the respondents' answers are vague or too general or incomplete, an effective probe is this: "That's interesting. Could you explain that a little more?" or "Let's see, you said . . . . Just how do you mean that?"

Throughout, the interviewer must be very careful not to suggest a possible reply. People sometimes find the questions difficult, and sometimes they are not deeply interested in them. In either case, they might welcome any hint from the interviewer that would enable them to give a creditable response. Interviewers must be thoroughly impressed with the harm that results from a leading probe, from any remark that "puts words in their mouth." To be safe, the interviewers should use repetition of all or part of the actual question or such innocuous nondirective probes as are suggested in the preceding paragraph.

The "don't know" reply is another problem for interviewers. Sometimes that response represents a genuine lack of opinion; other times it can hide a host of different attitudes: fear to speak one's mind, reluctance to focus on the issue, vague opinions never yet expressed, stalling for time while thoughts are marshaled, lack of comprehension of the question, and so on. It is the interviewers' job to distinguish among all these types and, when appropriate, to repeat the question with suitable assurances. In one case, for example, the interviewer might say, "Perhaps I didn't make that very clear. Let me read it again"; in another, "Well, lots of people have never thought about that before, but I'd like to have your ideas on it, just the way it seems to you." Or again, the interviewer might point out, "Well, I just want your own opinion on it. Actually, nobody really knows the answers to many of these questions."

Qualified answers to questions that have been preceded in terms of yes–no, approve–disapprove, or similar dichotomies are an interviewing problem that should be addressed as part of the questionnaire design process. As far as possible, the most frequent qualifications of opinion should be anticipated in the actual wording of the question. If very many people find it impossible to answer because of unspecified contingencies, the question is a poor one. Most qualifications can be foreseen as a result of the pretest, and those that are not taken care of by revisions of the wording should be mentioned in the instructions to interviewers, with directions on how to handle such answers. In some cases, special codes are provided for the most frequent qualifications; in other cases, the interviewers are instructed to record them as "don't know" or "undecided." In avoiding many qualifications inherent in the response to almost any opinion question, the interviewers might find it helpful to use phrases such as, "Well, in general, what would you say?" or "Taking everything into consideration" or "On the basis of the way things look to you now."

Sometimes the interviewers will react to respondents' answers by providing evaluative feedback. The interviewers can convey that the respondent's behavior is adequate by such phrases as "Uh-huh, this is the kind of information we want" or "Thanks, we appreciate your frankness." Or the interviewers can convey that the answer is inadequate by "You answered that quickly" or "You only mentioned two things." Such feedback helps respondents understand what is wanted in the interview and motivates them to perform well. Careful training is important so that the interviewers supply feedback appropriately. Interviewers who are not specifically trained often give the most positive feedback (e.g., "That's okay") after respondents refuse to answer a question, the worst possible respondent behavior. Interviewers do so to maintain a positive atmosphere despite the refusal, but the comments serve to reinforce inadequate answers.

Recording the Responses

There are two chief means of recording responses in the interview. Closed-ended questions require only that the interviewers check or circle a response code or press a computer key. Errors and omissions are possible even in these relatively simple tasks, but they can be reduced by clear questionnaire design, including appropriate use of typography and page layout.

Even the best interviewers occasionally make errors. The unforgivable sin is to turn in an interview as complete when it contains errors and omissions. The only certain way for the interviewers to avoid this is to form a habit of inspecting each interview immediately after its completion, before going on to another respondent, to make sure it has been filled in accurately and completely. Computer-assisted interviews are less prone to incompleteness or inaccuracy, owing to the checks executed by the software (e.g., the software will not move to the next item until an acceptable response is entered). Yet, even in computer-assisted interviews, responses to questions on sensitive topics might be gathered in written form. When the information is in written form, if any information is lacking, the interviewer can go back and ask the respondent for it. If the questionnaire contains any errors or omissions, the interviewer can correct them on the spot; if, in the case of paper-and-pencil recording, the respondent's or interviewer's handwriting is illegible in places or if the interviewer has recorded verbatim replies only sketchily, he or she can correct the information right there. If the interviewer waits until later in the day or until returning home at night, he or she will have forgotten many of the circumstances of the interview, or perhaps the prospect of editing the whole day's work will seem so forbidding that he or she will skip the matter completely.

In reporting responses to open-ended questions, interviewers should be aware of the importance of complete, verbatim reporting. Whether such responses are written or entered into a computer, it often is difficult to get down everything the respondents say in reply, but aside from obvious irrelevancies and repetitions, this should be the goal. Interviewers should be given some idea of the coding process so that they can see the dangers of summarizing, abbreviating, or paraphrasing responses. Unless coders can view the whole answer, just as the respondent said it, they are likely to classify it improperly or lose some important distinctions.

Interviewers should be instructed to quote the respondents directly, just as if they were news reporters taking down the statement of an important official. Paraphrasing the reply; summarizing it in their own words; or "polishing up" any slang, cursing, or bad grammar not only risks distorting the respondents' meaning and emphasis but also loses the color of their replies. Frequently, the verbatim responses of individuals are useful in the final report as illustrations of the nuances of attitudes, and they should not be abbreviated or distorted.

Even with closed-ended questions, if the respondents say anything to explain or qualify the coded response, the interviewer should note it verbatim. Such remarks by respondents often help the researcher evaluate the meaning of results and warn of any commonly held qualifications or differences in intensity of opinion.

Avoiding Bias

From the earliest days of survey research, it has been known that interviewers can influence the responses that are given. Rice (1929) had two interviewers administer a questionnaire to people living in poverty. In one interviewer's data, overindulgence in alcohol emerged as the most common cause of poverty, whereas the other interviewer's results showed social and economic conditions to be the most frequent cause. It turned out that the first interviewer was a prohibitionist and the second a socialist.

More formal research on the interview process has revealed several ways the interviewer can influence responses. Besides the interviewers' own attitudes, they might have expectations about what a particular category of respondents will say or think, which can bias responses. The respondents' perceptions of the interviewer's characteristics (age, sex, race, apparent social status, and so on) can also bias their responses; it is known, for example, that Blacks reveal less hostile attitudes toward Whites when interviewed by White as opposed to Black interviewers (Anderson, Silver, & Abramson, 1988). Such effects can occur no matter how conscientiously the interviewers attempt to be "unbiased." As might be expected, these effects are smaller in magnitude with telephone than with face-to-face interviewing; fewer cues about the interviewer are available over the telephone.

Not all interviewer effects operate through the respondents' perception of the interviewer, however. Indeed, some respondents appear to be totally immune to even the most flagrant biasing characteristics of the interviewer. Fully as important a source of bias are the interviewers' perceptions of the respondents. No matter how standardized the questionnaire or how rigidly interviewers are instructed, they still have much opportunity to exercise freedom of choice during the actual interview, and it is often their perception of the respondents that determines the manner in which they ask the questions, probe, classify equivocal responses to precoded questions, and record verbatim answers.

A final source of bias arises from interviewers' perception of the situation. If they see the results of the survey as a possible threat to personal interests or beliefs, for example, they are likely to introduce bias. Or if they regard the assignment as impossible, they are almost certain to introduce bias. Such difficulties can best be overcome by proper motivation and supervision.

Because interviewers are human beings, such biasing factors can never be overcome completely, although their effects can be reduced by standardizing the interview procedures. Thus, standard wording in questions serves to prevent the bias that would result if each interviewer worded the question in his or her own fashion. Similarly, if interviewers are given standard instructions on probing procedure, on the classification of doubtful answers, and so on, their biases will have less chance to operate.

Summary

In research that directly questions individuals about facts, beliefs, attitudes, or behaviors, careful attention must be paid to questionnaire construction. There is much accumulated experience available to a researcher today, in the form of guidelines and recommendations based on research, for decisions on question content, wording, and sequence. Often there is a need for multiple-item scales, or multiple questions, both closed-ended and open-ended, to operationally define key constructs in the study. No one item is likely to be reliable enough or multifaceted enough to stand alone, especially if dealing with beliefs and attitudes rather than facts. If a questionnaire is to be administered by an interviewer, then a number of significant concerns arise. Interviewing procedures must be carefully designed and standardized to avoid error and bias, with careful training of interviewers.

Key Concepts

closed-ended questions
context effects
double-barreled questions
filter question
floaters
forced-choice format
funnel principle
items
memory telescoping
open-ended questions
randomized response technique
responses
scales
sociometric questionnaire
split-ballot experiment

On the Web

http://marketing-bulletin.massey.ac.nz/article9/article3b.asp At this site is a detailed and informative essay on the activity of designing a questionnaire. "A Framework for Questionnaire Design" features many of the procedures outlined in this chapter but embeds them in a theoretical model of the questionnaire design process.

http://www.dssresearch.com/library/general/quesdesi.asp A technical paper posted by a marketing research firm on the basic considerations in designing a questionnaire and administering it as an interview.

http://www.unc.edu/depts/nnsp/viewtech.htm A detailed set of instructions for developing an interviewer training manual. Includes examples of good and bad probes for eliciting acceptable answers from respondents.

Further Reading

Dillman, D. A. (2000). *Mail and Internet surveys: The tailored design method* (2nd ed.). New York: Wiley.

Fink, A., & Kosecoff, J. B. (1998). *How to conduct surveys: A step by step guide* (2nd ed.). Thousand Oaks, CA: Sage Publications.

Schuman, H., & Presser, S. (1996). *Questions and answers in attitude surveys: Experiments on question form, wording, and context.* Thousand Oaks, CA: Sage Publications.

Seidman, I. (1998). *Interviewing as qualitative research: A guide for researchers in education and the social sciences* (2nd ed.). New York: Teachers College Press.

CHAPTER

7

Scaling and Multiple-Item Measures

In the previous chapter our focus was on writing and administering direct questions; we touched only briefly on issues that concern how respondents are asked to answer those questions. Although the wording of a direct question and the ways in which the respondents can answer it are not independent, in reality there are many possible ways to scale responses to a particular question. By **scaling,** we mean the assignment of scores to answers to a question so as to yield a measure of a construct. The range of possible answers to a given question constitute the **response scale.** Once a question has been written, the social scientist must decide what sort of response scale to provide respondents in order to best capture their standing on the construct the question was designed to measure. The focus of this chapter is scaling responses, with a particular focus on multiple-item measures.

Scaling techniques are of two basic types, which define the two major subdivisions of this chapter. Some scaling methods use global ratings—by the individual in question or by observers—to assign scores to people or other objects to reflect the underlying construct. For example, individuals might rate their own liberalism or conservatism in response to the single-item measure, "Do you consider yourself to be very liberal, liberal, middle of the road, conservative, or very conservative?" The response places the individual in a particular position on the scale, which might be associated with outcomes of interest, for example, voting choices. As another example, judges might rate news stories as "favorable," "neutral," or "unfavorable" with respect to a controversial issue. The judges evaluate the content and style of presentation of the story based on a standardized set of rules that they have been trained to use, assigning scores that locate the stories along a single scale from favorable to unfavorable.

Other scaling methods obtain multiple observations or ratings and combine them into a single score. For example, a congressional representative's positions on a number of roll-call votes might be combined to give a single score measuring the representative's overall liberalism or conservatism. Each individual response is assumed to be related to the underlying construct, and scaling techniques can combine them into a single overall measure of the construct. As another example, to measure a White person's attitudes toward desegregation, we might construct items such as "I would prefer to have Blacks as well as Whites in school classes," "Property values do not decline when Black people move into a neighborhood," and so on. An overall measure of favorability toward desegregation could be formed by summing the total number of "agree" responses. The total score would represent a general attitude toward desegregation, even though each individual item refers to a different specific aspect of the issue.

Advantages of Multiple-Item Measures

In common with single-item measures, multiple-item measures, or **scales,** serve the basic function of providing a usable measure of a theoretical construct; however, multiple-item scaling procedures offer additional advantages to the researcher. First, multiple-item scaling can reduce the complexity of a measure of a construct. Creating a single score to summarize several observed variables in a meaningful way can simplify the analysis. For example, it would be simpler to make predictions or test hypotheses about congressional representatives based on one total liberalism or conservatism score than on a large number of individual roll-call votes.

Second, some scaling methods allow researchers to test hypotheses about the nature of a construct, for example, to test whether liberalism or conservatism constitutes a single dimension or several different dimensions. The dimensionality of a construct that we wish to measure is one of its most important attributes. If a series of variables all measure a single general characteristic of an attitude or other construct, the variables should all be highly interrelated. The construct is then said to be **unidimensional;** however, low associations among some variables imply that several dimensions might exist, that is, the construct is **multidimensional.** Perhaps political liberalism or conservatism is not a unidimensional construct, for we might find that representatives who are liberal on social welfare issues are not particularly likely to be liberal on civil rights issues. That is, the pattern of associations among the variables might reveal strong associations among variables within each of the dimensions (e.g., between two votes on social welfare issues) but weaker associations between variables across dimensions (between a social welfare vote and a civil rights vote). We would then need to take account of at least two dimensions of overall political ideology, for instance, attitudes toward social welfare and civil rights.

The dimensionality of a construct is a research hypothesis that like any other is subject to empirical testing as well as theoretical consideration. In fact, dimensionality can change over time or vary from one population to the next. For example, consider political efficacy, defined as the individual's sense of power or weakness about his or her relations to government and the formation of public policy. Four political efficacy items were found to form a single dimension in several studies conducted on a variety of populations during the 1950s (Campbell, Converse, Miller, & Stokes, 1954). Thus, it was assumed that political efficacy constituted a fairly immutable, general, and unidimensional attitude, and it was found to be useful for explaining several aspects of political participation. Later, more refined analyses of the same items using responses gathered during the 1960s revealed that the four items had split apart so that they represented two distinct dimensions rather than one. One dimension appeared to reflect attitudes about one's personal power to affect political life, whereas the other dimension was related to attitudes about politicians' ability to bring about change (Balch, 1974). The set of items no longer measured what they once had because the interrelations of the items had changed. The dimensionality of the scale had changed from one to two dimensions.

Finally, the most important advantage of multiple-item measures is improved reliability and validity of measurement. A scale formed by combining multiple items or variables almost always has better reliability and validity than the individual variables that make it up. We use an example to introduce and illustrate this concept, which is discussed in detail later in this chapter. Suppose that we are considering a set of roll-call votes from the U.S. Congress, all related to issues of social welfare. If we want to determine which representatives are generally liberal and which are conservative on social welfare issues, this might best be done by assigning each representative one scale score based on how he or she voted on all the roll calls. The votes could be combined in a meaningful way, using one of the multiple-item scaling techniques to be described later in the chapter. This would provide a simplified description, one scale value for each representative instead of the long list of individual votes. More important, the scale value would most likely be more reliable and valid as a measure of liberalism or conservatism than any single vote. Any particular vote is surely influenced by many factors besides the representative's underlying liberalism or conservatism, such as the impact of the specific issue on the home district, lobbyists' influences, or pressure from party leadership to vote a particular way. But across a large number of votes, such varying influences would be expected roughly to cancel out, leaving the scale formed from all the votes as a purer measure of the underlying construct, the representative's liberalism or conservatism. This is a specific application of the logic of multiple operations initially outlined in Chapter 4.

In the remainder of this chapter, we follow an overview of levels of measurement with a discussion of the use of single-item rating scales and then the various approaches to combining multiple items to assign scores to individuals or other objects. For simplicity of presentation, most of our examples focus on measuring attributes of people and therefore on questionnaire responses as the basis for scaling; however, it is important to remember that any type of measurement—including all the modes of measurement discussed in Chapter 5—can be used as raw material for scaling procedures to improve the reliability and validity of measurement.

Levels of Measurement

Variables have different levels of measurement. Our coverage of measurement in the last three chapters has generally assumed that variables have numerical scales such as the familiar IQ score, on which higher numbers indicate more of the construct. But not all variables have scales of this type. Four levels of measurement are commonly distinguished.

Nominal Scales

Nominal scales contain qualitatively different categories to which we attach names rather than numerical meaning. The simplest are dichotomies, having only two values, such as male and female or home owners and renters. The categories are *qualitatively* rather than quantitatively different. If we were to use numbers like 1 and 2 to stand for male and female, respectively, the numbers would have no arithmetic value; we could have used the letters *m* and *f* instead. The number 2 would not mean that cases placed in that category have more of the quality than cases placed in the category numbered 1. Other examples of nominal scales are the following:

Types of Urban Stressors

1 = traffic noises

2 = air pollutants

3 = crowds

4 = bureaucratic harassment

5 = other

Living Arrangements for the Elderly

1 = own home or apartment

2 = relative's home

3 = retirement home

4 = other

The list of alternatives need not exhaust all possible categories, but it should include those categories relevant to the theory and the population tested and should allow for the classification of every case. For instance, there are many more living arrangements for elderly people than the three just listed. If, however, we designed a study to test the effects of living in one's own home, in someone else's, or in an institution, the three categories plus the unspecified "other" category would be sufficient for the purposes of that study. The inclusion of "other" ensures that every case can be classified.

Ordinal Scales

An **ordinal scale** contains categories that can be ordered by rank on a continuum. The categories have a rudimentary arithmetic meaning such as more or less of the quantity being measured. For instance, we could order occupations in terms of how much autonomy the workers have in their jobs.

1 = little autonomy (e.g., assembly line workers, keypunch operators, and checkout clerks in a large discount department store)

2 = moderate autonomy (e.g., construction workers, nurses, and taxi drivers)

3 = much autonomy (e.g., independent artists, jewelers, doctors, lawyers)

The scale states that 1 means an occupation permits less autonomy than 3 and that 2 is located in between. An ordinal scale gives only this information and does not provide any information about the interval, or degree of difference, between the values. The interval between 1 and 2 could be larger or smaller than the interval between 2 and 3. An ordinal scale does not imply anything about the arithmetic values other than that they are in ascending or descending order.

Interval Scales

When numbers attached to a variable imply not only that 3 is more than 2 and 2 is more than 1 but also that the size of the interval between 3 and 2 is the same as the interval between 2 and 1, they form an **interval scale.** Just because a scale contains values from 1 to 100, it does not automatically follow that the difference between 60 and 70 is the same as the difference between 90 and 100. For instance, if we made up a 100-item vocabulary test on which most people defined between 60 and 70 words correctly and only two people defined 90 and one person defined 100 correctly, the gap between 90 and 100 probably represents a greater difference in vocabulary level than the gap between 60 and 70.

If the intervals represent equal quantities of the variable measured, they constitute an interval scale. For every unit increase on the scale, there is a unit increase in the variable. The Fahrenheit scale measures temperature in equal intervals. The temperature difference between 33° and 34° is the same as the temperature difference between 36° and 37°. If this seems obvious, it is because we have grown accustomed to the Fahrenheit scale and take for granted that it represents equal intervals of physical heat and cold. We cannot take for granted that social science scales represent equal intervals.

Most constructs in the social sciences are measured by ordinal rather than interval scales. To return to an example used in Chapter 4, if we used families' annual income as a variable to measure the underlying construct social status, we could not assume that the dollar scale represented equal intervals of social status. (This was illustrated in Figure 4.1.) The status difference in the interval between \$20,000 and \$40,000 in annual income is much larger than the status difference in the interval between \$120,000 and \$140,000. As we go up the income scale, the \$20,000 difference makes less and less difference in social status. Two families with incomes of \$120,000 and \$140,000 are more likely to live next door to each other than are two families with incomes of $20,000 and $40,000 because the $20,000 interval represents a bigger difference in social status at the bottom end of the scale than at the top. Annual income, therefore, is not an interval scale measure of social status.

Unlike values on an ordinal scale, the numbers on an interval scale can be meaningfully added or subtracted because the properties of the scale are such that 20 − 10 = 40 − 30. But numbers on an interval scale cannot be multiplied or divided because the scale does not have a true 0 (i.e., none of the variable being measured). We can multiply and divide the values only if we have a ratio scale.

Ratio Scales

Ratio scales do have a true 0, and as a result the scale values represent multipliable quantities. Physical scales measuring length and weight are ratio scales: A 4-foot length of board is twice as long as a 2-foot piece; 10 pounds of feathers weigh twice as much as 5 pounds. For these physical scales, 0 is real and meaningful. Although we cannot point to anything that has 0 inches or 0 pounds, we know what those mean on our rulers or scales, and we do not arbitrarily locate 0 at just any point on the scale.

Some variables used to measure constructs in the social sciences look superficially like ratio measures because they have 0 as the lowest score. Money as a measure of social status, for instance, gives the appearance of being a ratio scale because the variable has an absolute true 0. A person can be penniless. This does not mean, however, that the penniless person has 0 social status, the construct we are operationally defining with this variable. A monk who takes a vow of poverty, for instance, has no money but has social status among people who respect religious orders. The most we can assume about social status measured in dollars is that more money represents more status, all other assets being equal.

Similarly, some variables used to operationally define constructs in the social sciences appear as if they could be meaningfully multiplied or divided. If we measured happiness by how often a person smiled, we might be tempted to say that someone who smiles 10 times is twice as happy as someone who smiles 5 times. True, 10 smiles are twice as many as 5 smiles. Our scale, however, is to be a measure not of smiling but of the construct happiness. Number of smiles is the variable we have chosen to measure the abstract construct happiness, and happiness probably does not double as smiles do.

Even standardized and copyrighted measures such as IQ scales do not produce scores with ratio properties. No psychologist would try to argue that someone with an IQ score of 150 is twice as intelligent as someone with an IQ of 75. Although the numbers can be added or multiplied and although a scale begins with 0, it does not mean that the underlying construct has those properties. It is difficult to imagine any social construct such as happiness, social status, or power for which there is a true 0 because it is always possible to imagine a case with a little less of the construct. For instance, if we devised a 10-item scale of happiness for which every answer that represented unhappiness received a 0, someone who answered all 10 items with 0s would receive a total happiness score of 0. Does that person truly have no happiness? Is it not possible to imagine someone else who might have even less happiness than that person? Social science constructs have this quality of an infinite regress at the bottom end of the scale. It is always possible to imagine a case of a little less status, a little less power, a little less happiness; and the scale, therefore, does not have a true 0. Without a true 0, a scale does not have ratios—it is not possible to say that a score of 10 represents twice as much of the construct as 5.

Summary

A key consideration in scaling either single- or multiple-item measures is level of measurement. The level at which a variable is measured is a function of both the response scales provided respondents and the nature of the construct the variable represents. We identified four levels of measurement, which vary in the way they distinguish respondents on a variable. The nominal level of measurement serves only to sort respondents into groups and affords no information about the direction or magnitude of difference between those groups with reference to the construct of interest. The ordinal, interval, and ratio levels of measurement provide increasing information about the direction and magnitude of differences between people who obtain different scores on the variables and, therefore, the construct of interest. As we shall see in the remainder of this chapter, most measures used by social scientists have ordinal or interval properties.

Rating Scales for Quantifying Individual Judgments

The proper use of rating scales rests on an understanding of exactly what demands they place on the respondent or judge. Most commonly, the judgment task is viewed as consisting of two steps: forming a subjective impression or judgment of the position of the stimulus object along the desired dimension and then translating that judgment into an overt rating, using the scale provided. For instance, in a study of toddler activity, observers must first reach a conclusion about what each toddler is doing, then assign a number to each toddler. Similarly, a group of participants who are asked how they would rate their physical appearance must reach a subjective judgment about their appearance and then translate this judgment into a rating.

As to the first step, researchers often simply assume that judges can be made aware of the desired dimension for judgment and can form an impression of each stimulus that corresponds to the object's position on that dimension, possibly with some degree of random error. As we shall see later (in discussions of "halo bias," for instance), this assumption is not always justified. The judges' impressions of the object on other dimensions can affect their judgments on the desired dimension. To the extent that this occurs, the ratings will be invalid, reflecting something other than the intended construct.

The second step is also problematic because the correspondence of a particular subjective impression (of the favorability of a newspaper article toward a particular policy, for instance) to a particular point on the rating scale cannot be explicitly defined for the judge (either an observer or a respondent). Therefore, the way judges use the rating scale to reflect their subjective impressions, and hence the ratings they assign to any given stimulus, can vary from judge to judge or from time to time. That is, the judges' frame of reference for using the rating scale affects their ratings. The frame of reference can depend on the particular set of objects that are being rated at the moment, the set of objects that the judges recall having seen in the past, or particular salient stimuli or reference points (such as the judges' own attitude or a neutral point of the scale) that serve to "anchor" the scale. We cannot understand the rating given to a single object without knowing something about the range of objects with which the judges are implicitly comparing it.

Classic studies by Sherif and Hovland (1961) on ratings of attitudes illustrate this principle. They demonstrated that individuals' own attitudes influence their ratings of attitude statements on a dimension of favorability versus unfavorability to an attitude object (e.g., civil rights). People tend to place items with which they disagree in a more extreme category than items with which they agree. In effect, individuals' own attitude is used as an anchor, a reference point with which other attitude statements are compared in order to rate them.

In light of these issues, several different types of rating scales have been used by social scientists. These rating scales satisfy the criteria for ordinal scales and, for certain constructs, take on interval properties. Each takes a different approach to the issues of reliability and validity.

Graphic Rating Scales

One of the most widely used scaling methods is the **graphic rating scale.** The judge indicates his or her rating by placing a mark at the appropriate point on a line that runs from one extreme of the attribute in question to the other. Scale points with brief descriptions can be indicated along the line, but their function is to serve as a guide to the judges in locating the rating on the scale rather than to provide discrete categories. Figure 7.1 shows an example, a "feeling thermometer" graphic rating scale. This scale can be used by respondents to rate their feelings toward some object, such as a political candidate, along a dimension from warm (favorable) to cold (unfavorable).

One of the major advantages of graphic rating scales is their ease of use. To use them effectively, though, we should take several precautions. For example, we should avoid end statements so extreme that they will rarely be used (e.g., "hot" and "freezing" on a feeling thermometer scale or "best job imaginable" and "worst job imaginable" on a scale of feelings about one's job). Graphic rating scales do not explicitly take account of the frame of reference problem, simply assuming that most judges will use the scale in the same way.

Itemized Rating Scales

Itemized rating scales, also called specific category scales and numerical scales, require the rater to select one of a small number of categories that are ordered by their

FIGURE 7.1 **FEELING THERMOMETER GRAPHIC RATING SCALE**

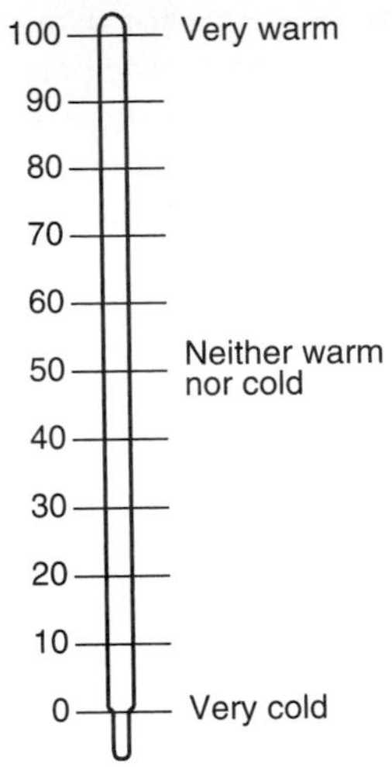

scale position. The number of scale positions or categories varies, depending on the research problem and the type of judgments required, but 5 to 11 categories are typical.

For example, respondents might be asked to rate their own liberalism or conservatism by choosing from categories such as "extremely liberal," "liberal," "moderate or middle of the road," "conservative," and "extremely conservative." The respondents are instructed to choose the category that best describes their own political viewpoint. The resulting rating could be used to predict voting behavior, preferences on specific political issues, and so on.

The verbal descriptions that specify the categories can be brief statements indicating only degrees of the attribute or elaborate descriptions including illustrations of behavior appropriate to the category. In general, it has been assumed that more clearly defined categories should decrease interjudge variability in the use of the scale and hence give greater reliability. It is likely that relatively vague categories like "liberal" or "conservative" are seen in different ways by judges with different frames of reference. For example, people who associate mainly with relatively liberal college professors might rate their political attitudes as moderate, whereas other individuals, whose daily contacts are mostly with conservative businesspersons, might rate the identical position as somewhat liberal—because of a different frame of reference. Even extensive and precise descriptions for rating categories, however, cannot completely eliminate context effects.

Comparative Rating Scales

Graphic and itemized rating scales do not require the rater to make explicit comparisons of the rated individual or object with others, although, as argued previously, all ratings are inherently comparative because of the effects of frames of reference. **Comparative rating scales**—as their name suggests—explicitly require the judge to make comparisons. The positions on the rating scale are expressly defined on the basis of a given population or social group or in respect to people of known characteristics. For example, a questionnaire used in selecting applicants for admission to a graduate school might ask judges to provide an estimate of each applicant's ability to do graduate work "as compared with the total group of graduate students you have known." Is the applicant more capable than 10% of them? 20%? 30%? Or the judges might be asked to indicate whether an individual's leadership skill most closely resembles that of person A, of person B, or of person C (all of whom are known to the rater and all of whom have been assessed in terms of their leadership skills). In the first example, to make a valid rating, the judges must have a clear conception of the range and distribution of the abilities of the total graduate student group. Scales of the second type are often difficult to construct, for there might not be sufficient variation in leadership behavior (or whatever attribute is being rated) among the people known to the judge for them to serve as examples for the various points on the scale.

Another comparative or relative rating procedure is the **rank-order scale.** Here the judges are required to rank individuals specifically in relation to one another; the judges indicate which person is highest in regard to the characteristic being measured, which is next highest, and so on, down to the one who is lowest. Such scales epitomize the ordinal level of measurement. Rank-order scales are used only when the investigator is concerned with a limited group of individuals. The rating an individual receives indicates simply his or her relative rank or position in the group being studied; it would not necessarily be of any use apart from the specific group whose members are being compared.

Self-Ratings Versus Ratings by Others

All these types of scales can be used to secure individuals' ratings of themselves or someone else's rating of each of them. (Collateral reports, described in Chapter 5, are an instance of the latter.) It seems reasonable to assume that individuals often are in a better position to observe and report their own beliefs, feelings, and fears than anyone else is. This assumption is valid, however, only if individuals are aware of their own beliefs and feelings and are willing to reveal them to others. If people are unaware, for example, of the fact that they have hostile feelings toward a particular minority group or if they are aware of such feelings but are afraid of the consequences of revealing them, the self-rating procedure is of little value. Another difficulty arises from the fact that even if individuals are capable of reporting their beliefs or feelings objectively, their concept of what constitutes a moderate or an extreme position can be quite different from those of others making comparable self-ratings. That is, because in most self-rating procedures each judge rates only one stimulus (i.e., himself or herself), it is difficult to ensure that the frame of reference and hence usage of the response scale is comparable across judges.

Despite the hazards involved, self-ratings have proven useful in the measurement of constructs of interest to social scientists. For beliefs and feelings that individuals can be expected to know and be willing to report—for example, attitudes toward specific television programs—self-ratings are probably the most useful source of information. In fact, self-ratings have been shown to be equal or superior to other types of assessments in predicting a wide range of criteria, including how people are viewed by friends on personality dimensions, the careers people will enter, and how people will function in school or in psychotherapy (Shrauger & Osberg, 1981).

Several precautions must be taken, however, to obtain reliable and valid self-ratings. The individuals should be told explicitly and specifically what attribute is to be rated, should be given an opportunity and incentive to recall their behaviors in past situations that are relevant to the judgment, and should be motivated to give accurate (rather than socially desirable) ratings (Shrauger & Osberg, 1981). The latter point is probably the most important. It is often assumed that when ratings are to be used to distribute valued resources (such as jobs or positions in training or therapy programs), self-raters will distort their responses rather than convey their honest assessments. Evidence for this assumption is limited, however, and studies of alcoholics and other drug abusers even suggest that these people are usually accurate in reporting their drinking and drug use—an area in which we might expect dishonest responses (Petzel, Johnson, & McKillip, 1973). The researcher should attempt to enlist the respondents' cooperation and active involvement in the rating task and should stress that accuracy is highly valued and will be checked. With precautions like these, self-ratings can give reliable and valid measures of a variety of constructs.

Construction and Use of Rating Scales: Some Cautions

Because a large element of subjective judgment enters into the use of rating scales, both random and systematic errors can influence ratings. A common form of systematic error is **halo bias,** which refers to the tendency for overall positive or negative evaluations of the object or person being rated to influence ratings on specific dimensions (Cooper, 1981). For example, Thorndike (1920) found that supervisors' ratings of teachers yielded a very strong association between rated intelligence and rated ability to discipline. Because the actual association (based on intelligence test scores) is probably only modest, Thorndike concluded that the raters were unable to judge each dimension independently. Instead, their global evaluations of the teacher influenced their ratings of both intelligence and ability to discipline, inflating the association. Another type of error, related to halo bias, is the **generosity error,** in which raters overestimates the desirable qualities of people that they like.

Other types of errors are related to the general frame of reference problem described earlier—that is, they reflect differences among raters in the translation of subjective judgments into overt rating scale responses. Some raters seem to avoid extreme response categories and assign ratings using only the more moderate categories. The **contrast error,** a tendency for raters to see others as opposite to them on a trait, arises from using one's own position on a dimension as an anchor for rating others. For example, raters who are very orderly tend to rate others as relatively disorderly and vice versa.

Besides systematic errors or biases like these, random errors can enter into any ratings and reduce their reliability. The most obvious source of random error is simple mistakes caused by rater fatigue, inattention, or improper training.

A number of steps can be taken in the construction and use of rating scales to minimize the impact of such biases and errors. Obviously, training and motivating the raters plays an important role. The use of multiple raters (e.g, two or more judges, collateral reports) and computation of a mean rating for each rated object almost always reduces the impact of random errors (unreliability) because the independent errors will tend to balance each other out in the averaging process. The use of multiple raters also reduces halo bias, compared to the use of a single rater (Kenny & Berman, 1980). Of course, combining multiple ratings is generally more feasible when the ratings are based on recorded material or observations of a sample of behavior. It is often impossible to have more than one rater on hand to observe live social behavior.

Increasing the judges' familiarity with the object or person being rated also reduces halo bias, although it can increase generosity errors. This effect might account for the fact that self-ratings (which are obviously made by a familiar rater) are less subject to the halo bias than are ratings by others (Thornton, 1980). Ratings made concurrently with observation of behaviors are less subject to the halo bias than are ratings made from memory after witnessing the behaviors (Shweder & D'Andrade, 1980). On the other hand, one frequently used technique does not seem to be effective in reducing halo bias: rating all objects or people on one category before going on to the next category instead of rating each one on all categories in succession (Cooper, 1981).

In terms of the construction of the rating scale itself, as opposed to the procedures involved in its use, certain precautions can reduce error and bias. Many precautions amount to efforts to give all the raters a common frame of reference so that they use the rating scale in the same way. For example, all raters could be asked to rate a common set of practice stimuli before proceeding to the actual ratings required by the research. Their ratings on the practice stimuli could be compared and training provided until the ratings are made in similar ways. Raters' tendency to avoid extreme positions could be counteracted by giving less extreme labels to these positions. People would be more likely to choose "I am well satisfied with my job" than "I am completely satisfied with my job" and would be more likely to choose "There are many things about my job that I do not like" than "There is nothing about my job that I like."

The use of a common frame of reference is also more likely if the scale (or the training procedure) provides clear, concrete definitions of the characteristic being measured, preferably including illustrations of behaviors or other responses that exemplify the various rating categories. (Many of the principles of clarity and precision in question writing from Chapter 6 apply here.)

The labeling of response categories should also take account of generosity biases. For example, in rating their instructors, college students rarely use any category worse than "good." Therefore, on a five-category scale, with "average" as the middle category, almost all the responses would fall in the upper two categories. Some universities therefore use asymmetrical wording, with "good" at the center of the scale, to obtain a more symmetrical response distribution: "superior," "very good," "good," "average," and "poor" (Dawes, 1972). This example also points out the common fallacy of interpreting rating scale responses literally. On a scale like this one, 80% to 90% of the responses might be above the "average" category, although it is obviously impossible for 90% of the instructors to be above average in their teaching effectiveness. The information in a rating scale response is not literally contained in the specific category label that the rater chooses (such as "good" or "average") but is implicit in the scale's demonstrated associations with other measures.

Finally, the number of categories on the response scale can influence reliability. Providing fewer than five categories seems to limit reliability, although increasing the number of categories over this number helps little, if at all (Masters, 1974).

Developing Multiple-Item Scales

When people indicate their own attitude or judges rate an object on some scale, a large element of intuitive judgment is involved, no matter how precise the rating instructions and no matter how well trained the judges. This fact brings both benefits and costs. First, judges can meaningfully rate objects even when they have no idea of what specific properties of the objects underlie the ratings; for example, judges could rate the emotionality of facial expressions in photographs or the physical attractiveness of the faces. Such ratings must be done on an intuitive basis because we do not presently know how else to do them. Second, ratings by judges often are easy, inexpensive to obtain, and probably the best way to measure some constructs, even if alternative methods are available, for example, in assessing the favorability of newspaper articles toward some issue.

However, as noted, the subjective judgment in the use of rating scales makes the ratings vulnerable to bias—different judges making ratings with different frames of reference, using different criteria, or even no criteria at all—and hence unreliability or invalidity of measurement. If we wanted ratings of the "honesty" of a series of faces portrayed in photographs, it is possible that judges' ratings might instead be most influenced by the attractiveness of the faces. We then would have a set of measurements that did not validly reflect the dimension in which we were interested, and in real life we would often not have any way to know that this was the case.

For these reasons, particularly for measuring attitudes, procedures have been devised that do not depend on single judgments or ratings of the construct of interest, either by the individual or by observers. Instead, individuals respond (usually with agreement or disagreement) to multiple statements relevant to the construct under study, and scores are assigned by numerically combining the responses. The process of constructing the standardized set of items establishes that the combined scale score is a reliable and valid measure of the underlying attitude.

The logic of domain sampling is relevant here. We can define a **domain** as the hypothetical population of all items (say, attitude statements) relevant to the construct we wish to measure. Then the "true underlying attitude" can be defined as the aggregate of the person's responses to all the items in the domain. Of course, this cannot be measured directly, but conceptualized in this way it is natural to think of measurement as an application of sampling. In **domain sampling,** we draw a sample of items from the domain and use the person's responses to those items to estimate the desired construct, the attitude as measured by the entire population of items. The reliability of the measurement is then defined as the expected error in estimating the population value on the basis of the sample observations, that is, as sampling error.

In practice, researchers cannot construct domains of items that measure attitudes or similar constructs (although in such cases as vocabulary or arithmetic ability tests, the domain could in principle be explicitly identified). Instead, researchers write a set of items that tap the desired construct and define the domain as the hypothetical population of items with characteristics equivalent to those that were written. Although this definition seems like a roundabout way of saying very little, it actually serves to put the construction of multiple-item measures in the framework of sampling theory. Two examples illustrate the implications that follow directly from this framework. First, the fact that measures with more items are more reliable follows immediately from the most basic principle of sampling: Larger samples produce smaller sampling errors (Chapter 8). A 10-item measure might have moderate reliability, whereas a 40-item test of equivalent items could have high reliability, simply because a larger sample permits better estimation of population values.

Second, the domain-sampling model permits the insight that the amount of variation in item content is the key determinant of a measure's reliability. The domain of items is not completely homogeneous in content; if it were, people would respond identically to every item. Instead, sampled items vary in ways that affect people's responses. An item such as "The government should see to it that discrimination against Blacks and other minorities is ended" might be intended to tap racial attitudes, but it might in addition pick up respondents' feelings about "big government." This would lower the association of responses to this item with other racial attitude items and thus lower the overall reliability of the attitude measure. In effect, items that have more in common will correlate more highly with each other, leading to a more reliable measure for a given length.

Item Construction

A number of considerations are important in constructing items for multiple-item scales. First, the items must be empirically related to the construct that is to be measured; otherwise, they can contribute nothing (except random error) to the measurement. The different types of scaling techniques to be discussed all ensure that this condition is met, although in different ways.

Second, the items must differentiate among people who are at different points along the dimension being measured. To discriminate not only between extreme positions but also among individuals near the midpoint of the scale, items that tap different points along the scale are generally included. Thus, a test of opinions about child-rearing practices to measure strictness versus permissiveness would contain some items representing a very strict approach, a very permissive approach, a position of moderate strictness, and so on. However, items representing the most extreme positions are often not worth including. For example, if a particular item elicits 97% agreement and only 3% disagreement, it would not be of much value in discriminating among people with different positions on the attitude dimension (especially considering that many of the 3% probably represent random errors).

Third, as noted in the previous chapter, it is important to avoid items that are "double-barreled" or otherwise ambiguous. Consider the item "Most people don't realize the extent to which their lives are governed by secret plots hatched in hidden places" (drawn from the authoritarianism scale of Adorno et al., 1950). Does a person who disagrees with this statement mean that most people do realize the extent to which their lives are controlled by secret plots, or does disagreement mean that secret plots do not govern people's lives? Obviously, interpreting responses to such items is problematic. Other types of ambiguity can create similar interpretive problems, for example, with items that use intrinsically vague words such as often, most, frequently, many, and so on. (Many points in Chapter 6, particularly concerning clarity and precision in question writing, are relevant to the construction of multiple-item measures.)

Finally, it is important to include items worded in both positive and negative directions so that the construct being measured is expressed by a "yes" or "agree" response approximately half the time and by "no" or "disagree" the rest of the time. This avoids confounding the measure of the construct itself with **acquiescent response style,** the general tendency to agree with statements regardless of their content. If a scale were composed of all positively worded items, a person who just tended to agree a lot would be wrongly classified as having a high level of the attitude. Although this bias is not as prevalent as once thought, it often requires little extra effort in the scale construction process to create balanced scales with roughly equal proportions of "agree" and "disagree" items.

Three Types of Multiple-Item Scales

Three general procedures for developing multiple-item attitude scales have been widely used. They differ most fundamentally in their assumptions about the association between people's underlying attitude and the responses they will give to the individual items that make up the scale. Other differences—in the types of item used, the way the individual responses are combined to produce a scale score, and so on—follow from this fundamental difference. All three scaling methods assume that attitude questions or statements can be thought of in terms of their position along the attitude dimension that ranges from favorable to unfavorable. For instance, "The Equal Rights Amendment should be passed immediately" represents a position favorable to the amendment, whereas "The Equal Rights Amendment will contribute to the breakdown of the traditional family" represents a position of opposition or unfavorability.

Differential Scales

Differential scales, developed initially by Thurstone (1929), include items that represent known positions on the attitude scale. Respondents are assumed to agree with only those items whose position is close to their own and to disagree with items that represent distant positions.

Construction and Example The scale is constructed by a complex multistep procedure. A large number of statements related to the attitude are gathered or constructed, and they are submitted to judges. Working independently, the judges classify the statements into categories (usually 11) on the basis of the statements' favorability toward the attitude object (or position on a dimension such as liberalism–conservatism). The first category includes the statements that the judge considers most favorable to the object; the second, the next most favorable statements; and so on. The scale value of each item, ranging from 1 to 11, is then calculated as its average category placement by the judges. Table 7.1 shows an example of Thurstone-type items with their scale values, drawn from Thurstone's (1929) study of attitudes toward the church. Items on which judges fail to agree are discarded as ambiguous or irrelevant. Finally, items representing a wide range of scale values are selected to form

TABLE 7.1 EXAMPLE OF A DIFFERENTIAL SCALE

Scale Value	Item
1.2	I believe the church is a powerful agency for promoting both individual and social righteousness.
2.2	I like to go to church for I get something worthwhile to think about and it keeps my mind filled with right thoughts.
3.3	I enjoy my church because there is a spirit of friendliness there.
4.5	I believe in what the church teaches but with mental reservations.
6.7	I believe in sincerity and goodness without any church ceremonies.
7.5	I think too much money is being spent on the church for the benefit that is being derived.
9.2	I think the church seeks to impose a lot of worn-out dogmas and medieval superstitions.
10.4	The church represents shallowness, hypocrisy, and prejudice.
11.0	I think the church is a parasite on society.

Note: On the actual questionnaire the items would appear in random order, not ordered by scale value as shown here.

the scale. They are presented to respondents, usually in a random order, with instructions to check each statement with which they agree. The respondents' attitude is calculated as the mean of the scale values of the items with which they agree.

In contrast to other scale types, differential scales require items that have a definite position on the scale—that is, items that will elicit agreement from people with positions near the item's scale value but disagreement from others whose attitudes are either more favorable or less favorable. For example, "Affirmative action is a necessary evil" will obtain agreement from people with a particular attitude position near the midpoint of the scale, but people who either strongly favor or strongly oppose affirmative action will disagree with the item. This is an example of a **nonmonotone item** of the sort that differential scales use. Cumulative and summated scales, in contrast, require **monotone items:** items that are either clearly favorable or unfavorable to the object. The probability of agreeing with such items should increase (or decrease) consistently as respondents move from one end of the attitude dimension to the other. For example, "Affirmative action programs increase the overall fairness of our society" would presumably elicit consistently more agreement from people who favor affirmative action than from those who oppose it.

Advantages and Disadvantages The differential scaling method offers certain advantages. For one thing, the responses offer a check on the scale's assumptions. Respondents are supposed to agree with only a narrow range of items around their own position (such as items with scale values of 6.7, 7.1, and 8.0). If a respondent checks a wide range of noncontiguous items (e.g., scale values of 3.3, 7.1, and 9.4), it might mean that the respondent does not have an attitude on this issue or that the attitude is not organized along the dimension assumed by the scale. For respondents who meet the assumptions of the scale, the **latitude of acceptance** (defined as the range of scale values that the subject agrees with) can be calculated from the responses. This measure is related to the degree of the respondent's involvement with the issue or the attitude: People who are more involved in an issue tend to agree with a narrower range of positions.

The differential scaling technique is little used today because of several disadvantages. Most obviously, the construction procedure is lengthy and cumbersome. Although the use of judges' ratings allows the discarding of items that are ambiguous or meaningless, other scaling techniques achieve similar results with less effort. And there is much evidence that the attitudes of the judges themselves influence their assignment of scale values to the items, which is undesirable in the context of this measurement technique. Finally, and perhaps most important, differential scales have generally lower reliabilities than summated scales with the same number of items. Because reliability is the first requirement of any scaling technique, this disadvantage is crucial.

Cumulative Scales

Cumulative scales also are made up of a series of items with which the respondent indicates agreement or disagreement. The special feature of cumulative scales, pioneered by Guttman (1944), is that items are associated in such a way that a respondent who holds a particular attitude will agree with all items on one side of that position and disagree with other items. As noted, cumulative scales thus require each item to be monotone: either clearly favorable or unfavorable to the object or issue.

Construction and Examples We use an analogy with a test of ability to illustrate the basis of cumulative scales. Imagine a mathematical ability test made up of three items: a simple addition problem like $3 + 4 = X$, a long division problem involving four- and five-digit numbers, and a complex problem in calculus. We would expect anyone who passes the long division problem to also pass the first problem, and anyone who passes the calculus problem to pass the other two problems as well. That is, people's level of mathematical ability can be thought of as a point on a scale, and they are expected to pass all items below their ability level but to fail all items above it. With "agree" and "disagree" substituted for "pass" and "fail," this is exactly the pattern expected in a cumulative scale. The scale score is simply defined as the total number of items passed or agreed with.

In the field of social attitudes, one of the earliest scales, the Bogardus Social Distance Scale (Bogardus, 1933), was intended to have this cumulative pattern. The scale lists a number of relationships and asks which would be acceptable between the respondent and members of a particular social or ethnic group. An example is shown in Table 7.2. Note that the items are monotone, and the expected cumulative pattern seems logical. That is, a person who circles number 4 in respect to some group, indicating willingness to accept them to employment in his or her occupation, also should be willing to allow them as citizens in the country (number 5) and should not circle 6 and 7 (because these two items are worded negatively). If the respondent did not circle 3, we would not expect him or her to circle 2 or 1.

TABLE 7.2 BOGARDUS SOCIAL DISTANCE SCALE

	To Close Kinship by Marriage	To My Club as Personal Chums	To My Street as Neighbors	To Employment in My Occupation	To Citizenship in My Country	As Visitors Only to My Country	Would Exclude from My Country
English	1	2	3	4	5	6	7
Black	1	2	3	4	5	6	7
French	1	2	3	4	5	6	7
Chinese	1	2	3	4	5	6	7
Russian and so on	1	2	3	4	5	6	7

Directions: For each race or nationality listed on the scale, circle each of the classifications to which you would be willing to admit the average member of that race or nationality (not the best members you have known or the worst). Answer in terms of your first feeling reactions.

Response patterns that allow the formation of cumulative scales occur in other domains as well. One such domain concerns the conditions under which physicians will recommend abortions (Koslowski, Pratt, & Wintrob, 1976). The items range from those conditions in which most physicians sampled would recommend abortion, such as the pregnancy constituting a threat to the mother's life (77% accept abortion), to those in which most would reject abortion, such as the pregnancy disrupting the mother's career or education (only 40% accept). For the most part, the physicians' acceptance of abortion under the 11 different circumstances studied followed the cumulative pattern of a cumulative scale. For example, physicians who accept abortion if the pregnancy disrupts the mother's career also accept abortion if the pregnancy threatens the mother's life.

Advantages and Disadvantages The most important advantage of a scale with this cumulative pattern is that a single number (the person's scale score) carries complete information about the exact pattern of responses to every item—under the crucial assumption that there is no random error in responses. For example, anyone with a score of 2 on the preceding ability test would be assumed to have passed the addition and division items and failed the calculus problem, rather than any of the other possible patterns of two passes and one failure. Anyone with a score of 5 for a particular group on the social distance scale (Table 7.2) would be known to favor allowing group members to his or her street as neighbors and into his or her country and occupation but not to a social club or to close kinship by marriage. Thus, the scale score from a cumulative scale is unusually informative.

Another advantage is that the scale provides a test of the unidimensionality of the attitude. Items that reflect more than one dimension generally will not form a cumulative response pattern; indeed, Guttman (1944) originally proposed his technique as a means of examining unidimensionality rather than constructing scales. This advantage is tempered by the fact that simple random error in responses can distort the perfect cumulative response pattern, making it difficult to determine whether the attitude domain is really unidimensional when error is present (as it usually is). Various measures of the "scalability" or "reproducibility" of a set of items have been developed in an attempt to answer such questions (Green, 1956; Guttman, 1944). Figure 7.2 illustrates some possible response patterns for a hypothetical four-item cumulative scale. The first five rows show the expected response patterns. If all respondents give these patterns, the scale has perfect reproducibility, indicating perfect unidimensionality. However, error in responses can result in patterns such as the examples in the last three rows, which do not fit the cumulative pattern. Measures of reproducibility use various assumptions to estimate the proportion of error responses and hence the degree of departure of the scale from unidimensionality.

Other disadvantages of the cumulative scaling technique are related to its limitation to unidimensional domains. First, unidimensionality should not be assumed to be a property of a set of items; rather, it is a pattern of an attitude within a given population of individuals. A particular set of items might show a unidimensional pattern for one group of individuals but not for another, or it might be unidimensional at one

FIGURE 7.2 **PATTERNS OF RESPONSES ON A CUMULATIVE SCALE (+ MEANS AGREE, – MEANS DISAGREE)**

Participant Number	Items 1	2	3	4	Scale Score
	Expected Response Patterns				
1	–	–	–	–	0
2	+	–	–	–	1
3	+	+	–	–	2
4	+	+	+	–	3
5	+	+	+	+	4
	"Error" Response Patterns: Examples				
6	+	–	–	+	
7	–	–	+	+	
8	–	+	–	–	

time but not later (as the example of a political efficacy scale at the beginning of this chapter illustrates).

Second, it is hard to find domains that are unidimensional. Consider attitudes toward government, for example. People might have attitudes toward government regulation of business that are distinct from their attitudes toward taxation, civil rights enforcement, and so on. No one of these dimensions would completely index the attitude toward the complex concept of government or provide the sole basis for predicting voting or other behaviors. The best approach in such cases is to accept the fact that the attitude of interest might be multidimensional and to measure it with summated scales, which do not require strict unidimensionality, rather than with cumulative scales. For these reasons, cumulative scales are less frequently used today than summated scales to measure complex social attitudes.

Summated Scales

Summated scales of the form developed by Likert (1932) are the most widely used in the social sciences today. Like differential and cumulative scales, a summated scale consists of a set of items to which the research participant responds with agreement or disagreement; however, there are a number of differences. Only monotone items are used in summated scales—that is, items that are definitely favorable or unfavorable in direction, not items that reflect a middle or uncertain position on the issue. Respondents ordinarily indicate a degree of agreement or disagreement to each item rather than simply checking those items with which they agree. For example, participants might respond to an item such as "A working mother can establish just as warm and secure a relationship with her children as a mother who does not work" by choosing either "strongly disagree," "disagree," "agree," or "strongly agree." The set of response choices might or might not include a middle position (e.g., "neutral," "undecided"). Each response option is either explicitly identified by a number (e.g., "strongly disagree" = 1, "disagree" = 2, and so on) or is numerically coded by the researcher.

Finally, the scale score is derived by summing or averaging the numerically coded agree and disagree responses to each item (with sign reversals for negatively worded items) rather than by averaging the scale values of the items with which the respondent agrees, as in a differential scale. As with any scaling method, the scale score is interpreted as representing the respondent's standing on the construct being measured. In the case of attitudes, the basis for the interpretation is that the probability of agreeing with favorable items and disagreeing with unfavorable ones increases directly with the degree of favorability of the respondent's attitude. (This is the definition of monotone items.) Thus, a respondent whose attitude is highly favorable will respond favorably to many items and be given a high score; a respondent who is ambivalent or holds a middle position will respond favorably to some items and unfavorably to others and be given an intermediate score; and a respondent whose attitude is unfavorable will respond unfavorably to many items and be given a low score. As noted in Chapter 4, the measured response to any single item is considered to reflect in part the error-free underlying construct and in part measurement error. The summation of many item responses into a single scale score allows the error components (some of which are positive, some negative) partially to be canceled out, while preserving and strengthening the common core of the "true" underlying construct reflected in each item.

Construction and Example The Mach IV scale of Christie and Geis (1970), a measure of Machiavelianism, or the desire to manipulate other people, is a summated scale. The items from this scale include those shown in Table 7.3. There, (+) and (−) indicate the direction of the item's contribution to the total scale score; they are included for the reader's information but would not appear on the scale as administered to participants. Respondents indicate agreement or disagreement with each item on a four-point scale ranging from strong agreement to strong disagreement. The sum of responses to the items labeled (+), minus the sum of responses to the items labeled (−), constitutes the scale score.

The procedure for constructing a summated scale involves several steps: (1) Based on a theoretical conception of the attitude or other construct to be measured, the investigator assembles a large number of items that are relevant to the attitude and that are either clearly favorable or unfavorable (i.e., are monotone). (2) The items are administered to a group of pilot participants drawn from a population that is similar to that for which the scale eventually will be used. The participants indicate their agreement on a multipoint response scale. (3) The participants' scale scores are computed, taking into account the direction in which each item is worded. (4) Finally, the

TABLE 7.3 **EXAMPLE OF A SUMMATED SCALE (CHRISTIE & GEIS, 1970)**

	(Circle One)			
Item	**Strongly Agree**	**Agree**	**Disagree**	**Strongly Disagree**
2. The best way to handle people is to tell them what they want to hear. (+)	SA	A	D	SD
10. When you ask someone to do something for you, it is best to give the real reasons for wanting it rather than giving reasons that might carry more weight. (−)	SA	A	D	SD
15. It is wise to flatter important people. (+)	SA	A	D	SD
17. Barnum was very wrong when he said there's a sucker born every minute. (−)	SA	A	D	SD
18. It is hard to get ahead without cutting corners here and there. (+)	SA	A	D	SD

responses are analyzed to determine which items contribute most to the reliability and validity of measurement.

This **item analysis** stage is the most important in the development of a scale. There are several available techniques. A simple approach is to calculate the association between the set of responses to each item and the set of total scale scores. Items whose responses are not strongly associated with the scale scores are not doing a good job of measuring the desired attitude dimension and should be discarded. More sophisticated and complex approaches also are available, for instance, **factor analysis**, which is used to evaluate the degree of statistical commonality in a set of items—that is, the degree to which responses to them appear to be influenced by the same underlying construct (Kline, 1994).

Dimensionality Besides being based on the analysis of responses from pilot participants, item analysis also calls on the investigator's theoretical conceptions of the construct to be measured. The most crucial issue is dimensionality. If the domain is considered to be unidimensional, responses to all the scale items should be moderately to strongly associated with each other and all at about the same level. On the other hand, the domain might be multidimensional. For example, political liberalism or conservatism is sometimes considered to comprise somewhat independent dimensions of economic liberalism and favorability to civil rights. The scale items should then divide into two subsets, called **subscales,** corresponding to the two content domains. Within each subset would be strong associations among items because each subset forms a small scale measuring its single dimension. Between subsets the associations would be weaker, although probably still positive. Factor analysis is particularly useful for detecting this type of pattern, so the researcher does not need to look for them by eye.

Thus, there is a strong interplay among the theoretical conception of the construct to be measured, the process of writing items to reflect the theoretically expected dimensions, and the analysis of the responses from pilot participants to verify the presence of the expected patterns. The final multiple-item scale generated by this process can be unidimensional or multidimensional depending on the informed decisions of the researcher. Even if several dimensions emerge, however, they should all be positively associated to some extent, as otherwise the concept of a single overall scale score makes no sense.

Advantages and Disadvantages The advantages of summated scaling methods are several. First, a summated scale is usually simpler to construct than a differential scale. Second, summated scales can be used in many cases in which differential or cumulative scales cannot (e.g., multidimensional constructs). Because many attitudes, such as favorability toward racial integration or political liberalism or conservatism, seem to be complex and multidimensional, this is a major advantage. Third, a summated scale is generally more reliable than a differential scale of the same length. Finally, the range of agreement–disagreement responses permitted with summated items might make respondents more comfortable in indicating their position than the simple agree versus disagree choice forced by differential items. The graded responses also can elicit more precise and reliable information about the respondent's opinion.

Summated scales also have disadvantages, though. Unlike differential scales, they do not yield information about the respondents' latitude of acceptance to measure the degree of issue involvement. Unlike cumulative scale scores, those from a summated scale do not carry information about the exact pattern of responses to all the individual items. The same scale score might be based on quite different combinations of responses to individual items; however, it is not clear that this should be seen as a disadvantage. The individual items in a unidimensional summated scale are considered to be basically interchangeable; their individual identity is not as important as the fact that each reliably reflects the underlying attitude. Some differences in response patterns that lead to a particular scale score can derive from simple random error, which it is desirable to ignore. The fact that the scale contains a number of items means that random variations on individual items tend to cancel each other out when the variations are not associated with the construct being measured.

On the other hand, when a scale is considered to be multidimensional, the same total score can derive from different response patterns in ways that are conceptually meaningful rather than simply due to random error. For example, two people could receive the same total liberalism score on the two-dimensional scale given as an example previously, one by being high on economic liberalism and average on civil rights attitude and the other by being quite favorable to civil rights and average on economic liberalism. These are meaningfully different response patterns that might yield the same total score. In such cases the researcher could use the subscale scores (i.e., civil rights liberalism and economic liberalism) as well as the total scale score to test hypotheses involving this construct. The subscale scores would differentiate the two patterns of responses. This point illustrates the advantages of the summated scale construction technique, in which multiple correlated dimensions can be included within a scale when it is empirically and theoretically meaningful to do so.

The Semantic Differential One specialized scaling method that has been applied to the measurement of social attitudes, the semantic differential, shares the basic characteristics of summated scales but also has some unique features. Respondents are asked, in effect, to make a series of ratings on multiple-point response scales. Total scores are then derived from the individual item responses by statistical techniques that might include factor analysis. In these ways the semantic differential resembles other summated scales.

The **semantic differential,** developed by Osgood, Suci, and Tannenbaum (1957), is a method for measuring the meaning of an object to an individual. It can also be thought of as a series of attitude scales. The respondent rates a given concept (e.g., "Irish," "Republican," "me as I am") on a series of seven-point **bipolar scales,** of the type shown in Figure 7.3. Any concept—a political issue, a person, an institution, a group—can be rated. Factor analyses have demonstrated that these scales generally group together into three underlying attitude dimensions: (1) respondents' evaluations of the object, corresponding to the favorable–unfavorable dimension of traditional attitude scales (fair–unfair, clean–dirty, good–bad, valuable–worthless);

FIGURE 7.3 EXAMPLE OF A SEMANTIC DIFFERENTIAL

Me as I Am

fair	1	2	3	4	5	6	7	unfair
clean	1	2	3	4	5	6	7	dirty
light	1	2	3	4	5	6	7	heavy
large	1	2	3	4	5	6	7	small
passive	1	2	3	4	5	6	7	active
strong	1	2	3	4	5	6	7	weak
slow	1	2	3	4	5	6	7	fast
bad	1	2	3	4	5	6	7	good

Note: The respondent is instructed to circle a number from 1 to 7 on each scale to rate the given concept.

(2) respondents' perceptions of the potency or power of the object or concept (large–small, strong–weak); and (3) respondents' perceptions of the activity of the object (active–passive, fast–slow, hot–cold). Responses to the individual bipolar scales can be summed to give scores that indicate the respondents' positions on these three underlying dimensions of attitude toward the object being rated. This use of semantic differential ratings thus resembles a summated scale with three subscales.

Osgood and his associates (1957) suggested that the semantic differential allows the measurement and comparison of diverse objects by diverse people because it is not greatly affected by the nature of the object being measured or the type of person using the scale. Although some of their results, including several cross-cultural studies, support this claim, other evidence indicates that the semantic differential is not completely comparable across concepts. The meanings of scales and their associations with the other scales vary, depending on the concept being judged. What is good, for example, depends on the nature of the concept: "Strong" might be good in judging athletes but bad in judging odors. The implication is that the rating scales do not always provide consistent measurements of the underlying dimensions independently of the concepts being judged.

Scaling and Levels of Measurement

Scaling methods are undergoing rapid development. This situation results in occasional disagreement among experts on particular issues. In particular, some authorities claim that particular scale construction methods necessarily give rise to scores representing different levels of measurement (Stevens, 1968). Usually, cumulative and summated scales are said to provide only ordinal data, whereas differential scales produce interval scale data. Some authorities even hold that certain useful methods of data analysis can in principle be meaningfully applied only to interval scale data.

However, other authorities disagree with all these claims (e.g., Dawes & Smith, 1985). Their basic argument is that the level of measurement of a particular set of data is an empirical question, to be settled—like other issues of scale validity—by examining the associations of the scores to other measurements. If the associations are essentially **linear associations**—they are the same at all points across the range of values the measures can take—the responses can be treated as interval scaled, and powerful data-analytic methods may be used.

The statement that this is an empirical question means that the level of measurement is not an intrinsic property of measures that is guaranteed by the use of a particular scaling method. Thus, any of the rating scale or multiple-item scaling techniques discussed in this chapter could be found to produce scores that have interval properties. There is no theoretical assumption that differential scale data will be "better" than any other type. Empirical studies have shown that even single-item rating scales often approach linear associations with physical measurements (such as height) remarkably well, and multiple-item scales do even better (Dawes, 1977). The results of these studies, then, provide empirical and logical justification for the common practice in social science research of analyzing responses to rating scales or summated scales using statistical methods that assume an interval or ratio level of measurement.

Summary

In this chapter we discussed various methods of scaling that distinguish among individuals (or other objects) in terms of the degree to which they possess a given characteristic or their position on an underlying construct. The methods range from the simple use of judgments quantified along rating scales to complex multiple-item scaling techniques. Here, as with other measurement techniques, we have raised issues related to reliability and validity, which are crucial determinants of the quality of any measurement. Investigating the validity of data is often difficult, posing both theoretical problems of determining what would be appropriate criteria for validity and empirical problems of gathering the necessary data. However, thousands of investigations using single-item ratings and multiple-item scales have demonstrated meaningful empirical associations between scores from such measures and other constructs. Each such association constitutes evidence for the general usefulness and validity of these measurement techniques, when properly applied.

Key Concepts

acquiescent response style
bipolar scales
comparative rating scale
contrast error
cumulative scales
differential scales
domain
domain sampling
factor analysis
generosity error
graphic rating scale
halo bias
interval scale
item analysis
itemized rating scale
latitude of acceptance
linear association
monotone item
multidimensional
nominal scales
nonmonotone item
ordinal scale
rank-order scale
ratio scale
response scale
scales
scaling
semantic differential
subscales
summated scales
unidimensional

On the Web

http://www.apa.org/science/faq-findtests.html Looking for a multiple-item measure? Check out the American Psychological Association's frequently asked questions page on finding information about psychological tests.

http://ipip.ori.org/ipip/ Lewis Goldberg's International Personality Item Pool, a list of 1,412 phrases that reflect personality attributes. An excellent example of the development of multiple-item measures of personality and other individual differences.

Further Reading

Devellis, R. F. (1991). *Scale development: Theory and applications.* Thousand Oaks, CA: Sage Publications.

Spector, P. E. (1992). *Summated rating scale construction: An introduction.* Thousand Oaks, CA: Sage Publications.

Tourangeau, R., Rips, L. J., & Rasinski, K. A. (2000). *The psychology of survey response.* Cambridge, England: Cambridge University Press.

PART

III

Sampling

CHAPTER

8

Fundamentals of Sampling

In every piece of research a crucial issue is whether the conclusions can be generalized beyond the immediate settings and samples that have been studied. In Chapter 2 we labeled this issue external validity. A piece of research that has high external validity is one from which we can confidently generalize the results to the population and settings that are of theoretical interest.

This chapter provides an introduction to the logical issues and goals of sampling. After giving some basic definitions and concepts, we describe how the process of selecting a sample from a population can affect the validity of generalizations from the sample to the population. Most of the discussion focuses on sampling people (e.g., to interview or to serve as research participants in some other way); however, in a final section of the chapter we discuss the considerations involved in sampling units other than people (e.g., newspaper stories).

A few general points about external validity might be helpful before we delve into the details of sampling. The first point is that the importance of external validity varies for different types of research. In most survey research, external validity is quite important. For instance, a national public opinion polling organization that conducts a survey to estimate the proportion of voters who favor one candidate or another in an election is naturally very concerned about external validity. It is not practical for this organization to interview all voters, and hence only a relatively small sample of voters is surveyed. Whether or not the sample is well chosen affects the success of the entire enterprise. However, for most laboratory research in psychology, for instance, external validity is less important. When we conduct laboratory research, we usually are more concerned about internal validity. Based on this concern, every effort is made to control extraneous variables that might affect the results—which is why randomized experiments are frequently conducted in laboratories. But not every prospective research participant is willing to come to a laboratory. Hence, laboratory researchers frequently must make do with whatever participants are available. For instance, as described in Chapter 3, participants might come from a pool of students who must participate in research as a course requirement. Because of the laboratory researcher's primary focus on internal validity, it might not be possible to engage in the kind of sampling procedures that would allow the researcher to generalize the research results directly to a target population.

A second point is that even when external validity is a concern, the nature of the desired generalization can take different forms for different types of research. (This point is elaborated on in Chapter 15.) Some research aims specifically at drawing conclusions about a given target population, which is specified in the research goals and hypotheses from the outset. Examples are a political survey (of which the goal is to make accurate statements about the distribution of opinions in the entire electorate) and a study of a new teaching method (of which the goal is to determine whether the new method, as implemented by this city's teachers, can aid the learning of this city's population of third-graders). For such **particularistic research goals,** external validity amounts to the ability to generalize the research results themselves from the studied sample to the target population, and sampling is a crucial step enhancing that ability.

On the other hand, some research aims at testing theoretically hypothesized associations, with no specific population or setting as the focus of interest. An example would be an investigation of the effects of frustration on aggression, in which the goal might be to test a theory that specifies conditions under which frustration does and does not lead to aggression. For such **universalistic research goals,** the consistency or inconsistency of the findings with the theoretically based hypotheses in the sample is the key outcome, for inconsistency implies that the theory is inadequate and requires revision (as outlined in Chapter 2). In such cases, the ability to extend the research findings from the sample to some population is of no interest. Instead, the applicability of the theory itself outside the research context is the central question, and sampling is of little or no concern.

In short, research can serve a variety of purposes. For some purposes (e.g., testing theoretical hypotheses of a causal nature) internal validity is crucially important. External validity becomes a theoretical question (i.e., how broadly applicable is the theory) rather than a methodological question. For other purposes, as illustrated by political polling, the extent to which the results apply directly to a larger population is the key concern, and sampling is the most important methodological contributor to external validity. The relative priority of the various research validities depends on what the researcher is trying to accomplish.

Having made these points, we now are ready to begin our introduction to the fundamentals of sampling. This chapter has three parts. First we provide some basic definitions and concepts that are used throughout this and the following chapter. Then we outline the two basic types of sampling: nonprobability and probability. Finally, a short section introduces ideas involved in sampling units other than people.

Some Basic Definitions and Concepts

A **population** is the aggregate of *all* of the cases that conform to some designated set of specifications. Thus, by the specifications "people" and "residing in the

United States," we define a population consisting of all the people who reside in the United States. We could similarly define populations consisting of all the shop stewards in a factory, all the households in a particular city district, all the boys in a given community under 16 years of age who deliver newspapers, or all the case records in a file.

By certain specifications, one population might be included in another. Thus, the population consisting of all the "men" residing in the United States is included in the population consisting of all the "people" who live in the United States. In such instances, we refer to the included population as a subpopulation, a population stratum, or simply as a stratum. A **stratum** is defined by one or more specifications that divide a population into mutually exclusive segments. For instance, a given population could be subdivided into strata consisting of males under 21 years of age, females under 21 years of age, males from 21 through 59 years old, and so on. Similarly, we could specify a stratum of the U.S. population consisting of White, male college graduates who live in New England and who have passed their seventy-fifth birthday; or we might have some reason for regarding this group of individuals as a population in its own right—that is, without reference to the fact that it is included in a larger population.

A single member of a population is referred to as a **population element.** We often want to know how certain characteristics of the elements are distributed in a population. For example, we might want to know the age distribution of the elements, or we might want to know the proportion of the elements who prefer one political candidate to another. A **census** is a count of all the elements in a population and/or a determination of the distributions of their characteristics, based on information obtained for each of the elements.

It is generally much more economical in time, effort, and money to get the desired information for only some of the population elements rather than for all. When we select some of the elements with the intention of finding out something about the population from which they are taken, we refer to that group of elements as a **sample.** We hope, of course, that what we find out about the sample is true of the population as a whole. Actually, this might or might not be the case; how closely the information we receive corresponds to what we would find by a comparable census of the population depends largely on the way the sample is selected.

For example, we might want to know what proportion of a population prefers one political candidate to another. We could ask 100 people from that population which candidate they prefer. The proportion of the sample preferring Jones might or might not be the same as the corresponding proportion in the population. For that matter, even the actual distribution of votes in an election might not correctly represent the distribution of preferences in the population. Unless there is a 100% turnout, the actual voters constitute only a sample of the population of people eligible to vote. A very high proportion of the people who prefer Smith might be overconfident about their candidate's chances and neglect to come to the polls; or they might be living in a rural area and be discouraged from coming to the polls by a heavy downpour. The election results will properly determine which candidate takes office, but they will not necessarily indicate which candidate is preferred by a majority of the population. Similarly, the early returns in an election can be taken as a sample of the population of returns; and as everyone knows, they can be thoroughly deceptive.

In the case of elections and in the case of early returns in a national election, there probably is not much we can do to guarantee that the samples correctly represent their populations. We usually accept on faith that the outcome of an election does reflect the popular will. And if we are misled by the early returns with respect to the final outcome, at least our errors are soon corrected. There are, however, situations in which we can to some extent control the properties of the sample. In these situations, the way we go about drawing the sample can, if not guarantee, at least increase the likelihood that the sample returns are not too far from the true population figures for our purposes. We can never guarantee that the sample returns reflect the population for the characteristics we are studying unless we have simultaneously conducted a complete comparable census. We can, however, devise sampling plans, which if properly executed can guarantee that if we were to repeat a study on a number of different samples selected from a given population, our findings would not differ from the true population figures by more than a specified amount in more than a specified proportion of the samples.

For instance, suppose that we frequently want to know what percentage of the population agrees with a certain statement. On several occasions we might put such a statement to a sample, compute the percentage who agree, and take this result as an estimate of the proportion of the population who agree. We could devise a number of **sampling plans** that would carry the insurance that our estimates do not differ from the corresponding true population figures by, say, more than 5% on more than, say, 10% of these occasions; the estimates will be correct within 5 percentage points (the **margin of error**) 90% of the time (the probability or **confidence level**). We could similarly devise a number of sampling plans that would produce correct results within 2 percentage points 99% of the time or within any other margin of error and any assigned confidence level. In practice, of course, we do not repeat the same study on an indefinite number of samples drawn from the same population. But our knowledge of what would happen in repeated studies enables us to say that with a given sample, there is, say, a 90% probability that our figures are within 5 percentage points of those that would be shown by a census of the total population using the same measures. Having set our level of aspiration for accuracy and confidence in the findings, we would select from the available alternatives the sampling plan that could be most economically achieved. Needless to say, the higher the level of aspiration, other conditions being equal, the higher the cost of the operation.

A sampling plan that carries such insurance is referred to as a **representative sampling plan.** Note that in this usage the word "representative" does not qualify "sample" but "sampling plan." What a representative sampling plan can do is to ensure that the odds are great enough so that the selected sample is, for the purposes at hand, sufficiently representative of the population to justify our running the risk of taking it as representative.

The use of such a sampling plan is not the only kind of insurance that can decrease the likelihood of misleading sample findings. Another involves taking steps to guarantee the inclusion in the sample of diverse elements of the population and to make sure (either by controlling the proportions of the various types of elements or by analytical procedures in the handling of data) that they are taken account of in the proportions in which they occur in the population. We consider this type of insurance at greater length in our discussion of quota sampling and of stratified random sampling in Chapter 9.

It should perhaps be emphasized that the dependability or accuracy of survey findings is affected not only by the sampling plan and the faithfulness with which it is carried out, but also by the measurement procedures used. This is one reason why sample surveys of a large population can, in practice, produce more dependable results on some matters than can a census. There simply are not enough highly skilled interviewers available to get anything beyond the most superficial information in a national census; a survey on a smaller scale puts less of a drain on the available supply of interviewers and also more readily permits a relatively intensive training program. Similarly, a smaller-scale survey can make it economically feasible to spend more time with each respondent and, hence, make it possible to use measurement procedures that could not be seriously considered for a census of a large population.

The basic distinction in modern sampling theory is between probability and nonprobability sampling. The essential characteristic of **probability sampling** is that one can specify for each element of the population the probability that it will be included in the sample. In the simplest case, each of the elements has the same probability of being included, but this is not a necessary condition. What is necessary is that for each element there must be some specifiable probability that it will be included. In **nonprobability sampling,** there is no way to estimate the probability each element has of being included in the sample and no assurance that every element has some chance of being included.

Probability sampling is the only approach that makes representative sampling plans possible. It makes it possible for the investigators to estimate the extent to which the findings based on their sample are likely to differ from what they would have found by studying the population. If investigators use probability sampling, they can specify the size of the sample (or the sizes of various components of complex samples) that they will need if they want to have a given degree of certainty that their sample findings do not differ by more than a specified amount from those that a study of the total population would yield.

The major advantages of nonprobability sampling are convenience and economy—advantages that can, for some research purposes, outweigh the benefits of probability sampling. Precise comparisons of the relative costs of the two approaches to sampling are, however, not available. Moreover, the comparative costs vary depending on the number of surveys contemplated. Thus, if a number of surveys of the same population are to be carried out, the cost of preparing and maintaining lists from which to sample (generally a necessary step in probability sampling) can be distributed over all of them.

Major forms of nonprobability samples are accidental samples, quota samples, purposive samples, and snowball samples. Major forms of probability samples are simple random samples, stratified random samples, and various types of cluster samples. Only simple random samples are discussed in this chapter; the other two types are discussed in Chapter 9.

Nonprobability Sampling

Accidental Samples

In **accidental sampling,** we simply reach out and take the cases that are at hand, continuing the process until the sample reaches a designated size. Thus, we might take the first hundred people we meet on the street who are willing to be interviewed. Or a college professor, wanting to make some generalization about college students, studies the students in his or her classes. Or a television station, wanting to know how "the people" feel about a given issue, interviews conveniently available shoppers, store clerks, barbers, and others who are presumed to reflect public opinion. There is no known way of evaluating the **biases**, systematic deviations of sample means from true population values, introduced in such samples. If we use an accidental sample, we can only hope that we are not being too grossly misled.

Quota Samples

Quota sampling (sometimes misleadingly referred to as "representative" sampling) adds insurance of the second type referred to earlier—provisions to guarantee the inclusion of diverse elements of the population and to make sure that they are taken account of in the proportions in which they occur in the population. Consider an extreme case: Suppose that we are sampling from a population that includes equal numbers of males and females and that there is a sharp difference between the two sexes in the characteristic we wish to measure. If we did not interview any females, the results of the survey would almost certainly be an extremely misleading picture of the total population. In actuality, females and minority group members are frequently underrepresented in accidental samples. In anticipation of such possible differences among subgroups, the quota sampler seeks to guarantee the inclusion in the sample of enough cases from each stratum.

As commonly described, the basic goal of quota sampling is the selection of a sample that is a replica of the population to which one wants to generalize; hence, the notion that it "represents" that population. If it is known that the population has equal numbers of males and females, the investigators attempt to include equal numbers of males and females. If it is known that 10% of the population lies within a particular age range, the investigators sample so as to ensure that 10% of the sample falls within that age range.

However, despite these precautions in the selection of the sample, quota sampling remains basically similar to the earlier described accidental sampling procedure. The part of the sample in any particular class constitutes an accidental sample of the corresponding stratum of the population. The males in the sample are an accidental sample of the males in the population; the 20- to 40-year-olds in the sample constitute an accidental sample of the 20- to 40-year-olds in the population. Even if the sampling procedure yields correct proportions of the compound classes (e.g., White males in the 20-to-40 age range), the sample cases in these classes are still accidental samples of the corresponding compound strata in the population. The total sample is thus an accidental sample.

Researchers who use quota sampling procedures tend to fall prey to several types of bias. They might include their own friends, who will tend to be rather like themselves and thus potentially nonrepresentative of the overall population. They might concentrate on areas in which large numbers of people are available—large cities, college campuses, airport terminals. Such samples would overrepresent the kinds of people who tend to gravitate to these areas and underrepresent those who seldom leave their homes. If, for instance, interviewers fill their quotas by home visits, they are likely to avoid rundown buildings in dangerous-looking neighborhoods and to pick more attractive homes (presumably building a socioeconomic bias into the sample). They might even avoid the upper stories of buildings without elevator service.

The point to be noted about selective factors such as these is that they are not easily corrected using statistical correction procedures. For many populations we know in advance the true relative proportions of the two sexes and of the various age groups and so can correct for disproportions in the sample, but what true proportion of what definable population is most likely to be found at an airport terminal during the course of a survey? The major control investigators have available for such variables is in the sampling process itself. They can try to make sure that important segments of the population are not entirely unrepresented in their sample; try to benefit from their experience and sample in such a way that many possibly relevant variables are not too grossly distorted in their sample; and hope that whatever disproportions remain will not have an undue bearing on the opinions, preferences, or whatever it is that they seek to know. Or, perhaps wisely, researchers can avoid the ambiguities and uncertainties introduced by quota sampling by turning to probability sampling plans instead.

Purposive Samples

The basic assumption behind **purposive sampling** is that with good judgment and an appropriate strategy, we can handpick the cases to be included and thus develop samples that are satisfactory in relation to our needs. A common strategy of purposive sampling is to pick cases that are judged to be typical of the population in which we are interested, assuming that errors of judgment in the selection will tend to counterbalance one another. Experiments on purposive sampling suggest that without an objective basis for making the judgments, this is not a dependable assumption. In any case, without an external check, there is no way of knowing that the "typical" cases continue to be typical.

Purposive samples selected in terms of assumed typicality have been used in attempts to forecast national elections. One such approach is as follows: For each state, select a number of small election districts whose election returns in previous years have approximated the overall state returns, interview all the eligible voters in these districts on their voting intentions, and hope that the selected districts are still typical of their respective states. The trouble with this method is that when there are no marked changes in the political atmosphere, we can probably do as well by forecasting the returns from previous years without doing any interviewing at all; when changes are occurring, we need to know how they are affecting the selected districts in comparison with other districts.

Snowball Samples

When the research question concerns a special population whose members are difficult to locate, researchers might resort to snowball sampling as a means of gaining access to members of the population. **Snowball sampling** is a multistage sampling procedure by which a small initial sample "snowballs" into a sample large enough to meet the requirements of research design and data analysis. The snowballing results from members of an initial sample from the target population enlisting other members of the population to participate in the study. If participants enlisted in this way bring additional people into the study, then the sample size grows geometrically, quickly reaching a size much larger than the initial sample.

The starting point for a snowball sample is the initial sample of population members, each of whom is asked to name all the other population members he or she knows. For instance, the population of interest might be prostitutes, and the initial sample might include 20 prostitutes who responded to strategically posted flyers. After these individuals complete the survey or interview, they would be asked to list as many fellow prostitutes as come to mind. The newly named prostitutes form the next "layer" of the snowball. Using the list generated by the initial sample, the investigators either directly contact and attempt to enlist new participants or, if it is unlikely that members of the research team could directly contact prospective new participants, offer an incentive for members of the initial sample to enroll individuals on their list in the study. If necessary, participants recommended or enlisted by members of the initial sample would be asked to provide names of additional prospective participants. This procedure continues until either no new prospective participants are listed or the sample of enrolled participants reaches a predetermined size.

As with all nonprobability sampling methods, for any given application of snowball sampling, it is impossible to know how representative the final sample is of the population from which it was drawn. Even if the initial sample is obtained using a probability method, the lists provided by members of the initial sample are accidental and, therefore, subject to the biases described earlier. Nonetheless, it is wise to begin with either a stratified random sample (though this would require a list of population members) or, minimally, a quota sample and seek the largest initial sample possible. Even when the initial sample is chosen carefully, inferences from information provided by samples obtained using the snowball method must be drawn with caution given the unknown association between the sample and the population. For this reason, when external validity is a priority, findings from snowball samples typically are taken as tentative and used as a basis for additional studies using some form of probability sampling.

Probability Sampling

Probability samples provide the first kind of insurance against misleading results that we discussed earlier—the ability to specify the likelihood that the sample findings do not differ by more than a certain amount from the true population values. They also provide the second kind of insurance—a guarantee that enough cases are selected from each relevant population stratum to provide an estimate for that stratum of the population. Here we describe only simple random sampling, the most basic form of probability sampling, for it will suffice to display the logic involved in generalizations from sample to population. Other, more complex types of probability sampling are discussed along with the practical issues of sampling in Chapter 9.

Simple Random Samples

Simple random sampling is the basic probability sampling design; it is incorporated in all more complex probability sampling designs. A simple random sample is selected by a process that not only gives each element in the population an equal chance of being included in the sample, but also makes the selection of every possible combination of the desired number of cases equally likely. Suppose, for example, that we want a simple random sample of 2 cases from a population of 5 cases. Let the 5 cases in the population be *A, B, C, D*, and *E*. There are 10 possible pairs of cases in this population: *AB, AC, AD, AK, BC, BD, BE, CD, CE*, and *DE*. Write each combination on a card, put the 10 cards in a hat, mix them thoroughly, and have a blindfolded person pick one. Each of the cards has the same chance of being selected. The 2 cases corresponding to the letters on the selected card constitute the desired simple random sample.

In this illustration, each of the cards (i.e., each combination of 2 cases) has 1 chance in 10 of being selected. Each of the individual cases also has the same chance of being selected—4 in 10 because each case appears on 4 of the cards. There are, however, many ways of giving each case the same chance of being selected without getting a simple random sample. For example, suppose we were to arbitrarily divide an illustrative population of 10 cases into 5 pairs as follows: *AB, CD, EF, GH, IJ*. If we write the designations for these pairs on 5 cards, blindly pick one of the cards, and take as our sample the 2 cases designated on this card, every case has 1 chance in 5 of being picked; but obviously not every possible combination has the same chance of being selected as every other—in fact, most of the combinations (e.g., *AC*) have no chance at all as they have not been included on the cards.

In principle, we can use this method for selecting random samples from populations of any size, but in practice it could easily become a lifetime occupation merely to list all the combinations of the desired number of cases. The same result is obtained by selecting each case individually, using a list of **random numbers** such as can be found in most textbooks on statistics or generated by computer. (These procedures are detailed in Chapter 9.) These are sets of numbers that were generated in such a way that there is no evidence of systematic order. Before using a list of random numbers, it is first necessary to number all the elements in the population to be studied. Then the list is consulted, and the cases whose numbers come up as one moves through the list are taken into the sample until the desired number of cases is obtained. The selection of any given case places no limits on what other cases can be selected, thus making equally possible the selection of any one of the many possible combinations of cases. This procedure, therefore, is equivalent to selecting randomly one of the many possible combinations of cases.

Without going into the mathematical argument, it is possible to illustrate only the underlying principles of probability sampling. Consider, for this purpose, a hypothetical population of 10 individuals, or cases, as follows:

Case	A	B	C	D	E	F	G	H	I	J
Score	0	1	2	3	4	5	6	7	8	9

The score represents some attribute of the individual, such as his or her performance on a test of mechanical aptitude. The mean score for this population of 10 cases is 4.5. If we did not know this figure, the problem would be to make an estimate of the population mean on the basis of the scores of the elements in the sample that is drawn. According to the definition of simple random sampling, the method of selecting the sample must give equal probability to every combination of the desired number of cases; in other words, over the long run, with repeated sampling, every combination should come up the same number of times. We can, therefore, figure out what will happen in the long run in our illustrative population by the simple device of considering all the combinations; that is, we take every combination of the desired number of cases and compute a mean for each combination. What results is a distribution of sample means—known as a **sampling distribution.** For example, there are 45 possible combinations of 2 cases in our hypothetical population of 10 cases. One, and only 1, combination (cases *A* and *B*) yields a sample mean of .5; there are 5 combinations (*A* and *J*, *B* and *I*, *C* and *H*, *D* and *G*, *E* and *I*) that yield sample means of 4.5; and so on. Similarly, there are 210 possible samples of 4 cases. One of these combinations (*A*, *B*, *C*, and *D*) yields a sample mean of 1.5; 1 (*A*, *B*, *C*, and *E*), a sample mean of 1.75; and so on.

Table 8.1 shows the sampling distributions for sample means based on simple random samples of 2, 4, and 6 cases from our illustrative population.

Notice that for samples of any given size the most likely sample mean is the population mean; the next most likely are values close to the population mean; the more a sample mean deviates from the population mean, the less likely it is to occur. (Because of the grouping of means, this pattern is obscured for samples of 2 cases, for which there are 5 possible samples with a mean of 4.5, 4 possible samples with a mean of 4.0, and so on.) Also, the larger the sample, the more likely is it that its mean will be close to the population mean. For instance, whereas 39% of the means for samples

TABLE 8.1 **MEAN SCORES OF SIMPLE RANDOM SAMPLES OF 2, 4, AND 6 CASES FROM ILLUSTRATIVE POPULATION OF 10 CASES WITH POPULATION MEAN SCORE OF 4.5**

	Sample Size		
Sample Means	**2 Cases**	**4 Cases**	**6 Cases**
.5	1		
1.0	1		
1.50–1.75	2	2	
2.00–2.67	5	10	2
2.75–3.25	3	25	10
3.33–4.00	8	43	52
4.17–4.83	5	50	82
5.00–5.67	8	43	52
5.75–6.25	3	25	10
6.33–7.00	5	10	2
7.25–7.50	2	2	
8.00	1		
8.50	1		
Total number of samples	45	210	210
Mean of sample means	**4.5**	**4.5**	**4.5**
Percent of sample means between 4.00 and 5.00	11	24	39
Percent of sample means between 2.67 and 6.33	60	89	98

Note: With the small number of different scores in the illustrative population, there are only a limited number of possible sample means. Thus, for samples of 2 cases, there is no combination that can yield a mean of 2.25; but there are 3 samples of 4 cases (ABDF, ABCG, ACDE) with a mean of 2.25. Similarly, a mean of 2.67 is not possible for 1 sample of 6 cases. For convenience of tabulation and to help bring out the characteristics of the sampling distribution, the means of the samples have been grouped.

of 6 fall between 4.00 and 5.00, only 11% of the means for samples of 2 fall within this narrow range centered around the population mean.

It is this kind of behavior on the part of probability samples (not only for means but also for proportions and other types of statistics) that makes it possible to estimate the population characteristic (e.g., the mean) as well as the likelihood that the sample figure differs from the true population figure by a given amount.

One interesting feature of simple random sampling ought to be mentioned, even though it is hard for most people to believe it without mathematical proof. When the population is large compared to the sample size (say, more than 10 times as large), the variabilities of sampling distributions are influenced much more by the ***absolute number*** of cases in the samples than by the ***proportion*** of the population that is included; that is, the magnitude of the errors that are likely depends more on the absolute size of the sample than on the proportion of the population it includes. Thus, the estimation of popular preferences in a national preelection poll, within the limits of a given margin of error, would not require a substantially larger sample than the estimation of the preferences in any one state in which the issue is in doubt. Conversely, it would take just about as large a sample to estimate the preferences in one doubtful state with a given degree of accuracy as it would to estimate the distribution of preferences in the entire nation. This is true despite the fact that a sample of a few thousand cases obviously includes a much larger proportion of the voters in one state than the same-size sample does of the voters in the nation.

Concluding Remarks About the Two Kinds of Sampling

Throughout the preceding discussion, we made it clear that only by using probability sampling do we have any basis for estimating how far sample results are likely to deviate from the true population figures. At the same time, we noted that the major claimed advantages of nonprobability sampling are its convenience and its economy. It is likely, therefore, that many investigators will continue to use nonprobability methods and to justify their use on the ground of practical experience, even while conceding the superiority in principle of probability sampling.

Of course, there are circumstances in which probability sampling is unnecessary or inappropriate. One such circumstance arises from the fact that we do not necessarily carry out studies of samples only for the purpose of being able to generalize to the populations that are being sampled. If we use samples for other reasons, the ability to evaluate the likelihood of deviations from the population values is irrelevant. For example, if our goal is to obtain ideas, good insights, and experienced critical appraisals, we select a purposive sample with this in mind. The situation is analogous to one in which a number of expert consultants are called in on a difficult medical case. These consultants—a purposive sample—are not called in to get an average opinion that would correspond to the average opinion of the entire medical profession. They are called in precisely because of their special experience and competence. Or the situation can be viewed as analogous to our more or less haphazard sampling of foods from a famous cuisine. We are sampling not to estimate some population value but to get some idea of the variety of elements available in this population.

Another example of sampling for ideas rather than for the estimation of population values is provided by the field of market research known as motivation research. The typical problem of motivation research is to find out something about motives, attitudes, and associations evoked by certain products, brand names, and package designs that might not be obvious even to the respondents themselves. The results of such studies are turned over to advertising agencies, which use them in developing advertising campaigns. Characteristically, the motivation researchers are quite happy with accidental samples or with purposive samples selected in such a way as to maximize the likelihood of differences among the elements in the sample. They are looking for ideas to transmit to the advertising people, not for correct estimates of population distributions. We might argue that they would be better off if they could establish not merely the variety of motives that are likely to become associated with certain products but also the precise distribution of these motives. At present, however, it is questionable whether the additional information would be worth the extra cost of getting it. At any rate, as long as these researchers deceive neither themselves nor their clients into believing that they are getting the second kind of information, no one can take exception to their application of accidental sampling.

Other reasons justifying the use of nonprobability samples arise from the fact that there are many important considerations in research in addition to the sampling design. In the introduction to this chapter, we discussed how, for some social scientists, the need for experimental control overrides sampling considerations. That is, social scientists who use experimental methods in a laboratory setting frequently trade some external validity for increased internal validity. There also are times when the claims of construct validity and external validity conflict. That is, it is necessary on occasion to decide whether we want a better sampling design or more sensitive and generally more informative measurements. Consider a study by Chein (1956) on the factors related to the use of drugs by boys in juvenile street gangs. Chein used group workers as informants (with complete protection of the anonymity of the individual gang member). These workers had spent months winning the confidence of the boys, convincing the latter that they were not confederates of the police, social reformers, or other things reprehensible in the eyes of the boys; and they had been working closely with the gangs for many more months—in some instances, for several years. As these informants were available only for the gangs that were being worked with, the sample of gangs—and hence of gang members—was an accidental sample. Assuming that (1) it would have been possible to get a probability sample of gang members and (2) the information obtained through the group workers was much more dependable than would have been information obtained through direct interview, what should the investigators have done?

The answer to such a question is not easy. The first thing to do, of course, is to assure ourselves that the dilemma is real. If convinced that it is, we must then decide whether the problem is, under the circumstances, worthy of investigation at all. If the answer is still in the affirmative, we must decide, in terms of the research purpose, whether it would be better to gather more useful information based on a not very sound sample or less useful information based on a sounder sample.

Sampling Elements Other Than People

Research sometimes requires representative samples of elements other than people or groups of people. We cover a significant subset of these elements—people's thoughts, feelings, and behaviors—in Chapter 10; however, in the interest of completeness, we touch on such sampling problems here. One example would be samples of time periods for an observational study in which the phenomenon of interest is to be observed at discrete times rather than continuously (see Chapter 15). For example, 30 five-minute observation periods might be randomly chosen over the course of a day. Another example is drawing samples of media content for content analysis (Chapter 15). It might be impractical or unnecessary to code all the content of a particular newspaper for an extended period of time, so only a sample of days or pages might be chosen for examination. In these situations, a clear goal of the research is to generalize the observations or analyses based on a sample of elements to the entire population—the whole day's activities in the case of the time-sampled observations; the whole content of the newspaper in the case of content sampling. Probability sampling is therefore the approach that should be chosen. In such cases, a simple random sample is likely to be both theoretically and practically satisfactory because of the ease of listing the elements of the population (e.g., all the five-minute time periods in a day, all the days and page numbers for the newspaper).

A more specific application of the logic of sampling to measurement theory has been developed (Nunnally & Bernstein, 1994). It makes use of the concept of sampling items to construct a multiple-item measure of a desired construct. Suppose that we could define a domain (population) of items that measures the construct of interest, for example, the domain of two-digit addition problems (e.g., 37 + 74) or the domain of statements describing positive or negative attitudes toward abortion. We could describe the theoretical goal of measurement as assessing the individual's responses to all the items in the domain. But doing so explicitly is impractical (we cannot generate all the attitude statements that would fall into the defined domain) and unnecessary (we probably do not need to administer all 10,000 arithmetic problems to get a good idea of the person's addition ability). Therefore, the domain can be sampled.

The logic of **domain sampling** is identical to the logic of sampling in general, then: The person's performance on the sample of items contained in a measure is used as a basis for estimating the desired construct, his or her hypothetical performance on the entire domain. The sample could in a few instances actually be a probability sample; for example, it would be easy for a computer to draw a simple random sample of addition problems from the domain described. More often the sample is a nonprobability sample because the boundaries of the domain (e.g., domains of attitude statements) are ill-defined. In practice, we simply construct a set of attitude statements and define the domain as being the hypothetical population of similar items. It should be clear, based on the principles of sampling, that a larger sample (i.e., a measure with more items) would permit a closer approximation to the desired construct (the person's responses to the entire population of items) by reducing sampling error. Indeed, as we showed in Chapter 4, measures with more items have higher reliability.

Summary

The focus of this chapter is sampling as a vehicle for maximizing the external validity of research. We started by arguing that for a sampling procedure to be representative, the first thing that must be done is to specify the population to which we want to generalize. Then we can proceed to use either probabilistic or nonprobabilistic sampling procedures. In the former, every element in the population has a known, nonzero probability of being included in the sample. In the latter, we do not know the probability of inclusion for each element and some of the elements have zero probability of inclusion. Only in probability sampling do we have a basis for estimating how far sample results are likely to deviate from the true population figures.

Four types of nonprobability sampling were defined: accidental, quota, purposive, and snowball sampling. The first involves gathering data from whoever is convenient, accessible, or otherwise accidentally encountered. Quota samples are also accidental samples; the only difference is that in quota samples we specify strata from each of which accidental samples are to be gathered. In purposive samples, we use our best judgment to decide which elements are most representative of the population and include them in the samples. Finally, snowball samples capitalize on the knowledge of and access to members of special populations by a small number of people from the population initially enrolled in the study to build a sample.

Probability sampling was illustrated through a description of the simplest form, simple random sampling. In such a sample, each element has an equal probability of being included in the sample, and the inclusion of each element is an independent decision. This property makes all possible samples of the desired size equally likely to be drawn. Simple random samples are commonly but not exclusively used in practical sampling situations, and in Chapter 9 we describe alternative methods of probability sampling that can be used in a wider range of situations.

In the concluding parts of the chapter, we discussed situations in which the confident ability to generalize to a larger population must be traded off to achieve other important research goals. Situations arise, for example, in which internal or other forms of validity are more important than external validity or in which probability sampling would conflict with sound measurement practices.

Finally, we briefly described ways in which the logic of sampling can operate on the selection of other types of elements besides people, an idea we cover in detail in Chapter 10. Time periods, elements of media content, and test items are all subject to sampling when the goal is to generalize results to a population that is the main focus of interest.

Key Concepts

accidental sampling
biases
census
confidence level
domain sampling
margin of error
nonprobability sampling
particularistic research goals
population
population element
probability sampling
purposive sampling
quota sampling
random numbers
representative sampling plan
sample
sampling distribution
sampling plan
simple random sampling
snowball sampling
stratum
universalistic research goals

On the Web

http://www.gallup.com/poll/faq/faq.asp In the "Frequently Asked Questions" section of the Gallup Organization's Web site is a detailed description of how samples are drawn by an organization that specializes in the use of samples to describe the U.S. population. Begin at the home page, http://www.gallup.com/, to read about results from Gallup's latest polls.

Further Reading

Henry, G. T. (1990). *Practical sampling.* Thousand Oaks, CA: Sage Publications.

CHAPTER

9

Probability Sampling Methods

Probability sampling is almost always involved in survey research and is often used in other types of research as well. An observational study, for example, might involve data collection during only a sample of time periods. This chapter describes in concrete terms the practical issues involved in several types of sampling plans, building on the general logic of probability sampling that was described in the Chapter 8.

Basic Probability Sampling Methods

Probability samples are those in which every element of the sampled population has a known probability of being included in the sample. It is not necessary that all elements have an equal probability, although that is frequently the case. Three types of sampling plans have been developed that fit this basic definition and, therefore, provide a probability sample that can support firm inferences about the population's characteristics. These three are simple random sampling, stratified random sampling, and cluster sampling. It also is possible to combine two or more of these strategies to form a multistage sampling plan.

Simple Random Sampling

Drawing a **simple random sample** requires either a list or some other systematic enumeration of the population elements. The list or other specification of the population from which elements are drawn to form a sample is referred to as the **sampling frame.** Perhaps the most important step in any type of probability sampling is establishing an accurate and complete sampling frame. This requirement is difficult to meet for many real populations (e.g., all the residents of a particular city), but lists exist for other types of populations (all currently enrolled students in a university or all the physicians licensed to practice medicine in a state). At times the list is explicit, such as the list of students that could be provided by a university. Other times, actually creating the list is unnecessary, if there is a clear and systematic way of enumerating all the population elements. For example, if we wish to sample 5-minute time periods from a population of 24 hours, there would be 12 × 24, or 288, time periods in the population. It would be easy enough to determine the specific time period corresponding to each population element that is sampled, so there would be no real need to list all of them in advance.

Given the availability of a list or other enumeration of population elements, the procedure for drawing a simple random sample is not complicated. Recall that this type of sample was defined as each population element having an equal and independent probability of being sampled. Independence means that the decisions about every population element are separate; the inclusion of one element depends not at all on the inclusion of any others. In combination, these properties mean that every possible combination of elements of a particular number has an equal probability of being drawn.

The procedure for drawing a sample would operate as follows. Suppose that there are 1,672 elements in the list of the population and that a sample size of 160 is to be drawn. Then random numbers from 1 to 1,672 would be drawn one at a time and the elements identified by the numbers added to the sample. A list of random numbers (such as appears in many statistics textbooks) could be used, as could a high-quality computer **random number generator** (illustrated in the next section). The latter has the advantage that it could easily be programmed to generate only numbers in the desired range, whereas choosing sets of four digits from a printed table would yield many numbers that are out of range and unusable. If a number corresponding to an element that is already in the sample comes up a second time, it is simply ignored and the next number drawn; this corresponds to **sampling without replacement**. When the desired number of elements is in the sample, the process stops. It is easy to see that the definition of simple random sampling is met in this way, for each choice of a number is random and independent (by the definition of what random numbers are), and therefore each population element has an equal and independent chance of being included in the sample.

Although this procedure sounds simple, there are two common pitfalls that should be avoided. First is the procedure of **systematic sampling,** which involves choosing elements in such a way that choices are not independent. For instance, noticing that the desired sample size of 160 is approximately 1 in 10 population elements, we might pick a random number between 1 and 10 (say, 6) and sample the sixth element, sixteenth, twenty-sixth, and so on—that is, every tenth element after the random start. Although this method would provide a sample in which every element has an equal chance of being chosen (because of the random choice of starting point), it is not a simple random sample because the selection decisions are not independent. If the sixth element is included, the sixteenth must be and the seventh cannot be. Systematic sampling can create important biases when the list involves regularities or systematic cycles. (Imagine what would happen if the population list in this example consisted of married couples always listed in the order husband followed by wife.) Because the correct procedure for drawing a simple random sample involves little additional effort in these days of widespread computer availability, it should be used in preference to systematic sampling.

Another pitfall involves the treatment of population elements that are ineligible for sampling. For example, we might have a list of graduates of a job training program, from which a sample is to be drawn for a follow-up study of the program's effects. The decision might be made to sample only people who completed the program a year or more ago. Thus, the list would include some eligible elements and some ineligible ones. It might seem appropriate simply to select the next element on the list when the sampling procedure comes up with an ineligible name; however, this method would introduce bias and violate the nature of a probability sample. Names that follow ineligible ones would have double the usual probability of selection (because they might either be drawn in their own right or selected because the previous element was drawn but found ineligible). Instead, the correct procedure is to draw a larger sample in the first place—a sample that is large enough to compensate for the loss of ineligible elements. For instance, if a final sample of 160 is desired and it is estimated that 20% of the listed population will be ineligible, we would draw an initial sample of size 160×1.20, or 200. After the expected 20% loss, the remaining sample would approximate the desired size. More important, it would retain the property of being a statistically correct simple random sample.

Obtaining and Using Random Numbers Before moving to descriptions of other probability sampling methods, we address in some detail the practical question of how best to obtain a list of random numbers. There are two categories of strategies—published tables and random number generators; random number generators can be distinguished according to whether they are software or hardware based.

Most statistics textbooks include a random number table in an appendix.[1] Typically, such tables include a series of numbers, usually four to six digits in length, arrayed in matrix format (i.e., columns and rows). Table 9.1 is a small random number table we created for illustrative purposes using numbers generated by Research Randomizer (Urbaniak & Plous, 2001), a Web-based randomization program. Note that columns and rows are numbered, a feature that facilitates movement through a large table such as those typically included in textbooks. The table is used as follows: Suppose our sampling frame included 500 people, and our goal was the selection of a simple random sample of 20 people. Our first step would be to array names or some identifier of the 500 people in a list and give each a unique number from 1 to 500. Next, we would select an arbitrary place in the table to begin. Perhaps we could drop a coin or some other small object onto the random number table from such a distance that we could not anticipate where it would land. We would begin with the number

[1]You can find random number tables on the World Wide Web as well. Two examples can be found at http:// www.ccm.edu/stw/witcookie/npd2rnt.htm and http://www.au.af.mil/au/hq/selc/smpl-d.htm.

TABLE 9.1 **EXAMPLE OF A RANDOM NUMBER TABLE**

	1	2	3	4	5
1	12580	31823	22653	27734	47**403**
2	29525	48**314**	58762	60704	50**241**
3	60798	76**190**	23514	29**173**	33917
4	71**407**	11789	76**269**	18456	16527
5	99**098**	52**177**	84710	11**274**	24956
6	36998	16917	53**341**	16**151**	02600
7	56802	06**327**	37**068**	69581	70**150**
8	56**315**	13969	98**018**	16**050**	86985
9	73**094**	57**414**	37955	87909	60581
10	49**390**	15**483**	30627	77**030**	59**252**

closest to the object. For purposes of illustration, let us pretend that this exercise pointed to column 1, row 5. Because our sampling frame includes only 500 people, we need only three of the five digits provided in the table. We could use either the first or the last three; we have chosen to use the last three. Beginning with the number in column 1 and row 5, we systematically move through the table (either across rows or down columns), consulting the last three digits of each number and looking for values from 1 to 500. We have highlighted numbers in the table that fall in this range. As you can see, our first number ends in 098; hence, the person assigned 98 in our sampling frame becomes the first member of our sample. Moving down the column, the last three digits of the next number, 998, falls outside our range, so we move to the next number and the next until we encounter another three-digit number within our range. (If we encounter 098 again, we ignore it and move on.) In the end, our sample of 20 comprises the people holding the following positions in the sampling frame: 98, 315, 94, 390, 314, 190, 177, 327, 414, 483, 269, 341, 68, 18, 173, 274, 151, 50, 30, and 403.

Because of the wide availability of statistical software and access to the World Wide Web, it is now commonplace to generate random numbers specific to the sampling situation rather than consulting generic random number tables. Before illustrating the use of a random number generator, we need to point out a distinction between types of generators. Software-based random number generators such as those provided in Microsoft Excel, SPSS, or SAS are, technically speaking, *pseudo*-random number generators. These generators begin with a seed, an arbitrary starting value (e.g., the time of day). The seed value is transformed according to some algebraic rule, then the outcome of that transformation is itself transformed. This process proceeds until the desired number of random numbers is generated (Marsaglia, 1984). Because one can document the process by which such numbers are produced, they are not genuinely random. *Genuine* random numbers do not involve algebraic manipulation, instead relying on some naturally occurring random process as the basis for generating numbers. For instance, the HotBits hardware (Web access information is provided at the end of the chapter) builds lists of genuinely random numbers based on the inherent randomness in the amount of time it takes the Krypton-85 nucleus to decay. The algebraic transformations that underlie pseudo-random number generators have become increasingly sophisticated, yielding numbers that approach genuine randomness and suffice quite well for random sampling.

Returning to the example of drawing 20 cases at random from a population of 500, we can illustrate the use of a Web-based pseudo-random number generator, Research Randomizer (http://www.randomizer.org). The input screen offers the user a number of choices that tailor the generated list to the specific requirements of the sampling situation. Reflecting the particulars of our hypothetical situation, we asked for one set of 20 numbers falling in the range from 1 to 500 with no repeats. We also asked that the generated numbers be ordered from lowest to highest. A screen shot of the output provided by Research Randomizer appears in Figure 9.1. The efficiency of this procedure compared to the manual search through a random number table should be apparent.

In summary, simple random sampling plans are indeed simple—provided that a list of the population elements exists. However, in some research situations other types of samples are used, either for reasons of efficiency (stratified samples) or practicality (cluster samples). These more complex probability sampling techniques are variations of simple random sampling. We turn to these next.

Stratified Random Sampling

In **stratified random sampling,** the population is first divided into two or more strata. The **strata** can be based on a single criterion (e.g., sex, yielding the two strata of male and female) or on a combination of two or more criteria (e.g., age and sex, yielding strata such as males under 21, males 21 and over, females under 21, and females 21 and over). In stratified random sampling, a simple random sample is taken from each stratum, and the subsamples are then joined to form the total sample.

To illustrate how stratified random sampling works, we refer to this population of 10 cases.

Case	*A*	*B*	*C*	*D*	*E*	*F*	*G*	*H*	*I*	*J*
Sex	*F*	*F*	*F*	*F*	*F*	*M*	*M*	*M*	*M*	*M*
Age	*Y*	*O*	*Y*	*O*	*Y*	*O*	*Y*	*O*	*Y*	*O*
Score	0	1	2	3	4	5	6	7	8	9

The first five cases are females; the last five, males. The cases designated *Y* are younger, and the *O*s are older. The score represents some attribute of the individual, such as his or her performance on a test of mechanical aptitude.

Consider samples of four with equal proportions of males and females. To satisfy this last condition, many samples of four that were possible under the conditions of

FIGURE 9.1 **RESULTS FROM WEB-BASED PSEUDO-RANDOM NUMBER GENERATOR, RESEARCH RANDOMIZER (HTTP://RANDOMIZER.ORG), WHEN GIVEN THE PROBLEM OF GENERATING 20 UNIQUE RANDOM NUMBERS FROM THE RANGE 1 TO 500**

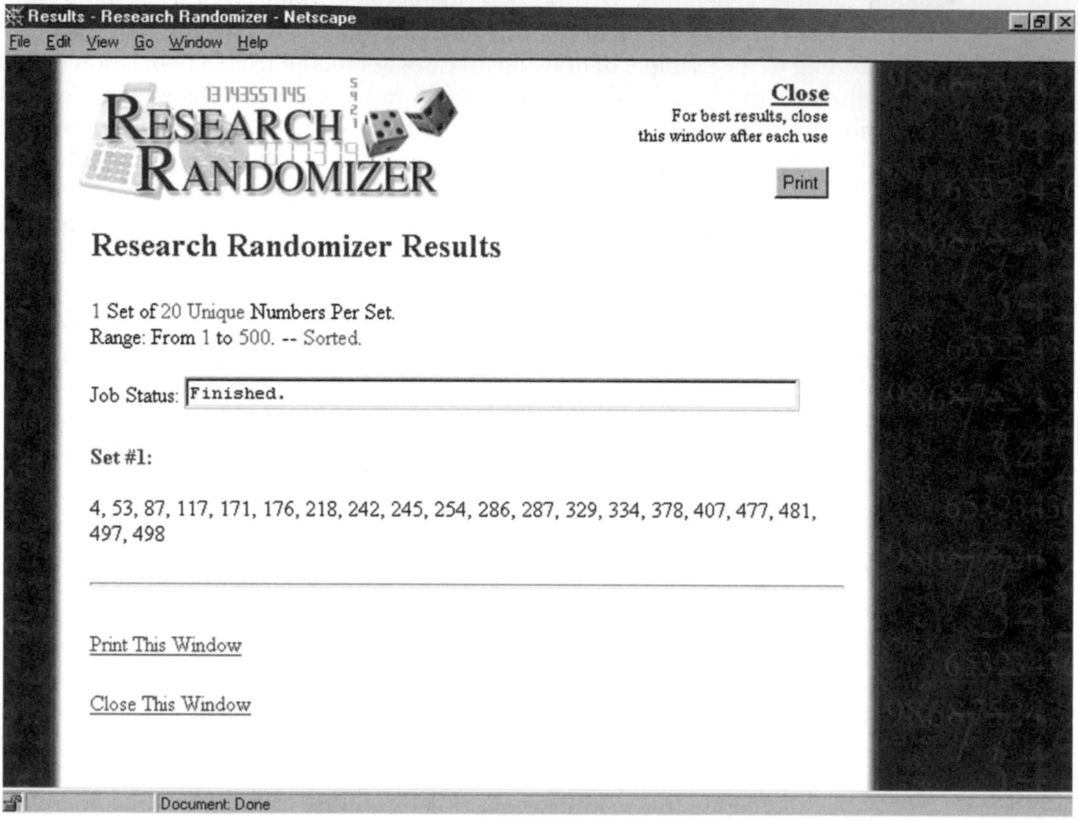

SOURCE: Reproduced with permission of the authors.

simple random sampling are no longer possible—for example, samples consisting of cases *A*, *B*, *C*, *D* or of cases *A*, *B*, *C*, *F* or of cases *D*, *F*, *G*, *I*—because they do not have two males and two females. In fact, there are now exactly 100 possible samples as compared to the 210 possible simple random samples. As in Chapter 8, we have computed the mean score for each of the possible samples and thereby obtained the sampling distribution of the mean. Table 9.2 compares the sampling distribution for samples of four obtained on the basis of simple random sampling, stratified sampling with sex as a criterion for stratification, and stratified sampling with age as a criterion.

TABLE 9.2

MEAN SCORES OF SAMPLES OF 4 CASES FROM ILLUSTRATIVE EXAMPLE OF 10 CASES WITH POPULATION MEAN SCORE OF 4.5 (SIMPLE AND STRATIFIED RANDOM SAMPLES)

	Type of Sample		
Sample Means	**Simple Random Sample**	**Samples Stratified by Sex**	**Samples Stratified by Age**
1.50–1.75	2		1
2.00–2.50	10		7
2.75–3.25	25	3	8
3.50–4.00	43	25	26
4.25–4.75	50	44	16
5.00–5.50	43	25	26
5.75–6.25	25	3	8
6.50–7.00	10		7
7.25–7.50	2		1
Total number of samples	210	100	100
Mean of sample means	**4.5**	**4.5**	**4.5**
Percent of sample means between 4.00 and 5.00	24	44	16
Percent of sample means between 2.50 and 6.50	89	100	84

Note: The means of the samples have been grouped.

There is a marked improvement over simple random sampling when the sampling is based on a stratification of our hypothetical population by sex; with this kind of stratification we get a marked increase in the number of samples that give means very close to the population mean and a marked reduction in the number of sample means that deviate widely from the population mean. When the population is stratified by age, however, there is no such marked improvement in the efficiency of sampling; in fact, the means of individual samples are somewhat less likely to be very close to the population mean.

In general, stratification contributes to the efficiency of sampling if it succeeds in establishing classes that are internally comparatively homogeneous with respect to the characteristics being studied—that is, if the differences between classes are large in comparison with the variation within classes. In our illustrative population, the difference in scores between the sex groups is relatively large and that between age groups relatively small; that is why stratification by sex is effective and stratification by age ineffective in this case. The general principle is that if we have reason to believe that stratifying according to a particular criterion or set of criteria will result in internally homogeneous strata, it is desirable to stratify. If the process of breaking down the population into strata likely to differ sharply from one another is costly, we have to balance this cost against the cost of a comparable gain in precision obtained by taking a larger simple random sample. The issues involved in the decision of whether to stratify have, basically, nothing to do with trying to make the sample a replica of the population; they have to do only with the anticipated homogeneity of the defined strata with respect to the characteristics being studied and the comparative costs of different methods of achieving precision. Both simple and stratified random sampling are representative sampling plans.

Except for a slight saving in arithmetic, there is no reason for sampling from the different strata in the same proportion; that is, even with respect to the criteria selected for stratification, it is not necessary for the sample to reflect the composition of the population. Thus, in sampling from a population in which the number of males equals the number of females, it is permissible (and might be desirable) to sample nine or five or two or some other number of females to every male. When this is done, however, it is necessary to make an adjustment to find the mean score (or the proportion of elements with a given characteristic or whatever measure is desired) for the sample that will be the best estimate of the mean score of the total population of males and females. This step is accomplished by "weighting" the figure for each stratum in such a way that it contributes to the score for the total sample in proportion to its size in the population, as in the quota sampling illustration previously mentioned. When the various strata are sampled in constant proportion, we are spared this bit of arithmetic because the various strata are already properly weighted.

There are several reasons for sampling the various strata in different proportions. Sometimes it is necessary to increase the proportion sampled from classes having small numbers of cases in order to guarantee that these classes are sampled at all. For example, if we are planning a survey of retail sales volume in a given city in a given month, simple random sampling of retail stores might not lead to an accurate estimate of the total volume of sales because a few very large department stores account for an extremely large proportion of the total sales, and there is no guarantee that any of these large stores would turn up in a simple random sample. In this case, we would stratify the population of stores in terms of some measure of their total volume of sales (e.g., the gross value of sales during the preceding year). Perhaps only the three largest department stores would be in our topmost stratum. We would include all three of them in our sample; in other words, we would take a 100% sample of this stratum. Any other procedure in such a situation would greatly reduce the accuracy of the estimate, no matter how carefully samples were taken from other strata. Again, of course, figures from the various strata would have to be appropriately weighted before estimating the total volume of sales in the city.

Another reason for taking a larger proportion of cases from one stratum than from others is that we might want to subdivide the cases within each stratum for further analysis. Let us say that in our survey of retail sales we want to be able to examine separately the volume of sales made by food stores, by clothing stores, and by other types. Even though these classifications are not taken into account in selecting the sample (i.e., the sample is not stratified on this basis), it is clear that we need a reasonable number of cases in each volume-of-sales stratum to make possible an analysis of different types of stores within each stratum. If a given stratum has relatively few cases, so that sampling in the proportion used in other strata would not provide enough cases to serve as an adequate basis for this further analysis, we might take a higher proportion of cases in this stratum.

One of the major reasons for varying the sampling proportions for different strata cannot be fully explained without going into the mathematical theory of sampling, but the principle involved can be understood on a more or less intuitive basis. Consider two strata, one of which is much more homogeneous with respect to the characteristics being studied than the other. For a given degree of precision, it will take a smaller number of cases to determine the state of affairs in the first stratum than in the second. To take an extreme example: Suppose there is reason to know that every case in a given stratum has the same score; we could then determine how to represent that stratum in the total sample on the basis of a sample of one case. Of course, in such an extreme case we are not likely to have this information without also knowing what the common score is. But in less extreme cases we can often anticipate the relative degrees of homogeneity or heterogeneity of strata before carrying out the survey. For example, if with respect to certain types of opinion questions, men differ among themselves much more than women, we would accordingly plan our sample to include a larger proportion of men. If it is the case that women would be expected to be more alike than men in these matters, they do not have to be sampled as thoroughly as do the men for a given degree of precision.

In general terms, we can expect the greatest precision if the various strata are sampled proportionately to their relative variabilities with respect to the characteristics under study rather than proportionately to their relative sizes in the population. A special case of this principle is that in sampling to determine the proportion of cases having a particular attribute, strata in which we can anticipate that about half the cases will have the attribute and half will not should be sampled more thoroughly than strata in which we would expect a more uneven division. Thus, in planning a stratified sample for predicting a national election, using states as strata, we should not plan to sample each state in proportion to its eligible population; it would be wiser to sample most heavily in the most doubtful states.

In summary, the reason for using a stratified rather than a simple random sampling plan is essentially a practical one: More precise estimates of population values can be obtained with the same sample size under the right conditions, as Table 9.2 illustrated. This result reduces the overall cost of the research. The "right conditions" involve relative homogeneity of the key attributes within each stratum and easy identification of the stratifying variables. The concrete procedure for drawing a stratified random sample does not need to be separately illustrated, for it simply amounts to drawing a simple random sample within each population stratum, treating each as a separate population list. The complexities involved in assigning unequal sampling probabilities for different strata and the like take us well beyond the scope of this chapter, although some of the major considerations were touched on.

Cluster Sampling

Except when dealing with small and spatially concentrated populations, there are enormous expenses associated with simple and stratified random sampling—for example, in the preparation of classified lists of population elements and in drawing participants from scattered localities. There also are other factors that often make it difficult or impossible to satisfy the conditions of random sampling. For example, it might be easier to get permission to administer a questionnaire to three or four classes in a school than to administer the same questionnaire to a much smaller sample selected on a simple or stratified random basis; the latter might disrupt the school routines much more. For such practical reasons, large-scale survey studies seldom use simple or stratified random samples; instead, they use the methods of cluster sampling.

In **cluster sampling,** we arrive at the ultimate set of elements to be included in the sample by first sampling in terms of larger groupings—clusters. The clusters are selected by simple or stratified methods; and if not all the elements in these clusters are to be included in the sample, the ultimate selection from within the clusters is also carried out on a simple or stratified random sampling basis.

Suppose, for example, that we want to do a survey of seventh-grade public school children in some state. We could proceed as follows: Prepare a list of school districts, classified perhaps by size of community, and select a simple or stratified random sample. For each of the school districts included in the sample, list the schools and take a simple or stratified random sample of them. If some or all of the schools thus selected for the sample have more seventh-grade classes than can be studied, we could take a sample of these classes in each of the schools. The survey instruments would then be administered to all the children in these classes or, if it is desirable and administratively feasible to do so, to a sample of the children.

Similarly, a survey of urban households might take a sample of cities; within each city that is selected, a sample of districts; within each selected district, a sample of households.

Characteristically, the procedure moves through a series of stages—hence the common term **multistage sampling**—from more inclusive to less inclusive sampling units until we finally arrive at the population elements that constitute the desired sample.

Notice that with this kind of sampling procedure it is no longer true that every combination of the desired number of elements in the population or in a given stratum is equally likely to be selected as the sample of the population or stratum. Hence, the kinds of effects we noticed in our analysis of simple and stratified random sampling of our hypothetical population of 10 cases (the population value being the most probable sample result and larger deviations from the population value being less probable than smaller ones) cannot develop in quite the same way. Such effects, however, do occur in a more complicated way, provided that each stage of cluster sampling is carried out on a probability sampling basis. We pay a price, however, in terms of sampling efficiency. On a per-case basis, effective cluster sampling is much less efficient in obtaining information than comparably effective stratified random sampling; that is, for a given number of cases, the probable margin of error is much larger in the former case than in the latter. Moreover, the correct statistical handling of the data is apt to be more complicated. These handicaps, however, are more than balanced by the associated economies, which generally permit the sampling of a sufficiently larger number of cases at a smaller cost.

The comparison of cluster sampling with simple random sampling is somewhat more complicated. Stratified sampling principles can be used to select the clusters, and what is lost in efficiency because of the clustering effects can be regained by this stratification. Depending on the specific features of the sampling plan in relation to the object of the survey, cluster sampling might be more or less efficient on a per-case basis than simple random sampling. But again, even if more cases are needed for the same level of accuracy, the associated economies generally favor cluster sampling in large-scale surveys.

In summary, cluster sampling, like stratified sampling, is also done for practical reasons—but the specific reasons are different. The costs of sampling (e.g., making a list) and of data collection (e.g., sending interviewers to scattered individual locations) can be reduced by sampling cases in clusters. However, sampling efficiency (the number of cases required to produce population estimates of a given quality) is reduced, so more cases are required. Clustering is a reasonable choice whenever the reduction in costs per sampled element outweighs the increased number of elements required. The optimum sample design depends on a number of properties of the population that might be only vaguely known or estimated (Sudman, 1976).

The actual procedures involved in cluster sampling are not described in detail here, for they are generally beyond the resources of a nonexpert. In principle, however, this type of sampling plan is relatively straightforward, as the preceding discussion suggests. First, clusters are sampled (e.g., schools) with either a simple or stratified sampling plan. (This implies that a list of clusters has to exist or be created.) Then, if necessary, a list of the population elements (e.g., students) within each selected cluster is created. Note that such lists need not be obtained or made for nonselected clusters; this cost avoidance is one of the advantages of cluster sampling. At last, the desired simple or stratified random sample can be drawn for each cluster.

Sampling Error

Even if our sampling frame is accurate and complete and our method of random selection is without error, our sample will not exactly match the population from which it is drawn on any given characteristic. This unavoidable discrepancy is referred to as **sampling error,** the difference in the distribution of characteristics between a sample and the population as a whole. Because we cannot measure the entire population, we can only estimate the extent of sampling error for a given sample. Inasmuch as any value we derive for sampling error is an estimate, we tend to cite such values according to degree of confidence. In the social sciences, the convention is to accept estimates about which there is 95% confidence that the estimate is correct.

(Occasionally, the more stringent 99% confidence criterion is used.) Thus, when speaking of sampling error, we tend to make statements such as, "With 95% confidence we can say that there is X% sampling error given the size of our sample."

It probably comes as no surprise that sampling error decreases—that is, characteristics of the sample more closely match characteristics of the population—as the size of a random sample increases. This property of random samples is easy to see in the formulas used to calculate margin of error. For instance, if we want to estimate with 95% confidence the margin of error associated with an estimate of a proportion (e.g., the percentage of registered voters who will vote for a particular candidate in an election), we can use the formula,

$$1.96 \times \sqrt{\frac{P(1-P)}{N}}$$

where N represents sample size and P represents the proportion of the sample that displayed the behavior of interest to us. For illustrative purposes, let use assume that $P = .50$ and $N = 100$. Substituting these values into the equation and solving it yields a value of .098. If we convert this to a percentage, then we find that the margin of error is 9.8%. Hence, if we are willing to accept a number of key assumptions, we can say with 95% confidence that the true percentage of the population who displayed the behavior of interest falls between 40.2% and 59.8%. With the same degree of confidence, if we boost sample size to 1,000, the range shrinks to 46.9% to 53.1%. If we need a higher level of confidence, say 99%, we increase the multiplier to 2.58, expanding our range for $N = 1{,}000$ to 45.9% to 54.1%. The important point for our purposes is that, because N is in the denominator, increasing N always reduces the estimate of sampling error.

The impact of sample size on sampling error is illustrated in Figure 9.2. On the x axis is sample size and on the y axis is sampling error expressed as a percentage. Consistent with computations described in the previous paragraph, the sampling error when sample size is 100 is about 10%. Note that increasing the sample size an additional 100 dramatically reduces the sampling error to just under 7%. Adding another 100 elements to the sample reduces the sampling error further but to a lesser degree. In fact, after sample size reaches about 600, sampling error is reduced very little by adding additional elements. (This explains why national polls rarely sample more than 700 people.) Another way of describing this pattern is to consider the proportionate increase in sample size required to achieve a specific reduction in sampling error. For instance, say we wanted to cut sampling error in half. To accomplish this for any given sample size, we would need to quadruple the number of elements. Referring back to Figure 9.2, note that the sampling error for $N = 400$ is about half the sampling error for $N = 100$. In order to realize this same reduction in sampling error for $N = 400$, we would have to increase sample size to 1,600. Clearly, there is a pattern of diminishing return in the association between sample size and sampling error.

FIGURE 9.2

Theoretical Percentage Sampling Error (95% Confidence) Associated with Estimates from Random Samples Ranging in Size from 100 to 1,600

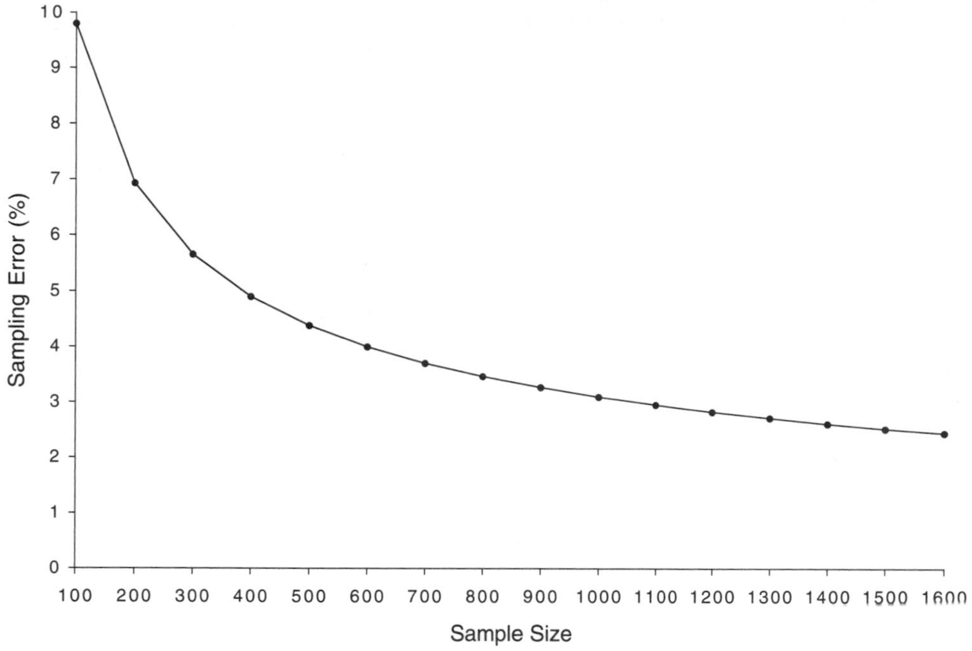

Before concluding our discussion of sampling error, we want to emphasize that sampling error and the oft-cited margin of error associated with public opinion polls are *estimates* based on a set of assumptions that rarely are met. Such estimates are idealized values that assume a truly random sample from the population and no extraneous influences associated with other aspects of the polling. Humphrey Taylor, Chairman of Louis Harris & Associates, Inc., who conduct the widely cited Harris polls, describes other sources of error associated with estimates based on real-world "random" samples:

> In theory, with a sample of this size, one can say with 95 percent certainty that the results have a statistical precision of plus or minus __ percentage points of what they would be if the entire adult population had been polled with complete accuracy. Unfortunately, there are several other possible sources of error in all polls or surveys that are probably more serious than theoretical calculations of sampling error. They include refusals to be interviewed (non-response), question wording and question order,

interviewer bias, weighting by demographic control data, and screening (e.g., for likely voters). It is difficult or impossible to quantify the errors that may result from these factors (Taylor, 1998).

Despite these drawbacks to estimating population opinions and behavior from samples, Taylor concludes with a twist on Winston Churchill's famous remarks about democracy: "Polls are the worst way of measuring public opinion and public behavior, or of predicting elections—except for all of the others."

Two Examples of Sampling Plans for a National Survey

As a way of illustrating probability sampling designs for a large-scale research project, a hypothetical national survey, we outline two procedures. One is a multistage area sample (a type of cluster sample) for use with personal interviews, and the other is a random-digit-dialing telephone sample.

Multistage Area Sample

In conducting a survey of the national population (or another broad population, such as all registered voters, all employed people, or the like) we immediately face the problem that no list of the total population exists, nor can one be created reasonably with available resources. Therefore, some version of cluster sampling is required. Clustering also will reduce travel costs because an interviewer can perform a number of interviews in a limited area. A **multistage area sample** is a cluster sampling plan that uses geographic areas as the initial sampling units, ending with a sample of households and then individuals within households at the final stage. The procedure for drawing such a sample, much simplified, is as follows:

1. **Primary sampling units (PSUs)** are selected from the population of counties and metropolitan areas in the United States. These geographical entities are listed in atlases and other reference sources, so drawing a sample of them is relatively simple in principle; however, a simple random sample of PSUs would be a poor design. It would give all the units an equal chance of selection, so that a desert county in Nevada with a few dozen residents would have the same chance of selection as the Los Angeles standard metropolitan statistical area (SMSA), with several million residents. The best procedure is to sample PSUs with probabilities proportionate to size so that the chance of each area being sampled is proportionate to its population, which can be estimated on the basis of U.S. Census figures. The detailed procedure for sampling in this way cannot be illustrated here. Complications can be introduced by stratification at this stage (and at stages 2 and 3). Areas might be stratified into urban versus rural, by region, economic status, or other variables.

2. Within each selected PSU, one or more smaller areas need to be selected. The areas might be cities, towns, townships, census tracts, or other smaller geographical areas within the PSU (county or SMSA). These smaller areas are also randomly sampled with probabilities proportionate to their sizes. The population of each area (individual residents or households) can be determined from census publications.
3. Within each of the selected smaller areas, one or more blocks are sampled in the same way, using similar procedures and data sources.
4. Now that a set of blocks (clustered within the areas selected at stage 2) has been identified, a list of households within the selected blocks must be obtained. A city directory or other available source can be used in some cases, although its completeness of coverage should be checked. In other cases the interviewer must create a list of households as a step in the sampling plan. Using a detailed map, the interviewer locates the boundaries of the selected area, generally one or a few contiguous blocks separated by streets in urban areas and areas demarcated by roads, rivers, or railroads in rural areas. The dwelling units within the area are then listed. The interviewer is cautioned to make sure to identify all units, including single houses, all apartments in apartment buildings, a separate basement or attic apartment within a single house, hotel rooms that are occupied permanently, mobile homes used as permanent residences, and so on. The objective of this stage is to create a list of all dwelling units in which households might be found, each identified by its address or a detailed description of its location.
5. At this point a simple random sampling procedure is used to select the desired number of dwelling units from the list. The interviewer returns to the selected units and attempts to interview the residents at that location. Of course, a dwelling unit might be unoccupied or not contain an eligible household for some other reason.
6. Finally, once a household is located, in most surveys the final goal is the sampling of an eligible individual. For instance, one of the residents who is over the age of 18 might be selected at random after the interviewer initially obtains a list of such eligible individuals from whatever household member is contacted first. In other cases, households rather than individuals are the desired population, as in a survey focusing on household income, expenditure patterns, and savings. Then this final sampling step would not be necessary, and the interviewer would simply try to locate a knowledgeable adult member of the household to serve as an informant.

Random-Digit-Dialing Telephone Sample

A telephone survey can involve much simpler procedures than a multistage area sample. As explained in Chapter 5, most telephone samples today are not drawn from phone directories, which would involve bias because of the omission of unlisted numbers and people who have recently moved, but by random-digit-dialing sampling plans. That is, random digits are used to create a list of telephone numbers to be contacted. The steps are as follows:

1. From telephone companies, a list of three-digit area codes and three-digit central exchange numbers is obtained.
2. Phone numbers are sampled by combining a randomly drawn valid area code–exchange combination (six digits) with a random four digits, giving a potential number within an existing exchange. The number is dialed, and if it is answered, screening questions are asked to determine whether an eligible household has been contacted (as opposed to, say, a business, a computer, or another type of nonhousehold number). Unfortunately, only one in five numbers created on this basis generally turns out to be a household (Sudman, 1976)—which means that much time is wasted on screening out ineligible numbers.

As an alternative, a phone directory can be used as a basis for random sampling of numbers in a way that avoids most of the problems of straight sampling of listed numbers. A household listing is drawn at random from the directory, and the last three digits of its phone number are replaced by three random digits. This procedure means that a much higher proportion (perhaps half) of sampled numbers will actually be households because phone companies seem to assign numbers in consecutive blocks of 100 or 1,000. At the same time, unlisted numbers and numbers of new residents not listed in the directory have the same chance of being called as numbers that are in the directory. Additional, more complex strategies used by survey research firms and facilitated by sophisticated survey software provide even greater sampling efficiency and accuracy (Frey, 1989).

Summary

In practice, sampling plans used in small-scale research ordinarily involve simple random sampling or stratified random sampling, which in simple cases is essentially identical to simple random sampling within each separate stratum of the population. Procedures for drawing such samples are not demanding, but a few common pitfalls should be avoided. Of particular concern is sampling error, and a key determination is the number of elements that must be sampled in order to achieve an acceptable theoretical margin of error. For large-scale research projects, such as a national survey, sampling becomes a much more complex and demanding issue. Cluster samples are required if personal interviews are to be used. For telephone interviewing, random-digit-dialing methods are convenient and offer good coverage of the population of households with phones.

Key Concepts

cluster sampling
multistage area sample
multistage sampling
primary sampling units (PSUs)
random number generator
sampling error
sampling frame
sampling without replacement
simple random sampling
strata
stratified random sampling
systematic sampling

On the Web

http://www.randomizer.org/ Home page for Research Randomizer, a JavaScript program for random selection and random assignment. Research Randomizer has a user-friendly graphical interface that allows considerable flexibility in specifying the characteristics of the list of random numbers it generates. Like most computer-based random number generators, Research Randomizer is a pseudo-random number generator.

http://www.fourmilab.ch/hotbits/ Home page for HotBits, Web-based applications for research that require a true random number generator. A hardware-based generator, HotBits capitalizes on the inherent randomness in the decay of a Krypton-85 nucleus.

http://www.pollingreport.com/ This Web site features highlights of national polls, including nonpartisan analysis.

http://www.ncpp.org/home.htm The National Council on Public Polls works to "promote better understanding and reporting of public opinion polls." In its Web pages are a variety of commentaries on the proper use of polling information (e.g., "20 Questions a Journalist Should Ask About Poll Results").

Further Reading

Levy, P. S., & Lemeshow, S. (1999). *Sampling of populations: Methods and applications* (3rd ed.). New York: Wiley.

CHAPTER

10

Experience Sampling

In Chapters 8 and 9 our primary focus was the activity of drawing samples of individuals from defined populations. In Chapter 8 we discussed the fundamental concerns that face social scientists, who can rarely obtain the information they need to address a research question from every member of the population to whom the question applies. We argued that a key concern in sampling is external validity, particularly when the goals of the research are to describe a specific population (i.e., particularistic). Building on this discussion, in Chapter 9 we presented the advantages of probability sampling and described procedures by which a relatively small number of individuals from a population can be used to draw firm conclusions about the characteristics of the population as a whole.

In this chapter we build on the material presented in Chapters 8 and 9 by coupling these principles of sampling with measurement. We discuss a novel approach to research on social experience called the **experience sampling method**, which we described briefly in Chapter 5 as one of the modes of measurement that involve direct questioning. Although there are various forms of experience sampling, all have as their primary goal the intensive study of people's naturally occurring thoughts, feelings, and behaviors as they unfold over short periods of time. Because, during waking hours, people are thinking, feeling, and behaving continually, making it impossible to record every thought, feeling, or behavior they experience, experience sampling methods make use of sampling procedures typically used to assemble representative samples of people to obtain representative samples of people's experience.

We introduced the experience sampling method as an approach to measurement in Chapter 5. In this chapter, we expand our coverage in two ways. First, we provide a series of examples that illustrate the range of topics that can be explored using experience sampling methods and the variety of sampling and measurement techniques used in applications of the method. Then we isolate and discuss a number of decisions that social scientists who use the experience sampling method must make. These decisions fall into two categories: sampling and measurement.

Applications of the Experience Sampling Method

During 1965 and 1966, more than 25,000 individuals in 12 countries used diaries to describe how they used their time in a 24-hour period (Szalai, Converse, Feldheim, Scheuch, & Stone, 1972). These individuals recorded the occurrence of more than 640,000 events that took place during the course of one day in their lives. For each event, participants provided contextual information such as when, where, and with whom the event took place. The Multinational Comparative Time-Budget Research Project provided rich, detailed information about aspects of people's lives not often studied by social scientists. For instance, at that time married men in Germany were substantially more likely to do the laundry than their counterparts in the United States. And women in every country surveyed spent more time than men transporting their children; U.S. women spent more time at this activity than women in any other country (Stone & Nicolson, 1987). A critical feature of the information generated by this study is that it was provided *in situ* at the time the activities took place. Thus, reports were not subject to many of the distortions and biases that can influence responses in surveys and interviews.

By the mid-1970s psychologists had begun to move beyond simply asking respondents to record what they were doing at particular points in time to asking them about the thoughts and feelings that accompanied their activity—aspects of inner experience. Current approaches to experience sampling are based on the pioneering work by Mihaly Csikszentmihalyi and colleagues during this period. They were interested in the experience of "flow," an optimal state of being that comes with full involvement with an activity (Csikszentmihalyi & Csikszentmihalyi, 1988). These researchers had been asking research participants to retrospectively report what they had been doing and feeling at randomly selected times during the day. A problem with this strategy was participants' inability to confidently reconstruct their experiences from memory. To solve this problem, Csikszentmihalyi and colleagues had participants carry a pager of the sort used by physicians. They paged participants at random times during the day. Participants carried copies of a brief questionnaire with them and completed one each time they were paged (Csikszentmihalyi, Larson, & Prescott, 1977). These researchers referred to their strategy as the experience sampling method.

Since the pioneering work of Csikszentmihalyi and colleagues, the experience sampling method has been used to study many phenomena of interest to social scientists (Wheeler & Reis, 1991). In the remainder of this section of the chapter, we describe applications of the experience sampling method to a diverse set of topics of interest to social scientists. These examples also illustrate the diversity in implementation of the technique.

Subjective Experience of Time

Although objectively speaking time passes at a constant rate, people's experience of the passage of time is not at all constant. Such expressions as "time flies when you're having fun" and "the watched pot never boils" suggest that people can experience time passing quickly or slowly relative to its objective rate. Conti (2001) reasoned that people who are intrinsically motivated, that is, motivated by the pleasure they find in working on tasks, routinely "lose track of time" and are therefore more likely to report the subjective experience of time moving quickly than people who are motivated by incentives external to the task (e.g., wages, grades).

To test this hypothesis, Conti (2001) equipped 75 college students who had provided information about their intrinsic motivation toward schoolwork with electronic planners, microcassette recorders, and small questionnaire booklets and sampled their experience of time for a period of five days. The electronic planners were programmed to randomly signal participants eight times each day. When signaled, participants were first to record a guess as to the time of day. Then they were to respond to a series of questions regarding time awareness (e.g., "When was the last time you looked at a watch or clock?"); the activity in which they were engaged (e.g., "What was the main thing you were doing?"); and their emotional state (e.g., happy versus sad, irritable versus cheerful). Participants either recorded responses using one of the pages in the small questionnaire booklet provided or, in the event their hands were not free (e.g., driving), audio-recorded their responses using the microcassette recorder. A small number of participants completed fewer than half of the 40 questionnaires they were to complete across the five days. In general, however, the response rate was very good, with participants, on average, completing questionnaires more than 80% of the time they were signaled. The study yielded information on 2,381 experiences.

The findings were consistent with Conti's (2001) reasoning. Intrinsically motivated students checked the time less often and reported being less aware of the time of day when they were signaled. Moreover, they tended to guess that the time of day was later than it actually was. Finally, analyses revealed that time awareness was negatively associated with positive emotions. In other words, the more aware participants were of the time of day when signaled, the less positive was their emotional experience at that time. Conti concluded that, although the design of her study did not allow for causal inferences, her research clearly demonstrated an association between intrinsic motivation and the subjective experience of time.

Age Differences in Emotional Experience

Life span developmental psychologists are interested in age-related differences and changes from infancy to old age. One aspect of experience that varies with age is the experience of emotions. Most research on the development of emotions has focused on the experience of young children. Carstensen, Pasupathi, Mayr, and Nesselroade (2000) were interested in whether emotional experience continues to develop and change throughout adulthood. Their particular focus was the experience of emotions in everyday life, a focus that is well suited to study using the experience sampling method.

Carstensen et al. (2000) enlisted 184 adults ranging in age from 18 to 94 to participate in an experience sampling study of emotional experience. For a period of seven days participants wore pagers that could be set to signal either by sound or vibration. They were randomly paged five times each day between the hours of 9 A.M. and 9 P.M. When paged, they were to press a button to signal that they had detected the page, then complete one of a set of brief questionnaires that were provided in a small booklet they were to keep with them during the hours when they could be paged. The questionnaire included a list of 19 emotion adjectives (e.g., anger, amusement) on which respondents were to rate their experience when paged. Each participant provided information on 35 occasions, yielding a total of 6,440 experiences.

Extensive analyses of the ratings on the adjectives revealed the following: Negative emotions are experienced with decreasing frequency from young adulthood to about age 60, at which point the frequency of negative emotional experience increases slightly from year to year. The intensity with which negative, positive, and specific emotions are experienced does not vary across the adulthood years. With increasing age, emotional experience is more stable and complex. That is, older adults experience a greater variety of emotions in a more sustained pattern than their younger counterparts. Finally, older participants were more likely to experience positive and negative emotions simultaneously than younger participants. This initial study of emotional experience across the adult years suggests that emotional functioning does not decline; indeed, it becomes richer with age.

Thinking . . . Day and Night

In an innovative application of experience sampling methods, Fosse, Stickgold, and Hobson (2001) examined the experience of thoughts and hallucinations during waking and sleeping. The impetus for their work was the general lack of research on the less sensationalistic aspects of experience during sleep; most research on thought during sleep has focused on extreme features such as nightmares or hyperawareness. As an initial foray into the cognitive experience during sleep, Fosse et al. used experience sampling methods to sample thoughts during states of waking and sleeping for a period of two weeks.

During waking hours, participants carried a pager and were signaled in a manner similar to that described in the first two examples. Readers might be wondering how Fosse et al. (2001) signaled and obtained questionnaire responses from participants during the time they were sleeping. While in bed, the 16 participants wore a "Nightcap," a cap connected to a computer programmed to signal and gather information about sleep state from participants. The computer was programmed to awaken participants at random intervals during the night, at which time participants were to answer the same series of questions to which they responded when signaled by the pager during waking hours. (Participants also were to answer the questions if they spontaneously awoke during the night.) The questions were open-ended and concerned the participants' location; the activity in which they were engaged; who else was with them; and their thoughts, feelings, and perceptions. All told, Fosse et al. received information on 1,576 experiences of thought by participants. Just over half of the experiences took place during active waking hours. The remainder were distributed across the night, from the time participants initially went to bed but before they went to sleep until they awoke to begin the next day. Participants' open-ended responses were coded by judges as evidencing thoughts, hallucinations, or both.

As might be expected, the primary pattern was for more thoughts during waking hours and more hallucinations during sleeping hours. Within this broad pattern, however, were some interesting variations. For instance, during waking hours, thoughts were more prevalent during the period when participants were in bed and not asleep (90%) than when they were awake and active (79%). During sleeping hours, thoughts occurred more frequently during the onset of sleep (64%) than during shallow (38%) or deep (22%) sleep. Hallucinations were scarcely reported at all during waking hours, peaking at 4% during the period just before sleep. The incidence of hallucinations increased during sleeping hours, from 35% at sleep onset to 60% during shallow sleep and 82% during deep sleep. The authors linked their findings to mechanisms in the brain known to vary in their functioning from waking to sleeping and at different times during the sleep cycle.

Motives for Drinking Alcohol

People consume alcohol for reasons that range from celebrating the best of times to bemoaning the worst of times. Sometimes they drink with other people, and sometimes they drink alone. Mohr, Armeli, Tennen, Carney, Affleck, and Hromi (2001) were interested in the typical situations in which moderate to heavy drinkers consume alcohol. They expected to find that such individuals would be more likely to drink alone at home on days when their social life went poorly and with other people away from home on days when their social life went well.

To test these hypotheses, Mohr et al. (2001) recruited men and women from the community who were moderate to heavy drinkers but did not meet criteria for lifetime alcohol dependence. The 100 participants carried handheld computers and completed a questionnaire each evening for 30 days. Because Mohr et al. were interested in specific events, those on which alcohol was consumed, they did not randomly signal participants. Rather, participants were to alert the handheld computer each time they anticipated drinking for a period of time. Then, they either recorded each drink on the computer after the drink was consumed, or they were prompted every hour after the initiation of a drinking episode to record how much they had drunk during the previous hour and the context within which they had drunk. Specifically, questions administered by the handheld computer concerned the location, the presence of other people, and information about the type of drinks consumed. In addition, each evening the participants completed a brief questionnaire about the quality of their social interactions during that day. These were mailed to researchers the following morning.

In line with Mohr et al.'s (2001) predictions, participants whose social life had been largely negative during the day drank more alone and at home. This was particularly true of individuals who were prone to instability of emotions. Furthermore, participants whose social life had been largely positive on a given day were more likely to drink away from home and with other people, particularly participants who were high on extraversion. The authors characterize their findings as compelling evidence for the role of social motives in drinking. That is, people drink for different reasons and, at least to some degree, those reasons involve the quality of their social life.

Sampling Strategies and Procedures

The distinctive features of the experience sampling method are a strategy for sampling experiences and a mechanism that is quick and efficient for obtaining information about those experiences. As the examples illustrate, there are multiple approaches to sampling and measurement using the experience sampling method. In this section, we take up the activity of sampling. We identify three general approaches to sampling and discuss the advantages and disadvantages of each.

In Chapter 8 we introduced our discussion of sampling people by distinguishing between two goals that motivate research—particularistic and universalistic. Recall that particularistic research goals are those that involve drawing inferences about particular populations; external validity is a critical concern in research motivated by particularistic goals. Universalistic research goals, on the other hand, involve drawing inferences about theories, and internal validity is the more critical concern. These same goals distinguish between approaches to sampling experience. In some cases, researchers are interested in accurately describing the subjective experience of participants; therefore, it is vitally important to obtain a *random* sample of participants' lives so that the sample of experiences on which measures were taken is representative of the "population" of participants' experience. In other cases, researchers are interested only in particular experiences; therefore, they need only to sample designated experiences. The sampling procedure is *purposive*, and the goal is to test theoretical propositions about the causes and effects of specific aspects of those experiences. In short, experience sampling can be random or purposive, and the particular strategy researchers use to sample will vary according to which type of sample their research questions require.

Signaling

In order to apply the experience sampling method, the researcher must develop a means by which participants will know they are to respond to a copy of the brief questionnaire they have been provided. The **signaling** of participants can take one of three forms. In the most rudimentary applications of experience sampling, participants are signaled by the clock. That is, they are instructed at the outset of the study to complete a questionnaire each day according to a set schedule, usually late in the day or just before retiring for the day. The prototypic signaling strategy involves alerting participants through some electronic device that they are to complete a questionnaire. In early applications of this strategy, participants wore pagers and were paged by members of the research team according to a schedule of which the participant was not aware. Because of the beeping sound emitted by pagers, experience sampling studies came to be known as "beeper studies." A third means of signaling participants is to instruct them to recognize the occurrence of something about themselves or their environment and to complete a questionnaire at every occurrence. In these applications, the researcher controls neither the timing nor the number of measurements. They are dictated by the unique experience of each research participant.

When the signaling is dictated either by the clock or by the occurrence of something in the person's experience, the actual implementation of signaling is straightforward. Otherwise, the research must decide what sort of electronic device will be used to signal participants according to a random schedule. The increasing popularity of the experience sampling method and the widespread availability of small electronic devices have given rise to a wide range of possibilities.

As noted at the beginning of the chapter, the earliest studies that used the experience sampling method were inspired by the physician, for whom the ubiquitous pager provides a means of signaling the need to return a call or report to a specific location (e.g., Csikszentmihalyi et al., 1977). A particular advantage of the pager is its relatively small size and light weight. Participants in experience sampling studies can carry a pager in a discrete fashion that does not invite the sort of queries from friends and acquaintances that would alter their ordinary comings and goings. Moreover, pagers can be set to signal by vibration, so that only the participants are aware that they have been paged. In the typical use of pagers, the researcher designates a period of hours during which experiences will be sampled (e.g., 9 A.M. to 9 P.M. as in the Carstensen et al., 2000, study described earlier); determines how many times participants will be sampled during that period (Carstensen et al. sampled five times); and then uses a random process to develop a schedule for each participant. Then either by computer or telephone calls from members of the research team, participants are signaled according to their individual schedules.

An alternative approach is programmable electronic devices that include an alarm system. The simplest device is an electronic wristwatch (e.g., Thomas & Diener, 1990), which has the additional advantages that it is relatively inexpensive and participants can wear it throughout the day without concern for misplacing or damaging it. Most wristwatches are not equipped with a means of randomly emitting signals; thus, as with pagers, the researcher must develop a random schedule and program it into the watch for each participant. A more sophisticated variation of this strategy is the use of an electronic planner (e.g., Conti, 2001). Electronic planners offer greater flexibility in programming and signaling, but they are more expensive and more difficult for participants to keep with them at all times than a wristwatch.

An even more sophisticated (and expensive) approach is the use of handheld computers (e.g., Mohr et al., 2001). Handheld computers (e.g., Palm Pilot, Handspring) offer two significant advantages over pagers, wristwatches, and planners. First, they do not need to be preprogrammed for each participant. Software can be installed that randomly samples according to parameters established by the researcher (e.g., seven times between 8 A.M. and 10 P.M. with a minimum of 30 minutes between signals). Second, as described in the next section, using readily available software designed specifically for experience sampling studies, they can be used to administer questionnaires as well. Thus, a single device can be used both to sample and to measure participants' experiences.

A novel and promising approach to signaling involves interrupting individuals navigating the World Wide Web using pop-up windows. Sampling of this sort is accomplished using a Web-based computer application developed by Chen and Nilan (1998) called "Auto Ask." Their software has all of the capabilities of software typically used for experience sampling on handheld computers, although its use is restricted to the sampling of experiences while participants are on-line. Despite the limited circumstances under which Auto Ask could be used, it is appealing because no other experience sampling procedure is well suited to the Web environment, wherein many individuals spend a significant portion of their time.

Apart from the particular mechanism used to signal participants are decisions regarding the specific schedule by which they will be signaled. These decisions fall into three categories: (1) during what hours will experience be sampled; (2) how many times during those hours will experience be sampled; and (3) are there other constraints that should be imposed on the sampling. We discuss these decisions with respect to the three primary approaches to sampling in experience sampling research.

The Daily Diary

The most straightforward application of experience sampling is the daily diary. In much the same way that an individual might settle in at the end of the day and write about his or her experiences in a personal diary, the **daily diary** approach to experience sampling uses end-of-day reporting to gather summary information about participants' experiences over the course of the day. For instance, at the end of each day Gable, Reis, and Elliot (2000) asked participants to state the occurrence of 22 events over the course of each day of a seven-day study. Often, participants are asked to seal or deliver each evening's responses to the researchers in order to prevent day-to-day comparisons (e.g., Mohr et al., 2001). The decision making with regard to sampling using the daily diary is minimal. By definition the samples are drawn once per day just before participants retire for the day. Although this highly purposive approach to sampling lacks the appealing quality of many experience sampling studies, in which information is obtained about events and experiences as they occur, it works well for studies that are concerned with the cumulative influence of events that transpire over the course of a day.

Sampling at Random

When researchers are interested in an accurate estimate of the quality or quantity of particular experiences or events participants experience, the standard procedure is to sample experience on random occasions throughout the day for a number of days.

Recall the example we described earlier comparing the incidence of thoughts and hallucinations during waking and sleeping hours (Fosse et al., 2001). The procedures for this sort of experience sampling were pioneered by Csikszentmihalyi and colleagues (e.g., Csikszentmihalyi et al., 1977) in the context of their research program on the experience of flow. This is a powerful approach to describing people's subjective experience because participants cannot anticipate when they will be signaled to describe their experience. As such, the signal to provide information should catch them thinking, feeling, and acting naturally.

The power of this approach to sampling comes at a cost. First, it requires a signaling device. As noted earlier in this section, these devices typically are electronic and can be costly. Second, signaling by these devices is not completely reliable. Unreliability might stem from a malfunctioning of the equipment itself (e.g., battery failure) or a failure on the part of the research participants to keep the device with them at all times. A second set of costs concerns the decisions that must be made regarding the random schedule itself. The researcher must reach a decision regarding all three scheduling concerns raised earlier. The first of these concerns the hours during which experience will be sampled. Although the innovative work by Fosse et al. (2001) sampled thoughts around the clock, most applications of experience sampling sample experience during waking hours (i.e., the researchers are interested in conscious experience). What constitutes waking hours for a particular population is not always clear. For instance, Carstensen et al. (2001), in their study of age differences in emotional experience, determined that the 12 hours from 9 A.M. to 9 P.M. would serve as the "population" of experience from which they would sample. If, for instance, the population is college students, then the period of sampling is not so easily defined because many of the most interesting aspects of their social lives take place after midnight, and the beginning and end of their waking hours can vary dramatically from one day to the next.

Once a time frame has been defined, the researcher must decide how many times to sample from experience. Carstensen et al. (2001) sampled five times during the 12-hour period each day when participants could be signaled. Conti (2001) sampled eight times each day for five days. If experience is sampled much more frequently than this, participants are likely to feel as if their normal experience has been altered by their participation in the research. Indeed, they might become frustrated and refuse to provide information every time they are signaled. Yet, there is a trade-off that must be weighed between the potential problem of overburdening participants and obtaining a large enough sample in order to adequately represent experience. If the researcher's goals are particularistic in nature, then external validity—that is, the degree to which the findings based on the sampled experiences generalize to all experiences for each participant—is a key concern. Although the randomness of the signal ensures no bias in the particular experiences that are sampled, if the number of experiences sampled is too small, there is no guarantee that inferences drawn from the sampled experiences will apply to the population of experiences. Moreover, if the experience or perception of interest is relatively rare, the researcher who does not sample experience frequently enough is likely to miss the very experiences in which he or she is interested. Indeed, there are situations in which random sampling is abandoned altogether in favor of the purposive sampling strategy described in the next section.

Beyond the question of when during the day to sample and how often to sample, the practicalities of experience sampling research often require the researcher to place additional constraints on the sampling schedule. For instance, if the signaling device determines the random schedule on the fly for each participant (as opposed to the researcher programming it into the device in advance), there is no guarantee that two or more signals will not occur only minutes apart. This is due to the fact that, if the sampling of time is truly a random process, the likelihood of every moment being chosen during the period of sampling is equal. Thus, if a participant is signaled at 9:05 A.M., if a truly random process is followed, he or she is just as likely to be signaled again at 9:06 A.M. as at 12 noon, 5:30 P.M., or any other time during the period of sampling. Moreover, it is possible that all signals could occur during the morning, afternoon, or evening. Neither of these scenarios is acceptable in experience sampling research; hence, researchers often place constraints on the sampling plan. For instance, using the logic of stratified random sampling discussed in Chapter 9, the researcher might stratify the day into two-hour blocks and program the device to sample only once within each block (e.g., Carstensen et al., 2001). Because this strategy does not guarantee that two signals will come within a few minutes of each other, the researcher might also specify that signals cannot occur within 30 minutes of each other. A strategy such as this ensures that participants are not annoyed at being asked to provide information two or more times within a short period of time. It also ensures that experiences are sampled over the course of the entire day.

Another constraint that might be placed on the random sampling schedule concerns periods of time when it might not be possible for respondents to provide information. For instance, a college student participant signaled during a final examination would not be expected to stop working on the exam and answer a series of research questions. To avoid such problems, researchers often provide participants with a list of circumstances under which they should feel free to disable or ignore the signaling device. Although this constraint compromises the randomness of the sampling schedule, it is a constraint that researchers often need to impose in order to make the experience tolerable for participants.

Event-Contingent Sampling

An alternative approach to sampling experience is to ask the participants to determine when they are to report on their experience (i.e., they are not signaled on a schedule determined by the researcher). This approach to experience sampling is particularly useful when the research question concerns people's reactions to specific aspects of their experience. Recall, for instance, the research described earlier by Mohr et al. (2001) on the conditions under which people drink alone or with other people. Rather than signal participants to provide information, the researchers described to participants the specific event of interest (a drinking episode) and instructed them to provide information when the event occurred in the course of their normal activity. In applications of experience sampling such as this, the term "event" refers to the aspect of experience of interest to the researcher, and, as noted, measures are completed only when the participant experiences the event. Hence, the sampling is **event contingent.**

A key concern in event-contingent sampling is the definition of "event." In everyday use, the term can be used to describe occurrences as different as a party and a soccer match. Of course, such vagueness is not permissible in scientific research. As such, researchers who sample experience using the event-contingent approach must clearly define, both for themselves and research participants, the event or events about which information is to be provided. In the generic sense, an **event** in event-contingent experience sampling research is any aspect of people's experience about which they are aware. Awareness is a key feature of this definition, for participants are in control of information gathering, and the provision of information about a particular experience will be reliable only to the extent that participants can recognize its occurrence. An event in the experience sampling sense might further be defined according to whether it is internal or external to the individual. **Internal events** are thoughts, feelings, and behaviors of the participant. **External events** are situations or stimuli that the participant might encounter during the course of everyday life. An internal event of interest to social scientists might be any occasion on which a participant in a long-distance relationship thinks about his or her romantic partner. The study of drinking by Mohr et al. (2001) is an example of an event-contingent experience sampling study focused on an external event.

The scheduling decisions that attend event-contingent sampling are not complex. As with random sampling of experience, the researcher must define the period of time during which participants are to provide information should the focal event take place. Because the participant is charged with detecting events, it is reasonable to simply ask participants to provide information should events occur any time during their waking hours, without bracketing those hours in any way. With event-contingent sampling, the researcher does not control how many times experience is sampled each day. Because participants report about their experience any time the focal event occurs, there is no way to know how many reports participants will provide in a day, and the number of reports provided in a day will vary from one participant to the next. Because measurement is event rather than signal triggered, there is little need to consider practical constraints that might need to be placed on the sampling schedule. As with signaling, it might be necessary to provide participants with a list of situations in which the event might occur, but they would not be expected to provide information. Recall the example of a college student sitting for an examination. If our focus was intrusive thoughts about one's romantic partner in a long-distance relationship, we would not expect participants to provide information should such thoughts occur during an examination.

Duration of the Study

A concern regardless of whether experiences are sampled on a daily basis, at random, or in an event-contingent fashion is the number of days on which sampling should take place. The standard duration is seven days. The rationale behind this choice is that many experiences in which social scientists have an interest systematically vary in their occurrence over the course of a week. By sampling across all seven days of a week, researchers do not miss experiences that might take place on the weekend but not during the week. Yet, there are various reasons why this reasonable strategy might not always be the best.

A rather obvious reason to choose a duration shorter than seven days is that the research questions might focus on experiences that only take place on certain days of the week. For instance, perhaps the researcher is interested in workers' experiences while on the job. Many workers are on the job Monday through Friday but not Saturday and Sunday. Similarly, students typically do not take classes on the weekend; hence, research on their classroom experience would not necessitate sampling over the weekend (e.g., Conti, 2001).

More frequently, researchers make the decision to sample for more than seven days. Often, researchers choose to sample for 14 days (e.g., Wheeler & Nezlek, 1977; Wheeler, Reis, & Nezlek, 1983). In so doing, researchers increase the reliability of their sampling by lessening the likelihood that the validity of their findings is compromised because some participants provided information during an atypical week. The increase in days of sampling also is useful when the event of interest does not frequently occur for all participants. In such cases, additional days of sampling might be necessary in order to obtain a sufficiently large sample of events for all participants to be able to use the information they provide in hypothesis tests.

One of the more ambitious experience sampling studies in terms of duration was the 30-day study by Mohr et al. (2001) on conditions under which people drink. One might ask why experience sampling ordinarily is not undertaken for this length of time. To hearken back to our discussion of how many times per day to randomly signal participants, a key concern is creating an exercise that participants can tolerate and will take seriously from beginning to end. For high-frequency events, it is unlikely that participants could be asked to participate in an event-contingent experience sampling study for 30 days. Indeed, so intrusive would be such a study that it is not clear whether the sampled experiences would reflect normal, everyday experience at all. On the other hand, if the study makes use of the daily diary, then it would not be unreasonable to ask participants to provide information for a month or more. So, as with the decision about how many times to signal participants when using a random schedule, the decision about how many days an experience sampling study should last involves balancing trade-offs. In the end, the best decision is one that maximizes the amount of information obtained from participants without intruding in their everyday lives in such a way as to alter them.

Measurement Strategies and Procedures

Once the researcher has decided how participants will be signaled to provide information about their experience in an experience sampling study, he or she must decide what to measure and how to measure it. In this section of the chapter, we first outline the general issues involved with measurement in the context of experience sampling. Then we discuss the advantages and disadvantages of the two primary approaches to measurement in the experience sampling method: paper-and-pencil and computer-assisted.

General Issues

Regardless of how measurements are taken in an experience sampling study, the questionnaire itself must manifest two qualities: It must be brief, and it must reference the experience of the participant at that moment or within a narrow time frame. We discuss each of these in turn.

Brevity As noted in Chapter 6, it is not uncommon for a face-to-face interview to last for more than an hour. Some paper-and-pencil questionnaires might require 30 to 45 minutes of respondents' time. In experience sampling studies, questionnaires must be dramatically shorter. The reason for this is twofold. First and foremost, participants will be asked to complete the same questionnaire on numerous occasions—wherever they might be when signaled or when the event of interest occurs—and the activity of completing the questionnaire must itself not alter in any significant way the ongoing experience of the participant. Second, the questionnaires themselves must be carried on the participants' person throughout the duration of the study. As such, the forms must be small, preferably small enough to fit into a trouser pocket or a small purse. (Computer-assisted approaches, described later, are not limited in this way.)

Given this need for brevity, questionnaires used in experience sampling research rarely are of the multiple-item variety discussed in Chapter 7. Rather, researchers must select no more than two or three items to represent each construct that is implicated in the hypotheses the data will be used to test. This limitation is not an absolute, for it varies somewhat as a function of the sampling plan. For instance, Gable et al. (2000), who used a daily diary procedure, asked participants to select which of 22 events they had experienced over the course of the day, then rate their mood using 20 adjectives. Conti (2001), who signaled participants eight times per day, asked only eight questions about participants' experience of time. As these examples illustrate, the upper limit in questionnaire length for experience sampling studies is around 40 if the questions are simple and the sampling strategy is a daily diary. As the number of times sampled per day increases, the number of questions that participants can reasonably be expected to answer decreases.

Frame of Reference Questionnaires typical of social science research refer to respondents' "typical" behavior, or what they have done during the past 30 days, 6 months, or the course of their entire lifetime. In experience sampling research, the focus is on the experience of the moment or very recent past and, as such, measures must be constructed that help participants adopt the appropriate frame of reference.

To some extent, the appropriate frame of reference is created during an initial session at which participants are trained in the use of equipment and questionnaires and instructed as to how they are to complete measures when signaled. Even when training has been extensive, it pays to provide abundant cues designed to help respondents answer questions appropriately. For instance, including qualifiers such as "right now" and "at this moment" can keep respondents from expressing their general dispositions rather than their subjective experience at the time they were signaled or when the event of interest occurs.

When a questionnaire of appropriate length and frame of reference is developed, a decision must be made regarding how the questionnaire will be administered. The traditional approach is an adaptation of the paper-and-pencil survey, whereas newer approaches take advantage of the increasing capacity of handheld devices to convey and receive information. In the remainder of this section, we describe and illustrate the administration of questionnaires in experience sampling research using paper-and-pencil and computer-assisted approaches.

Paper-and-Pencil Approaches

When considering the use of paper-and-pencil questionnaires in experience sampling research, there are two primary concerns: (1) the physical properties of the questionnaire document and (2) the process by which completed copies of the questionnaire will be delivered to researchers. The first concern is rather straightforward—the questionnaire forms should be as small as possible, typically no larger than 1/4 of a sheet of 8 1/2″ × 11″ paper. Usually, the necessary number of forms (with a few extras in the event of mistakes) are stapled together into a small booklet. Ideally, this booklet could be slipped into a jacket or trouser pocket or a small purse. The key concern is that participants need to be able to keep the booklet with them at all times during the period when their experience is being sampled. For instance, Conti (2001) provided participants with a 5″ × 4 1/2″ booklet that included 40 copies of the questionnaire. Hoyle (1988) provided participants with a set of 5 1/2″ × 4 1/4″ questionnaire booklets, one for each day of the study. The latter example raises a minor issue because, unlike Conti's study, in which the sampling schedule ensured that participants would be sampled 40 times, the event-contingent approach used by Hoyle provided no information about the number of forms a given participant would need over the course of the seven-day study. To deal with this ambiguity, Hoyle provided ample copies of the questionnaire booklet for participants to complete the first two days of the study and requested that they report to a designated office after two days in order to receive the necessary forms to complete the study. This strategy provided a means of estimating and providing the number of booklets each respondent needed to complete the study as well as offered the opportunity for clarification regarding any problems the participants might have encountered.

An additional concern when the paper-and-pencil approach to measurement is used in experience sampling research is how completed questionnaires will be returned to the experimenter. It might appear as if the obvious answer to this question is that participants should simply drop them off where they received them when the sampling period has ended. Although this procedure might work for some experience sampling studies, it has drawbacks for others. For instance, in repeated measures studies, of which experience sampling is an extreme example, it is important that information provided by respondents at each measurement is without consideration of information provided at previous measurements. When respondents hold completed questionnaires until sampling is complete, they are free to look back through completed questionnaires and even alter their answers if they have concerns about how answers given "in the heat of the moment" might make them look. Alternatively, they might feel a need to think, feel, and behave in a consistent fashion throughout the course of the study, and this motivation might lead them to reference prior responses when contemplating their response at a particular occasion. Carstensen et al. (2000) avoided problems such as this by providing preaddressed, stamped envelopes in which participants returned completed questionnaires at the end of each day.

It also is important that researchers establish a means by which participants remain motivated and by which problems are detected and corrected early. One means of accomplishing this when the paper-and-pencil approach to measurement is used is by providing participants with only a portion of the forms they need to complete the study, thereby requiring that they interact with a member of the research team after having completed a portion of the study (e.g., Hoyle, 1998). The potential payoff of this strategy is twofold. First, it affords the opportunity to catch mistakes or problems and address them, rather than detecting them after the study is complete. Second, it offers the opportunity for members of the research team to motivate participants by encouraging them or perhaps offering rewards for providing complete and accurate records each time they return.

In short, the paper-and-pencil approach to experience sampling is widely and effectively used. The key concerns are that the questionnaires can be carried by participants at all times and that there is an appropriate way for participants to deliver completed copies of the questionnaire to the researcher, preferably at the end of each day or two of sampling. These and other concerns associated with the use of paper-and-pencil questionnaires in experience sampling research are minimized or eliminated when the questionnaire is delivered and responses obtained by computer, an approach to which we now turn.

Computer-Assisted Approaches

Experience sampling studies were the first in the social sciences to make routine use of electronic devices, virtually always devices whose primary purpose was some activity other than research. Pagers, wristwatches, planners, and handheld computers, all initially designed to increase the efficiency of people at work and in school, have become the "tools of the trade" for experience sampling researchers. Earlier in this chapter, we discussed the use of such devices for sampling. Here, we focus on the use of electronic devices to administer questionnaires and process responses to them. After an overview of computer-assisted approaches, we illustrate an approach that uses handheld computers equipped with software specifically designed for experience sampling research.

The most rudimentary form of computer-assisted information acquisition in experience sampling studies is the use of desktop or notebook computers in daily diary studies. Recall that daily diary studies typically require participants to provide information only once per day, usually at the end of the day. Moreover, the information concerns their experience over the course of the day rather than their experience at the time they complete the measures. This situation lends itself to the use of computers that could not be carried around by the participant when experience is sampled randomly or in an event-contingent fashion. An example of this approach is the study by Gable et al. (2000) of the effects of daily experience on emotions. Participants were given a diskette that could be read using any PC-based computer. On the diskette was an executable file that administered the questionnaire when opened and recorded participants' responses. A key feature of this strategy was that the information, once keyed into the computer, could not be retrieved by participants. This feature ensured that, even though diskettes were not returned until the end of the seven-day sampling period, participants could not review or change earlier responses. Implementation of this strategy requires only that participants have access to a PC-based computer. Although it is not wise to assume such access with all populations, the study by Gable et al. involved college students, who either owned a computer or had ready access on campus.

For gathering data in their event-contingent sampling of adult drinking behavior, Mohr et al. (2001) used a small, programmable handheld computer. A significant advantage of handheld computers for experience sampling research is the ability to both signal and measure using the same device. Indeed, the signaling needs of Mohr et al. were such that standard approaches to signaling would have been difficult to use. Recall that, after participants prompted the computer that they were beginning a drinking episode, they were signaled once an hour thereafter to record what they had consumed. An additional benefit of using the handheld computer for such studies is that it can be programmed to record the time and date when each questionnaire is completed. For event-contingent studies, this capability is important because it relieves the participant of the necessity to provide such information while ensuring that the information is accurate. For studies that use a random signaling approach, the time-date stamp is useful because it allows the researcher to determine with precision how much time passed between the time participants were signaled and the time they provided information. Yet another benefit of the handheld computer approach to measurement is that information can be transferred with relative ease from most handheld computers to the desktop or notebook computers on which statistical analyses will be done. Thus, researchers avoid completely the onerous task of keying by hand information on what can be very large numbers of experiences.

To provide readers with a sense of what participants experience when using a handheld computer to answer questions in an experience sampling study, we now provide a concrete example. Our example is based on the use of a handheld computer (e.g., Palm Pilot, Handspring) that has been loaded with the Experience Sampling

Program (ESP). ESP is freely available for use and alteration (i.e., open source) by download from the Web (the address is provided at the end of the chapter). Although all handheld computers are, in principal, programmable, the virtue of a handheld equipped with ESP is that very little programming is required; the software was designed for experience sampling research. Moreover, the interface is intuitive and unintimidating for participants.

Suppose, for example, we had designed an experience sampling study that involved signaling at random and measurement using a handheld computer loaded with ESP. Here is what the research participant would see. (Images were downloaded from http://www2.bc.edu/~barretli/esp/palm/man-subject.html and are reproduced here with the permission of the authors.)

When the computer is on but the participant has not been called on to provide information, the screen looks like this:

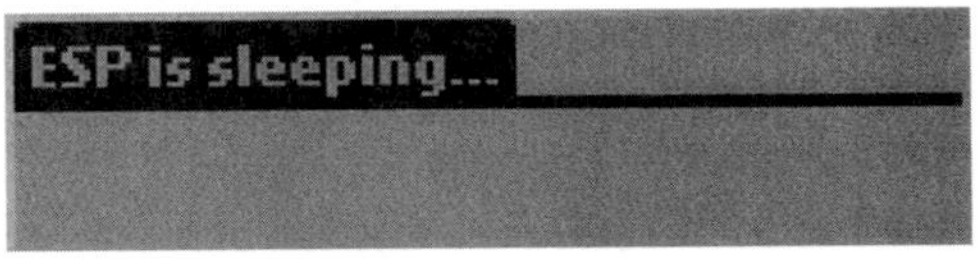

When the participant is signaled, he or she is prompted to begin responding to the questionnaire. (This is the resting screen for event-contingent studies.)

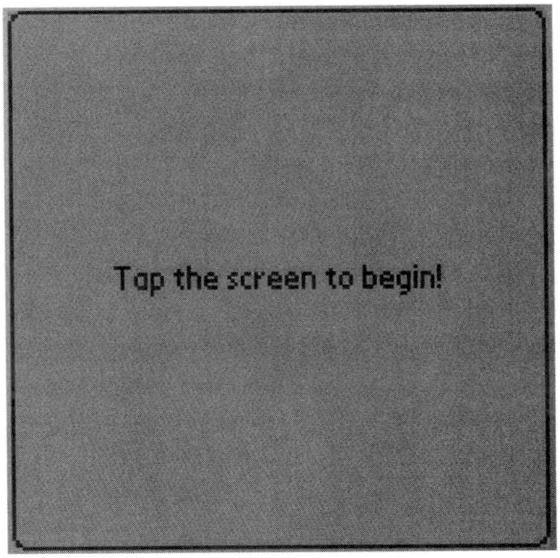

Once the participant indicates that he or she is ready to begin, the first question appears on the screen.

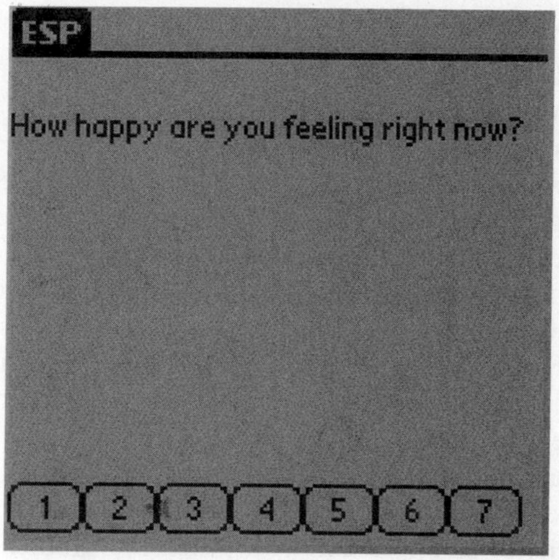

After the participant responds to all questions in the set, the handheld once again displays the "ESP is sleeping" screen. After the participant has been signaled and answers the questions for the final time, this screen appears:

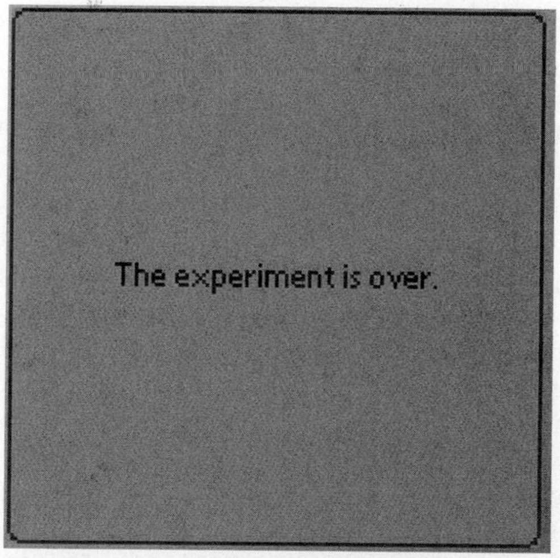

Although the equipment is expensive and somewhat fragile, relatively few problems arise in uses of the software or hardware involved in this implementation (Feldman Barrett & Barrett, 2001) And, as noted earlier, the ability to signal and measure with a single device is a major asset for studies that use a random signaling approach.

Other Approaches

Although the overwhelming majority of experience sampling studies use either paper-and-pencil or computer-assisted approaches to measurement, there are scattered instances of other approaches. For instance, in the study of thoughts and hallucinations during sleep and waking hours by Fosse et al. (2001), when participants were paged, they dictated their responses to open-ended questions. These responses were then transcribed and coded by trained judges. Although Conti (2001) primarily relied on the paper-and-pencil approach in her study of the subjective experience of time, she provided participants with a microcassette recorder by which they could indicate responses in the event they were driving when signaled. Although this approach is not widely used, it seems particularly appropriate when, as in the study by Fosse et al., the questions are open-ended.

As computing and communication become increasingly wireless, it seems likely that experience sampling researchers will seize on this technology in order to increase the efficiency and precision with which they gather data (Feldman Barrett & Barrett, 2001). As of this writing there are no examples to report; however, devices that integrate the computing power of handheld units with the communication power of mobile telephones are becoming more reliable and affordable. Given the experience sampling researchers' affinity for technology, we expect to see examples of wireless experience sampling research soon.

Summary

In the same way that people are sampled from populations, experiences can be sampled from the stream of people's lives. These experiences can be sampled in a variety of ways. People can be randomly signaled by an electronic device and asked to report about their experience at that moment. Alternatively, people can be instructed to attend to particular events in their lives and report about their experience when those events occur. Or people can be instructed to end each day during the period of a study by reporting on their experiences over the course of the day. These reports can be obtained either through the use of brief paper-and-pencil questionnaires or handheld computers. However implemented, the experience sampling method yields rich and detailed information about people's subjective experiences in the course of their everyday lives.

Key Concepts

daily diary
event
event contingent
experience sampling method
external events
internal events
signaling

On the Web

http://www2.bc.edu/~barretli/esp/ Information and download page for The Experience Sampling Program, software for conducting experience sampling studies using handheld computers such as Palm Pilot.

http://www.apa.org/psa/sepoct97/reis.html Read more about experience sampling in the on-line article, "Everyday Experience Matters," by Harry Reis, an authority in the use of experience sampling methods.

Further Reading

Hormuth, S. E. (1986). The sampling of experiences in situ. *Journal of Personality, 54*, 262–293.
Reis, H. T., & Gable, S. L. (2000). Event sampling and other methods for studying daily experience. In H. T. Reis & C. M. Judd (Eds.), *Handbook of research methods in social and personality psychology* (pp. 190–222). New York: Cambridge University Press.
Wheeler, L., & Reis, H. T. (1991). Self-recording of everyday life events: Origins, types, and uses. *Journal of Personality, 59*, 339–354.

PART

IV

Social Research Strategies

CHAPTER

11

Randomized Experiments

All research in the social sciences uses the logical principles of design outlined in earlier chapters to increase the validity of the research conclusions; however, this common logical framework is expressed in a great diversity of ways: Studies of different types, conducted in different settings, generally look very different. This chapter and the next five outline the issues that arise in the conduct of research of specific types: laboratory investigations, surveys, questionnaire and interview studies, and research in natural settings.

Recall from Chapter 2 that the research design of a study has a substantial effect on the study's internal validity, that is, the ability to reach causal conclusions about the impact of one construct on another. Of course, research designs differ in many other ways as well. Some are more efficient than others, some make fewer demands on the researcher or on the participant populations, and some take more time to implement. From the point of view of the research validities we are considering, however, the major distinction among designs is how effectively they rule out threats to internal validity. In this chapter, we consider the strongest sort of designs from this point of view, those that are known as randomized experiments.

Randomized experiments are highly specialized tools, and like any tool they are excellent for some jobs and poor for others. They are ideally suited for the task of causal analysis. No other method of scientific inquiry permits us to say with as much confidence as an experimenter, "This caused that to occur." In reading scientific reports, we find many guarded, qualified, and indirect causal statements such as "X seems to be a factor in determining Y" or "It would appear that there is an association between X and Y." The conclusions sound indirect and the words carefully chosen because the writers cannot make definitive causal assertions. They cannot make bold causal statements if they have not conducted randomized experiments.

Randomized experiments are used heavily in the social sciences for good reasons. Yet they have their weaknesses. In this chapter, we point out their strengths and their weaknesses and show how they differ from other research designs. The chief strength of randomized experiments is their internal validity, which is accomplished through the researcher's assumption of control over the independent variables in the design. That is, to use a randomized experiment, the researcher must be in a position to decide which participants are assigned to which level of the putative cause. Frequently, this sort of control, although maximizing internal validity, can compromise construct and external validity. The sort of control that is necessary for a randomized experiment is perhaps most easily achieved in laboratory settings. Such settings, discussed at length in Chapter 12, typically differ from real-life, everyday settings in a variety of ways that limit the researcher's ability to generalize his or her results to other settings. Accordingly, external validity can be compromised. To see this more clearly, let us examine what sort of control a randomized experiment requires.

Controlling and Manipulating Variables

All research requires the manipulation or measurement of variables. As defined in earlier chapters, variables represent the constructs that the researcher is interested in theoretically. They represent the things that he or she wants to study and draw conclusions about. For instance, if we want to study people's political behavior and understand why they vote as they do, their votes are a variable we must measure. Variables, as the name suggests, must vary and have at least two values. Therefore, to understand people's party preference, we must study people who vote for at least two different candidates or parties. If everyone in the study said he or she would vote for the Republican presidential candidate, vote or preference would no longer be a variable; it would be a constant.

For most research, we have not just one but at least two variables, and we look at the association between them. One of these is usually called the independent variable and one the dependent variable. The **independent variable** is the variable we believe to have a causal influence on our outcome variables. The **dependent variable** is the outcome variable; its values *depend* on the independent variables. In most cases, whether something is considered an independent or dependent variable depends on the research questions being asked. For example, if we wanted to demonstrate that teachers who hold high expectations for their students treat those students with greater nonverbal warmth, expectations would be the independent variable and teacher warmth would be the dependent variable. But if our research looked instead at the influence of teacher nonverbal warmth on students' subsequent achievement, teacher warmth would be the independent variable and student achievement would be the dependent variable.

Going back to our example of a voting behavior study, if we were interested in examining the effect of religious preference on voting, religion would be considered the independent variable and voting preference the dependent variable. Clearly there are many variables besides religion that also influence how a person will vote. A person's education, parents' party preference, income, and attitudes about specific issues such as abortion or gun control also determine how that person will vote. If we wanted to be able to predict people's votes, we would try to include as many of these variables as possible in our research. If, on the other hand, we wanted to understand the influence of a single variable, to see whether it exerts a causal effect on voting, we would try to control all the other variables. Isolating and controlling independent variables is the strategy followed in experimental research.

Experimenters ask such questions as "What is the effect of exposure to televised appearances by candidates on people's votes for candidates?" Notice that the question refers to a variable the experimenter can possibly control—televised appearances. Experimenters study variables that either they or someone else can manipulate, such as the timing or content or amount of televised political advertisements. Thus, they can decide who sees which particular television advertisement; that is, they can control its delivery to certain individuals and not to others. Variables that can be so controlled are called experimental independent variables. Other sorts of independent variables, such as religion, income, education, and parents' party preference, are all variables that people bring with them to a study and are virtually impossible to manipulate. These sorts of independent variables are called **individual difference variables.** They are properties that people already possess. In contrast, **experimental variables** are properties an experimenter can manipulate or expose people to. This is a major difference between experimental and nonexperimental or quasi-experimental research. Experimenters can control the variables whose effects they wish to study, or they can control who is exposed to those variables.

Why is it necessary to isolate and control or manipulate the independent variable to conduct a randomized experiment and to maximize internal validity? To answer this question, consider again the study of the influence of television advertising on voting behavior. Assume we were not interested in the effects of education, religion, and parents' party preferences, or any other independent variables on voters' choices. All we wanted to know was whether seeing a particular television advertisement influenced those choices. Now suppose we did not actually manipulate who watched the television advertisement and who did not. Suppose, rather, that we simply found some individuals who saw the advertisement and some who did not, and we asked them about their preferred candidate. But if we found a difference in candidate preferences between those who saw the advertisement and those who did not, we could never be sure that this difference was really due to having watched the advertisement or not. Instead, it might be due to a host of other individual difference variables on which the two groups happen to differ. For instance, those who saw the advertisement might tend to watch more television in general than those who did not, and because television watching might be related to education, the two groups might also reasonably differ in average levels of education. Thus, the candidate preference difference that we document between the two groups might be due to the educational difference between them.

Once we realized this problem, we might decide to redesign our research a little so that we looked at two groups of individuals, some who saw the advertisement and some who did not. This time, we would select individuals who all had the same education level and watched on average the same amount of television. That is, we would try to equate the two groups on these individual difference variables or control these variables by holding them constant.

This approach to controlling other variables is like that frequently used in the physical sciences. If we try to study the effects of some varieties of plant food on the growth of plants, we might select a field of white pine seedlings in a particular field in Maine and feed four varieties of plant food to trees in the four quadrants of the field. This would hold constant the soil type (assuming the field has the same soil type in its four quadrants), the climate, the plant variety, and the season. We know that all these variables affect how fast plants grow, but we would have controlled them in our study by limiting the experiment to one soil type, climate, plant, and season. This is an appropriate way to study the effectiveness of the four varieties of plant food because it seems reasonable that the only difference between plants in the four quadrants is the type of food they received.

In the social sciences, however, this way of controlling for other variables, by holding them constant, is never sufficient to be assured of internal validity. Consider again our efforts to determine whether watching the political advertisement influences voter choice. Even if we controlled education and television watching, there might be many other individual difference variables that influence candidate preference and that differ between the two groups. For instance, the two groups might also differ in how late they stayed up at night, in how many children they had, in their age, or in what they preferred to eat for breakfast. Any one of these other variables might be responsible for the difference between the two groups in candidate preference rather than whether or not the advertisement was seen. In other words, any preexisting difference between groups could serve as a plausible **alternative explanation** for our conclusion that exposure to advertisements affects voting behavior. Some alternative explanations are more plausible than others (it would be difficult to think of a reason why breakfast preference would determine voting behavior, for example), but the existence of *any* systematic difference between groups other than the experimental variables threatens our internal validity.

Even if we did our research in such a way that the four particular individual difference variables were controlled or equivalent in the two groups, there is a nearly infinite number of other individual difference variables that remain uncontrolled and that might influence candidate preference. This is in contrast to the plant food example, in which there is only a limited number of variables (such as climate, soil type, season, and plant variety) that influence plant growth, and these can easily be controlled or held constant by using different plant foods in the four quadrants of the same field. In contrast, there is an unknown, but surely large, number of variables that might be responsible for voting choices, and it is simply not possible to design our research to control for them all simultaneously.

Thus, in social science research one can never maximize internal validity or reach unassailable causal conclusions about the effect of an independent variable simply by making sure that the individuals in the research do not differ on a limited number of other potentially confounding variables. There are simply too many other variables that would need to be controlled.

The solution to this dilemma is to conduct a **randomized experiment,** and the defining condition for such a research design is that individuals are randomly assigned to the various levels of the independent variable. In our study of the effects of televised advertisements on political preference, we would randomly determine for each individual whether he or she did or did not watch advertisements featuring the political candidates. Obviously, to conduct this sort of randomized experiment, we must be the ones to decide who watches the advertisements and who does not. The researcher must be able to manipulate the independent variable.

Random Assignment

Random assignment is the only way to equate two or more groups on all possible individual difference variables at the start of the research. This step is essential for drawing causal inferences about the effects of an experimental independent variable because the experimenter must be reasonably confident that the differences that appear at the end of the experiment between two treatment groups are the result of the treatments and not of some preexisting differences between the groups.

Random assignment (also called randomization) is not the same as random sampling, which we covered in detail in Chapter 9. **Random assignment** is a procedure we use after we have a sample of participants and before we expose them to a treatment. It is a way of assigning participants to the levels of the independent variable so that the groups do not differ as the study begins. It is a "fair" procedure, whereby all participants have an equal chance of being assigned to the various experimental conditions. The randomization procedure must be truly random; dividing participants on the basis of their arrival to the laboratory or alphabetically does not ensure equal probabilities of assignment to condition and could introduce systematic biases in the data. For example, there are probably important personality differences associated with early versus late arrival to the laboratory, and thus we would not want our experimental groups to differ on those traits. The mechanics of randomization are discussed in greater detail in Chapter 12; for now it is important only to note that random assignment requires a truly random process of the sort reflected in random numbers tables and computerized random number generators.

Random sampling, on the other hand, is the procedure we use to select in the first place the participants we will study. Random sampling serves not to equate two or more experimental groups but to make sure the participant group we study is representative of a larger population. It is also a "fair" procedure, whereby all participants in a given population (e.g., the population of people over 21 living in North America) have an equal chance of being included in the study. As discussed in Chapter 9, random sampling allows us to say that what we have found to be true for a particular sample is true of people in the larger population from which it was drawn. It maximizes the external validity of research. Random assignment, on the other hand, enables us to say, "X caused Y" with some degree of certainty. It maximizes the internal validity of research. We do not discuss random sampling further in this chapter; we introduced it here only to distinguish it from random assignment, and it is the latter that defines randomized experiments.

To appreciate what random assignment accomplishes and why, consider a new example. Say we are hired by a distance learning company to determine whether students learn more about research methods through a traditional lecture format or through an interactive Web-based format. The company draws a random sample of undergraduate students from across the country, brings them together, and pays them to take part in our study. We therefore do not have to worry about the representativeness or cooperation of the students. Our only concern is to determine whether students learn more from traditional lectures or the Web-based format. The best way to design this experiment is to assign students randomly to one of two conditions: group L, which will take the traditional lecture-based course, and group W, which will take the Web-based version of the course. We measure how much they have learned by giving them all the same examination at the end of the semester. Assume for the sake of this example that the Web and lecture versions of the course cover exactly the same material and that the final examination is an accurate and fair measure of how much people know about research methods.

If our sample were large enough or if we did the study repeatedly, we could be confident, because of random assignment, that the two groups of students—those attending lectures and those doing the Web course—were equivalent in all possible ways. To appreciate this statement, suppose we randomly assigned the students by flipping a coin. About half of the students would get "heads" and about half would get "tails." With a large enough sample, would we expect all the students with light hair to be in one group and all the students with darker hair in the other? Of course not. Chances are that there would be a mixture of dark- and light-haired students in both groups. Would we expect all the men to get "tails" and all the women to get "heads"? Of course not. On average, the two groups would include both women and men. In fact, on average, the two groups through random assignment would be equivalent in *all* possible ways. We would not expect them to differ on any individual difference variables. Thus, random assignment and randomized experimental research designs control for all possible individual difference variables that could interfere with our ability to reach causal conclusions about the effect of the independent variable.

Of course, if we had only two students in the study, one male and one female, and we used random assignment, it would certainly be the case that in spite of random assignment, the student attending the traditional lecture course would be of a different gender than the student taking the Web course. But if we were to do this study over and over again (randomly assigning the two students each time), across the studies, gender would not be confounded with the independent variable. Thus, in explaining why random assignment allows us to reach causal conclusions about the effect of the independent variable, we have been very careful to say that it works *on average*, given a large enough sample or given a sufficient number of times that a given study is conducted. In any one study, with a limited sample size, there can be differences between the experimental groups by simple chance. But on average, if we did the study over and over again, all such differences would disappear. Thus, random assignment works only on average. Nevertheless, it is certainly the only procedure that will work on average to ensure internal validity.

Because random assignment works on average, it is important for researchers to be cognizant of the possibility of **failures of randomization.** In other words, for any given study, it is possible that particular kinds of participants will not be evenly distributed across experimental conditions (e.g., all the African-American participants might end up in one condition, or there might be disproportionately more women in one group and men in another). Failure of randomization is a problem for researchers because it means that even though randomization procedures were followed, the groups were not equivalent at the beginning of the study and therefore the internal validity of the study is potentially compromised. Thus, it is often a wise idea for researchers to measure important individual difference variables or administer pretests for important dependent measures. Analyses conducted comparing experimental groups on these individual difference and pretest variables should ideally reveal no differences between experimental conditions. If the analyses show that there was a failure of randomization, the researcher is in a difficult position. It would not be acceptable to shuffle the experimental assignment of some of the participants until the groups "looked" equivalent, as that undermines the whole point of randomization. Replicating the study with a larger sample is often the only satisfactory solution to a failure of randomization. Failures of randomization are significantly more likely to occur with small samples, making a powerful argument for designing one's research with a large sample to begin with.

Independent Variables that Vary Within and Between Participants

In the research examples presented so far in this chapter, the independent variable has varied between research participants. That is, some individuals were exposed to the political advertisements and some were not; some students went to lectures and some took the course on the Web. There are many independent variables, however, that can be manipulated *within* participants, and a more efficient research design might well result.

Consider a new example: We want to examine whether incidental noise induces stress in the workplace. We design a study in which we vary the noise level in the workplace and then measure employees' stress levels. Again, we assume that the sample has been chosen to maximize external validity and that the stress measure has very high reliability and construct validity. We now face the choice of how to manipulate the independent variable. Two options present themselves. Most obviously, we can assign some employees to the incidental noise condition and some other employees to the condition without incidental noise. With a total of 30 employees at our disposal in this study, we would then have data from 15 participants in each of the two conditions of the study.

But there is a second option for manipulating the independent variable. We might decide that we want to measure the stress levels of all 30 participants in both conditions, once while working with incidental noise and once while working without such noise. For instance, on one day a given participant might work with the incidental noise and on the next without it. We would then measure the stress level of the participant twice, at the end of each of the two days. In this case, the independent variable varies within participants rather than between them. Rather than some participants being in one condition and some in the other, all participants are in both conditions. This is called a within-participants or **repeated measures design.**

We introduce this distinction between independent variables that vary within participants and those that vary between participants because it helps to clarify the list of threats to internal validity that we consider in the next section of the chapter. At this point, it is only necessary to understand the distinction and also what random assignment means in the two cases. Remember that random assignment is used in order to be confident that the two sets of observations, those gathered under incidental noise and those gathered without it, are identical, on average, on all other variables. When the independent variable varies between participants, random assignment is accomplished by randomly assigning participants to one condition or the other. By so doing, the participants in the two conditions will not, on average, differ on any variables that are not part of the experimental procedure.

When the independent variable varies within participants, random assignment means that we randomly determine the order in which any given participant is exposed to the two levels of the independent variable. Suppose we did not do this. Instead, all 30 employees first worked with the incidental noise for a day and then they worked without it for a day. At the end of each of the two days, we measured all employees' stress levels. Now it might just happen that the temperature was warmer on the second day than the first, that rumors of impending layoffs circulated on the second day, or that the employees' lunch was more appetizing on one day than the other. All of these other things might influence the employees' stress levels in addition to the presence or absence of incidental noise. If we then found a difference in stress levels between the two days, we could not be sure that it was in fact due to the difference in levels of incidental noise between the two days. A host of other differences exists between the two days that might plausibly be responsible for differences in stress levels.

It is simple to overcome this problem. What we do is randomly assign half of the employees to spend the first day under incidental noise and the second day without it; the other half spends the first day without it and the second day with it. In this way, the measures of stress following incidental noise come equally from both days, as do the measures of stress following no noise. Thus, differences in weather or rumors or menus cannot account for the stress differences between the two levels of the independent variable. This practice of varying the order of experimental conditions across participants in a repeated measures design is called **counterbalancing.** Counterbalancing is important not only because it helps to assure internal validity but also because it controls for possible contamination or carryover effects between experimental conditions, for example, the possibility that the incidental noise creates so much stress in the employees that they are still stressed the next day even though there is no noise present.

To recap how random assignment differs for the two types of designs, when the independent variable varies between participants, we randomly assign each participant to one condition or the other. When the independent variable varies within participants, each participant is measured under each condition, and we must then randomly assign participants to experience or be exposed to the various conditions in different orders. Later we consider some of the advantages and disadvantages of using designs in which the independent variable varies within rather than between participants.

Threats to Internal Validity

Making causal inferences is what doctors do when they try to diagnose the cause of a patient's pain or what detectives do when they attempt to identify the cause of a crime. The researcher, doctor, and detective must each rule out a list of alternative explanations to arrive at the most probable cause. The alternative explanations are threats to the internal validity of the research proposition. The strength of randomized experiments is that through randomization these threats are, on average, eliminated. If we use a research design other than a randomized experiment, these threats make causal inference very difficult indeed. Six such threats to internal validity are defined in this section. Other threats exist as well; fuller discussions of them can be found in the classic primer on research design by Campbell and Stanley (1966) as well as more recent works by Shadish, Cook, and Campbell (2001) and Judd and Kenny (1981).

Selection

Selection refers to any preexisting differences between individuals in the different experimental conditions that can influence the dependent variable. As should be clear from our earlier discussion, selection is always a threat to validity any time participants are not randomly assigned to a condition. An extreme example makes it obvious why selection poses such a serious threat to internal validity: Pretend a researcher is interested in testing the hypothesis that bungee jumping has mental health benefits. The researcher explains the study to a group of prospective participants, and all those who want to try bungee jumping are placed in the experimental group, whereas the participants who decide they would rather not bungee-jump are placed in the control group. Of course, no experienced researcher would design a study in this manner. Clearly, the two groups differ in many important ways, including risk-taking tendencies and attitudes toward bungee jumping. It would be impossible to determine at the conclusion of the study whether any differences between the two groups were caused by the bungee jumping itself or these preexisting differences.

The threat posed by selection is obvious in cases like these in which participants *self-select* into experimental conditions. Less obvious, but just as much of a threat, are cases in which participants do not self-select, but rather preexisting groups are used that could differ on any number of characteristics. For example, a researcher might wish to test a new method of increasing sales productivity. The method might be used in one car dealership and monthly sales compared to those of a neighboring dealership using traditional sales techniques. The inferential difficulty is that the sales personnel at the two dealerships might differ in many respects that affect their productivity above and beyond the effects due to the experimental sales techniques.

In short, unless participants have been randomly assigned to an experimental condition, selection is always a threat, and in most cases no causal inferences about the independent variable can be drawn.

Maturation

Maturation involves any naturally occurring process within persons that could cause a change in their behavior. Examples include fatigue, boredom, growth, or intellectual development. A rather obvious example of the threat to internal validity caused by maturation would be a study testing the effects of intensive speech therapy on two-year-old children over a six-month period. At the conclusion of the study, the children are pronouncing words significantly more clearly than at the beginning. Of course, children of that age are experiencing rapid improvement in their speech as a natural function of language development, and they might have improved just as much without the speech therapy. Fortunately, such biases caused by maturation can be easily cured by including a control group (i.e., children who do not receive intensive therapy) in the design of a study. Normal developmental changes should affect participants in both the experimental and control groups to the same degree.

In addition to developmental changes that occur in individuals over extended periods of time, maturation also refers to short-term changes that can occur within an experimental session. If a participant is performing a reaction time task, for instance, in which he or she is instructed to attend to a complicated visual pattern and press a button whenever a certain stimulus shape appears, the participant is likely to become fatigued or bored after doing the task for 30 or 40 minutes. Reaction latencies probably will increase and more errors will be committed. This could pose an inferential problem if all of the experimental trials are located in the beginning or end of the session. This type of maturational bias, too, has a simple cure: Make sure to present stimuli in a counterbalanced order so that all types of stimuli are evenly distributed across the experimental session.

History

History refers to any event that coincides with the independent variable and could affect the dependent variable. It could be a major historical event that occurs in the political, economic, or cultural lives of the people we are studying, or it could be a minor event that occurs during the course of an experimental session—such as a disruption in the procedures because of equipment failure, a fire alarm going off, a participant in a group session laughing inappropriately while a stimulus videotape is being shown, or an interruption from any unwanted source. In short, history is anything that happens during the course of the study that is unrelated to the independent variable yet affects the dependent variable.

For example, imagine a researcher is conducting a study of attitudes toward the death penalty. If a well-publicized execution takes place during data collection, that could affect participants' attitudes in ways unintended by the researcher. History threatens both the internal and external validity of this study. The threat to internal validity caused by such events can be remedied by including a control group, as participants in both conditions should be aware of and affected by the execution to the same extent, so we can infer that any additional differences between the groups were caused by the independent variable. The threat to external validity, however, is not so easily removed. There is no way of knowing whether participants would have reacted similarly to the dependent measures if they had *not* been exposed to the publicity surrounding the execution.

With respect to unique events that occur during the course of a study, the degree of damage caused depends on how the data are gathered. If participants are run individually, such events would presumably affect only one participant, whose data could be dropped from analyses. At worst, the disruption would merely add a slight amount of noise or random error to the data. Intrasession history becomes more problematic when participants are run in group sessions, as is often done to gather data quickly and easily. Here, a malfunctioning computer or broken slide projector can disrupt or ruin a significant portion of a study, and the researcher is faced with the unfortunate choice of either dropping the affected data or contending with considerable noise in the data analyses. Moreover, if the data are gathered in such a way that all of the experimental participants are run in one group and the control participants in another, history becomes an insurmountable threat to internal validity. If any differences are obtained between conditions, we do not know if it is because of the independent variable or because of the unique events that occurred within each group. For that reason, if participants are run in groups out of necessity or convenience, researchers should ensure that the different experimental conditions are represented within each group if at all possible. If that is not possible (e.g., if the manipulation must be administered orally), then multiple groups for each condition—as many as possible—should be run so that any unique history effects for a given group will not contaminate the entire study.

Instrumentation

Instrumentation is any change that occurs over time in measurement procedures or devices. If researchers purposefully change their measuring procedures because they have discovered a "better" way to collect data, or if observers gradually become more experienced or careless, these changes could have effects that might be confused with those of the independent variable. As was the case with maturation, this problem is a particular threat to internal validity if the various experimental conditions are run at different times. Instrumentation is a bias that should not happen. The cure is careful training and monitoring of observers or measurement procedures and ensuring that the order of experimental conditions is counterbalanced or randomized throughout the course of the study.

Mortality

Mortality refers to any attrition of participants from a study. If some participants do not return for a posttest or if participants in a control group are more difficult to recruit than participants in a treatment group, these differential recruitment and attrition rates could create differences that are confused with effects of the independent variable. Take, for example, a study testing an experimental drug designed to help people quit smoking. The drug reduces the desire for nicotine substantially, but it has the rather distressing side effect of causing unrelenting diarrhea. As a result, 70% of the treatment group drops out of the study. At the conclusion of the study, the remaining 30% in the treatment group are smoking significantly fewer cigarettes than the participants in the control group (none of whom dropped out). Can we conclude that the new drug works? No, because the 30% who stayed in the study are almost certainly no longer equivalent to the control group participants on important variables such as motivation. Presumably, the people who are truly motivated and committed to quitting smoking are the ones who would keep taking the drug despite the troubling side effects.

Mortality is particularly problematic in longitudinal research, in which data are gathered at multiple points in time. Imagine an intervention study designed to improve school success for at-risk adolescents. At the five-year follow-up, 45% of the original sample could not be located. Analyses of the data showed significant gains in achievement test scores; however, the high mortality rate precludes us from drawing the causal inference that the gains were caused by the intervention. The adolescents who could not be located for the follow-up in all probability are the students whose performance was worse, and perhaps the reason they could not be located is that they dropped out of school or were even incarcerated.

Mortality always presents a threat to external validity; at the end of a study, we are only able to conclude that our results are representative for the kind of individuals who are likely to finish the study. The greater the mortality, the less representative our final participant sample becomes. On the other hand, when mortality rates are different for the various experimental groups—a state of affairs termed **differential mortality**—it creates a threat to internal validity. Because experimental groups are no longer equivalent except for the independent variable, we cannot determine whether it was the independent variable that caused any group differences or the other ways in which the groups differ. Thus, it is important that researchers always look for the possibility of problems caused by mortality and differential mortality. At the conclusion of data gathering, the researcher can count the number of participant dropouts and in particular look to see if the frequency of dropouts varies systematically across condition.

Unlike some of the other threats to internal validity, there is no easy cure for mortality. There are steps researchers can take to reduce mortality in a longitudinal study, such as keeping in close contact with participants by mailing them newsletters or birthday cards or obtaining the name and address of a contact person who would be expected to know how to find the participant over the duration of the study. With adequate preparation and effort, attrition in even a 10-year study can be kept to under 20%. Differential mortality is harder to prevent, especially if the experimental treatment involves aspects that make it substantially more or less desirable than the control group's experience. The antismoking drug with the unpleasant side effects would naturally result in more dropouts than the control condition, as would a study in which the experimental participants must agree to experience painful electric shocks. In such cases, the problem of differential mortality can be addressed by carefully designing the experience of the control participants to be equally desirable or aversive. For example, a placebo could be used in the drug study that causes similar degrees of diarrhea. Making such a change to the study's procedure could very well increase the total amount of participant mortality (as more people in the control group will likely drop out of the study), but external validity might be a necessary cost to pay for increasing the internal validity of the study. (See Chapter 12 for an extended discussion of the internal/external validity trade-off.)

Selection by Maturation

Selection by maturation occurs when there are differences between individuals in the treatment groups that produce changes in the groups at different rates. Differences in spontaneous changes across the different groups can be confused with effects of the treatment or the independent variable. For example, imagine we were conducting social skills training groups for preadolescents. If analyses showed significant improvements in girls but not in boys, we might be tempted to conclude that our treatment is effective for girls, at least; however, an alternative explanation is that girls simply mature socially earlier than boys and that our treatment had no effect at all.

Random assignment, if feasible, is a straightforward means of addressing this threat to internal validity. When participants are randomly assigned to treatment groups, any variability in rates of maturation is spread across all groups to an equivalent degree. When random assignment is not feasible, as in the social skills training example, the inclusion of control groups, one for each level of the independent variable (i.e., girls and boys), allows the researcher to determine whether apparent differences between groups are attributable to the variable of interest or to different rates of change between the groups. In short, the selection by maturation threat is addressed either by the strategy for addressing selection threats—random assignment—or the strategy for addressing maturation threats—inclusion of a control group.

Illustrating Threats to Internal Validity with a Research Example

Some of the threats to internal validity are particularly troublesome when the independent or treatment variable varies between participants (selection and selection by maturation). Others are likely to be more problematic when there is no control group or the treatment variable varies within participants (history, maturation, instrumentation, mortality). To help understand these threats and how they are in fact threats if a randomized experiment is not conducted, consider the following examples of nonexperimental research designs.

Imagine that a researcher has been asked to evaluate the effects of going to college on people's political attitudes. The trustees of an educational foundation would like to know whether receiving a liberal arts education actually makes people more liberal. The question is seemingly simple: "Does going to college make people more liberal?" The researcher decides to answer the question by comparing the people she knew in high school who went to college with those who did not. A high school reunion provided the opportunity to make some observations. These observations revealed that the researcher's high school friends who had not gone to college were more politically conservative than the people who had gone to college. Let us consider the type of research design on which this conclusion was based and then the extent to which the internal validity of the design is threatened.

The independent or treatment variable in this example is whether the participants went to college. The researcher wishes to ascertain whether this independent variable exerts a causal effect on political attitudes, the dependent variable. Because some of her classmates went to college and others did not, and because she was comparing the political leanings of these two groups of classmates, the independent variable varies between classmates. Obviously, classmates were not randomly assigned to the levels of the independent variable: The researcher did not flip a coin for each classmate at high school graduation to determine who went off to college and who did not.

The internal validity of this design is particularly threatened by selection and by selection by maturation:

Selection We need to consider the possibility that the people who did not go to college and the people who did were different types of people to begin with, with different political attitudes even before their educational paths diverged. Because they were not randomly assigned to the college and no-college groups but rather selected their own paths or had their paths selected for them by admissions committees, parents, school counselors, and other advisers, there is no guarantee that they were similar at the outset. Such selection effects are serious threats to the internal validity of studies in which there is not random assignment. Whenever people select their own treatments or are selected by others for treatments or end up in different treatment groups by some unknown process instead of by random assignment, we have no assurance that the people in different groups were equivalent before exposure to the independent variable. Chances are they were not because the very fact that they selected or were selected for different treatments indicates that they were different types of people, with different preferences, different abilities, or some other characteristics that made them seem more suitable for one treatment rather than another.

Selection by Maturation Now suppose the researcher had thought about the selection threat and tried to eliminate it. Perhaps she gathered some information from the past about her classmates in an attempt to show that the political leanings of those who went to college were the same as the leanings of those who did not go to college back when both groups were finishing high school. Suppose in fact she found some records of interviews about the then-current presidential election and became convinced that at that time the two groups of classmates had approximately the same political attitudes. The researcher then argued that selection was no longer a threat and that causal conclusions about the impact of college on political attitudes were more defensible.

But we need to consider the possibility that the two groups of classmates might have subsequently grown apart in their political leanings even if one of the groups had not gone to college. Even if the two groups were the same politically during senior year in high school, they probably still were very different groups in other ways, and their political attitudes might have been changing at different rates and in different directions even if, for some reason, the college-bound classmates had not in fact enrolled in college.

Realizing the impossibility of eliminating these two internal validity threats, the researcher decides to gather some more data, using a different sort of research design, one that she hopes will not be as subject to the threats of selection and selection by maturation. This time she decides to follow a group of students as they go to college for the first time. She initially measured their political leanings when they graduated from high school and then again two years later, after their sophomore year in college.

Again, the researcher found that the political attitudes after two years in college were more liberal than they were two years earlier. On the plus side, this research design has effectively eliminated the threats of selection and selection by maturation because this time the researcher is not comparing two different groups of individuals. Rather, she is looking at the political attitudes of the same students at two different times: before they went to college and after they had been there two years.

Note that the research design is now a repeated measures design in which the independent variable varies within participants. That is, the political attitudes of each individual are measured twice, once before and once during college. Obviously, the researcher has not randomly assigned individuals to different orders. That is, everyone's attitudes were measured the first time without having been to college and the second time after having been there for two years. This is an example of a study in which counterbalancing the order of experimental conditions is impossible. Thus, the design is not a randomized experimental one, and its internal validity is threatened in the following ways:

Maturation We need to consider the obvious problem that individuals might simply change in their political attitudes as they mature or grow older. Accordingly, the individuals followed for two years might have developed more liberal political attitudes even if they had not gone to college during those two years, simply as a function of growing older.

History We also need to consider the possibility that different sorts of historical events were taking place at the two times and everyone at the second time might have been more liberal than they were at the first, whether or not they went to college in the interim. It is well known that the American populace as a whole seems to change in its political leanings across time. The decade of the 1960s was characterized by relatively liberal sentiments throughout the country compared to the 1950s. Thus, historical events change everyone's outlook, and such events might have affected the outlook of the students over the two-year period that they were followed.

Instrumentation We need to consider whether the way in which the dependent measure was measured changed from the first time to the second. Perhaps after the first phase of data collection, the researcher thought of better ways to ask the political attitude questions for the second phase of data collection. If the measurement procedures were not exactly the same at the two times, differences in the measurement instruments could be responsible for the differences in attitudes observed.

Mortality In all probability, after a two-year period, the researcher was not able to gather data successfully from all of the individuals who participated in the first phase of the study. Some of them, despite the best efforts of the researcher to track them down, might have moved away, become ill, or for other reasons become unreachable. It is possible that these individuals happen to be those with the most conservative political attitudes. Thus, the relative liberalness of those from whom data were gathered the second time, after two years in college, might be due not to their becoming more liberal but to the fact that the most conservative individuals have not been included in the sample at the end of the study.

Construct Validity of Independent Variables in a Randomized Experiment

A randomized experiment requires the experimenter to be able to control or manipulate the independent variable so that a random assignment rule can be used. This is frequently most easily accomplished in laboratory settings such as those discussed in Chapter 12; however, randomized experiments can also be conducted in real-world settings. The use of one setting or the other does not define the type of research design used. That is defined by the use of a random assignment rule.

In order to control the independent variable, a researcher must first define and create an operational definition of it. As discussed in Chapter 4, an **operational definition** is the procedure used by the researcher to manipulate or measure the variables of the study. All research contains operational definitions of abstract concepts; they are not unique to laboratory experiments. Sometimes the operational definition of an independent variable is clear and straightforward. For example, if we are interested in the impact of jury size on verdicts, the independent variable is easy to conceptualize and manipulate: We simply compare juries composed of 6 versus 12 jurors. In many cases, however, the operational definition of a given independent variable is not so straightforward. Either the independent variable is fairly complex, requiring a complex operational definition, or the independent variable is a general construct that can be operationally defined in any number of ways, and the chore of the researcher is to choose an operational definition that is valid, practical, and convincing.

Take, for example, the concept of urban stress. Urban stress is a complex, abstract notion, and it could conceivably be measured or manipulated in a number of ways. We could ask people living in large cities to rate how stressed they feel on a 9-point scale. That might be an adequate measure of urban stress if we were interested in stress as a dependent variable, but we could not readily use that operational definition if we wanted to manipulate stress. Glass and Singer (1972), in their classic work on urban stress, manipulated stress in the laboratory by subjecting participants to noise that was either controllable or uncontrollable. Their reasoning was that uncontrollable noise in the laboratory is a noxious stimulus that could serve as a substitute for urban social stressors. In order for their findings to be compelling, however, they must convince us that it is reasonable to equate uncontrollable noise with the abstract construct urban stress.

In Chapter 4 we discussed the importance of **construct validity,** that is, making sure that our variables capture the construct we wish to measure. The same problems of assessing validity pertain to variables that we create by experimental manipulations. For instance, instead of measuring anxiety, a researcher might manipulate people's anxiety levels, creating high anxiety in some persons and low anxiety in others. Or rather than measure people's existing levels of motivation, an experimenter might manipulate motivation by giving some participants instructions that motivate them to do well on a task and giving others instructions that cause them to care little about their performance.

When researchers create rather than measure levels of an independent variable, we call it a **manipulated variable.** When independent variables are obtained by measurements rather than manipulations, a researcher uses the same logic for assessing reliability and validity that is used for dependent variables. With manipulated independent variables, however, the researcher must test the manipulation by subsequently measuring its effects to determine its construct validity. For instance, if a researcher tries to create high levels of motivation by telling some participants that their performance on a task is an indicator of their intelligence and create low motivation by telling others that the task is a measure of willingness to practice dull tasks, the researcher needs to know whether these instructions really created different levels of motivation. Perhaps they created no differences because the participants did not believe the instructions, for example. Perhaps they created no differences because all the participants wanted to do well regardless of the nature of the task. Perhaps they created differences—but in anxiety instead of motivation. To demonstrate the validity of the manipulation, the researcher must also *measure* the participants' levels of motivation after the instructions. If those who received the "intelligence test" message say the task is important and they intend to do well, this is partial evidence that the researcher has created a high level of motivation; however, the instructions might also have created different levels of anxiety along with levels of motivation. We would like to see evidence that only motivation, and not anxiety, was manipulated by the instructions. To do this, a researcher would have to demonstrate both the discriminant and convergent validity of the manipulation.

When researchers demonstrate the validity of their manipulated variables, they generally obtain a measure of the independent variable construct after they have manipulated it. This is called a **manipulation check,** and it gives evidence of the convergent validity of the manipulation. Researchers rarely take the further step of demonstrating discriminant validity by showing that their manipulation has not created different levels of some other variables, for example, that it has not changed participants' anxiety levels. Occasionally, however, when research includes this additional step, it becomes all the more persuasive. Manipulation checks are discussed in greater detail in Chapter 12.

Constructing good operational definitions requires appropriate and accurate procedures to measure and manipulate variables. The art of finding suitable procedures cannot be captured by a set of rules but is acquired through experience. And in addition to construct validity is the question of external validity. The real test of external validity for both measured and manipulated variables, however, rests on the confirmation of the findings in other settings. In short, the best test of external validity is a replication of a study—a demonstration that the results can be repeated with different participants, procedures, experimenters, and operational definitions.

Alternative Experimental Designs

We already have briefly discussed two alternative designs for randomized experiments. In one, the participants were randomly assigned to the levels of the independent variable and each participant was measured only once. In this case, the independent variable is said to vary between participants. In the other design, the independent variable varies within participants and each participant is measured under each level of the independent variable; the order of exposure to those levels is randomly determined. These two designs, both of which we talk about in more detail in this section, are not the only alternatives. A variety of other randomized experimental designs are also possible and useful. We use the following notation to describe different research designs:

X = a treatment, an independent variable, a cause
O = an observation, a dependent variable, an effect
R = participants who have been randomly assigned to the treatment condition

Design 1: Randomized Two-Group Design

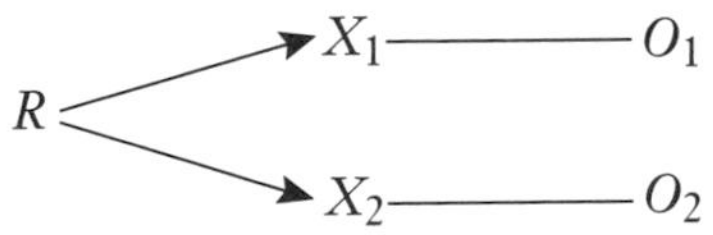

Participants are randomly assigned to the experimental treatment group (X_1) or to a comparison group (X_2). This is the design discussed earlier in which the independent variable varies between participants and has only two levels: treatment and control. The word "treatment" is simply verbal shorthand for the experimental manipulation or independent variable; it does not necessarily imply some kind of intervention designed to help people.

This design contains all the bare essentials for a randomized experiment: random assignment, treatment and no-treatment groups, and observations after the treatment. We must have at least two groups to know whether the treatment had an effect, and we must randomly assign individuals to groups so that the groups will be, on average, equivalent before treatment. Then we can attribute any posttreatment differences to the experimental treatment.

We can rule out several alternative explanations or threats to internal validity by using this design. We know that any posttreatment differences are not the result of a selection threat (barring any failure of randomization) because participants were randomly assigned rather than self-selected or systematically assigned to the two groups. We know also that the posttreatment differences are not a product of maturation because the two groups should have matured (e.g., aged or fatigued) at the same rate if they were tested at the same intervals after random assignment.

We can rule out other alternative explanations not just by referring to random assignment but also by looking carefully at the experimental procedures to see whether it is plausible that the treatment group might have been exposed to some other events (historical events in the outside world or events within the experimental session) that the no-treatment group did not experience. If not, we can eliminate history as an alternative explanation. If the two groups were tested or observed under similar circumstances, we can eliminate instrumentation differences as an explanation. Once we have eliminated these alternative explanations, we can feel quite confident that the experimental treatment caused any observed difference between the two groups (O_1 and O_2).

Design 2: Pretest–Posttest Two-Group Design

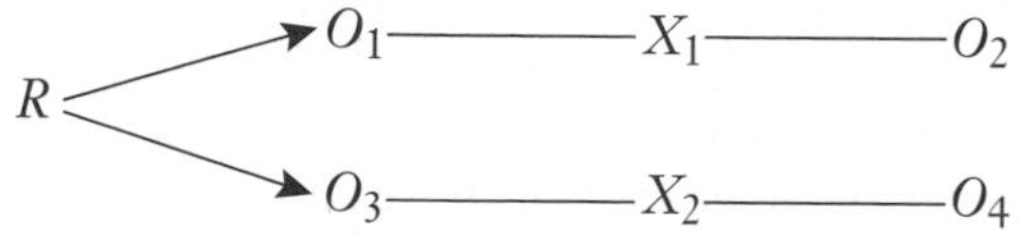

This design has an additional set of tests or observations of the dependent variable, called **pretests,** before the experimental treatment. Pretests have several advantages. They provide a check on the randomization and let the experimenter see whether the groups were equivalent before the treatment. Pretests also provide a more sensitive test of the effects of the treatment by letting each participant serve as his or her own comparison. Instead of comparing only O_2 and O_4, the experimenter can compare the difference between each participant's pretest and posttest scores. In other words, O_2 minus O_1 can be compared with O_4 minus O_3. Because participants' pretest scores all differ from one another and their posttest scores reflect some of these preexisting individual differences, the experimenter gains precision by making these sorts of comparisons rather than simply comparing O_2 and O_4.

To understand the benefits of this pretest design, suppose two people were randomly assigned to different groups in an experiment on weight loss; Person A was assigned to the no-treatment comparison group and Person B to the weight-loss treatment group. If Person A weighed 130 pounds on the pretest and 130 pounds on the posttest, it is clear that being in the comparison group did not affect his or her weight. If Person B weighed 160 pounds on the pretest and 150 pounds on the posttest, it is plausible that the treatment caused Person B to lose 10 pounds. However, if the experimenter did not take pretest measures and looked only at the posttest weights, Person B's 150 pounds compared to Person A's 130 would make the treatment look bad. Therefore, having pretest information in this pretest–posttest two-group design gives the experimenter a more precise measure of treatment effects.

The pretest also has some disadvantages, however. It can sensitize participants to the purpose of the experiment and bias their posttest scores. If this occurs for the experimental and control groups alike, their posttest scores should be equally elevated or depressed, and pretesting alone would not be an alternative explanation for a difference between O_2 and O_4. However, if the pretest affects the treatment group differently from the no-treatment group, this would appear as a difference on the posttest scores and would be indistinguishable from a difference produced by the treatment alone. In sum, when pretesting affects both experimental conditions equally, it is a threat to external validity; participants' responses to the second testing are not representative of how people would respond if they had not been given a pretest. When pretesting affects the experimental groups differentially, however, it becomes a threat to internal validity.

Unfortunately, this kind of differential effect of pretesting is common. Take, for example, a persuasion study trying to change people's attitudes toward capital punishment. A pretest asking for participants' attitudes about capital punishment probably will alert participants to the focus of the study and thus make them particularly sensitive to the persuasion manipulation. An alert participant might realize that the experimenter is interested in capital punishment and that the persuasive message is supposed to change his or her attitudes, and thus the participant might change his or her responses on the posttest in an attempt to please the experimenter. The participants in the control group, however, who do not receive a persuasive message on the topic of capital punishment, do not realize that this is the focus of the experiment and hence feel no demand to change their attitudes on the posttest.

Design 2 provides no solution to this problem. Experimenters must therefore decide whether this is a plausible occurrence for any particular study, and if it is, they should avoid this design in favor of the simpler Design 1 or opt for the more complex Design 3 described next.

Design 3: Solomon Four-Group Design

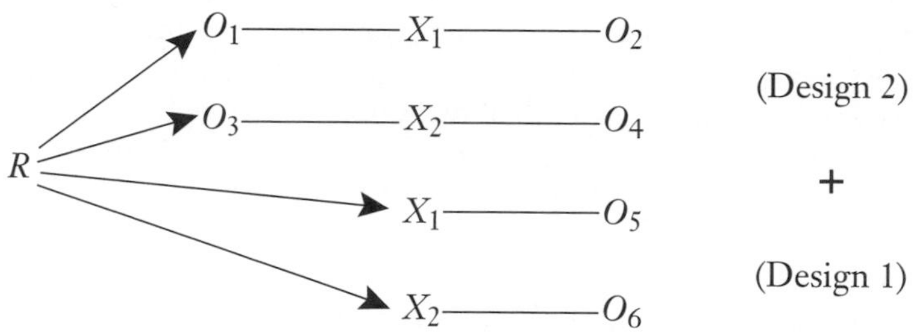

The third design combines Designs 1 and 2. With this design an experimenter can test decisively whether the posttest differences were caused by the treatment, the pretest, or the combination of treatment plus pretest. Design 3 is an expensive design because it requires four groups of participants to test the effects of only two levels of a treatment. The four groups are needed because in addition to the treatment and no-treatment groups, there are pretested and non-pretested groups.

This design offers the separate advantages of Design 1—no interference from pretesting effects—and Design 2—greater precision from the pretest scores as baselines against which to measure the effects of the treatment. In addition, it enables the experimenter to see whether the combination of pretesting plus treatment produces an effect that is different from what we would expect if we simply added the separate effects of pretesting and treatment. Such combinations, if they are different from the sum of the two individual effects, are called **interaction effects.** They are similar to what occurs when two natural elements combine to produce a new effect, as hydrogen and oxygen together produce a new compound, water. The whole is different from or greater than the simple sum of the parts. For many problems studied by social scientists, interaction effects are important. We need more than two-group designs to study these, and we need more than one independent variable because an interaction results from a combination of two or more causes, or independent variables. Designs with two or more independent variables are called factorial designs.

Design 4: Between-Participants Factorial Design

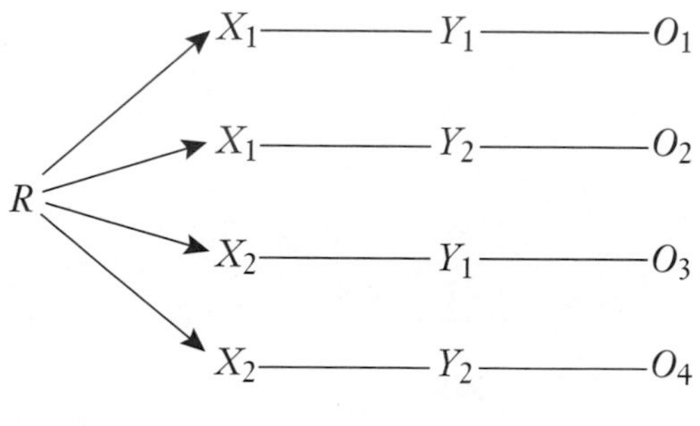

The *X* is one independent variable; the *Y* is another. In a **factorial design,** two or more independent variables are always presented in combination. The entire design contains every possible combination of the independent variables (also known as factors; hence the name, factorial design). If there are more than two independent variables and if each has more than two values, the design rapidly mushrooms because each additional variable or value greatly increases the number of conditions. We illustrate this fact using tables, which are the form most commonly used to diagram factorial designs.

Table 11.1 illustrates the combination of two factors, or independent variables. In the language of experimental design, we call this a 2 x 2 (where the "x" is read out loud as "by") factorial design, which means there are two factors and each has two values, or levels. In this particular example, the two factors are feedback (positive/negative) and confederate gender (male/female). If we added a third factor, we would double the number of conditions if the additional factor also had two levels, triple it if the new factor had three levels, and so on. For instance, if we added the relative status of the confederate as another factor to the two factors in Table 11.1 and used three status categories—lower, same, or higher than the participant—we would have a 2 x 2 x 3 design, with 12 conditions, shown in Table 11.2. This 12-cell design is much more complex than the original 2 x 2. It is triple the size and, therefore, either requires three times as many participants or spreads the same number of participants thinner, with one-third the number in each condition.

The advantage of a factorial design involving more than a single independent variable is that we can examine interaction effects involving multiple independent variables in addition to the separate or **main effects** of those variables by themselves. Suppose we were interested in two independent variables, *X* and *Y*, and their effects on some dependent variable, *O*. We could design two different experiments, one in which we randomly assigned participants to levels of *X* and then examined effects on *O*, and a second in which we randomly assigned participants to levels of *Y* and examined effects on *O*. Alternatively, we could create a factorial design and randomly

TABLE 11.1 A 2 X 2 FACTORIAL DESIGN

Factor *Y*	**Factor *X***	
Feedback	**Confederate Gender**	
	Male	**Female**
Negative	Male Negative	Female Negative
Positive	Male Positive	Female Positive

TABLE 11.2 A 2 x 2 x 3 FACTORIAL DESIGN

Factor *Y* Feedback	Factor *Z* Confederate Status	Factor *X* Confederate Gender: Male	Female
Negative	Lower		
	Same		
	Higher		
Positive	Lower		
	Same		
	Higher		

assign participants to all of the *X*-*Y* combinations of levels: X_1-Y_1, X_1-Y_2, X_2-Y_1, and X_2-Y_2. The advantage of this factorial design over the two separate single-factor experiments is that we can ask whether the effect of one of the independent variables is qualified by the other independent variable. If it does, the two independent variables are said to "interact" in producing *O*. Then, we cannot simply talk about the effect of *X* on *O* because the effect of *X* on *O* depends on the level of *Y*. Conversely, we cannot simply talk about the effect of *Y* on *O* because that effect depends on the level of *X*. We must talk about their joint or interactive effects on *O*.

To describe an interaction effect more concretely, we consider a published example of a 2 x 2 design (Sinclair & Kunda, 2000, Study 2). The study examined how participants responded to receiving either positive or negative feedback from a male or female manager. Participants were told that the study was a collaborative venture on the part of the university with local businesses to train personnel managers. The participants were asked to respond orally to an interpersonal skills test while a manager-in-training (actually a videotaped accomplice of the experimenter posing as a research participant) was allegedly listening from another room. Following the task, participants were then shown one of four videotapes showing the alleged manager-in-training giving an evaluation of the participants' interpersonal skills. Half of the time the person on the videotape was female and half the time the person was male. Half of the time the feedback given was positive and half the time the feedback was negative. Participants were then asked to rate how skilled the manager was at evaluating them.

Thus, the study had a 2 x 2 (Manager Gender x Feedback) factorial design, depicted in Table 11.1. Notice that the gender variable in this study refers not to the gender of the participants but to the people whom the participants rated. This is an important distinction. Participants' age and gender are characteristics they bring with them rather than experimental conditions to which people can be randomly assigned. The portion of a study that examines such individual difference variables is therefore technically not a true experiment because it does not feature random assignment.

The gender of an actor or stimulus person to whom participants respond is an experimental variable, however, because participants can be randomly assigned to interact with or observe a male or female actor.

The researchers combined two independent variables—manager gender and the valence of the feedback—because they were particularly interested in the effect of the combination. The dependent variable was the participants' ratings of how skilled they thought the confederate manager-in-training was. The experimenters believed the effects of the feedback given by the confederate would depend not only on whether the feedback was positive or negative but also on whether the feedback was delivered by a man or a woman. Therefore, it was important to look at all four combinations of feedback and manager gender.

Table 11.3 displays the results of the experiment. Higher scores mean that the participant evaluated the confederate's skill more positively. Let us now review the varieties of effects that we can examine with a factorial design. All factorial designs provide information about the separate main effects of each independent variable and the interaction effects among the independent variables. The main effect shows whether one independent variable has an effect when we average across the levels of any other variable. Do not be misled by the term "main effect"; it does not mean the most important or primary result but rather the effect of one independent variable ignoring the others. In Table 11.3, the main effects for each variable are shown in the margins. Looking first at the results for the feedback factor, we can see that participants who received positive feedback rated the confederate much more positively (average = 9.0) than did participants who received negative feedback (average = 7.4). And, indeed, statistical analysis confirmed that this difference was statistically significant (i.e., not likely a chance occurrence). Looking at the results for the confederate gender factor, we see that male confederates are rated slightly higher (average = 8.4) than are female confederates (average = 8.0), but the difference is small and in fact is not statistically significant.

TABLE 11.3 RATINGS OF MALE AND FEMALE CONFEDERATES WHO DELIVERED POSITIVE OR NEGATIVE FEEDBACK

	Confederate Gender		
Feedback	**Male**	**Female**	
Negative	8.0	6.8	Average for negative: 7.4
Positive	8.8	9.3	Average for positive: 9.0
	Average for male: 8.4	Average for female: 8.0	

The primary benefit of the factorial design is that in addition to telling us about the main effects of independent variables, it shows us how they interact in their effect on the dependent variable. The values inside the four cells of Table 11.3 show the interaction effect. Interactions are often depicted in graphical form for ease of interpretation. Figure 11.1 displays the data from Table 11.3 in the form of a figure. Inspection of Figure 11.1 reveals immediately that we would be remiss in concluding that just because the main effect of confederate gender was nonsignificant that it had no effect. Instead, it is clear that the effect of feedback was negligible when the confederate was a man but considerable when the confederate was a woman. In other words, if the confederate was male, participants rated him as being equally skilled whether he had delivered flattering or unflattering feedback about the participant. If the confederate was female, on the other hand, participants rated her as being skilled when she had just delivered flattering feedback but as significantly less skilled when she had delivered negative feedback.

Interaction effects require more complex theoretical explanations than main effects. The researcher must sufficiently develop his or her theory to explain why

FIGURE 11.1 **EFFECT OF THE INTERACTION OF CONFEDERATE GENDER AND VALENCE OF FEEDBACK ON PARTICIPANTS' EVALUATIONS OF THE CONFEDERATE'S SKILL AT PROVIDING FEEDBACK**

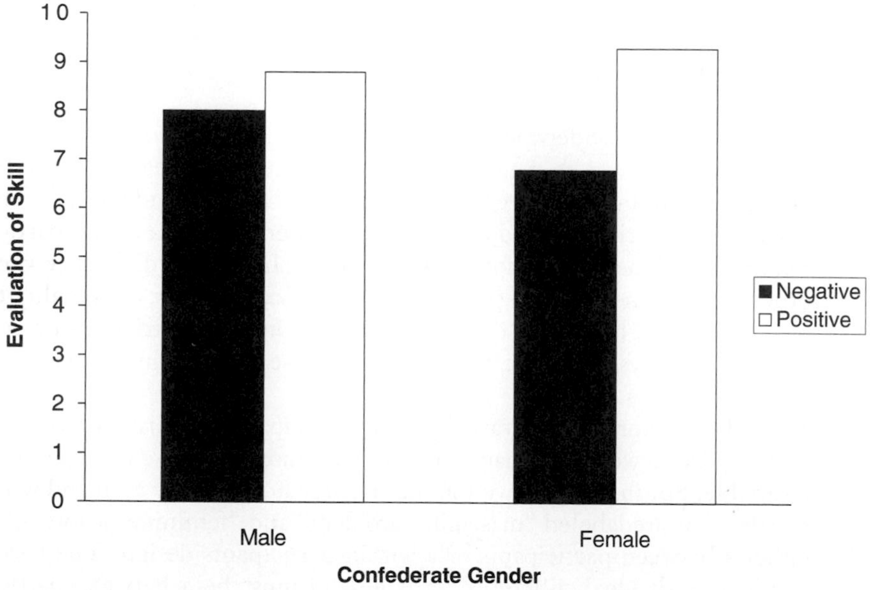

effects of one independent variable are different at different levels of the other independent variable. This complexity, however, is also one of the major strengths of factorial designs: By including more than one independent variable, the researcher is better able to identify and understand multiple causes of a behavior. Thus, a major reason to use factorial designs is to look for interaction effects. Another reason is to be able to generalize the effects of one variable across several levels of another variable. For instance, if we wanted to study the effects of being able to control noise (variable 1) on people's ability to solve puzzles, we might vary the type of puzzle as a second independent variable. This would enable us to demonstrate that people perform better on not just one but two types of puzzles (variable 2) when they can control the noise in their environment. We add the second variable not because we expect it to make a difference but to demonstrate that it makes no difference. A third reason to include more than one independent variable in an experiment is to study the separate effects of that variable. We might design a factorial study even if we expect to find only two main effects and no interaction because we can accomplish testing the two main effects more efficiently and with fewer total participants in a factorial design than we could with two separate studies.

Repeated Measures Designs

Earlier we discussed the fact that experimental independent variables could be manipulated within as well as between participants. Rather than assign different people to different treatments, the experimenter exposes the same persons to multiple treatments. Each participant is repeatedly treated and tested, and the variations caused by different treatments appear within the same person rather than between different groups of people. Such designs are, in fact, randomized experimental designs as long as we randomly assign participants to be exposed to the various conditions in different orders.

Not all independent variables can be used in repeated measures designs, just as not all variables can be manipulated experimentally. We earlier made the distinction between manipulated experimental variables and individual difference variables. Manipulated variables are designed by the experimenter, and any participants can be randomly assigned to manipulated treatments. Individual difference variables, on the other hand, come with the participant, such as age, height, personality traits, gender, race, and so on. Individual difference variables impose restrictions on research design as well as analysis because they cannot be used as within-participants or repeated measures factors.

When factors can be varied within participants, experimenters can use a design that requires fewer participants and provides more sensitive measures of the effects of a variable. For instance, if we wanted to study how quickly men and women can solve puzzles that are labeled "masculine problem" and "feminine problem," we could use either a between-participants or a within-participants design. The participants' gender is an individual difference variable and must be a between-participants factor. The label on the puzzle could be either a between-participants or within-participants

TABLE 11.4 ILLUSTRATION OF THE NUMBER OF PARTICIPANTS NEEDED FOR A BETWEEN-PARTICIPANTS DESIGN

	Gender Labeling of the Task	
Participant's Gender	**Masculine**	**Feminine**
Male	15 men	15 men
Female	15 women	15 women
	Total $N = 60$ participants	

factor. If it were between participants, we would have to recruit 60 participants for our study, using a rule of thumb that there be 15 observations in each condition as shown in Table 11.4. The 60 observations would come from 60 different people.

We could, however, make the gender labeling of the task a within-participants factor and have each participant solve both a "masculine" and "feminine" labeled puzzle. In this case, as shown in Table 11.5, we would need only 30 participants, 15 men and 15 women, to get the same number of observations in each condition because each person would solve two puzzles. The other efficient feature of repeated measures designs is the precision gained by using each participant as his or her own comparison. Like the pretest observations of the pretest–posttest two-group design, the repeated measures give us individual baselines for each participant. The 15 men who solve the "masculine" puzzle in Table 11.4 might vary widely in the time they require. One might solve the puzzle in 10 seconds and another might take 10 minutes. If each person takes one minute longer to solve the "feminine" than the "masculine" puzzle, it would not appear as a noticeable difference between the two puzzle groups if we used a between-participants design, but it might be a noticeable difference in a repeated measures design.

As noted earlier, individual difference variables cannot be used with repeated measures; not even all manipulated variables are suitable as within-participants or repeated measures variables. Some manipulated variables would arouse the participants' suspicions about the purposes of the experiment. For instance, suppose we tried to use the ethnicity or gender of job applicants as a within-participants variable. If we presented prospective employers with two hypothetical job applications and résumés in which everything was identical except the ethnicity or gender of the applicant, the prospective employers could see immediately that we were testing to see if they practice race or sex discrimination in hiring. Other variables are not suitable if they produce long-lasting effects that would carry over from one testing to the next. For instance, if we tried to compare the effects of alcohol and hallucinogenic drugs on drivers' reaction times, we would not have them drink a large dose of alcohol, give them a driver's test, and then give them hallucinogenic drugs an hour later for a

TABLE 11.5 ILLUSTRATION OF THE NUMBER OF PARTICIPANTS NEEDED FOR A WITHIN-PARTICIPANTS DESIGN

	Gender Labeling of the Task	
Participant's Gender	**Masculine**	**Feminine**
Male	15 men -------------	(15)
Female	15 women -----------	(15)

Total N = 30 participants

second test. In addition to the obvious ethical problems of administering drugs to experimental participants, we also would encounter practical problems. If we use repeated measures designs, we must be sure the effects of the first level of a treatment are gone before we try to administer subsequent levels.

Strengths and Weaknesses of Randomized Experiments

We have emphasized the strengths of randomized experiments. By randomly assigning people to experimental conditions, experimenters can be confident that the subsequent differences on the dependent variable are caused, on average, by the treatments and are not preexisting differences among groups of people. Manipulated experimental variables, unlike individual difference variables, enable experimenters to conclude "This caused that." No experimenter can be 100% sure that "this" experimental treatment was the cause of "that" effect, as there is always the possibility of a failure of randomization or undetected artifact, but randomized experiments can rule out many alternative explanations. Yet randomized experiments are not without their weaknesses. In this section we describe some of the major drawbacks of the experiment. When considering these criticisms, it is important that readers keep in mind that they are not inevitable condemnations of experimental designs. Not all experiments carry these limitations and not all nonexperimental research is beyond reproach on the same grounds. They really are criticisms of how laboratory research is typically conducted, regardless of the research design that is used.

Experimental Artifacts

One set of extraneous variables that continues to plague experimenters is artifacts. In the realm of research design, the word **artifact** refers to an unintended effect on the dependent variable that is caused by some feature of the experimental setting other than the independent variable. Even with selection, history, maturation, instrumentation, and the other threats to internal validity taken care of, some experimenters worry that the results of their research might not be true effects of the experimental treatment but instead might be artifacts, or effects of some extraneous variables. For instance, experimenters can unwittingly influence their participants to behave in ways that confirm the hypothesis, particularly if the participants want to please the experimenter. Findings that result from such attempts are artifactual in the sense that they do not represent the participants' true responses to the independent variables of interest. A detailed discussion of such artifacts and their potential threats is given in Chapter 12, where we consider laboratory research in detail. Artifacts can arise in laboratory situations regardless of whether or not a randomized experimental design is used. Thus, artifacts are not a necessary concomitant of an experimental design. In laboratory settings, artifacts are just as likely when nonexperimental or quasi-experimental designs are used. Artifacts can also occur in the field if, for example, the independent variable is confounded or covaries with some unintended aspect of the field setting.

External Validity

Experimental designs and procedures maximize the internal validity of research—they enable the researcher to rule out most alternative explanations or threats to internal validity. There can be a trade-off, however. Experimenters might maximize internal validity at the expense of the external validity or generalizability of the results. Because many randomized experiments are conducted in laboratory settings (although they need not be), we might ask whether the findings extend beyond the laboratory. Can the experimenter talk about these phenomena with reference to the world outside, or do they appear only in seemingly sterile conditions?

A common criticism of laboratory experiments in particular is that they are poor representations of natural processes. Some laboratory experiments, like Glass and Singer's (1972) studies of noise, use remote analogues of real-world variables, like urban stress. Although some readers criticize such analogues as being artificial, we also can argue that the artificial conditions in these experiments are more effective ways to study the problem than are some more realistic conditions. The laboratory noise and laboratory measures of physiological and cognitive effects are all substitutes for the real phenomena; they are analogues and therefore artificial. Being artificial is not necessarily a disadvantage, however. Some laboratory analogues are more effective than their realistic but mundane counterparts and therefore make the research more persuasive, an issue we revisit in Chapter 12. In the final analysis, how realistic or generalizable any treatments and effects are can be discovered only by trying to replicate the findings in another setting.

The Problem of College Sophomores in the Laboratory

A third major criticism of experiments questions the representativeness of the research participants, who often are college students participating in research to fulfill course requirements. Are college students representative of the larger population? For some research questions, yes; for others, no. For many research purposes college sophomores are no different from anyone else. For instance, to study a physiological variable such as the eye blink response, we can assume that what is true for 18-year-old college students is also true for 6-year-old elementary school students and 40-year-old employees. To study the effects of a more socially situated variable, however, such as the effects of politicians' campaign styles on people's support for candidates, we would be wise to include a more heterogeneous group of people. Or to study the effects of an economic variable, such as tax incentives for installing solar energy systems, it is necessary to include people with a range of incomes.

Methodologists have warned researchers in the social sciences regarding the dangers of overreliance on college students as participants in research, but these warnings have largely fallen on deaf ears. Perhaps the most compelling critique of current research practices is an article written by David Sears (1986), entitled "College Sophomores in the Laboratory: Influences of a Narrow Data Base on Psychology's View of Human Nature." Sears began by documenting social psychologists' overreliance on college students as participants. He read and classified all of the articles published in the three most selective and rigorous journals in social psychology. He found that fully 74% of the articles reported findings from studies that enlisted college undergraduates as participants, and 78% of the studies were conducted in the laboratory. What are the implications for theories about social behavior when the bulk of relevant research findings come from such a narrow range of participants?

Consider how college undergraduates differ from the rest of the population: Most obviously, they come from a very narrow age range and are concentrated at the upper levels of educational background. Most undergraduates that participate in research are between 17 and 20 years of age, a time of life developmental psychologists call "late adolescence." Late adolescence is characterized by a number of distinguishing psychological features. Individuals have a less than fully formulated sense of self, as manifested by variable self-esteem, feelings of insecurity, and depression; they have less crystallized social and political attitudes; they are more egocentric; they have a stronger need for peer approval, manifested in dependency and conformity; and they have unstable peer relationships. In addition to these differences from the general population associated with late adolescence, college students also differ from other late adolescents: They have higher levels of intelligence and cognitive skills; they have even more unstable peer relationships due to greater geographic mobility and delayed entry into the workforce and marriage; and they display greater compliance to authority because people who are rebellious or continually disobedient are unlikely to complete high school and get accepted into college (Sears, 1986).

How much do these differences matter? As we noted earlier, if we are looking at basic physiological or biological processes, the unique characteristics of the college student probably do not affect our findings; however, for many areas of the social sciences, these differences matter a great deal. Sears (1986) asks us to consider social psychology, for example. If we were to summarize the view of the human condition generated by 50 years of social psychological research, it would be that people have malleable self-concepts; that they are very easy to influence in terms of attitude change and persuasion; that they are highly conforming to peers and susceptible to group norms; that they display egocentric biases in their thinking; and that they are highly obedient to authority. If readers are thinking that this list sounds suspiciously like the list of differences between college students and the general population given in the preceding paragraph, they are correct. The representativeness problem in using college students as our primary source of data in the social sciences is indeed serious.

What can be done about this problem? The answer is simple and obvious, yet not likely to be heeded: Researchers should stop relying so heavily on college students and use other populations in their studies. The convenience of the college "subject pool" creates a siren song that is hard for researchers to resist, and many university-based researchers make the conscious decision to conduct more research more quickly and cheaply using undergraduates even at the cost of external validity. The attitude among many researchers appears to be "Well, I'll just see if my hypothesis holds true for this specialized population, and I'll let someone else demonstrate that it generalizes to the rest of the population." The problem is that "someone else" might never come along, partly because scholarly journals and university performance-review committees do not reward scientists for replicating studies using different samples, no matter how important it is to demonstrate such generalizability.

We are not suggesting that all areas of the social sciences are guilty of the college sophomore bias. Indeed, for many social science questions, the participant population in the research simply must be more heterogeneous than college students; participants must vary in age, income, education, or occupation if these are variables in the research. For instance, sociological research usually raises questions about demographic groups—people of different economic, ethnic, educational, and cultural backgrounds. Or if not different groups of people, sociologists study the effects of situations and social structures much more diverse than those typical of late adolescence and college campuses. Sociological questions, therefore, cannot usually be studied using undergraduates alone.

More important, there is nothing about experimental designs that *requires* studying college undergraduates. Although laboratory experiments are criticized for relying too heavily on college students, the truth is that the choice of design is independent of the choice of sample. The only requirement of a randomized experiment is random assignment; and with manipulable variables, ingenuity, and a little tact, experimenters are able to use random assignment in many places outside the college community. Thus, the college sophomore problem is not a weakness of experimental designs per se but rather an unfortunate feature of the preponderance of research in the social sciences that features randomization and manipulation of independent variables.

The Failure of Experiments to Provide Useful Descriptive Data

Another drawback of randomized experiments is that they rarely yield descriptive data about frequencies or the likelihood of certain behaviors that we can generalize to the rest of the population. For instance, if 20% of the people in the treatment group agree with a statement about the usefulness of therapy, it tells us nothing about the percentage of people who agree with this statement in the larger population unless we have recruited the participants for our experiment by selecting a representative sample from the larger population. In theory this can be done; in practice it is exceedingly rare.

An important difference between how probability surveys and experiments are usually conducted is that probability surveys enlist a random sample of respondents who are representative of some larger population (see Chapter 8). Therefore, if 80% of the people in a representative sample say they believe cigarettes cause cancer, we can generalize this result to the population from which they were drawn. Because the sample is a random selection of people from a population, the distribution of beliefs and preferences in that sample is approximately the same as the distribution in the population. The survey, therefore, provides descriptive data about the population. An experiment, on the other hand, usually does not make use of a representative or random sample because the purpose of the experiment is not to provide descriptive data about percentages of people in the population who profess certain beliefs; the purpose of an experiment is to provide information about causes and effects.

Summary

Randomized experiments are the best method for examining causal associations and concluding that "This caused that." The defining characteristic of such designs is that participants are randomly assigned to the levels of the independent variables. Randomized experiments enable a researcher to test and rule out the primary threats to internal validity: maturation, history, instrumentation, mortality, and selection. Experiments that comprise more than one independent variable provide tests of both the main effects and the interaction effects of those variables. The high internal validity of randomized experiments can sometimes be achieved at the cost of external validity, especially when randomized experiments are conducted in laboratory settings with relatively select samples of participants; however, two things must be kept in mind about this possible limitation. First, the limitation is not a necessary consequence of the use of a randomized design. Randomized experiments can be conducted in field settings using representative samples. Second, even if this is a limitation of some experimental designs, the goal of experimental research is not to maximize external validity; it is to maximize internal validity. We use the diverse designs of social science research to accomplish a set of diverse and partially incompatible goals. We should use randomized experiments for what they are particularly good at—that is, answering questions about causal processes—and we should rely on other sorts of designs to answer other sorts of questions.

Key Concepts

alternative explanation
artifacts
construct validity
counterbalancing
dependent variable

differential mortality
experimental variables
factorial design
failure of randomization
history
independent variable
individual difference variables
instrumentation
interaction effect
main effect
manipulated variable
manipulation check
maturation
mortality
operational definition
pretests
random assignment
randomized experiment
repeated measures design
selection
selection by maturation

On the Web

http://trochim.human.cornell.edu/tutorial/tutorial.htm A very nicely written and organized Web site that contains units on many concepts covered in this chapter, including operationally defining variables, experimental and nonexperimental designs, internal and external validity, repeated measures designs, and threats to internal validity.

http://www.une.edu.au/WebStat/unit_materials/c2_research_design/index.html A tutorial designed by the School of Psychology at the University of New England that has several relevant units, including a discussion of experimental and nonexperimental designs, internal and external validity, and between-participants and within-participants designs.

Further Reading

Campbell, D. T., & Stanley, J. C. (1966). *Experimental and quasi-experimental designs for research.* Chicago: Rand McNally.

Huck, S. W., & Sandler, H. M. (1979). *Rival hypotheses: Alternative interpretations of data based conclusions.* New York: Harper & Row.

Rosnow, R. L., & Rosenthal, R. (1999). *Beginning behavioral research: A conceptual primer.* Upper Saddle River, NJ: Prentice-Hall Canada.

Shadish, W. R., Cook, T. D., & Campbell, D. T. (2001). *Experimental and quasi-experimental designs for generalized causal inference.* Boston: Houghton-Mifflin.

CHAPTER

12

The Laboratory Setting

The laboratory is a unique setting for research in many ways. Perhaps the best way to understand its special features is to think of it not as a single type of environment for research but as a medium in which research settings can be constructed. The laboratory's uniqueness lies in its flexibility; like a skilled actor in a play, it can take on whatever character is called for by the script of the research plan. Its flexibility gives the researcher the ability to construct physical settings, tasks, social environments, and many other factors that influence human behavior.

Three underlying research goals can be served by using the laboratory in well thought-out research: attaining control, implementing an experimental manipulation, and constructing a setting for the experiment. **Control,** or the minimization of extraneous influences on whatever the research is designed to investigate, is made possible by the laboratory's isolation from external influences. Each participant in the research can be taken through a planned and consistent sequence of events, which should not vary materially from one participant to another. From the obvious fact that research participants' attention is not distracted by passersby or other activities, to the somewhat more subtle notion that participants might be isolated from their positions in social structures and networks (Sampson, 1977), the laboratory can help control variability in the dependent variable that would be present in other settings.

The control over extraneous variables that is possible in the laboratory increases statistical power and the precision of the conclusions that can be drawn from the research. That is, control increases the likelihood that a true effect of a given size can be statistically detected in a study (the logic of statistical inference is covered in Chapter 18), in comparison to the typical case in field or survey research, where many factors that affect the dependent variable are free to vary. In consequence, smaller effects are more easily statistically detectable in laboratory studies than in field studies—including effects that might even be too small to be of practical importance outside the laboratory.

Manipulation of independent variables, the defining characteristic of experimental designs as outlined in Chapter 11, is also facilitated by the laboratory research setting. Of course, much nonexperimental research is conducted in the laboratory (because certain types of observation are most easily conducted there, for example), and much experimental research is conducted outside the laboratory. But for practical reasons, it is particularly easy to implement experimental manipulations in the laboratory. In a way, manipulation is just another side of control. Instead of contriving a single controlled setting, task, and the like, two (or more) treatments are constructed that differ in only the intended ways, and participants are randomly assigned to experience one or the other treatment.

Various features of the setting that can influence the research participants' behavior or facilitate research in other ways can also be arranged in the laboratory. For example, researchers might wish to explore physiological reactions to some experimental stimulus. The physiological equipment requires a computer, psychophysiological recorders and accompanying finger/muscle leads, and in some cases, a specially constructed room that is electrically isolated. This kind of research could be conducted only in a laboratory setting.

The flexibility of the laboratory is used to attain control, implement a manipulation, and construct an appropriate setting in different ways for different research topics and goals. This fact implies that much practical advice concerning laboratory-based research is highly dependent on the particular procedures used to study a particular phenomenon. The set of factors that the wise researcher takes into account for a group interaction study has little in common with the set of factors that are important for a study of the effects of pornography on sexual aggression. The best advice for the researcher is to read carefully through published research reports to find studies that are similar to the one planned and to adopt or adapt from them the specific features that appear helpful. Nonetheless, some principles that hold across different types of laboratory research are described in this chapter.

When Should the Laboratory Be Used?

As is evident throughout this and the next four chapters, the particular strengths and weaknesses of the laboratory as a research setting make it more appropriate for some types of research topics and goals and less appropriate for others. Several conceptual contrasts define types of research that vary in their suitability for the laboratory. Although these contrasts are expressed as dichotomies, they actually are continua along which specific research studies fall at various points.

Universalistic versus Particularistic Research Goals

The goal of some research is to investigate hypothesized associations such as "use of pornography causes sex crimes." Such propositions, intended to have broad (though usually unspecified) limits of generalizability, contrast sharply with more local or focused questions, such as "Will the adoption of quality circles increase worker satisfaction at Acme Widget?" This contrast, which we discussed in Chapter 8 because of its relevance to sampling, has been labeled universalistic versus particularistic (Kruglanski, 1975).

Universalistic research is intended to investigate theoretically predicted associations between abstractly specified constructs (e.g., pornography and sex crimes). Tests of such hypotheses are important because they shed light on the validity of the theory from which the hypotheses were derived. The significant question is this: Can the hypothesized association be demonstrated at all? And for this purpose, the details of the setting, population, and other particulars of the demonstration are less crucial. Although the empirical universality of many associations has not been established (because of the difficulties of conducting cross-cultural and cross-historical research), the associations are tentatively assumed to apply to all humans, across all sorts of theoretically irrelevant conditions. Thus, the research focuses on detecting associations between general, abstract constructs; the particular operationalizations of the constructs used in a given study are in part arbitrary and chosen for reasons of practicality and convenience. Similarly, the participant sample is an essentially "arbitrary group from the general universe (e.g., the class of all humans) to which the hypothesis is assumed to apply" (Kruglanski, 1975, p. 105). Of course, if an association can be replicated—observed in many studies that use diverse operationalizations of the theoretical constructs and diverse participant populations—our confidence in the existence of that association is increased.

In contrast, the specification of a particular concrete setting, population, and time period to which the results are intended to apply is an intrinsic part of **particularistic research**. For example, we might not be interested in whether a new management technique produces good results in other places where it has been tried but only in whether it benefits our firm (with our particular production methods, corporate culture, and population of workers). Rather than general statements, a specific target of generalization for the research results is intended. Therefore, there is little or no interest in replication of the results across multiple settings, operationalizations, or populations.

Particularistic research goals often involve questions of how much, how often, or how many—quantitative questions of how large an effect is. Such questions are intrinsically particularistic, for they presuppose a population, setting, and other conditions as the intended target of applicability for the research findings. For instance, estimating how large the effects of pornography are would require knowledge about the types of people who are particularly susceptible to the effects and their relative prevalence in the population of interest; the size of effects associated with different types of pornographic material and the amount each type is used in the population; the ways in which the conditions of use influence the size of the effects; the conditions under which use takes place in the population; and many other similar questions. It is obvious that quantitative questions cannot be answered in the abstract but require substantial involvement with the details of the target setting and population.

When the research goals are universalistic, because a particular setting and population of participants are not crucial aspects of the hypothesis under study, a laboratory study might be appropriate. If a theory specifies that under conditions *X*, *Y*, and *Z*, outcome *C* should be observed, it might be possible to set up the required conditions in the laboratory and look for the predicted outcome. Whether the conditions actually co-occur *anywhere* in the "real world" outside the laboratory is not significant for the intended purpose of testing the validity of the theoretical prediction. The laboratory is less often suitable for pursuing particularistic research goals. It is difficult to answer questions about the impact of a program, or the effect of a variable, in a specific setting with specific people unless the research is actually conducted under those same conditions, implying the use of a field study, survey, or observational study.

Basic versus Applied Research

A distinction that overlaps partly but not completely with the preceding one is that between basic and applied research. This distinction is subject to several frequent misunderstandings. It is certainly not the case that research conducted in the laboratory is always basic, whereas nonlaboratory (field or survey) research is always applied. Instances of applied laboratory and basic nonlaboratory research are easy to find. Also, it is not that applied research is somehow less valuable or worthwhile than basic research, as many people seem to feel. In fact, many researchers would say that they find it difficult to separate the two and that their personal goals in conducting research are both to develop and refine new knowledge—**basic research**—and to use that knowledge for the improvement of the human situation—**applied research.** These goals are inextricably linked because, as Lewin (1951) noted, attempts to apply theoretically based knowledge to solve real social problems will almost always reveal new knowledge—even if it is only the knowledge that the theory is incomplete or inadequate. Lewin's famous dictum underscores this linkage: "There is nothing so practical as a good theory."

The distinction is probably best based on the use that is made of a research finding. Suppose we consider the empirically supported theory that says feelings of control improve people's ability to cope with stress (Glass & Singer, 1972). When research inspired by that theory is used to improve our understanding of the social and personality processes underlying coping and reactions to stress in general (Endler, Macrodimitris, & Kocovski, 2000), we are treating it as basic research. Or we might use the theory to develop an intervention for stroke patients to improve their coping following discharge from the hospital (Frank, Johnston, Morrison, Pollard, & MacWalter, 2000), in which case we are treating it as applied research. As another example, take the well-established finding in cognitive psychology that under very broad conditions, spaced study leads to better memory than massed or concentrated study. That is, studying some material for 10 minutes on each of three days leads to much better memory than studying the same thing for 30 minutes in a single session. This finding could be used to develop further basic theories of memory storage and retrieval (basic research) or to design instructional programs in classrooms, where memorization of studied material is an important applied goal (Dempster, 1988).

As noted earlier, the basic–applied and universalistic–particularistic distinctions are similar. Most basic research is universalistic, but basic research does not have to be, as, for example, would be the case in a study developing a theory of coping processes in a highly specific population such as patients infected with HIV from a tainted blood supply. Most applied research is particularistic, but again it does not have to be, as might be the case in research dedicated toward developing teaching techniques that are intended to be effective across a wide range of curricula and students. Perhaps the best way of understanding how the two distinctions differ is to consider the *goals* versus the *end use* of the results. The universalistic–particularistic distinction involves the researcher's underlying goals in conducting the study; the basic–applied distinction involves the use that is made of the study's results.

Examining What Does Happen versus What Would Happen

Some research is aimed at investigating what happens in a particular situation. For example, what is the structure of a naturally occurring "get-acquainted" conversation? How much, and when, do people self-disclose? To answer such research questions, we must find or construct the situation of interest, and the laboratory might or might not be appropriate. Pairs of college students who are strangers can have a "getting acquainted" conversation in the laboratory (Gable & Shean, 2000), although other situations (e.g., an organizational setting or a family) would be harder to investigate there. Obviously, the key concern would be to maintain the theoretically significant elements of the target situation, and the laboratory would often, though not always, be inappropriate for this purpose.

On the other hand, sometimes the goal of research is to see what would happen under specified circumstances. Many types of research fall under this heading, including most theory-testing research, in which the theoretical hypothesis specifies a set of circumstances and the goal is to create those circumstances and see whether the predicted phenomenon is observed. For example, consider the question of whether extensive equal-status interaction among prejudiced Whites and Blacks would reduce the prejudice (Pettigrew, 1998). It is necessary to create the setting and other conditions for such interaction, probably in the laboratory, for it would be relatively unlikely to occur otherwise.

Other examples of what-if questions include research in which the goal is to strip away many elements that occur in a natural setting to determine the minimal conditions for the occurrence of some behavior or event. Milgram's famous experiments on destructive obedience are perhaps the best example (e.g., Milgram, 1974). Motivated in part by the question of why seemingly ordinary people served as concentration camp guards and participated in other ways in Nazi atrocities, Milgram wanted to determine the limits of this phenomenon. Studying destructive obedience in natural settings (such as the military) poses serious inferential ethical problems, for people would risk job loss, prison, or perhaps execution if they refused to obey. Such powerful incentives would cloud any interpretations of their reasons for obedience. In order to simplify and clarify the situation, Milgram deliberately set up a situation in which no concrete penalties would stem from refusal. As is well known, his results showed that authoritative demands from a societally respected source cause many ordinary people to obey, even to the point of risking serious injury to an innocent fellow participant in the research. This important conclusion could not have been reached by studying natural settings (in which disobedience might be punished) but only by the deliberate creation of a simplified situation.

Another example along similar lines is research into intergroup behavior using the "minimal group paradigm" (Tajfel, 1982; Turner, 1987). It is easy enough to find real-life instances of negative intergroup interactions but difficult to explain them theoretically because multiple contributing factors, both present and historical, generally coexist. To remove the effects of historical antagonisms between groups, cultural stereotypes, concrete conflicts over economic rewards, and the like, we can bring individuals into the laboratory and divide them on some trivial basis into two groups. The division can even be explicitly random. Even in this highly simplified situation, in which social categorization is the only element, people have been found to discriminate in favor of the "group" to which they belong and against the other "group"; to develop stereotypes of the other "group"; and to believe that the other "group" is homogeneous ("They're all alike.")—all familiar components of real-life antagonistic intergroup relations. Without the ability to experimentally separate mere categorization from the other historical and cultural factors with which it usually covaries, we would not be in a position to discover its powerful effects.

As these examples illustrate, research aimed at determining what would happen under specific circumstances—whether or not those circumstances actually exist anywhere in concrete form—is important both for theory testing and for other reasons (e.g., exploring the limits of a phenomenon of interest). Such research, in contrast to research aimed at determining what actually happens in a real situation, is particularly well suited to the laboratory setting, where the circumstances required by the research goals can be constructed.

Manipulable versus Nonmanipulable Independent Variables

Of course, there are practical and ethical limits on the kinds of research that can be conducted in the laboratory, even if that were a desirable setting for other reasons. Certain types of independent variables cannot practically or ethically be set up and manipulated in the laboratory. So, for example, we cannot use the laboratory to study the psychological effects of learning that one has a terminal disease; the interested researcher would have to seek out a cancer treatment center or other natural setting in which this event occurs with frightening frequency. Some variables simply cannot be manipulated, as in the case of research looking at the consequences of experiencing a natural disaster. To give another example, for practical reasons such variables as position in an organizational structure cannot be manipulated and are difficult or impossible to investigate in the laboratory.

Short versus Long Time Frames

Related to the preceding point is the fact that laboratory research rarely extends beyond a relatively short time period. The great majority of laboratory studies are completed within an hour or two. A few might last as long as several weeks (e.g., Park, 1986). But many important phenomena in the social sciences develop only over weeks, months, or years, and the practical limitations of the laboratory force their study in other, more natural and less controlled settings. For example, research on determinants and consequences of peer victimization (Juvonen & Graham, 2001) could not practically be carried out in the laboratory.

Participants' Awareness of the Research

In a laboratory study, it is difficult if not impossible to keep people unaware of the fact that they are participating in research. As we explain later in this chapter, this fact can create problems for the validity of the research, as the participants might formulate hypotheses about how they are "supposed" to behave and act in ways that confirm these hypotheses rather than as they would in a more natural, less reactive situation.

However, even if participants are aware that they are in a research study, it is often possible to conceal from them the particular focus and goal of the research. For example, laboratory studies of helping behavior might involve staged "emergencies," which occur while participants are performing another task that is the ostensible focus of the research (e.g., filling out questionnaires). The participants are presumably unaware that their reactions to the emergency are of primary interest, for as far as they are concerned the emergency simply happened. By techniques like this, researchers aim to keep participants from guessing the true purpose of the study.

Moreover, even when participants know they are in a study, if they remain unaware of the particular behavior that is of interest, they are more likely to act naturally with respect to that behavior. For example, participants might realize that a study of the getting acquainted process is concerned with how much they like their partners, and their ratings on a self-report measure of liking might be higher than they should be due to social desirability concerns. However, the researchers might also measure liking by recording how close the participants choose to sit to their partners, a variable of which the participants are probably unaware and hence more likely to accurately reflect their true feelings about their partners. Chapter 15 describes the issues involved in designing and interpreting such nonreactive measures in greater detail.

Finally, we should note that nonlaboratory research can also involve participants who are aware of being studied. Except for innocuous observations of publicly accessible behavior, ethical considerations usually require that participants in field research be informed that they are being studied. Thus, although the laboratory setting obviously makes the individual's role as a research participant highly salient, awareness of such a role, and the validity problems it presents, is not limited to laboratory research.

Summary

Despite its popular association with such high-prestige scientific fields as physics and chemistry, the laboratory is by no means a perfect setting for social scientific research. Like every research setting, the laboratory has its own profile of strengths and weaknesses that make it more appropriate for some types of research than for others. The laboratory can be particularly useful for testing theoretical hypotheses of universalistic scope, to answer questions about what would happen rather than what does happen in some actual setting, and to investigate the relatively short-term effects of manipulable independent variables. It is less suitable for answering questions about what does happen in particular target settings, for describing particular populations in particular places, or for looking at long-term effects of fixed and nonmanipulable variables. The researcher who views the laboratory as an inappropriate setting for social science research across the board commits as serious an error as the researcher who adopts it unquestioningly for every type of research problem. Reality is more complex than either of these extreme and uncritical positions; the suitability of the laboratory for each individual research issue and goal must be judged on its own merits.

Types of Laboratory Study

Laboratory studies can be divided into categories, which differ in the nature of the independent variable and often in the participants' task as well. Aronson, Wilson, and Brewer (1998) distinguished between impact and judgment experiments, and we add a third category, observational studies.

Impact Studies

An **impact study** is one in which the manipulation in some sense actually happens to the participants. In this type of study, "people are active participants in an unfolding series of events and have to react to these events as they occur" (Aronson et al., p. 109). An example is a classic study of helping behavior in which the participants are unexpectedly confronted with a (staged) emergency while they are performing some mundane experimental tasks (Darley & Latané, 1968). The researcher actually is interested in how and whether the participants seek help. Impact studies in general require careful staging, for the event whose impact the researcher is studying must be taken as real by the participants.

Other examples include the following:

- The Milgram (1974) study of obedience to authority already described. This is perhaps the prototypical impact study in social psychology.
- A study of the effects of video game violence on subsequent aggression (Anderson & Dill, 2000). Undergraduates were asked to play either a violent ("Wolfenstein 3D") or nonviolent ("Myst") video game. These games had been

shown through pilot testing to be matched on a number of important variables such as ratings of game enjoyment, difficulty, frustration, action speed, and cardiovascular activation while playing. After playing the video games, participants completed a measure of aggressive thinking and then played a competitive reaction time game in which they had the opportunity to punish their opponents by administering an aversive blast of white noise. Analyses showed that participants who had played the violent video game thought and behaved more aggressively than participants who played the nonviolent game.

- A study of the effects of past success and persistence on organizations experiencing a dramatic environmental change (Audia, Locke, & Smith, 2000). In this study, management students played the Cellular Industry Business Game, a computer-based simulation that manipulated the amount of task knowledge available to participants and required them to make strategic decisions in several areas of activity. Results showed that greater past success led to more persistence, but such persistence could lead to performance declines. Dysfunctional persistence was related to greater satisfaction with past performance, greater confidence, higher goals and self-efficacy, and less seeking of information from critics.

All of these studies involve independent variables that were intended to have a direct impact on the participants' behavior.

Judgment Studies

Judgment studies are those in which participants are "more like passive observers; they are asked to recognize, recall, classify, or evaluate stimulus materials presented by the experimenter. Little direct impact on participants is intended, except insofar as the stimulus materials capture people's attention and elicit meaningful judgmental responses" (Aronson et al., 1998, p. 109). In general, effects of variations in the characteristics of the stimulus materials are the key focus of interest. An example is a study by Lee and Hallahan (2001), which looked at whether the explanations people offer for another person's behavior are influenced by the similarity between the observers' and target person's career goals and whether the observers are instructed to carefully think about their responses or simply give their initial reaction. The manipulation included short vignettes describing either a young doctor or lawyer facing work-related dilemmas. The contrast between this kind of study and an impact study is clear: Nothing is actually happening to the participants, who are simply supplying the researcher with their judgments and evaluations.

Other examples include the following:

- A classic study of person perception in which participants were given written information about a series of behaviors of a hypothetical stimulus person (Hastie & Kumar, 1979). For example, they might have read that he won the chess tournament and that he ate a cheeseburger for lunch. Participants were instructed to form an impression of the target person and to answer several questions about him. Finally, they were unexpectedly asked to recall as many as possible of the original behaviors that they had read; the researchers used these data to test a theory about how information about other persons is organized in and retrieved from memory.

- A study of children's perceptions of a teasing incident (Scambler, Harris, & Milich, 1998). In this study, children watched a videotape portraying three children working on a puzzle together. The children in the tape (actually actors following a script) are discussing where they go to school when one of the children reveals that he had repeated third grade due to a move. The other children commence teasing this child, calling him stupid. Three versions of the videotape were created, varying the victim's response to the teasing. In one version the child responds in a hostile manner; in the second, the child ignores the teasing and changes the subject; and in the third, the child responds with a humorous comeback. The child participants viewed one of the three versions and then responded to a questionnaire asking for their impressions of the children on the videotape and the effectiveness of the target child's response to the teasing.

In these judgment studies, in contrast to impact studies, events do not actually happen to the participants. Instead, the participants read, listen to, or watch stimulus materials and then make evaluations and judgments.

Observational Studies

A third category of laboratory research does not fall clearly into either of Aronson et al.'s (1998) categories because of their focus on experimental research. We label as **observational studies** those that use the laboratory mainly for its convenience in arranging controlled observation. The key element of such studies is intensive observation; although different experimental conditions might be used, there is not a strong emphasis on impactive manipulations. An example might be a study of group discussion, in which detailed records of interaction are made, perhaps including videotapes of the participants' nonverbal behaviors as well as transcripts of what is said to whom. Groups might be studied under different conditions (e.g., high-cohesiveness versus low-cohesiveness groups). In a sense this might be termed an impact study, for the cohesiveness manipulation directly affects the participants, but the focus is not on a high-impact manipulation such as the staged emergency in a helping study but on detailed observation of social interaction or other ongoing behavior under different conditions.

Examples include the following:

- Studies of group decision making. For example, Sommer, Horowitz, and Bourgeois (2001) had jury-eligible men and women participate in mock juries deliberating a negligence lawsuit. After hearing the evidence, juries deliberated to reach a verdict and assign a damage award. The deliberations were videotaped, and coders later rated the videotapes for references to evidence that favored the plaintiff, references to evidence that favored the defendant, and the presence of a "trigger person," someone who advocated disregarding the instructions to the jury in favor of doing what was "fair." Analyses indicated that jurors selectively raised and discussed evidence that would justify their decisions and that the presence of a trigger person who raised justice concerns was more likely to result in noncompliant juries.

- Studies in developmental psychology aimed at showing how children of a specific age play with each other and their parents, therefore making inferences about their social and cognitive structures and abilities (e.g., Farver & Howes, 1993).

In these examples, the focus is on detailed observation of interaction or behavior as it unfolds over time, rather than on the impact of some event on the participants.

Summary

Because laboratory studies are of different types, the key issues and concerns differ from one study to another. For example, in an impact study, the staging and pretesting of an "unexpected" event might consume most of the researcher's efforts, whereas in a judgment study, the careful, controlled construction of multiple stimuli might be the focus of the work. Anyone who is planning to conduct or evaluate laboratory research should carefully consider what the key issues are in the particular study of interest—depending on its type, its topic, the variables being manipulated, the special nature of the population, and so on. Unfortunately, there is little general-purpose practical advice that is applicable to all types of laboratory studies, as the great diversity of the examples provided suggests.

Artifact and Artificiality

Research has revealed several types of artifact that can contaminate the results of laboratory studies if appropriate precautions are not taken. Moreover, laboratory studies sometimes impress readers or observers as trivial or unnatural in various ways. The presumed "artificiality" of laboratory research has become a kind of catchword for critics who advocate increased use of more naturalistic types of research. Let us examine the merits of these concerns and criticisms to see what lessons we can learn about threats to the validity of laboratory research.

The Laboratory and Types of Validity

As noted in Chapter 2, all research—not just laboratory research—must be judged against three general questions, which correspond to three types of validity. The special considerations that arise concerning the laboratory setting affect each of these types of validity.

Internal Validity The laboratory setting in itself carries no positive or negative implications for internal validity; however, as noted, the laboratory facilitates random assignment and manipulation, and experimental design is the most important single factor in increasing the internal validity of research. In fact, a well-designed experiment, whether in the laboratory or in the field, allows few if any plausible threats to internal validity, as detailed in Chapter 11.

Construct Validity In the laboratory, we face questions about the extent to which concrete independent and dependent variables truly match their intended theoretical constructs. For the independent variable, at times there are no problems in capturing the intended causal construct in a laboratory manipulation. Consider a study on the effects of persuasive messages delivered by print versus television. A laboratory manipulation in which some participants read messages and others see messages on videotape certainly seems to correspond in all relevant ways to the intended theoretical construct. Yet, at times the issue is more difficult. We might wish to investigate the effects of authority relationships on social interaction, for example, by bringing pairs of college students into the laboratory and assigning one to a "supervisor" role and the other to the role of "subordinate." But serious questions could be asked about how well this manipulation captures the theoretical construct of "authority" as it exists in organizations or other nonlaboratory settings. The manipulation lacks such features as a history over time, actual control by the "supervisor" over significant outcomes for the "subordinate," differential access to organizational resources, and so on. For such reasons, we might wonder about the construct validity of some laboratory manipulations.

For the dependent variable, laboratory studies often rely on single-item pencil-and-paper measures, which can be criticized from the viewpoint of construct validity. (Of course, much survey and field research is subject to the same criticism.) However, as discussed in Chapter 6, questionnaire-based measures can be constructed with good reliability and validity. In addition, laboratory research often uses other types of dependent variables, including response latencies, physiological activity, and observations of real behavior. In fact, the ability to arrange settings, tasks, and instruments (e.g., cameras or physiological monitoring equipment) to record behaviors of theoretical interest, instead of having to depend on the participants' self-reports, is a significant advantage of the laboratory over most field settings.

How do we assess construct validity? The answer was given in Chapters 2 and 4, where we argued that any operationalization can be demonstrated to match its intended theoretical construct by showing that its associations with other variables follow theoretical predictions, both in the sense of convergent and discriminant validity. This strategy is as applicable in the laboratory as anywhere else. A good example of demonstrated convergent validity is found in Isen's research on the effects of moods on memory and judgment (e.g., Isen, 1984). Across a number of studies, she induced positive moods in research participants by giving them gifts, offering them cookies and soda as they enter the laboratory, having them read a series of positive statements about themselves, and showing them comedy films. The research seems to show that all these manipulations have similar effects, laying to rest most concerns about the construct validity of each.

Note that the construct validity of a manipulation or dependent measure is not assessed by examining its surface features. Strictly speaking, the degree of apparent similarity between a laboratory operational definition and some other instance of a construct is irrelevant to the construct validity of the operational definition. Aronson et al. (1998) underscore this fact by drawing a distinction between experimental realism and mundane realism. **Experimental realism** refers to the extent to which the manipulations or measures are truly perceived in the intended ways by the research participants—in other words, to their construct validity. **Mundane realism** refers to the degree of resemblance between the laboratory operational definitions and some target objects or events outside the laboratory. Mundane realism is not a precondition for experimental realism.

For example, the construct validity of the manipulation of authority in Milgram's (1974) experiments on obedience depends on the extent to which research participants perceive the experimenter's authority as real and valid—experimental realism. Its construct validity is to be judged by the demonstrated correspondence of its effects to theoretically expected patterns, not by its superficial resemblance to particular "real-life" instances of authority—mundane realism. The construct validity of the number of shocks participants deliver to a confederate on the "Buss aggression machine" as a measure of aggression cannot be assessed by asking questions such as "How often in real life do people give shocks to others when they are angry?" but rather by comparing the results obtained with this measure, over a series of studies, with those that are theoretically expected for a valid measure of the construct of aggression. Such comparisons speak well for the construct validity of this particular measure (Berkowitz & Donnerstein, 1982).

This discussion should make it clear that the construct validity of a laboratory operational definition cannot be assessed simply by examining the superficial aspects of the operational definition, for example, by asking whether it resembles anything that participants encounter in real life. Experimental realism is not the same as mundane realism. Nor can construct validity generally be assessed on the basis of the outcome of a single study. Instead, evidence of construct validity emerges as the results of multiple studies using the operational definition are found to concur with theoretical expectations: The empirical associations found using the operational definition match the theoretically predicted associations that the construct is expected to have.

In summary, in our view construct validity is the key question that must be asked about manipulations or measures used in laboratory research. The question ordinarily cannot command a definite answer in the short run, in contrast to internal validity, which can in many cases be confidently attributed to a particular study. Construct validity can be problematic more often in the laboratory than in field settings because operational definitions used in the laboratory often are simplified or abstracted from a situation of interest or devised to operationally define theoretical constructs. With the researcher's creative act of abstraction or construction comes the obligation to assess the correspondence between the operation and the construct of interest.

External Validity As defined previously, external validity refers to the range of settings, populations, and the like to which the research results can be generalized or applied. As with construct validity, external validity is an empirical question. Unlike construct validity, which is important in all research, the importance of external validity depends greatly on the specific research goals. Two cases can be distinguished using labels previously introduced: particularistic versus universalistic research.

The goal of all particularistic research is generalization from the laboratory or other research setting to a specific target setting and population. Research results are therefore of little use if they do not apply to the target setting. Thus, care is usually taken to make the research setting (and population and operational definitions of dependent and independent variables) as similar as possible to the target. Of course, absolute similarity cannot generally be attained, and an appeal to theory must be made to establish which variables are important and which ones are not. For example, the color of the walls in the research setting probably does not need to match the color of the walls in the setting of interest, unless theory or prior evidence demonstrates that wall color has a systematic effect on the phenomenon of interest. For particularistic research, external validity is a key goal, and researchers generally attempt to increase it by making consequential features of the research setting, population, and manipulations as similar as possible to those about which inferences are to be drawn.

In universalistic research, on the other hand, because there is no specific target setting, population, and so on, the issue of external validity takes a very different form. It makes little sense to ask to what settings and populations the specific results of the research will generalize, for the results in themselves are not really the point. Instead, the goal of the research is to test theoretically derived hypotheses. For example, a researcher might note that in a specific laboratory study the effect of a certain manipulation of frustration is to increase one measure of aggression by 9% in a given population. The researcher would be quite unjustified in extending this finding in quantitative detail to any larger population, for instance, by claiming that "frustration on the job increases the likelihood that parents will physically abuse their children by 9%." The nonrepresentative sampling of research participants (e.g., undergraduate volunteers) and the other arbitrary aspects of the experimental manipulation and setting rule out any effort at generalization in this form. But such generalization is not the point of universalistic research. The research was intended to support or falsify theoretical predictions about the conditions under which frustration increases aggression.

In universalistic research, the external validity question takes this form: To what range of settings and populations does the theory apply? External validity or generalizability is really a property of the theory, not of the research findings. From this perspective, consider the possible conclusions that could be drawn if a particular theoretical association is demonstrated in a laboratory study but is absent in a field setting: (1) Perhaps the operational definitions of the theoretical constructs used in the laboratory research were flawed, having poor construct validity. (2) The operational definitions that are being examined in the field setting might have the same problem. (3) The theory is inadequate, failing to specify the importance of one or more variables that differ between the laboratory and field setting. The theory has missed the existence of a qualifying condition that limits the range of situations in which the key association will apply. The external validity of a theory in this sense is most clearly demonstrated by **replication:** A finding that can be reproduced across a variety of settings, populations, and specific operational definitions of the theoretical constructs probably has a broad range of applicability.

In short, once construct validity has been established, external validity questions for universalistic research are not questions about the research results per se but about the adequacy and completeness of the theory. In the case of universalistic research, generalization from the laboratory to other settings and populations is not direct but indirect. The research is used to test and support a theory; the theory is used to generate predictions for other settings and populations of interest. This principle is schematically illustrated in Figure 12.1. The operative links are A and B, which correspond respectively to the construct validity of the research operations and to the predictive power and completeness of the theory. Link C, the extent of direct correspondence or similarity between the laboratory operational definitions and elements of the target situation, is of little or no importance in the logic of universalistic research; however, as noted earlier, C is the key link in particularistic research and is appropriate to emphasize in evaluating the external validity of research that investigates phenomena as they occur in specific settings or populations.

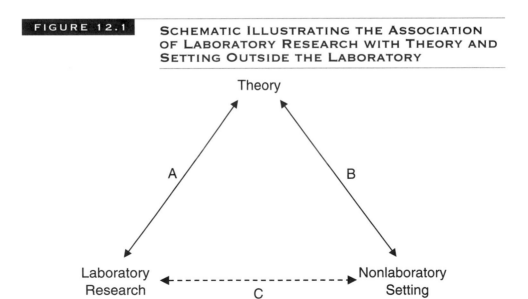

FIGURE 12.1 SCHEMATIC ILLUSTRATING THE ASSOCIATION OF LABORATORY RESEARCH WITH THEORY AND SETTING OUTSIDE THE LABORATORY

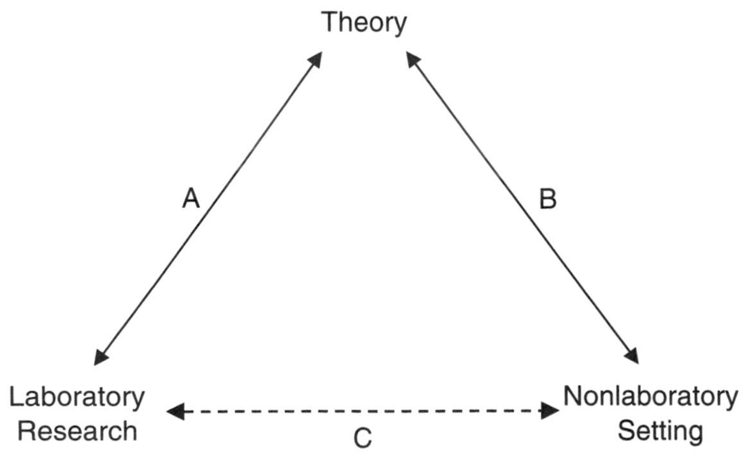

"Artificiality" of the Laboratory

Criticisms of laboratory research are often phrased in terms of the laboratory's artificiality. Of course, laboratory research is necessarily artificial in that the laboratory is used precisely because it permits the creation or construction of settings, tasks, and manipulations that are most suited to achieving the research goals. But critics take artificiality in a different sense, pointing to differences between events and tasks in a laboratory study and those that might be found outside the laboratory. For example, the Milgram (1974) studies on obedience to authority have been termed "artificial" because being ordered by a psychological researcher to deliver shocks to a helpless fellow participant is not an event within most people's everyday experience.

But as the earlier discussion indicates, resemblance to events in everyday life is not a criterion for the evaluation of universalistic research. The most problematic form of validity for laboratory research that is intended to test a theory is construct validity, which is established by careful comparisons between research results and theoretical expectations, not by examining the superficial attributes of the research operations. Artificiality in the critic's sense is irrelevant to the construct validity of universalistic research, and the critic is inappropriately applying a standard that is suited for evaluating particularistic research. However, artificiality in this sense can contribute to one particular kind of threat to construct validity, demand characteristics. This concern is discussed later in the chapter.

The message to the critic, then, is to look beneath the surface. A seemingly artificial manipulation might turn out to be a valid operational definition of the intended theoretical construct—or it might not. The question is an empirical one, not to be settled by pointing at superficial attributes of the research but by evaluation of the results of research, using the operational definition in question.

Overcoming Threats to Validity of Laboratory Research

Laboratory research is subject to many of the same threats to validity as other types of research. The main strength of the laboratory in this domain is its conduciveness to the randomized experiment, which rules out the most significant threats to internal validity. The most significant weaknesses of laboratory research involve construct validity, which can be threatened by several factors, including experimenter expectancies and demand characteristics.

Experimenter Expectancy Imagine that students walk into a laboratory to participate in a research project. The experimenter tells the students that they are going to be making judgments about photos of people's faces for a study of perception. The experimenter shows the students a series of photos, one at a time, and asks the students to judge how much each face reflects "success" or "failure." Unknown to the students, the experimenter was previously told by a supervisor that people generally judge these particular photos as highly successful (or in another condition, that they were generally judged failures). The remarkable findings of experiments like these, pioneered by Rosenthal and his collaborators (Rosenthal,1976; Rosenthal & Rosnow,

1969; Rosnow & Rosenthal, 1997), demonstrate that **experimenter expectancies** concerning people's typical responses can influence research participants' actual responses; in other words, the students believed by the experimenter to be "success perceivers" actually give success ratings that are significantly higher than students believed to be "failure perceivers," even though the label of success and failure perceiver was randomly assigned.

These hypothesis-confirming results do not occur because experimenters (or participants) consciously attempt to bias the results or cheat (Rosenthal, 1969). Instead, the influence stems from subtle, nonverbal cues that are not under the experimenter's conscious control but that can nevertheless be detected by the participants, affecting their behavior. For example, using the research strategy described in the above paragraph, studies have shown that differential vocal emphasis plays an important role in eliciting expectancy-consistent ratings from the participants (Adair & Epstein, 1968; Duncan & Rosenthal, 1968). That is, when reading the standardized script, experimenters expecting higher success ratings from their participants slightly and unintentionally stress such words as "success" and "positive." In turn, simply hearing a tape recording of experimental instructions with such words stressed leads participants to rate the target persons as more successful.

Laboratory research is particularly susceptible to experimenter bias for two reasons. First, the researcher is ordinarily in direct communication with the participants, which might not be the case in much survey or field research. Second, in the isolated and controlled environment of the laboratory, participants might be particularly attentive to subtle aspects of the researcher's behavior or the setting, trying to discover the purpose of the study and to act accordingly by giving "correct" or socially desirable responses (Rosenberg, 1969).

How can such subtle, nonconscious biases be eliminated? Clearly they must be, for otherwise research is in danger of seeming to confirm researchers' theories simply because of their expectations, not because the theories are accurate. Put another way, these biases constitute a threat to construct validity, for an experimental manipulation can represent not only a manipulation of the intended construct but also a confound—a dose of nonverbal messages from the experimenter. We could never be certain which of the two factors produced the results.

Fortunately, eliminating the possibility of experimenter expectancy effects is not as difficult as it might seem. Table 12.1 lists a number of strategies that might be undertaken in coping with expectancy effects. First are listed strategies that would prevent expectancy effects from occurring, of which the most important and effective is keeping the experimenter unaware of the experimental condition of the participants. Consider a study on mood and interpersonal judgment, designed to test the hypothesis that people in a good mood make more positive judgments about others than people in a neutral or bad mood. If the experimenter is aware that the current participant is in the good-mood condition, the experimenter might unintentionally give nonverbal signals that lead the participant to make positive judgments. But if the experimenter is unaware of the condition to which the participant has been assigned, there is no way that his or her cues can artificially bias the experimental results. The experimenter can know that good-mood participants are expected to make more

TABLE 12.1 **STRATEGIES FOR COPING WITH EXPERIMENTER EXPECTANCY EFFECTS**

Strategies that Prevent Expectancy Effects

- Keep experimenters unaware of participants' conditions.
- Eliminate experimenter–participant interaction, e.g., conduct study on the Internet or have participant respond to instructions delivered by computer or audiotape.

Strategies that Minimize Expectancy Effects

- Minimize experimenter–participant interaction, e.g., deliver crucial instructions, manipulations, or measures on paper or computer.
- Use multiple experimenters within sessions, one to deliver the manipulation who is not unaware of the participants' experimental conditions and one to administer the dependent variable who is kept unaware of participants' experimental conditions.
- Keep experimenters unaware of participants' conditions as long as possible.
- Keep experimenters unaware of experimental hypotheses.
- Use multiple experimenters across sessions.
- Train experimenters carefully and emphasize importance of adhering to standardization.

Strategies that Permit the Detection and Assessment of Expectancy Effects

- Observe experimenters' behavior, either on-line or through videotaping.
- Adopt an expectancy control group design.

---

positive judgments, but without knowing what mood condition a person is in, the experimenter cannot have firm expectations about the kind of responses the person will produce and thus cannot systematically bias the results.

Eliminating *all* experimenter–participant contact is the other surefire strategy for preventing experimenter expectancy effects. If expectancies are communicated subtly through the experimenter's nonverbal behaviors, then if the experimenter is not present, expectancy effects cannot occur. An increasing number of studies are conducted over the Internet, for example, and although these studies were not designed to avoid experimenter expectancy effects, they eliminate them altogether. Experimenter contact can also be avoided through the practice of having participants show up at the laboratory to find signs instructing them to start a tape recorder or computer program that delivers further instructions. Although such procedures are successful in preventing experimenter expectancy effects, they entail obvious disadvantages. With no experimenter present, there is no way to answer any questions participants might have. There also is no quality control over responding, including no way to ensure that the intended participant of the study is the person who actually provides the responses. Lastly, participant motivation can suffer under such automated procedures, leading to a corresponding drop in response quality. For these reasons, automated data gathering is not used often and is probably appropriate only for very short, simple studies.

In the second section of Table 12.1 are listed strategies that can minimize, though not prevent entirely, the occurrence of experimenter expectancy effects. Limiting experimenter–participant contact can help to reduce the opportunities for experimenters' nonverbal cues or reinforcement to influence participants' behavior. Having crucial instructions or manipulations handed to participants on a sheet of paper or delivered by computer not only reduces the potential for experimenter bias but also aids in enhancing the standardization of procedures, as it can be guaranteed that the instructions or manipulations are identical across participants. However, the disadvantage of this strategy is that written or computer-administered instructions often are less motivating and have less impact on the participants, thus reducing the experimental realism of the study.

As we have stressed, keeping experimenters unaware of the treatment condition to which participants were assigned is the best strategy for avoiding expectancy effects. However, there are situations in which it is not possible to keep experimenters unaware, for example, if the manipulation is one that must be delivered orally by the experimenter or cannot be enacted without the experimenter's awareness. There are nonetheless creative ways of preserving unawareness as much as possible in such situations. Clever experimental arrangements—including such tricks as the use of two experimenters, one to deliver the manipulation and the other, who remains unaware of what manipulation was given, to collect the dependent variable—can prevent experimenter expectancy effects in research. This strategy was used in a study by Harris, Milich, Corbitt, Hoover, and Brady (1992). Because the participants in this study were children as young as eight years old, whose reading and writing skills were thus uncertain, both the experimental manipulations and dependent measures were administered orally—a situation that could easily lead to experimenter bias. The researchers thus used multiple experimenters, one who interacted with the child only briefly to deliver the experimental manipulations and another who worked with the child for the remainder of the session, including gathering responses to the dependent measures. This second experimenter was kept unaware of not only the treatment condition to which the children had been assigned but also the goals of the study.

An obvious drawback to this solution is that it requires the use of multiple experimenters, which often is not feasible. When only a single experimenter can be employed, an alternative strategy is to keep that experimenter unaware of the experimental condition of the participant as long as possible. Using the mood and judgment study example discussed earlier, the experimenter could remain unaware while obtaining informed consent and delivering the cover story. At the point in the script when the manipulation is delivered, the experimenter would—only then—open an envelope revealing the participant's experimental condition and then insert the proper stimulus videotape to show. This solution works best for studies in which there is little need for experimenter–participant interaction during and after the manipulation.

A weaker form of unawareness is keeping the experimenter unaware of the research hypotheses. The experimenter could be aware that a person is in the good-mood condition but would not have been told that a good mood is hypothesized to lead to more positive interpersonal judgments. This measure hardly protects against experimenter expectancy effects, however, for the experimenter might well form his or her own idiosyncratic expectations for different conditions, regardless of whether they correspond to the actual research hypotheses. Using multiple experimenters throughout one's study helps to minimize that possibility and is another strategy for reducing expectancy effects. Having more experimenters running fewer sessions each makes it less likely that the experimenters will generate experimental hypotheses in the first place, as well as making it less likely that they will pick up on the subtle operant conditioning strategies that lead to participants yielding the expected results. It also has the benefit of increasing the generalizability of the research findings.

Training experimenters carefully and emphasizing the need to adhere to standardization in all aspects of the experimental procedure can help to minimize experimenter expectancy effects. If experimenters are educated about the potential for and danger of expectancy effects, they might be more conscientious about sticking to the script and monitoring their nonverbal behavior. Training and adherence to standardization is a wise strategy in general for increasing control and reducing error in laboratory research, but it is at best a weak strategy for preventing experimenter expectancy effects. It is simply impossible for experimenters to continuously monitor and control the subtle nonverbal behaviors through which hypotheses might be communicated.

Lastly, there are two strategies researchers can use that will not prevent expectancy effects from happening but would allow a determination of whether they are occurring and, if so, their magnitude. The first involves monitoring experimenters' behavior, either in the actual experimental sessions or afterwards by watching videotapes of the sessions. Naive observers could watch the tapes and rate the experimenters' behavior on relevant dimensions, and analyses could be done to see whether experimenter behavior varied systematically across conditions. For example, do experimenters look happier and smile more when they interact with participants in the good-mood condition compared to participants in the bad-mood condition? This strategy has the added benefit of probably working to reduce expectancy effects as well, because experimenters might adhere more closely to standardization if they know their behavior will be scrutinized later by the researcher. When observations are made on-line as the study is being run, experimenters who appear to be significantly biased in their behavior toward participants can be retrained or replaced. When these observations are made after the fact, it is too late to salvage the study, but at least the researcher has gained important knowledge about the source of the participants' behavior.

The second strategy for detecting and assessing the magnitude of expectancy effects is to use an **expectancy control group design,** also known as the balanced placebo design. In this elegant design, experimenters' expectancies are manipulated along with the major independent variable in a factorial design. We illustrate this

TABLE 12.2 HYPOTHETICAL EXAMPLE OF AN EXPECTANCY CONTROL GROUP DESIGN

Participants' Actual Experimental Condition	Experimenters' Expectancies About Participants' Condition	
	Happy Movie	**Sad Movie**
Happy movie	8.50	5.50
Sad movie	5.50	2.50

Note: Data represent positivity of interpersonal judgment, rated on a 9-point Likert scale.

design using the hypothetical mood and interpersonal judgment study introduced earlier. In the traditional design, half of the participants (say, $n = 60$) are placed in a good mood by watching a funny movie, whereas the other half are placed in a bad mood by watching a sad movie. In the expectancy control group design, the mood manipulation would occur just as described—half of the participants would watch a funny movie and half would watch a sad movie. However, in addition to this manipulation, the experimenter's *beliefs* about the condition of the participants would be manipulated. Of the 60 participants watching the happy movie, the experimenter would be led to believe that a randomly chosen 30 had watched a happy movie (consistent with their actual experience) and the other 30 had watched a sad movie (opposite to their actual experience). Similarly, the experimenter would be led to believe that half of the 60 participants who had watched the sad movie had in fact watched the sad movie but that the other 30 participants had seen a happy movie, which they had not. Table 12.2 displays in graphic form what this expectancy control group design would look like and shows some hypothetical results.

As can be seen in the table, the expectancy control group design yields four groups: two groups for which the experimenters' expectancies are consistent with the participants' actual experience and two groups for which the experimenters' expectancies are inconsistent with the participants' actual experience. The former two groups are those found in research conducted in the traditional manner, wherein experimenters are not kept unaware of participants' experimental condition. The latter two groups are not found in traditional research, but it is their inclusion in the design that allows researchers to detect whether and to what extent expectancy effects are occurring. Essentially, the expectancy control group design provides the answers to three questions: (1) What is the effect of the theoretical independent variable of interest? (2) What is the effect of experimenters' expectancies? (3) Is the expectancy qualified by the independent variable, that is, are the effects of experimenters' expectancies greater at one level of the independent variable than another?

Looking at the numbers in Table 12.2, we can see that there is an effect for the hypothetical independent variable: Participants who watch happy movies do in fact judge others more positively than participants who watch sad movies. But we see that there also is an effect (equal in magnitude, actually) for experimenters' expectancies: Participants whose experimenters believed them to have watched a happy movie—whether that belief was correct or not—give more positive judgments than participants whose experimenters believed them to have watched a sad movie.

This basic result, that the effect of experimenter expectancy can be significant and comparable in magnitude to the effect of the theoretical variable, is found frequently in the domains in which the expectancy control group design has been applied. A classic example is a study by Burnham (1966; cited in Rosnow & Rosenthal, 1997, pp. 60–61) that looked at the role of experimenter expectancies in a study of lesions in rats. Twenty-three experimenters each ran a rat through a maze. Half of the rats had received surgery that induced a lesion in a region of the brain; the other half had received sham surgery but their brains had not been lesioned. In addition to actual brain status, experimenter expectancy was manipulated such that about half of the experimenters were told that their rat's status was opposite to what it actually was. The dependent measure was performance on the maze task. Analyses revealed that rats whose brains had been lesioned ran the maze more slowly than did rats without lesions, an unsurprising result that tells us only that it is better to have an intact brain than not. The more surprising result was that there was also a significant effect due to experimenter expectancy: Rats whose experimenters *thought* they were lesioned ran the maze more slowly than rats whose experimenters thought they were not lesioned. Moreover, this effect was slightly larger in magnitude than the effect due to actual brain lesions. In other words, in terms of maze performance, it mattered more what the experimenter thought about the rat than whether or not the rat actually had an intact brain.

The advantage of the expectancy control group design is that it is the only strategy listed in Table 12.1 that allows a precise estimation of the magnitude of expectancy effects and comparison to the effects of the independent variable. This design is not without its limitations, however. First, it can be used only when it is possible to fool experimenters about the experimental condition of the participants. Second, the expectancy control group design is not a panacea for problems caused by expectancy effects: All it does is reveal whether expectancy effects are occurring; it does not prevent them from happening. Third, and more problematic, is that by adding the experimenter expectancy factor, researchers are essentially doubling the size of their design. Few researchers have the resources to double their data-gathering efforts for the sole purpose of detecting an effect that they do not want. Consequently, the expectancy control group design is underutilized in the social sciences and tends to be restricted to those research areas in which expectancies are of substantive interest, such as the large literature on behavioral effects of alcohol, in which both experimenter and participant expectancies about the participant's consumption of alcohol are often manipulated (e.g., Monahan, Murphy, & Miller, 1999).

Demand Characteristics Imagine a student walking into a laboratory to participate in a study. Cut off from the outside world, in a setting with few if any familiar elements, and confronted with a novel set of tasks, the student might be particularly motivated to try to make sense of the situation or to figure out what behaviors would make him or her appear psychologically "normal" or more likely to be evaluated positively by the researcher. This is the key idea behind the notion of **demand characteristics:** that participants attempt to pick up subtle cues in the researcher's behavior, the task, or the setting to use as guidance for their behavior. The danger to the validity of the research conclusions is that when participants act in response to their perceptions of the research purposes or in ways that are motivated by a desire to appear in a positive light, they are not responding as they naturally would to the experimental manipulations or stimuli.

A striking confirmation of this point is the fact that participants have complied with instructions to behave in seemingly dangerous ways, picking up a poisonous snake or taking a penny out of an acid solution that would presumably burn their bare hands. They were willing to heed the researcher's instructions because they believed that the research would not truly endanger the participants. (And of course, they were correct in this belief.) The experimental setting, therefore, contained demand characteristics that somehow conveyed to participants that there was no real danger (Orne, 1969).

Even innocuous studies, though, can be affected by demand characteristics. Orne's interest in demand characteristics, in fact, grew out of a frustrating experience he had in his research on hypnosis. Orne (1962) wanted to create a task that would demonstrate definitively that hypnosis is a qualitatively distinct psychological state. His original idea was to design a task that would be so tedious and dull that a non-hypnotized person would refuse to do it. So he brought participants into the laboratory and presented each of them with a huge stack of paper that had hundreds of thousands of simple arithmetic problems (adding two-digit numbers). Orne told the participants to work on the additions until he told them to stop. *Five and a half hours later* Orne himself gave up and told the participants to stop. When Orne made the task even more pointless by instructing the participants to tear each sheet of paper into no fewer than 32 pieces after they had finished it, the participants kept working for hours until Orne finally told them to stop. What could account for the participants' ceaseless toil? Orne (1962) concluded that the participants were reacting to the demand characteristics of the situation. Because the researcher obviously was not interested in mathematical ability (the problems were too easy, not to mention the pages were being torn up before the researcher could see them), the participants concluded the study had to be about something else. And the "something else" they came up with was that it involved task persistence, and because nobody wanted to score low on a measure of task persistence, they all kept working until they were told to stop.

There are two important morals to this story: The first is that research participants engage in an active search for meaning when they participate in an experiment. If the researcher does not provide them with the meaning of the experiment, or if the researcher's explanation blatantly contradicts what they actually experience, participants will generate their own meaning. The second moral is even more important: The meaning participants come up with on their own is not random. Rather, they react to the demand characteristics of the situation in similar ways. The vast majority of Orne's (1962) participants concluded that the boring task was in reality a test of task persistence. And therein lies the insidious danger of demand characteristics: Because they lead participants to behave in systematic ways, they undermine the construct validity of the experiment.

What can researchers do about the problem of demand characteristics? Because demand characteristics represent the totality of cues that participants use to guess the hypothesis of the study, researchers need to accept the reality that demand characteristics can never be eliminated. Unless participants go through the study completely unaware, incurious, and unquestioning, they will be reacting to something in the experimental setting and they will be using that something to guide their behavior. Thus, the strategy for experimenters is not to eliminate demand characteristics but to carefully control them. The first step is to identify the demand characteristics that are salient in a given study. This is best accomplished through extensive **pilot testing,** in which individuals taken from the same population as the eventual participants are led through the procedures and periodically queried as to what they think the hypothesis of the study is and which features of the setting led them to that hypothesis. Researchers should take care not to settle for the expedient practice of using their own reactions to the laboratory setting as a substitute for more time-consuming pilot testing, as they are too intimately familiar with the experiment and its goals and will not be able to view the procedures and setting as a naive participant would.

Second, the best defense against bias due to demand characteristics is careful attention to the details of the laboratory setting and procedures. Disguising the independent variable is often the key—for example, by exposing each participant to only one level of the variable rather than several or by making the independent variable appear to be an event unrelated to the experiment. Examples of some methods researchers have used to decrease the possibility of bias caused by demand characteristics are given in the next section. But demand characteristics remain a concern in any research in which participants are aware of their participation, even in nonlaboratory research settings. For example, it might be rare for people to complete a survey questionnaire or perform tasks while under research observation without asking themselves the question "What are they trying to find out here?" and the almost inevitable sequel, "What should I say?" or "How should I act?"

Elements of a Laboratory Study

Practical advice on a number of aspects of laboratory research has been developed and refined by experienced researchers over the years. Here we present some basic suggestions and guidelines.

Setting

The context or surroundings in which someone participates in an investigation, though easy to overlook, can play an important role in influencing his or her reactions and behavior. Although the physical context and setting can be important, perhaps the central element is the participant's overall interpretation of "what is going on" in the research. Ordinarily, researchers do not allow participants to construct such an interpretation freely but give them one, commonly called a **cover story.** This term suggests that the interpretation provided is often misleading or deceptive, and sometimes it is. More often, though, researchers give participants a truthful but nonspecific account of the research purposes.

For example, in a study focusing on the helping behavior of participants in response to a staged emergency, the cover story would be quite simple but in fact deceptive: Participants would simply be told that their task is to fill out a questionnaire about life in college. While they are doing so, smoke might begin to filter into the room. In an investigation of the effects of stereotypes on interpersonal judgment, the participants might be told that the researcher is interested in how people form impressions of others. The participant is told that he or she will be given some information about other persons and is to study it, form an impression of what the target individuals are like, and answer some questions about them. This is an example of a truthful but overly general cover story; the researcher accurately conveys the general focus of the study on interpersonal judgments but does not mention that the key manipulation embedded in the descriptions of the target persons is their ethnicity. Finally, studies of the effects of persuasive communications on attitude change often use deceptive cover stories to prevent participants from focusing on how they "should" react to the stimulus materials. They might be told, for instance, that they are going to be watching a videotape of a speaker delivering a message and are to judge it for technical quality or for the speaker's skill and eloquence in conveying his or her message.

In all cases, the primary purpose of a cover story is to give research participants the sense that they know what is going on, an overall framework in which to interpret the events and tasks called for by the research. A cover story is successful if it both satisfies participants that they understand the research purpose (and thus keeps them from speculating about what the researcher really wants) and keeps them interested and motivated. Obviously, for both ethical and practical reasons, it is best to avoid deception when possible. But in some instances, such as research on helping behavior or aggression, it is difficult to imagine how the research could be conducted without some measure of deception.

In most cases, the details of the physical setting are subordinate, intended to bolster the cover story. For example, in an investigation of the effects of anticipated group discussion on people's prediscussion opinions or attitudes, the cover story will certainly focus on the upcoming discussion. If the researcher simply states that a group discussion will follow as soon as the participant completes a questionnaire, the participant might believe it. But if the participant is taken through a room containing a table surrounded by several chairs, hears sounds that suggest the presence of other participants in adjoining cubicles, and sees other people's books and coats in the research waiting room, belief in the cover story becomes much more likely. Similarly, research on the effects of fear might involve telling participants that they will receive electric shocks. The chances of arousing fear would be increased by allowing the participant to catch sight of impressive electrical apparatus or even by having the researcher dressed in a white laboratory coat.

In summary, the setting for a laboratory study must provide a framework (1) in which participants can interpret the events they will be going through—to prevent their own interpretations, a possibility that leads to the influence of demand characteristics on their behavior—and (2) that keeps the participants interested and motivated. Physical details, task instructions, and above all a sensible, coherent cover story are essential for these purposes. The key test of a cover story and its related aspects is whether participants find it plausible or disbelieve it and seek to look deeper for the "true" purpose of the research.

Independent Variable

Laboratory research often is experimental in design, so that the independent variable is actually a manipulation to which participants are randomly assigned. Of course, nonexperimental laboratory studies are sometimes performed, as in observations of how different types of people (e.g., people high and low on power motivation) respond to a laboratory-constructed situation (e.g., a group discussion). In such cases the independent variable is a property of the participants rather than a manipulation. In this section we focus on the special considerations involved in creating a laboratory manipulation of an independent variable.

The first requisite for a manipulation is construct validity or experimental realism (Aronson et al., 1998). How that is attained, however, differs between impact and judgment studies. In an impact study, the believability of the manipulation is crucial; a carefully constructed cover story, corroborating physical details, and skillful acting by the experimenter might all be necessary. If the research goal is to make participants angry to investigate the effects of anger on interpersonal evaluations, it might be decided that a bluntly worded hostile comment by a **confederate,** an accomplice of the experimenter posing as a participant, is the best way to accomplish it. A cover story must be constructed to render the delivery of the comment believable—perhaps on the theme that the research topic concerns effects of evaluations by peers versus superiors and that in the condition the participant is in, he or she will write a paragraph that will then be evaluated by a fellow student. The stage has now been set for the desired manipulation, framed as an untactfully direct negative evaluation of the participant's writing. Obviously, the details could vary greatly, depending on the specific nature of the manipulation that is to be delivered, and the researcher's creativity can be exercised.

In other cases, a manipulation is contained in the experimental instructions rather than in an event that occurs to the participant. In one study on the effects of social interaction goals, the control participants were told simply to conduct a job interview with no special instructions (Neuberg, Judice, Virdin, & Carrillo, 1993). The experimental participants were given a "liking goal" manipulation, which stressed that job applicants' true abilities are more likely to be revealed when the applicant likes the interviewer and concluded with the sentence, "Thus, in order for this study to be a valid representation of interviews in real-life, we'd like you to try to get the applicants to like you" (p. 412). Analyses showed that interviewers who held negative expectancies about their applicants and no interaction goal elicited self-fulfilling prophecies, whereas the liking goal interviewers overcame their negative expectancies.

With a judgment study, different considerations come to the fore. Manipulations are typically embedded in stimulus materials that participants study and evaluate, and making the materials believable is the key. For instance, if the research concerns the effects of a job applicant's ethnicity on evaluations of his or her suitability for a job, materials (perhaps in the format of résumés) would be prepared that differed only in that one respect: the applicant's ethnicity. The rest of the material on the résumé serves mainly as a context for the ethnicity manipulation; its effects on judgments are somewhat beside the point, for it does not vary from one experimental condition to another. Of course, it might be well to use several different résumés to establish that the effects of the ethnicity manipulation are relatively constant regardless of the other information.

In the case of judgment studies, believability is relative. It might not be important for participants to think that the résumés were provided by real job applicants, although some researchers might prefer to use a deceptive cover story including this statement. As long as the materials are plausible, participants generally are able to make judgments and evaluations as if they describe real people, events or situations, much in the same way that the psychological impact of a well-written novel does not depend on readers' belief that it describes actually existing persons and events.

Across all types of manipulation, unintentional confounding must be avoided. A **confound** occurs when the levels of the independent variable vary directly with some other, nonessential factor(s). For example, if two experimenters administer the experiment to participants, it would be extremely unwise to divide the participants between them by condition, perhaps on the theory that each experimenter would only have to learn the procedure for one condition. The manipulation that is intended to constitute the sole difference between conditions would be confounded by any irrelevant differences between the experimenters and their respective treatment of the research participants, rendering any results from the study uninterpretable. Of course, this confound is quite obvious and would not be seen in any experienced social scientist's work. Unfortunately, other equally problematic confounds are more often encountered. Consider, for example, manipulating a job applicant's ethnicity by means of a photograph. A photograph of a White person or an African American could be attached to otherwise identical résumés to create stimulus materials for two different conditions. However, the ethnicity manipulation is confounded by any number of unique attributes of the photos: Their physical attractiveness, whether they are smiling, and any other characteristics on which the photos differ would confound the intended variable. The solution to problems like these is to use more than one representative of each desired level of the manipulation (e.g., five photographs of African Americans and five of Whites). Irrelevant characteristics of the photographs would then vary within as well as between groups, lessening the danger of confounding.

A question that can arise in any type of experimental design is whether to expose each participant to more than one condition. As noted in Chapter 11, the advantage of using more than one condition per participant is that more information can be gathered per unit of research effort, increasing statistical power and precision. The disadvantage is that a participant who sees more than one condition is in a better position to grasp the purpose of the experiment, possibly modifying his or her reactions accordingly. Also, in some cases it makes no sense for a participant to experience more than one condition. We would not want to stage a serious "accident" to measure participants' helping behavior and then turn around and stage a less serious one for the same participants. Nor could we show the same participant an identical résumé with the job applicant's gender varied. This decision has to be made with careful thought about the specifics of each research project.

Finally, with any experimental manipulation it is essential that participants understand what they are to do and pay attention to the stimulus materials, the manipulation, and their task. The instructions that participants receive at the outset of their participation are the key means by which researchers attempt to reach these goals. A researcher who states instructions too briefly or not clearly enough risks gathering essentially random data from participants who do not understand or do not care what they are doing. Repetition of key elements of the instructions, numerous examples, and probes to make sure that the participants understand all are desirable strategies in virtually any laboratory research. Also, pretesting of the entire experimental procedure, from cover story through instructions to manipulation, is important. Pretest participants can be taken through the procedure and then questioned about their reactions, their understanding of their task, their belief in the cover story, and so on. Only after thorough pretesting has established that the procedures work as intended should actual data gathering begin.

We have stressed in this section an independent variable that is experimentally manipulated and to which participants are randomly assigned. Because random digits are equally likely to occur at any position in a list of random numbers, we should end up with roughly equal numbers of participants in each of the conditions, or cells of the design, following this procedure. However, there can be differences in cell sizes, especially if the number of conditions is high and the sample size relatively low. Such disparities are more problematic when another independent variable or blocking factor is being considered. Say, for example, that we are interested in looking at sex differences across four treatment conditions. Here we would ideally like to have equal numbers of men and women in each of the four conditions. A variation on randomization can be used to assure equal cell sizes for any factor or combination of factors, and that variation is to randomly assign participants in blocks. Using the example of a manipulation with four conditions, this strategy would entail "randomizing without replacement" in blocks of four. Let us say that the random number for the first participant was 2, indicating that he or she would be in condition B. If the next random number that appears is also 2, we would not assign the participant to condition B because that condition is already taken for that block. Instead, we would go to the next eligible number, let us say 5, meaning that the participant should be in condition C. Let us imagine that the next random number is 1, so the third participant is assigned to condition A. Because we have now assigned three of the four participants in the first block (B, C, A), this means that the fourth participant is automatically assigned to condition D, without referring to the random number table. We then consult the table to determine the assignment for the next block of four participants. This procedure thus ensures equal numbers of participants per condition, assuming that the total sample size is an even multiple of the number of conditions. When another independent variable is involved, this procedure can be adapted to assure equal cell sizes simply by randomizing by blocks separately for each level of the other variable (e.g., randomizing within blocks of four separately for men and women).

Another practical aspect of random assignment is an issue when participants take part in a laboratory experiment in groups. For instance, if, as in a typical judgment study, the conditions are defined simply by variations in stimulus materials, the researcher might enlist as many participants as there are chairs in the room in which the study takes place. In such situations, it is desirable for all experimental conditions to be represented in each group. Otherwise, any special properties of that group's experience (e.g., the fact that many members of the group were annoyed by an inattentive participant who did not listen to the instructions and had to have them repeated) would be confounded with the condition. Of course, at times this representation is impossible because the procedure differs between experimental conditions. But in most judgment studies there is ordinarily no barrier to distributing the different versions of the materials at random within each group of participants who participate together, thereby ensuring that any effects of experimenter, time of day, or other session-specific differences are randomly distributed across all conditions.

Manipulation Checks

Certainly as part of the pretesting procedure, and in many cases during the actual study as well, researchers ask questions—termed **manipulation checks**—to assess whether the manipulations had the intended effects on the participants. For example, if the manipulation is intended to induce anxiety, participants could be asked to fill out a mood checklist, including such terms as "anxious," "fearful," and "afraid." Such manipulation checks are desirable for two reasons. First, they aid in establishing the construct validity of the manipulation. If the manipulation has the theoretically predicted pattern of effects on manipulation checks, a stronger argument can be made that it is truly operationally defining the intended construct. Second, manipulation checks are helpful in interpreting what has happened whenever a study does not produce the predicted results on the dependent variable. Without a manipulation check, the researcher is often uncertain whether (1) the manipulation simply failed to have any effect on the participants or (2) the manipulation worked but the independent variable failed to produce the predicted effects on the dependent variable. These two possibilities are different in important ways, in that the first possibility suggests the desirability of repeating the experiment with a stronger or better manipulation, whereas the second possibility means that the experiment has actually worked and that the results disconfirm the theory. A manipulation check is often the only way a researcher can confidently tell which of these two possibilities is responsible for negative results.

Some researchers advocate using manipulation checks as a rationale for omitting participants from the sample prior to analysis. The logic here is that if a mood manipulation, for example, is supposed to put participants in a happy mood, we really do not want to include them in that condition unless they are truly happy. If by some chance a participant is assigned to the happy condition but, just prior to arriving at the laboratory, had terminated a five-year-long relationship and hence is feeling truly miserable despite the funny movie, the manipulation check will reveal that the person is not feeling happy. Is it then a fair test of the hypothesis to keep that participant in the happy condition? Some researchers argue that a true test of the hypothesis is whether happy moods affect the dependent variable of interest, and the movie manipulation is simply the vehicle by which happy moods are achieved. As such, they argue further, science is better served if that person were dropped from the study. Other researchers adopt the position, "once randomized, analyzed," and argue that manipulation checks do not constitute an adequate rationale for deleting participants.

Our position is that because it is often too tempting and easy to drop participants who give us "inconvenient" data, manipulation checks should be used only rarely, if at all, to justify omission of participants. And in such rare cases, the analyses should be done twice, once using all participants and once omitting any participants with offending manipulation check data. Ideally, identical patterns of statistically significant results will be obtained, and the researchers need merely to indicate so in their written report. Should there be discrepancies across the two sets of analyses, with the most common case being nonsignificant findings when all participants are included and significant findings after omitting participants, the researcher should report the outcomes of both analyses. The chore of deciding which set of analyses to believe then falls on the readers, and their decision will probably depend on how much emphasis they place on issues of internal validity.

A related issue concerns the use of manipulation checks for **internal analyses.** In an internal analysis, the manipulation check responses are not used as a basis of dropping participants. Instead, the manipulation check becomes a new independent variable that is related to the dependent variable, in lieu of using the participants' randomly assigned conditions. Using the mood manipulation example again, participants would be randomly assigned to watch the happy or sad movie, as described earlier. A manipulation check would be administered, and instead of using a two-level treatment variable in analyses, the participants' scores on the manipulation check mood scale (e.g., 1 to 7) would be used. Again, the logic seems impeccable: If the hypothesis is that people in happy moods would form more positive impressions of others, does it not make more sense to use those individuals' true mood states, as reflected by their self-reports in the manipulation check, in predicting their subsequent impressions?

And when described in that manner, internal analyses do make a lot of sense and, in fact, they are often seen in the literature. There is a major drawback to such internal analyses, however, that should be obvious: When an internal analysis is done, the study is transformed from a true experiment, where random assignment allows causal inferences to be drawn, into a correlational study, with all the interpretational ambiguities that a correlational study involves. When the hypotheses are tested with respect to the participants' randomly assigned treatment conditions, if there is a significant effect due to movie condition, the researchers can safely conclude that watching the happy movie caused the differences in judgment. But when an internal analysis is performed, even if the correlation between mood and judgment is consistent with the hypothesis, the researchers can conclude only that mood and judgment are associated, not that the mood caused the differences in judgment. The inability to draw a causal inference is a serious drawback in universalistic research in which theory building is the goal. In sum, in most cases, the cost to researchers in terms of the increased threats to internal validity outweigh whatever benefits they obtain through conducting an internal analysis or omitting participants whose manipulation check responses indicate that the experimental treatment did not have the intended effect. We believe that manipulation checks are thus most useful in the early pilot-testing stages of research or to offer convincing evidence to readers that the manipulations truly were effective.

As a final thought, we also need to acknowledge that manipulation checks carry with them an added danger: the possibility that the manipulation check will arouse participants' suspicion by alerting them to the crucial independent variable. For example, in research on interpersonal expectancy effects, one participant is told something that is not true about his or her interaction partner, for example, that the partner scored very high or low on a problem-solving task or is either very extraverted or introverted. The purpose of such research is to see how the perceiver's expectancies about the target affects the interaction and, in particular, if the expectancies elicit self-fulfilling prophecies. For such a study to work, it is essential that the perceiver paid attention to the expectancy manipulation and believes the target to be either bright, dumb, extraverted, or introverted. However, a manipulation check that is administered prior to interaction with the target ("On a 7-point scale, how extraverted do you think the target will be?") quite easily could get the perceiver to thinking about why the researchers are so concerned with the target's extraversion. A participant who previously would have accepted the expectancy manipulation at face value without thinking twice might now be a participant who suspects the manipulation was not true. Researchers might therefore wish either to avoid manipulation checks in studies in which the independent variable is deceptive in nature or to constrain their use to the pilot-testing stage.

Dependent Variable

In some laboratory research, the measurement of the dependent variable does not receive the careful attention it deserves. Although the construct validity of the dependent variable should be developed and assessed with the same care that researchers typically allocate to their manipulations, all too often a carefully executed study is weakened by a one- or two-item paper-and-pencil measure having questionable reliability and validity, that is used as the dependent measure. In Chapter 7 we discussed some basic aspects of measurement that apply to laboratory dependent variables as well as surveys.

In this section, phrases such as "the dependent variable" should not be taken to suggest that an ideal study has only a single dependent variable. As we have argued previously, multiple measures are better than any single measure, and the greater the diversity among the measures (as long as they tap the same theoretical construct) the better, because error and invalidity in any one measure will be unlikely to be shared with another very different measure. Thus, common patterns of findings on the different measures will strengthen confidence in the study's construct validity: the inference that the results are produced by the intended theoretical construct rather than by extraneous factors.

There can, however, be too much of a good thing: Just as we would recommend that researchers not stake an entire study on a single dependent variable, we also would recommend that researchers not make the opposite—and all too common—error of including too many dependent variables. It is tempting to add more and more dependent variables, on the logic that as long as we have the participants in the laboratory, it only takes a minute or two to have them complete another measure, and maybe if a certain measure does not work out, another measure will. The problem is that having lots of dependent variables increases the number of analyses to be conducted and therefore the possibility of some results being significant by chance alone, a problem that is termed **capitalizing on chance.** Yet there is no way of telling which significant results are genuine and which are statistical flukes (i.e., not likely to replicate). Having a large number of dependent variables also increases the possibility of inexplicable patterns of findings—how can we explain to readers what it means if we got our predicted results for dependent variables A, B, and C but not for D, E, and F? Does it mean our theory is not correct? Not necessarily, but it is not as reassuring as if we had collected only A, B, and C and gotten significant results for all three. In sum, researchers are better off concentrating their efforts on coming up with two or three highly reliable and well-validated dependent measures than using a large number of measures of questionable reliability and validity.

Dependent variables in laboratory studies can be divided into two fundamental categories. (In Chapter 5 we discussed the different categories of measures in great detail; we focus here on some of the issues particularly relevant for laboratory studies.) Most laboratory studies use self-reports, elicited through questionnaires or interviews; the great majority of judgment studies fall into this category. Many considerations are important when self-report measures are employed, including the thoughtful wording of questions and careful conceptualization of what is to be asked. For instance, participants can be asked to report on their judgments, experiences, past behaviors, beliefs, memories, or attitudes (e.g., "What were you thinking about when you were rating the textbook?") but cannot be expected to make reliable inferences about their behaviors (Ericsson & Simon, 1984; Nisbett & Wilson, 1977). Therefore, questions such as "Why did you rate the textbook as highly as you did?" which call for inferences, should be avoided, unless the research interest is in people's theories about the causes of their behaviors. In Chapter 6 we described general principles of questionnaire construction, which apply equally to self-report dependent measures used in laboratory studies.

At times, laboratory dependent measures go somewhat beyond self-report, as usually defined, to elicit people's willingness to make commitments concerning future behavior. For instance, if a particular attitude change technique is hypothesized to increase people's motivation to help the poor, the dependent measure might be based on a sign-up sheet in which participants actually commit themselves to some number of hours of community service over the next month (ranging from 0 hours to 40 hours, say). Such measures are sometimes termed **behavioroid,** for intuitively they seem to fall somewhere in between a potentially meaningless pencil-and-paper report of how much the participant cares about the poor and an actual behavioral measure based on observation of the participant's volunteering over an extended period of time. They do not have the concreteness and realism of behavioral observations (for participants make a commitment that they might not keep), but they are vastly easier to measure. This type of procedure sometimes involves deception: The participants sign up for some activity, believing that they are making a true commitment—a belief that is essential for this type of measurement—but the experimenter has no intention of holding participants to it and terminates the research after the measure is completed. Of course, in some instances it would be ethically superior if researchers avoided deception and took the participants' commitment seriously, for example, by referring them to a community agency that actually needs volunteers.

Non-self-report measures could be broadly classed as observational or behavioral measures, but many distinct types of observation are used in laboratory research. Most commonly, research participants are given an opportunity to perform some behavior of interest, and observers or recording devices keep records of what they do. Research on small-group interaction or nonverbal behavior would typically use such methods. Observation of this sort is intrinsically not much different in the laboratory than it is in the field, except that the laboratory setting can make it easier to arrange for the appropriate type of observation, with one-way mirrors, carefully placed video cameras, and the like. The issues involved in the use of observation are described in detail in Chapter 15.

Other measures used in some laboratory studies are observational in that they do not depend on participants' reports about their internal states but make use of tasks that participants are instructed to perform. They might be called **performance measures** for this reason. One example is research on goal setting and performance, in which people in different conditions are induced to set different types of goals and then to perform some task as well as they can for a given period of time (Locke, 1996). Patterns of performance demonstrate which types of goal setting are most effective. Measures of memory are another example. In research in the field of social cognition, for example, the way information is organized in a perceiver's memory can be inferred from what the perceiver writes under instructions to reproduce exactly the previously studied stimulus materials (Hamilton, 1981). As these examples suggest, performance measures can have an advantage over other types of measures in their relatively low susceptibility to demand characteristics or other social desirability effects.

With any type of dependent measure, however, it might be necessary to disguise either its actual existence (e.g., a hidden camera) or its purpose (e.g., a questionnaire presented as being from an unrelated experiment). Disguise can be helpful or necessary to prevent demand characteristics or guesses about the purpose of the research. For example, consider a typical experiment on attitude change. After participants read a persuasive message on some topic, simply getting a questionnaire about their current attitude on that topic would be reactive, leading them to wonder whether the "right" response is to agree with the message they have just heard, to show consistency and firmness by not changing their original views, and so on. Any naturalness in answering the question would be lost. Instead, researchers can embed the questions on the key topic within a long questionnaire covering many diverse topics and headed "Social and Political Attitudes" or something equally broad. Alternatively, researchers can represent the purpose of the question as something other than what it actually is. For instance, the cover story in some studies on attitude change is that participants are to rate the audio or video quality of the presentation (the persuasive message). Researchers can then say to participants that people's attitudes on the issue advocated in the message might influence their ratings, so in order to control for this possibility the participant's opinion on the topic is being sought. Of course, deceptions such as these should be used only when necessary and participants should be fully debriefed regarding the deception.

As material in this section suggests, the dependent measures used in laboratory research are quite diverse. But in all cases, the underlying goal in the development of a measure is high reliability and validity, to be accomplished both through the properties of the measurement process itself (e.g., employing multiple measures instead of single items) and through controlling the participants' reactions to it (e.g., avoiding demand characteristics).

Debriefing

Debriefing ordinarily involves a two-way exchange of information in an interview with participants after the study is concluded, a process that is important for several reasons. Of course, if the experiment involved any deception or other stressful manipulations, it is of paramount importance to ensure that the participants leave in a psychologically positive state. Debriefing also is important to make participation in research a truly educational experience; finding out something about how and why research is conducted is often the most valuable payoff participants receive in return for their time. Finally, there is a benefit to the researcher. Participants are the best sources of information on whether the procedures, instructions, and tasks were clear; whether the manipulations were perceived as intended; and whether participants formulated hypotheses about the purpose of the experiment and tried to behave accordingly. Researchers who pass up the opportunity to question participants about these matters do so at the peril of their own research.

It is generally most natural to begin the debriefing by inviting participants to ask any questions they might have. Then participants can be asked to comment on matters that are important from the researcher's viewpoint: the comprehensibility of the instructions and the like. Finally, a detailed description of the methods and purpose of the study is given by the researcher so that participants can appreciate why the experiment was conducted as it was in terms of the researcher's hypotheses and goals. Often, participants do not have the background knowledge to understand fully the details of the research hypotheses, but it is almost always possible—and desirable—to convey the key ideas in terms that are meaningful to most people. The researcher should avoid saying, for example, "We are trying to test Hastie's theory that the formation of associative links between behaviors produces better memory for schema-incongruent compared to schema-congruent behaviors." Instead, he or she could explain, "You might learn that a person has performed some behaviors that are consistent, and some that are inconsistent, with an expectation that you initially had about the person. Then you are likely to think about the inconsistent behaviors in a special way, perhaps trying to explain them by comparing them with some of the person's other known behaviors. As a result, the inconsistent behaviors might actually be remembered better than the consistent ones when you later try to recall all of the behaviors."

For research that involves deception, special procedures are important, both for the researcher's and the participant's sake. The researcher generally wants to find out whether participants saw through the particular deception that was used or whether they were more generally suspicious about any aspects of the study. To accomplish this goal, **funnel questioning** is best, that is, initially asking such general questions as "What do you think the study was about?" and "Did you think there may have been more to the experiment than meets the eye?" Then the questions are narrowed down by stages, ending with questions focused on the specific deception, such as "Did you suspect that the questionnaire we said was unrelated was actually a key part of this research?" (Aronson et al., 1998). The disadvantages of beginning with a specific question or, even worse, simply telling participants that they have been deceived are that (1) participants might feel naive or foolish to learn in a very direct manner that they were victims of a deception and (2) to protect their self-image, they might say, "Of course, I knew it all along." This response prohibits distinguishing those participants who really had reasonably accurate suspicions and whose responses are therefore tainted.

Sensitive researchers make a special point of explaining why deception had to be used in the study to demonstrate to the participants that it was not undertaken lightly and was used only because no other available methods would serve the purposes of the research. And these statements should be true. Deception should not be used lightly, both for the obvious ethical reasons and for significant practical ones: Research that uses deception is generally more difficult and risky to conduct.

A debriefing generally ends with the experimenter urging the participant not to discuss the study with other people before it is completed. Participants have to be persuaded not to reveal the "clever" and potentially interesting details of the stage setting and deception to others who might become participants in the future. Even if no deception is involved, participants who enter the study forewarned about its overall purposes will be almost certain to behave differently than naive participants whose knowledge is limited to the cover story. A valid question, of course, is how much we can trust our participants when they agree to our request not to divulge the details of our studies. Fortunately, there is reassuring data on this question. In a clever experiment, Aronson (1966) enlisted three undergraduate confederates to approach individuals who were known to have participated in a previous experiment. Despite repeated pleas from the confederates to divulge the true purpose of the study, the participants steadfastly refused to say or merely repeated the cover story originally given to them.

In summary, debriefing is important for the researcher's purposes: to identify participants who were inattentive or held accurate suspicions and to learn whether the procedures were clearly understood and accurately followed or were confusing. But protection of the participant's interests is even more crucial. Ideally, debriefing accomplishes the purposes of uncovering and dealing with any negative reactions to the study, gently disabusing the participants who have been taken in by deceptive procedures in research, and making sure that the participants emerge from the study wiser—but no sadder—than when they entered it.

Summary

The laboratory is an appropriate setting for the investigation of certain types of research questions. When the independent variables are practically and ethically manipulable, the time period short, and the ability to draw inferences about causality central to the research goals, laboratory research is an obvious choice. On the other hand, research with particularistic goals involving generalization of findings to specific target populations or investigations of the effects of nonmanipulable variables over long time periods are generally best conducted in other settings.

Laboratory studies fall roughly into three categories: impact studies, in which something actually happens to the participants and their reactions are of interest; judgment studies, in which people's perceptions, judgments, or evaluations of stimulus materials are the focus of the research; and observational studies, in which the laboratory setting is used to facilitate detailed observation, with or without manipulation of independent variables.

With all types of laboratory studies, as with all research in general, the construction of the setting, manipulation of independent variables, measurement of dependent variables, and debriefing are specifically aimed at increasing the validity of research conclusions. Internal validity is the chief strength of laboratory-based research, for the setting facilitates randomized experimental designs. Construct validity can be strong, although the setting carries specific risks of artifacts (i.e., experimenter expectancy effects or demand characteristics) against which the researcher must guard. External validity in the sense of the generalizability of findings directly to specific target populations is often low with laboratory research. However, its external validity often takes a different form: Generalization to other populations and settings of the theory that is tested in the laboratory, rather than of the specific laboratory findings themselves, is the chief goal of the research.

Key Concepts

applied research
basic research
behavioroid measure
capitalizing on chance
confederate
confound
control
cover story
demand characteristics
expectancy control group design
experimental realism
experimenter expectancies
funnel questioning
impact studies
internal analysis
judgment studies
manipulation check
mundane realism
observational studies
particularistic research
performance measure
pilot testing
replication
universalistic research

On the Web

We do not provide addresses for specific Web pages relevant to the material covered in this chapter. Instead, we suggest that, using a search engine such as Google or Yahoo!, readers input the phrase "psychology laboratory," which will return hundreds of links, some providing access to pages featuring descriptions (even photographs) of laboratories in which work such as that described in this chapter is done.

Further Reading

Aronson, E., Wilson, T. D., & Brewer, M. B. (1998). Experimentation in social psychology. In D. T. Gilbert, S. T. Fiske, & G. Lindzey (Eds.), *The handbook of social psychology, Vol. 1* (4th ed., pp. 99–142). New York: McGraw-Hill.

Brannigan, G. G., & Merrens, M. R. (Eds.). (1993). *The undaunted psychologist: Adventures in research.* New York: McGraw-Hill.

Rosnow, R. L., & Rosenthal, R. (1997). *People studying people: Artifacts and ethics in behavioral research.* New York: W. H. Freeman.

CHAPTER

13

Nonrandomized Designs

Science does not begin and end with the randomized experiment. Science is a process of discovery, in which researchers use the best tools available to answer their questions. When random assignment is not feasible, either because the independent variables cannot be manipulated or because it would not be ethical to do so, researchers can choose from an assortment of research designs. There are circumstances under which these other designs are even preferable to randomized experimental designs.

In this chapter we discuss nonrandomized research designs, which differ from randomized experimental designs in that in the former the research participants are not randomly assigned to levels of the independent variable. Instead, the comparisons between levels, or between treatment and nontreatment conditions, must always be made with the presumption that the groups are *nonequivalent.* As a result, the internal validity of these designs is threatened by the full range of threats discussed in Chapter 11. Accordingly, causal inferences about the effects of independent variables on dependent variables are difficult to make.

Yet in many ways, these designs have distinct advantages over randomized experimental designs. The relative sacrifice in internal validity can well be worth the cost, depending on the aspirations of the researcher and the context in which the research is conducted. For instance, a primary goal of a researcher might simply be to explore the distribution of some variable in some population of interest. In this case, considerations about internal validity are not relevant. The researcher is not interested in determining what causes what. Rather, all he or she wants to know is how many people believe something or act in a certain way or have a certain characteristic. With such goals, a survey research design is an appropriate tool.

The wide variety of situations and purposes for the application of survey research designs can be seen in the following examples of their use:

- Sociologists gather information from a representative sample of male members of the U.S. labor force to study their training and occupational attainments.

- Public opinion polling organizations conduct studies of the popularity of various presidential candidates among potential voters.
- Market research organizations conduct studies of consumers to find out what kinds of soft drinks they prefer.
- Medical researchers survey the nation's population to determine the incidence of disease-related factors.
- Political scientists interview members of the U.S. House of Representatives to monitor their reactions to increasing public attention to the ethics of public figures.
- A national women's magazine asks its readers to answer a questionnaire that solicits information about their occupational aspirations.
- Political sociologists survey a sample of students in large universities to determine whether they support or oppose a military draft in the United States.
- A national broadcast rating organization uses electronic recording devices to measure the distribution of television watching each week.

In each of these cases, the researchers are not interested in establishing cause-and-effect conclusions. Rather, of central concern is measuring constructs well and gathering information from a representative sample of individuals. The designs that we discuss in this chapter are perfectly appropriate for answering these kinds of questions.

In other situations the researcher wants to do more than simply describe a sample of respondents. In addition, he or she might want to document or discover an association between two or more variables in some target population. In such a case, establishing causality still might not be the researcher's primary goal. Also, often it is much easier to secure a random sample of respondents from the target population if random assignment is not attempted. In still other cases, a researcher might simply be interested in the effects of independent variables that cannot be effectively manipulated. It would be impossible, for example, to design a manipulation that would allow researchers to examine people's reactions to a natural disaster. Yet psychologists are certainly interested in the behavioral and mental health implications of how people cope with natural disasters. The solution to this dilemma—that is, being interested in the effects of a variable that cannot be manipulated—is not to abandon empirical research strategies. Rather, the solution is to employ the best nonrandomized research design we can use, recognizing its internal validity limitations and attempting to overcome them as best we can.

Examples of Nonrandomized Designs

Before considering the formalities of alternative designs and their relative strengths and weaknesses, let us consider two examples of research that have made effective use of nonrandomized designs.

Starting in 1968, the Panel Study of Income Dynamics, a longitudinal study of a representative sample of American families, has been conducted by researchers at the Institute for Social Research at the University of Michigan. Information was gathered annually through 1997 and has been gathered biennially since then. By following the children of these families as they grew and formed families of their own, the sample size has grown from 4,800 to more than 7,000 families in 2001. By the end of the 2001 data collection effort, the Panel Study of Income Dynamics will have acquired information about more than 62,000 individuals spanning over 30 years of their lives. The interviews elicit information on a host of economic and social variables. A set of core variables is included in every interview. These address such topics as income sources and amounts; poverty status and whether the family receives any public assistance; family structure and basic demographic variables; employment, housing, and socioeconomic background; and general health status. Other supplemental topics are addressed at different time periods and include such things as housing and neighborhood characteristics, education, savings and retirement plans, health expenditures, and child care issues.

The massive amounts of information accumulated in this panel study can be and have been used to address many important social scientific questions. Many different researchers have approached these same data from different vantage points and with different theoretical interests and yet have found them a rich source of information. Since the beginning of the study, more than 2,000 research reports have been written to communicate findings from the data set.

Consider the strengths of this study. First, the sample is obviously large and representative. Regardless of one's theoretical interest, it is difficult to imagine any randomized experiment in which a representative sample of 7,000 respondents could be used. Second, considerable amounts of time were spent interviewing each family and refining the questions that were asked. Therefore, hundreds of constructs were measured and issues of reliability and validity of measurement could be addressed relatively easily. Again, it is difficult to imagine a randomized experiment within which such massive amounts of information about family life in America could have been gathered. Third, because the survey was administered in a **panel design,** meaning that the same families were reinterviewed regularly, it is possible to document variations in economic conditions both between families in any given year and longitudinally within the same families over time.

Consider this last advantage in more detail. Suppose we were interested in examining the association between employment status and family composition variables. For instance, we might believe that when the parents in a family are unemployed, stress within the family increases, which in turn might lead to divorce and family breakup. It would be impossible to conduct a randomized experiment to examine this hypothesis. Manipulating employment status is not something that even the most devout experimentalist would choose to do. Yet this panel design permits us to look at the hypothesized association in a variety of different ways. First, within any given year, we can compare the family compositions of employed and unemployed respondents. This **cross-sectional comparison** can be done for each year of the panel study. Second, we can make the same sort of comparison within individual families when the employment status of the parents changes over the course of the study. Thus, we can find families in which the parents either become newly unemployed or employed during the course of the study and then examine whether their family composition changes accordingly. If both sorts of comparisons lead to the same conclusion—that is, that employment status of parents is associated with family composition variables both between families and within families over time—we can have increased confidence in the correctness of our hypothesis in spite of the fact that a randomized experimental test of it is not feasible.

Consider now a nonrandomized design that involved an intervention. Researchers have long been interested in designing public service announcements (PSAs) that would be effective in reducing drug use. This is another topic that would be difficult to address experimentally. Although it would be possible to bring people into the laboratory and randomly assign them to watch either an experimental (antidrug) PSA or a control (neutral topic) PSA, such a limited onetime exposure probably would not work, nor would it be representative of the real world in which the PSAs would ultimately be employed. Thus, a quasi-experimental field study was deemed to be a more appropriate approach to answering the question of the effectiveness of antidrug PSAs (Palmgreen, Donohew, Lorch, Hoyle, & Stephenson, 2001). In **quasi-experimental designs,** one or more independent variables are manipulated but participants are not randomly assigned to levels of the manipulated variables. In this quasi-experimental study, the researchers created PSAs that were designed to be particularly effective for high sensation seekers, who were identified as a population at high risk for drug use. (In Chapter 16, we revisit the Palmgreen et al. 2001 study when we discuss how focus groups were used to create the PSAs.) The PSAs were then shown at different points in time in Fayette County, Kentucky, and Knox County, Tennessee, two counties that were deemed comparable on demographic and cultural variables (but to which participants obviously were not randomly assigned). During a 32-month interval, individual interviews were conducted each month with samples of 100 randomly selected adolescents in grades 7 through 10 from each of the two counties. The main dependent variable was whether respondents had used marijuana during the previous 30 days. The independent variable was whether the antidrug PSAs were running on local television. The PSAs were televised between January and April 1997 in Fayette County and between January and April 1998 in both Fayette County and Knox County. Because drug use was tracked continuously starting 8 months before the first Fayette County PSA campaign, and because adolescents in Knox County were not exposed to the PSAs at the time of the first campaign in Fayette County, the researchers could determine whether self-reported marijuana use appeared to be affected by the presentation of antidrug PSAs.

This study is an example of an **interrupted time-series design.** "Time series" refers to the strategy of measuring a set of variables on a series of occasions (e.g., monthly) during a specified period of time (32 months in the example). "Interrupted" refers to the strategy of introducing the stimulus or event (the PSA campaign) during the period of assessment in order to evaluate its effect on the variables being measured (e.g., 30-day marijuana use). This design conveys several important advantages. First, it controls for trends in marijuana use prior to the PSA campaigns in both counties by providing a long baseline period before the campaigns were initiated. Second, the fact that three separate campaigns were used (two in Fayette County, one in Knox County) helps to rule out threats due to history effects; it would be highly unlikely that any given external event would coincide exactly with the three PSA campaigns. The fact that Knox County serves as a control for the first campaign in Fayette County further helps to rule out history effects that might be occurring at a national level; in other words, if a federal antidrug campaign coincided with the first PSA campaign in the Palmgreen et al. (2001) study, it should affect marijuana use equally in both Fayette and Knox Counties. The design also controls for maturation effects, again because Knox County acts as a control group. Lastly, the design includes elements of both a between-participants design (Fayette versus Knox County) as well as repeated measures design (the two administrations of the campaign in Fayette County), thus providing the advantages of both types of design.

Figure 13.1 shows the results for the Palmgreen et al. (2001) study. We provide more detail about interrupted time-series designs later in the chapter, but the main results should be obvious to readers simply by looking at the pattern. The top half of Figure 13.1 displays the data for the Knox County samples; as readers can see, marijuana use increased steadily from May of 1996 to December of 1997, but when the PSA campaign was introduced in January of 1998, marijuana use declined. In Fayette County (bottom half of the graph), however, the pattern of drug use was quite different. Again, we see a steady increase of marijuana use at the beginning of the study, but the first peak occurs in January of 1997, at the introduction of the first PSA campaign. Marijuana use declined steadily until the fall of 1997, when it started increasing again. But with the introduction of the second PSA campaign in January of 1998, marijuana use again declined.

These results illustrate the strength of a carefully designed and well-executed quasi-experiment. Although participants were not randomly assigned to condition, thus precluding a definitive causal inference, it would be difficult to imagine any alternative explanation that could account for the pattern of marijuana use that was obtained in the two counties. Thus, we can feel fairly confident that the PSAs were in fact effective in reducing marijuana use among high-sensation-seeking adolescents.

Alternative Nonrandomized Designs

There are a wide variety of nonrandomized research designs (for comprehensive treatments, see Campbell & Stanley, 1966; Shadish, Cook, & Campbell, 2001; Judd & Kenny, 1981). In the remainder of this chapter we illustrate some of these designs and discuss the major threats to internal validity that are posed by each one. Remember that in general the hallmark of nonrandomized designs is the inability or failure to assign individuals randomly to the levels of the independent variable.

FIGURE 13.1

EXAMPLE OF FINDINGS FROM AN INTERRUPTED TIME-SERIES DESIGN

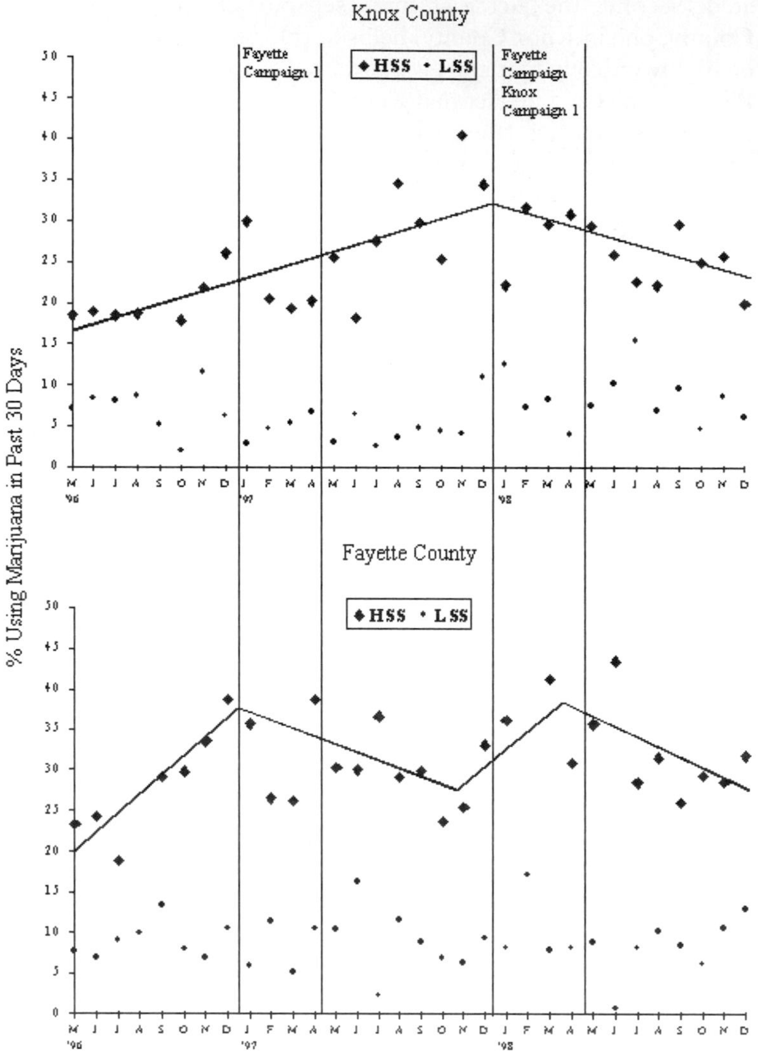

SOURCE: From "Television Campaigns and Adolescent Marijuana Use: Tests of Sensation Seeking Marketing," by P. Palmgreen, L. Donohew, E. P. Lorch, R. H. Hoyle, and M. T. Stephenson, 2001, *American Journal of Public Health, 91,* p. 294. Copyright 2001 by the American Public Health Association. Reprinted with permission.

As in Chapter 11, a fundamental distinction to be made among designs concerns the way in which the independent variable varies. It can vary either between participants or within them, just as it did in randomized experimental designs. Recall that in the former case, different individuals are measured under the different levels of the independent variable. That is, those research participants who are exposed to the treatment are not the same as those who are in the control group. When the independent variable varies within participants, each one is observed under all of its levels. That is, the same individual is observed both in the treatment and in the control condition. As we will see, there are different threats to internal validity depending on whether the independent variable varies within or between participants in nonrandomized designs. Finally, in some designs, such as the one used in the Palmgreen et al. (2001) study discussed previously, independent variables of interest vary both between and within participants. In that study, exposure to the PSA campaign varied between counties during the first year of the study, but, because adolescents in both counties ultimately were exposed to the campaign during the time series, it varied within each county as well.

As in Chapter 11, we use the following notation to describe different research designs:

X = a treatment, an independent variable, a cause
O = an observation, a dependent variable, an effect

(Note that the R used in Chapter 11 to denote randomization is not needed here.)

Static-Group Comparison Design

Group 1 X ———— O_1

- -

Group 2 not-X ——— O_2

The dashed line separating the two groups indicates that people were not randomly assigned to group 1 and group 2; instead, these are either naturally occurring groups or groups to which people are assigned for some reason other than a random one (e.g., self-selection).

If we imagine the **static-group comparison design** with a naturally occurring X having several levels (e.g., socioeconomic status—low/medium/high), it becomes the following:

Group 1 X_1 ———— O_1

- -

Group 2 X_2 ———— O_2

- -

Group 3 X_3 ———— O_3

This design has as many groups as there are levels of the independent variable. As such, the independent variable varies between participants.

Because participants have not been randomly assigned to the groups, selection is a serious threat to the internal validity of this research design. Suppose *X* represents education (no college, some college, college graduate) and *O* represents income. If the groups differ in income, it is tempting to interpret this difference as the effect of education on income. Such an interpretation would be analogous to our interpretation of the effects of *X* in a randomized experiment. The difficulty with interpreting the results of a static-group comparison is the possibility that there are other differences between the education groups that might also affect income. For example, the education groups probably differ on intelligence or parental socioeconomic status. Such differences are plausible **alternative explanations** for any differences in income between groups.

There are three criteria for inferring causality: (1) that *X* and *O* covary, (2) that *X* precedes *O* in time, and (3) that there are no alternative explanations of the group differences in *O*. Two variables covary (i.e., they are associated) when certain values or levels of one variable occur with particular values or levels of the other variable. For example, to say that education and income covary is to say that lower levels of income tend to occur with lower levels of educational attainment and that higher levels of income tend to occur with higher levels of educational attainment. Data from the static-group comparison design can be used to meet the first of these three criteria. Readers will remember the uncompromising dictum from Chapter 2: "Correlation does not imply causality." To that truism should be added the statement: "Causality *does* imply correlation." Thus, the demonstration of an association between two variables using different populations and different research conditions certainly lends credence to a causal hypothesis involving the two variables. Each such instance is a test of the hypothesis that could disconfirm it; however, each such instance has to be examined for plausible alternative explanations before even tentative causal interpretation is reasonable.

A comment should be made about the assumption of temporal order in this design. It is usually the case that *X* and *O* are measured at approximately the same time; that is, each is likely to be measured by responses to items in a questionnaire. In this sense it cannot be said that *X* comes before *O* in time. The researcher must assume that *X* as measured in the questionnaire has influenced the respondent as part of his or her prior life experiences. Sometimes it can be determined that *X* preceded *O* in time. For example, for most Americans, the end of schooling comes before the beginning of their first full-time employment. If we used survey data to study the occupational attainments of American workers, we could say that for most Americans, educational attainment came before occupational placement. Even so, this temporal order does not describe part of the population. Some people who ultimately attain college degrees work on a full-time basis at a job they consider to be permanent before they attend or complete college. To the extent that respondents are not uniform regarding the ordering of education and the first job, there is ambiguity in the interpretation of the association between them. Such ambiguity is another reason for researchers to exercise caution in making causal inferences from this sort of research design.

If our purposes are limited to assessing the incidence or distribution of characteristics, say, the number or proportion of men and women in a given occupation, the static-group comparison design is perfectly adequate. Even when we wish to assess the degree of covariation among variables, this design is adequate to the task. Thus, using this design, we could readily gather data from which to calculate the degree of association between family background measures (income and parents' educational attainments) and performance in school (grades and grade point average). It is when we wish to go beyond the *estimation* of associations to the *interpretation* of them that the limitations of the static-group comparison design are met.

In the physical sciences there are cases in which the threat of selection is relatively improbable even when random assignment has not been used. Recall the example from Chapter 11: studying the effects of different plant foods in the four quadrants of a field. Because the same field is used and all four plant foods are used during the same growing season, we can be fairly confident that all the other things that affect plant growth have been controlled and cannot be responsible for observed differences between quadrants of the field. In this case, even without random assignment, a persuasive case for internal validity can be made simply because there are no alternative explanations for any differences found. In essence, the selection threat to internal validity has been eliminated simply by controlling for all plausible alternative differences even without the use of random assignment. In principle, we might contemplate cases in which such control is possible in the social sciences. In practice, however, it is never possible to have sufficient confidence in the belief that all competing explanations for group differences on the dependent variable have been eliminated.

Pretest–Posttest Nonequivalent Control Group Design

The **pretest–posttest nonequivalent control group design** is an extension of the static-group comparison design that includes measures of the dependent variable at multiple points in time. Each group is given both a pretest and a posttest, measuring the dependent variable both before and after exposure to the independent variable:

Group 1 O_1 ——— X ——— O_2

- - - - - - - - - - - - - - - - - - - -

Group 2 O_3 ————————— O_4

With three or more levels of the independent variable, this design is simply extended to additional groups, as in the static-group comparison design:

Group 1 O_1 ——— X_1 ——— O_2

- - - - - - - - - - - - - - - - - - - -

Group 2 O_3 ——— X_2 ——— O_4

- - - - - - - - - - - - - - - - - - - -

Group 3 O_5 ——— X_3 ——— O_6

Like the static-group comparison design, in this design the independent variable varies between participants, but a random rule for assigning individuals to its levels has not been used. There are two advantages of this design over the static-group comparison design. First, because the pretest measurement is taken before exposure to the independent variable, and because the posttest measurement is taken afterward, the temporal precedence of the independent variable to the dependent variable can be firmly established. Unlike the static-group comparison design, then, the longitudinal nature of this design helps us argue that the independent variable is responsible for variation in the dependent variable, rather than the other way around.

The other advantage of this design is that we measure (rather than randomize away) preexisting differences between groups on the dependent variable, which can help us argue against the selection threat to internal validity. Consider the hypothetical results in Figure 13.2, comparing consumption of electricity in two groups—individuals who installed solar panels after the pretest and individuals who did not. In spite of nonrandom assignment, the results are fairly interpretable, thanks to the added pretest. It is quite likely, as Figure 13.2 shows, that people who install solar panels use energy more sparingly than other people to begin with. Their interest in solar energy is a further expression of their preexisting inclinations. Therefore, if we had only the posttest information, we would not know whether the difference reflected the natural conservation tendencies of the people who installed solar panels or whether it reflected the savings produced by the panels. When we look at the pretest differences, we see that those who installed the panels were conservers to begin with. They used less electricity even before they installed the panels. This difference became even larger after the treatment, however, which suggests that the solar installations had an effect.

FIGURE 13.2 **EFFECTS OF SOLAR HEATING PANELS ON ELECTRICITY USE**

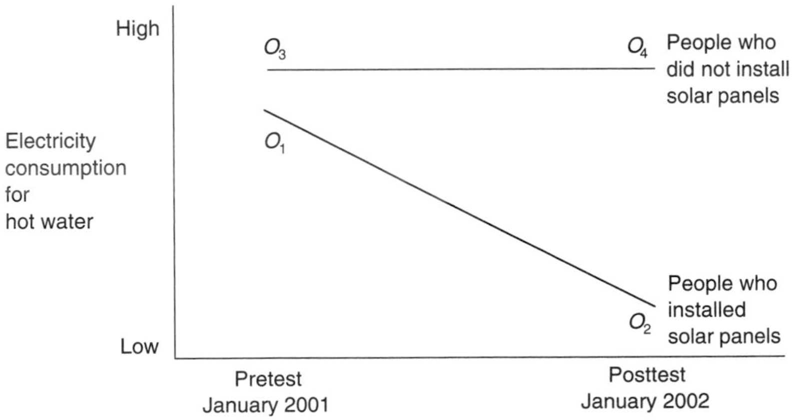

Are there any alternative explanations? We might suspect that the people who became interested in solar energy would naturally have decreased their electric consumption even if they had not installed the panels; because they were conscious of the need to conserve energy, they might have naturally used less hot water at the time of the posttest than at the time of the pretest. This design does not provide the information necessary to rule out this possibility—a selection by maturation threat to internal validity. Only if we had a longitudinal series of observations, including many observations taken before the solar panels were installed and many taken after, could we see whether the treated group was on a natural downward trend both before and after the solar panel installation.

This example illustrates how we must consider not only the design but also the content of a study and the pattern of results when ruling out alternative explanations. For some topics we might not consider it plausible that the treated group would have changed to become increasingly different from the control group without the intervention of the treatment.

For some patterns of results, the most plausible explanation is that the treatment produced the effects. Imagine an energy conservation program imposed on people who live in states that use the most air-conditioning. Suppose the imposed conservation program consisted of higher electric rates for people in the high-consumption states. To study the effects of this program we could compare the electric consumption by people in those states with consumption by people in neighboring states who had not consumed as much electricity for air-conditioning. We know that the treatment group initially consumed more electricity than those in the comparison states, so their pretest levels would look like O_1 and O_3 in Figure 13.3. If the posttest showed that the treatment group reduced their consumption below the level of the control group, the most plausible explanation is that the program worked. A crossover pattern such as the one in Figure 13.3 is more difficult to explain with any of the alternative explanations, such as a selection by maturation threat. In this example, the constant trend of the control group can be considered the normal trend; the downward trend of the treatment group can be reasonably attributed to the treatment. To explain away the apparent treatment effect by calling it differential maturation (or differential development of energy consciousness), we would have to regard the people in the formerly high-electric-consumption states as an extraordinary group of late-blooming conservationists, who not only met but also surpassed the conservation levels of the people in the neighboring states. This is so unlikely for this case, and most others, that the crossover pattern shown in Figure 13.3 usually can be interpreted as a treatment effect.

One-Group Pretest–Posttest Design

Both of the designs we have discussed so far are those in which the independent variable varies between individuals. Thus, comparisons between treatment and control conditions involve comparisons of average scores on the dependent variable between different groups of individuals. The **one-group pretest–posttest design,** also

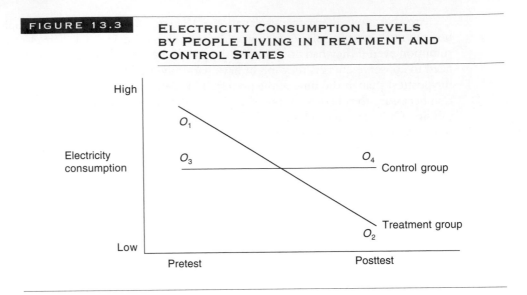

FIGURE 13.3 **ELECTRICITY CONSUMPTION LEVELS BY PEOPLE LIVING IN TREATMENT AND CONTROL STATES**

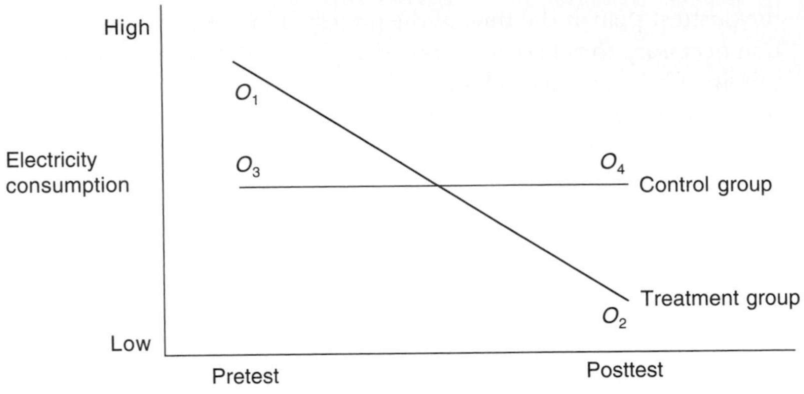

known as a simple panel design in survey research, is based on within-individual treatment comparisons. The design is represented schematically as

$$\text{Group 1} \quad O_1 \text{———————} X \text{———————} O_2$$

One group of individuals is observed (O_1), exposed to the treatment, X, then given a posttest (O_2) measurement. The treatment effect is then estimated simply by examining the average difference between O_2 and O_1.

Although this design is not threatened by selection, it is subject to the internal validity threats of history, maturation, testing, and instrumentation. To see these threats, consider a design in which we want to evaluate the effects of taking yoga classes on an individual's serenity. We develop a measure of serenity and administer it to individuals both before and after they have taken yoga classes. Suppose we find higher average serenity scores after classes than before. Can we attribute this difference to the practice of yoga? No. The following alternative explanations are threats to this conclusion:

- *History:* Because the posttest observations are made after the pretest, the difference between them could be a result of historical events intervening during the period. For instance, the nation might have ended a war, a new presidential candidate might be talking about Eastern philosophies, or popular culture might be advertising new forms of meditation. Any of these historical events could be responsible for the increase in serenity instead of the yoga classes.
- *Maturation:* During the course of the study, the individuals became older. They might also have become more relaxed, retired from work, or matured in other ways that affected their serenity apart from any effect of the yoga classes.

- *Testing:* If the pretest measurement of serenity sensitized the people we were studying and made them believe that they should relax or slow down, the pretesting alone could have produced higher serenity scores on the posttest. The shorter the time between pretest and posttest, the more plausible are testing effects.
- *Instrumentation:* If we changed our serenity questions or scoring system between the pretest and posttest, these changes in the measuring instrument could account for a difference between pretest and posttest levels of serenity.

As discussed in Chapter 11, these threats to internal validity are all eliminated on average if participants are randomly assigned to different orders of treatment exposure. This can be done only with independent variables whose effects dissipate or wear off over short time periods. Presuming, for instance, that the effect of taking yoga classes on serenity occurs only for one week following the classes, we might measure the serenity of some individuals immediately after yoga classes and then again one week later (first treatment, then control), whereas for other individuals we would measure their serenity prior to classes and then immediately after (first control, then treatment). If we randomly decided which individuals to measure in which sequence, the preceding four threats to internal validity would be eliminated. Employing such a randomized experimental design is simply not feasible in this example because we would not expect such short-lived treatment effects.

Interrupted Time-Series Design

Group 1 O_1——O_2——O_3——O_4——X——O_5——O_6——O_7——O_8

Time-series designs are an extension of the one-group pretest–posttest design. They extend the design simply by having numerous pretests and posttests, spread out before and after exposure to the treatment. This extension of the design sometimes enables the researcher to argue against the internal validity threats of maturation, testing, and history. Thus, this design is substantially stronger, from the point of view of internal validity, than the simple one-group pretest–posttest design.

Consider the maturation threat. Suppose we find a marked difference between O_4 and O_5 and wonder whether the difference is truly a result of the treatment (X) or of maturation; we can inspect all the intervals before and after that point to look for maturation trends. Presumably, if maturation were occurring, it would show up as a long-term trend, producing similar differences between O_1 and O_2, between O_2 and O_3, and so on, along the entire series. If none of the other intervals shows such a trend and the only difference lies between O_4 and O_5, maturation is not a very plausible explanation, unless, of course, we are studying some phenomenon that happens to coincide with a particular maturational change such as puberty and that could also plausibly be affected by puberty. Only under such a special set of circumstances and coincidences would maturation pose a threat to the validity of a time-series study.

The same reasoning applies to testing as an alternative explanation. If we suspected that the difference between O_4 and O_5 resulted not from the treatment but from the sensitizing effects of the pretest (O_4), we could examine all the preceding and succeeding intervals to see whether the repeated testing produced similar differences along the entire series. If there were no differences at any other points, it would be highly implausible that the testing at O_4 alone would have created an effect at O_5.

Eliminating history as a threat to internal validity is a little more difficult because historical events that affect observations can have precipitous effects similar to exposure to the treatment (i.e., between O_4 and O_5). In such cases, the history threat is insurmountable. Many historical events, however, unfold slowly, with slowly accumulating effects rather than precipitous ones. These can be effectively argued against using an interrupted time-series design.

Sometimes the X occurs only once, and its effect is presumed to persist forever or for some specified time. A measles inoculation should last forever; a flu shot might have a limited period of effectiveness. Sometimes the X signals a permanent change in the situation—as when a state changes its divorce laws to permit no-fault divorce or when the federal government introduces new air pollution standards. In cases like these, when the treatment occurs not only at a single time but also continues in force, the time series is more rightly diagrammed as follows:

$$\text{Group 1} \quad O_1—O_2—O_3—O_4—X—O_5—X—O_6—X—O_7—X—O_8$$

In either case, with a one-shot treatment or a continuing treatment, the virtue of time-series designs is that we can examine the trends in the data before the treatment, at the time of intervention, and after the treatment. This allows us to assess the plausibility of maturation, testing, and history as alternative explanations.

How easily we can interpret a time series and rule out alternative explanations depends not on the formal features of the design alone but also on the pattern of results. Some results are relatively easy to interpret—we can rule out most of the threats to validity and conclude that the treatment caused the effect. Other patterns are more vulnerable to alternative explanations. For instance, in Figure 13.4 three hypothetical patterns of results are plotted for an interrupted time-series design. The graph at the top of the figure is readily interpretable and probably shows an effect of the treatment. The pattern of results shown in the graph in the center of the figure is ambiguous. The pattern illustrated in the remaining graph is a clear case of no effect of the treatment.

With results like those shown in the graph at the top of Figure 13.4, many alternative explanations can be eliminated. It appears that the treatment caused the shift in scores from the pretest level to the posttest level. There are no maturational trends in either the pretest (O_1 to O_4) or posttest (O_5 to O_8) observations, so maturation is not a persuasive alternative explanation. The most problematic and plausible threat is history—some event that coincided with the treatment. How plausible it is depends on the problem under study. If we were studying the effects of a foreign relations film

FIGURE 13.4

Some Possible Outcomes Resulting from the Introduction of a Treatment (*X*) into a Time Series of Measurements

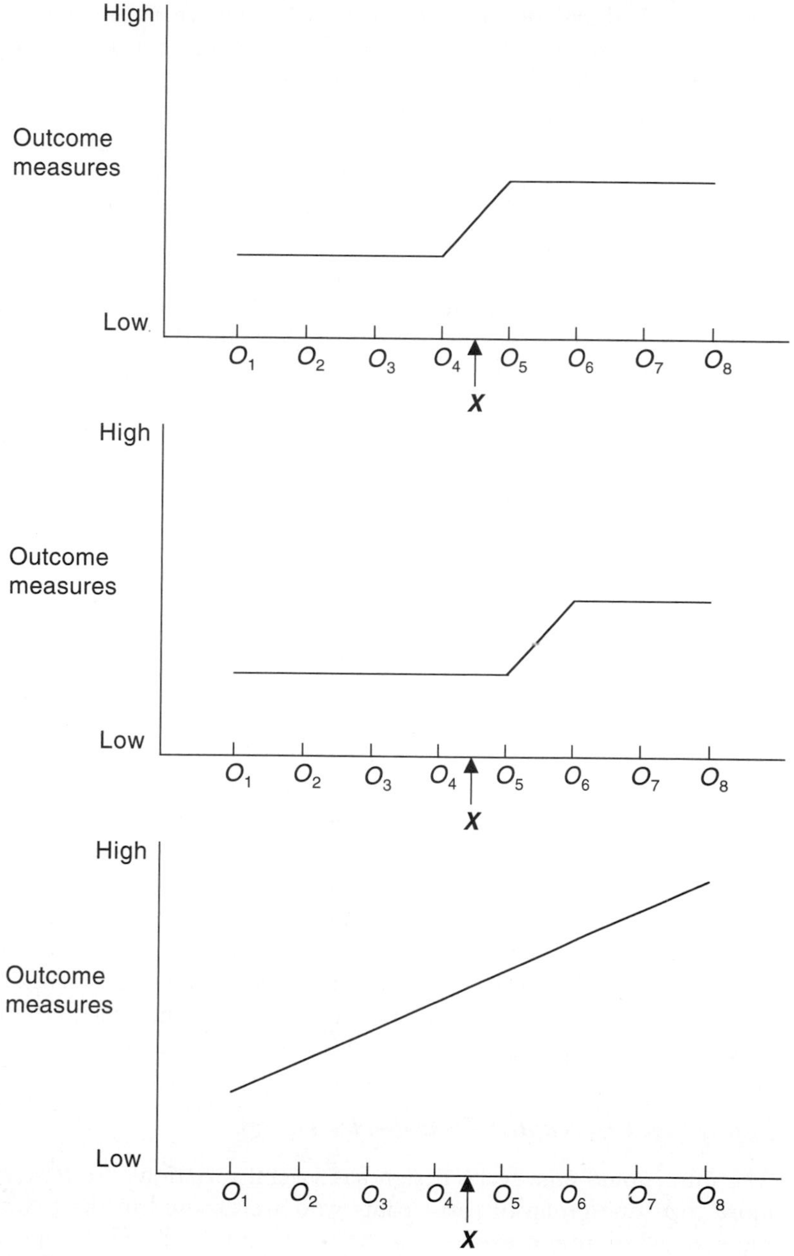

on American students' attitudes toward people of other countries, and if the showing of the film coincided with international agreements about sharing the world's energy resources or with an international incident in which Americans were suddenly held hostage by another country, these historical events would be plausible alternative explanations. If there are no obvious external events that coincide with the treatment and could have produced the same effects, history presents less of a problem.

With results like those depicted in the center of Figure 13.4, it is not clear that the treatment caused the shift upward because the shift does not coincide with the treatment; it lags behind by one time interval. In some cases, there would be reason to expect such a lag and, therefore, to attribute the effect to the treatment. For instance, a rise in the world's petroleum export prices might not be felt immediately in domestic gas prices at the pumps because of an oil reserve that was bought at lower prices. Therefore, if we were studying the effects of world export oil price increases on American car pooling, the effect is likely to lag some months behind the cause. If, for instance, there was a six-month lag in the effect, and the time-series observations were made at three-month intervals, the effect would appear not in the first observation following treatment but in the second, and the pattern in the graph would be a convincing demonstration of the effect of the price increase on car pooling. If there is no such plausible mechanism and therefore no plausible lag for the cause to have its effect, the graph is more difficult to interpret, and other alternative explanations might be plausible. These alternative explanations would probably fall under the heading of history—other events that followed the treatment and produced the effect.

The pattern shown in the graph at the bottom of Figure 13.4 is the clearest case of no effect. The higher levels of O after the treatment merely reflect the prevailing trend that also produced increasingly higher levels of O before the treatment. This graph also shows most clearly why the time-series design is far superior to the one-group pretest–posttest design. If the pattern seen in the bottommost graph in Figure 13.4 were studied with only one pretest and one posttest (points O_4 and O_5), we would be tempted to conclude that the treatment had an effect—causing O_5 to be higher than O_4. Without the other data points, it would be impossible to distinguish between a real effect and the prevailing trend that we see in the graph.

By the addition of a series of pretest and posttest observations, the time-series design is much more interpretable than the one-group pretest–posttest design. Even though it lacks random assignment, it is a useful quasi-experimental design because the additional observations allow the investigator to test the plausibility of several alternative explanations. The chief threat to internal validity with this design is history, although on occasion this too can be eliminated as a threat.

Replicated Interrupted Time-Series Design

The interrupted time-series design has several variations. In these variations there is more than one group of participants who are exposed to the treatment at different times or who are not exposed to the treatment at all. Thus, the **replicated interrupted time-series design** subsumes the following designs:

Design 1

Group 1 $O_1 — O_2 — O_3 — O_4 — X — O_5 — O_6 — O_7 — O_8$

- -

Group 2 $O_9 — O_{10} — O_{11} — O_{12} ——— O_{13} — O_{14} — O_{15} — O_{16}$

Design 2

Group 1 $O_1 — O_2 — O_3 — O_4 — X — O_5 — O_6 — O_7 — O_8$

- -

Group 2 $O_9 — O_{10} — O_{11} — O_{12} — O_{13} — X — O_{14} — O_{15} — O_{16}$

In the first design we have two groups of participants, the first of which is exposed to the treatment following O_4, whereas the second is never exposed to it. In the second design, both groups are exposed to the treatment although at different times. The Palmgreen et al. (2001) antimarijuana PSA study we described earlier was of this design. It is important to remember that participants have not been randomly assigned to groups in these designs.

Although these are not randomized experimental designs, they are quite strong from the point of view of internal validity. As in the one-group interrupted time-series designs, threats of maturation, instrumentation, and testing can usually be eliminated as alternative explanations for treatment effects. In addition, the replication of the design with more than a single group permits most alternative explanations associated with history to be eliminated. If the treatment coincided with some historical event in one of the groups and if the various groups were presumably exposed to the same historical conditions, the effects of that historical incident should appear in both groups as a difference at the same time. In the first group it might be coincident with the treatment, but in the second it would not be.

Note that part of the strength of these replicated interrupted time-series designs comes from the fact that comparisons between treatment and control conditions can be made both within the same participants over time and between different groups of participants at the same time. Consider the first design shown above. There are numerous pairs of observations that can be used to estimate a treatment effect. Looking only within participants, we can treat the design as a single-group interrupted time-series design and estimate the treatment effect by comparing O_4 and O_5. If this difference is large and if the differences between adjacent pretests or adjacent posttests are relatively small (e.g., the topmost graph in Figure 13.4), we have evidence within participants of a treatment effect. Because this estimate of a treatment effect is within participants, a selection threat is eliminated.

To eliminate history, maturation, testing, and instrumentation threats, we would also like to estimate the treatment effect by examining the difference between treated and untreated participants at the same time. Thus, we can estimate the treatment effect between participants by comparing O_5 and O_{13}, O_6 and O_{14}, O_7 and O_{15}, and O_8

and O_{16}. Because each of these between-participant comparisons involves information gathered at the same time, presumably threats due to maturation and history can be eliminated. Of course, because participants have not been randomly assigned to groups, it could be that the two groups of participants are differentially sensitive to historical events that might intervene and cause changes in the posttest measures. In other words, in the absence of random assignment, we cannot eliminate all threats to internal validity. Nevertheless, this sort of replicated time-series design, because it permits both within- and between-participant treatment comparisons, is a very strong design.

Note that this design is the one used in the Panel Study of Income Dynamics described earlier. Longitudinal panel surveys permit comparisons both within individuals over time and between individuals at the same time. Such survey designs are particularly informative about the development of social behavior, particularly when the researcher is unable to control assignment to levels of the independent variable. Thus, in the Panel Study of Income Dynamics, we might well be interested in the effects of unemployment, but we are surely unable to manipulate it experimentally. By observing numerous individuals over time, some of whom become unemployed during the course of the panel study, we have in essence a replicated time-series design that permits relatively strong inferences about the effects of employment status.

Matching as a Mistaken Strategy in Quasi-Experimentation

Researchers often are tempted to use a **matching** strategy in many nonrandomized research designs. Suppose we have a treatment and a control condition and we plan on using a pretest–posttest nonequivalent group design. We are not able to assign individual participants randomly to the treatment and control groups, but we intend to gather pretest data. We might consider the possibility of trying to eliminate preexisting group differences by matching the otherwise nonequivalent groups on their pretest scores. Although this might sound logical, we warn readers against trying to match groups unless people can subsequently be randomly assigned from the matched pairs to a treatment and control group. The problem with matching is that even if researchers believe they have matched perfectly on a pretest, the preexisting group differences are likely to reappear on the posttest and make it impossible to determine whether the differences observed after the treatment are the result of the treatment or are the resurgence of the preexisting difference.

To show how this can happen, we must introduce another threat to internal validity: regression toward the mean. **Regression toward the mean,** or statistical regression, as it also is called, refers to the phenomenon that extreme scores are not likely to be as extreme on a second testing. Regression toward the mean appears whenever two sets of scores are not perfectly correlated, that is, when a person's score on one variable cannot be perfectly predicted from their score on the other. Two sets of scores are never perfectly correlated if there is any error in the measurement of either one. There is always error in measurement (recall Chapter 4). Therefore, there always will be regression toward the mean.

Let us imagine giving a midterm and a final exam to a group of 58 students. The midterm we shall call our pretest and the final our posttest. In general, the students who scored in the upper half of the class on the pretest score in the upper half on the posttest, and the students who score in the lower half score there again, although there is some shifting of scores from the first to the second test. The correlation is not perfect. This means that the students who received the highest pretest scores do not all receive the highest posttest scores, and those who received the lowest pretest scores do not all receive the lowest posttest scores. Figure 13.5 shows what scores these students received on the pretest and posttest. Of the four students who scored 100 on the pretest, only one received 100 again on the posttest. The other three students obtained scores of 90, 80, and 70. Therefore, the average posttest score of those students is closer to the mean than their pretest scores were. A similar movement toward the mean appears for the students who received the lowest pretest scores. They all received 40 on the pretest, but on the posttest their scores ranged from 40 to 70. At both extremes of the pretest, we find that the group's average posttest scores are closer to the mean. This is what we mean by regression toward the mean.

Regression toward the mean occurs whenever there is an imperfect correlation. To see this, compare Figure 13.5, which shows two measures that are imperfectly correlated, with Figure 13.6, which shows two measures that are perfectly correlated. There is no regression toward the mean in Figure 13.6 because everyone who received the highest score on the pretest also received the highest score on the posttest, and everyone with the lowest pretest score has the lowest posttest score. We never see perfect correlations such as this in reality because all our measurements contain a random error component—which means that observed scores are not perfectly reliable and will show fluctuations from one testing session to the next. Such fluctuations reduce the correlation, and the lower the correlation the more we find regression toward the mean as it appears in Figure 13.5.

The fact that extreme scores regress toward the mean does not imply that students become more homogeneous over the course of a semester. If we work backward and begin with final exam scores, we find the same regression effect of final exams on midterm scores. The students who received the highest scores on the final exam would not all receive identical midterm scores, and those who received the lowest scores on the final would not all receive the lowest scores on the midterm. If we turn Figure 13.5 on its side, we can see that the same regression toward the mean occurs when we look first at posttest scores and second at pretest scores.

Regression toward the mean occurs, therefore, not as a result of a homogenization process but as a result of scores being less than 100% reliable. Any change of the most extreme scores is of necessity a regression toward the mean.

To see how regression toward the mean is a threat to internal validity when a matching strategy is used, consider the evaluation of a program like Head Start. Head Start is what is known as a compensatory program—an educational program specifically targeted to groups of children from relatively deprived backgrounds. When such compensatory programs are evaluated, a regression artifact can mistakenly make the program look detrimental in the following way. If children are not randomly

FIGURE 13.5 SCATTERPLOT SHOWING REGRESSION TOWARD THE POSTTEST MEAN FROM PRETEST SCORES

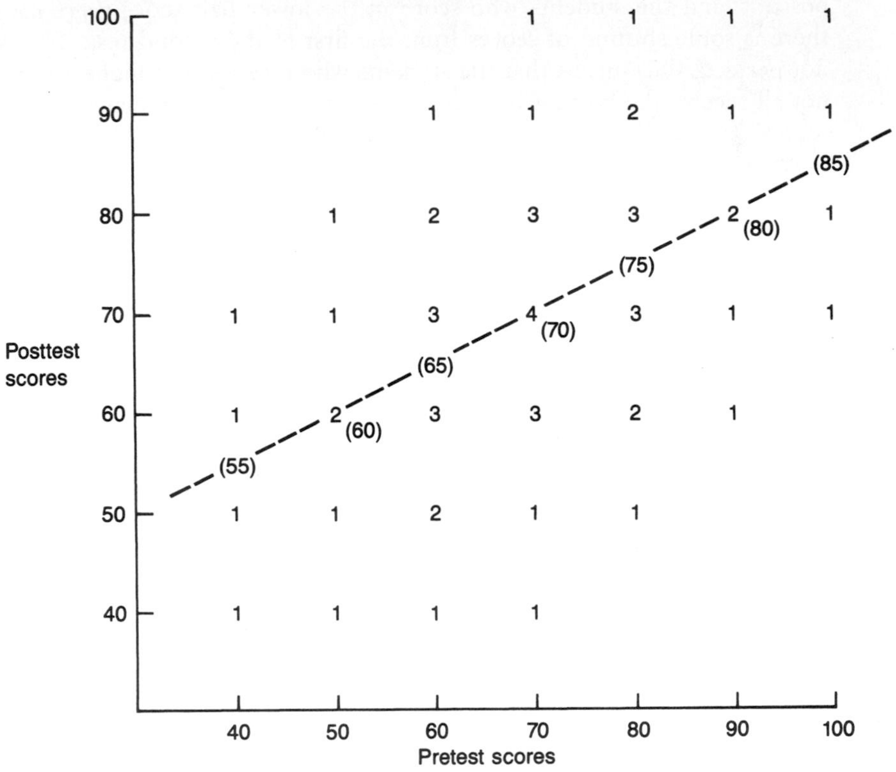

Note: The numbers inside the graph (1, 2, 3, and 4) indicate how many students received each score on the two tests. The dashed line represents the average posttest score for each group of students who received a particular pretest score. The figures in parentheses are those averages. Turning the figure on its side shows the average pretest score for each group of students who received a particular posttest score. Regression toward the mean operates in both cases.

assigned to the treatment and control groups but are selected on the basis of some qualifications, we cannot assume that the children in the two groups come from the same population. In fact, the more reasonable assumption is that they come from two different populations or social groups, those who qualify and those who do not. In the case of a compensatory program, those who qualify must usually demonstrate a disadvantage, such as having a low income. The children who qualify for the program come from a group considered disadvantaged; the comparison children come from a group considered advantaged. These two groups obviously differ in their income levels and in the many other advantages that accompany income. They also differ in

FIGURE 13.6

SCATTERPLOT SHOWING NO REGRESSION TOWARD THE MEAN WHEN THERE IS A PERFECT CORRELATION BETWEEN PRETEST AND POSTTEST SCORES

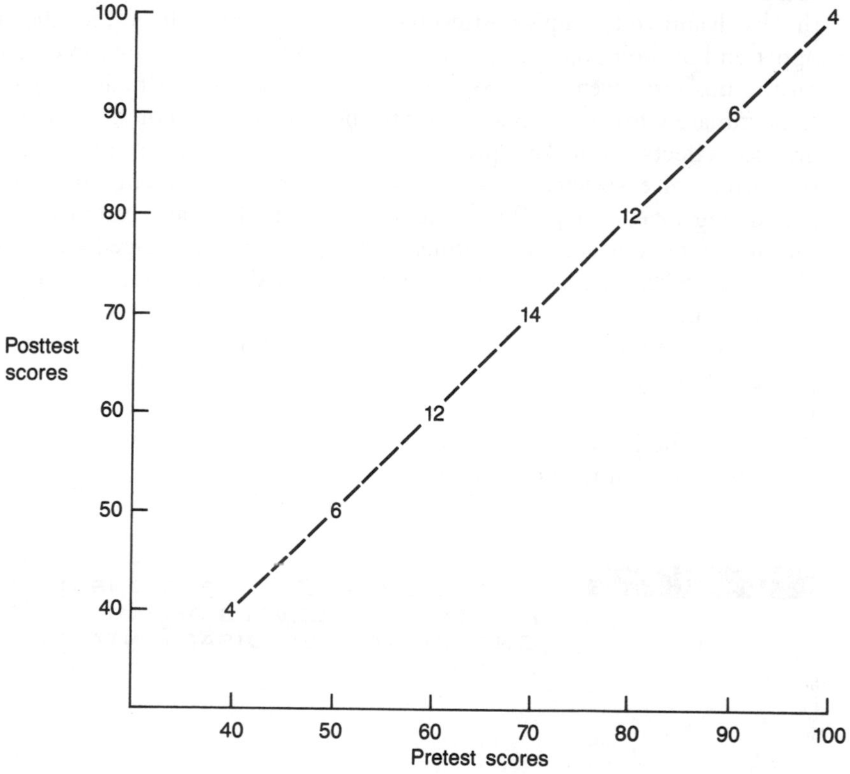

Note: The numbers along the dashed line indicate how many students received each score on the two tests. The dashed line with all scores falling exactly on the line has no "scatter" of points around it. Therefore, there is no regression toward the mean. The posttest score is the same as the pretest score for each group of people.

their average pretest achievement levels, a difference that the evaluators might try to remove by matching on pretest scores. In the process of matching, a researcher sets the conditions for regression artifacts to operate. Figure 13.7 shows the distributions of pretest scores for two hypothetical groups—one an advantaged comparison, the other a disadvantaged treatment group. The distributions overlap, but they have different means or averages. In an attempt to match individuals from the two groups, the researcher draws from opposite ends of each group—from the upper end of the disadvantaged group and the lower end of the advantaged group. The darker region of Figure 13.7 shows the matched portion of each group.

These two "matched" groups represent extreme scorers from their respective populations. Because the pretest scores are not 100% reliable, we know that the posttest scores of these children will not be equally extreme—they will regress in opposite directions, toward their population means. The advantaged group's posttest scores will be slightly higher, for they represent the bottom end of their population; the disadvantaged group's posttest scores will be slightly lower, for they represent the upper end of their population. Thus, regression artifacts alone can create a difference on the posttest, even if no compensatory program had actually been implemented. Unfortunately for researchers trying to show benefits of compensatory programs, regression effects can make a program look detrimental if the treatment and comparison groups are selected in such a way that they represent opposite ends of two preexisting social groups. The same regression artifacts also can make a program look mistakenly beneficial if the treatment is given to the advantaged group and a presumably matched comparison group is drawn from a disadvantaged group.

Matching, therefore, is inadequate for removing preexisting group differences. Unless we randomly assign individuals from a common pool to treatment and control groups, it is always likely that the two groups represent different populations with different means. Attempts to match on either pretest scores or other variables are destined to be imperfect, and regression toward the mean is a potential explanation for subsequent differences. Because of the problems associated with matching, an

FIGURE 13.7 **HYPOTHETICAL DISTRIBUTIONS OF PRETEST ACHIEVEMENT LEVELS OF TWO POPULATIONS, ONE CONSIDERED DISADVANTAGED AND ONE ADVANTAGED**

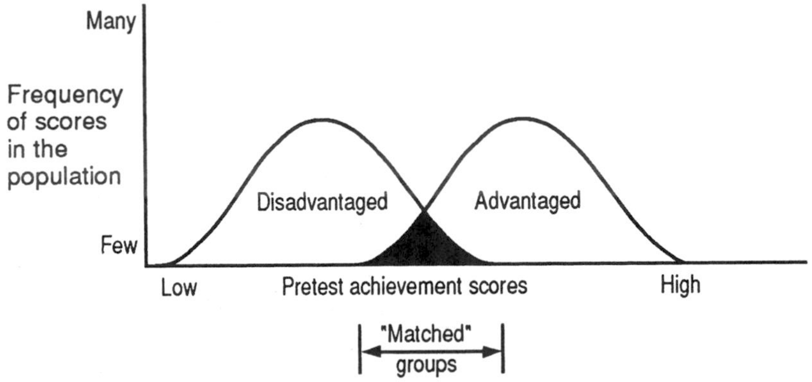

Note: The darker region represents the "matched" groups from the two populations.

expert panel appointed by the U.S. Secretary of Health and Human Services issued a report in 1999 recommending that all future evaluation studies of Head Start include random assignment of children to Head Start and control conditions.

Researchers can try to match nonequivalent groups either on pretest measures of the dependent variable or on other variables known to be associated with the dependent variable. Both of these strategies fail to eliminate preexisting group differences. Matching on variables known to be associated with the dependent variable always errs in the direction of **undermatching** and, therefore, fails because we can never know when we have matched on enough variables to be sure the two groups represent the same population. For instance, Head Start evaluators might match the treatment children with a comparison group on the basis of age, sex, race, kindergarten attendance, and parents' social status. Yet the children might still differ in the kinds of television programs they watch, in their grandparents' education levels, in the number of books in their homes, in the achievement levels of their friends, and so on. The numbers of variables on which they were not matched is infinite. As compensatory social programs are usually designed for populations that are defined as disadvantaged, the children from the treatment group had fewer natural "head starts" than the comparison group on many other variables. Therefore, because they were not matched on grandparents' education, kinds of television programs watched, and many other variables, the treatment group probably would have scored lower on these unmatched variables. The two groups were undermatched, with the advantage probably going to the control group. Therefore, matching on variables known to be associated with the dependent variable is inadequate because it is always incomplete. In studies of compensatory social programs, the resulting undermatching will usually favor the control group and make the program look harmful solely as a result of the failure to equate groups.

Summary

Nonrandomized designs are the methods of choice either when establishing causality is not a primary concern in the research or when we cannot randomly assign participants to levels of manipulated independent variables of interest. In the former case, we might simply be interested in documenting the distribution of some variable of interest in some population. We also might be interested in establishing whether two variables are associated, regardless of whether that association is causal. For these sorts of goals, nonrandomized designs are perfectly suitable. Indeed, they might be more appropriate than randomized experimental designs because random sampling and other procedures to ensure external and construct validity sometimes are more easily accomplished in nonrandomized designs.

In other cases, we might wish to infer causality about the effects of an independent variable on a dependent variable, but we might not be able to manipulate the independent variable and randomly assign individuals to its level. In these cases, we use a quasi-experimental design and attempt to rule out threats to internal validity.

Quasi-experimental designs are subject to a variety of different threats, such as selection, history, maturation, testing, and regression toward the mean. Alternative designs differ in their susceptibility to each one of these threats, with perhaps the strongest design, from the point of view of internal validity, being a replicated interrupted time-series design.

Although we might get discouraged by the threats to internal validity that characterize these research designs, we must remember that the designs are nevertheless very useful tools. Research does not begin and end with randomized designs. For many purposes, nonrandomized designs are tools of choice rather than simply less desirable alternatives.

Key Concepts

alternative explanation
cross-sectional comparison
interrupted time-series design
matching
one-group pretest–posttest design
panel design
pretest–posttest nonequivalent control group design
quasi-experimental designs
regression toward the mean
replicated interrupted time-series design
static-group comparison design
undermatching

On the Web

http://www.isr.umich.edu/src/psid/index.html The Web site for the Panel Study of Income Dynamics.

http://trochim.human.cornell.edu/kb/quasnegd.htm Detailed discussion of the pretest–posttest nonequivalent control group design, emphasizing the threats to causal inference entailed in the design. Part of the Research Methods Knowledge Base Web text written by William Trochim.

http://trochim.human.cornell.edu/kb/quasioth.htm Another part of Trochim's Research Methods Knowledge Base, this is a very nicely written description of variations of quasi-experimental designs, including some not described in this chapter.

http://www.fammed.ouhsc.edu/tutor/qexpdes.htm Another site with clear descriptions of various types of quasi-experimental designs, including research examples.

http://www.fmarion.edu/~resdes/design/basicdes.htm Brief and easy-to-follow checklist of various types of experimental and quasi-experimental designs and which threats to validity they control.

http://www.ed.gov/databases/ERIC_Digests/ed421483.html Nice summary of the distinction between experimental and quasi-experimental designs.

Further Reading

Shadish, W. R., Cook, T. D., & Campbell, D. T. (2001). *Experimental and quasi-experimental designs for generalized causal inference.* Boston: Houghton-Mifflin.

Trochim, W. M. K. (Ed.). (1986). *Advances in quasi-experimental design and analysis.* San Francisco: Jossey-Bass.

West, S. G., Biesanz, J. C., & Pitts, S. C. (2000). Causal inference and generalization in field settings: Experimental and quasi-experimental designs. In H. T. Reis, & C. M. Judd (Eds.), *Handbook of research methods in social and personality psychology* (pp. 40–84). New York: Cambridge University Press.

CHAPTER

14

Applied Research

In this chapter we examine applied social science research, with an emphasis on evaluation research. **Applied research** is any social scientific research designed to answer practical questions. Applied researchers also can be testing theories while they are answering practical questions, and they can be more or less directly involved in a practical or real-world setting, but ultimately they are interested in answering some question with practical implications. They are interested in gathering information that can be useful in affecting, implementing, or changing some social policy. Ultimately, then, applied researchers in the social sciences are interested in speaking to a somewhat different audience than are researchers who conduct more **basic research,** which focuses on the development and testing of theories about social behavior. Applied social scientists ultimately wish their work to be used by those who make or change social policy. They are interested in affecting how legislators, judges, and administrators think about some social problem or issue.

The distinction between applied and basic research is not a distinction among different research methods and research designs. Applied researchers use randomized experiments, quasi-experiments, and surveys, just as basic researchers do. They gather information through questionnaires, interviews, and observational methods. They are concerned with construct validity, internal validity, and external validity. All the issues discussed in this book are of concern to both applied and basic researchers. The distinctions between the two are more practical than methodological.

First, because applied research is typically conducted in the real world, real-world problems can intervene and make researchers change their plans and procedures. Participants might not always be available when and where researchers would like. Information can be relatively hard to gather. Historical events can intervene and affect our conclusions. A program or treatment that is being evaluated might change during the course of the research because administrators decide that some change in a program is necessary. In sum, practical problems can arise in carrying out a chosen research design and successfully gathering and analyzing the data.

Second, applied research differs from basic research in the audience to which it must appeal. Applied researchers must often justify their claims and demonstrate the utility of their empirical work, not to fellow social scientists, who usually take for granted the value of empirical research, but to policy makers and administrators who might be more skeptical about the value of questionnaire, interview, or observational data. Because applied research takes place in a political world and ultimately seeks to affect policies that result from political processes, it must appeal to those processes in ways that more basic research cannot. One of the hardest steps in conducting applied research is translating the empirical findings into a language and form so that their policy implications are both clear and useful.

Before shifting our focus to evaluation research, we present three examples to give the flavor of applied research, the social problems and issues it occasionally addresses, and the political realities it inevitably must confront.

Varieties of Applied Research

Laboratory Simulation—Survivors' Reactions to Layoffs

How do "survivors" react when they see coworkers laid off from work? A team of researchers set out to answer this question with a laboratory experiment designed to simulate the conditions under which workers get to know each other and then learn that some of their number have been laid off (Brockner, Grover, Reed, DeWitt, & O'Malley, 1987). The "workers" in the simulation were college students who volunteered to participate in what they thought was a test validation study. When they came to the laboratory, they were told each person would receive $5 in payment along with a chance to win a $75 raffle.

The experimenters tested the effects of two variables on workers' reactions to layoffs. They wanted to see whether a survivor's *identification* with someone who was laid off and the *fairness* of the circumstances surrounding the layoff would affect subsequent commitment to work. Each participant completed a brief survey that measured attitudes about a number of social and political issues. The experimenters used the survey to inform participants how similar their attitudes were to those of a coworker. By manipulating the perceived similarity of coworkers, the experimenters hoped they were simulating various levels of identification among workers.

After learning about how similar their coworkers' answers were to their own, the participants were asked to do the actual "work" for which they had volunteered, proofreading pages of text. They worked for eight minutes on seven pages and were then given a brief rest before beginning the next batch. During the rest period an experimenter came in to announce the layoff, which he said was caused by a room scheduling problem. The person who would be laid off was chosen by drawing straws, but the drawing was rigged so that an experimenter's confederate was laid off and the participants "survived." The layoff was then presented in two different ways that the experimenters hoped would seem either fair or unfair. In the unfair condition the laid off worker was told he would receive neither the $5 payment nor the chance at the $75 raffle. In the fairer condition, he was offered a $3 payment and retained his chance at the raffle.

The researchers were interested in how the circumstances surrounding the layoff would affect the survivors' subsequent work performance. The second work period was identical to the first—proofreading seven pages in eight minutes—and the experimenters measured the change in performance from the first to the second period. The workers who felt they were similar to someone who had been laid off and who saw that person as unfairly compensated produced the least work during the second period relative to the first. This result was as the researchers predicted.

The results of this experiment were clear. The question remaining for the researchers, however, was this: Do real workers who survive real layoffs react as these research participants did? To address this question, the researchers turned to the field to conduct a survey of workers who had survived layoffs.

Survey Research—Survivors' Reactions to Layoffs

A chain of retail stores had closed many of its outlets in the preceding year, and the employees in the remaining stores were all considered survivors by the researchers. Of the 773 remaining stores, Brockner et al. (1987) randomly selected 300 and contacted the store managers of each to ask for their assistance. They mailed the required number of surveys to each manager for distribution to employees and asked the employees to return their answers in envelopes addressed to the researchers' university address. About one-third of the 1,602 surveys were completed and returned.

What had been experimental manipulations in the laboratory simulation became questions on the survey. Two items assessed identification: "I have (or had) a close personal relationship with at least some of the laid off people" and "I had a close working relationship with at least some of the laid off people." The fairness of compensation to the victims was measured by four survey items: (1) amount of severance pay, (2) efforts by management to find other employment in the company, (3) continuation of health and insurance benefits after the layoff, and (4) help from management in finding work elsewhere. The dependent variable, commitment to work, which was measured by proofreading in the simulation, was measured by an 18-item scale asking about pride in the company before and after the layoffs. The scale included items such as "I am proud to tell my friends I work for this company."

Before examining the results of this survey, what can we say about the research design? We know that workers were not randomly assigned to be laid off or to survive, so this sample of people was already preselected in some way. That is not a serious threat to the external validity of the study, however, because it is by definition a study of those who survived. The 300 stores were randomly chosen from the 773 stores that had remained open, so the results can be generalized to the employees who survived layoffs in the other 473 stores in this chain and quite possibly to employees in other chain retail businesses of this size. The external validity, therefore, is high.

What can we say about internal validity? All three variables—identification with laid off workers, perceived fairness of the layoffs, and commitment to the organization—are individual difference variables. They come prepackaged, with no random assignment to levels of the first two and no way of knowing how prior commitment to the organization might affect the survivors' identification with laid off workers or perceptions of fairness. As with any nonrandomized research design, this condition raises the difficult issues associated with selection as an alternative explanation. Perhaps people who are strongly committed to the organization also are more inclined to say that layoffs were handled fairly and to downplay their ties with laid off workers. These are plausible alternative explanations because we have no way of knowing how the three variables were associated even before the layoffs occurred.

Let us place this survey back in its context, however, as a companion piece to the laboratory experiment. The experiment has high internal validity; the survey, high external validity. If they arrive at the same conclusions about the associations among identification, perceived fairness, and work commitment among survivors, we are more assured about their validity than if we had only one type of study.

The survey did show the same pattern of results as the laboratory simulation. Workers who identified with colleagues who had been laid off and who thought the compensation was unfair said they were much less committed to the organization after the layoffs than before. This pair of studies presents a strong case for using multiple research methods.

Intervention—The Jigsaw Classroom

The ideal applied research study would be a truly randomized intervention in a real-world setting. Such a study would have high internal and external validity.

Classrooms are ideal settings for such studies. Because teachers often experiment with innovative educational methods, a research intervention is not out of the ordinary experience of teachers or students. Students are accustomed to taking tests or filling out questionnaires, so using a test or questionnaire as a dependent variable is consistent with what occurs in classrooms. If teachers, parents, students, and school administrators want to choose whether to participate in an innovation, the selection of treatment and control groups might be voluntary rather than random, and the research would be quasi-experimental. In some instances, however, they might consent to random assignment, permitting the researchers to conduct a true randomized experiment in a real-world setting.

Students and teachers in Austin, Texas, took part in a series of randomized and nonrandomized experiments designed to change the nature of the American classroom. Eliot Aronson and his colleagues (1978) worked with teachers to develop classroom conditions that were cooperative rather than competitive and that would facilitate peer teaching. They wanted to create a climate in which Black, Latino, and White children would all participate and benefit.

The cooperative classroom activities were modeled on the activity of piecing together a puzzle. Children worked in small groups of five or six and were given assignments for which each child had one piece of the solution. The students were to piece together the whole solution by learning from and teaching each other. For instance, in one assignment the students were expected to learn about the life of Joseph Pulitzer. His life story was divided into six periods, each described in a paragraph written by the researchers. They cut and distributed the separate paragraphs to fifth-grade students, who had been put into interdependent learning groups of six children each. Each child in the group had a different paragraph describing one of the six periods in Pulitzer's life, and they were not allowed to pass their paragraphs around or read one another's. Instead, they were to teach and learn from one another. This meant the other five needed to pay close attention to the one who was speaking because that person had valuable information and was an important resource. Each child was essential for the others' solutions; no one could be dismissed as unimportant or unintelligent. And no one could benefit from studying all alone, trying to be the "best," independent of the others in the group.

The students who were in these interdependent jigsaw groups liked each other and liked school better than children who were in traditional classrooms. They also came to like themselves better—they developed higher self-esteem. These positive effects were evident across ethnic boundaries. For example, in some of the predominantly White classrooms there were Latino children who had previously remained silent in class. When they had been called on to speak in the traditionally competitive classrooms, they had sometimes been embarrassed, so they and their teachers learned it was safest for them to be silent. With the jigsaw problem, these children had information essential for the solution, and what they said became valuable to others. The transition was not easy for them or their classmates, but their role in the class did change and so did their performance. The grades of ethnic minority children went up almost a whole letter, as did their self-esteem and that of all the students who participated. Most of the teachers also liked what they saw happening in the interdependent groups, and many continued to use the technique after the intervention ended.

The first of these jigsaw classroom interventions was a quasi-experiment. Ten teachers who had participated in a weeklong workshop with the researchers volunteered to use the jigsaw method in their classrooms. The school administrators then identified three other teachers who were known as very competent and committed to their own methods of teaching to serve as a control group. The teachers were, therefore, self-selected rather than randomly assigned into the treatment and control conditions.

At the end of six weeks, the researchers found that students in the jigsaw classrooms had higher self-esteem, liked school more, were more convinced they could learn from one another, and had higher grades than did students in the regular classes (Blaney, Stephan, Rosenfield, Aronson, & Sikes, 1977). The only problem with these glowing results was that no one could be sure it was the jigsaw method itself that was responsible because the teachers in the jigsaw classrooms were self-selected rather than randomly assigned. Perhaps those teachers who volunteered to use the new method were doing all sorts of other things differently. Could it have been their personal enthusiasm, their expectations that the "experiment" would succeed, their commitment to do something (anything) for which they had volunteered?

To rule out these alternative explanations, the researchers next obtained permission to assign classrooms randomly to the jigsaw method or to a control group that would conduct business as usual (Lucker, Rosenfield, Sikes, & Aronson, 1977). In the randomized experiment among 11 fifth- and sixth-grade classes, 6 classes used the jigsaw method and 5 classes were taught by equally competent teachers using their traditional methods. At the end of just two weeks, students in the jigsaw classrooms showed gains in their test scores compared with students in the traditional classrooms; this was particularly true for ethnic minority students.

These examples illustrate how applied researchers can affect what actually occurs in the real-world settings they study.

Qualitative Research—Everything in Its Path

Social scientists sometimes participate in court cases on behalf of persons who have suffered not just physical but also psychological and social damages from environmental disasters. In 1972, after a mining company dam burst and sent 100 million gallons of mud through a narrow mountain hollow of a community in West Virginia, sociologist Kai Erikson was asked by a law firm to recommend someone to assess the social and psychological damages. After going to the hollow, he was so struck by the damage and the need to report it that he volunteered to do the research, and he wrote his analysis in a moving book titled *Everything in Its Path* (Erikson, 1976).

Erikson (1976) viewed the physical damage left behind by the flood of mud and water and listened to the stories people told about the flood and their lives during the weeks and months since. His research report contains many stories like the following:

> I have the feeling that every time it comes a storm it's a natural thing for it to flood. Now that's just my feeling, and I can't get away from it, can't help it. Seems like every time it rains I get that old dirty feeling that it is just a natural thing for it to become another flood.
>
> Why, it don't even have to rain. I listen to the news, and if there's a storm warning out, why I don't go to bed that night. I set up. I tell my wife, "Don't undress our little girls; just let them lay down like they are and go to bed and go to sleep and then if I see anything going to happen, I'll wake you in plenty of time to get you out of the house." I don't go to bed. I stay up. (p. 143)

Some people talked of trying to move from the valley; some talked of suicide; everyone talked of recurrent fears, nightmares, and other symptoms.

> It was as if every man, woman, and child in the place—every one—was suffering from some combination of anxiety, depression, insomnia, apathy, or simple "bad nerves," and to make matters worse, those complaints were expressed in such similar ways that they almost sounded rehearsed. (p. 136)

Two years following the flood, residents of the hollow remarked on their inability to rebuild their lives. People whose homes had been swept away were placed in trailer camps provided by the U.S. Department of Housing and Urban Development. Thirteen camps were scattered throughout the valley, and people had been placed in them almost at random. A young woman living in one of the camps observed,

> Perhaps the communities people were placed in after the disaster had a lot to do with the problem. If there had been time enough to place people [near] the same families and neighbors they were accustomed to, it might have been different . . . . I have conflicts with people I don't even know. It seems like everyone's on edge, just waiting for trouble to happen. Things like that just didn't happen in Lundale. Everybody knew you and your personality. (p. 149)

Many people talked of the loss of community:

> Everybody was close, everybody knowed everybody. But now everybody is alone. They act like they're lost. You can't go next door and talk. You can't do that no more, there's no next door . . . . You can't laugh with friends . . . because there's no friends around to laugh with . . . . There's nobody around to even holler at and say "Hi" and you can't help but miss that. (p. 196)

Erikson (1976) documented people's individual traumas, their state of shock, fear, and depression, which persisted for at least two years after the flood, and he examined what he called the collective trauma, the loss of community. His testimony became part of a lawsuit, which two years later won $13.5 million from the mining company. The day the money was distributed, wrote Erikson, "was a cruel time as well as a comforting one."

> The people of the hollow, some of them, in any event—have been compensated financially for the loss of their property and symbolically for the emotional injuries they had to bear. But they have not been compensated for the loss of their communal base, and to that extent they are still stranded in the same uncomfortable spot, suspended vaguely in midair. (p. 249)

Evaluation Research

Evaluation research is one type of applied research. Its purpose is to answer practical, real-world questions about the effects of some policy or program. Although applied research can serve more broadly to define a social problem or explore alternative policies or programs that might be implemented to solve some problem, evaluation research has as its primary goal the description and evaluation of some existing social policy or program.

What is a program? In the broadest sense, a **program** is a set of procedures put in place by an organization in order to provide services to its constituents (e.g., patients, customers, clients). In not-for-profit organizations (e.g., schools, social services), programs often map directly onto the goals of the organization. In for-profit organizations, programs often are circumscribed efforts aimed at introducing a new product or line of products. In either case, programs and the organizations that underwrite them can benefit from evaluations that draw attention to their strengths and needs.

Summative and Formative Evaluations

There are two general categories of evaluation research, summative and formative. **Summative evaluations,** otherwise referred to as outcome evaluations, examine the effects of a program and ask, "Does it work?" **Formative evaluations,** sometimes called process evaluations, ask, "What is it?" and "How does it work?" Summative evaluations use experimental, quasi-experimental, and survey research designs. Formative evaluations use techniques more like the observational methods discussed in the next chapter. Summative research usually uses statistical analysis of quantitative data. Formative research is usually qualitative research and uses case histories rather than statistics to make a point. Summative evaluations are used to decide whether programs should continue or cease, and for this reason administrators might resist and evaluators find it difficult to implement a summative evaluation. Formative evaluations seem more benign because they are used to help the administrators develop their programs, revise them, and improve them. Formative evaluators provide feedback to the program director about how the participants react to the program, how the implementers are carrying out the program, and whether the actual program resembles the intended program. They define the program as it appears in action and describe how it works. This feedback often takes place during the early stages of a program, when there is still room for change and improvement—hence, the name *formative* evaluation. By contrast, summative evaluations are done at the end of a program or after it has been in existence long enough to have produced some measurable effects that provide a fair test of the program's success. In this chapter we focus primarily on summative evaluations; in the next chapter we describe strategies that can be used in formative evaluation research.

Criteria for a Sound Evaluation

Because of the potential real-world impact of the findings from an evaluation study, it is important that the evaluation be sound in every respect. The Directorate for Education and Human Resources of the National Science Foundation, which provides funds for evaluation studies of programs designed to improve science, mathematics, engineering, and technology education, has established a set of criteria that must be met by any evaluation conducted using their funds. These criteria likely apply to any sound evaluation of a program or organization. The criteria fall into three categories: evaluation plan, evaluation instruments, and evaluation report.

Evaluation Plan Before an evaluation study can begin, a detailed plan that has been reviewed by all concerned parties must be developed. The plan should include the following information:

- What are the purposes of the program or organization to be evaluated? Without a clear understanding of the philosophy, goals, and procedures of the program, it is not possible to evaluate its performance in a fair and meaningful way.
- What is the purpose of the evaluation, and how will it be done? The justification for and procedure by which the evaluation will be done needs to be explained to all parties who might be affected by the results of the evaluation.
- Who are the **stakeholders?** That is, who stands to gain or lose from the evaluation? This might include program staff, clients served by the program, or the policy makers who will determine the future of the program.
- What is the scope of the evaluation? Will it focus on the overall performance of the program, or will it focus on specific goals or procedures within the overall purpose of the program? The evaluation can vary in the depth and breadth of its scope, characteristics that sometimes are influenced by the amount of resources available to conduct the evaluation.
- From whom within the organization will information be gathered, and how will it be gathered? Will the evaluation focus on management or other personnel within the organization, or will it focus on the clients for whom the program was designed? In what way will stakeholders be involved in developing a strategy?
- What measures will be put into place to ensure that the information obtained as part of the evaluation is of high quality? These concerns are not different from those for any type of empirical research; however, there is the additional concern that the measures suit the context in which the program is implemented. Also, it is important that ethical considerations, such as confidentiality of responses, are adequately addressed.
- Will the evaluation study include both qualitative and quantitative measures? Although quantitative measures are well suited to an evaluation of the productivity or performance of a program, qualitative measures can provide important information about how these outcomes are achieved.

Evaluation Instruments The second set of criteria concerns the means by which information will be obtained regarding the performance of the program that is being evaluated. These criteria focus primarily on the way in which respondents will be sampled and the approach to measurement that will be taken.

- The measures should be defensible. That is, they should evidence high construct validity in the context of the evaluation. It is important that the measures can be defended clearly and persuasively to all stakeholders and decision makers.

- The measures should be comprehensive. They should not be biased in their coverage of the various goals, functions, and procedures of the program.
- The procedures for administering the measures should be standardized. Because respondents are likely to come from various constituencies associated with the program, the settings within which information will be gathered likely will vary. This variability must be overcome by strategies for administering the measures that ensure no influence of setting.
- The measurement strategy must be practical. Because the measurement process will be disruptive for some respondents, it is important that the procedure for administering and responding to the measures be as straightforward and efficient as possible.
- The measures should be balanced. They should be designed to detect both strengths and weaknesses of the program being evaluated.
- The measurement process must be done in such a way that respondents' rights are not violated. Although evaluation research varies in terms of goals and participants from most of the research described in this book, all of the ethical principles outlined in Chapter 3 apply. A particular concern in evaluation research is confidentiality of responses. Respondents cannot be expected to provide honest and meaningful answers to questions about the program if they worry that their honest opinions could get them in trouble.

Evaluation Report Perhaps the most critical feature of an evaluation study is the final report. As noted earlier, unlike research reports, which are intended for a relatively homogeneous audience of the researchers' peers, reports produced by evaluators must be appropriate for a heterogeneous audience. This audience can include program staff, clients, government officials, or other policy makers in whose hands the future of the program rests.

- The evaluation report begins with an **executive summary,** a succinct document that provides essential information about the evaluation report in a style that is easily understood by stakeholders. It should clearly summarize the primary content of the full report.
- The evaluation report should describe in detail the program that has been evaluated. The description should include the goals and objectives of the program, the procedures by which the program attempts to realize its goals and objectives, the rationale for the evaluation, and the stakeholders.
- The report should identify prevailing forces that need to be understood in order to interpret the results of the evaluation. These forces can range from timing to economic, political, and social conditions impinging on the organization during the period covered by the evaluation.

- The report should identify the stakeholders in the program and describe the different perspectives they will bring to a reading of the report.
- A proportionately large section of the report should describe in detail the procedures used in the evaluation. It is this section of the report that most resembles a research report typical of social science research. Measures should be described and justified, procedures detailed, and results of statistical analyses presented.
- Perhaps the most critical aspect of the evaluation report is "the bottom line"—the conclusions and recommendations offered by the evaluator based on the findings from the evaluation study. This section of the report should be balanced and circumspect. Both strengths and needs identified by the study should be highlighted. And potential limitations to the evaluation should be disclosed and discussed.

Viewed as a whole, these criteria make clear the distinction between applied and basic research. Although the principles of sampling, measurement, and research design discussed so far in this book apply equally to applied and basic research, applied research such as program evaluation involves additional considerations, some of which are in conflict with the principles of good sampling, measurement, and design. In the end, the evaluation researcher must balance principles of good science and the practicalities of conducting research in an arena in which many, often conflicting, personal and political agendas are at play.

Randomization—Pro and Con

This balance between principles and practicalities is perhaps nowhere more apparent than in the decision regarding whether a program should be evaluated using a randomized experimental design. From the perspective of solid scientific practice, the randomized experiment, when feasible, is highly desirable. Recall, for instance, the early jigsaw classroom studies that were evaluated in nonrandomized studies. Although the evaluations appeared to favor the program, there were too many compelling alternative explanations to confidently assert that the program was effective. Only when the program held up under the scrutiny of a randomized experiment was it reasonable to assert its effectiveness.

Despite the allure of randomized experiments, practical considerations specific to the evaluation context often argue against their use. Critics have made the following arguments against randomized experiments as a strategy for program evaluation:

1. They are not feasible.
2. They have a narrow scope and are limited because they "fail to include qualitative information . . . [and] are unable to recognize subtle human reactions to a social program" (Boruch, 1975, p. 122).
3. They are useless in providing information on how to make a program better.

4. They are unethical because they either deprive the control group of a desirable treatment or subject the treatment group to a questionable treatment.

In response, Robert Boruch, an evaluator, has addressed each of the criticisms as follows.

1. Randomized social experiments are feasible because more than 200 evaluations of social programs have successfully used random assignment. This does not mean that it is easy to implement true experiments, but it is proof that they are feasible. Boruch's (1975) list of over 200 evaluations using an experimental design shows a wide range of programs that include job training, education, mental health, social welfare, medical care, economic incentives, criminal justice, the mass media, and many others. Random assignment is possible in more places than the critics believe.

   The critics might still have a point, however, if we ask whether there are some special conditions that make random assignment particularly difficult and other conditions that make it easy. Boruch (1975) gives us some insight on this subject:

   > The examples . . . serve as a basis for examining conditions under which controlled tests appear to be most readily mounted. For example, many such tests compare the effects of various material products, such as two different income subsidy plans, rather than the effects of social programs which are based heavily on personal skills or program staff, such as two rehabilitation programs for the mentally ill.

   It is conceivable that experimental tests of the latter sort are more difficult to conduct because we do not know enough about designing tests that are especially sensitive to staff skills or that do not threaten the status of program staff. Program administrators often resist random assignment and true experimental designs because they do not want an evaluation that looks foolproof—and they could be right. We might not know enough about designing treatments and measuring the effects of social as opposed to material programs to conduct a truly fair test of an idea; and well-intentioned program administrators do not want to jeopardize a good idea by having a rigorous evaluation conducted on an inadequate implementation of it.

2. Randomized experiments need not preclude gathering qualitative data, and gathering quantitative data need not preclude discovering "subtle human reactions to a social program." Data in true experiments can be either quantitative or qualitative; what matters is that they be systematic: "systematic and reliable information is essential for dispelling erroneous ideas generated by casual observation, dramatic anecdote, and unchecked impressions. That systematic information may be quantitative, or qualitative, or both" (Boruch, 1975, p. 122).

Another part of the second criticism is that experiments are narrow and limited in scope because they are "one-shot affairs." Boruch (1975) replies that "nothing in experimental design methodology demands one-shot tests, and, for a variety of reasons, sequential assessment should ordinarily be the rule rather than the exception" (p. 125). Both the critics and the defenders of experiments are correct. Experiments and evaluations often are one-shot tests and do not follow the program or the participants over many months or years, but they need not be so limited. The 30-year follow-up evaluation of the Cambridge–Somerville experiment described later in this chapter is a notable exception. Most summative or outcome evaluations are not longitudinal studies because the answer to the question "Does it work?" cannot wait for years.

3. The third criticism, that experimental evaluations are not useful because they provide little guidance on how to make the program better, also has a grain of truth. If we discover that job-training programs do not succeed in getting higher wages for the trainees, we do not know what will succeed. All we know is that this attempt failed. Experiments do not necessarily provide ideas for innovations, but they do provide clear answers about whether a particular innovation worked. Whenever it is possible to compare two innovations, an experimental test will show which one is better. If we accept experiments for what they are—tests of effects—they do enable us to make decisions about whether a program is good and which of several alternative programs is the best.

   Another part of the third criticism is that "rigorous evaluations of social programs, including experiments, can destroy any incentive to be creative in program development" (Boruch, 1975, p.128). Boruch answers that experimental design and evaluation cannot guarantee creativity but that there is also no reason why they must stifle it. The experimental approach is very compatible with creativity—people who are willing to experiment are innovative and creative. And those who experiment generally want to know the results of their experiments.

   Barriers to innovation can arise when the results of the innovation threaten the innovator's career, and in this sense, experimental evaluations can stifle creativity. For this reason, Campbell (1969b) says the ideal strategy is to compare two innovations, with the program administrators' jobs guaranteed no matter what the evaluation reveals, so that administrators and evaluators can be impartial judges of the value of social programs. "This is a useful strategy to the extent that multiple comparisons inhibit premature emotional endorsement of what might be thought of as the solution to a complex social problem, and that they reduce the staff anxieties usually associated with a test of only one solution" (Boruch, 1975, p. 129).

4. The fourth criticism of randomized experiments in evaluation research concerns the ethics of experimentation, and it takes several forms. On the one

> hand, critics say that the untreated or control group is unfairly deprived of a potentially good program. On the other hand, critics also say the treated or experimental group ("guinea pigs") are unfairly subjected to questionable treatments that might not help and might even harm them. Whether the treatment be helpful or harmful, experimentation is called unfair. Boruch (1975) has a simple answer: "Failure to experiment . . . [can be] unethical" (p. 135) because we will never know if a treatment is good or bad if we do not put it to a rigorous test.
>
> In those cases in which we know that a program will not be harmful and we doubt only whether it is helpful or simply ineffective, we ideally want to permit as many people as possible to participate. The limit on how many people can participate is usually determined not by any principle of experimental design but by budgets. If this is the case and if more people volunteer or express an interest in a program than can be served, randomization is a fair way of deciding who can participate in the program and who will be in the control group (Brickman et al., 1981; Wortman & Rabinovitz, 1979). Some people participate in lotteries for pleasure and profit. They might also be willing to participate in lotteries for access to social programs for which there are more volunteers or applicants than there are places available. Social psychologists who examined the fairness of lotteries found that people regard random assignment as fair when all the people in the participant pool are equally deserving (Brickman & Stearns, 1978). If prior screening of people's merits or needs still leaves a pool of people larger than the number who can receive a special program (e.g., scholarships), a lottery seems fair, and a lottery is random assignment.

Seligman's research on energy conservation is a good example of how it is possible to conduct randomized experiments in the real world. Seligman and his colleagues wanted to see whether home owners would reduce their energy consumption if they were given feedback about how much energy they were consuming (e.g., Becker & Seligman, 1978; Becker, Seligman, & Darley, 1979; Seligman & Hutton, 1981). They randomly assigned home owners to two groups; one received conservation feedback and the other did not. They first recruited a large number of potential participants, more than they could accommodate. The home owners who were willing to participate were told that if they were selected for the experiment, they would have a small device installed in one wall of their home. They also were told that the experimenter might not have enough devices for everyone who was interested, in which case the devices would be allotted randomly. After the random assignment was made and the participants were informed of their luck, all remained willing to participate. Those who did not receive the feedback meters remained in the experiment as a control group. They were willing to answer questionnaires and have their energy consumption monitored because they shared an initial commitment to the goal of energy conservation. This feature, of course, makes the entire sample a special one, not a randomly selected sample. It limits the external validity of the experiment.

Nonetheless, it gives the evaluation high internal validity, and it demonstrates the willingness of people in the real world to participate in randomized experiments.

A True Experiment—The Cambridge–Somerville Youth Study

The Cambridge–Somerville Youth Study is a unique piece of evaluation research because it did what many social program evaluations ideally should do. It examined the long-term effects of a childhood treatment program. In 1939 a social philosopher and physician named Richard Clark Cabot began a program that he hoped would prevent delinquency among boys in Boston. He located over 500 boys aged 5 to 13 through recommendations of teachers, clergy, police officers, and welfare agencies. Some of the boys were considered "difficult" or predelinquent, and others were identified as "average." Half were assigned to the treatment program, and the other half were designated "controls." The assignment was made by the toss of a coin, making this a randomized experiment.

Boys in the treatment program were visited by counselors on the average of twice a month. The counselors worked with both the boys and their families and encouraged the families to seek assistance from the program. The assistance and counseling included tutoring for the boys, medical and psychiatric attention, summer camps, youth activities, and access to other community programs. Boys in the control group participated only by providing information about themselves. The program lasted five years.

Over 30 years later, in 1975 and 1976, Joan McCord (1978) and her research team traced 488 of the original 506 members of the experiment "through court records, mental health records, records from alcoholic treatment centers, and vital statistics in Massachusetts. Telephone calls, city directories, motor vehicle registrations, marriage and death records, and lucky hunches were used to find the men themselves" (pp. 284–285). Both the program and its evaluation are remarkable. The implementation of the program is notable for its truly experimental nature with random assignment and its magnitude—506 boys were studied for five years. The evaluation is remarkable for its long-term follow-up and its thoroughness—95% of the men were located and their records traced 30 years after their original assignment to the treatment and control groups. In McCord's follow-up she compared the men who had been in the treatment group with "matched mates" from the control group. She used official records and statistics from courts, mental hospitals, and alcohol treatment centers, as well as the men's self-reports from a questionnaire, which was returned by 113 men in the treatment group and 122 in the control group.

The results of these comparisons are surprising and controversial. Many of the records show no differences between the men who received "treatment" and those who received none, and in those instances in which there were differences, the differences often show the treatment to have been harmful rather than helpful. McCord (1978) divided the treatment and control samples into those who had been described as "difficult" and "average" at the beginning of the treatment to see whether treatment was more beneficial for boys who originally seemed "difficult"; she again found no beneficial effects. Instead, 34% of the "difficult" boys in the treatment group and 30% of the "difficult" boys in the control group had juvenile records.

Adult criminal records reinforced the finding of no difference. Equal numbers of both treatment and control group men had been convicted for crimes as adults. The one significant difference between the two groups' criminal records showed the treatment to have been harmful. Whereas 78% of the men with criminal records in the treatment group committed two or more crimes, only 67% of the men with criminal records in the control group committed at least two crimes.

Comparisons of health statistics also made the treatment group look bad. In response to questionnaire items that asked whether they were alcoholic, 17% of the treatment group responded yes, compared with 7% of the control group. On some other measures, the groups were equal: 21 men in each group had "received treatment in mental hospitals for disorders other than alcoholism" (p. 286). But the general mental and physical health of the treatment group appeared worse than the control's. Of the 24 men in each group known to have died, those in the treatment group died at earlier ages, and in response to questions about stress-related illnesses such as ulcers, asthma, high blood pressure, and the like, more men from the treatment group reported having had at least one of the ailments.

Comparisons of the family relations, occupations, and leisure-time activities of the treatment and control groups again showed few differences—and the differences that did exist made the treatment look harmful. Roughly equal percentages of the two groups were married, divorced, remarried, and never married. Approximately equal proportions were unskilled workers. They differed in their numbers of white-collar or professional workers, however—43% of the control group and 29% of the treatment group had white-collar or professional jobs. A comparison of the prestige ratings of the occupations of the two groups with National Opinion Research Center ranks showed that the control group men were in positions with higher prestige.

The only measure on which the treatment group indicated that the program was successful was a questionnaire item that asked for their subjective evaluation of the program: "In what ways (if any) was the Cambridge–Somerville project helpful to you?" A full two-thirds of the men indicated that the program had been helpful to them. They wrote comments such as, "helped me to have faith and trust in other people," "helped prepare me for manhood," and "better insight on life in general" (p. 287).

McCord's (1978) evaluation of the Cambridge–Somerville experiment received much attention and comment, particularly because it contradicts many other beliefs about the value of social programs. The only explanation McCord (1979) found for the harmful effects of the experiment is that the men in the treatment group developed unrealistically high expectations. The unsolicited help and attention they received as boys could have led them to expect more of themselves and of other people than they were able to realize. Critics of McCord's conclusions warn against overstatement; they ask for further research before we decide that programs like the Cambridge–Somerville project be abandoned (e.g., Sobel, 1978).

Because the research design was a randomized experiment, with boys randomly assigned to treatment and control groups, we might be reasonably confident that the effects McCord (1978) reported were a result of the treatment and not preexisting group differences. However, as in all randomized experiments conducted in the real world, there always are questions about how successfully the experimental design was implemented. Was the social program actually delivered as designed to boys in the treatment condition and not in fact delivered to boys in the control condition? In real-world research, issues of treatment implementation, generalization of aspects of the treatment to the control group, and some sort of compensatory treatment of the control group always are threats. Overall, however, in spite of these potential threats, the evidence seems quite clear that the treatment hurt more than it helped. The only redeeming feature of the program appears in the men's subjective evaluations. We return to this point later in the chapter when we consider the role of the client's satisfaction in program evaluation.

Quasi-Experiments—Compensatory Education

Head Start preschool education programs began in the 1960s on the assumption that "if children of poor families can be given skills and motivation, they will not become poor adults" (Economic Report of the President, 1964). Social critics have argued that this assumption is tantamount to "blaming poverty on the inadequacies of the poor versus blaming the poverty condition on the inadequacies of society" (Levin,1978, p. 523). We agree and would argue that erasing the economic disparity between rich and poor requires much more than preschool educational programs. Nonetheless, we can ask some simpler questions of compensatory educational programs: Do they improve children's subsequent academic achievement or self-esteem, and what do children and parents think of the programs?

The actual evaluations of Head Start and other preschool programs did not, in fact, use measures of poverty to judge the programs' success or failure. They used children's subsequent academic achievement—a short-term rather than long-term goal of the programs.

The evaluations of Head Start programs included three types: (1) summative evaluations of the overall effectiveness of all Head Start programs, (2) comparisons of different strategies and curricula within Head Start, and (3) on-site monitoring or formative evaluations of individual programs (Williams & Evans, 1972). We describe the first type of evaluation—summative evaluation of the overall effectiveness of the programs—and discuss some of the criticisms of it.

The first and most widely publicized evaluation of the overall effectiveness of Head Start was made by the Westinghouse Learning Corporation (Cicirelli & Granger, 1969). The evaluation included a sample of 104 Head Start centers from across the country and a sample of children from those centers who were then in first, second, and third grades. A comparison group was formed of children from the same grades and the same schools who had not been in preschool Head Start programs. These comparison children were selected to be similar to the Head Start children in age, sex, race, and kindergarten attendance. The evaluators tested both groups of children with a series of standardized tests to measure scholastic abilities and self-concepts. They also had teachers rate the children's achievement and motivation, and they interviewed the parents of both groups of children. The comparison group was not formed by random assignment, making this a quasi-experiment rather than a randomized experiment. The researchers tried to match the children in terms of their backgrounds; we discussed in the last chapter how such attempts to match fail to eliminate group differences.

The results of this evaluation received wide attention because the findings were negative. The major conclusions were that (1) the summer programs were ineffective in producing gains that persisted in the elementary school years; (2) the full-year programs were marginally effective in producing cognitive gains and ineffective in producing gains in how the children felt about themselves; (3) Head Start children remained below national norms for standardized tests of language and scholastic achievement but approached national norms on school readiness in grade one. The most positive finding came from parents' testimonials: "Parents of Head Start enrollees voiced strong approval of the program and its influence on their children. They reported substantial participation in the activities of the centers" (p. 78). The Westinghouse report concluded that

> the Head Start children cannot be said to be appreciably different from their peers in the elementary grades who did not attend Head Start in most aspects of cognitive and affective development measured in this study, with the exception of the slight, but nonetheless significant, superiority of full-year Head Start children on certain measures of cognitive development. (p. 78)

The criticisms of this study, even though it was not a true experiment with random assignment, include some of the criticisms made of randomized experiments: "the study is too narrow. It focuses only on cognitive and affective outcomes. Head Start is a much broader program which includes health, nutrition, and community objectives, and any proper evaluation must evaluate it on all these objectives" (Williams & Evans, 1972, p. 257). The authors of the evaluation answered that "in the final analysis Head Start should be evaluated mainly on the basis of the extent to which it has affected the life-chances of the children involved. In order to achieve such effects, cognitive and motivational changes seem essential" (p. 257).

Another criticism was that the test instruments used to measure the cognitive and motivational changes were not developed for disadvantaged children and were therefore insensitive and inappropriate. The evaluators conceded that this was possible but that they had used the best instruments available.

A third criticism is that the study looked only for long-term effects by testing children in first, second, and third grades and ignored the immediate benefits that children might have derived from being in a preschool program. "Rather than demonstrating that Head Start does not have appreciable effects, the study merely shows that these effects tend to fade out when the Head Start children return to a poverty environment" (p. 259). The evaluators admitted that this, too, could be true, but they said the program must be judged not by its short-term effects alone if those effects disappear in a year or two; ". . . the fact that the learning gains are transitory is a most compelling fact for determining future policy" (p. 259).

One other major criticism is the one we discussed in the last chapter. The results were probably contaminated by a regression artifact; because the children were not admitted to Head Start by a lottery, the "control" group of comparison children was not equivalent, making this a nonequivalent control group design. The researchers tried to match the Head Start and comparison children on age, race, sex, kindergarten attendance, and parents' social status, but matching does not eliminate the effects of preexisting differences between two populations. Matching is a good strategy only if it is followed by random assignment. If the investigators had originally tried to match pairs of children and then from within each pair randomly assigned children to Head Start and the control group, they would have created equivalent groups. But matching alone is no substitute for random assignment.

Let us compare the results of the randomized experiment in the Cambridge–Somerville Youth Study and the quasi-experimental Head Start evaluations. The results of the Cambridge–Somerville experiment are difficult to dispute because the randomized experimental design made the treatment and control groups equivalent to begin with. Some aspect of the well-intentioned treatment hurt the life chances of the recipients. The question that remains unanswered about that evaluation is why did the treatment hurt more than it helped? In the Head Start evaluation, the apparently negative results are not so convincing because there is an alternative explanation—regression artifacts alone could have made the program look ineffective. It could be the evaluation research rather than the compensatory program that failed in this case. Without random assignment, the Head Start researchers could not conclude that a treatment did or did not produce the intended effects.

Subsequent evaluations of elementary school compensatory education programs have yielded more positive and interpretable results. Follow-Through is an elementary education program designed to continue the work of Head Start. It was conceived as a large-scale, federally funded program to provide for teacher training, parental involvement, and new instructional models of education for children from low-income families. When the funds needed to serve large numbers of schools and children were not made available, the program continued on a much smaller scale, including a research component to evaluate the effectiveness of 15 model programs (Wang & Ramp, 1987). The evaluation was based on a nonrandom assignment of students to Follow-Through and control groups. Because participation in Follow-Through was based on being "in need," the students in the comparison group most likely began with higher achievement scores and living conditions, favoring their subsequent scholastic achievement. The impossibility of equating the treatment and control groups persists in this research, as it did for the evaluation of Head Start. If the results had shown no differences between the two groups or had shown the Follow-Through students performing less well than the comparison group, it would again be difficult to know whether their preexisting differences overshadowed any gains, but this was not the case.

The results of more than a dozen evaluations were positive and interpretable. Measures of the long-term effects showed that students from the Follow-Through classes achieved higher academic scores; had better school attendance; and were less likely to drop out of school, repeat grades, or require special educational placement (Wang & Ramp, 1987). Given these results, the nonrandom assignment did not present problems in interpreting the effects of the Follow-Through program.

The Politics of Applied and Evaluation Research

We started this chapter by stating that applied research, and particularly evaluation research, differs from basic research in the extent to which it can affect people's lives. The applied researcher designs studies with the ultimate hope of being useful in changing or affecting social policies and programs that have an impact on people's lives. Because policy change and formation are inevitably a political process, applied research must necessarily address the political realities within which it is conducted.

One of the most pressing political concerns in the conduct of evaluation research is the question of for whose benefit the research is conducted. The issue here is one of deciding what dependent variables the research should examine. What defines whether or not a program or policy is "successful"?

Results with Immediate Impact

Because it is carried out to evaluate ongoing programs, evaluation research is designed with a shorter time span than basic research. The social problems are not solved immediately, but decisions about programs are made immediately because budget allocations and personnel decisions are frequently based on demonstrable "results." Lynn (1977) points out that "social problems are seldom solved by a single decisive act or policy declaration; rather, policies to deal with them are fashioned incrementally over time in a series of measures which are partial and not necessarily reversible" (p. 72). However, policy makers often have "short time horizons" and wish to see research results to justify continuing or terminating a program. The press for quick and definite answers makes most evaluation research different from basic research.

Although evaluation research is intended to produce immediate results and have an immediate impact, two circumstances often prevent this from happening. The first arises when results are equivocal or contradictory so that it is not clear what the policy decision should be. For example, there have been many evaluations of preschool Head Start programs, and they do not all agree about the program's success or failure (Campbell & Erlebacher, 1970; Cicerelli & Granger, 1969). If the planners and decision makers are to use these results, which set should they use?

The second circumstance that interferes with using the results of program evaluation arises when the real effects of social programs are not immediately visible. For instance, Head Start preschool education was originally introduced to "break the cycle of poverty" by educating three- and four-year-old children so that they would become achieving, self-sufficient adults. Educational planners do not intend to wait 20 or 30 years for an evaluation, however, before they decide whether to continue with the preschool programs. Instead, they use immediate outcomes—the children's subsequent academic achievement in elementary school—and assume that adult occupational achievement will follow from childhood scholastic performance. In reality, there is a positive but weak connection between the two.

Weiss (1972) calls these immediate or short-term effects "proximate" goals and the long-term desired effects "ultimate" goals. She says short-term effects suffice when previous research shows a direct and strong connection between proximate and ultimate goals. For instance, "in evaluation of a Smokers' Clinic, it is probably enough to discover that the program led participants to stop smoking. It is not essential to investigate the ultimate incidence of lung cancer" (p. 38). Many of our more ambitious social programs, however, are designed to have long-range effects. Proximate outcomes in such cases are unsatisfactory, but they are all that we have.

Vested Interests and Competing Criteria

The choice of dependent variables—the criterion for evaluating a program—makes evaluation researchers face this issue: In whose interests is the research? It is not sufficient to say "in the interests of science" because the outcome will influence more than science. Because the results of evaluation research are used to make funding decisions, there are vested interests in the criteria chosen for success. The evaluation could affect some people's jobs, education, or health; and the results could be in the interests of some people and perhaps to the detriment of others.

The scientific questions of selecting dependent variables become political questions in evaluation research. Whose criteria will prevail? It is not always clear that one set of criteria is "better" than another. All evaluation research must address the question of whose values, whose criteria for success or failure, will prevail in judging the outcome of a program. Different stakeholders have different perspectives and different goals. Evaluation researchers, therefore, even more than basic researchers, must ask themselves, "Whose side are we on?" (Becker, 1967).

Technical Decisions with Ideological Consequences

The technical issues involved in finding measurable criteria have ideological consequences. "Applied social researchers are more technically proficient in the study of individuals than in the study of organizations, and therefore, social research tends to be more social psychological than social structural" (Berk & Rossi, 1977, p. 81). The technical ease with which we can measure problems and outcomes determines which ones we recognize or attend to. Crime-prevention programs provide a case in point. One criterion for success is reduction in crime rates, which can be accomplished or attempted in several ways. If we consider the events leading to crime as forming a long causal chain, we could intervene at any point along that chain to prevent or reduce crime (Kidder & Cohn, 1979). We could intervene in the childhood experiences of "potential delinquents" and try to prepare them for noncriminal careers (McCord, 1978). Or we could focus on adult employment problems and provide job skills for the unemployed. Or we could seek alternatives to unemployment and layoffs as industrial options. Or we could focus on the doorsteps of victims of crime and promote better home-security measures, such as locks and burglar alarms. All these are reasonable starting points for explaining and preventing crime. Yet, they all suggest very different goals or solutions for crime-prevention programs, some of which would be much easier to implement successfully than others. Programs to install door locks and burglar alarms have higher success rates (if we simply count numbers of locks and alarms distributed) than do programs to restore community cohesion or job security; and as Berk and Rossi (1977) point out, "outcomes that can be counted easily tend to be listed as the outcomes desired" (p. 81). The technical decision—to count burglar alarms installed—has the ideological implications that the way to reduce crime is to prevent victimization.

Clients' and Other Stakeholders' Participation in Evaluations

In any program evaluation, there are likely to be numerous parties with different stakes in the program and its outcomes: funders, administrators, frontline staff, and clients. Efforts to include stakeholders in the development of evaluations reveal the very political nature of the research (Farrar & House, 1986; Weiss, 1986). Each group of stakeholders has a different type of decision to make and considers different results to be relevant. Policy makers who decide whether to continue funding the program want to know whether the program caused the intended effects. Program administrators who are interested in improving the program want to know whether to change personnel, techniques, or clients. The frontline staff wants to know how they can help particular clients. And the clients themselves, if they have a choice, want to decide whether or not to continue participating in the program (Weiss, 1986). Each group considers different information relevant for its decision.

Bush and Gordon (1978) valued client participation in their research on children's placements in foster homes, institutions, or their families of origin. In going through records, they came across the description of a woman described as a pyromaniac—a mother who set fire to her apartment and whose child was subsequently taken from her and placed in an institution as a ward of the state. When Bush and Gordon interviewed the child, they heard another version of that incident. The child said that during a cold winter, when the apartment heating was inadequate and the mother had repeatedly requested that it be repaired, the mother lit a fire in a wastebasket, which tipped over and set fire to the apartment. From an agency's point of view, this was pyromania; from the child's point of view, it was an effort to keep warm. Whichever version of the story you believe, there are at least two—and one is the client's.

Bush and Gordon (1978) advocate including clients' preferences not only in the evaluation of social programs but also in the decision of what treatment they should receive. Letting clients choose their own treatments naturally obviates random assignment, but we present the case because it also tells us something about using clients' satisfaction as a criterion for program evaluation. Bush and Gordon make three points: (1) that clients have more information about their past and present needs and a greater stake in choosing the right treatment than do "outsiders"; (2) that clients who exercise such choice are more pleased with their treatments (in this case, foster placements for children) than clients who are denied the choice; and (3) that for the choice to be a real choice, it must be an "informed" choice. Two factors sometimes limit people's ability to make an informed choice: Small benefits can look good to someone who has previously had no benefits at all, and restricted experience with alternative treatments in the past can limit people's ability to make an informed judgment about which treatment to choose. Some of the children in Bush and Gordon's study who could "only remember one kind of placement, institutions, were very reluctant to choose other forms of care when given a variety of options" (pp. 26–27). Only when the researchers made it clear to the children what the other placements were like were the children able to make an informed choice between living in an institution or a foster family.

Applying this logic to the McCord (1978) evaluation of the Cambridge–Somerville social program casts doubt on the validity of the participants' subjective evaluations of the treatment. Would two-thirds of them still have said positive things about the treatment had they known about the subsequent criminal records, poor health, lower occupational standing, and earlier deaths of the treatment group? For clients' satisfaction to be a useful evaluation, it must be an informed evaluation, with hindsight about the objective consequences of the treatment and not a simple judgment of whether it made the clients feel good. It is fair and reasonable to include clients as judges and evaluators of the services they receive, but if they are not fully informed, they might err in their judgments. Like McCord's findings that clients' testimonials were contradicted by objective evidence, other researchers report inflated and sometimes misguided testimonials in evaluations of educational programs: "Studies of compensatory education programs have one 'universal finding': regardless of the type of program, duration, or actual results, parents are enthusiastic" (McDill, McDill, & Sprehe, 1969, pp. 43–44). Perhaps the participants in the Cambridge–Somerville experiment and the parents of children in compensatory education programs are telling us that they appreciate the special attention—the investment of resources and the good intentions.

We face a dilemma: We want to take into account clients' evaluations, criteria, ratings of effectiveness, and satisfaction; but those ratings do not always agree with objective indicators. If we resort to objective indicators, we face another problem: "The more any quantitative social indicator is used for professional decision making, the more subject it will be to corruption pressures and the more apt it will be to distort and corrupt the social process it is intended to monitor" (Campbell, 1979, p. 69). Moreover, objective indicators measure something quite different from satisfaction. The association between objective indicators such as absenteeism or job turnover and subjective ratings of satisfaction is weak. Gutek (1978) concludes, therefore, that we should not abandon subjective measures because "people live in a subjective world as well as an objective one . . . . Satisfaction may not take the place of objective indicators, but neither can objective indicators take the place of subjective indicators such as satisfaction" (p. 50).

Can We Afford Not to Do Applied Research?

Psychological Effects of Nuclear Accidents

After the nuclear reactor accident at Three Mile Island in Pennsylvania in March 1979, many research teams of psychologists tried to assess the psychological effects, particularly on people living near the reactor (Hartsough & Savitsky, 1984). That accident led lawyers and social scientists to ask whether psychological effects could also be considered environmental ones. If so, the future construction and operation of nuclear plants could be subject to environmental impact statements that include an assessment of potential psychological damage. Research on the psychological effects of disasters shows that sleep disturbances, anxiety, psychosomatic symptoms, fatigue, and depression are common short-term effects. The long-term effects are as yet uncertain.

Many studies were conducted after the Three Mile Island accident, using a great variety of measures and designs. Two telephone surveys of 2,748 people compared the stress reactions of persons living close to the reactor and those living more than 40 miles away. The stress levels of those living near the reactor were very high in the month following the accident and then began to decline; however, nine months after the disaster, about 15% of those people still reported higher than normal stress-related symptoms (Houts, 1980a, 1980b).

One group of investigators was particularly concerned about the psychological effects on mothers of preschool children, nuclear power plant workers, and clients in community mental health centers (Bromet, Parkinson, Schulberg, Dunn, & Gondek, 1982; Bromet, Schulberg, & Dunn, 1982). Their study included comparison groups of people who lived near another nuclear reactor in a different part of the state. The researchers found that mothers of preschool children suffered greater effects than the nuclear power plant workers or mental health center clients. They were five times more likely to feel anxiety and depression immediately after the accident and also had higher levels of symptoms a year later. The power plant workers and mental health clients had higher stress symptoms than the comparison groups living near a distant reactor, but the effects were not as marked as those felt by the mothers of young children.

The authors of such "environmental impact" studies have encountered resistance from the courts, primarily on the grounds that psychological stress cannot be adequately measured. Judges and lawyers have argued that psychological claims can too easily be fabricated, and they fear a rash of fraudulent claims. Nonetheless, an appeals court decision *(PANE v. United States Nuclear Regulatory Commission,* 1982) did suggest that psychological stress could be a factor in environmental impact statements provided it (1) "is severe enough to threaten physical health" and (2) "can be reliably measured" (Hartsough & Savitsky, 1984, p. 1120). Therefore, the impact of applied social science research hangs on basic principles of measurement—it must be reliable and valid.

Living Downwind of Nuclear Reactors

Rosalie Bertell, a mathematician and medical researcher, examined environmental influences on the survival of low-birth-weight infants in Wisconsin between the years 1963 and 1975 (Bertell, Jacobson, & Stogre, 1984). Bertell and her colleagues chose Wisconsin because the state has routinely tested milk for radioactive materials, and these tests provide a measure of radioactive contamination of pasturelands. The researchers chose six regions based on their proximity to nuclear power plants. Three regions—Eau Claire, La Crosse, and Green Bay—are close to and downwind of nuclear power plants. The other three—Rice Lake, Wausau, and Madison—are distant from or upwind of nuclear power plants. They studied the effects on low-birth-weight infants (weighing less than 5 1/2 pounds, or 2,500 grams) because those infants are very fragile and sensitive to environmental influences that might threaten human health or life.

To assess the health effects of nuclear power plants, one must take into consideration not only proximity but also prevailing wind patterns. For instance, the three downwind regions were affected by the start-up of seven nuclear power plants, four in Wisconsin and three in Minnesota. The prevailing winds are from the west or northwest, so the residents of Eau Claire are downwind of the Minnesota nuclear plants.

The power plants whose effects Bertell and her colleagues examined were started up between 1969 and 1974. Therefore, the researchers compared the death rates of low-birth-weight infants for three time periods: 1963 to 1966, 1967 to 1970, and 1971 to 1975. They used the first two time periods to see whether there was an overall upward, downward, or level trend in the infants' death rates. They then compared the death rates during the third time period with those during the previous two to see whether there was a change after the start-up of the nuclear power plants.

During the period from 1971 to 1975, which was after the start-up of the nuclear power plants, the death rates in two of the remote or upwind regions were below the state level. The death rates in the regions downwind and close to the nuclear power plants were all above the state level. After the start-up of the nuclear reactors, death rates in all three downwind regions were higher than in the upwind regions. Figure 14.1 summarizes the effects by showing the average death rates for infants in the downwind and the upwind or remote regions.

Before the introduction of the reactors, the death rates declined between the first and second time periods in both sets of regions. This decline probably resulted from advances in health care and medical technology. The decline in death rates continued in the upwind or remote regions from the second to the third time period. In the downwind regions, however, the death rates rose again after 1970. This rise in deaths corresponds with the start-up of the seven nuclear reactors between 1969 and 1974.

FIGURE 14.1

AVERAGE DEATH RATES OF LOW-BIRTH-WEIGHT INFANTS PER 1,000 LOW-BIRTH-WEIGHT BIRTHS FOR THREE DOWNWIND REGIONS AND THREE REGIONS UPWIND OR REMOTE FROM NUCLEAR PLANTS THAT WERE STARTED UP BETWEEN 1969 AND 1974

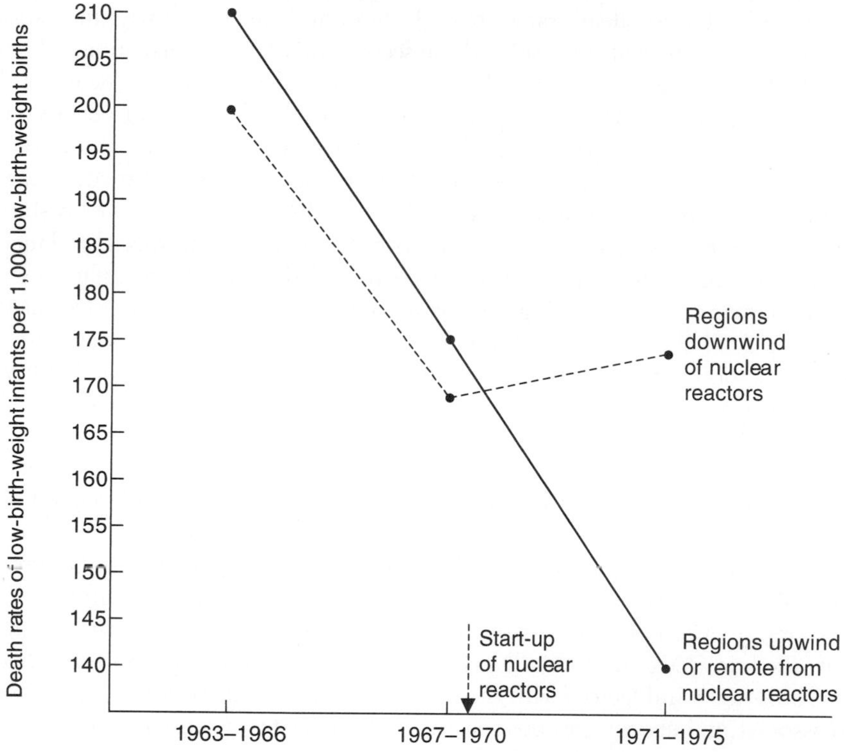

Before concluding that the increased death rates of these infants were caused by the nuclear power plants, Bertell and her colleagues examined some potentially confounding variables to see whether there were plausible alternative explanations. The researchers were rightly concerned about the internal validity of their research, for the results could alarm people in Wisconsin and elsewhere and so must be carefully scrutinized before being made public. They considered several sets of potentially confounding variables. We consider two here: (1) the existence of other environmental pollutants that could adversely affect the health of infants and adults, such as waste products from chemical plants and fossil fuel plants, and (2) the availability of quality medical facilities, particularly infant intensive care units, which are known to affect the survival rates of low-birth-weight infants.

In examining the effects of chemical and fossil fuel plants, the researchers found no association between the existence or operation of those industries and the infant death rates. For instance, in Eau Claire, a downwind area where infant death rates increased, there are only 2 fossil fuel generators, whereas in Madison, where the infant mortality rates decreased, there are 11 fossil fuel generators. So fossil fuel plants cannot be implicated in the infants' deaths. The same pattern appears for chemical plants. In Eau Claire there are only 2 chemical companies and in Madison there are 28, but the death rates are higher in Eau Claire and lower in Madison.

The researchers also considered the second alternative explanation—that the availability of medical facilities, particularly infant intensive care units, is the major determining factor in the infants' deaths. The evidence on the existence of perinatal care units shows that all three downwind regions, with the increased death rates, are served by perinatal care units, so the deaths cannot be attributed to lack of medical care. In fact, within one of the downwind areas, La Crosse, the highest rates of low-birth-weight deaths were in those parts of the county with the best access to specialized medical care. In contrast, of the three upwind regions, two had no perinatal or infant intensive care units, so their better survival figures could not be attributed to better medical care.

As a final check on their findings and interpretations, the researchers examined the association between reports of radioactive gases released and low-birth-weight infant death rates. They encountered several difficulties with this analysis. The first is that not all gaseous releases are reported by the operators of nuclear power plants. The Nuclear Regulatory Commission does not require operators to report the gases released during start-up and testing phases (Bertell et al., 1984). A second difficulty is that there are seasonal shifts in prevailing winds. Eau Claire, for instance, is downwind of one nuclear reactor about 50% of the year and downwind of another reactor 25% of the year, so the gaseous releases that affected Eau Claire came from different reactors at different times of the year. The researchers, therefore, had to proceed with the knowledge that not all gaseous releases were reported, and they had to combine seasonal wind factors with the timing of reported gaseous releases. They did find an association between gaseous releases and infant death rates and concluded:

> In spite of the many unknown factors, such as exact dates of "batch" releases of radioactive gases, wind direction at release times and probable doses to the downwind population, there is a discernible trend with greater excess in low birth weight infant deaths coinciding with years of larger radioactive gaseous releases, and fewer excess low birth weight infant deaths occurring during years with smaller radioactive gaseous releases. (p. 19)

If this research had not been done, no one would know about the connection between infant deaths and the location of nuclear power plants. These deaths would still be attributed to other causes. It took the empirical research to demonstrate that living downwind of nuclear power plants causes a rise in the deaths of these infants.

This research did not set off great alarms, perhaps because it was not widely publicized and perhaps because the persons most directly affected were not informed.

Why use low-birth-weight infant death rates as the indicator of how nuclear power plants affect human health? These infants provide such sensitive indicators because they are very fragile. And being fragile, they are more vulnerable to respiratory infections that other infants survive. The radioactive gases and particles released into the atmosphere by nuclear power plants suppress the immune systems of the infants and make them more vulnerable to respiratory diseases than they already are. When these infants contract respiratory infections, they are more likely to die, and their death records usually state the cause of death as "pneumonia."

This scenario raises several questions. Does the fact that fragile low-birth-weight infants die when they are born downwind of nuclear reactors mean that hardy adults are also affected? Does the hospital record, which says the cause of death is "pneumonia," accurately identify the cause? Might it not as well be said that the child died from "radioactive gaseous releases" or from "living downwind of a nuclear reactor"?

We come back to a question that we raised in Chapter 1 and that has been implied elsewhere in this book. Is it possible to conduct social science research—research that examines human relations and human welfare—without considering questions of social values? Does applied, and perhaps also basic, research not force us to consider whose purposes are served by an intervention or an evaluation or even a research question? And must we not usually choose sides?

Summary

Applied research has all the same problems and solutions in design and measurement as does basic research. It differs from basic research in its purposes and its connection with social policy. The connection with policy and public welfare presents challenges to applied social scientists that require personal, political, and philosophical decisions. The biases inherent in the questions asked and the criteria used to determine a program's success or failure do not simply get buried in libraries. They influence decisions and affect people's lives. Thus, applied and evaluation research are particularly relevant to social behavior and human welfare.

Key Concepts

applied research
basic research
evaluation research
executive summary
formative evaluations
program
stakeholders
summative evaluations

On the Web

http://www.eval.org/ Home page of the American Evaluation Association, "devoted to the application and exploration of evaluation in all its forms."

http://members.home.net/gpic/evalwebindex.htm Home page for Government Performance Information Consultants, whose goal is to "put all the Web links on the topic of evaluation in one place."

http://www.jigsaw.org/ A Web site devoted entirely to the Jigsaw Classroom. Includes material on more recent work by Eliot Aronson aimed at reducing prejudice and violence in schools.

http://www2.acf.dhhs.gov/programs/hsb/index.htm The official U.S. government site for Head Start. This extensive site provides detailed information about the interaction between policy makers and evaluators in the development and maintenance of this controversial program.

Further Reading

Chelimsky, E., & Shadish, W. R. (Eds.) (1997). *Evaluation for the 21st century: A handbook.* Thousand Oaks, CA: Sage Publications.

Rossi, P. H., & Freeman, H. E. (1993). *Evaluation: A systematic approach* (5th ed.). Thousand Oaks, CA: Sage Publications.

CHAPTER

15

Observational and Archival Research

Despite the wide usefulness of survey and laboratory techniques in the social sciences and their popularity in practice, many research questions are not well suited to study by these methods. For example, we might want to draw conclusions about Thomas Jefferson's political ideology, about the links between social integration and suicide, or about the degree to which lovers gaze into one another's eyes during conversations. Observational techniques and archival data often provide the only avenue of approach to such issues. For example, we might observe couples to record the frequency and duration of gaze during conversations, examine government records to determine suicide rates in social groups with differing levels of social integration, or examine Jefferson's writings to note the relative frequency of references to different ideological themes.

In addition, observational and archival methods often carry advantages of their own. The data are often "there for the taking," easily accessible to the researcher without great physical or financial costs. Archives often provide aggregated measurements, often over time, of significant constructs drawn from millions of individuals, hundreds of organizations, or dozens of different societies—data that would be almost impossible to obtain in other ways. And archives provide our only access to the thinking of people who are dead or otherwise unavailable for direct questioning.

Finally, and perhaps most important, some forms of observation and most archival research avoid potential problems caused by the respondents' awareness of being studied; that is, they can be unobtrusive or nonreactive measures. Laboratory research and survey studies inevitably run the risk that respondents might behave in unnatural ways; give socially desirable or otherwise biased responses rather than valid ones; attempt to guess the research hypothesis; or otherwise respond to the very fact of being studied rather than acting as they normally would. Concern about these possibilities has led to an emphasis on naturalness in research, which involves several issues that are discussed in the first section of this chapter. The remainder of the chapter is organized into two major sections, the first concerned with observational methods and the second with the use of archival data and other records.

Naturalness in Research

Observational and archival research, in different ways, often emphasize unobtrusiveness or nonreactiveness of research procedures. With these methods, participants either are unaware of being observed (with unobtrusive observation or archival data) or are thought to habituate quickly to the presence of open observers. Alternatively, they might be aware of being observed but unaware of the particular behavior they are emitting that is of interest. For example, studies of attraction among individuals might use as an indicator of liking how closely the participant sits to the target. Although participants are presumably acutely aware of being observed, they do not realize that interpersonal distance is being measured and, therefore, are unlikely to modify their own behavior in that regard. By using a **nonreactive measure,** the researcher hopes that participants' responses will not be shaped by such considerations as a desire to impress the researcher or a belief that certain behaviors would support the research hypothesis. The drive for "naturalness" in research thus derives from the belief that participants are more likely to behave in the same way that they would in "real life" if they can be studied in the circumstances in which they are ordinarily found. In contrast, survey and laboratory-based research is more likely to elicit behaviors that are specific to the unnatural research context such as socially desirable responses and behavior.

Relying on nonreactive forms of research to enhance the external validity or generalizability of results leads to a strategy of seeking naturalness in research. Three dimensions of naturalness have been generally emphasized: the behavior being studied, the setting of the behavior, and the event eliciting the behavior (Tunnell, 1977). Different researchers place different emphasis on these three dimensions, and the three do not always go together. The purest conception of natural research might involve all three dimensions, as for example was found in a study by Kraut and Johnston (1979): unobtrusive observation of a natural behavior (smiling) as it happened in its natural setting (a bowling alley) as the result of a naturally occurring event (getting a strike).

Natural behaviors are those that are "not established or maintained for the sole or primary purpose of conducting research" (Tunnell, 1977, p. 426). They reflect a concern with naturalness in the *dependent variable* in research. For example, committing suicide, gazing into one's lover's eyes, or smiling after bowling a strike are natural behaviors because they would have occurred without the researcher's presence. Conversely, questionnaire or interview responses occur only as a result of the researcher's questions and would not be considered natural behaviors. An example of a study of a natural behavior but neither a natural setting nor a natural event is one by Berry and Hansen (2000). Undergraduate women were videotaped while waiting in a psychology laboratory. The tapes were later coded for a wide variety of natural nonverbal behaviors, including gaze while speaking and listening, positive and negative facial expressions, gesture, and body orientation toward partner. Analyses showed that participants who devoted more visual attention to their partners, gestured more often, and oriented their bodies more toward their partners were deemed to have interactions of higher quality.

Natural settings are contexts that are not established for research purposes, such as shopping centers, private homes, racetracks, commercial aircraft, churches, or hospitals. For example, observation in the Kraut and Johnston (1979) study took place in a bowling alley, a natural setting. All forms of field research, by definition, occur in natural settings.

Finally, a **natural event** is an incident that is not arranged for research purposes and that has some human consequences, that is, a natural *independent variable* in research. Examples of natural events include natural disasters, economic fluctuations, heat waves, and surgery. Note that "natural" here does not mean that the independent variable cannot have been produced by human beings, only that the independent variable was not produced solely for research purposes. In an archival study of the impact of a natural event, Anderson and Anderson (1996) examined the "long, hot summer" hypothesis to see if there was an association between temperature (a natural event) and the incidence of violent crimes. Drawing data from government archives of weather and crime statistics, they found a strong positive association between increases in air temperature and incidence of violent crime.

Benefits and Costs of Naturalness

Natural behaviors, settings, and events are three distinct facets of naturalistic research, although they can go together in various combinations in practice. Naturalness in any of these forms can afford advantages for the social scientist. In particular, studying natural behaviors in natural settings can lead to greater external validity of research results because participants will not alter their behavior to take account of being studied. Naturalness can also contribute to construct validity because unobtrusively observed behaviors (such as racially integrated seating patterns in a lunchroom) are likely to reflect the desired construct (unprejudiced attitudes) to a greater extent than survey or interview responses obtained for obvious research purposes, which might be more subject to response biases.

Nevertheless, naturalness is not the sole criterion—or even the most important one—by which to evaluate research. Every study, not just those using observational or archival methods, must meet the fundamental criteria of reliability and validity of measurement, and naturalness in research can have drawbacks and costs in these and other respects. Conducting research in a natural setting often limits the researcher's ability to control extraneous factors that introduce error into observations and hence reduce reliability. Some research topics, such as the examination of patterns of gaze, might require an unnatural laboratory setting where precise measurement procedures such as carefully placed video cameras, observers behind one-way glass, and freedom from outside interruptions can be arranged.

The relative importance of the advantages and disadvantages of naturalness in research depends on the type of research question. Questions that concern rates or patterns of natural behaviors in natural settings obviously require naturalistic research to answer them. For example, we might wonder about sex differences in the practice of "civil inattention" (aversion of one's gaze from the other person's face) when strangers pass each other on the sidewalk. Results from laboratory research on this behavior might not generalize to real street settings; however, we must remember that nonlaboratory settings differ among themselves also. Results obtained on Broadway in New York City—however natural that setting—might not generalize to other locales (e.g., side streets of small towns) any more than results obtained in a laboratory might. Ultimately, whether results obtained in one setting, natural or unnatural, will generalize to another setting is an empirical question, not one that naturalness in research can answer automatically.

Research questions concerned with causal associations among constructs or with hypothetical (if-then or what-if) questions often require specifically unnatural research settings and treatments. To estimate the causal effects of exposure to violent television programming on aggressive behavior among adolescents requires the participants to be given unnatural treatments (some caused to watch and others prevented from watching violent programming). Attempts to answer this research question with nonexperimental methods (e.g., simply correlating people's reports of their television viewing with their aggressiveness) have low internal validity. We cannot be confident of the causal nature of the association unless random assignment to an experimental manipulation—unnatural by definition—is used. In short, advantages of natural research in external validity are often counterbalanced by costs in internal validity.

An example of how a hypothetical, or what-if, question might require an unnatural setting is the question of whether extensive experience cooperating with a Black person on some task would reduce anti-Black attitudes among initially prejudiced Whites. Waiting for a prejudiced person to show such cooperative behavior spontaneously might take a long time. In sum, although answering questions about the natural prevalence or patterning of behavior calls for natural settings, answering causal or hypothetical questions usually calls for the creation of an unnatural setting or treatment (Mook, 1983).

The importance of naturalness also depends on the target population of individuals, settings, or behaviors to which we wish to generalize. This involves the distinction between particularistic and universalistic research goals introduced in Chapter 8 and elaborated on in Chapter 12. The goal of drawing conclusions about a particular situation—for example, determining whether goal setting will improve the productivity of workers at the Acme Widget factory—is best attained by studying those particular workers performing their natural tasks in their natural setting. Many research questions do not so narrowly specify the target population or setting, however. For example, researchers who study helping behavior often have in mind a very broad intended target of generalizations (e.g., any person in any setting). For such research, naturalness is often irrelevant, and because it often interferes with experimental control and other important goals, it is often absent. The chief requirement in such research is experimental realism, the meaningfulness and impact of the situation for the participant, rather than mundane realism, the resemblance of the situation to some aspect of everyday life (Carlsmith, Ellsworth, & Aronson, 1976). Thus, helping has often been studied in an artificial laboratory setting with unnatural behaviors by the staging of accidents or emergencies that occur while the participant is working on some task (e.g., Latané & Nida, 1981). The researchers assume that the participant's interpretation of his or her behavior, setting, and surroundings, rather than their naturalness per se, influences generalizability. That is, it is argued that the theories supported by this research should apply in other situations in which people think that help is required despite differences in the setting, type of accident that necessitates help, and so on.

Perhaps the most articulate and entertaining discussion of these issues is Mook's (1983) classic article, "In Defense of External Invalidity." In this article, Mook notes the heavy pressures on researchers to demonstrate validity: "Who wants to be invalid—internally, externally, or in any other way? One might as well ask for acne" (p. 379). But he argues that the emphasis on external validity is often misplaced and that what we really want to generalize is not participants or experimental settings or tasks but rather *theories*. Mook uses as an extended example the important and well-known studies by Harlow showing that baby monkeys reared in isolation prefer a terry-cloth "mother" to a wire "mother" that provided food. As Mook points out, Harlow's studies (e.g., Harlow, 1958) fail to satisfy virtually any criterion of external validity one might impose: The monkeys were not a representative sample, having been born and orphaned in the laboratory. The experimental setting itself was highly reactive. And there certainly are no examples of terry-cloth or wire mothers in the jungle. But Mook argues that we do not care whether wild monkeys in the jungle would prefer terry-cloth to wire mothers; instead, all that is important is to know that it happens in the laboratory. Harlow's findings were important because they disproved traditional drive-reduction theories of attachment that led to the prediction that baby monkeys would prefer the food-providing wire mother. In short, Mook argues that for many, if not most, theory-testing purposes, we do not need to show how people would behave in the real world, only that they behave in predictable ways in the laboratory.

In summary, naturalness has an important place in the design of research to answer certain types of questions. For other questions it is irrelevant. Just as it might be a mistake to create an unnatural setting for research if our goal were to assess a target behavior as it naturally occurs in everyday life, it would be a mistake to view naturalness as an overriding criterion for the validity of all research. Dipboye and Flanagan (1979) reviewed hundreds of laboratory and field studies in industrial–organizational psychology and concluded that the ability to generalize from research is not related to its degree of naturalness. "Too often the assumption is made that because a study was conducted in a field setting, it is inherently more externally valid than a laboratory study" (p. 388). The generalizability of any research finding is ultimately an empirical question, to be settled only by replication of the research using different participants, behaviors, and settings. No specific feature of a study can guarantee generalizability.

Although we have focused on external and construct validity, which are usually the chief concerns of advocates of naturalistic research, other important goals might also be served by naturalistic research. It might lead to new hypotheses, which can be tested in more internally valid ways, perhaps by laboratory experimentation. It might reveal previously unsuspected empirical associations. And it might identify limitations of theories. All these purposes are important for the advancement of knowledge in the social sciences.

Observation

Some of the observations made by social scientists appear to be mundane at first glance. For example, it has been noted that some restaurant diners salt their food before tasting it and others salt only after they have had a first bite (McGee & Snyder, 1975); that some jail inmates socialize, whereas others perform isolated behaviors that are either active (e.g., reading or cleaning) or passive (e.g., just sitting or sleeping; Wener & Keys, 1988); and that some billiard players show their tongues while making difficult shots, whereas others keep them out of sight (Smith, Chase, & Lieblich, 1974). These observations become scientific when the data are gathered systematically and are related to other data also systematically gathered for the purpose of uncovering a general principle of human behavior. As to salting food, McGee and Snyder predicted that the more individuals ascribe stable traits to themselves, as opposed to seeing their behavior as varying with context, the more likely they are to salt their food before tasting it. Results confirmed their prediction. People who see their behavior changing with the situation are more likely to taste the food before seasoning it. Wener and Keys found that increased crowding in one jail unit led to decreases in active isolated behaviors and increases in passive behaviors, as well as to increases in sick-call rates. These findings are consistent with previous research demonstrating negative physical and psychological effects of population density among both humans and nonhuman animals. And finally, Smith, Chase, and Lieblich observed that tongue showing occurs when one is engaged in some demanding activity and signals an unwillingness to interact. Good billiard players showed their tongues more often on hard than on easy shots and showed the tongue less than did unskilled players overall.

Observation thus becomes scientific when it (a) serves a formulated research purpose, (b) is planned deliberately, (c) is recorded systematically, and (d) is subjected to checks and controls on validity and reliability. There are two major categories of observational techniques: physical trace measures, which involve assessing evidence of the behavior of interest after it has been expressed (e.g., counting beer bottles in a garbage can to estimate how much drinking went on during a party), and systematic observation, which involves structured or nonstructured assessment of the behavior of interest as it is occurring (e.g., posting an observer during the party to record the number of beers consumed). In the next two sections, we describe and give examples of these two categories of observational techniques.

Unobtrusive Measures Involving Physical Traces

Unobtrusive measures involving **physical traces** rely on "pieces of data not specifically produced for the purpose of comparison and inference but available to be exploited opportunistically by the alert observer" (Webb et al., 1981, p. 5). There are two major types of physical trace measures: erosion and accretion. **Erosion measures** look at the degree of selective wear on some material. The usual inference is that the greater the degree of erosion, the greater the popularity or liking for the object. One often-cited example is the finding that floor tiles around a museum exhibit featuring live, hatching chicks had to be replaced about every six weeks, whereas tiles around other exhibits in the same museum went months or years without replacement (Webb et al., 1981). This measure of erosion appears to show differences in the popularity of the exhibits. Note, however, that this inference might be in error. For example, viewers, possibly children, might move around and scuff their feet more at the chick-hatching exhibit, wearing out the tiles. Thus, the exhibit might not be seen by more people or for a longer time than other exhibits; it might just be seen by people whose feet are more active. Or, possibly, the erosion might have been caused by a small number of individuals who stay at the chicken-hatching exhibit for long periods of time. These alternatives highlight one of the major disadvantages of physical trace measures—their interpretation is considerably more ambiguous than more direct forms of observation.

Another classic anecdote of an erosion measure is found in the work by Friedman and Rosenman (1974), cardiologists who first proposed the existence of the Type A Behavior Pattern, or coronary-prone personality. They relay the story of an upholsterer who came to redecorate the chairs in their waiting room. The upholsterer asked them what kinds of doctors they were because he wondered why only the front edges of the upholstery were worn. The uneven pattern of wear on furniture in this instance served as an indicator of the time-pressured, hyper-alert, and tense characteristics of the coronary-prone patients.

Accretion measures are the opposite of erosion measures and look at the selective deposit of materials. Going back to the museum example, a possible accretion measure of the popularity of the chicken-hatching exhibit would be to count the number of fingerprints and nose prints on the glass wall surrounding the exhibit. Measuring the heights of the fingerprints could even provide a means of estimating age differences in exhibit popularity. The inference is that the greater the accretion of fingerprints, the more popular the exhibit, although once again this inference could be in error if all of the fingerprints were contributed by one individual who loved chickens.

Physical trace measures such as erosion and accretion can show the frequency or extent of some behavior. Such measures have not been widely used despite their inherent interest value; however, imaginative researchers have used physical trace measures on occasion and such measures appear to have much potential. One major impediment to using these measures is the lack of a standardized set of trace measures for which reliability and validity have been established. If a researcher wants a questionnaire measure of self-esteem, a large number of self-report measures is readily available. But where would a researcher go to find a physical trace measure of self-esteem? At first blush, the task of finding physical trace measures for constructs typical of the social sciences seems daunting if not impossible; however, a bit of creativity, ingenuity, and a few moments of hard thought often bring to mind several potential physical trace measures for complex constructs. We invite readers to participate in the following exercise. Take a few minutes to imagine possible erosion and accretion measures for the following constructs: hunger, anxiety, sadness, and liking for another person. Do the exercise first, and then turn to Table 15.1 (page 370) to see some of the responses we came up with when we did the exercise ourselves. As our list would attest, finding physical trace measures is not as difficult as it seems.

However, inspection of Table 15.1 further illustrates the limitation we spoke of earlier regarding the inferential problems inherent in physical trace measures. Yes, there might be many tissues in a wastebasket if someone is feeling sad and thus crying a great deal. But it also is possible that the person just has a bad cold that day and is not feeling sad at all. In sum, physical trace measures can suffer greater validity problems than more direct self-report measures.

One should not conclude, however, that physical trace measures are necessarily less valid than self-report measures. In some cases, for example, when dealing with socially undesirable behaviors, physical trace measures can actually be more valid than self-reports of those behaviors. Compelling evidence in this regard was reported by Rathje and Hughes (1975), who compared estimates about beer consumption obtained by interviews and by sampling the same households' garbage and counting beer cans. The "front door" interview data estimated that beer was consumed in only 15% of the homes, with eight cans per week being the maximum consumption reported. The "backdoor" data from garbage cans, on the other hand, found evidence of consumption in 77% of the households, with 54% of the homes having more than eight cans per week. Clearly, there was considerable underreporting of beer consumption in the self-report data.

In summary, physical trace measures such as erosion and accretion present both important advantages and disadvantages. They are generally anonymous, completely nonreactive, and involve low data-collection costs. On the negative side, they require considerable imagination and often pose significant validity problems. Thus, we recommend using physical trace measures as a complement to rather than a substitute for more traditional measures. In so doing, we echo a position we elaborated on in Chapter 4—the best approach to measurement is *multiple operationism*, measuring a variable using more than one approach, each of which is imperfect in different ways.

Systematic Observation

Systematic observation involves the selection, recording, and encoding of a set of natural behaviors or other naturally occurring phenomena. In other words, systematic observation involves relatively objective measures of behavior (e.g., checklists, detailed coding systems for movements), often in conjunction with a systematic procedure for sampling time intervals or other units for observation. The observer can be open or hidden but usually makes an effort to avoid interfering in any way with the ongoing behavior that is being observed. In contrast, participant observation, discussed in detail in Chapter 16, involves unstructured recording techniques, such as open-ended verbal descriptions of behavior, and the observer's participation in the ongoing behavior is accepted. It is considered to be a method of hypothesis generation rather than of structured data collection.

Systematic observation has been used to study a wide range of behaviors such as interactions between general and special education students (Hughes et al., 1999); parents' verbal behavior during their children's sporting events (Kidman, McKenzie, & McKenzie, 1999); nurses' interactions with AIDS patients (Siminoff, Erlen, & Sereika, 1998); the sentencing of defendants in a magistrate's court (Hedderman, 1994); and shoplifting behavior (Buckle & Farrington, 1994). In the field of nonverbal communication, there is evidence that several types of subtle but observable behaviors signal whether the speaker is being deceptive (Zuckerman, DePaulo, & Rosenthal, 1981).

Systematic observation studies differ considerably in how the behaviors or observations of interest are recorded and encoded (Weick, 1985). At one end of the continuum are methods that are relatively unstructured and open-ended. The observer tries to provide as complete and nonselective a description as possible. On the other end of the continuum are more structured and predefined methods, which itemize, count, and categorize behavior. Here the investigator decides beforehand which behaviors will be recorded and how frequently observations will be made. The investigator using structured observation is much more discriminating in choosing which behaviors will be recorded and precisely how they are to be coded.

Relatively Unstructured Methods: Ethological Approaches The most unstructured and nonselective method of observation would be a complete descriptive account of everything that surrounded an event. This is not only an impossible goal but also not a desirable goal. The basic goal of any observational technique is that it summarize, systematize, and simplify the representation of an event rather than provide a complete replay of it. Even films and videotapes do not provide exact reproduction, for they are subject to biases introduced by camera angle, lighting, microphone placement, and lens. Nor is a "complete" description ever a perfect carbon copy because of investigators' expectations, language structure, or other cultural biases that might unintentionally affect what is recorded. These issues will be discussed further but are noted here to alert the reader to the fact that all observational techniques involve selection and editing decisions. The issue is to make these decisions as explicit as possible.

Yet **ethological approaches** opt for as little prior categorization as possible. Ethologists attempt to enter a scene to discover what is there. The object is to derive a detailed and comprehensive description about the nature of an animal's or person's behavioral repertoire. A basic assumption for ethologists is that the natural world is best approached through careful exploratory studies aimed at the generation of hypotheses rather than the testing of them (Blurton-Jones, 1972). Moreover, ethologists are concerned with the naturalistic behavior of the animal species being studied in its own right, whereas other scientists study animals primarily as a means for ultimately understanding human behavior (Lyman-Henley & Henley, 2000). Thus,

TABLE 15.1 **EXAMPLES OF POSSIBLE EROSION AND ACCRETION MEASURES FOR ASSORTED CONSTRUCTS**

Construct	Erosion Measure	Accretion Measure
Hunger	• Pieces of candy eaten • Amount of food consumed	• Number of candy wrappers discarded • Size of food portion placed on plate • Milliliters of saliva generated
Anxiety	• Extent to which fingernails chewed off • Degree of wear on hospital waiting room floor • Indentations from fingers on some soft surface • Amount of alcohol consumed	• Accumulation of fingernails torn or chewed off • Sweat stains on clothing • Cigarette butts in ashtray or on floor
Sadness	• Number of tissues taken from box • Number of antidepressant pills taken	• Number of tissues in wastebasket • Quantity of tears
Liking	• Wearing down of speed-dial button for target • Wearing down of tile in hallway to target's room	• Fingerprints on speed-dial button of target • Number of e-mail messages sent to target • Number and size of gifts sent to target • Number of photographs of target in room • Lip prints on photographs of target

ethologists are concerned with questions that have application only for animal behavior, as seen, for example, in the study by Phillips and Morris (2001) showing that cows avoid walking through dark passageways but do not mind walking through slurry- or excrement-coated passageways. This study has important implications for dairy farmers (they do not have to worry about cleaning their walls but should add lights to cows' walkways to improve their welfare), but benefits for understanding human behavior are neither obvious nor intended.

Ethologists concentrate on **molecular behaviors**, that is, behaviors tied to specific motor or muscular phenomena, and avoid descriptions that involve inference. For example, ethologists would not describe someone as looking "very pleased." That would entail too much interpretation. They would instead describe such details as facial expression, body movement, speech content, and the behavioral results of such a display rather than allude to some underlying state or intention. An example of this approach is seen in a study by Fridlund (1991), who measured the extent to which people smiled while watching a pleasant videotape under various conditions of sociality (alone, alone but friend nearby, alone but friend watching same videotape in another room, or friend present). Smiles were measured not through observers' judgments but rather quite precisely through muscular movements detected via electromyograph. Analyses indicated that participants displayed moderate to strong smiling while watching the tape with a friend or believing that the friend was watching the same tape, but only weak smiles were displayed in the other two conditions. Interestingly, though, participants' self-reported happiness did not differ across the four viewing conditions, leading the author to conclude that smiling is better predicted by the social context than by the emotion felt (Fridlund, 1991).

Another example of an unstructured type of systematic observation is **ecological observation.** Ecological psychologists assume that all behaviors depend heavily on settings. In their view, the best way to predict a person's behavior is to know where he or she is: "In a post office, he behaves post office, at church he behaves church" (Willems, 1969, p. 16). Thus, these researchers are centrally concerned with characterizing behavior settings in terms of such dimensions as their geographical character (rural, urban); practical functions (drugstore, garage); typical objects (chairs, blackboards); primary behavioral displays (singing, discussing); and temporal domain (morning, evening).

According to ecological psychologists, to understand behavior one must account for two qualities of the behavior setting, *constraints* and *affordances*, and two qualities of the behaving person or persons, *attunements* and *abilities* (Greeno, 1994, 1998). With regard to the behavior setting, constraints are those aspects of the setting that prescribe specific behaviors that result in predictable outcomes (e.g., rules and norms of appropriateness). Affordances are those aspects of a behavior setting that present opportunities for action by people in the setting. Attunements are tendencies on the part of a person to behave in particular ways given particular constraints and affordances associated with behavioral settings. Finally, abilities are aspects of the person that contribute to their behavior in settings. Using these four qualities, the ecological psychologist can describe in rich detail the interactive forces that bring about behavior by a person or group of people in a particular setting.

An example of ecological observation is a study of social support in children's friendships by Rizzo and Corsaro (1995). These researchers positioned themselves as participant observers, then "peripheral participants," in a university preschool, a Head Start center, and a first-grade classroom. Their goal was to evaluate the degree to which the dynamics of childhood friendship are shaped by the settings in which friends interact. Their analysis made use of dozens of videotaped interactions among children during free play and copious field notes. Rizzo and Corsaro illustrate the use of friendship to get what one wants in this excerpt from field notes:

> Jenny and Betty are seated at a worktable with several other children drawing pictures.

> Jenny tells Betty that she is copying her picture. Betty says: "I am not!" which leads Jenny to claim: "Yes you are, you always copy me." Betty then replies, "I do not and if you keep saying that, then I don't like you any more and you're not my friend." "OK," says Jenny, "I won't say it any more."

From this and other instances recorded during intense observations, Rizzo and Corsaro concluded that children adapt their behavior to fit the constraints of the behavior settings in which they interact with peers, an adaptation the authors refer to as "ecological congruence."

Other ecological studies focus more on behavior settings themselves, with the goal of cataloging and organizing the many behavior settings that a person or group of people might inhabit. For instance, Barker and Schoggen (1973) comprehensively described all the behavior settings of a particular community, which were then organized in hierarchies of types and subtypes. The final step in this **behavior setting survey** is the description of the settings in terms of whichever of their many attributes and characteristics are of interest. Individuals are known then by the settings they inhabit as they conduct their daily lives. For the ecological psychologist, the lifestyle of an individual can be accurately grasped by listing the behavior settings that he or she inhabits. The listing of behavior settings is called the behavior range. For example, the behavior range for a particular person or group of persons is informative about how active they are in community life, what interests they have, and where they spend most of their time.

Ecological observation is thus a type of systematic observation that emphasizes full and impartial recording of behaviors in their specific setting and context. As in participant observation (Chapter 16), the goal is the discovery of ecologically valid base-rate information rather than hypothesis testing. In contrast to participant observation, but like other forms of systematic observation, the emphasis is on the objective observation of specific actions rather than the inference of underlying processes.

Structured Methods: Checklists or Coding Schemes The major difference between unstructured and structured observational methods is that in the latter, investigators know what aspects of social activity are relevant for their purposes before starting and deliberately set forth a specific and explicit plan to record them.

Most structured observational methods require an observer to code the appearance of the behavior, but some technological devices can record even in an observer's absence. For example, television meters note how many and what television programs are turned on, and pedometers calculate the territory covered by people on foot during any given day. As another example, the electronic scanners in many grocery stores actually gather extensive data continuously, recording all the items bought by each customer at what times, thus allowing market researchers to uncover trends in buying behavior. For example, are diaper sales greater in the morning or evening? What other products are people who buy diapers likely to purchase?

Checklists or **category systems** can range from simply noting whether or not a single behavior has occurred to multiple behavior systems (see Weick, 1985, for examples). As an example of the first, Perrine and Heather (2000) recorded whether individuals contributed more money to a donation box that displayed the phrase "even a penny will help" compared to boxes that did not display that phrase. As an example of the latter, Strayer and Strayer (1976) classified initiation of antagonistic behavior by children in a playground into one of several categories: bite, chase, hit, kick, push–pull, and wrestle.

The construction of a reliable and valid checklist is crucial to its usefulness as an observational tool. First, a critical feature of a good checklist is the explicitness with which the behavior is defined. For example, in observing antagonistic behavior, observers would need to know when a friendly tap becomes a hit. This is accomplished more easily when the behaviors are classifiable on objective grounds rather than on inferential ones. The observer would code a behavior as a hit only if it actually met the explicit description for the act and not if it only appeared that the child "wanted" to hit. Second, each behavior of interest must be able to be classified into one and only one category. A behavior would be either a "push–pull" or "wrestle" but not both. Third, the total set of categories for classifying a particular kind of behavior such as fighting or greeting should be exhaustive of the type but limited in distinctions. The code should cover the sphere of interest but be sufficiently finite to allow meaningful assessments to be made.

Group processes and classroom interaction are enduring targets for checklist observational systems. Two systems that have received substantial use by social scientists are Bales's (1970) Interaction Process Analysis for studying group interaction and Flanders's (1970) system for analyzing teacher behavior. In Bales's (1970) system, each act by a group member is categorized into 1 of the 12 categories shown in Figure 15.1. Bales's checklist system uses a modified version of continuous time sampling; that is, each act by a person is coded into 1 of the 12 possible types, and an act is defined as "a communication or an indication, either verbal or nonverbal, which in its context may be understood by another member as equivalent to a single simple sentence" (p. 68). In Flanders's system, classroom behavior is classified according to the 10 categories shown in Table 15.2. The Flanders system, in contrast to the Bales system, uses very small interval time-point sampling to maintain a rendering of the original behavioral sequence in the classrooms. An observer codes ongoing behavior into one of Flanders's 10 categories every three seconds.

Structured methods such as checklists are particularly appropriate for testing specific hypotheses after the behaviors have been described and hypotheses generated, perhaps by less structured observational methods. Checklists also vary with respect to how general or specific they are. One of the advantages of Bales's (1970) coding scheme is that it can be used to code virtually any group interaction. More specific checklists might be constrained to a certain context, but that can be an advantage if the specific checklist contains behaviors of direct theoretical interest. In sum, the choice of checklist should be theoretically driven. If an existing checklist encompasses the desired behaviors, by all means use it. If not, a new checklist tailored to the research questions being investigated might need to be devised.

Software programs exist that can greatly facilitate the use of a checklist. These programs generally allow the user to customize the coding scheme, specifying what

FIGURE 15.1

BALES'S (1970) INTERACTION PROCESS ANALYSIS CODING SCHEME FOR INTERACTION IN GROUPS

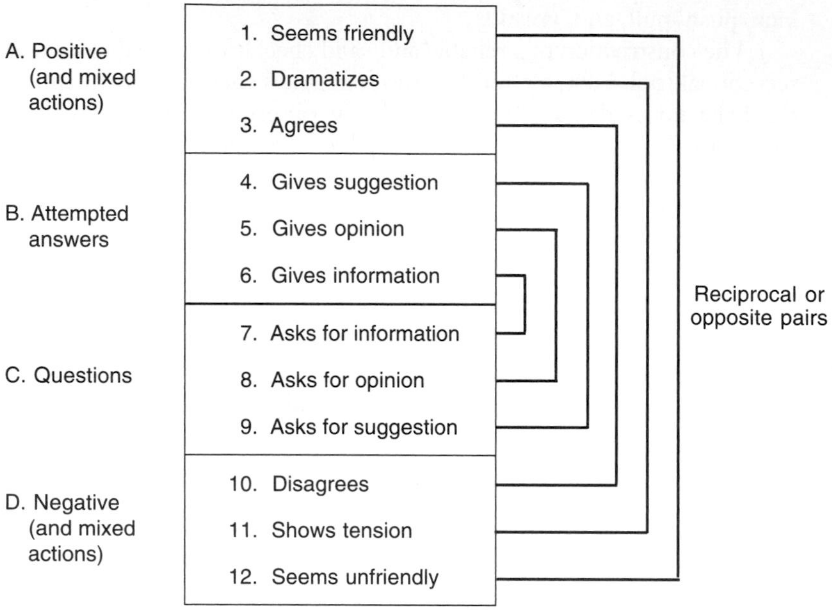

behaviors and how many targets are to be coded. The coder sits at the computer and strikes various keys corresponding to the behavior categories when appropriate. The computer keeps track of the time and records precisely at what times a given behavior occurs and for how long (if duration is being coded). Figure 15.2 shows such a coding entry screen from The Observer, one of the commercially available coding programs for observational data. As shown in the figure, this particular configuration is set up to code six separate activities (eat, kick, scream, avert, play, and other) and five types of position (sit, stand, walk, run, and other) expressed by a child. The coder strikes the appropriate key ("e" for eat, etc.) every time the behavior occurs. The program also allows the entry of modifiers that allow the recording of sequential data; for example, when the behavior "kick" is recorded, a modifier indicating who was kicked ("Derek") can be entered. These kinds of software programs possess several important advantages: First, they allow for much more organized, efficient, and hence more reliable coding than manual procedures. Rather than having to fumble with sheets of paper listing columns and memorizing special codes for each type of behavior, the coder merely needs to strike the appropriate computer key. Second, timing of events is done automatically and without error. Third, observations are entered directly into

TABLE 15.2 FLANDERS'S (1970) CATEGORY SYSTEM FOR CLASSROOM BEHAVIOR

Teacher Talk	Response	1. Accepts Feeling 2. Praises or Encourages 3. Accepts or Uses Ideas of Pupils
		4. Asks Questions
	Initiation	5. Lecturing 6. Giving Directions 7. Criticizing or Justifying Authority
Pupil Talk		8. Pupil-Talk Response 9. Pupil-Talk Initiation
Silence		10. Silence

the computer, removing the need for manual data entry and thus avoiding an important source of error.

Steps in Conducting an Observation

Any study using observation follows a general sequence of steps, which we outline here to summarize the decisions that must be made:

Step 1: Arrive at Operational Definitions of the Desired Construct(s) This step can be the most difficult, as it can require considerable imagination or creativity on the part of the researcher to decide to observe "fidgetiness" in doctors' waiting rooms as a measure of nervousness or floor-tile wear to measure an exhibit's popularity in a museum. The selection of the behaviors or physical traces to observe is guided both by the focus of interest and by practical and ethical concerns that limit what is observable. It is also important that the target of observation should be unambiguously definable, so that reasonable reliability and validity in measurement can be attained.

Step 2: Select the Setting and Mode of Observation Because settings exert a powerful influence on behavior, we must choose a setting in which the trace or behavior can be expected to occur with sufficient frequency to make observation

FIGURE 15.2

EVENT RECORDER SCREEN FROM THE OBSERVER® OBSERVATIONAL CODING PROGRAM

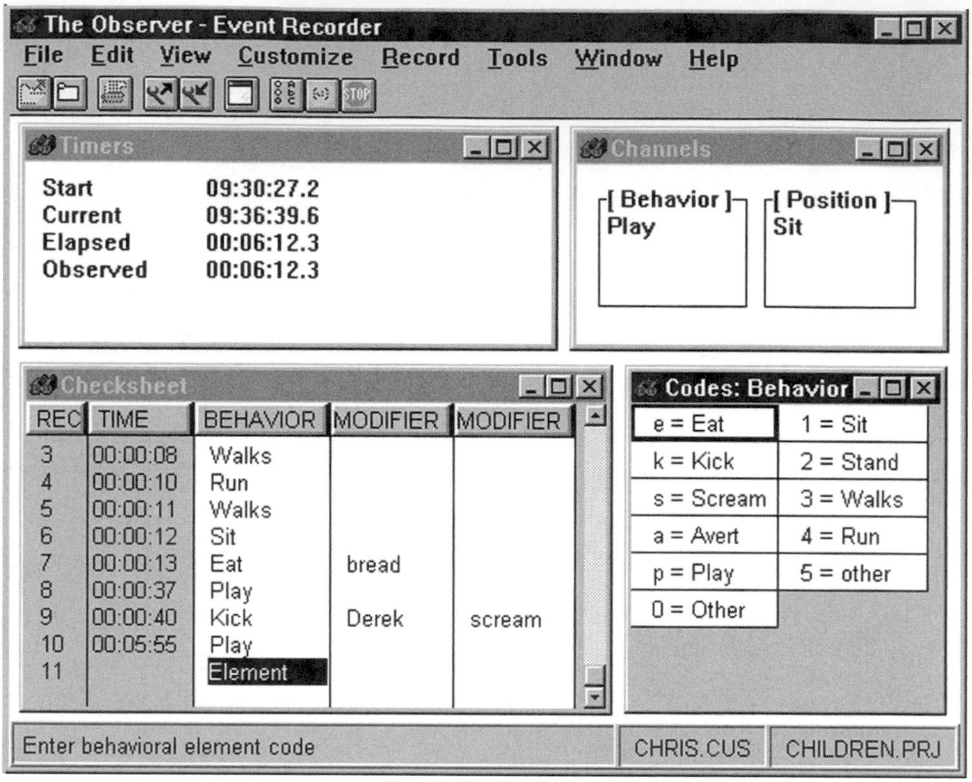

SOURCE: Copyright 2000 by Noldus Information Technology. Reprinted with permission.

worthwhile. For example, we would not try to code the time children spend running around during a religious service, though we probably would if we were observing the children at a park. The setting should, if possible, also permit relatively unobtrusive but reliable observations by an in-person observer or recording instrument (such as videotape equipment). For example, if fine, small behaviors are to be coded, the setting should permit the observers to be physically close to the participants or else permit the use of binoculars or telephoto lenses.

Mode of observation refers to whether the behavior will be coded on-line (i.e., live) or from videotapes. The choice between live coding and permanent recording for later coding is crucial. Videotaped and other recorded information facilitate the use of multiple coders for each behavior and therefore increase the reliability of measurement. Videotapes also carry the great advantage of producing a permanent record so that researchers can go back and code additional variables when desired. With on-line coding, the researcher must identify all the variables to be coded in advance of observation, and no changes can be made to this list. A permanent record such as videotape also allows the research team to review the behavioral information to resolve discrepancies between coders. Thus, if an initial reliability analysis indicates that coding is not sufficiently reliable, the coding scheme can be refined and observers trained until adequate reliability is reached. If the coding were done on-line, though, the researchers are stuck with any poor reliability that results. For all of these reasons, videotaping or otherwise permanently recording the behavior to be coded is preferred whenever possible. On-line coding should be used only when permanent recording is not feasible. For example, researchers wishing to code children's play behavior at a park would perhaps find videotaping too difficult. The camera angle would have to be very wide to capture all of the park activities, and the resulting video images of children running about would be so complex that coding of the behavior of individual children would be difficult. On-line coding using a large number of coders responsible for circumscribed sections of the park or individual children might be the only option in such a study.

Following recording, the next step entails encoding the observations. **Encoding** is the process of simplifying the observations through some procedure, such as categorization, and quantifying the categories for statistical analysis. Sometimes recording and encoding can involve a single operation, as when an observer counts whether a specific behavior has occurred when making a live observation. The observations are thus already encoded by virtue of being recorded. Sampling according to time-point procedures in vivo would yield this type of situation. In contrast, the recording of single or multiple behaviors through continuous time measurement would allow different types of encoding, such as frequency, rate, duration, percentage duration, and sequential analysis. The distinction between recording and encoding is a critical one in that the same recorded observations can be encoded according to different systems. In this regard at least, observations do not speak for themselves. The question that the researcher has in mind guides the encoding of the observations. Consider gaze behavior: Two pairs can look at each other for comparable total duration, thus seeming very similar; however, the first pair might have done so through one or two relatively extended periods of eye contact, whereas the second pair brought it about through frequent but brief looks.

Step 3: Select a Sampling Strategy The major decision here involves whether the entire interaction or event will be coded continuously or whether only portions of the interaction or event will be coded. The former method of coding is called **continuous real-time measurement** (Sackett, 1978). Continuous measurement occurs when every onset of a behavior (frequency) or elapsed time of a behavior (duration) is recorded during the observational session. For example, researchers interested in coding friendliness during an interpersonal interaction might code the frequency of smiles. The entire interaction would be observed and the total number of smiles expressed by each participant recorded. In later analyses, the researchers probably would want to convert the frequency measure to a rate measure by dividing by interaction length so as to correct for any variation in interaction length. Otherwise, a person who smiled 10 times might be deemed twice as friendly as a person who smiled only 5 times, yet if the first interaction were twice as long as the second, the actual rate (and level) of friendliness would be the same.

The second major approach to deciding what parts of an event or interaction to code is called time sampling. There are two variations of time sampling. In **time-point sampling,** recording is done instantaneously at the end of set time periods, such as every 10 seconds or every sixth minute or every hour on the hour, with the number and spacing of points selected to be appropriate to the session length. This is like freezing time and then recording whether a particular behavior is present at that moment in time. Through film or videotape, the time point is literally accomplished by stop action on one frame. In contrast, **time-interval sampling,** like continuous measurement, records behavior in real time; but as in time-point sampling, each observed behavior, such as smiling, is scored once and only once during successive intervals of the session (e.g., 60 seconds) regardless of the number of actual occurrences in each interval.

A third variation on sampling behavior is to use a combination of continuous and time-interval sampling. In this approach, only a portion of the total interaction or event is coded, but that portion is coded in a continuous fashion, that is, rather than scoring a given behavior only once if it occurs during the sampled time interval, the total frequency is tallied. This approach is particularly useful when the total amount of material to be coded is prohibitively large. Take, for example, a study looking at therapist and client behavior during a social skills training group that met weekly for 2 hours across a 12-week span. Assuming a rather small-scale study of 10 groups, consisting of 2 therapists and 8 clients each, we would be looking at 24 hours of coding per person, for a total of 2,400 coding hours if each person were coded independently. A reasonable alternative would be to code only a subset of those 24 hours, say, 3 hours randomly taken out of the 24 possible hours. Or, the times to be sampled could be deliberately chosen to be representative of the entire course of therapy, for example, 1 hour each from the beginning, middle, and last third of the group sessions.

Although some researchers initially express reluctance to such time-sampling methods ("What? You mean you want me to throw out most of the data?!"), there often is no choice but to adopt such an approach. Moreover, research indicates that the information obtained from sampled subsets of an event or interaction represent well the information obtained from continuous sampling over the entire session. Indeed, Ambady and Rosenthal (1992) have shown that nonverbal ratings taken from extremely short video clips, even as short as 30 seconds, have impressive validity coefficients. They also found that studies using longer periods of coding (e.g., 5 minutes) did not differ in their accuracy of predictions compared to studies based on observations of less than 30 seconds in length.

The decision whether to use continuous or time-sampling methods thus depends partly on practicality concerns and partly on theoretical concerns. Continuous real-time observation allows the determination of the actual frequency or duration of particular behaviors, whereas time-sampling strategies require less coding effort and allow estimation of total frequencies and comparisons of subgroups. Time-sampling methods are thus particularly useful when there is a large number of behaviors to code, long observational sessions to be recorded, or quick changes in the relevant behaviors. Time sampling tends not to be appropriate for behaviors that occur infrequently or briefly, when the sequence of the behavior amid other behaviors is significant, or when actual frequencies or durations are important to know. Consequently, continuous recording in real time is the method of choice when these concerns are paramount in the research.

Step 4: Train the Observers Observers need to be trained to code objects or events similarly and to avoid errors of commission and omission in scoring. Training can proceed in conjunction with the development of coding categories or checklists. Before actual coding begins, observers practice on sample behaviors until they reach acceptable levels of agreement (i.e., high reliability). As detailed in Chapter 4, the reliability of observational measures is usually assessed by documenting the extent to which two or more independent observers agree in their ratings of the same events or objects, expressed in statistics such as the inter-rater reliability coefficient or Cohen's (1960) kappa, which is based on the percentage of scored units on which the observers agree. If adequate reliability cannot be attained, the coding system or checklist needs to be revised, probably in the direction of more specificity in the definitions of the coding categories. Furthermore, **observer drift,** a decline in observer reliability or validity over time, is a common phenomenon. Because of fatigue or habituation, the use of coding categories can vary randomly or systematically over time so that behaviors are not coded in the same way. We cannot assume that high reliability at the beginning of a study implies high reliability at the end. When coding is done from videotapes or other permanent records, researchers can avoid a systematic bias due to observer drift by having participants coded in a random order that is different for each coder.

Observers also are subject to a number of biases (such as halo effects) that are characteristic of raters in general (see Chapter 7) and that can only be reduced, not totally eliminated, by careful training. The best control of such biases involves videotaped records of behavior and keeping observers as unaware as possible of potential biasing factors. It is sometimes possible to edit videotapes in a manner that would prevent halo and other potential biases through editing out information that identifies the conditions under which the observation was made. For example, if the research hypothesis is that male participants smile more while conversing with females than with males, and if the observers can see the other party to the conversation, their ratings of the participant's smiles might be influenced by their knowledge of the circumstances of the observation. This bias might even falsely lead to a seeming confirmation of the hypothesis. A strategy for dealing with this possible bias would be to record or edit videotaped observations so that the coders could see and hear only the participant, not the partner, removing any possibility of this form of bias. This also can be accomplished in some cases by the low-cost strategy of placing a piece of cardboard over half of the television monitor, obscuring the other person. When interactions are audiotaped, a simple approach is to record each person's comments on separate tracks, thus facilitating preparation of editing tapes that contain only one participant's voice. As should be clear, it is often easier to arrange for naive coding when videotape or other recording techniques are used than with live observers. In either case, it is crucial that observers are kept unaware of the hypotheses guiding the study. It is for this reason that researchers should almost never code their own observations.

Step 5: Analyze the Data After the coding system has been found or created, good reliability and validity have been achieved, and observations have been recorded on the research participants, analysis of the data is the final step. A common analytic approach is simply to use the coded behavior (i.e., frequency, rate, or duration of specific behaviors) as dependent variables in standard statistical analysis procedures such as those described in Chapters 17 and 18. More sophisticated procedures are available, however, for the investigation of behavior streams and sequences (e.g., Bakeman & Gottman, 1997; Hall & Oliver, 1997). Although the statistical nuances of these strategies are beyond the scope of this book, essentially what they do is to analyze the conditional probabilities of a given behavior predicated on a prior or subsequent behavior. In other words, given that Person A smiled, how likely is it that Person B smiled in return? An example of this kind of approach is given by Wehby, Symons, and Shores (1995), who coded a variety of prosocial and aggressive behaviors in classrooms for children with emotional and behavioral disorders. Analyses showed that students who displayed more aggressive behavior received fewer positive social interactions from their teachers. Teacher use of social or instructional commands elicited more aggressive behavior from students, whereas peer-directed aggression was usually precipitated by other peer aggression. Thus, a **sequential analysis** provides information not only on differences in mere frequencies of behavior but also on how certain behaviors relate to one another across time. Through sequential analysis, the Wehby et al. (1995) study was able to identify not merely which students were more aggressive but the precise events that elicited their aggression. In sum, as is the case with any form of social science data, the decision of what analytic strategy to pursue is a joint function of the conceptual questions that guided the research strategy and the nature of the information it generates.

Some Notes on the Ethics of Observation

Observational studies and nonreactive measures raise complex ethical issues. The primary goal of research in natural settings is to obtain behavior that is as natural as possible. That goal is best achieved by using measures and procedures that are nonreactive, that is, not affected by the measurement process. Unfortunately, often the best way to achieve nonreactivity is for the participant not to realize that he or she is being studied. And there is the ethical problem: Gathering information on participants who do not realize that they are under observation violates the principle of obtaining fully informed consent among individuals. Informed consent is not, however, absolutely required in all cases. The federal regulations allow waiving informed consent in research involving the observation of public behavior as long as the participants are not identifiable or—if they are identifiable—the behavior being observed is not of a sensitive nature. In other words, informed consent is not necessary as long as disclosure of the behavior would not place the participants at risk of criminal or civil liability or be damaging to participants' financial standing, employability, or reputation. The primary concerns are how identifiable the "participants" data are and whether the information is of a sensitive nature. Physical trace measures that are anonymous in nature—meaning that it is impossible to determine which particular individuals were responsible for the erosion or accretion in question—therefore do not pose any special ethical concern. Observational measures of characteristics that are identifiable but benign (e.g., recording individuals' hair color) also do not pose ethical concerns. On the other hand, observational measures of characteristics that are both identifiable as well as involving sensitive topics or constituting an invasion of privacy (e.g., recording estimates of women's bra sizes) are ethically more problematic, and researchers generally would not be able to dispense with informed consent in such cases. Moreover, even if the "participants" are not *individually* identifiable, if they come from a small group of people whose reputations would suffer if the information were made public (e.g., showing that the rest room of one particular small business showed a high level of racist graffiti), the research might be deemed as posing more than minimal risk and thus requiring informed consent. These issues are discussed in more detail in Chapter 3.

Summary of Observation

As with other methods of research on social behavior, observation of physical traces, naturally occurring behaviors, or other phenomena demands rigorous training of observers, careful construction of checklists or coding schemes, careful sampling, and caution in interpreting results. The special strengths of observational research are its ability to describe naturally occurring events in natural settings, avoiding problems that can arise with questionnaire measures or other methods that make respondents aware of participating in research. Thus, observations can be particularly informative about activities that cannot be talked about because of ignorance or inability (such as nonverbal behaviors) or will not be talked about because of fear or embarrassment (such as drivers' compliance with traffic laws).

Archival Research

Statistical archives and written records are kept by all literate societies for a variety of purposes, of which research is by no means the most important. However, such archives can be used by imaginative researchers for purposes that were never envisioned by the originators of the archives or documents, often in a way that takes advantage of the strengths of archival data. These strengths are the potential for (1) spanning long periods of time (including the ability to look *back* in time, which is not possible with other research methods); (2) covering large populations of people or other units of observation; and (3) quantifying reactions to events, such as earthquakes, riots, or factory closings, that researchers cannot intentionally impose for practical or ethical reasons.

This section of the chapter is divided into three parts, based on the nature of the archive that is the source of information. First we consider statistical records and other government or institutional records, such as those on hospital admissions, unemployment rates, daily temperatures, or population growth. Next, survey archives of data collected for research purposes by standard survey methods (usually by telephone or personal interviews) are considered; they generally include a range of sociodemographic information as well as attitudes on social and political topics, drawn from very large probability samples. Finally, the research use of written records, ranging from private diaries to mass-circulation newspapers, and the associated techniques of content analysis are presented.

Statistical Records

Many available **statistical archives** include socioeconomic information about age, sex, family size, occupation, residence, and other characteristics. Health statistics give birth and death rates and the like; federal, state, municipal, and private economic institutions collect and publish information on wages, hours of work, productivity, absenteeism, strikes, financial transactions, and so on. Many voluntary organizations have records not only of their own membership but also of groups of people whom they serve. In addition, a small but steadily increasing body of information is being collected by various institutions on psychological characteristics such as IQ, personality, anxiety, and attitudes. For example, schools, hospitals, social service agencies, personnel departments in businesses, and similar institutions frequently administer psychological tests of various kinds to their entire populations.

The variety of research questions that can be addressed using statistical archives is staggering. For example, Rubinstein and Caballero (2000) used archival data on the height and weight of Miss America pageant contestants to track social changes in standards of beauty. Fogg and Rose (2000) examined archival data on 2,288 astronaut applicants and determined that the best predictors of being accepted into astronaut training were undergraduate and graduate grade point averages and aviation experience. Intentions to remain in the military and their relation to family characteristics were examined in a study by Lee and Maurer (1999). Finally, archival analyses in South Africa of violent crime statistics and representative national surveys showed that although politically motivated violence had declined precipitously by the end of 1994, the levels of fear reported by citizens remained high (Barbarin, Richter, de Wet, & Wachtel, 1998).

Suicide is an example of a research topic that is difficult to study by any approach other than archival. Durkheim's (1897/1951) classic study of suicide tested the hypothesis that a basic cause of suicide is lack of integration into a social group. He examined three major kinds of social group integration: religious, familial, and political. He found suicide rates were lower among Catholics than among Protestants, lower among married people than among single people, lower among those with children than among those without children, and lower during periods of national fervor. All these findings, he argued, supported the hypothesis that belonging to a cohesive social group is a deterrent to suicide. A century later, Phillips, Carstensen, and Paight (1989) used statistical archives to document the "copycat effect" in suicides. There is a marked increase in suicides and traffic fatalities (which often reflect suicidal decisions) following a publicized suicide, but this effect is primarily restricted to individuals who are similar to the publicized suicide victim. In other words, more teenagers commit suicide after a teen suicide story is publicized, and more elderly people commit suicide after a story about an elderly suicide.

Available statistical records are used as social indicators to chart the status and change in the quality of life. The U.S. government gathers and reports statistics detailing various social indicators of human well-being, including employment levels, housing availability, and crime rates. Previously only accessible as heavy volumes with fine print in reference libraries, these reports can now be easily accessed on the World Wide Web. For example, the FedStats site listed in the "On the Web" section at the end of the chapter provides links to a cornucopia of statistics from over 100 federal agencies, including information on social and economic conditions in the United States, national trends in educational statistics, birth and death rates, life expectancy, risk factors, and other health-related topics. The U.S. Census Bureau also publishes the *Statistical Abstract of the United States*, available on the Web at http://www.census.gov/prod/www/statistical-abstract-us.html. Table 15.3 lists the over 30 types of statistical tables that are available through the *Abstract*. Just about anything one might want to know about the lives of Americans can be found here; for example, we can find out that housing costs in Lexington, Kentucky, for the third quarter of 1996 were 82.2% of the national average or that in 1998 Americans spent an average of \$540 on physician payments and \$183 on payments to dentists. These reports are compiled to monitor present social conditions and to chart societal changes. Therein lies one of the singular advantages of using existing records. Many of these are collected regularly, thus enabling the user to measure associations among social variables across time. For example, is the socioeconomic standing of various racial or sex groups declining, rising, or sustaining the status quo, and to what other social factors is there a systematic tie?

The U.S. Census, a truly massive data gathering effort undertaken every 10 years, produces a variety of statistical records that are suitable for many research purposes. The variables include a fairly narrow range, being limited to basic characteristics of people (such as age, sex, race, ethnic background, education, occupation, and income) and housing units (such as location, value, inclusion of indoor plumbing, and occupants per room). The Census Bureau publishes a number of tabulations of data (e.g., income broken down by race and sex) for the United States as a whole and for states and smaller areas, and using these data for research is as simple as looking up

TABLE 15.3 **CATEGORIES OF STATISTICS AVAILABLE IN THE STATISTICAL ABSTRACT OF THE UNITED STATES**

Population	Vital statistics
Health and nutrition	Education
Geography and environment	Law enforcement, courts, and prison
Parks, recreation, and travel	Elections
State and local governments	Federal government finances and employment
National defense and veteran affairs	Social insurance and human services
Labor force, employment, and earnings	Income, expenditures, and wealth
Prices	Banking, finance, and insurance
Business enterprise	Communications and information technology
Energy	Science and technology
Transportation—land	Transportation—air and water
Agriculture	Natural resources
Construction and housing	Manufacturers
Domestic trade and services	Foreign commerce and aid
Outlying areas	Comparative international statistics
20th century statistics	Industrial outlook
1997 economic census	

the appropriate table. Kasarda (1976) has long argued that the information provided in various national censuses offer opportunities for secondary analyses that are limited only by the imagination of the researcher. Among these opportunities Kasarda mentions the chance to analyze educational attainment, ethnic and racial segregation, poverty, marriage and divorce, social mobility, and commuting patterns.

However, often the particular associations in which a researcher is interested are not among those tabulated by the government, so the researcher must turn to the original information. Public Use Microdata, samples of a tiny percentage of the actual census responses, are released by the government, coded in relatively gross geographic areas so that individual respondents' privacy is not threatened by the release of the actual data. From the original information, any desired tabulation or analysis of the existing variables can be prepared by an appropriate computer program.

Despite their unparalleled coverage of the U.S. population, census data have important limitations for research. Although the repetition of the census every 10 years provides a good basis for research over time, the researcher must be wary of changing conceptual and operational definitions that render some year-to-year comparisons problematic. For example, the entire scheme for coding occupations changed between 1970 and 1980; some change is necessary as new occupations appear and old ones vanish, but the changes can make comparisons over time inexact. The boundaries of census areas within which information is accumulated (tracts and metropolitan areas) also change over time as population patterns shift. Again, examining social or economic changes within a city or other area can be difficult because of these noncomparabilities. Finally, social change can affect the way people respond to survey items, even when data-gathering procedures remain unchanged. Between 1970 and 1980, it appears that a large number of people of Spanish origin shifted from indicating "White" to "Other" on a question about ethnicity; in 1970, 90% of this group indicated "White" compared to 58% "White" and 38% "Other" in 1980. Ethnic breakdowns across years would be confounded unless special precautions were taken because the "White" and "Other" groups would contain varying proportions of Spanish-origin respondents. The addition of the "multiracial" category to the 2000 census makes ethnic group comparisons across time even more difficult.

The relatively small number of variables measured by the census has already been mentioned, and it is this feature that poses the most important limitation on research content. No attitude or belief variables are included. Yet, for whole fields within the social sciences, including the study of fertility, educational and occupational differences in income, or characteristics of different areas within cities (e.g., residential segregation by race or income), the census is the single most valuable data source.

Characteristics of Archival Research Archival studies have a number of common characteristics. First, they rely entirely on the analyses of information gathered for purposes other than those of particular studies of social behavior. Consequently, they require familiarity with known sources of information, such as the *New York Times Index*, and skill in uncovering less well known material, such as cemetery records. Second, archival studies often call for ingenuity in translating existing records into quantifiable indices of some general concepts. For example, objective public records of social integration do not exist, so Durkheim's (1897/1951) resourcefulness is evident in using existing material to indicate more general social psychological processes. Third, although the explosion of information archived on the Web makes it more likely that the statistics one needs are only a mouse-click away, the sheer volume of information available is overwhelming, and it can take hours of frustrating searching before relevant information is identified.

Fourth, archival studies are particularly susceptible to alternative interpretations for the natural events and their effects. What is required, then, is care in using multiple measures or ruling out other explanations. For example, Durkheim (1897/1951) examined a number of alternative hypotheses—that suicide is the result of psychopathic states, imitation, racial or hereditary factors, or climate. He then demonstrated that the statistics are not in accord with any of these hypotheses. For example, in considering the hypothesis that suicide is influenced by climate, he started with the observation that in all countries for which statistics are available over a period of years, the incidence of suicide increases regularly from January until June and then declines until the end of the year. This observation had led other writers to conclude that temperature has a direct effect on the tendency to suicide. Durkheim examined this possibility in great detail and demonstrated that the statistics did not support it. He argued, for example, that if temperature were the basic cause, suicide would vary regularly with it, but this is not the case. There are more suicides in spring than in autumn, although the temperature is slightly lower in spring. Moreover, suicide reaches its height not in the hottest months (July and August) but in June. By a series of such analyses, Durkheim demonstrated that the seasonal regularities in suicide rates could not be accounted for by temperature and suggested the alternative hypothesis that social activity is seasonal and that the rate of suicide is related to the extent of social activity.

Research Survey Archives

An alternative source of information on social behavior is archives created specifically for research—**research survey archives**. Several organizations (including the Roper Center of the University of Connecticut, the Interuniversity Consortium for Political and Social Research, and the National Opinion Research Center at the University of Chicago) maintain and distribute data files drawn from large-scale surveys, often based on high-quality probability samples of the general U.S. population.

One research survey archive, the General Social Survey (Davis & Smith, 1992), illustrates the types of information that are available. This survey, conducted by the National Opinion Research Center, began in 1972 and has gathered face-to-face interview data on an annual or biennial basis since then. To date, over 40,000 randomly chosen respondents have answered more than 3,500 questions on a host of variables relevant to social behavior. Each sample is a national area probability sample of 1,500 to 3,000 noninstitutionalized adults. Response rates average 77% for the 20 administrations of the General Social Survey since 1972, an impressively high rate given the length of the survey and reflective of the great methodological care that has gone into designing and implementing the survey.

The General Social Survey contains a standard core of demographic and attitudinal variables that remain the same from year to year, and others appear in rotation every two or three years, offering valuable opportunities to make comparisons over time. The questions cover a range of standard social and demographic characteristics of the respondent, including age, sex, education, income, religion, urban or rural residence, occupation, and marital status. In addition, many questions about beliefs, attitudes, and behaviors relevant to social and political topics are included, for example, reported vote in the most recent presidential election, preferences for government spending on a range of programs, interracial attitudes, sexual behavior, political alienation, attitudes toward labor unions, gun ownership and attitudes toward gun control, and abortion.

Many excellent studies have been conducted using the General Social Survey or other research survey archives; the National Opinion Research Center's bibliography lists over 5,000 studies published using the General Social Survey alone. Some examples include studies of changes in sex-role attitudes among men and women from 1972 through 1978 (Cherlin & Walters, 1981); race and social class differences in support for the use of force by police (Arthur & Case, 1994); and the incidence of high-risk sexual behavior in the general population (Anderson & Dahlberg, 1992).

The use of such archives for research has obvious advantages and disadvantages. The advantages include the availability of extensive information obtained from high-quality samples over time, which would be beyond the ability of any researcher to collect for himself or herself. Low cost is also a benefit; at many colleges and universities such archives are available through the campus computing center, and the cost to obtain them is typically low if they are not already available. Finally, in contrast to most archives, research survey archives are created and maintained for research use so that they do not have many of the problems that must be faced by the user of government or institutional archives, with regard to which research use is often a mere afterthought.

The main limitations are, of course, those imposed by the method (sample surveys, clearly not an unobtrusive or nonreactive form of data gathering) and the topics. Although the questions cover a wide range of topics, a researcher who is interested in an issue that is not covered by the survey is simply out of luck. In addition, some older archives have annoying problems such as incomplete or inaccurate codebooks (the documentation describing what variables are recorded where and what codes are used in the data; see Chapter 17) and obsolete recording methods (such as "multiple punched columns" in punched cards). Newer archives are largely free of these problems.

Verbal Records

Public and Private Documents **Verbal records** also provide a rich source of information about social behavior. For example, public documents such as the speeches made by Arab and Israeli political decision makers have been coded (Astorino-Courtois, 1995). This analysis revealed that, in contrast to popular impressions of the Mideast conflict, the speeches tended toward cautious decision making and restraint during times of uncertainty. Moreover, Arab and Israeli leaders attempted to minimize perceived conflict escalations by moderating their behavior. Similarly, an analysis of the public speeches by Presidents Bill Clinton and George H. Bush indicated that Clinton used a more flexible and cooperative approach to foreign policy, whereas Bush was relatively less cooperative (Walker, Schafer, & Young, 1999).

Personal documents, including autobiographies, letters, diaries, school essays, and the like are also open to social scientific observation once obtained. For example, a classic study by Thomas and Znaniecki (1918) used letters sent between Poland and the United States, along with other information sources, to draw conclusions about Polish peasants who immigrated to the United States and, more broadly, the effects of culture on beliefs and attitudes. Snowden and his colleagues (1996) used diaries written by nuns in their early twenties to predict their cognitive functioning 50 years later.

Ideally, the research use of personal documents can achieve for inner experiences such as beliefs and attitudes what observational techniques can achieve for overt behaviors: reveal them to the social scientist without the use of reactive questionnaires or other research instruments. However, personal documents are relatively rare and often pose problems for the researcher. Their authenticity can be uncertain—were the letters from Polish peasants actually written by the person in question or by somebody else (such as a village scribe)? If the latter, that person might have influenced the content. In addition, available samples of documents might be biased. If not all peasants are literate, conclusions about their thinking based on letters probably pertain to a biased sample of individuals, underrepresenting those who do not write.

Mass Communications In addition to statistical records and autobiographical documents, every literate society produces a variety of material intended to inform, entertain, or persuade the populace. Such material can appear in the form of literary productions, newspapers and magazines, film, radio, television broadcasts, and the Internet. Mass communications provide a rich source of information for investigating a variety of questions. They can be used to shed light on some aspects of the culture of a given group, to compare different groups in terms of some aspect of culture, or to trace cultural change. For example, Lusk (1999) analyzed images of patients in 446 advertisements displayed in four nursing magazines and found that more men than women were portrayed, and most patients were White and under 65 years old. Men were shown more frequently as being critically ill or having heart disease. Lusk noted that these portrayals do not reflect actual patient demographics and that, more seriously, the underrepresentation of minorities and the elderly in such advertisements negates their health care presence and needs.

Television commercials often have been the topic of study. Moore and Cadeau (1985) performed a content analysis of 1,733 commercials and found that over 88% used a man for the voice-over. For commercials with an identifiable central character, only 54% had a female as the central character and fewer than 2% had an elderly person as the central character. Minority group members were shown in fewer than 4% of all commercials, and when present, they were usually males playing secondary roles. A similar type of analysis was performed by Greenberg and Brand (1993), who analyzed Saturday morning cartoons and commercials targeted toward young children.

All these studies document trends in content in the mass media. All utilize a technique called **content analysis,** which is "any technique for making inferences by systematically and objectively identifying specified characteristics of messages" (Holsti, 1969, p. 601). This is similar to the definition of systematic observation of natural behavior. Both techniques require objectivity of coding categories to ensure reliability, systematic application of these coding systems across a representative sample of material to control observer bias, and consistency in theoretical aims so that the findings can be related to some relevant variable.

Although content analysis is covered in depth in Chapter 16, we summarize here the steps involved in doing a content analysis on mass media communications, which are very similar to the steps in systematic observation: (1) The phenomenon to be coded, such as the presence and portrayal of elderly people in the print media, must be chosen. (2) The media from which the observations are to be made must be selected.

The issue here, as in systematic observation, is the selection of media that are typical or representative of what is available and with which people have contact. The issue is to find out what is out there and not to select so as to enhance or inhibit the possibility of obtaining particular findings. (3) In deriving the coding categories, as was the case with systematic observation, content analysis categories can range from a simple binary system, in which the presence or absence of people of a certain age are noted, to multicategory systems using mutually exclusive and exhaustive categories in which distinctions are made on a range of phenomena, such as the status of the portrayed character (e.g., high, middle, or low), background physical attractiveness (attractive, neutral, unattractive), or evaluation of context (positive, neutral, negative). (4) The distinctions in deciding on the sampling strategy are roughly comparable to the decisions involved in systematic observation. The task is to choose among strategies that code every reference to the phenomenon in question or to select a discontinuous though regular method of sampling, such as every other issue of several magazines over a year's period. (5) Training the coders ensures reliability of content analysis, an important consideration, particularly so when inferences are required to decide, for example, whether the portrayal of an elderly person is cast positively or negatively. (6) Sometimes the most straightforward statistical analysis is the tabulation and presentation of the characteristics in summary form such as frequencies and percentages.

Sampling material from mass communications requires much time and thought. The first task is to define the population—newspapers, magazines, radio, television, or the Internet. But even if we limited ourselves to newspapers, it would not be satisfactory to list all the newspapers published in a given country and draw every tenth or twentieth one. Even if we were also to introduce controls to ensure that newspapers representing different geographic areas, political orientations, economic groups, and ethnic groups were included in the proportion in which they are represented in the total population of newspapers, there would be a problem. The difficulty arises from the fact that newspapers vary tremendously in size and influence, and a realistic sample should not weight an obscure journal equally with a metropolitan daily. The situation is not the same as that of drawing a representative sample of a voting population, each member of which has equal influence at the polls—namely, one vote.

A study by Graber (1971) illustrates the complexity of decisions involved in sampling mass media sources. Graber wished to represent a cross section of the newspapers used by the general public as sources of information in one study. She developed a complex sampling scheme that reflected where these newspapers would be found. First, it was decided that newspapers in each of the major regions in the country should be included in the sample. Cities in each region were then divided into three groups by population: over 1 million, 500,000 to 1 million, and fewer than 500,000. She decided to draw three-fourths of the sample from the most populous states in each region and the remainder from the less populous states to reflect voting power on the basis of population. Further decisions narrowed even more the potential newspapers that could be included in the sample. Half the newspapers were selected from states in which the Democratic Party was stronger; half from states in which the Republican Party was stronger. Newspapers were selected, moreover, to represent monopolistic as well as competitive newspaper market situations. Finally, two types of newspapers, appealing to either special or general audiences, were included in the sample. Graber then coded all the campaign stories in the newspapers included.

Frequently, then, the sampling procedure in content analysis of mass communications consists of three stages: sampling of sources (which newspapers, which radio stations, which films, and so on are to be analyzed); sampling of dates (which time period is to be covered by the study); and sampling of units (which aspects of the communication are to be analyzed). In the sampling of units, decisions are often arbitrary and based on tacit assumptions about which feature of a medium best characterizes it. For example, is it the headline, the human interest story, the editorial, or some other feature that best indicates the policy of a newspaper?

To avoid such arbitrariness, content analysts frequently follow one of two possibilities: They analyze on the basis of several different units (e.g., they take samplings of headlines, of human interest stories, and of editorials and then count how many times a target person, behavior, or event is mentioned in each), or they disregard these "natural" units completely, dividing the issues of a newspaper mechanically into lines or inches of space from which they draw a sample. Note here the similarity to the distinctions among types of time sampling.

In summary, content analytic methods applied to verbal records, either personal communications or the mass media, constitute an underused resource for research on social behavior. Content coding schemes for a variety of psychological states (such as anxiety, positive and negative feelings, and hostility) already exist and have been shown to have adequate reliability and validity (Viney, 1983). As we discuss in Chapter 16, content analysis can also be done via computer programs, with benefits of both lower cost and higher objectivity and reliability compared to human coders. As the previous examples illustrate, the range of issues that can be approached by content analytic techniques is wide indeed.

Issues in Archival Research

Archival research offers important advantages for some research questions. The use of archives is often economical, for the researcher is spared the time and cost involved in gathering and recording information. This advantage can be offset, though, by the effort involved in finding the relevant information as well as the search for materials that would allow the researcher to rule out alternative interpretations. Another important advantage is that much information is gathered by governments and other organizations as part of their everyday operations, and it is often collected repeatedly. This helps to avoid the difficulties associated with people's awareness of being participants in research (reactivity) and often makes possible the analysis of trends over time. Finally, archival research is particularly well suited to the investigation of large-scale or widespread social or natural phenomena that are not amenable to study in other ways.

Archival records give the opportunity to assess the impact of natural events and investigate many other issues. They are obviously strong on external validity because of the participants' unawareness of the research or its aims; however, they also characteristically offer certain problems of interpretation, centering on internal and construct validity. To give an oft-cited example, records are available on the two variables of ice-cream sales and crime rates, which turn out to be positively associated (i.e., as one increases the other increases as well; Kasarda, 1976). Can we conclude that eating ice cream increases the propensity to commit crimes? Obviously not, and this is an example of a **spurious association:** The two variables are associated only because they are both influenced by a third variable. Here, the variable is probably weather conditions—increasing temperature increases both ice-cream sales and crime, but the latter two variables probably do not affect each other. When using archival records, we must allow for the possibilities of internal invalidity or spurious associations (caused, for instance, by common influences of increasing population, inflation-induced price rises, or weather or other seasonal effects). This can require the collection of additional information, such as temperature records in this example, to rule out threats to internally valid causal inferences. We can never be sure we have ruled out all potential threats to internal validity, and thus it is difficult to arrive at a firm causal inference using archival methods.

Another major issue in archival research is the construct validity and reliability of the data for research purposes. The researcher does not control the gathering of information in archival research, so it can be subject to various sources of unreliability, bias, or invalidity. For example, organizations might keep records haphazardly, with little attention to consistency in recording similar events in the same way over time. Records also can be subject to systematic biases; for example, the crime reports published by universities under new reporting laws have been frequently criticized as reflecting an underreporting bias. Similarly, samples of written documents from some societies might overrepresent the literate (and therefore those with higher status) and underrepresent the illiterate. Even the *Congressional Record*, a rich source of information on speeches and official proceedings in government, is edited after the fact by the speakers, so that what appears in the record is not always what was spoken on the floor.

Finally, archives are subject to gaps and incompleteness that make it difficult to determine whether the available information adequately represent the population of interest. A demographer interested in the life span of ancient Romans investigated tombstones to find birth and death dates—but found biases. Tombstones that survive to the present are more likely to represent the middle and upper classes than the poor, and it even appeared that "a wife was more likely to get an inscribed tablet if she died before her husband than if she outlived him" (Durand, 1960). Researchers have examined suicide notes for clues to the mental states of suicide victims, but the majority of suicide victims do not leave notes. Are their mental states the same as those of note writers? And archives can contain information that is simply wrong. Stamp (1929) offered a friendly warning about the accuracy of archival records that is just as timely today as when he first said it:

> The government is very keen on amassing statistics. They collect them, add them, raise them to the *n*th power, take the cube root and prepare wonderful diagrams. But what you must never forget is that every one of these figures comes in the first instance from the *chowty dar* (village

watchman), who just puts down what he damn pleases (Stamp, 1929, pp. 258–259).

Summary

A concern with naturalness is the main defining feature of most of the research methods considered in this chapter. In contrast to laboratory and survey research, many forms of observation and archivally based research stress natural behaviors, treatments, and settings so that some of the potential problems stemming from the respondent's awareness of being a research participant can be avoided. For certain types of research questions, particularly those dealing with the naturally occurring rates or patterns of behaviors, methods like those described in this chapter are the most appropriate. Observational methods give particular stress to natural behaviors and settings, although the specific methods vary in their emphasis. Archival methods (with the exception of research survey archives) also emphasize the use of records that are kept by or about individuals in the natural course of their activities, so they similarly offer access to natural behavior that is unaffected by the research process. Archives are particularly well suited for the analysis of the effects of natural treatments, such as natural or human-created disasters or social changes.

In this chapter, as elsewhere in the book, we emphasize the use of appropriate research techniques to improve the validity of findings. The specific technique that is most appropriate depends on the nature of the question as well as other factors, but for a wide range of research questions, observational and archival methods are certainly strong candidates for adoption. Naturalness in research can increase the external and construct validity of results, as many examples cited indicate, especially with respect to participants' awareness of research and associated problems like social desirability biases in responding. Yet, these methods are characteristically weaker on internal validity and other aspects of construct validity; we often cannot be certain that a measure is affected by only the single desired construct rather than multiple possibilities. It is when a research hypothesis has been tested, with converging results, by both observational or archival methods and laboratory, questionnaire, or other more reactive methods that we can be most confident of its validity.

Key Concepts

accretion measures
behavior setting survey
checklists/category systems
content analysis
continuous real-time measurement
ecological observation
encoding
erosion measures
ethological approach
mode of observation
molecular behaviors
natural behaviors
natural events
natural settings
nonreactive measures
observer drift
physical traces
research survey archives
sequential analysis

spurious association
statistical archives
systematic observation
time-interval sampling
time-point sampling
verbal records

On the Web

http://www.nara.gov/ The Web site for the National Archives and Records Administration, an independent federal agency that oversees the management of all federal records. Includes links to the Federal Register, history/genealogy sites, and veterans' services archives.

http://dmoz.org/Reference/Archives/Government_Archives/ Links to over 50 national and international government archives, including the Bureau of Transportation statistics, Code of Federal Regulations, Supreme Court decisions, National Security archive of declassified documents.

http://www.fedstats.gov/ This site bills itself as "the gateway to statistics from over 100 U.S. Federal agencies." Very easy to navigate, allows searching by topic, state, or federal agency.

http://www.norc.uchicago.edu/homepage.htm The official Web site of the National Opinion Research Center, including information about the General Social Survey as well as other large-scale sample surveys conducted by the National Opinion Research Center.

http://www.noldus.com/ Web site for the Noldus Company, originators of The Observer and other software programs for observational research.

Further Reading

Bakeman, R., & Gottman, J. M. (1997). *Observing interaction: An introduction to sequential analysis* (2nd ed.). New York: Cambridge University Press.

Bakeman, R., & Quera, V. (1995). *Analyzing interaction: Sequential analysis with SDIS and GSEQ*. New York: Cambridge University Press.

Hill, M. R. (1993). *Archival strategies and techniques.* Thousand Oaks, CA: Sage Publications.

Mook, D. G. (1983). In defense of external invalidity. *American Psychologist, 38*, 379–387.

Russell, C. H., & Megaard, I. (1988). *The General Social Survey, 1972–1986: The state of the American people.* New York: Springer-Verlag.

CHAPTER

16

Qualitative Research

Qualitative research takes many forms and is called by many names. One form consists of open-ended questions embedded in a structured interview or questionnaire; we covered this form of qualitative research in Chapter 6. The other forms rely almost entirely on open-ended explorations of people's words, thoughts, actions, and intentions. This kind of research includes narrative analysis, focus groups, oral history, and participant observation. Although these research strategies vary in their goals and methods, they all share the critical defining characteristic of **qualitative research**: Instead of researchers imposing their own hypotheses, themes, and categories on the participants' responses, the participants relate stories about their lives that enable the researcher to generate hypotheses and themes. In this chapter, we describe several of the major forms of qualitative research used frequently in the social sciences, beginning with the most structured form of qualitative research—narrative analysis—and concluding with the least structured—participant observation. In doing so, we hope to communicate a sense of the atmosphere of creativity, spontaneity, and genuineness that qualitative research entails.

Narrative Analysis

Narratives are oral or written accounts of personal experience, told either to oneself or somebody else. Narratives can be distinguished from simple responses to open-ended questions in that they have the structure of a story: There is a beginning and an end, protagonists and antagonists, and a plot. Narratives can even be fictional, as in the case of fairy tales or myths, although in social science research we are normally concerned with narratives that are accounts of actual events in people's lives.

Narratives can be accounts that are produced specifically for a given research study, or they can be derived from preexisting archives, for example, collections of letters, diaries, or autobiographies. In the former case, the researcher has considerable control over the conditions under which the narratives are obtained and can focus the narrative in a direction that best suits the goals of the research. In the latter case, there is less control in terms of both sampling and content of the narratives; however, one benefit of archival narratives is that they are generally less likely to be biased by demand characteristics. Moreover, there might be some research questions or populations for which archival narratives are available, as in studies of suicide notes (e.g., Osgood & Walker, 1959). Archival narratives might also be relied on when the research questions are longitudinal in nature. For example, a group of researchers analyzed the diaries written by nuns when they were in their twenties (Snowden et al.,1996). Remarkably, a measure of "idea density" as reflected in the diaries predicted which nuns were likely to develop Alzheimer's disease over 50 years later. This kind of longitudinal evidence is both impressive and convincing, considering the fact that Alzheimer's disease was not even known as a separate diagnosis at the time the diaries were written.

Researchers use narrative analysis because they believe that narratives yield information that is not accessible by more traditional methods. Questionnaires using traditional Likert-type response scales are not optimal for eliciting people's innermost thoughts, hopes, and feelings, nor for capturing complex mental phenomena such as moral reasoning or cognitive styles (Smith, 2000). Narratives can reveal themes that researchers did not even think to ask about. As such, narrative analysis may be particularly helpful in the early stages of a research program, when the researcher is trying to identify the variables that are critical to understanding a phenomenon.

Research Example of Narrative Analysis

The richness and beauty of narrative data is nicely illustrated in a study by Laura King and her colleagues on parents' adaptation to having a child born with Down's syndrome (King, Scollon, Ramsey, & Williams, 2000). The advantages and perhaps even necessity for narrative analysis in a project of this nature become immediately obvious. It would be difficult, if not impossible, to capture the range and complexity of emotions felt by parents upon learning of their child's diagnosis with Down's syndrome using a traditional paper-and-pencil questionnaire. An item such as "On a scale of 1 to 7, how distressed were you when you found out that your child had Down's syndrome?" seems both naive and insensitive.

In King et al.'s (2000) study, 87 parents of children with Down's syndrome were recruited from mailing lists of various Down's syndrome support groups. Participants first filled out a variety of questionnaires measuring subjective well-being, ego development, and stress-related growth. Next, parents were asked to write a narrative "about the moment when you first were told that your child had Down's syndrome." These narratives were subsequently coded by judges for various features of the stories, such as the presence of foreshadowing, happy beginnings, happy endings, degree of closure expressed, and degree of negative emotion experienced. Two years later the participants were mailed another packet including the same questionnaires. The primary goal of the study was to determine whether features of the narratives written by parents were associated with changes in subjective well-being, ego development, and stress-related growth.

Analyses produced several interesting findings. Foreshadowing and happy endings in the stories were associated with greater subjective well-being at both time periods. A strong sense of closure and accommodation in the stories, on the other hand, was associated with greater stress-related growth. In other words, the parents who felt best about their experience are not necessarily the ones who grew the most personally from it. The divergence among these findings led the authors to conclude that "the stories we tell about our life experiences may illuminate two pathways—one to satisfaction and one to maturity" (King et al., 2000, p. 530).

The great advantage of narrative analysis is that researchers can provide excerpts from the narratives written by participants to illustrate important conclusions in addition to reporting more standard quantitative analyses from the coded variables. For example, King et al. (2000) provided quotes illustrating a happy ending in the story:

> I know my daughter is quite special. It's as if she's part of another race or from another planet. She's definitely wired differently. And I think those wires are hooked directly to God. She's the closest I've come to an angel on Earth. (p. 519)

Here is an excerpt from a narrative showing a sad ending:

> We were given an *Exceptional Parents* magazine . . . . I found a picture of a crib with a lid on it, like a cage. I remember wondering, what do we have? What are we faced with? I also remember thinking that now we'll never be normal. (p. 519)

Here is an example of a narrative showing the parents' attempt to accommodate to the diagnosis:

> I cried a lot. The pain was so deep. I felt cheated—I could hardly function. I was so absorbed with my own fears. But I did regroup. I did grow. And I did learn to accept the situation. That opened the door for me to bond and love my child. But it took time. (p. 521)

In each case, the narrative excerpts provide an impression that is much more informative than the mere variable labels of "happy ending," "sad ending," or "accommodation." Narrative analysis thus aids importantly in demonstrating construct validity because the meaning of a variable is clearly communicated through the judicious reporting of narrative excerpts.

Analyzing and Reporting Narrative Data

Narrative analysis is unlike the rest of the qualitative research methods we discuss in this chapter in that most social scientists who collect narrative accounts ultimately code them for variables that can be subjected to traditional quantitative analyses. As we saw in the King et al. (2000) study, excerpts from narratives are quoted to make points or illustrate important conclusions, but the primary analyses tend to be quantitative in nature.

To perform such analyses, the qualitative narratives must be translated into quantitative information using a content analysis. **Content analysis** is the process of extracting desired information from a text by systematically and objectively identifying specified characteristics of the text (Smith, 2000). Content analysis takes one or both of two major approaches: coding the narratives according to discrete themes or categories and rating the narratives on continuous dimensions.

The King et al. (2000) study provides examples of both approaches to content coding. First, three coders read each narrative for the presence of foreshadowing, happy beginning, or happy ending—variables that are on a nominal scale. A narrative received a score of 1 for each category if the feature (foreshadowing, etc.) was present and a 0 if it were not. In addition to these nominal variables, the narratives were rated on several interval-scaled variables. For example, raters scored each narrative using 7-point scales on such variables as how active the participant was in the story, how traumatic the experience was, and how much denial was present in the narrative.

The number and type of variables that are coded in a given study depend on the goals of the research. Variables can be identified on theoretical grounds before the narratives are obtained, or they can be derived after reading the narratives over and detecting recurring themes. In general, it is better not to fall into the trap of "over-coding" the narratives; if too many variables are coded, the researcher is in danger of capitalizing on chance in the analyses, meaning that some of the results will appear to be statistically significant but would not likely replicate using another sample from the same population. A better strategy is to outline a concise list of hypotheses prior to obtaining the narratives and to choose a limited number of coded variables that would test those hypotheses.

A critical aspect of content analysis is the reliability of coding. As described in Chapter 15, at least two raters should code all of the narratives, and the reliability among the raters should be estimated and reported. Raters should be carefully trained prior to working with the actual narratives. Variables should be explicitly defined, examples of categories should be provided, and raters should practice coding a sample set of narratives until satisfactory agreement has been demonstrated. Interval-scaled ratings are generally more subjective than nominal-scaled coding, and depending on the judgment being made, as many as five or six raters might be needed to attain adequate reliability. Raters should make their judgments independently, and they should be unaware of the status of the participant on any relevant independent variable.

Another approach to content analysis is to use computer software specifically designed for that purpose. Examples are General Inquirer, Linguistic Inquiry and Word Count (LIWC), ATLAS.ti, Non-numerical Unstructured Data with powerful processes of Indexing Searching and Theorizing (NUD*IST), and Ethnograph. What these programs do in general is to compare the text in question to **dictionaries,** which are either provided by the software or created by the researcher for a particular study. For example, the LIWC program (Pennebaker & Francis, 1996) processes the target text one word at a time and compares it against the program dictionary. If the target word matches one of the entries in the dictionary, the corresponding word category is increased by one count. The LIWC program thus provides frequencies for up to 85 linguistic variables, falling into four basic categories: linguistic dimensions (e.g., word count, personal pronouns, number of questions); psychological constructs (e.g., positive and negative emotion words, sensory-related words, social processes); relativity in time and space; and personal concerns (e.g., leisure activities, work and household-related words). Table 16.1 lists the LIWC variables grouped into the four categories.

TABLE 16.1 VARIABLES CODED BY THE LIWC CONTENT ANALYSIS PROGRAM (PENNEBAKER & FRANCIS, 1996)

	Standard Linguistic Dimensions	
Word count	Total pronouns	Negations
Words per sentence	First person singular	Assents
Number of questions	First person plural	Articles
Unique words	Total first person	Prepositions
% words in dictionary	Total second person	Numbers
% words > 6 letters	Total third person	
	Psychological Processes	
Affective Processes		
Positive emotions	Positive feelings	Optimism and energy
Negative emotions	Anxiety or fear	Anger
Sadness or depression		
Cognitive Processes		
Causation	Insight (e.g., think)	Discrepancy (e.g., should)
Inhibition	Tentative (e.g., maybe)	Certainty (e.g., always)
Sensory and Perceptual Processes		
Seeing	Hearing	Feeling
Social Processes		
Communication	Friends	Other references to people
Family	Humans	

(Continued)

TABLE 16.1 VARIABLES CODED BY THE LIWC CONTENT ANALYSIS PROGRAM (PENNEBAKER & FRANCIS, 1996) (CONTINUED)

	Relativity	
Time		
Past tense verb	Present tense verb	Future tense verb
Space		
Up Down	Inclusive	Exclusive
	Personal Concerns	
Occupation		
School	Job or work	Achievement
Leisure Activity		
Home Music	Sports	Television and movies
Money and Financial Issues		
Metaphysical Issues		
Religion	Death and dying	
Physical States and Functions		
Body states Sleeping, dreaming	Sex and sexuality Grooming	Eating, drinking, dieting

As with any methodology, computerized content analysis has its advantages and disadvantages. A major advantage of programs like LIWC is that they can perform a large amount of tedious work very quickly. It would take a crew of research assistants weeks to code the 85 LIWC variables from an average-sized sample of narratives. The main disadvantage is that the variables provided by the program might not correspond exactly to the researchers' need. Also, the content coding performed by the computer is crude; it essentially tabulates words that fall into various categories and cannot handle verbal subtleties such as sarcasm. A phrase like "Man, that show was bad," meaning that it was actually good, would be coded as a negative emotion instead by the computer. Lastly, programs such as LIWC might provide too much of a good thing; researchers might be tempted to analyze all 85 LIWC variables when only a few are theoretically relevant. Performing 85 analyses without compelling theoretical reasons for doing so is likely to result in nonreplicable findings.

An additional means of generating information using narratives is to have participants respond to a set of questions after they have finished writing their narratives. An example of this approach is seen in a study of how teasing is used in different relationships (Bollmer, Harris, & Dotson, 2001). Participants were asked to write three narratives about occasions on which they teased a friend, a romantic partner, and a family member. Immediately following the writing of each narrative, the participants completed a 10-item paper-and-pencil measure asking them to give, on 9-point scales, their impressions of their own motives for teasing in that particular incident and how the target of the teasing responded. For example, participants were asked how hurt and annoyed the target was, how humorous the teasing was, how much they regretted the teasing now, and to what extent they teased the target for each of three motives: to "put them in their place," to point out a weakness, or to gain their attention.

There is an important advantage to obtaining this kind of information in addition to the content analysis provided by objective judges. Having participants respond to standardized questions following a narrative ensures that comparable information is obtained from everybody in the study. Researchers typically have very little control over exactly what will be written in the narratives. Although a researcher can provide explicit instructions to the participant that request specific kinds of information, such instructions obviously cannot be enforced. For example, in the Bollmer et al. (2001) study, the researchers wanted a measure of the regret felt by the teaser. Many of the participants spontaneously mentioned feeling regret ("I feel really bad about it now"), but many did not. Does that mean they did not feel regret? Not necessarily; maybe it simply did not occur to those participants to write about their regretful feelings in describing the incident. Having all participants explicitly rate how much regret they felt ensured that all participants considered the issue and that information would be obtained to allow direct comparisons among them.

Of course, there is nothing preventing researchers from conducting both an objective content analysis as well as having participants complete standardized questionnaires about their narratives; in fact, having both kinds of information can be informative as well as provide valuable evidence of convergent validity. That was the case in the Bollmer et al. (2001) example. In addition to the 10-item questionnaire completed by the participant, a group of four judges read each narrative and rated it on how hurt and angry the target was, how much regret was shown by the teaser, how much the teaser enjoyed the teasing, how the target responded behaviorally to the teasing, and the overall positivity of the consequences of the teasing. Note that there was some overlap between the constructs rated by the judges and the items completed by the participants. This enabled the researchers to assess the degree of convergence among self-reports and judges' ratings, as well as to identify areas of intriguing difference. For instance, what does it mean when the objective judges deem the target to have been hurt badly by the teasing but the teaser rates the target as not having been hurt at all?

Asking participants to relate stories from their lives that illustrate a given research question is a highly effective yet curiously underutilized research tool. The stories told by participants convey emotion and detail that is impossible to reduce to numbers. It is this richness of emotion and detail that makes narrative analysis so appealing and informative. Given the minimal time investment involved in obtaining narrative accounts, there is no real reason for not collecting narratives in any research endeavor. The question is therefore not whether or why narrative analysis should be conducted but rather why so few researchers in the social sciences avail themselves of this rich source of information.

Focus Groups

Focus groups are structured group interviews. They bring together a small group of interacting individuals who discuss, under the guidance of a moderator, the topic of interest to the researcher. The first documented use of focus groups occurred soon after World War II when groups were assembled in an effort to evaluate audience response to radio programs (Stewart & Shamdasani, 1990). Since that time, focus groups have enjoyed immense popularity in market research; they are, perhaps, the bread and butter of market research firms. However, in the past decade the use of focus groups has spread to other areas of social science research. In this section, we describe the typical format and process of a focus group, provide examples of how focus groups might be used to study social behavior, and conclude with a discussion of the advantages and disadvantages of using focus groups.

How Focus Groups Are Structured and Conducted

A typical focus group consists of 6 to 10 individuals. Fewer than 6 makes it less likely that the desired diversity of opinions will be elicited; more than 10 makes it difficult for everyone to express their opinions fully. In most cases, it is desirable for focus group members to be previously unacquainted with one another. Lack of familiarity promotes free expression of ideas and opinions that might not be forthcoming if members feel constrained by what they have said in the past to others in the group. However, there are times when it is not practical to have unacquainted members in the focus group. For example, suppose we wanted to conduct a focus group of high school principals to generate ideas for preventing school violence. Depending on the size of the city, most principals within a city would know each other. Conducting a focus group in which principals are flown in from a variety of cities would achieve the goal of unfamiliarity, but it probably would be prohibitively expensive.

Focus group members usually are selected because they share something in common that is relevant to the topic being researched. In market research, for example, the focus group might be composed of individuals who use the product in question or who constitute the target population for the product (e.g., female teenagers). Theory-testing research using focus groups often has specialized populations in mind such as breast cancer patients, lesbians and gay men, military personnel, teachers, African Americans, depressed people, and so forth. Research looking at the interactions between members of different groups might require several different focus groups. For example, a study looking at the quality of doctor-patient interactions might arrange separate focus groups for doctors and patients as well as a few mixed doctor-patient groups.

In short, the membership of a focus group tends to be more homogeneous than a random sample of the population. As such, focus groups are not representative of the general population, and findings that emerge from a focus group cannot be assumed to be true for the rest of the population, or indeed, for anybody else. We return to this point later in the chapter when we discuss the limitations of focus groups as a research tool.

All focus groups are led by a **moderator,** the researcher or a hired professional, and it is the presence and activities of the moderator that distinguish a focus group from an unstructured group discussion. The moderator is the key to the success of a focus group. Because leading a focus group appears to be easy, one might be tempted to conclude that all a moderator has to do is bring a group of people together, give them snacks, and have them talk about a topic. But it is not as easy as it seems, and the quality of information obtained from a focus group is directly tied to the skills of the moderator in monitoring and controlling the discussion and eliciting insights and revelations from the group members. A useful analogy is that of psychotherapy: One can tell another person about one's personal problems, but real therapeutic progress is only likely to take place when the other person is a skilled clinician who is trained to bring about insight and behavior change.

The moderator must engage in considerable advance preparation to make a focus group successful. First, the research objectives must be identified and clarified. In applied research, the objectives are often provided by the client ("Find out why nobody is buying our widgets!"), but in any case the objectives usually need to be redefined and narrowed. In a research context, considerable expertise with the topic of interest is required to define the objectives in a way that will elicit theoretically useful information from participants. Along with identifying the objectives of the focus group, a **focus group guide** is developed. The guide consists of the major topics and questions that will be raised in the focus group discussion. The number of questions that can be asked in a focus group is surprisingly small. The recommended maximum duration of a focus group is $1\frac{1}{2}$ to 2 hours (even shorter with children)—much beyond that and the group members' attention wanders. Thus, only two or three major issues with two or three subissues each can be considered by any focus group.

The phrasing and sequencing of questions in the guide is also critical. For obvious reasons, moderators should avoid closed-ended, yes-no questions. Not nearly so obvious is the fact that moderators should also avoid asking "why" questions. The reason is that "why" questions almost always elicit rationalizations, particularly socially desirable rationalizations. Participants might feel pressured to give what they perceive to be the response expected by the moderator or that will cast them in a positive light. More generally, "why" questions might be less fruitful because people might not be consciously aware of the motives underlying their choices and behavior (Nisbett &

Wilson, 1977). A better way to get at participants' motivations is to ask about what they do and how they feel about it. From a detailed description of these actions, thoughts, and feelings, the reasons for behavior can be more easily and accurately inferred.

Table 16.2 shows an example of an interview guide that could be used in a focus group of adolescents aimed at discovering factors that encourage and discourage teenage alcohol use. Note that all questions are open-ended and grouped in a logical manner. Note also that the questions regarding the factors that encourage drinking among teenagers are asked before the questions regarding the factors that discourage drinking; often it is more productive to discuss the emergence of a problem before discussing how to solve it.

Once the focus group guide has been developed, participants are recruited. Because focus groups are not intended to be representative samples, convenience samples often are used. Unless the topic of the discussion is of special interest or relevance for the members (e.g., if a group was conducted for victims of spouse abuse), incentives might be necessary in order to get people to participate. The discussion itself is held in a comfortable meeting room, often equipped with one-way mirrors through which the researcher or sponsoring client can observe the proceedings.

Most focus groups begin with the moderator making introductions and describing the ground rules for the discussion. These **ground rules** include explaining the purpose and format of the focus group; emphasizing that everybody's ideas count and

TABLE 16.2 EXAMPLE OF A FOCUS GROUP INTERVIEW GUIDE

Major Objective: Determine what encourages and discourages teenagers from drinking alcohol.

Question 1: What factors encourage or pressure teenagers to drink?

Subissue 1: What do your friends think about teenage drinking? What do kids at your school typically do for fun? How is alcohol viewed by your friends and the other kids at school?

Subissue 2: How is teen drinking portrayed in movies or on TV? What usually happens when teenagers drink in movies or on TV shows?

Subissue 3: Under what circumstances is a teenager likely to have the opportunity to drink? When is a teenager likely to feel pressured to drink?

Question 2: What factors discourage teenagers from drinking?

Subissue 1: What do your parents think about teenage drinking? What are your family rules? How does that affect your behavior?

Subissue 2: What kinds of things have you learned about the effects of alcohol from school or the media? What are your school's rules regarding drinking?

Subissue 3: What do you think parents or teachers could do to prevent teenagers from drinking? What do you think they *should* do?

that the moderator wants to hear from everybody; that only one person should speak at a time; and that people should refrain from criticizing others' opinions. Perhaps the most important aspect of the ground rules concerns confidentiality. The moderator assures participants that only group-level information will be reported and nobody will be individually identified. Participants also are requested to keep what they hear during the focus group confidential; however, because the researcher does not have control over what the participants say after the session is over, it should be made clear to the participants that their confidentiality cannot be guaranteed. Most focus groups are either audiotaped or videotaped, and participants sign a consent form in which they are told that the session will be recorded.

Once the preliminaries are out of the way, the focus group session begins. The moderator generally follows the focus group guide, but the discussion is not entirely scripted. Part of what makes the moderator's role so difficult is that he or she must be able to guide the conversation while carefully processing what is being said. The moderator needs to be able to identify when follow-up questions are needed and what those follow-up questions should be. It is through the careful probing and following up of statements that focus groups generate the most useful information; a moderator who sticks completely to the guide is likely to obtain only superficial material. Depending on what is said, the moderator might need to abandon the guide to pursue a promising avenue of discussion. Many focus groups include an observer who takes notes on the process and records impressions so that the moderator can devote full attention to guiding the conversation.

One of the main tasks of the moderator is to make sure the conversation stays on track; with only 60 or 90 minutes to achieve its goals, a focus group cannot afford to digress often or for any length of time. In the event of digression, the moderator must refocus the conversation without annoying the person who digressed. The moderator also must prevent one or two individuals from dominating the conversation as well as make sure that even the shyest participant speaks up. The moderator therefore should be skilled at interpreting nonverbal behavior. There can be considerable conformity pressure operating in a focus group, and the moderator needs to be able to identify the subtle nonverbal signs of discomfort that indicate that a participant does not agree with what is being said. Prompts such as, "There might be other ways to view that issue. So-and-so, what do you think?" might be needed to elicit the dissenting opinion. Throughout the discussion, it is important that the moderator establish friendly rapport with the participants but take care to avoid appearing to approve or disapprove of particular statements being made. Participants generally desire to please the moderator, and any kind of verbal or nonverbal reinforcements (head nods, "uh-huhs," or "goods") might quickly bias the direction of the discussion and compromise the quality of the information.

Once the main discussion is completed, a "cooling down" exercise is often helpful. The moderator might ask each participant to describe the most important thing they heard during the discussion. The moderator then reminds participants to keep the discussion confidential and thanks them for their help. Immediately following the session, the moderator might consult with observers to ensure that they record their impressions of the discussion while it is fresh in their minds.

Generally, more than one focus group is conducted for a given objective. One rule of thumb is to keep having focus groups until few or no new insights are volunteered; this usually happens after four or five groups. The information yielded by focus groups rarely is in a format that can be subjected to inferential testing or statistical analysis. Rather, the comments made in response to each of the questions are classified according to broad themes, and a report is written summarizing the contents. Thus, focus groups capture the true spirit of qualitative research—the emphasis is on hypothesis generation rather than hypothesis testing.

Case Study of the Strategic Use of Focus Groups

We turn now to a real-world example of using focus groups in social science research. The goal of this research was to develop televised public service announcements (PSAs) for use in an antidrug campaign (Palmgreen, Donohew, Lorch, Hoyle, & Stephenson, 2001). Past media campaigns featuring prevention PSAs have revealed disappointingly small effects (Rogers & Storey, 1987). One possible reason for this is that the PSAs have not effectively targeted the population most at risk. Therefore, a major goal of the research program by Palmgreen and his colleagues was to create antidrug PSAs that would appeal to high-sensation-seeking adolescents, a population that previous research has identified as being especially susceptible to drug experimentation and abuse (Zuckerman, 1994).

Sensation seekers are people who like to go hang gliding or bungee jumping or who will eat chocolate-covered grasshoppers for the fun of it. Sensation seekers are also more likely to be attracted to the altered states of consciousness that alcohol and drug use cause. Because they are a population at increased risk of drug use, it would be particularly beneficial to design PSAs that would appeal especially to high-sensation-seeking teens.

Palmgreen and his colleagues chose a focus group methodology to answer the question of what kind of PSAs would appeal to high-sensation-seeking adolescents (Palmgreen et al., 2001). Three sets of focus groups were conducted; members were students in the eighth through eleventh grades. Participants in the focus groups had previously been administered a paper-and-pencil measure of sensation seeking, and only adolescents who scored highest on the measure were recruited to take part in the focus groups. The first set of focus groups was devoted to discussing the kinds of risks associated with using drugs. For any kind of educational campaign to be effective, the recipients of the campaign must believe that the consequences of drug use portrayed in the campaign are credible and perceived as deterrents. A good example of how a portrayal can backfire if that is not the case is the movie *Reefer Madness*, which was originally designed as an antimarijuana film but is now regularly shown in college towns to the great hilarity of the audience. Thus, the first set of focus groups addressed two major questions: (1) What are the specific kinds of risks—physical, legal, social, economic—that are realistic for particular drugs? (2) To what degree do these risks influence people like themselves to use or not use drugs?

The goal of the second set of focus groups was to identify features of PSAs that would appeal to high-sensation-seeking teens. To accomplish this, focus group members were shown a variety of advertisements and PSAs that had been previously produced and were asked to comment on specific features of the spots that did or did not appeal to them. The researchers used these focus groups to derive high sensation value criteria for producing PSAs; these criteria included characteristics such as novelty, drama, surprise, and strong emotional appeals.

The last set of focus groups used in the Palmgreen et al. research was to help in selecting the final antidrug PSAs to be produced. Using the results from the first two sets of focus groups, the research team and a professional television producer created storyboards sketching a variety of possible PSAs. These storyboards (rough impressions of what a PSA would look like, describing the scenes that would be shown and the verbal content but not entailing the full costs of a polished production) were then shown to a new set of focus groups, whose members commented on the aspects they liked most and least about each ad. Focus group members were also asked about the perceived attention value of each of the possible PSAs, as well as their emotional impact, perceived realism, and effectiveness in deterring drug use.

The PSAs identified as most effective by the focus groups were then professionally produced and aired in a large field experiment involving two metropolitan areas. Over a 32-month period, face-to-face interviews with randomly selected teenagers indicated that the targeted PSAs were highly effective in decreasing marijuana use among high-sensation-seeking teenagers; as predicted, marijuana use among low-sensation-seeking teenagers was at a very low rate and not affected by the media campaign (Palmgreen et al., 2001).

For several reasons the Palmgreen et al. (2001) antidrug campaign study is a good example of how focus groups can be used in social science research. First, it highlights the primary strength of focus groups, which is that they are best used in the hypothesis and idea generation stage of research. Palmgreen et al. used them to discover the best ways of creating an antidrug message. Second, this example shows just how cost-effective focus groups can be. Focus groups are an economical way of doing research; even if one is paying participants (usually $15 to $25 per participant is sufficient) and a moderator to conduct the groups, a full set of focus groups can be conducted for under $2,000. Contrast that amount to what it costs to prepare antidrug PSAs professionally and then buy television time to air them (hundreds of thousands of dollars at least). With so much money at stake, it was crucial that the researchers only produce PSAs that were likely to be effective, and the focus groups enabled them to do that. Thus, focus groups are highly recommended at the formative stage of any large-scale or expensive treatment or intervention.

What Focus Groups Can and Cannot Do

The foregoing discussion should make clear a primary appeal of focus groups: They are quick, easy, and cheap. Why run hundreds of participants in a months-long study when one can run three focus groups for a total of 20 participants in one weekend and get the same answers? Phrased that way, the growing popularity of focus groups as a research tool is easy to understand. The catch, of course, is in the assumption that focus groups yield "the same answers" as do other research methods. The reality is that focus groups are very good at generating certain kinds of information but not at all good for certain other purposes.

We already have stressed the primary practical advantages of focus groups—their convenience and ease of use. We would be remiss if we did not stress the theoretical advantages of focus groups as well—their ability to explore ideas and suggest hypotheses. The best uses of focus groups are in the early stages of a research project or product development. Focus groups can be especially helpful in these early stages because researchers tend to latch onto favorite ideas early on and often cannot see other possibilities or drawbacks to their favored hypothesis or plan. A quick and decisive dashing of an idea in the context of a focus group discussion ("Who are you trying to kid? There's no way that would work.") can end up saving the researcher considerable time and energy from pursuing an ultimately doomed hypothesis or product.

Focus groups also are invaluable for gaining access to the unique concerns and perspective of the target audience, which can sometimes be difficult for the researcher to grasp. Trying to figure out what kind of persuasive appeal would work best for a 10-year-old boy can be challenging for a 40-year-old female researcher, as it would be to guess the deepest hopes and fears of a 70-year-old. Rather than trying to second-guess the 10-year-old's preferences or the 70-year-old's fears, it is easier and more accurate to bring them in for a focus group session. When such groups are conducted, the researcher almost always gains new insights and discovers where his or her preconceptions were wrong. For example, researchers conducting one focus group discovered that some young children interpreted the phrase "alcohol-free" to mean free beverages that contained alcohol, a miscommunication that could have serious ramifications if not detected.

Focus groups also are helpful when designing experimental materials or questionnaires for a more traditional laboratory or survey study. The researcher can discover how to phrase questions using the everyday language of the target population, and this process can be quicker than the traditional procedure of creating a questionnaire, pilot-testing it on a small sample, and revising the questionnaire when ambiguities are identified in pilot testing. Focus groups can be helpful in more than just the beginning stages of research, though. For example, focus groups have been used extensively in evaluation research, by which researchers attempt to determine whether a given program or intervention has been effective.

Lastly, there is another advantage of focus group methodology that is not normally considered, and that is the benefits that accrue to the participants: Focus groups can be an empowering experience for many participants. Members of focus groups are treated not as low-status experimental "subjects" but rather as full partners in the research enterprise, working collaboratively with the researcher to address an important question. Most participants greatly appreciate being considered and treated as though they hold expertise on the topic in question, and they are gratified to feel that they are involved in something in a way that can make a real difference. In sum, participants generally leave focus groups feeling better about the scientific process than do participants in more traditional forms of research.

Every research methodology has limitations, and focus groups are not without theirs. The major limitation is one we touched on earlier in the chapter, the problem of generalizability. Unless members of a focus group are randomly selected, a focus group is not representative of the population, and conclusions drawn from the focus group cannot be safely generalized to the population. In this respect, market research firms perhaps rely too heavily on focus groups. They use focus groups to make decisions about which products are likely to be successful, yet that is a question that can best be, and maybe only, answered through careful sampling and surveying. For example, the first set of focus groups discussing the newly designed Ford Taurus reacted quite negatively, calling it a "jelly bean" on wheels (Market Navigation, Inc., 2000). If Ford had stopped right there, they would have abandoned one of the best-selling models in automotive history.

Moreover, focus groups are even less likely to be representative than other convenience samples found in social science research. This is because focus group sessions involve social groups and are thus vulnerable to all the biasing dynamics that can occur in groups. Although moderators attempt to encourage equal participation from all group members, one or two individuals can dominate a focus group discussion and set the tone for others' contributions. The results of a focus group could therefore reflect only one person's opinions rather than the desired-for diversity of opinion. Yet researchers or marketing firms who would never dream of going along with a single person's judgment often do not hesitate to accept the conclusions of a focus group.

Another disadvantage of focus groups is that the researcher has substantially less control over the information obtained than in other research contexts. In a questionnaire study, or even an individual interview, the researcher can set the agenda and specify exactly the questions that will be responded to and the data that will be elicited. In a focus group, however, the participants can and do talk to and ask questions of each other that wander far astray of what the researcher intended. Of course, the very feature of focus groups that results in less control for the researcher also produces the synergy that makes focus groups such a powerful tool. Researchers who use focus groups thus make the conscious choice to surrender control in order to gain insight.

Oral History

Oral history is a method for learning about the past by interviewing individuals who have experienced that past. Oral histories might center around important historical events, for example, the civil rights movement or the Holocaust, or they might center around important life roles or rites of passage, for example, what it means to be African American or becoming a parent. Interviews usually are tape-recorded, and the tapes or transcripts of the interviews are usually deposited in archives, libraries, or special collections so that other researchers can access them in the future. By examining what people have to say about their past, it is possible to gain insights about universals of human experience as well as an appreciation of how human nature has changed.

As with other forms of qualitative research, no attempt is made to select a random or representative sample in oral history, although in a few notable cases (e.g., the oral history of Holocaust survivors), researchers might attempt to interview the entire population, that is, every relevant individual. Usually, however, a smaller and nonsystematic subset of potential respondents is selected for interviewing, often using snowball sampling methods (see Chapter 8). The researcher generally contacts the respondent ahead of time, describes the project, explains why the respondent was chosen, and requests permission to conduct and record the interview. The researcher often mails the respondent an outline of the questions to be covered in the interview in advance so that the respondent will have had the chance to think about and mentally prepare for the interview.

On the day of the interview itself, the respondent signs an informed consent form and a **deed of gift form** that allows the researcher to use the interview tapes and transcripts for research purposes and to place the tapes in an archive for public use. The information obtained in oral history is unlike that usually obtained by social scientists. Instead of guaranteeing anonymity or assuring participants that their responses will never be individually identified but rather aggregated and presented in group form, the whole point of oral history is to preserve each individual's story in its unique form. Participants generally are offered the opportunity to have their identities concealed in transcripts and to have sealed those portions of the interview tapes that identify them, but many respondents choose to remain fully identifiable. It is important for researchers to explain clearly to interviewees what their choices and rights are regarding their identification and to document carefully the choices that were made. In many cases the respondents choose not to sign the deed of gift until after they review the transcript of their interview and are satisfied that the transcript faithfully reproduces their experience. Table 16.3 contains a sample deed of gift form that could be used in oral history research.

We illustrate oral history methods using extended quotes from a study by Barbara Levy Simon (1987) on the lives of women who were never married. Fifty women talked with Simon about their never-married lives, and from their stories she examined their views of being single, of family, intimacy, and work. The women's names were omitted or changed when their accounts were published, but their words remained in their original voices. For example:

> How dare I fail to marry? How peculiar. How brazen. How sad. Or so many believe. Were I weak in the knees, I might believe that too. But fortunately, my knees are steady and hold me up fine when people give me those patronizing looks and commiserating tones.
>
> As an eighty-two-year old, it's easy to ignore the labels attached to those of us who stayed single. It used to be harder. For example, when I was about forty, my boss asked me out of the blue if I was still in love with my father. By then, I knew enough to make jokes about such foolishness. The

TABLE 16.3 EXAMPLE OF A DEED OF GIFT FORM FOR ORAL HISTORIES

Deed of Gift Form

I, [name of respondent], hereby give to [name of sponsoring organization] for scholarly and educational use the recordings of the interview(s) conducted with me on [date of interview], and I grant to [sponsor] all of the rights I possess in those recordings, including all intellectual property rights. I understand that [sponsor] grants me a nonexclusive license to make and to authorize others to make any use of the content of those recordings, and that [sponsor] will, at my request, make available a copy of those recordings for such use.

If I wish to remain anonymous in any interview transcript or reference to any information contained in this interview, I will specify this restriction here. The foregoing gift and grant of rights is subject to the following restrictions:

This agreement may be revised or amended by mutual consent of the parties undersigned.

Accepted by:

[interviewer's signature] ____________________ Date: __________

[interviewee's signature] ____________________ Date: __________

[interviewee's address and telephone number] ____________________

SOURCE: From the Indiana University Oral History Research Center. Copyright © 1999 by the Trustees of Indiana University. Adapted with permission.

> only alternative to humor that I could think of was committing mayhem or worse. And how could I explain to the judge that I killed my boss because he saw me as a silly spinster? (p. 1)

The women did not all tell the same story, but neither did they give 50 unrelated accounts. Thirty-eight women told of being voluntarily single, as illustrated in this quote:

> I loved my job running that office. I did it for twenty-seven years. It was not my whole life, certainly, but it was a highly significant portion. They wouldn't have fired me if I had gotten married. But I would have been unable to be a good wife and also do that job. It required nights, weekends, early mornings, and lots of disrupted plans. I didn't meet men in those days who would have understood my insistence that the job was as important to

> me as anything else. Now, I know that such men exist. But back then, they were nowhere to be found, at least not in my circles. (p. 44)

Among the 12 women who described themselves as involuntarily single, seven said that their responsibility for taking care of elderly parents conflicted with the demands of fiancés and the former took precedence:

> Finally, he [fiancé] told me that I had to put my father in a home if he was going to marry me. The only homes we could afford were disgusting. I refused, and, after a while, Joe stopped coming by. (p. 52)

Simon (1987) did not use the discovery that 38 out of 50 women in her study described themselves as voluntarily single to conclude that 76% of never-married women are voluntarily single. Hers is not a random sample, and she did not set out to estimate a frequency distribution in the population. Instead, her research describes the ways never-married women have constructed their lives and formed relationships with friends and family. The women were between the ages of 65 and 105 when they were interviewed, so they were able to report on their old age as well as youth. Simon undertook this study to reveal the diversity in the lives and views of women who might otherwise be considered "old maids." This diversity is vividly expressed in their own words:

> I am the first to bristle when married people or youngsters bandy about old ideas about "old maids." I set them straight right away about what single women are like. Mostly I make sure that they comprehend that ten single women present at least ten different approaches to living.
>
> But I also know that we single women do share some qualities in common out of necessity. For example, we tend to plan ahead; we're good savers; and we initiate lots of things. Emily Post, you see, never devised a trail guide for the single woman. One has to devise that trail guide for herself at each step. So we do. From the outside, that looks like we are independent in the extreme. From the inside, I would say instead that we are heavily dependent on ourselves as well as on those select ones we choose to lean on. (p. 151)

Simon (1987) concludes with the observation that these women enter retirement and old age not simply as self-reliant individuals. Each woman has learned throughout her lifetime to create her own mixture of independence and reliance on others, and "this mix has proved to be invaluable in the last third of her single life" (p. 182).

In many respects, oral history is a logical extension of narrative analysis. The primary difference is that narrative analysis usually centers on short stories (one to two pages) about specific events in a person's life. Oral history is much more ambitious in scope; a typical 60-to-90-minute oral history interview can translate into 15 to 20 double-spaced pages of typed transcript. The intent, moreover, is usually to capture a much broader and more comprehensive story of a person's life, with more detail about the people, context, and events leading up to the topic of interest.

A second difference between oral history and narrative analysis concerns how the stories are subsequently analyzed. In narrative analysis, as we have described, the stories told by participants are usually objectively coded and quantitatively analyzed. In oral history, on the other hand, the stories told by the participants often are the final product. The researcher might try to identify major themes evident in the life stories and draw conclusions about the factors that shaped the respondents' lives, but statistical analyses are generally absent and unnecessary. For example, in the report of her study of never-married women, Simon (1987) presented excerpts from her notes to show how the concept of a "spoiled identity," borrowed from Goffman's (1963) study of stigmas, is useful in understanding the lives of her sample of older women who had never married. She noted that 8 of the women had wished to marry and lead "normal" lives, 20 remained ambivalent about their "deviant" status, and 22 resisted in various ways the definition of themselves as "not normal." She did not draw any conclusions from the fact that 22 is greater than 20 or 8. The numbers are less important than the fact that the concept of "managing a spoiled identity" provides a useful framework for understanding the lives of these women. This theoretical construct and the various ways the women react to their marginal status provide a set of lenses through which to view the women. These are not the only possible frameworks or lenses, but they are useful for summarizing Simon's data.

Often there is an exciting sense of urgency associated with oral history. The job of the oral historian is to capture the firsthand experiences of an important group of people while they are still alive and able to report on their experiences. The memories of individuals who lived through major historical events and times are irreplaceable; once these individuals die, an important source of information regarding the event is lost forever. After an interview takes place, though, and the tapes are placed in a permanent archive, the memories live on and can be used for research in generations to come.

Participant Observation

In **participant observation** the researcher joins the social group that is the topic of study. As a participant observer, the researcher moves outside the controlled settings typical of experiments and interviews to the **field,** the uncontrolled, sometimes unpredictable, settings in which people live out their lives. Thus, in contrast to the experimenters and interviewers who try to maintain a professional distance from their participants or respondents, participant observers become engaged in the conversations, actions, and lives of the people they study. And unlike the standardized questions and procedures used by experimenters and interviewers, the questions and actions of a participant observer vary from one person and setting to the next. Instead of approaching each respondent with the same list of questions, as does an oral historian, a participant observer engages in conversations and observations that might continue for several days, weeks, or months. The conversations move in directions that cannot be anticipated, so the researcher's questions cannot be duplicated from one person to the next. To the extent that the researcher participates in the lives of the people under study, each day provides new opportunities as a result of the previous day's activities.

Some participant observers participate fully in the lives of the people they study, by being or becoming members of the group. Others remain outsiders, purely observers. Between these two extremes are countless possibilities, with more or less emphasis on being a participant. A common arrangement in participant observation is for an outsider to become a limited participant in the lives of others. Someone who cannot become a bona fide member of a group can still become accepted as a trusted friend and confidante. William Foote Whyte, a member of the Harvard Society of Fellows, conducted research in the field by hanging out with the Norton Street Gang (Whyte, 1943). He bowled with them, intervened when he thought he could help one of them, and benefited greatly as a researcher from their acceptance of him—he could go anywhere with them and observe and ask questions at will.

Sometimes a complex exchange occurs between the researcher and researched. Carol Stack (1975), a White researcher, became accepted in a family and circle of friends in a Black community she called "The Flats." She studied how family and friendship networks helped residents of that community cope with illness, unemployment, and housing evictions. The following description of how she became a participant observer is from her book, *All Our Kin:*

> I first came by the Walters' home in the summer of 1968 . . . . [They] were sitting in the living room on a red velvet couch, which Magnolia had covered herself. The eight were methodically folding several piles of newspapers for Lenny's five evening paper routes . . . . After a lesson from a seven-year-old on how to make the fold, I joined in . . . . I told them I would like to begin a study of family life in The Flats . . . . Several months later Magnolia told me that she had been surprised that I sat with them that first day to fold papers, and then came back to help again. "White folks," she told me, "don't have time, they's always in a rush, and they don't sit on Black folks' furniture, at least no Whites that come into The Flats." (p. 10)

Such immersion in the lives of the people one studies is very different from the distance maintained by experimenters and survey researchers. The latter often do not know or ask for the names of their research participants, trying instead to assure them of anonymity and to treat all participants alike. Participant observers do the opposite; they become well acquainted with the people they study and consequently treat no two people alike.

This degree of immersion in the research setting is at odds with the distance and anonymity of experiments and surveys. Does it make participant observation more vulnerable to distortion? Not necessarily; in fact, the lack of anonymity of respondents can ensure that the researcher observes phenomena as they are and not as the respondent or the researcher wishes they were. Participants in laboratory experiments and anonymous respondents in surveys are freer to distort reality than are people whose identities are known and whose actions are observed in their natural setting. The people studied by participant observation are constrained to act as they normally would, particularly if the research continues over many weeks or months. They cannot put on an act and continue to function with their friends, families, or fellow workers. Even if a participant observer could not recognize an act or a distortion, the associates of the people being observed would, and the participant observer would probably hear about it. Thus, we have a paradox: The more time a participant observer spends with the people he or she studies, the less influence the observer exerts as a researcher because although the research participants might wish to appear a particular way in the researcher's eyes, they cannot act in unnatural ways if the observer stays with them very long. The more the participant observer is immersed in the research setting, therefore, the less likely the research participants are to distort the research.

However, it should be apparent that the same thing is not necessarily true from the perspective of the researcher: The more the participant observers are immersed in the research setting, the more likely they are to affect (and therefore distort) what transpires within the group. Participant observers thus face a difficult challenge: They must become sufficiently integrated into the group to gain access to high-quality information, yet they must remain sufficiently detached that they do not unduly influence the activities of the group.

This dilemma is beautifully described in Festinger, Riecken, and Schachter's (1956) classic account of participant observation, *When Prophecy Fails*. Readers might be familiar with this study, which involved several researchers joining a small cult that had predicted the imminent flooding and destruction of the world and subsequent salvation by extraterrestrial beings. The major goal of the study was to describe how the cult members adapted when the prophecy of worldwide destruction did not come true. As Festinger et al. (1956) explain, "We tried to be nondirective, sympathetic listeners, passive participants who were inquisitive and eager to learn whatever others might want to tell us," but as it turned out, "our initial hope—to avoid *any* influence upon the movement—turned out to be somewhat unrealistic" (p. 237). The first problem was that the simple act of gaining entry into the cult altered its dynamics; having four new members (the observers) join the small group within a short period of time—which they had to do in order to gather information prior to the predicted date of the flood—considerably boosted the confidence of the cult members, who interpreted the sudden rush of new members as evidence that their prophecy was correct. The second, more serious, problem was learning how to juggle appearing friendly and interested enough in the group so as to be a fully accepted member while still avoiding any act of commitment or proselytizing that would change the direction of the group. This was very difficult, for as the authors describe, the observers were often directly pressured to take some kind of action in the group. For example, during one meeting, the cult leader insisted that one of the participant observers "lead the meeting" that night. The observer, thinking admirably under duress, suggested that the group "meditate silently and wait for inspiration" (p. 244). As another example, the observers were all variously pressured to quit their jobs as the predicted flood date approached and spend all their time with the group. Although the observers tried to be evasive when asked about their plans, these evasions and failures to quit their jobs might have raised doubts in the true cult members who had quit their own jobs. In short, as Festinger et al. (1956) concluded, "the observers could not be neutral—any action had consequences" (p. 244).

Field Notes

How can research in the field be systematic if the procedures vary from one person or day to the next? The systematization occurs not by following uniform procedures but by recording faithfully what is seen and heard. The records are stored as **field notes,** that is, detailed records of everything the participant observer hears and sees, and the researcher subjects them to systematic scrutiny and analysis. Thus, as with narrative analysis, focus groups, and oral history, the distinctive feature of participant observation is its reliance on the words and voices of the people being studied. Instead of recording people's thoughts and feelings on scales or in categories, the researcher records their actual words, through notes or tape recordings. The goal of a participant observer is to record with as much detail as possible the people's voices, actions, intentions, and appearances.

This requirement might strike the beginning participant observer as an impossible task, which in a sense it is because the term "everything" sets no limits. It can include endless details about the time and location of an interview or observation, including descriptions of the building, the furnishings, the decor, the level of cleanliness, the amount of noise, the number of other people present, the facial expressions of the persons being observed, their appearance and dress styles, their behaviors, and so on. Only some of these details are relevant to the purposes of the research, but when the participant observer begins, he or she does not know what form the final report will take. The rule, therefore, is to try to remember "everything" and write notes that are as complete as memory allows.

Recording everything that is said is an equally arduous task. Participant observers generally do not record conversations on tape because a tape recorder would inhibit the researcher's participation in many situations. When a tape recorder would interfere with participant observation, the researcher must rely on memory to write the field notes as soon after the observations as possible.

Not all the details in these notes will become usable information. Nonetheless, it is important to record them for two reasons. First, by trying to write down as much as possible, the researcher stands a better chance of having useful information available for analysis later on; deciding which information is useful should be done during the analysis rather than during the writing of the field notes. Second, writing even those details that seem irrelevant at the time helps the researcher recall other details that are clearly relevant; each piece of information acts as a cue for recalling other pieces of the setting and is, therefore, worth recording as a means of triggering memory.

Analyzing Field Notes

Analysis of information obtained by participant observers is markedly different from analysis in quantitative research. In quantitative research, analysis is often predictable in advance and straightforward once the data have been gathered: The researcher knows the design of the study, and there is generally a small set of optimal ways of analyzing the data. It is hard to improve over analysis of variance when one has a 2 x 2 factorial design, for example. In participant observation research, the situation is different, and analysis involves considerable creativity and insight. The first step is to organize and transform field notes into a visual record, which the researcher can scan repeatedly and mark in some way to identify recurring events, themes, and explanations. Before the widespread availability of computers, participant observers would write or type their notes and then use color codes, make notes in the margins, or excerpt portions onto index cards, which could then be sorted into categories. Word processors now enable participant observers to enter key words into the text of their field notes to identify instances of various categories or themes. Using a search procedure, the researcher can easily locate all instances of any category and print them, see in what contexts they appear, note how they are related to other events, and begin to piece together an argument about what the observation reveals. The computer facilitates the physical search for categories and themes, but it does not perform the conceptual work. The researcher still does the work of reading through the notes many times, constructing and assessing themes or categories, revising hunches, testing ideas against the notes, and finally piecing together the story that he or she wants to tell.

Rather than design a study to test a hypothesis, participant observers gather information to generate hypotheses. Hypothesis testing is an example of **deductive research.** Experimenters generally work deductively, beginning with a theoretical framework, formulating a hypothesis, deducing what the results should be if the hypothesis is correct, and gathering information to test the hypothesis. Participant observers work in the opposite direction—generating rather than testing hypotheses. Theirs is called **inductive research.** They begin with observations and generate hypotheses that fit the information they obtain. In practice, no one works either purely deductively or purely inductively. Most social scientists use a combination of inductive and deductive logic. Nonetheless, we can still characterize research methods as being predominantly deductive or inductive, and participant observation is predominantly inductive. Participant observers might begin their research with some preliminary hunches and crude hypotheses, but as they proceed, they revise their hypotheses by the method of negative case analysis, a procedure that takes the place of statistical analysis in participant observation.

Negative case analysis requires the researcher to look for information that would disconfirm the hypothesis. When a single negative case is found, the participant observer revises the hypothesis so that it accounts for that case. Cressey's (1953) classic study of embezzlers illustrates how negative case analysis works. He revised his hypothesis five times before he completed his analysis of what leads embezzlers to use other people's money. For example, one version of his hypothesis was that "positions of trust are violated when the incumbent defines a need for extra funds or extended use of property as an 'emergency' which cannot be met by legal means . . . " (p. 27). However, after interviewing inmates convicted of embezzling, Cressey discovered that although some embezzlers admitted this was true, others said that there had been no financial "emergency," yet they had still taken the money. Thus, Cressey developed new versions of his hypothesis, each time checking them not only against subsequent interviews but also against previous ones. If cases were found that violated his hypothesis, he revised the hypothesis so that it could account for the negative case. This process resulted in the final version of Cressey's hypothesis:

> Trusted persons become trust violators when they conceive of themselves as having a financial problem which is nonshareable, are aware that this problem can be secretly resolved by violation of the position of financial trust, and are able to apply to their own conduct in that situation verbalizations which enable them to adjust their conceptions of themselves as trusted persons with their conceptions of themselves as users of the entrusted funds or property. (p. 30)

Cressey (1953) developed and tested this hypothesis with all cases of embezzlement found in one state prison. He then tested the hypothesis in three additional ways. He searched the literature on embezzlement to see if his hypothesis was consistent with other studies. He examined 200 cases of embezzlement collected by another researcher. And he went to a federal penitentiary and interviewed people convicted of federal bank and post office embezzlement. In each of these sources he looked for negative cases that would contradict his hypothesis and concluded that in all of the cases he identified, his hypothesized process was present.

Cressey's (1953) book is atypical because few other published reports reveal so clearly the process of forming, revising, and retesting hypotheses. It is typical, however, in its use of negative case analysis to revise and generate hypotheses. What makes qualitative research systematic, therefore, is not standardization but negative case analysis. Cressey revised and developed his hypothesis and his conclusion by testing each revision against information he already had gathered and information that he would subsequently gather. Each time he found a negative case, he revised his hypothesis to incorporate the new evidence. He did this until there were no more disconfirmations. To conduct systematic participant observation research, therefore, means making a thorough search for cases that might disconfirm the hypothesis. The search and the information gathering are not routinized; in fact, they usually require asking new and different questions in each search. The measurements are not standardized, the data are not uniform, and they do not yield numbers that can be added or averaged. But the *procedure* is systematic.

Generalization

Participant observers study how people behave in specific organizations, communities, or circumstances and conclude that anyone would behave similarly in those situations. It is important to realize that this is not the same thing as concluding that people in other organizations, communities, or circumstances would behave in the same way. Unlike survey researchers, participant observers rarely ask, "What percentage of persons in the population would respond in this way?" Instead they say, "What I have found true of the people in this study is likely to be true of any people placed in this situation." Participant observers are like laboratory experimenters in this respect. Both assume that the environmental forces or situational constraints they have studied would affect most people the same way. Experimenters and participant observers share this assumption even though they conduct their research in dramatically different ways and places.

Although participant observation might seem to have a priori external validity simply because it takes place in the external world, participant observers must demonstrate that their conclusions are valid beyond the specific conditions of their study. They are rarely content to say that the processes observed are true only for the people and places named in the study. If they set such limits, few readers would be interested in their conclusions. Participant observers, as much as experimenters and survey researchers, need to demonstrate that their research has wider validity. External validity is acquired by gathering and analyzing field notes so that the similarities to other persons or situations become clear. In the final analysis, the ultimate test of the believability of findings from participant observation is replicability, just as it is with any kind of research. If no one can replicate the research and reach the same conclusions, the research is not believable, no matter how vivid the data.

Ethical Concerns

More than any other type of qualitative research, participant observation raises serious ethical dilemmas, some possibly intractable. Because participant observers by definition become integrated into the lives of the people they are studying, invasion of privacy and confidentiality become important issues to consider. Participant observers witness events occurring in people's homes or other private settings, and they often hear sensitive information. There is almost never anonymity, so guaranteeing confidentiality becomes an ethical imperative. As we discussed in Chapter 3, these concerns can be largely met through a thorough informed consent process, during which participants are told of the study, the kinds of information that would be gathered, and the degree of access the observer wishes to gain. Assuming the participant still wishes to participate in the study, the researcher has fulfilled his or her ethical obligation. Confidentiality is preserved by changing names and all identifying information when findings from the study are reported.

However, some instances of participant observation entail considerable deception, namely, those studies in which the researcher joins the group "undercover," as it were, and does not inform the participants that he or she is a researcher and recording information about the group. Such was the case in the Festinger et al. (1956) study described earlier. The ethical concerns in this situation are not so easily addressed. The current federal regulations allow researchers to avoid informed consent only if (1) the research involves no more than minimal risk, (2) the rights of the participants would not be adversely affected, and (3) the research could not feasibly be carried out without waiving informed consent. Given the degree of deception and invasion of privacy involved in undercover participant observation studies, it is highly unlikely that Institutional Review Boards today would consider those conditions to have been met, and most would not approve such a study.

In sum, the classic form of participant observation, in which the researcher does not inform the individuals being studied that they are in fact being observed, would not pass ethical scrutiny in most cases today. That limits participant observation to those cases in which the researcher joins the group with the full knowledge and consent of those being observed. The trade-off, of course, is that participants might not behave as they normally would once they realize their actions are being recorded for research purposes. More problematic from a research standpoint is that there might be some groups—especially those involved in illegal or socially undesirable behavior—that would not grant access to researchers under open consent processes. The burden then falls on the researcher to create rapport with such group members and convince them of the benefits of participating in the research. In the final analysis, though, any conflict between the goals of the researcher and the rights of the participant must always be resolved in favor of the participant.

The involvement of participant observers in the lives of the people they study raises yet other ethical issues. For instance, Stack (1975), a White researcher, participated extensively in the lives of the Black women she studied. She provided some services:

> Once I had the car, people continually asked me to run errands—taking children, goods and gossip between households. For a while all I seemed to be doing was taking half a pot roast from one house to another, picking up the laundry from a home with a washing machine, going to the liquor store for beer, or waiting with mothers in the local medical clinics for doctors to see their sick children. (p. 18)

She also developed genuine friendships, not for the purpose of observing but as a consequence of being there. Did her services and her friendship make her observations more ethically correct or less so? In a laboratory or classroom context, giving or accepting favors is normally regarded as a conflict of interest that must be avoided. In participant observation research, on the other hand, the researcher becomes a genuine part of the social network of the group being observed, and to refuse to do or accept such favors would be to violate the ethical rules of friendship. The bottom line is that participant observation involves a tangled web of roles and relationships, as opposed to the detached and relatively simple experimenter–participant relationship of the laboratory, and participant observers must balance the natural consequences of friendship and involvement in the lives of their participants with their responsibilities as researchers.

Summary

Qualitative research differs from traditional formats in that the researcher does not impose structure or questions on the participant but rather learns from listening to the participant discuss issues in his or her own voice. There are different forms of qualitative research, varying with respect to the degree of structure. In narrative research, participants provide short narratives, or stories, of important life experiences that objective judges later code on theoretically meaningful dimensions. Focus groups bring several participants together to discuss the research question of interest. They are particularly helpful in the early stages of research to help guide the preparation of experimental materials and questionnaires; they also are useful in program evaluation. Oral history is a method for recording extended life stories of individuals, usually individuals who have undergone some culturally important event or in some other way serve as an important witness to history or national consciousness. The least-structured form of qualitative research is participant observation, in which researchers immerse themselves in the research setting and in the lives of the people they study. Participant observers generate and revise their hypotheses as they gather information, and they use negative case analysis to arrive at conclusions that hold true for every observation without exception.

Key Concepts

content analysis
deductive research
deed of gift form
dictionaries
field
field notes
focus group guide
focus groups
ground rules
inductive research
moderator
narratives
negative case analysis
oral history
participant observation
qualitative research

On the Web

http://www.baylor.edu/Oral_History/Introduction.html Published by the Institute for Oral History at Baylor University. Excellent overview of oral history methods, including a Web-based workshop full of useful tips for conducting oral histories.

http://www.indiana.edu/~ohrc/pamph1.htm A pamphlet on oral history techniques, written by Dr. Barbara Truesdell, assistant director of the Indiana University Oral History Research Center. Includes useful hints as well as sample informed consent and deed of gift forms.

http://www.mapnp.org/library/evaluatn/focusgrp.htm This is a short description of the nuts and bolts of conducting a focus group, from preparation and recruitment of members to running the group.

http://www.mnav.com/cligd.htm An entertaining and well-written summary of what focus groups are and how best to use them, written from an applied marketing perspective.

http://ag.arizona.edu/fcr/fs/cyfar/focus.htm Describes logic and rationale for focus groups, how to conduct them, their advantages and disadvantages.

http://www.gsu.edu/~wwwcom/ Provides many links to resources for conducting content analyses. Includes a comprehensive listing of software as well as an up-to-date bibliography.

Further Reading

Festinger, L., Riecken, H. W., & Schachter, S. (1956). *When prophecy fails.* Minneapolis: University of Minnesota Press.

Krueger, R. A. (1988). *Focus groups: A practical guide for applied research.* Thousand Oaks, CA: Sage.

Popping, R. (2000). *Computer-assisted text analysis.* Thousand Oaks, CA: Sage.

Ritchie, D. (1994). *Doing oral history.* New York: Twayne.

Smith, C. P. (2000). Content analysis and narrative analysis. In H. T. Reis & C. M. Judd (Eds.), *Handbook of research methods in social and personality psychology* (pp. 313–335). Cambridge: Cambridge University Press.

PART

V

Analysis and Writing

CHAPTER

17

Data Management and Exploration

Research in the social sciences generates information, or **data,** that must be prepared for analysis, analyzed, and interpreted. Activities concerned with preparing data for analysis are collectively referred to as **data management.** Data management involves putting the information generated by research into a form that can be subjected to statistical analyses of one sort or another. In addition, data management involves ensuring that records are kept and the data are stored in such a way that they can be referred to and used in the future. Once data management is complete, data analysis proceeds. In **data analysis** researchers arrange and portray the data in ways that help detect patterns or problems, explore associations that exist in the data, and generally see if the data are consistent with their hypotheses and theories.

This chapter and the next cover the important issues in data management and analysis. In this chapter we describe the nuts and bolts of data management and provide an introduction to graphical and statistical procedures used to check the integrity of and detect patterns in a data set.

The Data Matrix

It is useful to view a set of information that is collected in a study, a **data set,** as being arranged in the form of a large matrix or spreadsheet. To illustrate, we can think of a spreadsheet used by an instructor to keep track of attendance and grades on tests and assignments. The spreadsheet is rectangular in shape, and its dimensions are described in terms of the number of rows and columns that comprise information. In the instructor's spreadsheet, each row would be dedicated to a student, and in the columns would be the various pieces of information the instructor needed to track. Each intersection of a row and a column creates a cell in which resides a datum, a particular piece of information for a particular student. We call such a configuration of students and information about them a **data matrix.**

Now let us imagine how we could put social science data in the same matrix form. Suppose we have interviewed 1,000 individuals from a cross section of the adult electorate in the United States regarding their attitudes on current social and political issues. On our survey we asked 100 questions, including many about attitudes on a variety of topics ranging from abortion to school busing to local and national political candidates. We have asked about the respondent's age, education, background, income, occupation, past voting record, and political party preference.

Let us array each of the people whom we interviewed down the rows of the matrix so that each person is assigned one and only one row. The rows represent the **units of analysis,** or **cases,** which in this instance are individuals whom we have interviewed. Data on the first case is placed in the first row, the second case in the second row, the third case in the third row, and so on until data on the thousandth case is placed in the thousandth row of our data matrix.

We now assign one column to each of the variables about which we have collected data in our survey. Because information on 100 different aspects of each individual was collected, we need 100 columns to accommodate all the information from our survey; each column in the data matrix represents one variable. Let us say that the first variable concerns the report of which candidate the respondent voted for in the 2000 presidential election. Thus, information about respondents' votes would be placed in column 1 for each case. Column 2 is assigned information about the respondents' preference for the upcoming presidential election. Each variable is assigned one column in this manner until the hundredth variable—let us say, the respondents' income level—is assigned to column 100.

We have now defined the layout of the data matrix, which in this case is a 1,000 x 100 matrix. The values that fill the cells of the matrix are the next thing we need to specify. These values represent a particular piece of information gathered from a particular individual on a particular variable. For instance, the first individual might have voted for George W. Bush in the 2000 presidential election. Assuming that the first variable was the respondent's reported presidential vote in 2000, the first cell of the data matrix (i.e., row 1, column 1) contains a value that stands for or means George W. Bush. Similarly, if the third individual's reported income was $15,000, and if reported income was the one hundredth variable, the cell in the third row, one hundredth column of the matrix would contain a value representing $15,000.

To construct the data matrix, three questions need to be addressed. First, the variables or columns of the matrix must be defined. Defining the variables in a study amounts to deciding on how the theoretical constructs of interest are to be measured. This topic was thoroughly covered in the second section of this book. The second question in constructing the data matrix concerns the definition of the rows of the matrix—that is, what is the unit of analysis in this particular study? Answering this question raises a number of complex issues that have not been dealt with in previous chapters. The final question concerns how the values on specific variables are defined—what values are used to represent different responses to each variable.

Units of Analysis

In the example we have been using, in which 1,000 people are interviewed about their political attitudes and behaviors, the question of defining the unit of analysis is apparently easily answered. Individuals naturally constitute the rows of the data matrix because each individual presumably has a value on each of the variables; however, there is no requirement that individuals must always be the unit of analysis. In fact, there are many studies in which the unit of analysis is at some other level; for instance, in cross-cultural or cross-national research, the unit of analysis is quite likely to be a nation (e.g., Glick et al., 2000). Likewise, smaller groupings of individuals can be the unit of analysis. For instance, in studies of marital relationships, dyad might be the unit of analysis. In looking at how social informal groups that are structured in different ways interact, we could treat group as the unit of analysis (e.g., Bales & Cohen, 1979). In all of these examples, the unit of analysis has been defined as aggregates or groupings of individuals. The unit of analysis might also be defined in any particular study within individuals. For instance, a psychophysicist might be interested in examining how different temperatures are perceived when different parts of the body are exposed to them. In such a study, all of the data might be collected from a single individual and the unit of analysis becomes body part. Similarly, in time-series designs characteristic of experience sampling studies (Chapter 10), a single individual might be repeatedly observed over time and then the unit of analysis is defined as each individual observation.

All of these examples illustrate the fact that there is no single appropriate unit of analysis that should be used in any and all studies. Viewed differently, it is not the case that rows of a data matrix must always correspond to individuals. Rather, the choice of the unit of analysis depends on the research questions that are being addressed and the level at which the researcher wishes to generalize. If generalization to individuals is sought, the individual is most appropriately the unit of analysis. If we are interested in group processes, generalization across groups might be desired and groups are the appropriate unit of analysis.

Errors of generalization often occur when the unit of analysis is not at the same level as the unit to which we seek to generalize. For instance, assume that a set of data about voting trends and income is gathered from different counties. Here county is the unit of analysis. Assume further that wealthier counties tend to be on average more Republican and less Democratic. If we attempt to generalize these results, which apply to counties, to the individual level, we might well commit what is called the **ecological fallacy.** It is inappropriate to assume, on the basis of these group-level data, that the individuals within the counties necessarily behave in a way that is analogous to the way their counties behave. Wealthier individuals might indeed be inclined to cast Republican ballots, and less affluent individuals might well be inclined to cast Democratic ballots. But the individual and the ecological (group) associations are not necessarily the same. Typically, associations that are found when the unit of analysis is a group of individuals are stronger than the same associations would be if the individual were the unit of analysis. So, for instance, in this example, the association between counties' wealth and voting trends is likely to be considerably stronger than that between individuals' wealth and their voting records.

Sometimes it makes sense to employ multiple levels of analysis within the same study. This was the case in the Glick et al. (2000) study cited earlier. Glick and his colleagues were interested in cross-cultural differences in hostile and benevolent sexism. They had over 15,000 individuals from 19 countries complete the Ambivalent Sexism Inventory. Some of their research questions were aimed at the individual unit of analysis; for example, they tested differences between men and women within each country, for a total of 19 analyses. Other research questions asked by Glick et al. (2000) used country as the unit of analysis; for example, they computed the average hostile and benevolent sexism scores for each country and then correlated those scores with two United Nations indices of gender equality for each country.

In sum, the decision regarding the appropriate unit of analysis is a joint function of the nature of the data (we cannot use individual as the unit if all we have are group-level data) and the research question being asked. The only critical determinant is that units of analysis should be **statistically independent;** in other words, the data from one case should not influence or have been influenced by the data from another case. Take, for example, a study looking at marital conflict negotiation in which non-verbal expressions of anger were coded from 50 couples as they discussed a current problem in their relationship. We could not use individual as the unit of analysis (i.e., setting up a data set with 100 participants and their corresponding anger scores) because the anger expressed by the husband in a discussion surely affects the anger expressed by the wife. The proper unit of analysis in this hypothetical example is therefore the dyad. Independence of units of analysis is a critical assumption for most of the statistical analyses used in the social sciences, and violating this assumption can lead to badly biased results.

The issue of the appropriate unit of analysis is even more complex than we have portrayed it, for it raises statistical issues that are beyond the scope of this book. The important points for our purposes is that generalization should always be at the same level as the unit of analysis and units should always be statistically independent. Hence, to define what constitutes the rows of the data matrix, we need to think about whether we wish to generalize to individuals, groups, nations, or some other meaningful entity.

Defining Values for Variables

The cells of the data matrix contain the data that are to be analyzed. Returning to our example in which 1,000 individuals were asked about political preferences, each cell contains information about an individual's response to a given question. Normally, those responses are coded in numeric form. Thus, if the first question is which presidential candidate the respondent voted for in 2000, a response of "Bush" might be coded as 1, a "Gore" response might be coded as 2, and so forth, reserving a particular number, say 9, for no response. Responses are coded numerically rather than as "Bush," "Gore," and so forth because certain statistical procedures (e.g., multiple regression) require numerical data even for variables measured on a nominal scale.

For some variables, the choice of numbers for different responses is arbitrary. For other variables the choice is not at all arbitrary. In the previous example, in which the variable is presidential vote, the choice of numbers to represent the different candidates is purely arbitrary. A "Bush" response might be coded as 1 or 2 or whatever, as long as we are consistent in our use of the values assigned to different responses. By consistent, we mean that if the "Bush" response is coded as a given number, it is always given that value and no other response is given that value.

A consistent but arbitrarily defined coding scheme is used whenever the variable is measured on a nominal scale. Recall from Chapter 7 that measurement on a nominal scale means that responses can be sorted into different groups but cannot be rank-ordered. Thus, variables such as gender of respondent, hair color, and presidential vote would all be coded with arbitrary numeric values.

Variables measured on ordinal, interval, or ratio scales cannot be coded arbitrarily. Because all of these scales contain information about the rank order of different responses, at the least that rank order must be preserved in the values used for coding responses. In addition, for interval and ratio scales, the units of measurement have meaning. Thus, coding schemes must preserve not only the rank order of responses for variables measured on these scales but also the relative differences between responses. Finally, for ratio scales, zero has a meaningful definition, and hence the scale values are fixed or anchored there.

Let us illustrate each one. If we measure the respondents' gender (a nominal variable), we could code males 0 and females 1. We could also code females 0 and males 1. Or females 84 and males 27. As long as we use a coding scheme consistently, it makes no difference which numbers we use. For an example of a variable measured on an ordinal scale, suppose we had the rank order of the heights of 10 individuals. Thus, we knew that a given person was, for instance, the third tallest, but we did not know how much taller he was than the fourth tallest individual. We could code the tallest person 1 and the shortest 10. The only thing that matters is that we preserve the rank order in our coding scheme.

Now, suppose we knew how many inches separated everyone even though we did not know their actual heights. Our coding scheme would then have to preserve the relative differences between people as well as the rank order. Finally, when we know their height in inches, we have a ratio scale at our disposal and height should be coded as actual inches, with a fixed zero value and a meaningful unit of measurement.

Putting It All Together

An example of a typical data matrix is presented in Figure 17.1. In this matrix, individual is the unit of analysis; hence, the 15 rows indicate that data were gathered from 15 people. The eight columns indicate that we have included eight pieces of information for each participant. As is typical, the first column includes an identifier, in this case the last six digits of each participant's Social Security number. The second column carries information about sex; in this data set, female was coded as 1, male was coded as 2, and no response was coded as 9. The remaining six columns include data

FIGURE 17.1 A TYPICAL DATA MATRIX

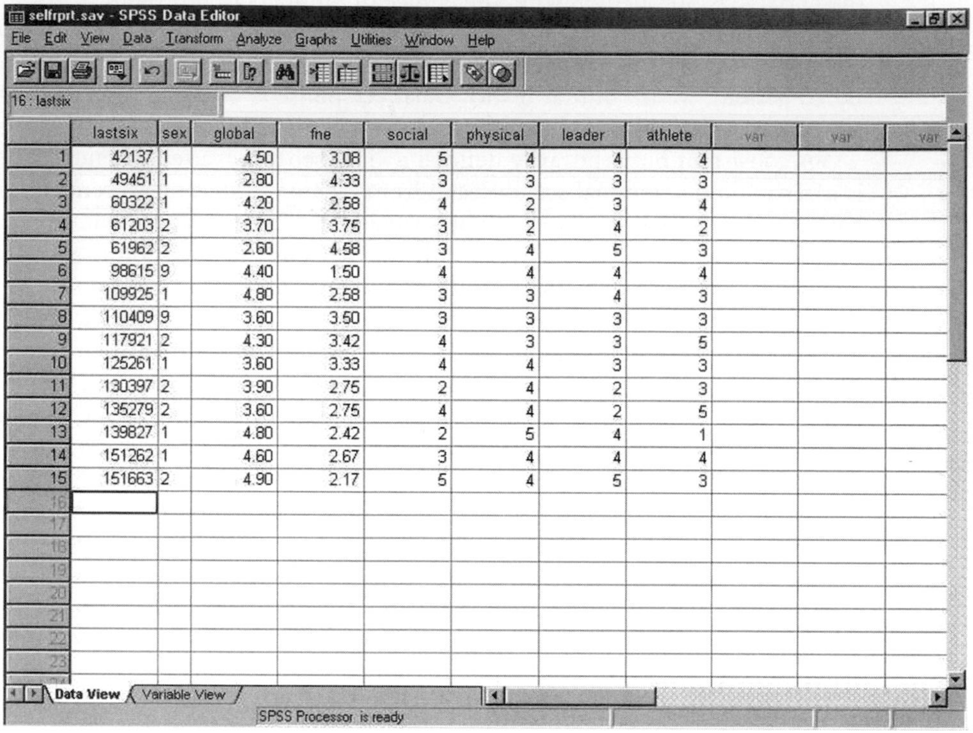

	lastsix	sex	global	fne	social	physical	leader	athlete	var	var	var
1	42137	1	4.50	3.08	5	4	4	4			
2	49451	1	2.80	4.33	3	3	3	3			
3	60322	1	4.20	2.58	4	2	3	4			
4	61203	2	3.70	3.75	3	2	4	2			
5	61962	2	2.60	4.58	3	4	5	3			
6	98615	9	4.40	1.50	4	4	4	4			
7	109925	1	4.80	2.58	3	3	4	3			
8	110409	9	3.60	3.50	3	3	3	3			
9	117921	2	4.30	3.42	4	3	3	5			
10	125261	1	3.60	3.33	4	4	3	3			
11	130397	2	3.90	2.75	2	4	2	3			
12	135279	2	3.60	2.75	4	4	2	5			
13	139827	1	4.80	2.42	2	5	4	1			
14	151262	1	4.60	2.67	3	4	4	4			
15	151663	2	4.90	2.17	5	4	5	3			

on variables relevant to hypotheses the study was designed to test. The variable "global" in column 3 includes scores on a measure of global self-esteem; "fne" stands for fear of negative evaluation, which was measured using a brief self-report instrument. Note that scores in these two columns include decimal values, indicating that they are composite scores produced by taking an average of a set of items. Scores in the remaining columns came from single items and indicate participants' self-evaluations in particular domains.

Although the data matrix shown in Figure 17.1 is properly organized, even with the commentary provided in the previous paragraph it would not be very useful to a data analyst unfamiliar with the specific measures from which the numbers were drawn. For instance, what do the values for "fne" mean? For that matter, what does the shorthand label "social" represent? Questions such as this would be answered in an accompanying codebook.

The Codebook

As scoring and coding decisions are made and as the values are entered in the cells of the data matrix, it is essential that the researcher keep a record of the organization of the data matrix and of all scoring procedures and coding decisions. This record, called the **codebook,** is essential to guarantee that in the future the coded data can be interpreted. All too often, researchers fail to maintain an adequate and detailed codebook. As a result, when they attempt to return to a set of data after some interval, perhaps as short as a few days or weeks, they have a difficult time reconstructing what the numbers in the data matrix actually mean. Without a codebook, the data matrix is as meaningless as a table of random numbers. Codebooks should therefore be complete and detailed, listing names and locations of computer files containing the data as well as coding decisions, the meaning of variable labels, and the like. Furthermore, multiple copies should be made and securely stored.

To illustrate the essential ingredients of a codebook, we return to the data matrix example used earlier in which 1,000 people were interviewed about their political opinions and actions. The codebook contains information about the columns of the data matrix. More specifically, it identifies the variable that occupies each column and then defines the values used to code that variable. Suppose the first variable in the matrix is the respondent's ID number; the second variable is the respondent's presidential vote in 2000; the next variable is the respondent's age; the fourth variable is the respondent's gender; the fifth is his or her party preference; and the sixth is the respondent's rating on a 7-point Likert scale of how satisfied he or she is with the current president. Table 17.1 illustrates the essential components of the codebook for these six variables.

There are a number of things in this table that deserve comment. First, notice that a single variable can occupy more than a single column in the matrix because, outside of the statistical software environment, columns are a single digit wide.[1] Thus, because the maximum ID value takes four digits, it must occupy columns 1 through 4 in the matrix. ID numbers less than 1000 should include leading zeroes (e.g., the first respondent would be coded as 0001; respondent 50 as 0050) to preserve the column locations of all other variables.

Second, we need to specify both the variable name and its full description. Many statistical software packages have an eight-character limit on variable names, which can force researchers to come up with creative abbreviations. The codebook should include both the name of the variable as it will be used by the statistical software as well as a fuller description of the variable that will be understandable by people who work with the data at a later time. Without a fuller description, researchers can be

[1]Contrasting this example with the example illustrated in Figure 17.1 points up a potential problem with the use of the term "column." In Figure 17.1, each column includes a *variable*. In Table 17.1, each column includes a *digit*. The different uses of the term reflects the transition in statistical software packages from the early procedure of writing programs to "read" data in columns and ranges of columns to the increasingly common procedure of keying data into spreadsheets such as the one illustrated in Figure 17.1. Because codebooks usually describe data in their "raw" form, that is, before they have been processed by statistical software, the term "column" refers to digit in that context.

TABLE 17.1 CODEBOOK EXAMPLE

Column(s)	Variable Name	Description	Values
1–4	ID	Respondent ID number	1–1,000
5	VOTE	2000 presidential vote	1 = Bush 2 = Gore 3 = Other 7 = Don't know 8 = Didn't vote 9 = No response
6–7	AGE	Respondent's age	18–95 99 = No response
8	SEX	Respondent's sex	1 = Male 2 = Female
9	PARTY	Respondent's party preference	1 = Democrat 2 = Republican 3 = Independent 4 = Don't know or no response
10	SATISF	How satisfied respondent is with current president	1–7 Likert scale 1 = not at all satisfied 7 = extremely satisfied

stumped a year later when they go back and see a variable named PNVFRND1, not being able to recall that it means "perceiver nonverbal friendliness at Time 1."

Third, wherever there is the possibility of missing data, one or more missing data values are included. For most variables, only a single missing value is necessary; however, there are times when it is helpful to preserve information about why respondents failed to answer a question. Thus, for the second variable in Table 17.1, three missing data values are defined to differentiate among respondents who do not remember for whom they voted, respondents who say they did not vote, and respondents who fail to answer for any other reason.

Fourth, it is important that the values used to code for missing information be numbers or responses that could not occur naturally as legitimate responses on the variable. Notice that for the missing value on the age variable, this is not the case. The value of 99 is used to represent any missing data, yet a respondent could in fact be 99 years old. The value of 99 was chosen here as the missing value because it is sufficiently unlikely that a respondent would be that old. Should one be encountered, his or her age would be recorded as 95 rather than as 99. Thus, the value of 95 stands for anyone whose reported age is 95 or more.

Once all of the coding decisions have been made and a detailed codebook constructed, the data can be entered into a computer file and prepared for analysis. As the data are entered, it is essential that they be checked thoroughly and repeatedly for errors. To do so, it is sometimes most efficient to enter the data twice and then use the computer to check for inconsistencies between the two versions of the data matrix. A tedious though also effective method of proofing is to print out the data set as entered on the computer and have one person check the printout as another person reads the values aloud from the original data. Another way of checking for some types of errors is provided by using statistical software, which allows the user to specify what the permissible values are for each variable. The software then flags impermissible values in the data matrix. Because this type of error checking will not flag a value that is incorrect but nevertheless a permissible value for the variable (e.g., a 3 entered as a 4, when both 3 and 4 are legitimate values for a variable), this approach should not be the sole form of data proofing.

Proofing data is not a pleasant activity, but it is an essential step in the data management process. Although we might think we are entering data carefully, it is practically impossible to enter a large data set in a computer file without initially making at least a few errors. Rosenthal (1969) examined a series of data sets from the psychological sciences and discovered that the error rate in recording data was about 1%. More problematic, examination of the nature of the errors that were made revealed that over two-thirds of the errors were biased in the direction of the researcher's hypothesis. We are more likely to catch errors that contradict our hypothesis than those that confirm it, which makes careful proofing even more essential.

Once the data are entered into the computer, data exploration and analysis can begin. In addition to computer storage of data, the original forms (e.g., questionnaires or observational records) should be kept by the researcher in a safe place. Above all, the researcher should know where the data are, how they can be read by others, and what the values in the data matrix mean. Once again, we emphasize the need for a detailed and complete codebook.

Statistical Software

The late statistician John Tukey often spoke of "airplane statistics," that is, analyses that could be computed on a tray table in an airplane using nothing more than a pencil and a pocket calculator. In these days of ready access to powerful desktop computers and user-friendly software, however, even the simplest data analyses are done by computer. Most colleges and universities offer students access to one or more of the comprehensive statistical software packages listed in Table 17.2. MINITAB Statistical Software, generally viewed as the most straightforward, easy-to-use statistical software, is widely used as a teaching tool in high school and undergraduate statistics courses. (The company Web site boasts, "We believe it is safe to say that more students worldwide have been taught statistics using MINITAB than any other statistics software package.") SYSTAT, one of the first statistical software packages available

TABLE 17.2 **THE MOST WIDELY AVAILABLE COMPREHENSIVE STATISTICAL SOFTWARE PACKAGES**

SAS (**S**tatistical **A**nalysis **S**ystem)	http://www.sas.com/
SPSS (**S**tatistical **P**roduct & **S**ervice **S**olutions)	http://www.spss.com/
BMDP (**Biomed**ical **P**ackage)	http://www.statsol.ie/bmdp/bmdp.htm
MINITAB	http://www.minitab.com/
SYSTAT	http://www.spssscience.com/SYSTAT/index.cfm

Note: An extensive, annotated list of statistical software can be found on the Web at http://www.galaxy.gmu.edu/papers/astr1.html.

for Macintosh users, is somewhat more nimble and specialized than the other major packages; a strength of SYSTAT is in the area of graphical displays of data. SAS, SPSS, and BMDP are the workhorse packages used by academic researchers and other professionals. BMDP is favored by researchers in biomedical disciplines, whereas SAS and SPSS are widely used by social scientists.

Throughout this chapter and the next, we illustrate practical aspects of data management and data analysis. Because SAS and SPSS are so widely used by social scientists, we always use one of these two software packages in our illustrations. Indeed, we already introduced you to the SPSS computing environment through the presentation of a typical data matrix in Figure 17.1. Later in this section, we discuss the use of statistical software for reading data using the SAS System.

Before introducing you to the SAS environment, we need to highlight an important difference in the way statistical software can be used. Historically, data management and data analysis using statistical software were done from terminals (or, in the early days of computing, card readers) connected to mainframe computers. During this era, the user wrote programs in the language of the software being used that were executed by the computer. These programs are referred to as **command files** or, in the case of SPSS, **syntax files.** When properly written, command files produce **output,** which reviews the commands that were executed, flags any programming errors or inconsistencies, and, most importantly, includes the results from execution of the requested analysis. As desktop computers became more powerful, statistical software publishers, using their mainframe-oriented programs as a starting point, began providing statistical software for desktop computers. In the early going, this software had the look and feel of the mainframe environment. Users still produced command files and fielded output in much the same way as they did in the mainframe environment.

Capitalizing on the graphical, point-and-click interface originally available on Macintosh computers and now widely available on desktop computers, most statistical software packages allow users to execute analyses without producing an explicit command file. Instead, pull-down menus much like those in word processing programs allow the user to, in effect, produce an unseen command file by choosing from lists of options. Despite the allure of this approach, many users still prefer to work with command files, which can be edited and rerun with relatively little effort and transported from one platform to another (e.g., desktop to mainframe) and used after minor edits. An example SAS command file is shown in Figure 17.2. The commands are written to take the data listed between the commands CARDS and PROC, convert them to a **system file** on which the program can operate, and print the results.

Because both the command file and pull-down menu approaches are widely used, our examples in this chapter and the next illustrate both. Also, rather than advocate

FIGURE 17.2 ENTERING AND DEFINING THE POLITICAL ATTITUDES DATA SET IN SAS

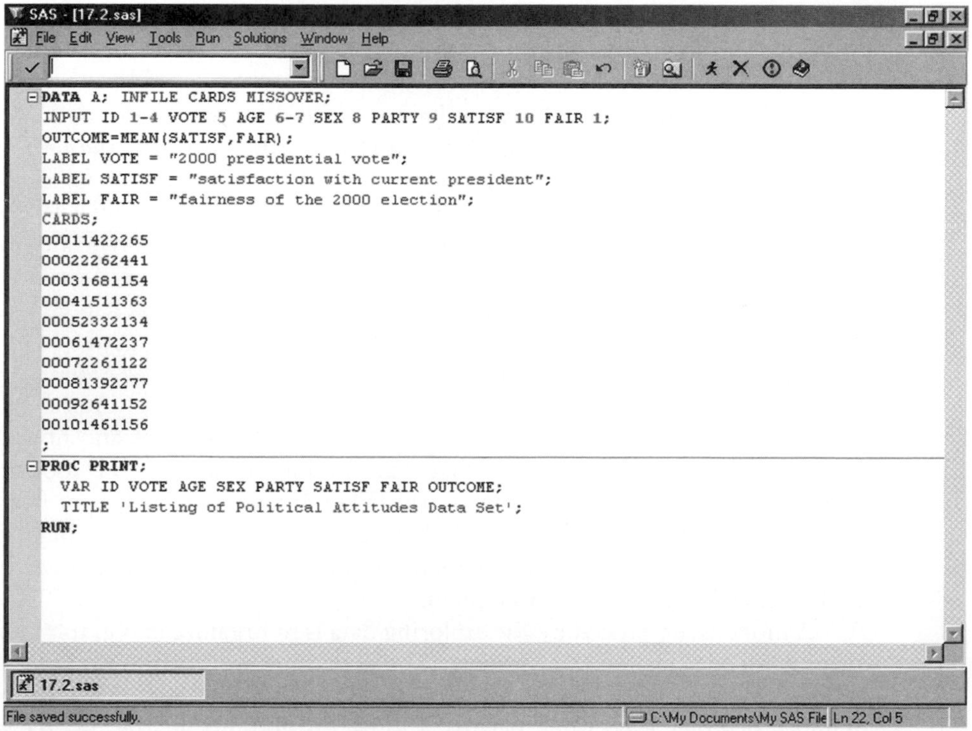

SOURCE: Created with SAS® software. Copyright © 2001, SAS Institute, Inc., Cary, NC, USA. All rights reserved. Reproduced with permission of SAS Institute, Inc., Cary, NC.

one statistical software package over another, we use both SAS and SPSS to illustrate the use of statistical software to accomplish the data management and data analysis steps we describe.

Exploring Data

After the data have been collected, a codebook created, and the data read into a statistical software package, social scientists turn their attention to data analysis and interpretation. In the remainder of this chapter and the next, we describe data analysis procedures. Our goal is not only to describe the procedures but also to discuss what kinds of questions the procedures can answer. By making clear how these procedures can be used to answer interesting questions about a data set, we hope to communicate an appreciation of the inherent interest that lies in data analysis. Data analysis is fundamentally like detective work (Tukey, 1969). Potential answers to many interesting questions lie hidden in a set of data. The goal of data analysis is to figure out what the data can tell us, what those answers might be, as well as to use the findings to pose new and interesting questions.

Data Displays

Table 17.3 presents the data matrix that we use to illustrate various data-analytic and interpretational issues in this and the next chapter. In these data, the unit of analysis is the state. For each of the 48 contiguous states there are values for each of three variables: 1979 birthrate (number of live births per 10,000 residents); 1979 marriage rate (number of marriages per 10,000 residents); and 1979 divorce rate (number of divorces per 10,000 residents). These three variables are measured on a ratio scale. (Most of the procedures that we discuss in the remainder of this chapter assume ratio or interval measurement scales.) These demographic data were gathered by the U.S. Census Bureau and reported in the *Statistical Abstract of the United States.*

Suppose we had collected these data because we were interested in how birthrates, marriage rates, and divorce rates varied across states and how they were associated with one another. The first thing we might want to do is look at the data themselves and see what we might learn. What impressions do we get from looking over Table 17.3? Other than seeing that marriage rates seem to be higher than divorce rates, and birthrates higher than the other two, it is hard to conclude much about these data just by scanning them.

A more useful procedure for exploring data is to organize and graph them. Let us do this for the divorce rate variable. The first thing we need to do is sort the data so that they go from the lowest divorce rate to the highest. We then count the number of times each value occurs. Table 17.4 presents all the divorce rates that were in Table 17.3, reordered from lowest to highest, along with how frequently each divorce rate was observed in a state. Thus, for instance, only a single state, Massachusetts, had a divorce rate of 30 per 10,000 residents. Three states, however,

TABLE 17.3

MARRIAGE RATES, DIVORCE RATES, AND BIRTHRATES FOR 48 CONTIGUOUS STATES

State	Marriage	Divorce	Birth	State	Marriage	Divorce	Birth
Alabama	129	70	166	Nebraska	89	40	167
Arizona	121	82	191	Nevada	1,474	168	176
Arkansas	119	93	167	New Hampshire	102	59	145
California	88	71	167	New Jersey	75	32	132
Colorado	118	60	170	New Mexico	131	80	206
Connecticut	82	45	124	New York	81	37	134
Delaware	75	53	153	North Carolina	80	49	150
Florida	117	79	137	North Dakota	92	32	179
Georgia	134	65	172	Ohio	93	55	156
Idaho	148	71	221	Oklahoma	155	79	170
Illinois	97	46	164	Oregon	87	70	165
Indiana	110	77	162	Pennsylvania	80	34	135
Iowa	96	39	161	Rhode Island	79	39	128
Kansas	105	54	165	South Carolina	182	47	173
Kentucky	96	45	167	South Dakota	130	39	189
Louisiana	103	38	197	Tennessee	135	68	156
Maine	109	56	149	Texas	129	69	190
Maryland	111	41	140	Utah	122	56	301
Massachusetts	78	30	122	Vermont	105	46	152
Michigan	97	48	157	Virginia	113	45	148
Minnesota	91	37	161	Washington	120	69	164
Mississippi	112	56	189	West Virginia	94	53	159
Missouri	109	57	157	Wisconsin	84	36	155
Montana	104	65	179	Wyoming	144	78	217

had a divorce rate of 39 (namely, Rhode Island, Iowa, and South Dakota). The third column of Table 17.4 adds up the frequencies as we proceed from the lowest to the highest values; the last number in this column must be the total number of states from which we have data. When the data are sorted, counted, and displayed in this way, the result is a **frequency distribution.**

TABLE 17.4

Frequency Distribution of 1979 Divorce Rate

Value	Frequency	Cumulative Frequency
30	1	1
32	2	3
34	1	4
36	1	5
37	2	7
38	1	8
39	3	11
40	1	12
41	1	13
45	3	16
46	2	18
47	1	19
48	1	20
49	1	21
53	2	23
54	1	24
55	1	25
56	3	28
57	1	29
59	1	30
60	1	31
65	2	33
68	1	34
69	2	36
70	2	38
71	2	40
77	1	41
78	1	42
79	2	44
80	1	45
82	1	46
93	1	47
168	1	48

From frequency distributions, it is easy to graphically display the data in a **frequency histogram.** In such a graph, we put the values along the horizontal axis, the frequencies along the vertical axis, and we draw a vertical bar for each value to indicate how frequently it occurs. If we did this from the frequency distribution of Table 17.4, we would observe a lot of bars one unit high, some two units high, and a few three units high. In other words, the frequency histogram would consist of a series of small bars all spread out across the possible values. A more informative frequency histogram might result if we first grouped values together in some way. Suppose, for instance, that we grouped together values from 30 to 39, 40 to 49, 50 to 59, and so forth. Such a grouping results in the frequency distribution shown in Table 17.5 and the frequency histogram shown in Figure 17.3.

Notice the gap between the last two bars along the horizontal axis in this graph. In these data there is one very extreme value: Nevada has a divorce rate of 168 per 10,000, whereas no other state's rate exceeds 100. A case with an extreme value on a variable, such as Nevada on this variable, is known as an **outlier.** As we demonstrate later on, outliers can have a disproportionate and unfortunate effect on certain statistics that are computed on the data set as a whole. Therefore, it is important to look for outliers in a data set and assess whether they are unduly influencing the results of any analysis.

TABLE 17.5 **GROUPED FREQUENCY DISTRIBUTION OF 1979 DIVORCE RATE**

Value	Frequency	Cumulative Frequency
30–39	11	11
40–49	10	21
50–59	9	30
60–69	6	36
70–79	8	44
80–89	2	46
90–99	1	47
100–109	0	47
110–119	0	47
120–129	0	47
130–139	0	47
140–149	0	47
150–159	0	47
160–169	1	48

FIGURE 17.3 **Grouped Frequency Histogram of the 1979 Divorce Data**

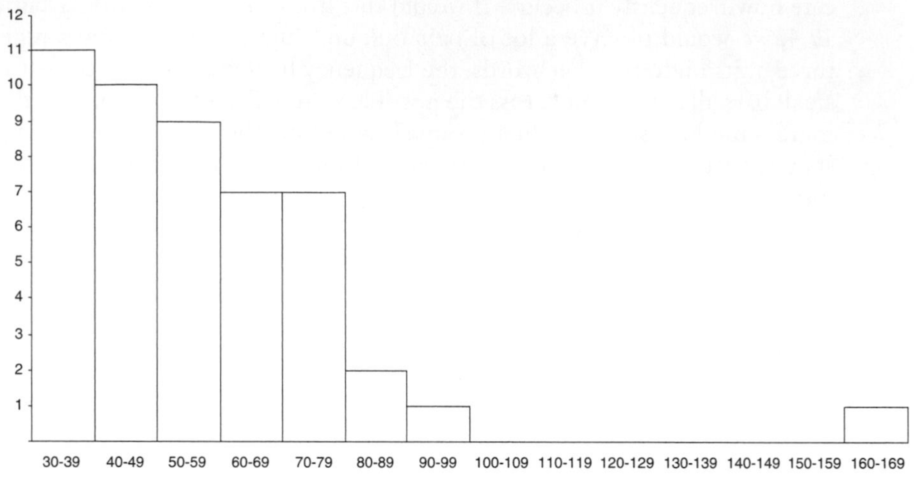

Frequency distributions and their associated histograms are useful for looking at the shape of a distribution of data on a variable. For instance, by examining the graphed frequency distribution, we can easily form some impressions about the variable. It seems as if the typical rate is somewhere in the range of 50 to 60. In addition, the distribution appears to be sloping downward to the right. That is, there are a lot of states in the 30 to 50 range, fewer in the range of 50 to 80, still fewer from 80 to 100, and only a single one after that. Most of the states seem to be bunched in the 30 to 80 range, and those that do not lie in that range are all above it.

Another procedure for graphing the data, invented by Tukey, gives the same sort of information as a grouped frequency histogram and, in addition, presents the actual scores at the same time. This procedure is called a **stem-and-leaf diagram** and is illustrated for the divorce rate data in Table 17.6. This stem-and-leaf diagram is constructed as follows: First, the first digits for all observed values are written in a column on the left side of the diagram. This column is called the "stem," and in this case the numbers represent increments of 10 units. For each case, the second digit of that case's value on the variable is written to the right of its stem. This digit is called the "leaf." Thus, the numbers in the first row in Table 17.6 tell us that one case had a value of 30 (stem of 3 and leaf of 0), two cases had the value 32 (stem of 3 and leaf of 2), and so forth. In this way, the actual scores for all 48 cases are contained in the diagram. In addition, if we turn the diagram on its side, it has exactly the same shape as the frequency histogram in Figure 17.3. Thus, we can graphically examine the shape of the distribution from this diagram, while presenting all of the scores as well, which is the major reason for preferring the stem-and-leaf diagram over the frequency histogram.

TABLE 17.6 STEM-AND-LEAF DIAGRAM OF 1979 DIVORCE RATES

3	0	2	2	4	6	7	7	8	9	9	9
4	0	1	5	5	5	6	6	7	8	9	
5	3	3	4	5	6	6	6	7	9		
6	0	1	5	5	8	9	9				
7	0	0	1	7	8	9	9				
8	0	2									
9	3										
.											
.											
16	8										

Descriptive Statistics

Although frequency distributions, histograms, and stem-and-leaf diagrams are useful in forming impressions about the shape of a distribution, it would be advantageous to be able to characterize the data in a more precise manner. In order to achieve this precision, we compute **descriptive statistics,** numbers that describe the different characteristics of a distribution of scores on a variable.

Central Tendency of a Distribution The first way in which we might like to characterize a distribution of scores on a variable is by identifying what seems to be a typical value. In other words, we would like to find a single value that is in some sense the most typical or representative of all the observed values. Such typical values are called the **central tendency** of a distribution.

There are a variety of ways to define the central tendency of a distribution. The two most frequently used definitions are the mean and the median. The **mean** is the average value of the variable, computed across all cases. It is defined by the following formula:

$$\overline{X} = \frac{\sum_{i-1}^{N} x_i}{N}$$

In this formula, $\overline{X}$ is the mean. The $\sum_{i=1}^{N}$ simply means that we add up the values on variable X for each case, adding from the first case (i = 1) to the last case ($i = N$). We then divide that sum by the total number of cases, N. Using this formula for our divorce rate data, we compute the mean as

$$\overline{X} = \frac{2{,}758}{48} = 57.46,$$

where 2,758 is the sum of all the divorce rates contained in Table 17.3, and 48 is the number of states for which we have data. Thus, one way of identifying the central tendency of the distribution of the divorce rate variable is to say that the mean divorce rate is 57.46 per 10,000 residents.

Whereas the mean is defined as the average value of a variable, the **median** is defined as the middle-most score on a variable in the data set. It is the value that separates the top half of the cases on the variable from the bottom half. The median is easily determined by counting cases, using the stem-and-leaf diagram in Table 17.6. To do so, we first have to divide the number of cases (i.e., N) by 2 and then take the number that the result of this division "grows to." "Grows to" is a fairly simple idea suggested by the inventor of the stem-and-leaf diagram. Any number that is not an integer (e.g., 10.5, 10.01, 12.9) "grows to" the next highest integer. Thus, 10.5 grows to 11, as does 10.01, and 12.9 grows to 13. Any integer grows to that number plus one-half, so 15 grows to 15.5, 20 grows to 20.5, and so on. Do not confuse "grows to" with rounding because they are slightly different.

In our example, when we divide 48 by 2, we get 24, which grows to 24.5. We now want to count cases in the stem-and-leaf diagram until we get to the twenty-fourth case. The median is the value that is halfway between the values of the twenty-fourth and twenty-fifth cases. In the divorce rate data, using Table 17.6, and counting from the lowest value, the twenty-fourth case has a value of 54. The twenty-fifth case has a value of 55. So the median for this distribution of data is 54.5. (If the "grows to" concept is confusing, an alternative way to conceptualize locating the median is to take the number of cases plus 1 and divide by 2; the resulting value is the case number corresponding to the median. If the resulting value ends in .5, one takes the average of the two adjacent cases.)

Now we have two different ways of identifying a typical value or central tendency for this distribution of data. The median value is 54.5 and the mean value is 57.46. One might wonder why these values differ and, given that they differ, which one better represents the central tendency of the distribution. The answer to the first question is that they differ because they are two alternative definitions of the central tendency. The median is the "middle-most" value, obtained by counting cases. In finding this value, we do not care by how much cases are above it or below it; we simply want to find the value that separates the top and bottom 50% of the cases. The mean, on the other hand, is the average value, and one way to think about what it means is as follows: Suppose we took all of the cases that have values above the mean, and we added up how far they were above the mean. Suppose now we did the same thing for all cases below the mean; we added up how far they were below the mean. By the definition of the mean, it turns out that these two sums must exactly equal each other. Therefore, whereas the median is defined by counting cases, the mean is defined by taking into account not the number of cases above it or below it but the degree to which cases are above it or below it.

Which of these two measures of central tendency is preferable? The answer is that they are both useful. The mean is used more frequently, primarily because it can be manipulated algebraically with greater ease than the median. As a result, the mean is used in computing many other useful statistics. A disadvantage of the mean, however, is that it is relatively less **robust** than the median. That is, the mean is affected more than the median by relatively extreme values, or outliers, in a distribution of data. A single extreme case in a distribution of scores can have a dramatic effect on the mean, whereas it might have little or no effect on the median. To illustrate, let us drop the outlier in the divorce rate data that we have been examining and recompute the mean and median. Recall that the state of Nevada, with its divorce rate of 168, was a clear outlier, that is, considerably different from all other states. If we delete Nevada from the distribution and recompute the mean and median, they turn out to be 55.11 and 54, respectively. Compare these values with the mean and median computed earlier and based on the full data set, including Nevada:

Including Nevada	***Deleting Nevada***
Mean = 57.46	Mean = 55.11
Median = 54.5	Median = 54

You can see that the presence of the outlier has a much larger effect on the mean than on the median. With the outlier deleted, the mean and median are in fairly good agreement about where the central tendency of the distribution lies.

Spread of a Distribution A second characteristic of a distribution that we might like to describe is how spread out it is. In other words, we might like to know whether the values are all bunched together closely around the central tendency or whether they are relatively spread out above and below it.

Just as we discussed two ways of characterizing the central tendency, we also discuss two ways of assessing how spread out a distribution of data is. The first way is based on counting cases, as was the median. This measure of spread, called the **inter-quartile range,** is defined as how far apart the twenty-fifth and seventy-fifth percentile scores are. What is a percentile score? The median is the fiftieth percentile score: It separates the bottom 50% of the distribution from the top 50%. Thus, the twenty-fifth percentile score is that score that separates the bottom 25% of the cases from the remaining 75%, and the seventy-fifth percentile score is that score that separates the top 25% of the cases from the remaining ones. The difference between these two percentile scores is the inter-quartile range.

To compute the inter-quartile range on the divorce rate data, we need to compute the twenty-fifth and seventy-fifth percentile scores. To do so, we divide the total number of cases by four and then take the number that this result grows to. In this case, 48/4 = 12, which grows to 12.5. To get the seventy-fifth percentile score, we count down from the top of the distribution of data in the stem-and-leaf diagram and average the twelfth and thirteenth values from the top. The seventy-fifth percentile score is thus (70 + 69)/2 = 69.5. The twenty-fifth percentile score is obtained analogously, by counting up from the bottom of the distribution of data and averaging the twelfth and thirteenth scores from the bottom. For these data, the twenty-fifth percentile score is (40 + 41)/2 = 40.5. The inter-quartile range is the difference between these two values:

$$\text{inter-quartile range} = 69.5 - 40.5 = 29$$

Because 25% of the cases have values less than 40.5 and because 25% of the cases have values greater than 69.5, the inter-quartile range defines the range within which lies the middle 50% of the distribution of scores. Clearly, if one distribution of scores is more spread out than another, the inter-quartile ranges will differ.

Notice that like the median, the inter-quartile range is a relatively robust measure of spread. Because we are only counting cases in computing it, it makes no difference whether Nevada has a divorce rate of 100, 168, or 2,000. It is still the case with the highest value and would appear in the highest 25% of the cases regardless of its actual value. Hence, the inter-quartile range is unaffected by the extremity of such outliers.

The second way of assessing the spread of a distribution of data is by asking how far, on average, the typical or average case is from the central tendency of the distribution. If, on average, cases have values quite discrepant from the center of the distribution, the distribution is more spread out or variable than if the cases are, on average, tightly bunched around the center.

The statistic we compute to estimate the variability of data around the mean is called the **variance,** and it is defined by

$$\frac{\sum_{i=1}^{N}(x_i - \overline{X})^2}{N-1}.$$

In other words, we take each observation (X_i), subtract the mean ($\overline{X}$), and square that difference. We then take the next observation, subtract the mean, and then square the difference. After we have summed all these squared deviations, we divide by $N - 1$ to obtain the variance. You might wonder why we are squaring the differences between each score and the mean and why we are dividing by $N - 1$ rather than N. We square the deviations because, if we did not, the sum of the deviations would necessarily be zero, as that is by definition a property of the mean. The reason for dividing by $N - 1$ is somewhat less intuitive. For now, all that is important to know is that when estimating the variance of a sample, dividing by N results in values that are slightly too small, so we divide by $N - 1$ instead.

Let us compute the variance for the divorce rate data, using the raw data from the stem-and-leaf diagram. We know that the mean value for all 48 cases is 57.46. For each case, we want to take the difference between that case's value and this mean, square the difference, and then total all those squared differences. Finally, we will divide by the number of cases less one:

$$\text{Variance} = [(30 - 57.46)^2 + (32 - 57.46)^2 + (32 - 57.46)^2 + \cdots + (168 - 57.46)^2] / 47 = 520.08$$

What does this number mean as a measure of how spread out this distribution is? By definition, the variance is the average squared difference between the cases in a distribution and the mean of the distribution. It is how far, in squared units, the average case is from the mean. Because most of us have trouble thinking in terms of squared units, the square root of the variance is frequently used as a measure of spread. The square root of the variance is known as the **standard deviation** and is defined as

$$\sqrt{\frac{\sum_{i=1}^{N}(x_i - \overline{X})^2}{N-1}}.$$

For the divorce rate data, the standard deviation equals 22.81.

We now have two measures of how spread out a distribution of data is: the inter-quartile range and the variance (or equivalently, the standard deviation). The former is based on counting cases, much like the median is as a measure of central tendency. The variance, on the other hand, is based not on counting cases but on how far cases are on average from the middle of a distribution. Which of these two measures is preferable?

There is no simple answer to this question, as there was none in choosing between the mean and median as measures of central tendency. Like the mean, the variance or standard deviation is used as a measure of spread more frequently than is the inter-quartile range. As we will see in the next chapter, the variance is used in computing other statistics that estimate the association between variables; however, the variance suffers from the same problem as the mean does: Relative to the inter-quartile range, it is not a very robust statistic. It tends to be affected by outliers more than does the inter-quartile range. To see this, let us compute the inter-quartile range and the variance for our data, first including and then deleting Nevada because of its relatively extreme divorce rate.

Including Nevada	*Deleting Nevada*
Variance = 520.30	Variance = 260.18
Inter-quartile range = 29	Inter-quartile range = 29

Clearly, the effect of deleting the outlier is much greater on the variance; the inter-quartile range in this example remains unchanged.

Other Characteristics and Other Distributions One of the things we noticed earlier about the divorce rate distribution is that it generally sloped down and to the right when we examined the shape of the frequency histogram or the stem-and-leaf diagram. Whether or not a distribution has an especially long tail in one direction or another is referred to as its **skewness.** A distribution that is positively skewed has more extreme high values than extreme low values; its long tail is at the upper end. A distribution that is negatively skewed has more extreme low values than high values; hence, its tail is at the lower end. A distribution that is completely symmetrical, with equally long tails at both its upper and lower ends is symmetric. Figure 17.4 shows the shape of skewed and symmetrical distributions.

We have now discussed three major characteristics of distributions: their central tendency, their spread or variability, and their skewness. All three of these can be determined by examining the stem-and-leaf diagram for the distribution of scores on a

FIGURE 17.4 **DISTRIBUTIONS ILLUSTRATING SKEWNESS**

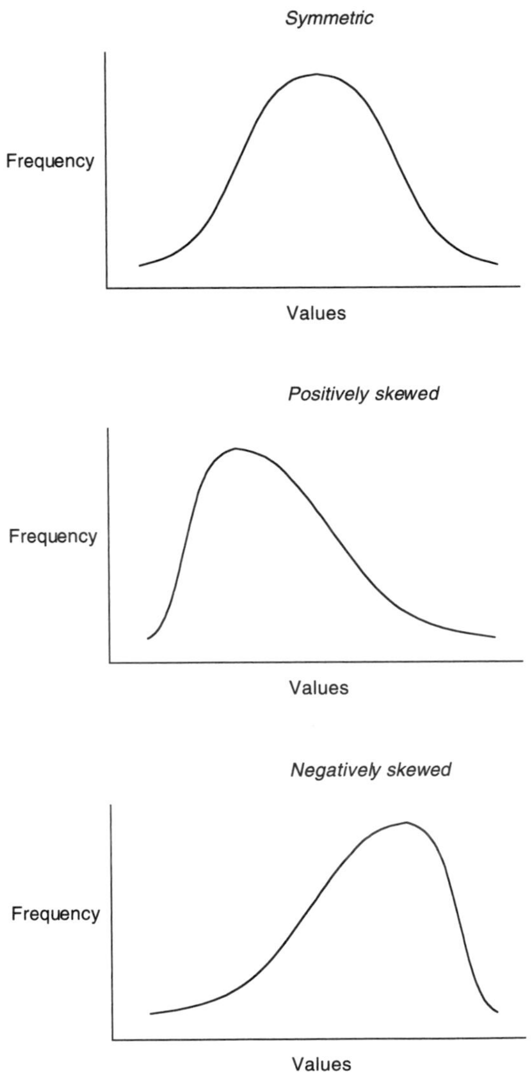

variable. So far, we have relied on the divorce rate data to illustrate these characteristics. We invite readers to return to Table 17.3 and generate stem-and-leaf diagrams for the marriage rate and birthrate data.

When that is done, one thing will be immediately clear. If the state of Nevada is an outlier in the divorce rate data, it is even more so in the marriage rate data. Whereas the majority of the states have marriage rates per 10,000 residents in the range of 80 to 180, Nevada's marriage rate is 1,474. Interestingly, however, Nevada is not relatively extreme on the birthrate variable.

Table 17.7 presents descriptive statistics for all three of the variables, both including Nevada in the distributions and excluding it. Examining these statistics makes clear the undue influence a single case can have on some measures of central tendency and spread when it is an extreme outlier. The effect of including Nevada in the marriage rate distribution is to increase the mean rate from 107.47 to 135.94. The effect on the variance is even more marked—from 543.38 to 39,436.19. Clearly, these two statistics are not robust to the presence of this outlier. Notice, however, that the median and inter-quartile range are hardly affected. This should teach us a lesson:

TABLE 17.7 STATES' MARRIAGE RATES, DIVORCE RATES, AND BIRTHRATES PER 10,000 RESIDENTS

	Including Nevada		
	Marriage Rate	**Divorce Rate**	**Birthrate**
Mean	135.94	57.46	166.35
Median	105.00	54.50	164.00
Inter-quartile range	31.50	29.00	23.50
Variance	39,436.19	520.08	878.91
Standard deviation	198.59	22.81	29.65
	Excluding Nevada		
	Marriage Rate	**Divorce Rate**	**Birthrate**
Mean	107.47	55.11	166.15
Median	105.00	54.00	164.00
Inter-quartile range	32.00	29.00	23.00
Variance	543.38	260.10	895.96
Standard deviation	23.31	16.13	29.93

Look for outliers. When they are present, rely on the median and inter-quartile range rather than the relatively less robust mean and variance. If for other reasons the mean and variance are to be used to assess central tendency and spread, do so only with extreme caution when outliers are present. Our recommendation is to compute and report the analyses twice, once including all data and once deleting outliers.

Although the computations involved in generating the descriptive statistics presented here are fairly straightforward, when sample size is large the computations can become onerous. Fortunately, these statistics and others can be obtained even for large data sets in minutes using statistical software. We used the SAS program to generate descriptive statistics for the divorce rate variable; the output is shown in Table 17.8. As you can see, this output provides a substantial amount of information, much useful but some rather esoteric. The top two sections provide the basic descriptive statistics we have been talking about such as the mean, median, variance, standard deviation, and inter-quartile range. Note that we also are given the value for an index of the skewness of the distribution. (The value would be zero if the distribution were symmetrical.) The section labeled "Tests for Location" provides a test for the significance of the difference of the mean from zero, a test that occasionally can be meaningful (for example, if the underlying data were change scores) but not in the current data set. The section labeled "Quantiles" is very useful; here the output provides values for the median and quartiles along with other percentile scores often deemed of interest. Finally, in the bottom section of the output we are given information about potential outlying scores. Such information is useful in terms of

TABLE 17.8 **OUTPUT FROM PROC UNIVARIATE SHOWING DESCRIPTIVE STATISTICS FOR DIVORCE VARIABLE**

```
Univariate Statistics for the Divorce Variable

The UNIVARIATE Procedure
Variable: divorce

Moments
N                        48    Sum Weights              48
Mean             57.4583333    Sum Observations       2758
Std Deviation    22.8053356    Variance         520.083333
Skewness         2.49103293    Kurtosis         10.6985587
Uncorrected SS       182914    Corrected SS     24443.9167
Coeff Variation  39.6902143    Std Error Mean   3.29166667

Basic Statistical Measures

     Location                  Variability
Mean     57.45833    Std Deviation           22.80534
Median   54.50000    Variance               520.08333
```

(Continued)

TABLE 17.8 OUTPUT FROM PROC UNIVARIATE SHOWING DESCRIPTIVE STATISTICS FOR DIVORCE VARIABLE (CONTINUED)

```
Mode        39.00000    Range                   138.0000
                        Inter-quartile Range    29.00000

NOTE: The mode displayed is the smallest of 3 modes with a count
                         of 3.

              Tests for Location: Mu0=0
      Test         -Statistic-    - - - p Value- - -
      Student's t  t  17.4557     Pr > |t|   <.0001
      Sign         M       24     Pr >= |M|  <.0001
      Signed Rank  S      588     Pr >= |S|  <.0001

               Quantiles  (Definition 5)

                  Quantile   Estimate
                  100% Max     168.0
                  99%          168.0
                  95%           82.0
                  90%           79.0
                  75% Q3        69.5
                  50% Median    54.5
                  25% Q1        40.5
                  10%           36.0
                  5%            32.0
                  1%            30.0
                  0% Min        30.0

                 Extreme Observations

       - - - Lowest- - -        - - Highest- -

         Value       Obs        Value        Obs

          30          19          79          34
          32          32          80          29
          32          28          82           2
          34          36          93           3
          36          47         168          26
```

identifying outliers, and knowing the specific scores allows us to go back to the data set and check for possible errors or otherwise figure out what makes these particular scores so atypical. In short, a very brief command file and a few clicks of the mouse produced a wealth of information to help us begin working with our data.

Summary

Once data have been collected, they must be put in a form to permit analysis. To do so, the researcher must construct a data matrix, in which the columns are variables, the rows are the units of analysis, and the cells are the actual data. All coding decisions should be recorded in a codebook. Above all, careful records should be maintained of the data matrix and how it was constructed to permit the researcher who collected the data, as well as others, to use them in the future. Statistical software can then be used with relative ease to produce tables, graphs, and descriptive statistics for each variable in the data set.

In exploring data for each variable, we discussed how frequency histograms and stem-and-leaf diagrams allow us to form impressions about the shape of a distribution. The median is a measure of central tendency based on counting cases: It is the value that separates the top and bottom 50% of the cases. The mean is the average value of a distribution and, as such, takes into account not how many cases are below it or above it but by how much cases are below it or above it. Measures of spread include the inter-quartile range, the variance, and the standard deviation. The inter-quartile range gives the range of values within which the middle 50% of a distribution lies. The variance tells us how far on average cases are from the mean of the distribution, measuring distances in squared units. The standard deviation is simply the square root of the variance.

Throughout this chapter we have paid particular attention to the undue influence that outliers can have on particular statistics. We will continue to emphasize that point in the next chapter as well.

Key Concepts

cases
central tendency
codebook
command/syntax files
data
data analysis
data management
data matrix
data set
descriptive statistics
ecological fallacy
errors of generalization
frequency distribution
frequency histogram
inter-quartile range
mean
median
outlier
output
robust
skewness
standard deviation
statistical independence
stem-and-leaf diagram
system file
units of analysis
variance

On the Web

http://www.galaxy.gmu.edu/papers/astr1.html "A Guide to Statistical Software." A Web page that provides detailed descriptions of a large number of statistical software packages, including links to vendor and user support sites.

http://www.stat.sc.edu/webstat/ A free Web-based application for obtaining descriptive statistics, it generates graphical displays that can be downloaded and imported into manuscripts or reports.

http://www.sas.com This is the SAS Institute's Web site. It contains information about SAS, technical support, and items of interest to both new and advanced users.

http://www.spss.com The home page for the SPSS statistical software package. The site includes descriptions of other statistical software packages owned by SPSS such as SYSTAT and Sigma Plot.

Further Reading

Abelson, R. P. (1995). *Statistics as principled argument.* Hillsdale, NJ: Erlbaum.

Dilorio, F. C., & Hardy, K. A. (1996). *Quick start to data analysis with SAS.* Belmont, CA: Wadsworth.

Green, S. B. Salkind, N. J., & Akey, T. M. (1999). *Using SPSS for Windows: Analyzing and understanding data* (2nd ed.). Upper Saddle River, NJ: Prentice Hall.

CHAPTER

18

Estimates and Tests of Association

Most of the phenomena that social scientists study involve associations between variables. For instance, a researcher might want to know whether political party affiliation is associated with age; whether educational attainment is associated with subsequent earnings; whether birth, marriage, and divorce rates are interrelated; or whether one personality trait is associated with another. When social scientists analyze their data, then, not only do they want to describe the distributions of single variables but they also want to estimate associations between two or more variables. In this chapter we discuss procedures for estimating and testing associations between two variables. Although our primary concern is the simple association between two variables, we also touch on estimates and tests that consider the influence of a third variable on such associations.

Associations Between Dichotomous Variables

When we say two variables are associated with each other, what exactly do we mean? What does it mean to hypothesize that marriage and divorce rates are associated across states? To answer this question initially, let us simplify considerably. Rather than having a whole range of possible values for marriage and divorce rates, let us make the simplifying assumption that these two variables can each take on only two values: high and low. In other words, the marriage and divorce rate data for any particular state are recoded simply as relatively high or relatively low, rather than as specific numbers per 10,000 residents as in the previous chapter.

To make our simplifying assumption that these variables have only two values, we have to translate the raw data from Table 17.3 in the previous chapter into these new values. Because the median is the measure of central tendency that divides the sample in half on a given variable, let us use the median to define the new values: Any state whose marriage or divorce rate exceeds the median will be coded "high" on that variable. Any state with a value below the median will be coded "low." If there are states whose value is exactly at the median, we will arbitrarily assign them to the high group.

Before we proceed, there is an important caveat that we must state regarding the use of this procedure. We are creating these new variables by performing a **median split** on the divorce and marriage rate variables because we think it is helpful to illustrate different measures of association and test statistics using a common data set. In actual practice, if our raw data are initially in the form of continuous variables as is the case here, we would want to analyze them using statistics appropriate for continuous variables, such as the correlation coefficient described later in the chapter. It is

TABLE 18.1 DICHOTOMOUS MARRIAGE AND DIVORCE DATA FOR 48 CONTIGUOUS STATES

State	Marriage	Divorce	State	Marriage	Divorce
Alabama	high	high	Nebraska	low	low
Arizona	high	high	Nevada	high	high
Arkansas	high	high	New Hampshire	low	high
California	low	high	New Jersey	low	low
Colorado	high	high	New Mexico	high	high
Connecticut	low	low	New York	low	low
Delaware	low	low	North Carolina	low	low
Florida	high	high	North Dakota	low	low
Georgia	high	high	Ohio	low	high
Idaho	high	high	Oklahoma	high	high
Illinois	low	low	Oregon	low	high
Indiana	high	high	Pennsylvania	low	low
Iowa	low	low	Rhode Island	low	low
Kansas	high	low	South Carolina	high	low
Kentucky	low	low	South Dakota	high	low
Louisiana	low	low	Tennessee	high	high
Maine	high	high	Texas	high	high
Maryland	high	low	Utah	high	high
Massachusetts	low	low	Vermont	high	low
Michigan	low	low	Virginia	high	low
Minnesota	low	low	Washington	high	high
Mississippi	high	high	West Virginia	low	low
Missouri	high	high	Wisconsin	low	low
Montana	low	high	Wyoming	high	high

unwise to simplify or **coarsely categorize** variables measured on an interval or ratio scale, as this can reduce the estimate of association and the sensitivity of our statistical tests substantially.

Keeping that caveat in mind, Table 18.1 presents the recoded marriage and divorce rate data for all 48 states. A portion of this same data set as it would appear in an SPSS data file is shown in Figure 18.1. With only two possible values for each of our variables, the variables are **dichotomous.** Now, how might we tell if the marriage and divorce variables are associated?

An examination of Table 18.1 reveals that states that have a "low" value on the divorce variable tend also to have a "low" value on the marriage variable. Similarly, states with a high divorce rate tend also to have a high marriage rate. Clearly, there are exceptions to this generalization: New Hampshire, Vermont, Ohio, South Dakota, Kansas, Maryland, Virginia, South Carolina, Montana, Oregon, and

FIGURE 18.1 A PORTION OF THE DATA SET DISPLAYED IN TABLE 18.1 AS IT APPEARS IN AN SPSS DATA FILE

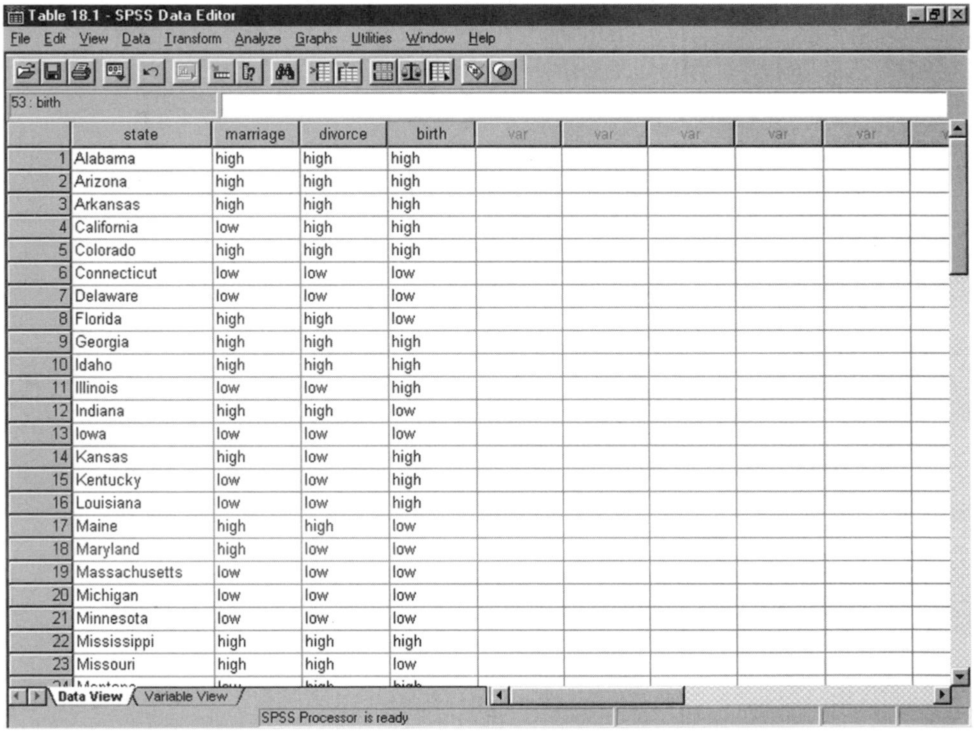

	state	marriage	divorce	birth	var	var	var	var	var
1	Alabama	high	high	high					
2	Arizona	high	high	high					
3	Arkansas	high	high	high					
4	California	low	high	high					
5	Colorado	high	high	high					
6	Connecticut	low	low	low					
7	Delaware	low	low	low					
8	Florida	high	high	low					
9	Georgia	high	high	high					
10	Idaho	high	high	high					
11	Illinois	low	low	high					
12	Indiana	high	high	low					
13	Iowa	low	low	low					
14	Kansas	high	low	high					
15	Kentucky	low	low	high					
16	Louisiana	low	low	high					
17	Maine	high	high	low					
18	Maryland	high	low	low					
19	Massachusetts	low	low	low					
20	Michigan	low	low	low					
21	Minnesota	low	low	low					
22	Mississippi	high	high	high					
23	Missouri	high	high	low					

California are all high on one of the two variables and low on the other. But out of the 48 states, 37 of them are either high or low on both.

An easy way to display these dichotomous data for the two variables is by putting them into what is called a **contingency table.** To construct such a table, we lay out all the possible pairs of values that states might have on these two variables: high–high, high–low, low–high, and low–low. We make one variable—say, divorce rate—the columns of the contingency table and the other variable the rows. There are thus two columns and two rows to the table because each variable only has two possible values. We then count the number of states that fall into each of the four possible cells of the table. For instance, Maine is in the high–high cell, New Hampshire is in the low–high cell, and so forth. The resulting contingency table as generated by SPSS is presented in Figure 18.2.

Eighteen states, or 37.5% of the 48 states in the sample, are low on both variables. Five states (10.4%) are high on divorce and low on marriage. Six states (12.5%)

FIGURE 18.2 CONTINGENCY TABLE OF MARRIAGE AND DIVORCE VARIABLES FROM TABLE 18.1

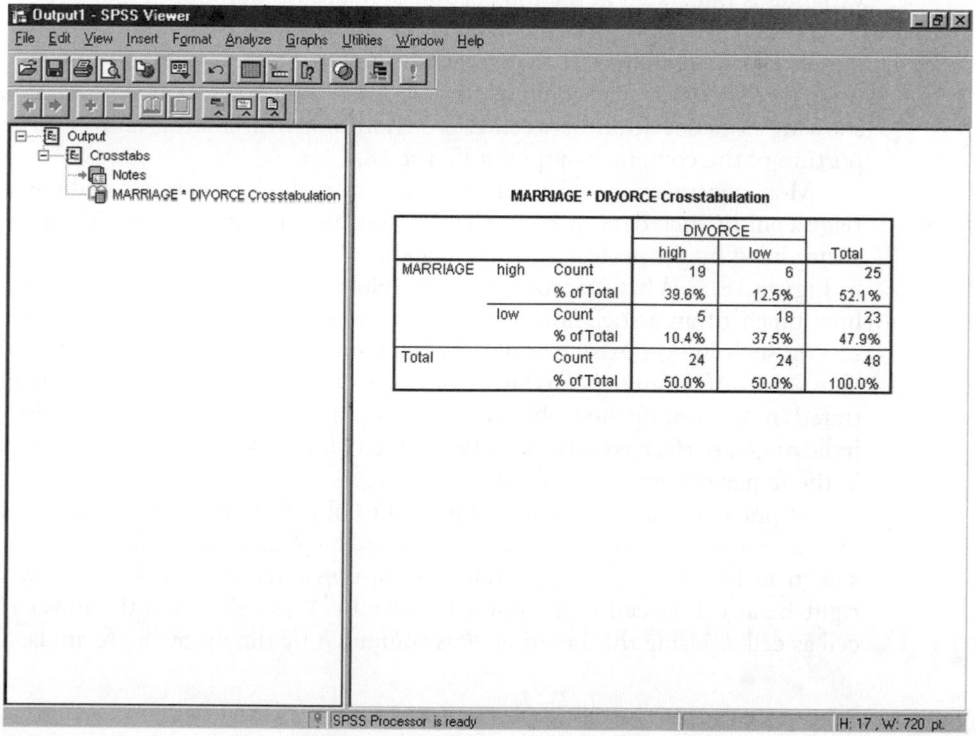

MARRIAGE * DIVORCE Crosstabulation

			DIVORCE		
			high	low	Total
MARRIAGE	high	Count	19	6	25
		% of Total	39.6%	12.5%	52.1%
	low	Count	5	18	23
		% of Total	10.4%	37.5%	47.9%
Total		Count	24	24	48
		% of Total	50.0%	50.0%	100.0%

are low on divorce and high on marriage. And finally, 19 states (39.6%) are high on both. The other numbers in the contingency table, outside of the numbers in the four cells just described (in the column and row labeled "Total"), are called the **marginal frequencies.** They tell us how many states have a given value on one of the variables, ignoring their value on the other. Thus, for instance, 23 of the 48 states, or 47.9%, are relatively low on marriage. The grand total number of states, 48, is indicated at the bottom right of the table.

The question of whether marriage and divorce rates are associated in the 48 states is really a question about our ability to predict a state's value on one of the two variables from knowledge of its value on the other variable. In terms of the contingency table, the question of association between the two dichotomous variables is whether we can predict which column a state falls into once we know which row of the table it is in. Or, equivalently, can we predict which row a state is in, given that we know which column it is in?

If the two variables were perfectly associated with each other, we should be able to perfectly predict columns from rows or vice versa. Thus, states might all be low on both variables or high on both variables, and the low–high and high–low cells would have zero frequencies. A hypothetical perfect association between two dichotomous variables is illustrated in the top portion of the SPSS output in Figure 18.3.

If two variables were completely unassociated with each other, we could not predict rows from columns at all. Knowing which column a state falls in would not give us any information that could be used in predicting rows. A hypothetical set of data showing no association between two dichotomous variables is shown in the bottom portion of the computer output in Figure 18.3.

Most contingency tables constructed with real data, such as our divorce-by-marriage contingency data in Figure 18.2, show associations between the two extremes exemplified by the perfect association and the total absence of an association depicted in Figure 18.3. What we would like, therefore, is some way of indexing or assessing how much of an association there is between two dichotomous variables. Although several such indices exist, one of the most commonly used is Φ (pronounced fī or fē). The values of Φ range from 0 to ± 1.0, with 0 indicating no association at all (as illustrated in the contingency table in the lower portion of Figure 18.3) and $+1.0$ or -1.0 indicating a perfect association between the two variables (as in the contingency table in the upper portion of the figure).

In practice, statistical software is used to obtain Φ. It is also, however, quite simple to compute by hand. Looking back at the four cells in the contingency table shown in Figure 18.2, we can refer to the upper left-hand cell as cell *a*, the upper right-hand cell as cell *b*, the lower left-hand cell as cell *c*, and the lower right-hand cell as cell *d*. Using this notation, Φ is computed by the following formula:

$$\phi = \frac{(ad - bc)}{\sqrt{(a + b)(c + d)(a + c)(b + d)}},$$

where *a*, *b*, *c*, and *d* refer to the number of states in each cell.

FIGURE 18.3 **CONTINGENCY TABLES ILLUSTRATING HYPOTHETICAL PERFECT ASSOCIATION (TOP) AND TOTAL ABSENCE OF AN ASSOCIATION (BOTTOM) BETWEEN VARIABLES *X* AND *Y***

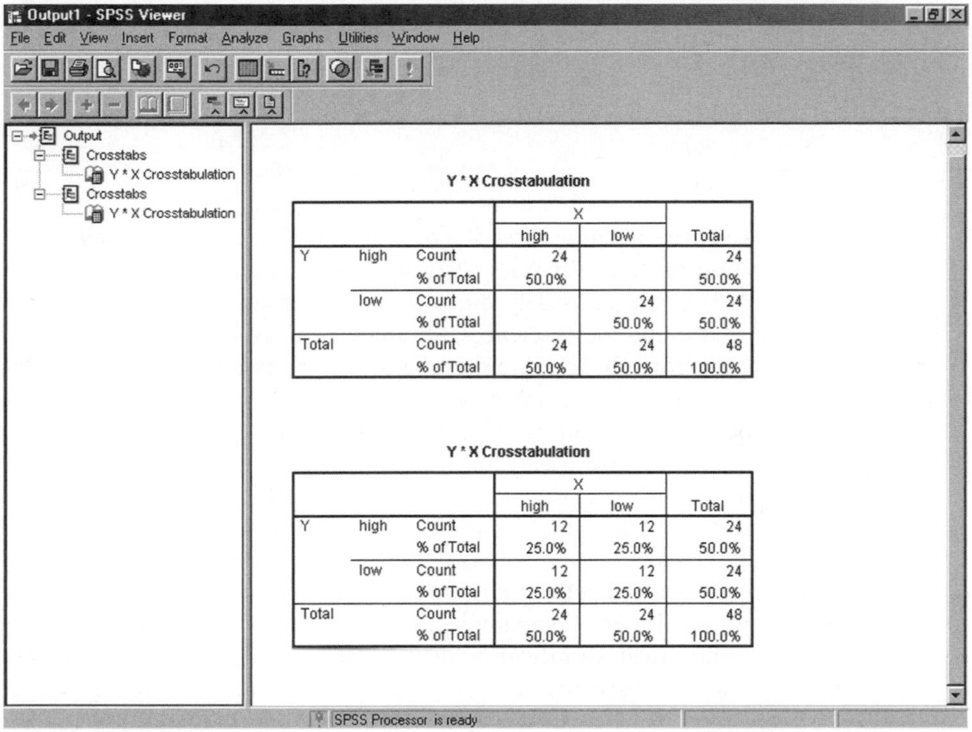

Y * X Crosstabulation

			X		
			high	low	Total
Y	high	Count	24		24
		% of Total	50.0%		50.0%
	low	Count		24	24
		% of Total		50.0%	50.0%
Total		Count	24	24	48
		% of Total	50.0%	50.0%	100.0%

Y * X Crosstabulation

			X		
			high	low	Total
Y	high	Count	12	12	24
		% of Total	25.0%	25.0%	50.0%
	low	Count	12	12	24
		% of Total	25.0%	25.0%	50.0%
Total		Count	24	24	48
		% of Total	50.0%	50.0%	100.0%

For our data, then,

$$\phi = \frac{((19 \times 18) - (6 \times 5))}{\sqrt{(19 + 6)(5 + 18)(19 + 5)(6 + 18)}} = .54.$$

In Table 18.2 are Φ values for all associations between the dichotomously coded marriage, divorce, and birthrate variables. (The values of 1.00 on the diagonal do not figure into this discussion.) As we can see from this table, all three variables seem to be associated with each other in dichotomous form. The strongest association of the three is between the states' divorce and marriage rates.

TABLE 18.2 **Estimates of Association (ϕ) Between Dichotomously Coded Marriage, Divorce, and Birthrate Variables**

Variable	Marriage Rate	Divorce Rate	Birthrate
Marriage Rate	1.00		
Divorce Rate	.54	1.00	
Birthrate	.33	.38	1.00

How can we interpret these Φ coefficients? We know that as Φ approaches an absolute value of 1.0, it implies a stronger association between the two variables. Cohen (1977) offered a widely used set of criteria for interpreting values of Φ; he suggested that in the social sciences, Φ values from .10 to .30 indicate a weak association; Φ values from .30 to .50 indicate a moderate association; and Φ values greater than .50 indicate a strong association. Using these criteria, our estimate indicates a strong association between states' divorce and marriage rates.

Cohen's criteria are useful for determining the strength of association signified by values of Φ, but we usually are interested in another question as well. We want to know if our finding that states' divorce and marriage rates are associated would replicate in another sample; in other words, we want to know if our estimate is reliable or whether it is merely a reflection of the peculiarities of our sample. To answer that question, we need more than simply an index of association: We need to compute a test of the **statistical significance** of the result—that is, an index of the degree of confidence we can have that an association we observe in a sample would emerge if we were to replicate the study using another sample from the same population. In the next section, we describe the logic underlying tests of statistical significance and how we go about computing a test of significance in our sample.

Inferring Associations in Populations from Sample Data

Beyond simply calculating the magnitude of an association in a set of data from a sample, we generally want to ask questions about what that association tells us about the population of observations from which we have drawn a sample. This brings us back to some fundamental notions of sampling that were introduced in Chapter 8. Recall from that chapter that the population consists of all those objects, elements, or individuals to which we would like to be able to generalize our results. Yet because it is inefficient to gather data from the entire population, we proceed to gather data from a sample of respondents drawn from the population of interest.

In light of this need to generalize from our samples to populations of interest, we frequently want to know whether an observed association between two variables in a sample of data can be generalized to the population from which that sample has been drawn. In other words, just because we estimate from some set of data that X and Y are strongly associated, does that mean we can necessarily conclude that if we gathered data on X and Y from the entire population we would find an association between them? Can we infer an association in a population from the observation of one in a sample of data? That is the question to be answered in this section.

The logic of statistical inference starts with what is called a **null hypothesis,** a statement that specifies what we hope is *not* true in the population. In the case of an association between two variables, we usually want to argue for theoretical reasons that the two variables are associated with each other. That is, based on Φ, or some other index of association that we calculate from some sample of observations, we hope to be able to conclude that the two variables are associated not only in the sample but also in the population from which the sample was drawn. Therefore, our null hypothesis would be that the two variables are unassociated in the population or, in other words, that the value of Φ in the population, if we could measure X and Y for everyone, is 0. By looking at our sample data, we hope to be able to conclude that this null hypothesis is in error; we would like to reject the null hypothesis.

It probably seems odd that when we are interested in one hypothesis (that two variables are associated), we start with its opposite (that they are unassociated) in statistical inference. But the logic behind this curious approach is not difficult to follow. There is a direct analogy with criminal trials. A jury must decide whether a defendant is guilty of the crime of which he or she is accused. Before the trial begins and any arguments are heard, the defendant is entitled in the U.S. legal system to a "presumption of innocence," that the defendant did not commit the crime. The prosecutor would like the hypothesis of guilty to be confirmed by the jury, but the prosecutor must provide enough evidence to overrule this presumption of innocence beyond a reasonable doubt. Our legal system recognizes that it is not possible to prove the lack of innocence, or guilt, of a defendant conclusively, without any doubts whatsoever. So the requirement is that the prosecution must disprove innocence beyond a reasonable doubt.

Social scientists are engaged in a task quite analogous to that of the prosecutor. When they collect data from a sample, they wish to conclude that the hypothesis that motivated the research is correct (i.e., that two variables are associated). So they start out with the presumption that their hypothesis is not true—the null hypothesis. They must then demonstrate, based on their sample of data, that this presumption is unlikely to be true in the population. Only then can they have reasonable confidence that their research hypothesis is potentially true in the population. Just as in the courtroom, however, there always will remain the possibility that, although the null hypothesis is incorrect, the particular explanation proposed by the researcher is incorrect (i.e., there is an alternative explanation for the findings).

The null hypothesis of no association between two variables is either in fact true in the population or it is not. That is, if we could gather data from everyone in the population, we would either find an association or we would not. In the latter case, the null hypothesis would not be rejected; in the former, it would be rejected. Based on our sample data our task is to decide whether the null hypothesis ought to be rejected as false or not. That is, we attempt to distinguish between the two states of reality in the population on the basis of our sample data. The two possible states of reality and the two possible conclusions we could reach based on our sample data set up the decision matrix in Table 18.3. The columns of this matrix represent the states of reality; the rows represent decisions we might reach. The cells, defined by the intersections of rows and columns, inform us about the quality of our decision. Two cells, the upper left and lower right, indicate a correct decision. In the upper left-hand cell, the null hypothesis is in fact true—that is, the two variables are in fact not associated—and on the basis of our sample data we did not reject the null hypothesis. In the lower right-hand cell, the null hypothesis is in fact false—that is, the two variables are in fact associated in the population—and, based on the sample data, we rejected the null hypothesis.

If we end up in the other two cells of the decision matrix (lower left or upper right), we have reached an erroneous conclusion. In the lower left-hand cell we make what is called a **Type I error.** As defined by the row and column of this cell, we can see from the matrix that this outcome results when we reject the null hypothesis of no association in the population erroneously when in fact there is no association. In other words, our sample data led us to conclude that there is an association when in fact there is none. The other erroneous cell of the matrix defines what is called a **Type II error.** If we end up in the upper right-hand cell, we failed to reject the null hypothesis based on our sample data when in fact that null hypothesis is false and should have been rejected. In other words, we failed to realize that X and Y are associated in the population when in fact they are. We failed to realize that the hypothesis that motivated the research in the first place could be correct.

Now that we have defined the decision to be made and its possible outcomes, let us proceed to examine how the decision is to be made. Remember we start with the null hypothesis as the presumption, much as the jury is supposed to start with the presumption of innocence. Only if the evidence encountered subsequently is sufficiently compelling or surprising will we abandon this presumption. Let us then assume that the presumption of no association in the population is correct. Under this presumption, what would constitute compelling or surprising evidence in our sample? In other words, what sort of results in our sample would be sufficiently compelling to cause us

TABLE 18.3 STATISTICAL INFERENCES DECISION MATRIX

	Null Hypothesis in Fact True	**Null Hypothesis in Fact False**
Decide Not to Reject Null Hypothesis	Correct	Type II error
Decide to Reject Null Hypothesis	Type I Error	Correct

to abandon the null hypothesis? If we drew a random sample of 10 cases and we observed a Φ of .10, would that constitute sufficiently compelling evidence to cause us to abandon our presumption of no association? What if we drew a random sample of size 10 and the sample value Φ was .80; would that be sufficiently compelling?

To answer the question of what constitutes improbable sample results if the null hypothesis of no association is true, we need to compute the statistical significance of the association. There is a large number of different statistical tests one can compute. The significance test most commonly associated with contingency tables and Φ is called $\boldsymbol{\chi^2}$ (pronounced kī square). χ^2 can be computed easily from Φ:

$$\chi^2 = \phi^2 \times N$$

For our example, with $\Phi = .54$ and $N = 48$, χ^2 is equal to 14.0. Alternatively, χ^2 can be computed directly from the data in the contingency table using this computational formula:

$$\chi^2 = \frac{N(ad - bc)^2}{(a + b)(c + d)(a + c)(b + d)}$$

Note the similarity between this formula for χ^2 and the formula for Φ; what this shows us is that measures of association and statistical tests are, in many ways, two sides of the same coin. They are related to each other in meaningful and important ways, a theme we explore further in Chapter 19.

Of course, the χ^2 value of 14.0 by itself does not tell us what we want to know, which is the probability that our "presumption of innocence" (the null hypothesis) is false. Fortunately, statisticians long ago worked out the probability of obtaining any given significance test value in samples of varying sizes. Statistical software such as SAS or SPSS compute and report the probabilities associated with a given χ^2 value automatically; most standard statistics textbooks also provide probability tables for common statistics. In our example, a χ^2 of 14.0 and an N of 48 is association with a probability level of .0001. This means that the probability of obtaining a χ^2 of 14.0 or higher in our sample, if the null hypothesis of no association between the two variables in the population were correct, would be only .0001, a highly improbable result indeed.

The notion of a population in this example is admittedly a little strange because the data from the 48 states constitute nearly the complete set of data for that given year. Nevertheless, we can still ask the question about whether this association is different from zero (the null hypothesis) in the population, recognizing that this population is in some sense a hypothetical entity. Our real question here is whether this association between the two variables would hold up if we did the study over and over again, for many different years and conceivably using different subsamples of states. In a formal sense the population remains undefined, yet we still want to know whether the association between the two variables that we observe in our data is reliable, that is, one that we can count on and expect to see again when using data from future years and other samples of states.

A χ^2 with a probability level (or, as it is often referred to, ***p*-value**) of .0001 is clearly a value that would give us grounds to reject the null hypothesis because it suggests that, given our estimate of association ($\Phi = .54$), there is only a 1 in 10,000 chance that we have incorrectly rejected the null hypothesis of no association. A χ^2 associated with a high *p*-value, say, $p = .50$, is also unambiguous. A *p*-value of .50 tells us that we have a 50–50 chance of obtaining the χ^2 value that we did if the null hypothesis were true, and obviously we would not want to reject the null hypothesis if there was a 50% chance it was correct. But at what point between the two extremes of .0001 and .50 do we decide that the null hypothesis should be rejected? In the social sciences, we have adopted the probability value of .05 (i.e., 1 in 20) as the cutoff for rejecting the null hypothesis. In other words, if the probability that we would obtain a given value of a particular statistic if the null hypothesis were true is .05 or less, we conclude that the null hypothesis can be rejected.

Just as in a criminal trial, there is, of course, no guarantee that we have reached the right verdict. It is entirely possible that the null hypothesis is in fact true and that we have simply observed a rare or unusual sample value of χ^2 (i.e., we made a Type I error). Because we have defined a surprising sample result as one that would occur less often than 1 time in 20 if the null hypothesis is true (i.e., $p < .05$), the probability that in fact such a surprising bit of evidence occurs when the null hypothesis is true is 1 in 20. In other words, once we decide to reject the null hypothesis as a result of observing a sample value of χ^2 that would occur less often than 1 time in 20 if the null hypothesis were true, we are risking a 1 in 20 probability of a Type I statistical error. The odds are in fact 1 in 20 that such a sample value of χ^2 would occur when the null hypothesis of no association is in fact true in the population.

It is important, however, that readers understand that the cutoff of $p < .05$ is a scientific convention and nothing more. There is nothing intrinsically meaningful or valuable about the .05 *p*-value; it is merely an arbitrary decision made by social science researchers that we are willing to tolerate making a Type I error 5% of the time. It is tempting to take the .05 cutoff too seriously; many students make the mistake of concluding that if their *p*-value = .04, they have "found something" but that if their *p*-value = .06, there is no support for their hypothesis. Many wise statisticians and methodologists have decried this kind of all-or-none thinking (see, for example, Cohen, 1994; Hunter, 1997; Meehl, 1978), and perhaps Rosnow and Rosenthal (1989) put it best when they said, "surely, God loves the .06 nearly as much as the .05" (p. 1277). When we cover meta-analysis in Chapter 19, we revisit this issue and stress the importance of always computing and reporting estimates of association in addition to significance tests.

Associations Between Continuous Variables

We have talked about how to estimate associations between two dichotomous variables and how to test those associations for their statistical significance. We turn now to a discussion of how to estimate the association between two continuous variables. Many of the underlying principles are the same, but there are differences in how we present the data and compute our measures and significance tests. For example, with dichotomous or nominal data, it is most efficient to present data in terms of a contingency table that lists the frequencies of cases that fall into the various combinations of levels of the two variables. With continuous variables, however, there is a large number, indeed infinite in theory, of possible values a variable can take. As a result, it is unlikely that any two cases have exactly the same values on the two variables. Hence, rather than counting frequencies in the cells of the table, we construct a table in which each case is represented by a single point in a two-dimensional graph, positioned according to its values on the two variables. Such a graph is called a **scatterplot.**

Let us make such a graph for the raw data on states' divorce and marriage rates from Table 17.3. We will array the possible values on the divorce variable along the horizontal axis of the scatterplot and the possible values on the marriage variable along the vertical axis. To do so we need to identify the lower and upper extremes of the values we need to include for each variable in order to represent all cases in the scatterplot. For the divorce variable, the lowest rate is 30 (Massachusetts) and the highest is 168 (Nevada). For the marriage variable, the lowest rate is 75 (both New Jersey and Delaware) and the highest is 1,474 (again Nevada). Hence, our horizontal axis has to at least encompass values from 30 to 168 and our vertical axis from 75 to 1,474. Once the two axes are laid out, we draw a symbol for each state in the graph, positioned so that its divorce rate is indicated by where it falls on the horizontal axis and its marriage rate by where it falls on the vertical axis.

In Figure 18.4 is a scatterplot of these two variables generated by SPSS. It is apparent that the axes required to include the Nevada data in the scatterplot leave a plot that is not very useful for visually examining the association between the two variables. All of the points, representing states, are clustered in the lower left-hand portion of the graph, with one exception. The state of Nevada is positioned in the far upper right-hand corner of the scatterplot. What has happened is that when we include Nevada in the graph, the scale values of the axes must be so compressed that differences among the other states seem to be inconsequential. An extreme case, such as Nevada is on these two variables, can make a scatterplot useless in examining associations between continuous variables and can greatly distort measures of association.

Why did this issue not come up earlier in this chapter when we were examining the association between these two variables by using a dichotomous contingency table and Φ? The answer is that under the dichotomous recoding of the variables, Nevada appeared simply in the "high" category on both variables. The fact that its raw values were considerably different from the raw values of other states in the "high" categories was lost. The implication is that measures of association between variables are relatively more resistant to the effect of outliers when those variables are treated as if they were measured on a nominal or ordinal scale rather than an interval or ratio scale.

In Figure 18.5 we have generated a new scatterplot for these data, omitting the state of Nevada. Each point in this scatterplot represents a different state (if one

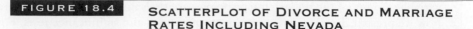

FIGURE 18.4 SCATTERPLOT OF DIVORCE AND MARRIAGE RATES INCLUDING NEVADA

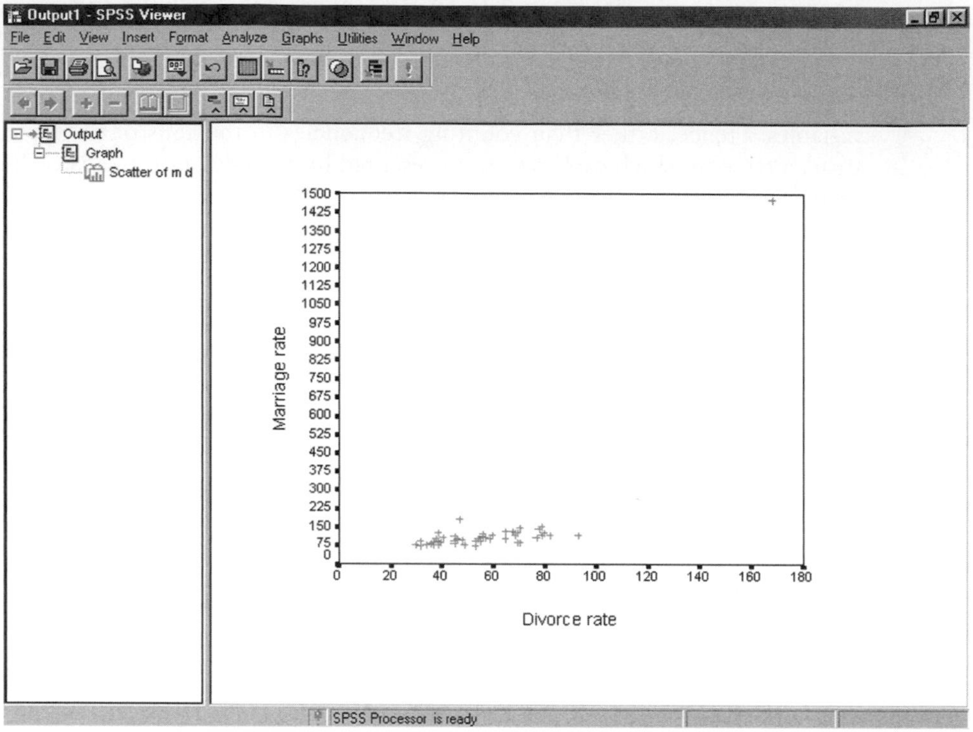

should count them, there are 47 points), and all the information about states' divorce and marriage rates in Table 17.3 is contained in this scatterplot as well. Remembering from earlier in the chapter that an association between two variables means that we can predict one from the other, we see from this scatterplot that there is an association between the two variables. The points have a clear upward trend from the lower left of the plot to the upper right. Higher marriage rates seem to be found with higher divorce rates, and at the opposite end of the scatterplot, lower marriage rates seem generally to go with lower divorce rates.

To be more precise about predicting values on one variable from the other, we could draw a straight line through the points in the plot so that the line summarizes the association between the two variables. We could then use this straight line to generate predictions of one variable from the other. In other words, once we had a straight line that summarized the association between the two variables, we could predict a given marriage rate from a given divorce rate based on this idealized depiction of the association.

In Figure 18.5 we have asked SPSS to insert a line into the scatterplot that best captures the association between marriage and divorce rates. To see how such a line can be used to predict values of one variable from the other, suppose we wanted to predict, in light of these data, what value on the marriage rate variable seems to go with a divorce rate of 60 per 10,000. We would go up from the horizontal axis at 60 until we hit our prediction line, and then we would see at what value on the vertical axis we found ourselves. As this table shows, our predicted marriage rate would be about 115 per 10,000.

Of course, a straight line is just one possible form that a prediction function could take. For some data, when we look at a scatterplot, it might appear that a

FIGURE 18.5

SCATTERPLOT AND SUMMARY LINE OF DIVORCE AND MARRIAGE RATES EXCLUDING NEVADA

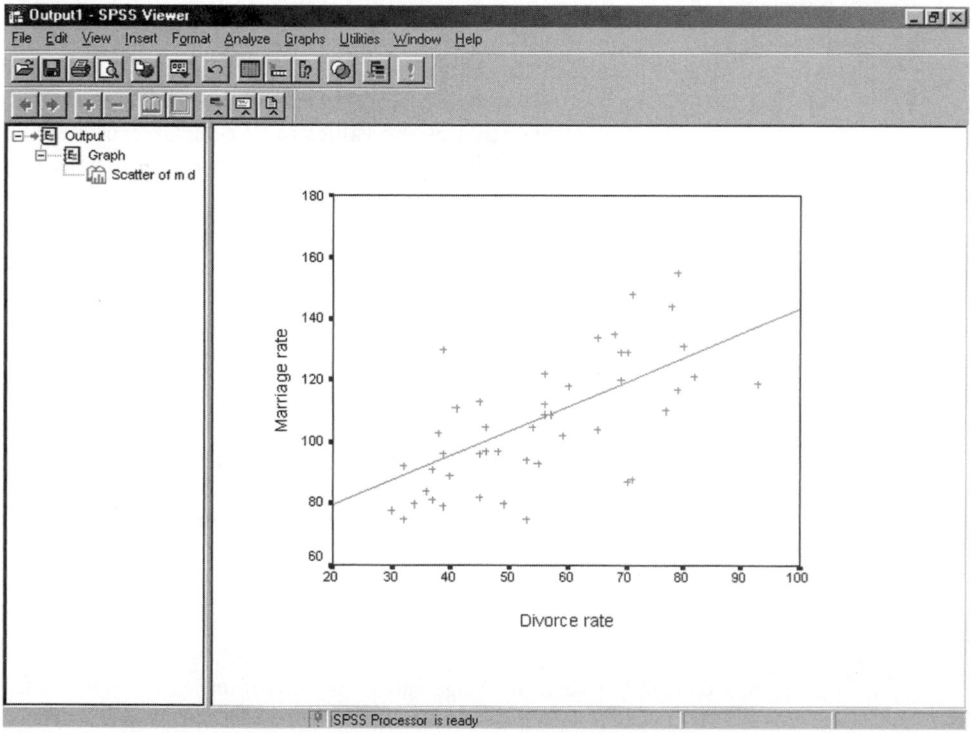

SOURCE: Created with SPSS® software.

curved rather than a straight line best summarizes the association between the two variables. By convention, however, we normally use a straight line as the prediction function, and thus we normally refer to associations between variables as **linear associations.**

Although scatterplots are effective at presenting pictorially the association between two variables, we would like to be able to represent the magnitude of the association with a single number as we did with Φ for dichotomous variables. The most widely used index of association between continuous variables is the **Pearson product moment correlation coefficient**, or r, as it is more commonly known. As with Φ and χ^2, statistical software can be used to compute r with ease; however, it also can be calculated more painstakingly by hand using the formula,

$$r = \frac{N\sum X_iY_i - (\sum X_i)(\sum Y_i)}{\sqrt{N\sum X_i^2 - (\sum X_i)^2}\sqrt{N\sum Y_i^2 - (\sum Y_i)^2}},$$

where N indicates sample size, and X_i and Y_i indicate each participant's scores on the two variables. As with Φ, r ranges between -1.0 and $+1.0$, with 0 meaning no association at all between two variables and ± 1.0 meaning a perfect association. (In fact, Φ is a special case of r computed on two dichotomous variables.) Positive values of r mean that as the values of one variable increase, so do the values of the second variable. Negative values of r mean that as the values of one variable increase, the values of the other variable decrease. When we compute the correlation between marriage and divorce rates from our example data set, we obtain an r of .57. Note that this value is slightly different from (and higher than) the Φ value of .54 we obtained earlier in the chapter. This difference results from the loss of precision when continuous variables are converted into coarsely categorized variables, and it shows us why we should leave our data in continuous form whenever possible.

When we square the value of r, we get a statistic known as $\boldsymbol{R^2}$. The interpretation of R^2 is that its values indicate the proportion of variability in one variable accounted for by the other variable; in other words, it tells us by what proportion our predictions of one variable improve when we base those predictions on knowledge of the other variable. For our example, $R^2 = .57^2 = .32$. This means that 32% of the variability in divorce rates between states can be explained by knowledge of states' marriage rates.

Returning once again to our example, we also can calculate r and R^2 for the remaining pairs of variables:

Association between marriage rates and birthrates:	$r = .50$ $R^2 = .25$
Association between birthrates and divorce rates:	$r = .35$ $R^2 = .12$

All three associations were calculated by using the data from only 47 states because Nevada's position as an outlier distorts the association considerably. Notice that all three associations are positive: States with higher values on one of the variables tend to have higher values on the others.

As was the case with Φ, we usually want to compute a test of the statistical significance of the correlation coefficient we obtain. The test statistic associated with r is the t statistic, and it can be computed quite easily as follows:

$$t = \frac{r}{\sqrt{1 - r^2}} \times \sqrt{N - 2}$$

Thus, the t corresponding to the r of .57 we obtained between states' marriage and divorce rates is 4.65. When we look up the t value of 4.65 in the appropriate probability table in any statistics textbook, we discover that the probability of obtaining a t that large or larger if the null hypothesis were true is only .00005, or 5 in 100,000. As with the χ^2 test of the association between these variables in dichotomous form, we reject the null hypothesis of no association between the two variables.

Associations Between a Continuous Variable and a Dichotomous Variable

We frequently encounter the case in which the two variables in whose association we are interested are measured at different levels of measurement. For instance, one of the variables might be interval or ratio, and the other might be nominal or ordinal, having only two values. In the case of the example we have been exploring, suppose we had full information about states' marriage rates—that is, we knew the exact numbers—but for divorce rates we knew only whether a given state was relatively high or low, not each state's actual divorce rate. In this case we might think that the procedures we have presented for examining whether two variables are associated might not work. Using a contingency table and calculating Φ clearly would not work because we cannot create a contingency table when one of the variables is continuous. We also might think that the use of correlation for examining the association between two variables would not work because these procedures were presented when both variables were measured continuously. In fact, however, the Pearson product moment correlation generalizes to the case of one continuous variable and one dichotomous variable quite easily, as we demonstrate in this section. In other words, the procedures developed for assessing associations between two continuously measured variables also are appropriate when only one of the two is measured continuously and the other is a dichotomy.

We most frequently want to examine the association between one continuous and one dichotomous variable in experimental and quasi-experimental research, so let us develop a new example to illustrate the process. Suppose we were interested in different leadership styles in small working teams, and we wanted to see whether they affected the team's productivity, a topic that has long been of interest to researchers in the social sciences. Suppose we had 10 teams, and in 5 of them the leaders tended to be quite autocratic and directive, telling team members what they should work on and how they should work and setting work goals and schedules with little or no consultation. In the other 5 teams, the leaders operated much more democratically, asking team members how they thought the work should be structured, who should work on what, and so forth. Now suppose each team worked for some number of hours at a given task—for instance, attempting to solve a series of logical puzzles—and at the end of that time we had a measure of how successfully each team had accomplished its task, the number of puzzles correctly solved by each team. In Figure 18.6 some hypothetical data that might have resulted from this study are presented as they would appear in a SAS input file.

We are interested in whether the teams who had one type of leader were more or less productive than the teams with the other type of leader. In other words, we are interested in whether a dichotomous variable, namely, leadership style, is associated with a continuous variable, namely, team productivity in these data.

With experimental designs that use two groups, such as this one, the most natural analytic strategy is one that compares the difference in the average scores on the dependent variable between the two groups: Do the democratic teams fare better than the autocratic teams? The statistic for comparing the significance of the difference between two means is *t*, and it is computed by,

$$t = \frac{\overline{Y}_1 - \overline{Y}_2}{\sqrt{S^2_{pooled}\left(\frac{1}{N_1} + \frac{1}{N_2}\right)}},$$

where S^2 pooled is the pooled variance of the two groups. (When group sizes are equal, as in this case, the pooled variance is equal to the average of the two variances.)

Using the SAS output shown in Figure 18.7, we can compute the *t* for our hypothetical study as follows:

$$t = \frac{11.0 - 9.6}{\sqrt{3.4\left(\frac{1}{5} + \frac{1}{5}\right)}} = 1.20$$

When the probability associated with obtaining a *t* of that value or higher is looked up, we see that it is only a $p < .30$. Because it does not meet our conventional criterion of $p < .05$, we cannot regard this sample *t* as sufficiently compelling evidence to cause us to reject the null hypothesis. In other words, based on these sample data, we cannot reject the null hypothesis that team productivity and leadership style are unassociated. To state our conclusion somewhat differently, we cannot conclude, based on these sample data, that there is a reliable difference between the mean productivity of autocratically led and democratically led teams in the population represented by our sample.

FIGURE 18.6

HYPOTHETICAL DATA FROM STUDY OF LEADERSHIP STYLES AND TEAM PRODUCTIVITY EMBEDDED IN AN SAS PROGRAM WRITTEN TO CREATE VARIABLES AND GENERATE MEANS AND VARIANCES FOR THE TWO TYPES OF TEAMS

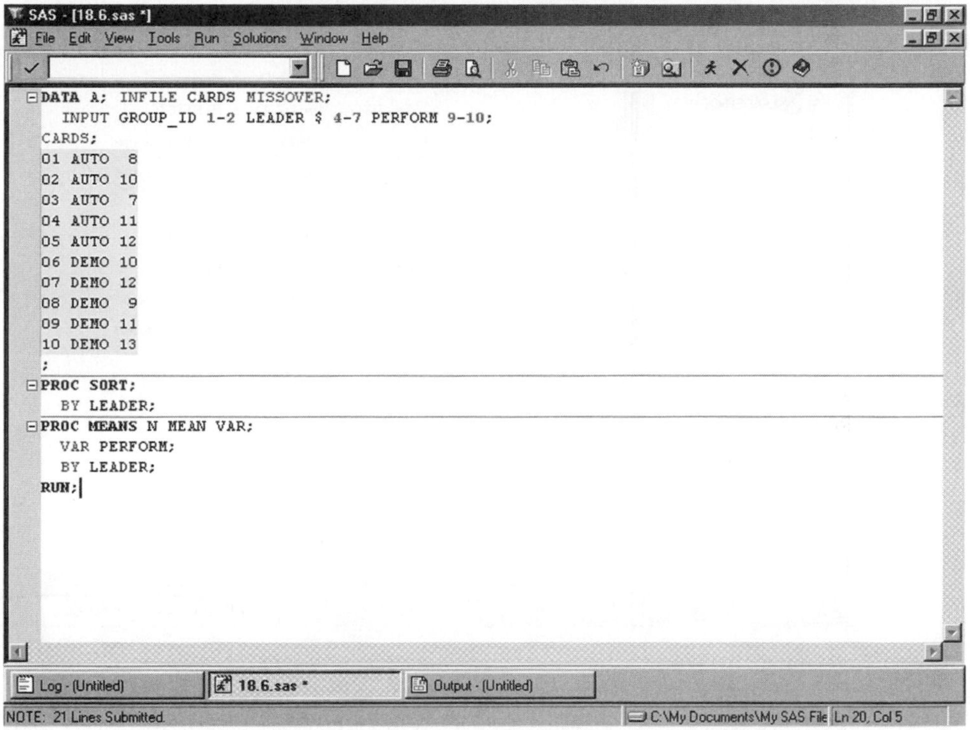
SAS - [18.6.sas *]
File Edit View Tools Run Solutions Window Help
DATA A; INFILE CARDS MISSOVER;
INPUT GROUP_ID 1-2 LEADER $ 4-7 PERFORM 9-10;
CARDS;
01 AUTO 8
02 AUTO 10
03 AUTO 7
04 AUTO 11
05 AUTO 12
06 DEMO 10
07 DEMO 12
08 DEMO 9
09 DEMO 11
10 DEMO 13
;
PROC SORT;
BY LEADER;
PROC MEANS N MEAN VAR;
VAR PERFORM;
BY LEADER;
RUN;
Log - (Untitled)
18.6.sas *
Output - (Untitled)
NOTE: 21 Lines Submitted.
C:\My Documents\My SAS File
Ln 20, Col 5

We also can approach the association between a dichotomous and continuous variable using correlational techniques. Before we can do so, we must code our leadership style variable numerically. A frequently used convention for coding a dichotomous variable like leadership style is to use **dummy coding.** (Note that this is a different, and more appropriate, strategy than the one we used earlier to recode the marriage, divorce, and birthrate variables into dichotomies.) Under this convention, we arbitrarily assign a value of 1 to one level of the variable and a value of 0 to the other level. For instance, in our example, we would create a variable representing leadership style. Let us call it X because it is the variable from which we will predict.

FIGURE 18.7 MEAN AND VARIANCE GENERATED BY SAS FROM HYPOTHETICAL DATA FROM STUDY OF LEADERSHIP STYLES AND TEAM PRODUCTIVITY

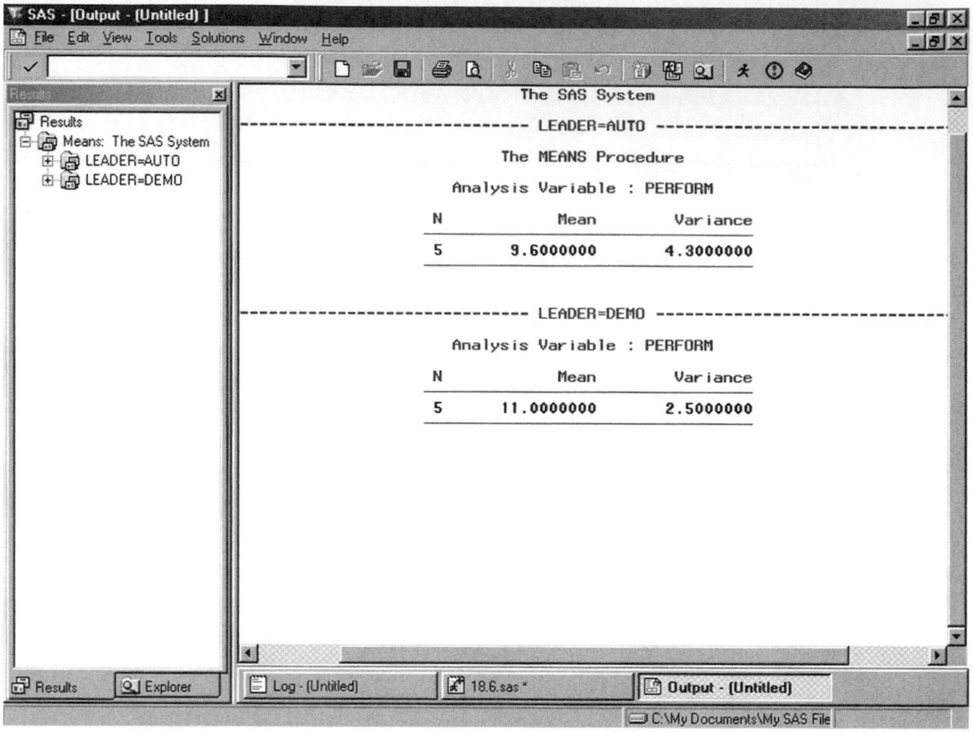

SOURCE: Created with SAS® software. Copyright © 2001, SAS Institute, Inc., Cary, NC, USA. All rights reserved. Reproduced with permission of SAS Institute, Inc., Cary, NC.

If leadership style is democratic, we will define X equal to 1. If leadership style is autocratic, we will define X equal to 0.

For each of our 10 teams we now have values on two variables, productivity and leadership style, with the former continuously measured and the latter a dummy variable that codes a dichotomous distinction. Table 18.4 shows what the data look like when recoded in this manner. We can now proceed to use the formula presented earlier in this chapter for computing the Pearson product moment correlation coefficient between the two variables.

As can be seen toward the bottom of the table, the correlation between dummy-coded leadership style and group productivity is .39. Although the magnitude of this correlation is moderate, our sample size is very small, so we might wonder whether the obtained correlation is statistically reliable, that is, whether we might expect to observe an association in other samples of this size drawn from the same population. Recall that we can test the significance of a correlation coefficient using the formula,

$$t = \frac{r}{\sqrt{1 - r^2}} \times \sqrt{N - 2}$$

Substituting the appropriate values we get

$$t = \frac{.39}{\sqrt{1 - .39^2}} \times \sqrt{8} = 1.20$$

The obtained t of 1.20 does not reach the conventional $p < .05$ level of significance; thus, we are not able to reject the null hypothesis despite the moderate size of our correlation, a lesson to us that we should always strive to achieve adequate sample sizes in order to avoid potential Type II errors.

Readers will no doubt notice that the t of 1.20 looks highly familiar; it is identical to the t we obtained when we used the standard computational formula for testing the significance of the difference between two means (page 468). This is not an accident. The two approaches—testing the difference between means and computing the

TABLE 18.4 ANALYZING THE TEAM DATA THROUGH THE CORRELATIONAL APPROACH

Group (i)	Dummy-Coded Leadership Style (X)	Team Productivity (Y)
1	0	8
2	0	10
3	0	7
4	0	11
5	0	12
6	1	10
7	1	12
8	1	9
9	1	11
10	1	13

$$r = \frac{N\sum X_i Y_i - \left(\sum X_i\right)\left(\sum Y_i\right)}{\sqrt{N\sum X_i^2 - \left(\sum X_i\right)^2}\sqrt{N\sum Y_i^2 - \left(\sum Y_i\right)^2}} = .39$$

correlation between dummy-coded group membership and the dependent variable—ask the same question and should always provide the same answer. This is because, unlike median splitting interval or ratio variables, dummy coding of nominal or ordinal variables does not result in a loss of information on the recoded variable. As such, estimates of association and tests of their statistical significance are indeed two sides of the same coin.

Interpreting Associations

Now that we have the tools to estimate associations between variables and to infer from sample data whether these associations are reliable, a few warnings are in order about how these statistical tools are used and interpreted.

First, as we have seen, a few unusual and extreme cases can distort estimates of association, particularly when the variables are assumed to be measured on interval or ratio scales. In examining associations between variables, it always makes sense to examine the data in a graph. Doing so might well point to unusual cases that exert undue influence on our statistics. Recall that when we drew a scatterplot of states' divorce and marriage rates (Figure 18.4), the state of Nevada plainly stood out.

Second, it is important to emphasize once again that an association between two variables does not mean that one of them causes the other. As we have said before, a necessary condition for a causal association between two variables is that they be associated. But it certainly is not true that because two variables are associated we can infer that one causes the other. As we have seen, states' birthrates and divorce rates are reliably associated. But this result does not mean that higher birthrates result in higher divorce rates. Similarly, in our hypothetical example, we saw that democratically led groups were somewhat more productive than autocratically led ones. By itself, this result does not necessarily mean that a group's style of leadership affects its productivity.

As we discussed in Chapter 2, in the presence of a simple association between two variables, for instance, states' birthrates and divorce rates, there are at least three causal alternatives consistent with the observed association. First, it might in fact be true that birthrate affects divorce rates:

Birthrate → Divorce rate

It might also be that the effect is in the opposite direction:

Birthrate ← Divorce rate

Finally, and most probably for these data, there might be other variables that affect both birthrate and divorce rate and are therefore responsible for the association we observe between the two. In other words, if these two variables share one or more common causes, we might observe an association between them that is uninformative about the causal effect of one on the other. For instance, it is quite likely in these state data that states with higher marriage rates have both higher divorce rates and higher birthrates. That is, states' marriage rates are a cause of both their divorce rates and birthrates, and the association that we observe is not a causal one; rather, it is a **spurious** one.

Partial Associations

The most powerful tool for discriminating among competing causal explanations is the randomized experiment. But frequently it is impossible to conduct an experiment that would reliably discriminate between the competing explanations. In such cases, we often can begin to discriminate between them by using techniques discussed in this final section of the chapter.

In general, whenever we have a causal hypothesis that X causes Y, and whenever we are unable to do a randomized experiment, randomly assigning participants or units to levels of the independent variable, X, it makes sense in quasi-experimental and nonexperimental designs to see if X and Y continue to be associated when we account for the influence of third variables that might explain their association. If the X-Y association is in fact a causal one, not a spurious one produced by the common cause Z, X and Y (e.g., birthrate and divorce rate) should continue to be associated even when the association of Z (e.g., marriage rate) with X and Y is accounted for. The association that persists between two variables when a third variable that might explain their association is held constant (i.e., its influence is removed) is called a **partial association.** Although statistically controlling for third variables can be informative, doing so can never conclusively demonstrate a causal association because it is not possible to hold constant all the variables that might produce a spurious association between the two variables of interest. Nonetheless, estimates and tests of partial association can be used to rule out specific variables that might account for an apparent association between two variables.

Partial Associations with Contingency Tables

Let us look at the association between birthrate and divorce rate by using the dichotomously coded forms of these variables. The contingency table for these data is displayed in Figure 18.8. The strength of association between these two variables as indexed by Φ is .38. Now what we want to do is see what happens to this association if we control for whether a state is high or low in its marriage rate. If the partial association is considerably smaller than the simple association between the two, we have evidence that the causal explanation that having children results in divorces is at least partly in error.

How might we hold constant whether or not a state has a high or low marriage rate? A rough approximation might be to look at the association between birthrate and divorce rate twice: once looking only at states that are relatively low on the marriage rate

FIGURE 18.8 **Contingency Table of Dichotomously Coded Birth and Divorce Variables from Table 17.3**

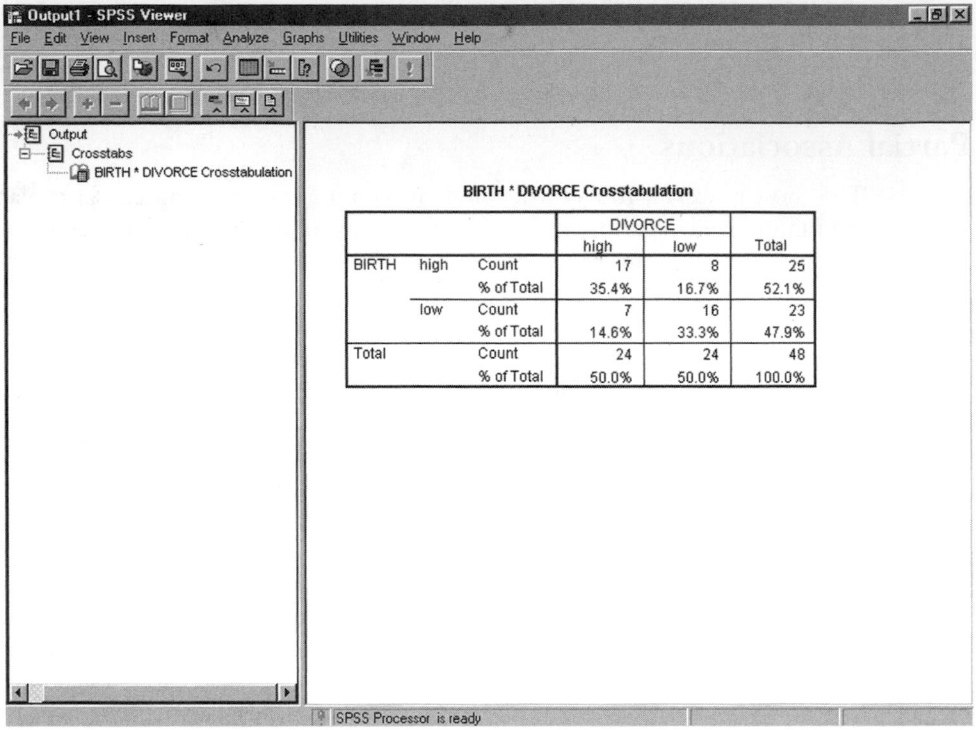

BIRTH * DIVORCE Crosstabulation

			DIVORCE high	DIVORCE low	Total
BIRTH	high	Count	17	8	25
		% of Total	35.4%	16.7%	52.1%
	low	Count	7	16	23
		% of Total	14.6%	33.3%	47.9%
Total		Count	24	24	48
		% of Total	50.0%	50.0%	100.0%

SOURCE: Created with SPSS® software.

variable and once looking only at states with relatively high marriage rates. In Figure 18.9 we present a three-way contingency table, one in which birth- and divorce rates are cross-tabulated separately for the high- and low-marriage-rate states. We can now assess the association between birthrate and divorce rate within each of these groups of states.

Our ability to predict whether a state is high or low on its divorce rate based on its birthrate declines markedly when we control for whether the state is high or low in its marriage rate. If we compute separate Φ statistics for the upper and lower halves of the table, we obtain values of .22 for the 25 high-marriage-rate states and .28 for the 23 low-marriage-rate states. These values are well below the Φ of .38 we observed for the simple association, and neither of the two values of Φ is significant (p-values are .28 and .18 for high- and low-marriage-rate states, respectively).

FIGURE 18.9

Three-Way Contingency Table of Dichotomously Coded Birth and Divorce Variables Controlling for Marriage Rate

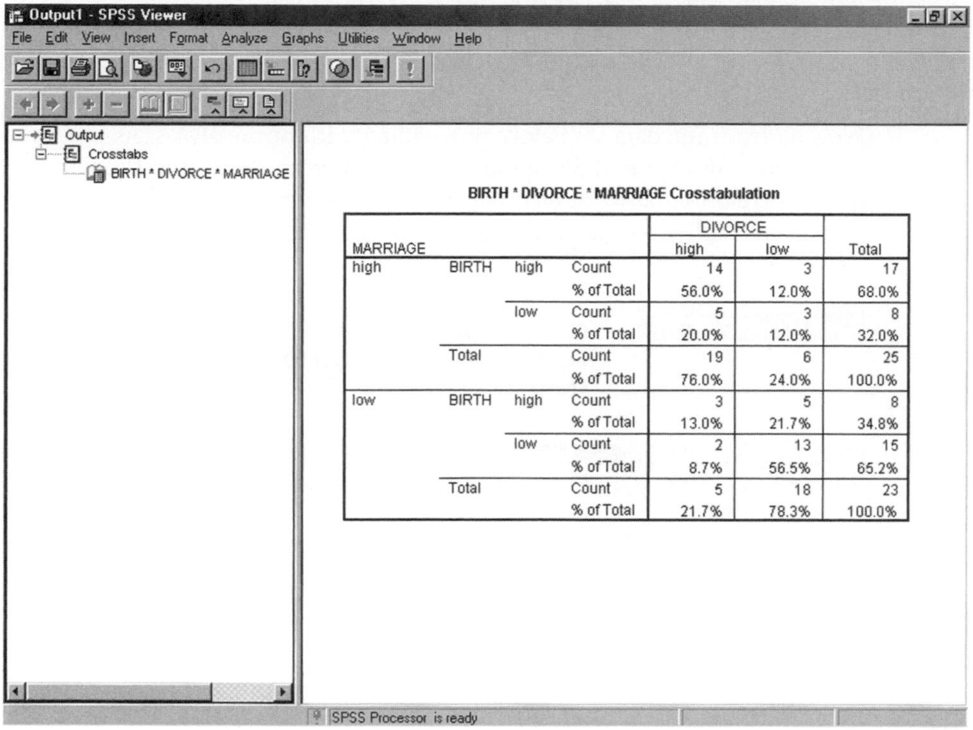

BIRTH * DIVORCE * MARRIAGE Crosstabulation

MARRIAGE				DIVORCE high	DIVORCE low	Total
high	BIRTH	high	Count	14	3	17
			% of Total	56.0%	12.0%	68.0%
		low	Count	5	3	8
			% of Total	20.0%	12.0%	32.0%
	Total		Count	19	6	25
			% of Total	76.0%	24.0%	100.0%
low	BIRTH	high	Count	3	5	8
			% of Total	13.0%	21.7%	34.8%
		low	Count	2	13	15
			% of Total	8.7%	56.5%	65.2%
	Total		Count	5	18	23
			% of Total	21.7%	78.3%	100.0%

Rather than two values of Φ, we can compute a single value to index the partial association between birthrate and divorce rate, controlling for marriage rate. The value of this partial coefficient is .25, which clearly is lower than the value of .38 we observed for Φ when marriage rate was not controlled. This partial coefficient is not statistically reliable (p-value = .10), and therefore we conclude that the dichotomously coded birthrate and divorce rate variables are spuriously associated.

Partial Associations with Continuous Variables

Now that we have the general notion of what it means to control for a third variable, let us return to the original data for the three variables (Table 17.3) and attempt to do the same thing with continuous variables. It might seem a little strange with such data to talk about examining the association between birthrates and divorce rates within levels of the marriage rate variable because there are so many levels of the original marriage rate variable. But in fact, we can use exactly the same principles that we did with dichotomously coded data to examine partial associations with continuous variables.

Recall that, when these variables are analyzed in continuous form, the outlying Nevada data distort the pattern of associations (see Figure 18.4). Thus, we remove Nevada from the data set before proceeding with our analyses. As can be seen in the upper portion of the SPSS output shown in Figure 18.10, the Pearson product moment correlation between birthrate and divorce rates is .34. This value is statistically significant with a *p*-value of .02. In the lower half of the output is information about

FIGURE 18.10 **SIMPLE AND PARTIAL ASSOCIATIONS BETWEEN BIRTH AND DIVORCE VARIABLES IN CONTINUOUS FORM**

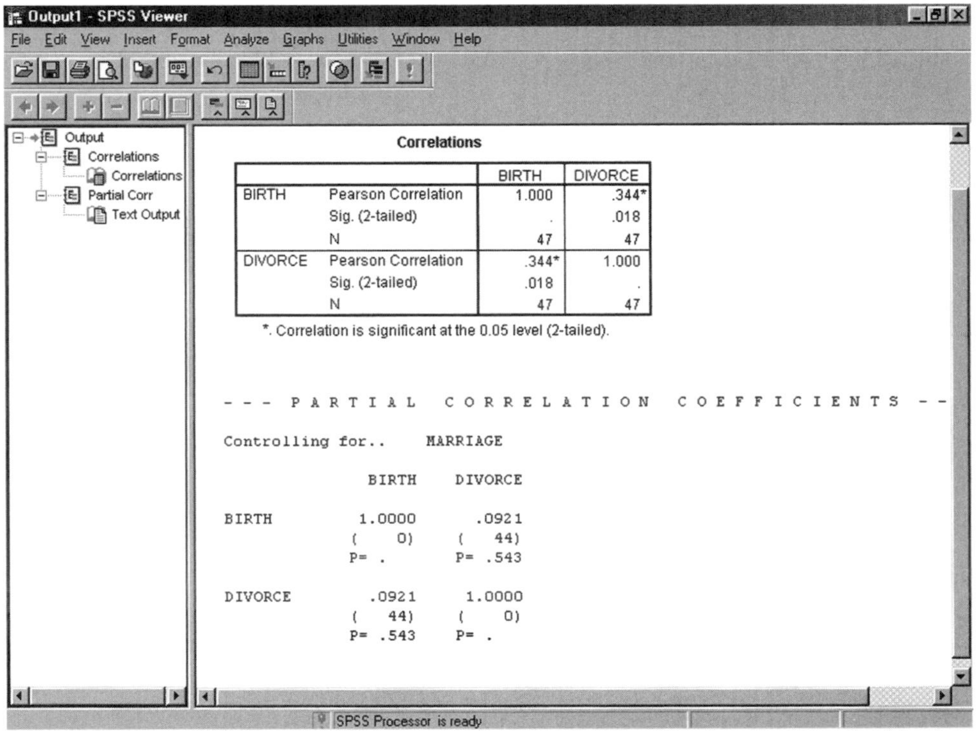

Correlations

		BIRTH	DIVORCE
BIRTH	Pearson Correlation	1.000	.344*
	Sig. (2-tailed)	.	.018
	N	47	47
DIVORCE	Pearson Correlation	.344*	1.000
	Sig. (2-tailed)	.018	.
	N	47	47

*. Correlation is significant at the 0.05 level (2-tailed).

```
- - -  P A R T I A L   C O R R E L A T I O N   C O E F F I C I E N T S  - -

Controlling for..     MARRIAGE

                  BIRTH     DIVORCE

BIRTH            1.0000       .0921
                (     0)    (   44)
                P= .        P= .543

DIVORCE            .0921     1.0000
                (   44)     (     0)
                P= .543     P= .
```

the association between birthrate and divorce rate controlling for marriage rate. As the output reveals, the partial correlation coefficient is only .09 with a *p*-value exceeding .50. If we square the partial coefficient to obtain a partial R^2, we find that less than 1% of the variability in divorce rate can be attributed to birthrate (and vice versa) when controlling for marriage rate.

Based on this analysis with the original data, we reach exactly the same conclusion as we did with the dichotomously coded data. Let us review the argument here. The simple correlation between states' birthrate and divorce rate is .34. At least two causal interpretations exist for this association. It could be that having lots of children increases the probability of divorce, and hence the association is a causal one. It also could be that the association is a spurious one, resulting from the fact that states with a higher marriage rate should tend to have a higher birthrate and divorce rate. The two explanations have rather different implications for the partial association between birthrate and divorce rate, controlling for marriage rate. If births produce divorce, the two should be associated even when we control for marriage rate. On the other hand, if the association is spurious, it should vanish when we hold marriage rates constant. The partial correlation and R^2 strongly suggest that the simple association is not due to a causal connection between birthrate and divorce rate. Although we are unable to conduct a randomized experiment, randomly assigning states to different birthrates, we can use partial associations to help us choose between these two alternative causal explanations.

Partial Associations with Continuous and Dichotomous Variables

In the section of the chapter on simple associations we saw that the procedures used to assess associations between two continuous variables can be generalized to the case in which one of the two variables is measured dichotomously. When we are predicting a continuous dependent variable with a dichotomous independent variable, we code the dichotomous distinction with a dummy variable. That is, we assign the value of 1 to some observations and the value of 0 to others, according to whether observations are grouped together on the dichotomous independent variable. Indexes of association such as the Pearson product moment correlation and R^2 can then be computed between this dummy variable and the continuous dependent variable, just as it was in the case of two continuous variables.

The generalization from the case of two continuously measured variables to that of one continuous and one dichotomous variable continues with partial associations. Specifically, we can use the partial correlation coefficient to assess the association between a continuous variable and a dichotomous one when controlling for a third variable. Such a procedure is used with great regularity in the analysis of data from quasi-experimental research designs, although it is not a general procedure for ensuring the validity of causal conclusions from such designs. Recall again that internal validity is maximized only through a randomized experimental research design.

Consider an expanded version of the example discussed earlier in the chapter. Using hypothetical data, we explored the association between team leadership style and productivity. Five teams were run autocratically and five were run democratically. We found that there was a moderate, although not statistically significant, association between leadership style and productivity, with democratic teams showing higher productivity. If those data had been gathered using a randomized experimental research design, in which teams had been randomly assigned to one of the two leadership styles, that difference in productivity could have been interpreted as a causal effect of leadership style, had it been statistically reliable. Suppose, however, that a quasi-experimental design had been used, one defined in Chapter 13 as the pretest–posttest nonequivalent control group design. Under this design, teams would not have been randomly assigned to one or the other style of leadership, and hence differences that we observed in productivity might not have been due to the different leadership styles. Productivity differences, for instance, might have been due to differences in productivity levels between the different kinds of teams that existed long before their leaders ever assumed an autocratic or democratic leadership style. Recall that this kind of preexisting difference is called a selection threat to internal validity: The teams in the control and experimental conditions are found to differ on the dependent variable not because the independent variable exerted a causal effect but because the two groups of teams differed prior to the start of the study.

In the pretest–posttest nonequivalent control group design, we attempt to overcome this selection threat by measuring the dependent variable as a pretest as well as a posttest. We then attempt to equate the two experimental and control groups on the basis of their pretest performance so that any differences induced by the independent variable will be revealed over and above any differences that existed at the time of the pretest. This is the purpose, then, of controlling for third variables in quasi-experimental research designs. Given that we have an independent variable that is dichotomous—that is, autocratic versus democratic leadership style—and that participants, or in this case, teams, have not been randomly assigned to the levels of this variable, we want to see whether the independent variable is associated with the dependent variable, or the posttest, after we have equated the two groups of teams for any pretest difference. In the language of partial associations that has been used in this section of the chapter, we want to see whether the dichotomous independent variable is still associated with the continuous dependent or posttest variable once we have controlled for the pretest variable. Again, we remind the reader that controlling for a pretest difference does not totally eliminate threats to internal validity. It can, however, lend support to causal interpretations.

We have all the tools necessary for this sort of analysis, based on the earlier discussion of procedures for assessing partial associations with continuous variables. The only difference is that the dichotomous independent variable must be recoded as a dummy variable to use these procedures, just as we were forced to do earlier in the chapter. Figure 18.11 presents in the context of a SAS program the hypothetical data from our leadership style study expanded to include a dummy-coded version of the independent variable as well as pretest scores. Assuming these data came from a pretest–posttest nonequivalent control group design, our goal now is to determine whether the independent variable of leadership style is associated with the posttest

FIGURE 18.11 **HYPOTHETICAL DATA FROM STUDY OF LEADERSHIP STYLES AND TEAM PRODUCTIVITY WITH PRETEST AND POSTTEST PRODUCTIVITY SCORES**

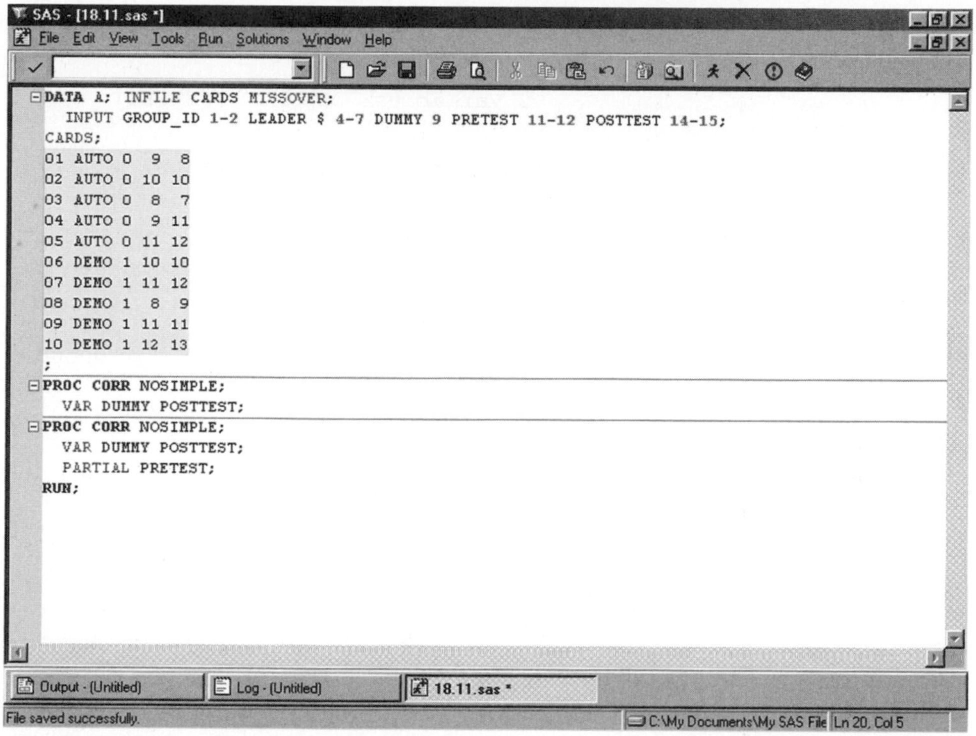


```
DATA A; INFILE CARDS MISSOVER;
  INPUT GROUP_ID 1-2 LEADER $ 4-7 DUMMY 9 PRETEST 11-12 POSTTEST 14-15;
CARDS;
01 AUTO 0  9  8
02 AUTO 0 10 10
03 AUTO 0  8  7
04 AUTO 0  9 11
05 AUTO 0 11 12
06 DEMO 1 10 10
07 DEMO 1 11 12
08 DEMO 1  8  9
09 DEMO 1 11 11
10 DEMO 1 12 13
;
PROC CORR NOSIMPLE;
  VAR DUMMY POSTTEST;
PROC CORR NOSIMPLE;
  VAR DUMMY POSTTEST;
  PARTIAL PRETEST;
RUN;
```

Note: Leadership style has been dummy coded. The data are embedded in a SAS program written to create variables and generate the simple association between leadership style and posttest productivity as well as the partial association controlling for pretest productivity.

measure of productivity when we control for the pretest measure of productivity. By equating teams on their pretest levels of productivity, we hope to remove partially the selection threat to internal validity in these data.

The results of simple and partial analyses are displayed in Table 18.5. In the top portion of the computer output is information about the simple association between leadership style and posttest productivity. Note that the value of the Pearson product moment correlation coefficient is .39. Although this coefficient is moderate in magnitude, it is not statistically reliable due in large measure to the very small

TABLE 18.5 **OUTPUT FROM TWO SAS PROC CORR RUNS SHOWING SIMPLE AND PARTIAL ASSOCIATION BETWEEN DUMMY-CODED LEADERSHIP STYLE AND POSTTEST PRODUCTIVITY**

```
                 The SAS System
               The CORR Procedure

           2 Variables:  DUMMY   POSTTEST

       Pearson Correlation Coefficients, N = 10
             Prob > |r| under H0: Rho=0
                     DUMMY              POSTTEST
       DUMMY        1.00000              0.39070
                                          0.2643

       POSTTEST     0.39070              1.00000
                     0.2643


               The CORR Procedure


1      Partial Variables:      PRETEST
2              Variables:        DUMMY        POSTTEST

     Pearson Partial Correlation Coefficients, N = 10
         Prob > |r| under H0: Partial Rho=0
                     DUMMY              POSTTEST
       DUMMY        1.00000              0.12260
                                          0.7533
       POSTTEST     0.12260              1.00000
                     0.7533
```


sample size. Moving to the lower half of the table, observe that, when pretest productivity scores are partialed from the association between leadership style and posttest productivity, the association drops to .12 with a *p*-value of .75. From these results, we infer that our estimate of a moderate association between leadership style and posttest productivity can be attributed to differences in the average productivity of the groups in the two conditions prior to the manipulation. Our findings can be explained by selection and, therefore, we cannot interpret them with reference to the theory that inspired the study.

Although controlling for a pretest, as we have done, can be quite informative about the selection threat to internal validity in quasi-experimental research designs, it is not a general strategy for eliminating all threats to internal validity that we encounter in quasi-experimental research. Statistical procedures such as controlling for third variables are useful for examining causal hypotheses with data from nonexperimental and quasi-experimental designs. Ultimately, however, the validation of causal hypotheses depends on data from randomized experiments.

Summary

In this chapter we considered procedures for estimating and testing associations between two variables. We started with the simplifying assumption that the two variables were measured on nominal or ordinal scales, with only two values each. The data from the two variables could then be displayed in a contingency table. In the case of two dichotomous variables, the Φ coefficient expresses the magnitude of the association between the variables. The concept of significance testing was introduced as a means of determining whether an obtained measure of association is statistically reliable. With data measured on interval or ratio scales, an association between two variables is best seen by drawing a scatterplot rather than a contingency table. The Pearson product moment correlation coefficient is the index of the magnitude of association between two continuous measures. In the case of one dichotomous variable and one variable measured on an interval or ratio scale, we can assess associations using the same correlational procedures as for two continuous variables. In this case, the dichotomous variable can be dummy coded and the correlation computed between the dummy-coded variable and the continuous variable. We also can compute t, a statistic that assesses the significance of the difference between the means of the two groups. We discussed pitfalls in interpreting associations between two variables. More specifically we cautioned against using standard measures for assessing associations when there are extreme outliers in the data. And we warned about the dangers in interpreting an association as indicative of a causal effect of one variable on the other. We illustrated the use of third variables to test for spurious associations and selection threats to validity in quasi-experiments. Although third-variable strategies do not rival randomized experiments for ensuring internal validity, they can be used to evaluate potential alternative explanations when randomized experiments are not feasible.

Key Concepts

coarse categorization	dichotomous variables	linear association
contingency table	dummy coding	marginal frequencies

median split	Φ	t
null hypothesis	R^2	Type I error
p-value	scatterplot	Type II error
partial association	spurious association	χ^2
Pearson product moment correlation coefficient	statistical significance	

On the Web

http://www.execpc.com/~helberg/pitfalls/ Provides the full text of "Pitfalls of Data Analysis (or How to Avoid Lies and Damned Lies)," an article in which Clay Helberg points out how the interpretation and presentation of results from data analyses can be risky.

http://davidmlane.com/hyperstat/ The *Hyperstat Online Textbook*, a very well organized site with lots of helps and links.

http://www.statsoft.com/textbook/stathome.html An on-line statistics textbook provided by StatSoft, who publishes STATISTICA, a comprehensive graphics-rich statistical software package.

Further Reading

Abelson, R. P. (1995). *Statistics as principled argument.* Hillsdale, NJ: Erlbaum.
Cohen, J. (1994). The earth is round ($p < .05$). *American Psychologist*, 49, 997–1003.
Kanji, G. K. (1999). *100 statistical tests* (2nd ed.). Thousand Oaks, CA: Sage Publications.
Rosnow, R. L., & Rosenthal, R. (1989). Statistical procedures and the justification of knowledge in psychological science. *American Psychologist*, *44*, 1276–1284.

CHAPTER

19

Reviewing Research Reports and Literatures

Part of being a good researcher is being able to evaluate and summarize the work of others. As we discussed in the introductory chapters, science and theory are cumulative, with later studies adding to and building on the results of previous studies. Progress is made through this cumulation, and reviews of the empirical literature are an essential part of this process. Periodic assessments of a given research area provide an evaluation of what has been found so far, point out weaknesses and limitations in this accumulated knowledge, and provide direction for future studies. Literature reviews thus are an integral part of doing science. In this chapter, we focus on two main topics: how to read and evaluate individual research reports and how to summarize the results of a group of studies bearing on the same topic.

Reviewing Research Reports

Most students experience something of a culture shock upon their initial foray into the social science literature. Students are accustomed to reading textbooks, which tend to distill empirical research into a few pithy conclusions accompanied by color photographs or humorous cartoons. Methodological detail is limited, and statistical results are practically nonexistent. Contrast this approach with typical research reports in the social sciences, which are generally packed with jargon, methodological detail, and dense statistical results that are virtually incomprehensible to those without training in graduate-level statistics. No cartoons or color photographs are to be found, only figures displaying three-way interactions or structural equation models that look like a Jackson Pollock painting.

Students generally get little practice reading original research reports. Our first goal, therefore, is to provide some pointers for getting the most out of reading empirical research reports, as one must be able to read and understand a single report before one can summarize a group of reports on a topic.

Step One: Read the Abstract

This recommendation may seem like common sense, but many readers actually skip over the abstract. It is useful, however, to read it, because it summarizes the study succinctly in nontechnical language and usually provides a short, "take-home" message for the study. Knowing ahead of time in general terms about the procedure and findings makes it easier to follow the more detailed description to come. However, readers must keep in mind that abstracts typically cast a study in the most positive light, and the actual findings might not be as impressive as conveyed in the abstract.

Step Two: Read the Introduction

The purpose of the introduction is to provide the theoretical background for the study and to review relevant past research. Thus it will—or should—tell why the questions being asked are interesting. A good introduction makes clear how the study builds on the previous literature and why this particular study is important. The introduction provides suggestions for other relevant articles to find and read. The introduction also usually points out weaknesses in the past literature and makes the case for any unusual methods or measures being introduced. Although the introduction should allow the reader to anticipate the hypotheses being tested, a well-written introduction states these hypotheses explicitly. Lastly, many articles conclude the introduction with a summary of the methodology employed in the study. This paragraph can be very helpful, as it provides a sketch of the subsequent method section.

Step Three: Read the Method Section with a Fine-Tooth Comb

It is essential to read the method section with a critical eye. There can be considerable slippage between the hypotheses stated in the introduction and the methods used to test them. It is not unusual for an introduction to convey rather grandiose goals for the study, only for the reader to discover in the method section that a narrow subset of those goals is actually addressed. Here is a list of questions readers should ask themselves as they read the method section:

Participants How many people participated in the study? If the number seems very small given the research design, then **statistical power,** that is, the likelihood of finding an effect that exists in the population (this is the opposite of Type II error, discussed in Chapter 18), is probably too low and the validity of the study is in doubt. This is particularly the case if the authors try to interpret any nonsignificant findings as being substantively meaningful. More rarely, samples that are extremely large (e.g., more than 1,000 or so participants) make it so easy to find statistically significant differences that one cannot rely on a mere finding of statistical significance as indicating that anything theoretically interesting is going on.

For studies using clinical or field samples, inclusion/exclusion criteria should be stated explicitly. For example, what cutoff score on the Beck Depression Inventory was used in determining if somebody qualified as depressed enough to be included in the study? For all studies, a relevant question is from how many participants were data excluded from analyses? And why were they excluded? In most studies at least a few participants are dropped from the sample, usually for failure to follow instructions. What one does not want to see is a large proportion of participants being dropped ("large" can be defined as over 10%), especially if the reason has potential implications for interpreting the findings. For instance, if, in a randomized experiment, participants are dropped because of their suspicion regarding the experimental manipulations, that indicates the manipulation was not executed in a believable manner and casts doubt on the entire study. Similarly, if, in a nonrandomized study, the initial sampling plan was not equally effective across groups or if there was greater attrition in one group versus the other(s), then apparent group differences might reflect a problem with the representativeness of the groups rather than real differences between the groups. In short, one does not want to see **differential mortality,** that is, a higher percentage of people being dropped from one group compared to the others, as that can pose a threat to the internal validity of the study.

Who are the participants? If they are college students, as is the case with most of the laboratory-based research in the social sciences, is the topic of the study one that is meaningful to address with a population of such limited generalizability? For example, if the study addresses the formation of political attitudes, a college student sample is highly appropriate. But if the study concerns factors that predict employee satisfaction, a sample of college students who are asked to role-play employer and employee roles would not be optimal.

Measures or Apparatus In this section, authors describe the paper-and-pencil measures, observational procedures, or—less commonly—the equipment by which scores on their independent or dependent variables were obtained. With respect to paper-and-pencil measures, questions to ask are: What is the name of this measure or scale? Is it a standardized measure, that is, one that was created earlier and has been extensively validated, or is it a measure that was created by the authors exclusively for this study and lacks independent validation? In the former case, the authors should provide a full citation for the measure so that it can be looked up if desired, as well as a summary of its basic **psychometric properties.** In the latter case, the authors need to provide more detail to demonstrate the adequacy of the measure. What is the reliability? Has it been shown to be valid? If this information is not included, it could mean merely that the authors were pressed for space or overlooked it—or it could mean that the measure has not been sufficiently validated. Measures that were created for a given study should achieve minimum standards of reliability, which is normally around .75 for internal consistency indices such as coefficient alpha.

Procedure Here, the major questions concern construct validity and the avoidance of methodological artifacts. If the study is an experiment, have the authors convinced readers that they did in fact manipulate the construct they wanted to manipulate? In other words, if the study involved making one participant feel envious of a target person, does it seem reasonable after reading the procedure that the participants did in fact feel envious? Is it clear that only envy was manipulated, for example, rather than simply negative mood? Were participants and experimenters kept unaware of the experimental condition and/or hypotheses? In some cases, experimenters cannot be kept unaware (if, for example, they are administering the crucial manipulations orally). If that is the case, do the authors make a good case that experimenter bias is not operating? If the study is a survey, what were the conditions under which the data were collected? In general, one trusts questionnaire data less that were provided by participants at home, under unknown conditions, than data collected under more controlled conditions. What kind of data were participants asked to provide? Retrospective reports (e.g., How many times have you been sick over the past year? What kind of attachment did you have with your mother as a child?) are less accurate and useful than concurrent reports.

Step Four: Evaluate the Results

What was the design of the study? Were participants randomly assigned to experimental conditions? If not, are the authors appropriately cautious in their conclusions about the findings? Are any **manipulation checks** reported to indicate that participants experienced the manipulation in the intended manner? For example, if a mood induction manipulation was used, do the authors demonstrate that the participants who were supposed to be in a good mood did in fact feel better than participants who were supposed to be in a bad mood? How many analyses were conducted, and roughly what percentage of those analyses yielded significant results? An unfortunate but common tactic for researchers is to mention only those variables in the results section for which there were statistically significant results without bothering to mention the other dependent variables for which there were none. Yet this is important to consider: One's confidence in the validity of a conclusion is considerably strengthened if, say, effects involving all three of the relevant dependent variables are significant compared to if only 3 of 15 effects are significant.

The results section is generally the most difficult section for students to read, especially if the analyses reported go beyond correlation analysis or a basic one-factor comparison of means. Skip over the numbers if you must, but do at least skim the results section and try to evaluate whether the authors' hypotheses were supported by statistically significant results. Well-written results sections usually explicitly restate hypotheses and provide a bottom-line assessment as to whether they were supported; be on the lookout for such summary/transition sentences.

Step Five: Take the Discussion Section with More than a Grain of Salt

Most students who are intimidated by statistical detail in the results section tend to rely on the discussion section as a verbal summary of the findings of the study. Such a reliance can be unwise. Authors tend to wax poetically in their discussion sections, and there can be many a slip between the statistical results and the conclusions drawn. Results sometimes are exaggerated, and inconvenient results (those that are nonsignificant or, worse, in the opposite direction) are often either summarily dismissed or completely ignored. A good analogy is carving a diamond: In the discussion section, rough edges are smoothed out, the original stone is cut down so that flaws and blemishes are excised, and everything is polished until it shines brilliantly. Pay close attention to the limitations section that most articles contain; one occasionally encounters what we call the "mea culpa" strategy where authors acknowledge a fatal flaw (e.g., lack of a critical control group or addressing a longitudinal question with cross-sectional data), but then—having pointed out the shortcomings of their study—they go on to draw firm conclusions as if the flaw did not exist. The discussion should be more than just a summary of the results but also provide an explanation of the why and how of what was found. The authors should relate their findings to the previous literature; are the results consistent with past research, and if not, why? Most discussion sections also include a section on directions for future research (and more flaws of the current study might be revealed in this section), as well as a discussion of the implications of the study for the field.

The review of individual research reports is often part of the larger exercise of reviewing the entire body of research on a particular topic. Such **literature reviews** begin with a thorough search for all research conducted on the topic. The 1980s and 1990s witnessed a proliferation of new publication outlets as well as increases in federal research funds committed to social and behavioral science research. As a result, the research literature devoted to many social science topics has burgeoned, making the task of finding and retrieving research reports on a given topic daunting. Fortunately, the increasing power and accessibility of computers has made the task more manageable. High-speed computers are no substitute for thoughtful planning and execution of a literature search, however, and the quality of a literature review is more a tribute to the thoughtfulness and care of the scholar who produced it than the power and accessibility of computers.

Searching the Literature

The first step in any review of the literature is to search the relevant literature and locate and retrieve all of the research reports pertaining to the topic of interest. In many respects, this is the most important step, because a literature review is only as good as the coverage of the literature it provides. A literature review that summarizes only 10 studies when over 100 exist does not make any useful contribution. This is not meant to imply that all literature reviews must include every single research report on the topic; there might be very sound reasons to restrict the number of reports included in a review. For example, it is not unusual to see reviews of established literatures that include only those reports published since the last major review of the topic. Or a review might be restricted to only those studies that used a particular operational definition or measure of key variables. The point is that the decision to restrict the population of studies to be included in a review should be made for sound theoretical reasons, not out of laziness or an incomplete search.

The good news is that searching and retrieving the literature has become much easier as access to electronic databases has become more widespread. In the days before ready access to computers, searching the literature meant doing a manual search of available databases. For example, using *Psychological Abstracts* was a time-intensive effort that required looking a topic up first in one book, then looking at one- or two-line summaries in a second book, and finally looking up the complete abstract to a given article in yet a third book. Today, one can type in a key word in an **electronic database** such as PsycINFO or MEDLINE from one's office or home and obtain within seconds the full abstracts to hundreds or thousands of articles.

Such electronic searches are deceptively easy, however. There actually is an art to conducting a literature search, and the steps involved in an effective search of electronic databases are often arcane. Too often students report that they have searched the literature but found nothing on a topic that has been heavily researched. Also common is the opposite problem that occurs when a student enters a popular term (e.g., "aggression"), obtains thousands of abstracts (7,149 in PsycINFO at the time this chapter was written, to be exact), and does not know how to proceed from there. Thus, perhaps the best piece of general advice we can offer for searching the social science literature is to solicit the help of a reference librarian. These individuals can be most helpful in identifying the best combination of key words and Boolean operators (e.g., *and, or, not, near*) to get the articles needed.

The first step in a **literature search** is to identify the relevant electronic database, as specialized databases exist for each major discipline, for example, PsycINFO for psychology, *Sociological Abstracts* for sociology, *Social Work Abstracts* for social work, ERIC for education, and so forth. Again, a reference librarian can be helpful. Depending on the topic, it might be fruitful to search more than one database. For example, the key words "teacher expectancy effects" would elicit a large number of articles (overlapping, but some unique) in both PsycINFO and ERIC.

The next step is the most critical—deciding on the key words to be used in the search. When an electronic database is accessed, the search can be conducted by author, title, or subject. **Key words** are those words entered when one searches by subject, and it is the key words selected that contribute most to the success or failure of a search. A short primer on abstracting services is in order here. Each electronic database or abstracting service compiles the abstracts published in the set of journals that is covered by the particular abstracting service. PsycINFO, for example, covers over 1,300 periodicals in over 25 languages, tracking articles published since 1887. Standard information is coded from each article that is abstracted, such as the author(s), journal title, article title, volume, page numbers, language, complete abstract to the article, and the descriptors (key words) associated with the article. Sometimes the descriptors are determined by the authors of the article, and sometimes they are chosen by the employees of the abstracting service following a close reading of the article. In either case, the descriptors are taken from a set of terms specified by the thesaurus for that particular abstracting service.

The **thesaurus,** which lists the "official" phrasing for a key word topic and variations on the descriptor, is perhaps the most underused tool in the arsenal of a literature reviewer. Knowing the proper terms used for descriptors can make searching the literature much more accurate. Say, for example, one wanted to look up references on computing the reliability between two coders or judges. If one were to enter the phrase "interjudge reliability" in a PsycINFO search, only 44 abstracts would be retrieved (at the time this chapter was written); however, perusal of the thesaurus would reveal that the official descriptor terminology preferred by PsycINFO is "interrater reliability." Entering the official descriptor would yield 1,651 abstracts.

Thus, one should consult the thesaurus associated with a particular abstracting service prior to doing an electronic database search and compile a list of possible descriptors to enter. Depending on the topic of interest, the search might need to be narrowed (e.g., searching for "television violence and aggression" rather than merely "aggression") or widened (specifying broader terms—supplied by the thesaurus—if an insufficient number of abstracts is elicited). Most literature searches require several iterations of specifying different key words and combinations of key words before one can feel confident that the vast majority of the relevant published literature has been found. And, as we noted earlier, one might need to repeat this process on multiple databases.

Once a stack of abstracts has been amassed, each one must be read carefully to determine its appropriateness for the literature review. Searches are actually done in a rather crude manner; the computer scans the article abstract and descriptor fields for the relevant key words. It is possible to have an abstract retrieved that merely contains the words "teacher," "expectancy," and "effect" interspersed throughout it but which actually has nothing to do with the topic of interest, teacher expectancy effects. Searches might also retrieve articles that discuss the topic in general terms but do not report empirical data, articles that might be helpful as a source for identifying other references but not for the review. Other decisions about the scope of the review need to be made. Will it exclude articles written in foreign languages? Will it include articles from all sources or only peer-reviewed journals? It is okay to restrict a review, but the authors need to make explicit and justify to readers the criteria used to restrict the search and, equally important, authors need to apply those criteria consistently across all research reports. For example, if it were decided in general not to use doctoral dissertations in the review, it would not be appropriate to include a certain dissertation just because it obtained particularly strong results in the favored direction.

Other Ways of Locating Articles A quick search of a relevant database is generally sufficient for writing term papers or empirical research reports that do not pretend to be exhaustive reviews of the literature. However, if one's primary goal is to summarize and review the existing literature on a given topic, one cannot rely solely on electronic searches. The major problem in doing so is that the electronic databases, by definition, include only the published literature in a field. Yet there are generally many relevant studies "out there" that are not detected by electronic searches for several reasons. Perhaps they are conference presentations that have not been published in journal form; perhaps they are still undergoing the journal review process; or perhaps they could not get published because the results were not statistically significant or because they merely replicated a previous finding.

Relying on the published literature therefore results in **publication bias,** which is the tendency to overstate the magnitude of a given effect because relevant nonsignificant findings or failures to replicate are not included in the review. A good literature reviewer makes every attempt to gather *all* the existing literature on a topic, not just the published literature. There are several ways to go about this, none of them particularly easy. First, one should use what is called the **ancestry approach**, in which the reference lists of all the articles obtained so far are checked to see if they cite any potentially relevant manuscripts that the search missed (Cooper, 1984). Second, one can search *Dissertation Abstracts International* for relevant studies. *Dissertation Abstracts* can be a good source for three reasons. First, it often includes reports of relevant studies that were never written up for publication because the student chose to go into a career other than academia and lost interest in writing for publication. Second, dissertations are written up whether or not the results were statistically significant, so dissertations can be a good source of failures to replicate that never make it into the published literature. Third, dissertations tend to be of relatively high methodological quality (the study must pass muster of a doctoral advisory committee), so they are sources a literature reviewer would generally want to include.

Practically speaking, though, it is difficult to include dissertations in a review. The abstracts provided in *Dissertation Abstracts* rarely give sufficient detail to rely on them alone, and most libraries are reluctant to send dissertations through the mail. One possible solution is to write the authors of the relevant dissertations (tracking them down can be difficult enough in itself) and ask either for the relevant results or to borrow a copy of the dissertation. When one of the authors of this book attempted to secure copies of relevant dissertations for a literature review, only 5 of the 40 or so dissertation writers contacted were willing to do this.

A third approach to supplementing an electronic literature search is to rely on what is called the **invisible college,** the network of researchers working on the topic (Price, 1966). Every research area involves a cadre of scholars who have been writing regularly on the issue; the preliminary literature search should readily identify who those individuals are. Reviewers should write to each of them, explain that they are working on a literature review in the person's area of expertise, and request copies of all unpublished papers and manuscripts in press (i.e., accepted for publication but not yet in print). (**Publication lag**—the interval between manuscript acceptance and actual publication—often exceeds a year, but authors usually are willing to provide preprints of in press reports.)

An approach somewhat broader than using the invisible college would be to solicit the help of individuals through an electronic mailing list of people belonging to a relevant professional organization. In social psychology, to give one example, there are two LISTSERVs (one affiliated with the Society of Experimental Social Psychology and one affiliated with the Society of Personality and Social Psychology). Such LISTSERVs often reach a high proportion of active researchers in the field and represent a quick and easy way to request copies of unpublished material.

Reviewing the Literature—"Traditionally" and Meta-Analytically

Once all the relevant articles bearing on a given topic have been located, the task is to summarize or integrate the findings in a comprehensive, comprehensible, and accurate manner. The first decision is whether to conduct a traditional, or narrative, literature review versus a meta-analysis, or quantitative literature review. In a **narrative literature review,** studies are described and summarized verbally. Usually, the review is organized among major theoretical themes or questions; for example, is psychotherapy effective? Which types of therapies are most effective? What kinds of therapist training result in the best outcomes? Often, a "box score" summary table is provided giving the frequencies of studies reviewed whose results significantly supported the hypothesis, were nonsignificant, or significantly opposed the hypothesis. Table 19.1 shows an excerpt from a narrative review by Leventhal and Brooks-Gunn (2000) on the effects of neighborhoods on child and adolescent outcomes that illustrates how such a review might summarize and describe relevant studies.

In a **meta-analysis,** on the other hand, the results of studies are combined and analyzed quantitatively. In other words, the individual studies themselves become the "participants" or units of analysis. As we explain later in the chapter, standardized effect-size indices are coded from the results of all studies, as well as other methodological and theoretical features of the studies, and these are subjected to statistical analyses that aim to show an overall combined effect size as well as conditions under which the effect is strongest and weakest.

From the first appearance of meta-analytic techniques, social scientists have debated the relative merits of narrative and meta-analytic reviews (e.g., Harris, 1991; Hoyle, 1993; Sharpe, 1997; Strube, Gardner, & Hartmann, 1985). In the early going, each side had strong proponents and opponents, and passion ran high, as shown by the title of Eysenck's infamous critique of meta-analysis, "An Exercise in Mega-Silliness" (Eysenck, 1978). Critics of meta-analysis did not like the apparent number-crunching nature of meta-analysis and felt that it often "mixed apples and oranges"—too many disparate studies of varying quality using different operational definitions and dependent variables were being combined together without sufficient appreciation of these differences. Proponents of meta-analysis countered that "[o]ne compares apples and oranges in the study of fruit" (Glass, 1978, p. 395) and pointed to studies showing that meta-analyses were less biased and more likely to reach accurate conclusions regarding the presence and magnitude of an effect than were narrative reviews (Beaman, 1991; Cooper & Rosenthal, 1980).

In our opinion, asking which is better, a narrative literature review or a meta-analysis, poses a straw man. A meta-analysis is also a narrative review and can and should do everything a narrative review does, only it adds more detail through combining results quantitatively in addition to discussing the articles narratively. For some research topics, there might not be enough studies all bearing on the same focused hypothesis, in which case a meta-analysis is not really practical; thus, a narrative literature review might be the best one can do. However, in most of the cases in which a literature review is warranted, a meta-analysis of that literature is possible

TABLE 19.1 **EXAMPLE OF DESCRIBING STUDIES IN A NARRATIVE REVIEW (ADAPTED FROM LEVENTHAL & BROOKS-GUNN, 2000)**

Study	Design	Sample	Neighborhood Data	Findings from Published Studies
National Longitudinal Survey of Youth	Children born to women in nationally representative study	673 children aged 3–4 and 5–6 (approximately 40% African American)	1980 census tract data; 70% only study child in tract	*Chase-Lansdale & Gordon (1996):* SES positive association with 5–6-yr.-olds' internalizing problems; male joblessness positive relation with 5–6-yr.-olds' internalizing and externalizing (African American only) problems. *Chase-Lansdale et al. (1997):* High SES positive association with girls' internalizing (ages 5–6 only) and externalizing behavior problems; low SES negative association with 5–6-yr.-old boys' internalizing behavior problems; ethnic diversity negative association with 3–4-yr.-old African Americans internalizing behavior problems and positive association with 5–6-yr.-old-boys' internalizing problems.
Drug Abuse Resistance Education Program	Students drawn from 36 Midwest schools	747 5th and 6th graders	1990 census block data	*Ennett et al. (1997):* Residential instability negative association with school rates of lifetime alchohol use.
Infant Health and Development Program	Early intervention for premature infants at 8 sites	Approximately 1,000 children, diverse backgrounds	1980 census tract data; average 1.1 cases per tract	*Brooks-Gunn et al. (1993):* Managerial/ professionals negative association with 3-yr.-olds' behavior problems. *Chase-Lansdale et al. (1997):* Male joblessness negative association with 3-yr.-olds', African Americans', and girls' internalizing and externalizing behavior problems. *Duncan et al. (1994):* Low-income negative association with 5-yr.-olds' externalizing behavior problems.

SOURCE: From "The Neighborhoods They Live In: The Effects of Neighborhood Residence on Child and Adolescent Outcomes," by T. Leventhal and J. Brooks-Gunn, 2000, *Psychological Bulletin*, *126*, p. 319.

and probably should be conducted in addition to a narrative review. Thus, in the discussion to follow, we concentrate on meta-analytic literature reviews, bearing in mind that a good meta-analysis also incorporates the best features of a narrative review.

Understanding the Concept of Effect Size: The Foundation of Meta-Analysis

The goal of a meta-analysis is to combine—statistically—the results of a group of studies all asking the same, focused question, for example, Does psychotherapy work? Is this intervention for reducing employee turnover effective? Does parental involvement reduce substance use among teenagers? The importance of having a **focused question** cannot be overstated; meta-analysis works only if the group of studies all address the same hypothesis. In other words, one cannot do a meta-analysis on, say, aggression in general; one needs to choose a specific hypothesis about aggression on which to focus: Does media violence lead to aggression? Does frustration lead to aggression? Does aggression in schools lead to lower student achievement?

In order to combine the results of several studies quantitatively, the results must be comparable to one another, that is, transformed to a standardized index. We cannot simply take the raw means of the assorted treatment groups, for example, across studies and compare them to the raw means of the corresponding control groups. Different studies use different dependent measures, and so a score of "20" could mean a positive outcome for one study but a poor outcome for another study using a different dependent variable. Thus, the first step in a meta-analysis is to convert the obtained results of each study into a **standardized effect-size index** that puts the results of all the studies on the same scale and therefore allows the reviewer to combine and compare results across studies meaningfully.

The term **effect size** can be defined as the strength or magnitude of an association in the population, or the degree of departure from the null hypothesis (Rosenthal & Rosnow, 1991). There are many ways of expressing the magnitude of an association; the Pearson correlation coefficient r is one of the most common. As we discussed in Chapter 18, a correlation coefficient expresses the degree to which two variables are linearly associated, that is, as values of one variable increase, to what extent do the values of the other variable also increase? To review, the value of r can range from -1.0 to $+1.0$, with 0 meaning no association between the two variables and $+1.0$ and -1.0 meaning a perfect positive and negative association, respectively. As noted in our discussion of Φ in Chapter 18, conventional standards for interpreting the magnitude of a correlation were given by Cohen (1977); in the social sciences, an r of .10 is considered to be a "small" effect; an r of .30 is considered "moderate;" and an r of .50 is considered to be "large."

Another popular effect-size index that is intuitively easy to understand is **Cohen's *d***, which is computed by subtracting the mean of the control group from the mean of the experimental group and dividing by the pooled standard deviation of the two groups:

$$d = \frac{\overline{X}_1 - \overline{X}_2}{\sigma}$$

Readers who are familiar with *Z*-scores will notice the similarity between the formulas for *Z* and *d*; both express values in standard deviation units. The main difference is that *Z* compares an individual score against the group mean in standard deviation units; *d* compares the difference between *two* group means in pooled standard deviation units. According to Cohen's (1977) standards, *d*s of .20, .50, and .80 correspond to small, medium, and large effects, respectively. In other words, if an intervention raised the experimental group's mean by half a standard deviation (i.e., $d = .50$), we could infer that the intervention had a medium effect.

When doing a meta-analysis, it does not really matter which effect-size index is computed as long as the same index is used across all studies. Rosenthal (1991) recommends *r* over *d* for several reasons, primarily because of its flexibility and relative ease of calculation when *d* cannot be calculated (to compute *d* accurately one needs exact numbers of participants per condition, and authors do not always provide this information). However, *d* is more common and accepted in certain fields (e.g., medicine), and if the literature review is asking a question that is naturally suited to a two-group format (e.g., comparing treatment and control groups), then *d* is a logical choice of effect size. If the review is asking a more correlational question (is teacher warmth associated with student achievement?), then *r* is probably more appropriate.

Some authors report effect sizes in their research reports; however, most of the time a meta-analyst must compute effect sizes from other information provided in the report. Fortunately, it is fairly easy to extract effect sizes from research reports because effect sizes, significance levels, and sample sizes are all related to one another in a straightforward way. This basic relation has been termed the **fundamental equation of data analysis** and can be expressed as:

$$\text{Significance Level} = \text{Size of Effect} \times \text{Size of Study}$$

In other words, how statistically significant something is can be determined by two factors: the magnitude of the effect in the population and the sample size. This equation thus makes clear a couple of important points: First, we should not rely on significance levels alone to tell us whether an effect or association is practically important. Because significance is driven so much by sample size, a *p* value by itself is not very informative. A study with a very small effect can still be statistically significant if the sample is large enough, as is the case with the U.S. Census, for example. The Census Bureau does not bother computing significance tests in its analyses because every test would be highly significant. On the flip side, a large effect, one that might be very important, could fail to produce a significant *p* value if the sample is very small.

The second major conclusion to draw from this equation is that as long as we know two pieces of the equation, we can calculate the third. Thus, effect sizes can easily be computed from the significance tests and sample sizes reported in the original research reports. So, for example, we could rewrite the general equation,

Significance Level = Size of Effect × Size of Study,

to reflect specific statistical tests:

$$t = \frac{r}{\sqrt{1 - r^2}} \times \sqrt{df}$$

$$F = \frac{r^2}{1 - r^2} \times df_{error} \qquad \text{(with 1 df in the numerator)}$$

$$\chi^2 = \phi^2 \times N$$

Using such equations, it is only a matter of minor algebraic manipulation to solve for effect size, for example:

$$r = \sqrt{\frac{t^2}{t^2 + df}}$$

$$r = \sqrt{\frac{F}{F + df_{error}}} \qquad \text{(when } F \text{ has 1 df in the numerator)}$$

$$d = \frac{t\,(n_1 + n_2)}{\sqrt{df}\,\sqrt{n_1 n_2}}$$

Textbooks on meta analysis contain these and other equations for computing *r*, *d*, *g*, and other effect-size indices from a host of statistics, for example, *t*, *F*, χ^2, *Z*, and so on (Rosenthal, 1991). Thus, once the appropriate statistical test(s) to include in a meta-analysis has been identified, the actual computation of effect sizes is generally straightforward. The word "generally" conveys an important caveat, however: In any meta-analysis one will encounter a significant minority of studies in which the necessary information is not provided in a direct fashion. There will be many cases, especially in reports published before standards for reporting statistical results became widely implemented, in which the desired information (e.g., sample sizes, standard deviations) is not provided. There also will be cases in which the desired focused comparison is embedded in a larger design containing irrelevant conditions, and the meta-analyst will be forced to carry out secondary analyses to obtain the effect size of interest.

For these reasons, although the actual computations involved in a meta-analysis are not complicated, a fair amount of statistical sophistication is nonetheless required to do a meta-analysis. A meta-analyst needs to be able to understand exactly what the authors did and be able to extract what is needed from the results they reported. The meta-analyst also needs to be able to detect when the authors made mistakes in their statistical analyses, which happens with surprising frequency. Errors are more likely to emerge in older research reports and those published in journals with lower publication standards, but meta-analysts must be vigilant when coding all studies.

Coding Studies for a Meta-Analysis

The second stage in conducting a narrative or meta-analytic review is reading each research report and coding it for effect size and other relevant methodological and theoretical variables. One of the most difficult and subjective challenges in meta-analysis is deciding what results from a given report to include. On the surface, it seems simple enough: One knows ahead of time the focused hypothesis of interest in a meta-analysis, so all one needs to do is read the research report, find the appropriate statistical test, and compute an effect size. However, it is never that straightforward. Many subjective judgments are required, both on the independent variable side (Does a particular study even belong in the meta-analysis? Which of possibly many experimental groups correspond to the hypothesis of interest?) and the dependent variable side (Which dependent variables should be used in computing effect sizes?).

Decisions are particularly subjective with respect to the issue of deciding what dependent variables to include. Very few studies include and report findings for only one dependent variable, and generally there is a large number from which a meta-analyst must choose. The first challenge is to decide which dependent variables are relevant. This is harder than it appears. Take, for example, a meta-analysis of the effects of using quality circles in management on employee satisfaction. Obviously, we would want to include all dependent variables that are explicitly labeled "employee satisfaction." But should we include or exclude a study that measured employees' level of "happiness" with their work? Is "happiness" appreciably different from "satisfaction"? How about employees' intentions to remain in their job? What if a study included both a "satisfaction" *and* a "happiness" variable? As should be readily apparent, nearly every research report will confront the reviewer with such decisions. Ideally, criteria for including dependent variables should be established prior to coding the studies, and they should be explicitly described in the report so that readers can see and evaluate the scope of the review.

The second challenge, once the relevant dependent variables have been identified, is to decide how to treat them in the meta-analysis. Some authors (particularly in older meta-analyses) treat individual effect size as the unit of analysis and thus allow studies with multiple dependent variables to contribute more than one effect size to the meta-analysis. This is not a good idea, for two main reasons: (1) It disproportionately weights studies with more dependent variables more heavily in the meta-analysis, yet there is usually no compelling theoretical reason for doing so. (2) It violates the independence assumption underlying many of the statistical tests that are carried out in a meta-analysis (Rosenthal, 1991).

How, then, to treat multiple results from a single study? Some people select the dependent variable that most closely fits the topic of the meta-analysis. The danger here, of course, is that it is too tempting to define "best" as the result that yields the largest effect size. A more defensible strategy, and the one that is used most often, is to compute the average of all relevant effect sizes and use that average to represent the study. Less commonly used, but statistically more powerful, are approaches that compute average effect sizes or significance levels taking into account the degree of dependence or interrelation among the multiple results (Rosenthal & Rubin, 1986; Strube, 1985). Another strategy is to conduct separate meta-analyses for each type of dependent variable (behavioral, self-report, etc.). Many meta-analyses use a combination of these approaches, reporting not only the overall mean effect size but also mean effect sizes at different levels of important variables. The key is that for any given analysis performed in a meta-analysis, each study should contribute only a single effect size.

A related topic involves how to handle results for variables described in the method section but for which no results are reported or effects are described simply as "nonsignificant." It is tempting to ignore those variables in a meta-analysis, as insufficient information is provided to compute an exact effect size. But it would be misleading to do so because excluding nonsignificant effects could result in a greatly biased mean effect size. Thus, if an article reports that results for a given variable were nonsignificant, the meta-analyst must enter an *r* or *d* of zero in the meta-analysis. The true effect size is probably not exactly zero, but the average of all nonsignificant effects probably is close to zero, as some of the nonsignificant results will be in the predicted direction and some will be in the opposite direction. Thus, zero is our best estimate of the effect size for a nonsignificant result, and it is better than not including the study at all.

A trickier situation is those studies that mention collecting data on a relevant dependent variable in the method section, but the variable is not mentioned in the results section. This can mean one of three things: The authors measured the variable but did not analyze it; they analyzed the variable and it was involved in significant effects but they did not report it; or they analyzed the variable and it was involved in no significant effects. The first two cases are unlikely, but one cannot rule them out entirely. In such cases, perhaps the best course of action for the meta-analyst is to contact the author and ask for the results concerning the variable of interest. Such requests are often granted, but in some cases, especially with older studies, the authors either cannot be located or they no longer have access to the original data to perform the analysis. A conservative solution in those cases would be to code the effect size for that variable as zero and include it in the meta-analysis.

We hope that this discussion has made clear just how subjective an "objective" quantitative literature review can be. The decisions made in the coding process can greatly influence the magnitude of effect sizes computed from studies and the ultimate results of the meta-analysis. This influence was documented by Matt (1989), who compared the results obtained when several common decision rules for a meta-analysis were applied to the same set of 25 studies. Matt found that the obtained mean effect size varied widely depending on the decision rule adopted. Matt's pessimistic conclusion was that "average effect estimates derived from meta-analyses may depend heavily on judgmental factors that enter into how effect sizes are selected within each of the individual studies considered relevant to a meta-analysis" (p. 106).

What does this subjectivity mean, practically, for practitioners and consumers of meta-analysis? First and foremost, it does not mean that we should abandon meta-analysis. Just because the estimates that are obtained can vary depending on who is doing the coding and what subjective decision rules are used does not mean that the estimates are not useful; a quantitative effect size estimate that has some error associated with it is still better than no quantitative estimate. And, it is important to remember that these subjective judgments affect narrative reviews to the same extent that they do meta-analyses; a narrative reviewer also must decide which variables are relevant and how to weight them when describing a study narratively. The main lesson to be drawn here is that meta-analysts and readers of meta-analyses need to be cognizant of the subjectivity that enters into the coding process. Decision rules should be stated explicitly so that readers know what judgments were made and how. Ideally, a person should be able to read the method section of a meta-analysis and extract the exact same effect sizes (or close to it) from original sources as those extracted by the authors. Equally important, more than one person should code the articles, and the reliability between the coders should be computed and reported.

Readers should be cautious in their interpretation and use of meta-analytic results. There is a danger of reification in meta-analysis; the obtained effect size is treated as "the" population effect size, with little consideration for the factors—such as the nature of the literature search and the decision rules for including effect sizes—that might affect the values that are obtained. Meta-analytic results are only imperfect estimates of population values that reflect a host of subjective decisions; they are not and should not be treated as some sort of "objective" truth.

Coding Other Features of Studies In addition to extracting effect sizes from an article, relevant theoretical and methodological features should be coded. A good literature review does more than simply report the mean effect size for a focused hypothesis. We want to know more; we want to know what factors are associated with larger or smaller effects. The choice of methodological and theoretical variables to be coded depends on the topic being studied. For example, in the developmental literature, whether a study was cross-sectional or longitudinal in design would probably be an important methodological feature to code, but it would not be useful to code in other areas in which longitudinal studies are rare (e.g., cognitive psychology). Mean effect sizes can then be calculated for the separate subcategories of the **moderator variables.** For example, Table 19.2 shows the output of a meta-analysis by Turkheimer and Waldron (2000) of the research literature on the role of nonshared environment in determining sibling similarity. In the table, median and weighted mean effect sizes are reported separately for two different kinds of study design (genetic versus nongenetic) and for longitudinal versus cross-sectional studies.

It is essential that meta-analysts have a good grasp on the literature prior to starting the review so that they know the important methodological issues relevant to the topic and the theoretical issues that remain unexplained. Variables that need to be coded should be identified prior to beginning the coding process; clearly, a reviewer would not like to finish coding 482 articles on a topic only to realize that he or she

TABLE 19.2 EXAMPLE OF REPORTING MEAN EFFECT SIZES BY LEVELS OF MODERATING VARIABLES (ADAPTED FROM TURKHEIMER & WALDRON, 2000)

	Environmental Correlation			
Study Design	**Median**	**Weighted Mean**	**Range**	**k**
Genetic vs. nongenetic				
Genetic	.354	.340	.05–.83	5
Nongenetic	.523	.510	−.08–.96	12
Longitudinal vs. cross-sectional				
Longitudinal	.655	.440	.05–.78	3
Cross-sectional	.430	.460	−.08–.96	17

SOURCE: From "Nonshared Environment: A Theoretical, Methodological, and Quantitative Review," by E. Turkheimer and M. Waldron, 2000, *Psychological Bulletin, 126*, p. 89. Copyright 2000 by the American Psychological Association. Adapted with permission.

should have coded whether participants were randomly assigned or self-selected and thus have to read the articles again.

Because the choice of methodological and theoretical variables is so context dependent, it is impossible to offer a definitive list of variables to code from studies; however, certain methodological features are applicable to a majority of possible research questions in the social sciences and are thus good candidates for coding. These include such things as: information on the participants (age, SES, gender composition); nature of the dependent variables (reliability, self-report versus behavioral, standardized versus created specifically for the study); nature of the independent variable(s) (experimentally manipulated versus naturally occurring, type—social, instructional, or environmental); presence of threats to internal validity; and type of experimental design used. The meta-analyst also can provide a subjective rating (e.g., on a 7-point scale) of the overall methodological quality of the study; this overall score of study quality can then be entered into later analyses to assess the association between effect size and methodological quality. As always, definitions for variables to be coded should be stated explicitly, and a second coder should code at least a subset of the studies so that reliability of coding can be estimated and reported.

Basic Meta-Analytic Tests: Combining and Comparing Studies

The literature has been searched and the relevant articles read thoroughly and coded. What next? Here is where a narrative literature review and a meta-analytic review part ways. In a narrative review, the authors attempt to organize and summarize the articles in a thematic manner, concentrating on questions of theoretical importance. Often, individual studies are described and criticized in detail. In a good meta-analysis, the authors also organize and summarize the articles in a thematic manner, but they go beyond verbal summary to offer quantitative analyses that yield mean effect sizes and tests of theoretical and methodological moderator variables. It also is less common (but not, in principle, impossible) for a meta-analyst to describe and discuss individual studies in great detail.

Rosenthal (1991) offered a useful framework for categorizing the various analytic approaches that are possible within a meta-analysis (see Table 19.3). He noted that the results of studies can be defined in terms of either effect sizes or significance levels. We have restricted our discussion of meta-analysis so far to effect sizes, for two compelling reasons. First, as we argued earlier, significance levels are driven so heavily by sample size that they are relatively uninformative. Second, the majority of meta-analyses report only effect sizes or, more rarely, effect sizes and significance levels. Very few report significance levels alone.

Most of the time we are concerned primarily with the magnitude of an effect, and thus effect sizes are the proper index of the results of a study to meta-analyze. However, there are some cases in which a meta-analysis of significance levels is both useful and necessary. These include cases in which considerable controversy reigns over the very existence of a phenomenon or, relatedly, in research areas marked by numerous

TABLE 19.3 FRAMEWORK OF META-ANALYTIC TECHNIQUES AND FORMULAS

	Results Defined in Terms of: Effect Sizes	Significance Levels
Combining studies	$\bar{z}_r = \frac{\sum z_r}{k}$	$Z = \frac{\sum Z}{k}$
Comparing studies (Tests of heterogeneity)	$\chi^2(k-1) = \sum(N_j - 3)(z_{r_j} - \bar{z}_{r_w})^2$ where $\bar{z}_{r_w} = \frac{\sum(N_j - 3)z_{r_j}}{\sum(N_j - 3)}$	$\chi^2(k-1) = \sum(Z_j - \bar{Z})^2$
Comparing studies (Focused contrasts)	$Z = \frac{\sum \lambda_j z_{r_j}}{\sqrt{\sum \frac{\lambda_j^2}{N_j - 3}}}$	$Z = \frac{\sum \lambda_j Z_j}{\sqrt{\sum \lambda_j^2}}$

failures to replicate. For example, research on expectancy effects was initially met with great resistance by scholars who doubted that teachers' and experimenters' expectations about their targets' behavior could result in self-fulfilling prophecies. Opponents of expectancy effects pointed to well-publicized failures to replicate as support of their doubts. Rosenthal and his colleagues thus were obligated to demonstrate not only the magnitude of expectancy effects but also their statistical significance, that is, to show that the obtained effects could not have occurred on the basis of chance alone (Harris, 1991; Rosenthal, 1968; Rosenthal & Rubin, 1978). Another example of an area in which a meta-analysis of significance levels was deemed critical is seen in Bem and Honorton's (1994) meta-analysis of ESP studies using the Ganzfeld technique, given the widespread and heavy skepticism of the existence of ESP.

Again, the main point is that significance levels and effect sizes are related to each other in a fundamental way and that a meta-analysis can be performed on either type of index. We focus on effect sizes for the reasons given earlier, but readers should bear in mind that the same analyses can be carried out on significance levels that are conducted on effect sizes using formulas adapted for p values.

The second dimension in Rosenthal's framework for categorizing meta-analytic techniques is whether the studies are being combined or compared. **Combining studies** refers to arriving at an overall, bottom-line answer to the focused hypothesis of interest: Does psychotherapy work? Is teacher warmth related to student achievement? Statistically, what is involved is simply the computation of a mean effect size, either unweighted or weighted by some index of choice, for example, sample size or methodological quality. (Some meta-analysts argue that effect sizes should always be corrected for unreliability prior to averaging. The arguments for and against such corrections are beyond the scope of this chapter, but interested readers can consult Hedges & Olkin, 1985, for a discussion of the issues and procedures involved.)

Because r is not normally distributed (having $+/-$ 1.00 as its boundaries), when the effect-size index being used is r, one should normalize the rs using Fisher's r-to-Z transformation prior to any analyses. (Tables or formulas for doing the r-to-Z transformation are found in most meta-analytic textbooks, e.g., Rosenthal, 1991; computer software available for doing meta-analysis do the transformation automatically.) Following the transformation, finding the mean effect size is simple:

$$\bar{z}_r = \frac{\sum z_r}{k} \quad \text{or} \quad \bar{z}_r = \frac{\sum w_j z_{r_j}}{\sum w_j},$$

where k is the number of studies, z_r is the Fisher-transformed correlation coefficient, and w is the desired weight, for example, sample size. The resulting mean Fisher z_r can then be transformed back to a Pearson correlation coefficient for presentation purposes.

The concept of **comparing studies** refers to analyses that seek to document and explain variability among the effect sizes of the group of studies. Rosenthal (1991) further differentiates between diffuse and focused tests. In **diffuse tests,** also known as **tests of heterogeneity,** the goal is to determine whether there is significant variability among a group of effect sizes. This can be tested quite simply using a χ^2 test:

$$\chi^2_{(k-1)} = \sum (N_j - 3)(z_{r_j} - \bar{z}_{r_w})^2,$$

where

$$\bar{z}_{r_w} = \frac{\sum (N_j - 3) z_{r_j}}{\sum (N_j - 3)}.$$

What do such diffuse tests of variability tell us? Variability among effect sizes is akin to the individual difference variability one normally finds among people in a single study. Tests of variability in meta-analyses are more often significant than not, and essentially all they are saying when significant is that there is variability among the effect sizes that needs to be explained. The diffuse test does not identify for the meta-analyst the reason for the variability. Indeed, because heterogeneity tests are usually significant, it almost becomes noteworthy when they are not, for it suggests that a given effect is so robust that it is not influenced substantially by variations in study design and methodology.

More useful from a theoretical standpoint are **focused tests** that explicitly test hypotheses about the reasons for variability among effect sizes. These analyses can take several forms. Rosenthal (1991) advocates the use of a Z test:

$$Z = \frac{\sum \lambda_j z_{r_j}}{\sqrt{\sum \frac{\lambda_j^2}{N_j - 3}}},$$

where λ refers to the contrast weight applied to a given study. For example, if a meta-analysis consisted of 20 studies, half of which used college students as participants and half of which used children, one could compute a contrast comparing the effect sizes from studies involving college students versus those involving child participants, with the contrast weights being $+1$ and -1. (The category to which the positive contrast weight is assigned should be the one predicted in advance to yield the largest effect sizes.)

There are other ways to approach focused tests of effect sizes. If the moderator variable of interest is continuous in nature, a logical analysis would be simply to correlate the moderator variable with effect size. For example, one could correlate obtained effect sizes with the meta-analyst's rating of methodological quality. A positive correlation would mean that better studies yielded larger effect sizes. As another example, if one wanted to test the hypothesis that a given effect should increase with age, one could correlate obtained effect sizes with the mean age of the sample. Figure 19.1 shows a scatterplot of such an analysis that was conducted in a meta-analysis by Gray-Little and Hafdahl (2000) of racial differences in self-esteem.

FIGURE 19.1 **EXAMPLE OF A SCATTERPLOT OF EFFECT SIZE AND PARTICIPANT AGE**

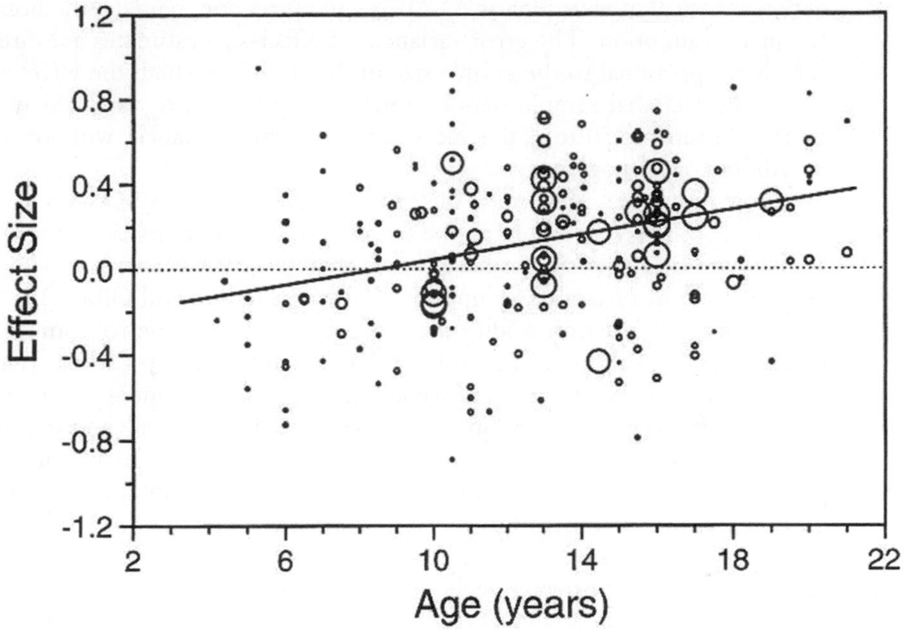

SOURCE: From "Factors Influencing Racial Comparisons of Self-Esteem: A Quantitative Review," by B. Gray-Little and A. R. Hafdahl, 2000, *Psychological Bulletin, 126*, p. 35. Copyright 2000 by the American Psychological Association. Reprinted with permission.

Another common approach to conducting focused tests of effect sizes is to conduct analyses of variance (ANOVAs) or regression analyses, using study as the unit of analysis, effect size as the dependent variable, and the coded methodological and theoretical variables as the predictor variables. An example of this type of analysis would be a meta-analysis that had coded studies with regard to the type of dependent variable reported, say, self-report, behavioral, and peer-report. A one-way ANOVA might be conducted on the effect sizes, yielding an *F* statistic for the effect of type of dependent variable. Mean effect sizes for each category could be reported, and follow-up contrasts could be conducted among the three groups, showing, for example, that effect sizes are larger in studies utilizing self-reports versus studies utilizing behavioral measures. This approach has some advantages, the most important being that it uses statistical procedures with which most readers are familiar; thus, readers can understand and interpret the results more readily than results from some of the more specialized meta-analytic techniques. The analyses also can be conducted quite easily using standard statistical software packages such as SPSS or SAS.

There is, however, one important disadvantage to using standard inferential statistics on meta-analytic effect sizes. This is the not so trivial problem that using effect sizes as the basic data in these types of analyses violates one of the major assumptions of the statistical models such as ANOVA and regression, namely, the homogeneity of variance assumption. The error variances of effect-size estimates are directly and inversely proportional to the sample size of the study on which the effect size is based. Given the fact that sample sizes in a meta-analysis tend to vary widely, often by as much of a ratio as 50 to 1, this means that the error variances will not be identically distributed or homogeneous.

How much of a problem is this? Based on how often ANOVA and regression is used in meta-analysis, one might be tempted to conclude that it is not a big problem at all. After all, many studies have shown that ANOVA is robust to violations of the homogeneity of variance assumption. However, Hedges and Olkin (1985) point out, first, that the simulation studies that have demonstrated the robustness of ANOVA typically test violations of the assumption that are much less severe than the violations found in meta-analysis, and second, that in ANOVA one is usually talking about homogeneity of variance within groups, whereas in meta-analysis the problem is homogeneity of error variance across individual cases (studies). In sum, Hedges and Olkin (1985) provide this grim conclusion: "There does not appear to be any rigorously defensible argument for the conventional use of *t* tests, analysis of variance, or regression analysis to analyze effect sizes or correlations" (p. 12).

However, the throwing of this gauntlet by Hedges and Olkin (1985) has not affected standard meta-analytic practice, as meta-analysts continue to perform standard statistical tests on their effect sizes with no apparent deference to the statistical violations involved. Hedges and Olkin provide multivariate models for testing hypotheses on effect sizes that do not violate the homogeneity of variance assumption. Their approach, however, is statistically complex and beyond the scope of this chapter. Our goal, instead, is simply to alert readers to the problem of conducting traditional analyses on effect sizes so that such analyses are interpreted with caution when encountered in the literature.

That said, it is not our intent to cause readers to shy away from focused tests of effect sizes. Indeed, it is our belief that such focused tests are at the heart of a meta-analysis. Through the judicious coding of methodological and theoretical variables and subsequent contrast analyses, meta-analysis can help advance theory by testing new hypotheses and uncovering associations previously unknown in the literature. In many ways, meta-analysis is even better suited for theory testing than are individual studies because individual studies cannot capture as many different levels of an independent variable or control variables as can a meta-analysis that encompasses hundreds of studies.

Writing and Reading Meta-Analyses

Once all analyses have been completed, the remaining chore is to report the results of the meta-analysis. Because the writing of research reports in general is addressed in Chapter 20, our remarks here are brief and restricted to concerns unique to meta-analysis. The first general recommendation is one to which we have alluded throughout this chapter, namely that the meta-analyst must be detailed and precise in describing how the meta-analysis was conducted. The literature search should be described in detail, including what databases were searched using which key words. Criteria for excluding studies should be specified in detail, and the numbers of studies excluded for each reason should be given. Variables coded from the studies should be named and defined in detail. The method of extracting effect sizes should be described, as well as the decision rules for determining which dependent variables to use. Reliability of coding needs to be documented. Full citations for all studies used in the meta-analysis should be included in the reference section.

In terms of presentation of the results, a table listing all the studies and their corresponding effect sizes, as well as values on important methodological and theoretical moderators, is invaluable. Table 19.1 illustrated that format for a narrative review; Table 19.4 shows an analogous layout for a meta-analysis by Langlois et al. (2000) on judgments of attractive and unattractive children. For meta-analyses involving hundreds of studies, such a table might not be feasible, but one should be included whenever space permits. For smaller meta-analyses, a table or appendix can be prepared that provides even more detail about all the studies; for example, each study could be evaluated in a paragraph summarizing the methods, major findings, and contributions and limitations.

The organization of the results depends in part on the nature of the meta-analysis, but one general approach that works well in most cases is to start off with global summary analyses (mean effect size, tests of heterogeneity) and then move to more specific analyses that compute mean effect sizes by category or present tests of moderator analyses. Stem-and-leaf diagrams (as described in Chapter 17) or other graphic displays of effect sizes (overall or broken down by relevant categories) are helpful in conveying quickly and visually a gestalt of the findings in the area. Table 19.5 shows an example of such a stem-and-leaf diagram of effect sizes for a meta-analysis by Miller and Downey (1999) of the association between self-esteem and weight. On the left-hand side of the diagram is the stem-and-leaf plot for studies looking at the association between self-esteem and self-perceived weight; the right-hand side of the diagram gives the corresponding plot for studies looking at the association between self-esteem and actual weight. Stacking stem-and-leaf diagrams side by side in this manner is an effective means of dramatically illustrating important points about differences across groups of effect sizes.

The discussion of the meta-analysis should summarize the basic findings and discuss in depth their theoretical implications. Limitations of the typical methods used in the area should be pointed out, and suggestions for improving research studies on this topic in the future should be offered. Revisions or extensions to the existing theoretical framework involving the topic should be made. In sum, a literature review, whether narrative or meta-analytic, ideally will make a significant contribution to the theoretical understanding of a research question.

Conducting a literature review, especially a meta-analytic one, is not an easy enterprise. It can take months or even years to gather the literature, code the studies, perform the meta-analysis, and write the report. And this does not even account for

TABLE 19.4 **EXAMPLE OF TABLE LISTING STUDY FEATURES AND EFFECT SIZES (ADAPTED FROM LANGLOIS ET AL., 2000)**

Study	Sample Size	Target Gender	Perceiver Gender	Rater Type	Perceiver Age	Attract-iveness Measure	*d*
Dion & Berscheid (1979)	71	B	B	I	C	F	0.53
Felson & Borhnstedt (1979)	209	F	B	I	C	F	1.12
Felson & Borhnstedt (1979)	207	M	B	I	C	F	1.56
Kenealy, Frude, & Shaw (1987)	503	F	B	I	A	F	1.22
Kenealy, Frude, & Shaw (1987)	503	M	B	I	A	F	1.25
Lippitt (1941)	15	B	F	N	A	G	−0.66
Lippitt (1941)	21	B	F	N	A	G	−0.54
Lippitt (1941)	9	B	F	N	A	G	4.50
Rieser-Danner et al., (1987)	23	B	F	I	A	F	−0.14
Weisfeld, Block, & Ivers (1983)	50	M	F	N	C	G	0.94
Weisfeld, Weisfeld, & Callaghan (1984)	25	M	B	N	C	G	−0.18
Weisfeld, Weisfeld, & Callaghan (1984)	8	F	B	N	C	G	0.16
Weisfeld, Weisfeld, & Callaghan (1984)	24	F	B	N	C	G	0.75

Note: M = male; F = female; B = both; I = independent; N = nonindependent; A = adult; C = child; F = facial measure; G = global measure.

SOURCE: From "Maxims or Myths of Beauty? A Meta-Analytic and Theoretical Review," by J. H. Langlois et al., 2000, *Psychological Bulletin, 126*, p. 417.

TABLE 19.5

Example of a Stem-and-Leaf Diagram of Effect Sizes (Adapted from Miller & Downey, 2000)

Self-Perceived Weight Leaf	Stem	Actual Weight Leaf
0	−2.2	
	−2.1	
	−2.0	
1	−1.9	
5	−1.8	6
	−1.7	
	−1.6	
4 0	−1.5	4
2 2	−1.4	
2	−1.3	
8	−1.2	
5 2 2	−1.1	
9 6 4	−1.0	3
0	−0.9	1 3 3 9
7 2 0	−0.8	5 7
7 **7** 5 0	−0.7	0 0 1 7 8
5 3	−0.6	0
8 4 0 0	−0.5	6 6 9
9	−0.4	1 2
9 7 7 0	−0.3	0 0 2 2
	−0.2	0 0 3 3 4 5 5 **6** 6 6 6 8
2	−0.1	1 2 6 7 8 8 9
6 0	−0.0	0 0 0 0 0 2 4
	.0	0 0 0 0 1 4 6 9
2 0	.1	0 0 0 8
9	.2	0
	.3	3 3
1	.4	

Note: Median effect sizes for each distribution are indicated.

SOURCE: From "A Meta-Analysis of Heavyweight and Self-Esteem," by C. T. Miller and K. T. Downey, 2000, *Personality and Social Psychology Review, 3*, p. 75. Copyright 2000 by Lawrence Erlbaum Associates. Adapted with permission.

the general high level of expertise that must be attained with respect to a research area before one can adequately review it. However, writing a literature review that is well received can be one of the most rewarding accomplishments of a social scientist's career. Literature reviews often are among the most frequently cited contributions in a research area, and a well-written review can influence the direction of an entire field (Garfield, 1992). Indeed, reviews hold the potential to change the face of a research area more than do individual studies. Thus, although the effort involved is enormous and the challenges great, the potential rewards are tremendous.

Summary

Reviewing the empirical research literature involves critically evaluating individual studies and summarizing multiple studies on a topic. Care should be taken in reading individual research reports, and readers need to determine that the authors' hypotheses were tested with methodologically sound designs and that the conclusions drawn by the authors reflect the actual statistical results obtained. The first step involved in reviewing a body of literature is to conduct a thorough literature search to identify all the relevant articles. The literature search is accomplished largely through searches of electronic databases and abstracting services. Specifying the right combination of key words or descriptors is critical to a successful search. Electronic searches should be supplemented by other means of locating studies, particularly unpublished studies, such as circulating requests for manuscripts around the invisible college of researchers working on the topic or on relevant LISTSERVs.

Studies on a given research topic can be summarized via a traditional (narrative) review or meta-analytic (quantitative) review. Both types of review provide a summary of the main findings of a body of research and a critical evaluation of the methodologies employed in that area. Meta-analyses provide additional information from quantitative analyses of standardized effect-size indices extracted from the individual studies. A typical meta-analysis report includes an overall effect-size estimate for the group of studies as a whole, as well as moderator analyses that identify the important theoretical and methodological factors that significantly affect the magnitude of the obtained effect sizes.

Key Concepts

ancestry approach
Cohen's *d*
combining studies
comparing studies
differential mortality
diffuse tests
effect size
electronic database
focused question
focused tests
fundamental equation of data analysis
invisible college
key words
literature reviews
literature search
manipulation checks
meta-analysis
moderator variable
narrative literature review
psychometric properties
publication bias
publication lag
standardized effect-size index
statistical power
tests of heterogeneity
thesaurus

On the Web

http://www.apa.org/psycinfo/ From this site you can get a personal subscription to PsycINFO®.

http://www.ncbi.nlm.nih.gov/PubMed/ PubMed, a service of the National Library of Medicine, provides access to over 11 million citations from MEDLINE® and additional life science journals. PubMed includes links to many sites providing full text articles and other related resources.

http://www.mnsinc.com/solomon/MetaAnalysis.html Offers an overview of meta-analysis, how to do a meta-analysis in the Hedges and Olkin tradition, and links to other meta-analysis sites.

Download free software for doing meta-analyses on your PC at the following sites:

http://www.fu-berlin.de/gesund/gesu_engl/meta_e.htm

http://www.spc.univ-lyon1.fr/%7Emcu/easyma/

http://www.cdc.gov/epo/dpram/epimeta/epimeta.htm

http://nw3.nai.net/~dakenny/meta.htm

http://www.ebstor.com/test/lyons/macalc/index.htm You can obtain a free piece of software for computing effect sizes at this site.

Further Reading

Bem, D. J. (1995). Writing a review article for *Psychological Bulletin. Psychological Bulletin, 118*, 172–177.

Rosenthal, R. (1991). *Meta-analytic procedures for social research* (rev. ed.). Thousand Oaks, CA: Sage Publications.

Rosenthal, R. (1995). Writing meta-analytic reviews. *Psychological Bulletin, 118*, 183–192.

CHAPTER

20

Writing the Research Report

You have conducted a study and analyzed the data. Now it is time to tell the world what you have learned, to write the research report. Even if your report is not for a professional audience, we suggest that you adopt the format used for research reports in the professional journals. This format permits readers not only to read the report from beginning to end, as they would any coherent narrative, but also to scan it for a quick overview of the study or to locate specific information easily by turning directly to the relevant section. Despite the standardized format, your individual style will find ample opportunity for expression. The report is divided into the following sections:

1. Introduction (What problem were you investigating and why?)
2. Method (What procedures did you use?)
3. Results (What did you find?)
4. Discussion (What do your findings mean? Where do we go from here?)
5. Summary or Abstract (A brief summary of points 1 through 4.)
6. References (An alphabetical list of books and articles cited in the report.)
7. Appendix (optional) (Copies of questionnaires, scales, or stimulus materials used in the research or tables of data too extensive or too peripheral to include in the body of the report.)

In this chapter we provide a step-by-step procedure for filling in the details of this outline as well as some stylistic suggestions for achieving maximum clarity in your report.

This chapter was written by Daryl J. Bem of Cornell University.

Some Preliminary Considerations

Which Report Should You Write?

There are two possible reports you can write: (1) the report you had in mind when you designed your study or (2) the report that makes the most sense after you have seen the results. They are rarely the same, and the correct answer is (2).

According to the popular view of the research process, an investigator begins with a formal theory, derives one or more hypotheses from that theory, designs and conducts a study to test these hypotheses, analyzes the data to see if they were confirmed, and then chronicles this sequence of events in the research report. If research actually proceeded according to this plan, most of the research report could be prepared before the data were collected. The introduction and method sections could be completely written beforehand, and the results section could be prepared in skeleton form, leaving spaces to be filled in by the specific numerical results obtained. The investigator could even prepare two possible discussion sections, one for positive or confirming results, the other for negative or disconfirming results. Research, however, does not usually go according to this plan even when that was the plan the investigator had in mind at the outset. Accordingly, we suggest you start thinking about your report by thinking about your data.

As we noted in Chapters 17 and 18, data analysis consists of more than simply checking to see if your original hypotheses were confirmed or disconfirmed. It also involves exploring the data thoroughly to see if there are any interesting results that might not have been originally anticipated. For example, by looking at the data separately for men and women, you might discover an unexpected gender difference. You may even find some results that are far more informative than the confirmation or disconfirmation of your original hypotheses. Statistical tests can help you decide just how much faith you should put in such discoveries. Perhaps you will only be able to mention these findings tentatively in your report and to suggest further research for following them up. On the other hand, you might be justified in deciding to center your report around these new findings and to subordinate or even ignore your original hypotheses.

This is not advice to suppress negative results or findings unfavorable to your theory. If your study was genuinely designed to test hypotheses derived from a formal theory or if the original hypotheses are of wide general interest for some other reason, the confirmation or disconfirmation of these hypotheses should remain the central focus of your report. The integrity of the scientific enterprise requires an investigator to report negative or disconfirming results no matter how personally disappointing this outcome might be.

But this requirement assumes that somebody out there cares about the disconfirmation of the hypotheses. Many, if not most, studies in the social sciences are launched from some personal speculations or idiosyncratic questions of the "I wonder if . . ." variety. If your study is of this type, nobody is likely to care if you were wrong. Contrary to the conventional wisdom, science does not care how clever or clairvoyant you were at guessing your results ahead of time. Your report should not be a personal history of your stillborn thoughts. Scientific integrity does not require you to lead your readers through all your wrongheaded hunches only to show—voila!—they were wrongheaded.

Your overriding purpose is to tell the world what you think you have learned about human behavior from your study. That might or might not be the same as telling the world about what you thought about human behavior before you began your study. If your results suggest an instructive or compelling framework for the presentation of your study, adopt that framework, making the findings that tell us the most about human behavior the centerpiece of your presentation. An appropriate metaphor here is to think of your data as a jewel. Your job is to cut and polish this jewel, to select the facets to highlight, and to craft the best setting for it. Good report writing is largely a matter of good judgment; despite the standardized format, it is not a mechanical process. So, think about your report by thinking about your data. You might even find that the easiest way to begin is to write the results section first.

The "Hourglass" Shape of the Report

An experimental report is usually written in the shape of an hourglass. It begins with broad general statements, progressively narrows down to the specifics of your particular study, and then broadens out again to more general considerations. Thus:

The introduction begins broadly:	"Individuals differ radically from one another in the degree to which they are willing and able to express their emotions."
It becomes more specific:	"Indeed, the popular view is that such emotional expressiveness is a central difference between men and women. . . . But the research evidence is mixed . . ."
And more so:	"There is even some evidence that men may actually . . ."
Until you are ready to introduce your own study in conceptual terms:	"In this study, we recorded the emotional reactions of both men and women to filmed . . ."
The method and results sections are the most specific, the "neck" of the hourglass:	"(Method) One hundred male and 100 female undergraduates were shown one of two movies . . ."
	"(Results) Table 1 shows that men in the father-watching condition cried significantly more . . ."
The discussion section begins with the implications of your study:	"These results imply that sex differences in emotional expressiveness are moderated by two kinds of variables . . ."
It becomes broader:	"Not since Charles Darwin's first observations has psychology contributed as much new . . ."

And more so: "If emotions can incarcerate us by hiding our complexity, at least their expression can liberate us by displaying our authenticity."

This closing statement might be a bit grandiose for some scholarly journals—we're not even sure what it means—but if your study is carefully executed and conservatively interpreted, you deserve to indulge yourself a bit at the two broad ends of the hourglass. Being dull only appears to be a prerequisite for publishing in the professional journals.

Introduction

What Is the Problem Being Investigated?

The first task of the research report is to introduce the background and nature of the problem being investigated. Even if your study were only asking a simple empirical question about human behavior or were directed toward a practical problem or policy issue, you must still place the question or issue into a larger context so that readers know why it is of any general significance. Here, for example, is an introduction to an article entitled "Does Sex-Biased Job Advertising 'Aid and Abet' Sex Discrimination?" (Bem & Bem, 1973):

> Title VII of the 1964 Civil Rights Act forbids discrimination in employment on the basis of race, color, religion, national origin and sex. Although the sex provision was treated as a joke at the time and was originally introduced in an attempt to defeat the bill, more than 40 percent of the complaints warranting investigation in the first year of the Act were sex discrimination complaints. Nearly 6000 charges of sex discrimination were filed in 1971 alone.
>
> Title VII extends as well to practices that aid and abet discrimination. For example, the Act forbids job advertisements from indicating a preference for one sex or the other unless sex is a bona fide occupational qualification for employment. In interpreting this provision, the Equal Employment Opportunity Commission (EEOC) has ruled that even the practice of labeling help-wanted columns as "Male" or "Female" should be considered a violation of the law.
>
> Nevertheless, a large number of employers continue to write advertisements that specify a sex preference, and many more write advertising copy clearly intended to appeal to one sex only. Moreover, many newspapers continue to divide their help wanted advertisements into sex-segregated columns.
>
> Do these advertising practices aid and abet discrimination in employment by actually discouraging applicants of one sex or the other from

applying for jobs for which they are otherwise well qualified? The two studies reported in this article sought to answer this question empirically. Both were conducted and presented as part of legal testimony, the first in a suit filed by the EEOC against American Telephone and Telegraph Company, the second in a suit filed by the National Organization for Women against *The Pittsburgh Press.*

Note how this introduction conforms to the "hourglass" shape of report writing by beginning with the 1964 Civil Rights Act in general and then successively narrowing the focus to the sex provision of the act, the aiding and abetting clause, and finally to the specific practices that are the subject of the studies to be reported. The same reporting strategy is employed if your study was designed to contribute to some theory of social behavior. In this case, you need to summarize the theory or conceptual framework within which you are working. But no matter how theoretical or esoteric your study is, an intelligent nonprofessional—perhaps your grandmother—should still be able to grasp the nature of the problem and understand why he, she, or anyone should care. Here are four rules of thumb for helping that reader out:

1. Write in English prose, not disciplinary jargon.
2. Don't plunge the unprepared reader into the middle of your problem or theory. Take the time and space necessary to lead the general reader up to the formal or theoretical statement of the problem step by step.
3. Try to open with a statement about human behavior, not the behavior of social scientists or their research. (This rule is almost always violated in the professional journals. Don't use them as a model here.)
4. Use examples to illustrate theoretical points or to help introduce theoretical or technical terms. The more abstract the theory, the more important such examples become.

The following are examples of opening statements:

Wrong: Recent research in the forced-compliance paradigm has focused on the effects of predecisional choice and incentive magnitude.

Wrong: Festinger's theory of cognitive dissonance has received a great deal of attention during the past 15 years.

Right: The individual who holds two beliefs that are inconsistent with one another may feel uncomfortable. For example, the person who knows that he or she enjoys smoking but believes it to be unhealthy may experience a discomfort arising from the disharmony or inconsistency between these two thoughts or cognitions. This feeling of discomfort has been called *cognitive dissonance* by social psychologist Leon Festinger (1957), who

> suggests that individuals will be motivated to remove this dissonance in whatever way they can . . . .

The Literature Review

After you have set the stage in your opening statement, summarize the current state of knowledge in the area of investigation. What previous research has been done on this problem? What are the pertinent theories of the phenomenon, if any? You should have familiarized yourself with previous work on the topic before you designed your own study, and hence most of your literature search should have been done by the time you are ready to write your report. Nevertheless, your results might have led you to recast your study in a slightly different framework or to introduce a new aspect of the problem. In this case, you might need to cite references you had not previously consulted. Suppose, for example, that you did discover an unanticipated gender difference in your results. You should then go back to the literature to see if other investigators have found such a difference or to see if there are any related findings that might explain your unexpected result.

If you plan to make the gender difference a central feature of your report, you should discuss the topic of gender differences in the introduction, including citations to the relevant previous findings. If you plan to mention the gender difference only as a subsidiary finding, however, postpone any discussion of gender differences until the discussion. (You should now begin to appreciate why you cannot really begin your report until you have a clear view of the results already in mind.)

In reviewing previous work, you need not describe every study ever done on your problem. Cite only articles pertinent to the specific issues with which you are dealing; emphasize their major conclusions, findings, or relevant methodological issues and avoid unnecessary detail. If someone else has written a review article that surveys the literature on the topic, you can simply refer your own readers to the review and present only its most pertinent points in your own report. Even when you must describe an entire study, try to condense it as much as possible without sacrificing clarity. One way of doing so is to describe one variation of the procedure in chronological sequence, letting it convey the overview of the study at the same time. Here, for example, is a description of a very complicated experiment on attitude change designed to test Festinger's theory of cognitive dissonance (Festinger & Carlsmith, 1959):

> Sixty male undergraduates were randomly assigned to one of three conditions. In the $1 condition, the participant was first required to perform long repetitive laboratory tasks in an individual experimental session. He was then hired by the experimenter as an "assistant" and paid $1 to tell a waiting fellow student (a confederate) that the tasks were fun and interesting. In the $20 condition, each participant was hired for $20 to do the same thing. In the control condition, participants simply engaged

> in the tasks. After the experiment, each participant indicated on a questionnaire how much he had enjoyed the tasks. The results showed that $1 participants rated the tasks as significantly more enjoyable than did the $20 participants, who, in turn, did not differ from the control participants.

This kind of condensed writing looks easy. It is not, and you will have to write and rewrite such summaries repeatedly before they are both clear and succinct. The preceding paragraph was the eighth draft.

Books and articles are cited in the text of the report by giving the author's last name and the date of publication; for example, "According to Festinger (1957), people find cognitive dissonance uncomfortable. Not everyone, however, agrees with this conclusion (e.g., Abelson, 1968; Bem, 1967; Kermit, 1979). Nevertheless, direct evidence for internal discomfort has actually been demonstrated in at least one study (Zanna, Freud, & Theophrastus, 1977)." Note that footnotes are not used for references or citations.

Your Study

As you come to the end of the introduction, it often is useful to introduce your own study in a brief overview. The purpose is not to discuss procedural details but to provide a smooth transition into the method section, which follows immediately. The following example could have ended the introduction to the previously cited sex-biased advertising study:

> The question, then, is whether or not such advertising practices discourage potential applicants from applying for jobs. The present study sought to answer this question by asking male and female high school seniors to read several telephone job advertisements and to rate their interest in each job. The interest ratings were analyzed to see if advertisements written in nonsexist language would increase the interest that men and women would show in jobs stereotyped for the "other" sex.

Method

What to Include

Readers need to know in considerable detail how the study was carried out. What was its basic design? If the study was an experimental one, just what were the experimental manipulations? (For example, was "threat" established by telling the participants that they were about to take a very difficult test that would determine their grades in a course or by shouting "Fire!"?) At what point or points were the measurements taken?

If the data were gathered through questionnaires or interviews, exactly what questions were asked? (The questionnaire or interview schedule often is reproduced in an appendix.) How much and what kind of experience had the interviewers had, and how were they trained for this particular study? If the measurements were based on observation, what instructions were given to the observers?

Readers also need to know how the observations or replies to questions were translated into measures of the variables with which the study was concerned. (For example, which questions were taken into account in estimating "alienation"; or what kinds of bystanders' behavior were classified as "helping"?)

Regarding the sample used in the study, readers should be told the following: Who were the participants? How many were there? How were they selected? These questions are crucial for estimating the probable limits of generalizability of the findings. Are elaborate conclusions being drawn on the basis of responses of 10 college sophomores, selected because they happened to be friends of the investigator? Were only women interviewed? If so, is there any basis for extending the findings to people in general? Intensive study of a small number of cases that do not constitute a representative sample of any specifiable population can be quite valuable. Nevertheless, the number and characteristics of the participants on which the findings are based should be clearly stated so that readers can draw their own conclusions about the applicability of the findings to other groups.

If you conducted a fairly complex experiment in which there was a sequence of procedures or events, it often is helpful to describe the study as it was seen from the participant's point of view. First give an overview of the study, including a description of the participants, the setting, and the variables assessed; but then describe the sequence of events in chronological order so that the reader is carried through the experience as a participant was. Provide summaries or excerpts of what was actually said to the participant, including any rationale or cover story that was given. Show sample items from questionnaires, labels on attitude scales, pictures of apparatus or stimulus materials, and so forth, even if you also include the complete questionnaires or rating scales in an appendix to your report. If you administered a standard personality test, describe its general properties and give a sample item even if it is a fairly familiar instrument; for example, "Participants then filled out the Marlow-Crowne Social Desirability Scale, a true-false inventory that taps the degree to which a person describes himself or herself in socially desirable terms (e.g., 'I have never lied')." The purpose of all this is to give the readers a "feel" for what it was like to be a participant. This factor often bears importantly on the interpretation of your results, and readers should be in a position to arrive at their own judgments about your conclusions.

Name all operations and variables with easily recognized and remembered labels. Don't use abbreviations (The AMT5% group) or empty labels (Treatment 3). Instead, tell us about the sex-biased ads and the sex-neutral ads, the success group versus the failure group, the teacher sample versus the student sample, and so forth. It also is better to label groups or treatments in operational rather than theoretical terms. It is difficult to remember that it was the high-dissonance group that was paid $1 and the low-dissonance group that was paid $20. So tell us instead about the $1 group and the $20 group. You can remind us of the theoretical interpretation of these variables again later when it is necessary. And finally, it often is helpful in a complicated experiment to end your description with a one- or two-sentence summary of the procedure and its purpose.

An Example

The following example is excerpted from the method section of the sex-biased advertising study cited earlier.

> **METHOD**
>
> **Participants**
>
> One hundred twenty seniors from a racially integrated high school in the San Francisco Bay area served as participants. Half were male and half were female. Few planned to go on to any four-year college. Students who were not planning to go on to college were purposely sought as participants so that they might be both appropriate for and interested in jobs like those advertised by the telephone company. (As seniors, many would even be preparing for jobs like these in the near future.)
>
> **Procedure**
>
> Each student was given a booklet containing 12 job advertisements and was asked to indicate on a 6-point scale how interested he or she would be in applying for each job. The scale ranged from "very uninterested" to "very interested" and was labeled at each point. The 12 advertisements included four telephone jobs and eight nontelephone jobs. In order of appearance, the jobs were: appliance sales, telephone operator, photographer, travel agent, telephone frameman, dental assistant, taxicab driver, telephone service representative, assistant buyer, keypunch operator, telephone lineman, and public relations/advertising. The cover sheet introduced all 12 jobs as follows: "All of the jobs have a starting salary of between $100 and $120 per week with regular raises after that. None of the jobs requires any previous training or experience beyond high school graduation; all of them provide paid on-the-job training." The phrase, "An Equal Opportunity Employer m/f," appeared at the end of every job advertisement.
>
> *Sex-Biased Job Advertisements* One-third of the booklets advertised the telephone jobs in the sex-biased format used by AT&T. In other words, these ads were copied verbatim from AT&T ads and brochures furnished to us by the EEOC. The four sex-biased telephone advertisements were worded as follows:

> *Telephone Operator*
>
> **WHO SAYS IT'S A MAN'S WORLD?**
>
> **Behind every man's telephone call, there is a woman. She's a smart woman. She's efficient. She has to be. She places the complex long distance calls people cannot place themselves or helps them locate telephone numbers.**
>
> **Hers is a demanding job. But we make it worth her while. We can make it worth your while too. Not only do we pay a good salary to start, but also offer group life insurance, group medical coverage, good vacations with pay and free pensions.**
>
> **A stepping stone to management positions.**
>
> **Pacific Telephone**
>
> **An Equal Opportunity Employer m/f**

[The other advertisements and conditions were similarly described and illustrated.]

Summary of Procedure The same four telephone jobs were thus presented in three different formats: the sex-biased format used by AT&T, a sex-unbiased format, and a sex-reversed, "affirmative action" format. All eight nontelephone ads were worded in sex-unbiased fashion and remained constant in all booklets. In other words, only the wording of the telephone jobs changed from condition to condition. For purposes of analysis, a participant was defined as "interested in applying" for a job if he or she checked any of the following three categories: slightly interested, moderately interested, or very interested. A participant was defined as "not interested" if he or she checked slightly uninterested, moderately uninterested, or very uninterested.

Ethical Issues

The participants in our studies are human beings and, as detailed in Chapter 3, should be accorded respect and gratitude for their partnership in the research enterprise. Accordingly, after you have described your procedures, it is appropriate to tell us how you compensated them for their time and effort and how you dealt with any ethical problems. If the research design required you to keep participants uninformed or even misinformed about the procedures, how did you tell them about this afterward? Did you obtain written consent from your participants for their participation? Were they free to withdraw their participation at any time? Were they subjected to any embarrassment or discomfort? Were you observing people who were not aware of that fact? What steps were followed to protect the anonymity of your participants? If your study raises any of these ethical issues, you should be prepared to justify your procedures and to assure readers that your participants were treated with dignity and that they left your study with their self-esteem intact and their respect for you and social science enhanced rather than diminished.

Results

In short articles or reports of fairly simple studies, the results and discussion sections are often combined into a single section entitled "Results and Discussion." The results are discussed as they are presented, and the section ends with two or three paragraphs that state the conclusions reached, mention qualifications imposed by problems encountered in executing or analyzing the study, and suggest what further research might be appropriate. Most empirical studies can be handled in this fashion. If, however, you need to present many different kinds of results before you can integrate them or draw any inferences or if you wish to discuss several different matters at length in the final discussion, you should separate the results and discussion sections. Even in this case, however, there is no such thing as a pure results section without any accompanying discussion. You cannot just throw numbers at readers and expect them to retain them in their memory until they reach the discussion section. In other words, the results section is still part of an integrated linear narrative about human behavior. It, too, is to be written in English prose, not numbers and statistical symbols.

Setting the Stage

Before you can present your main results, two preliminary matters must be handled. First, you need to present evidence that your study successfully set up the conditions for testing your hypotheses or answering your questions. If your study required you to produce one group of participants in a happy mood and another in a sad mood, here is the place to show us that mood ratings made by the two groups were significantly different. If your study involved a mail survey, here is where you need to tell us how many people returned the survey and to discuss the possibility that those who did not respond differed in some important way from those who did. If you divided your sample of participants into groups, you need to assure us that these groups did not differ on some unintended variable that might bear on the interpretation of your results (e.g., social class, race, sex, age, intelligence). If your study required observers to record behavior or judges to score written materials, you should present quantitative evidence for interobserver agreement or interrater reliability. If your study required that you misinform the participants about the nature of the procedures, you should have some evidence that they were not suspicious, that participants who participated earlier had not informed participants who participated later, and that your cover story produced the state of belief required for the test of your hypotheses. If you had to discard certain participants, either at the time of the study or later in the data analysis, you need to tell us why and how many and to discuss the possibility that this action limits or qualifies the conclusions you can draw.

Not all these matters need to be discussed at the beginning of the results section. Some of them might already have been mentioned in the method section (e.g., interrater reliabilities of scoring), and others might better be postponed until the discussion section, when you are considering alternative explanations of your results (e.g., the possibility that some participants became suspicious). In some cases, you might not have any hard evidence to cite, and you might have to fall back on plausible argument: "The possibility that those who did not return the survey were politically more conservative than those who did seems unlikely because surveys were returned in approximately equal numbers from the dormitories, the cooperatives, and the fraternities. If the survey had alienated conservatives, we would have expected a smaller return from the fraternities; moreover . . . ."

The decision of what to include at the beginning of the results section to assure the reader that you have successfully set the stage for adequately testing your hypotheses or answering your questions is very much a matter of judgment. It is an important step, but don't overdo it. Get it out of the way as quickly as possible, and then get on with your story.

The second preliminary matter to deal with is the method of data analysis. First you need to describe any overall procedures you followed in converting your raw observations into analyzable data. How were the responses to your mail survey coded for analysis? How were observers' ratings combined? Were all measures first converted to standard scores? (Some of these, too, may have been discussed in the method section and need not be repeated. Similarly, data-combining procedures that are highly specific can be postponed. For example, if you combined three measures of anxiety into a single composite score for analysis, you can tell us about that later when you are about to present the anxiety data.)

Next you need to tell readers about the statistical analysis itself. If it is quite standard, it can be described in very few words (e.g., "All data were analyzed by two-way analyses of variance with sex of participant and mood induction as the independent variables."). If your analysis is unconventional or requires certain statistical assumptions that your data might not meet, however, you need to discuss the rationale for it, perhaps citing an article or book for the reader who wishes to check into it further.

And finally, this is the place to give readers an overview of the entire results section if it is complicated or divided into several parts; for example, "The results are presented in three parts. The first section presents the behavioral results for the men, followed by the parallel results for the women. The final section presents the attitudinal and physiological data for both sexes combined."

Presenting the Findings

The general rule in reporting your findings is to give the forest first and then the trees. This is true of the results section as a whole: Begin with the central findings, and then move to more peripheral ones. It is also true within subsections: State the basic finding first, and then elaborate or qualify it as necessary. Similarly, discuss an overall measure of aggression or whatever first, and then move to its individual components. Beginning with one of your most central results, proceed as follows:

1. Remind us of the conceptual question you are asking (e.g., "It will be recalled that the men are expected to be more expressive than the women." Or, "We turn first to the question: Are the men or the women more expressive?"). Note that this is a conceptual statement of the question.

2. Remind us of the actual operation performed or the actual behavior measured (e.g., "Do the men produce more tears during the showing of the film than the women?"). Note that this is an operational statement of the question.

3. Tell us the answer immediately and in English. "The answer is yes." Or, "As Table 1 reveals, men do, in fact, cry more profusely than women."

4. Now, and only now, speak to us in numbers. "Thus, the men in all four conditions produced an average of 14 cc more tears than the women: $F(1,112) = 5.79, p < .025$."

5. Now you may elaborate or qualify the overall conclusion if necessary. "Only in the father-watching condition did the men fail to produce more tears than the women, but a specific test of this effect failed to reach significance: $t = 1.58, p < .12$.

6. As shown in the preceding examples, every finding that involves a comparison between groups or an association between variables should be accompanied by its level of statistical significance. Otherwise, readers have no way of knowing whether the finding could have emerged by chance. But despite the importance of inferential statistics for deciding which results are to be presented as genuine findings, they are not the heart of your narrative and should be subordinated to the descriptive results. Whenever possible, state the result first and then give its statistical significance, but in no case should you ever give the statistical test alone without indicating its meaning in terms of the substantive results. Do not tell us that the three-way interaction involving sex, esteem, and parent condition was significant at the .05 level unless you tell us immediately and in English that men are less expressive than women in the negative conditions if father watches but only for men with low self-esteem.

7. In selecting the descriptive indices or statistics, your purpose should be to show us the behavior of people as vividly as you can, to be as descriptive of the actual behavior observed as possible. If children in your study hit a Bobo doll, tell us how many times they hit it or the percentage of children who hit it. If an aggression score represents the mean on a 5-point rating scale, remind us that 3.42 lies between "slightly aggressive" and "quite aggressive." Just as the

method section should give us a "feel" for the procedures employed, so, too, the results section should give us a "feel" for the behavior observed.

8. Every set of findings that is sufficiently important to be stressed should be accompanied by a table, graph, or figure showing the relevant data (unless the entire set of findings can be stated in one or two numbers). The basic rule here is that readers should be able to grasp your major findings either by reading the text or by looking at the figures and tables. This implies that tables and figures must be titled and labeled clearly and completely, even if that means constructing a very lengthy title or heading (e.g., "Mean number of tears produced in male and female participants by the heart operation movie as a function of participant sex, parental observation, and self-esteem"). Within the text itself, you must lead the reader by the hand through the table to point out the results of interest: "As shown in the first column of Table 2, men produce more tears (7.58) than women (6.34) . . . . Of particular interest is the number of tears produced when both father and mother were watching (rows 3 and 4) . . . ." Don't just wave in the general direction of the table and expect the reader to ferret out the information.
9. End each section of the results with a summary of where things stand: "Thus, except for the father-watching condition, which will be discussed later, the hypothesis that men cry more than women in response to visually depicted grief appears to receive strong support."
10. Lead into the next section of the results with a smooth transition sentence: "Men may thus be more expressive than women in the domain of negative emotion, but can we assume that they are also more willing and able to express positive emotions? Table 3 shows that we cannot . . . ." (Note, again, that you should give the reader the bottom line immediately.) As the results section proceeds, you should continue to summarize and update the reader's store of information frequently. The reader should not have to keep looking back to retrieve the major points of your plot line.

By structuring the results section in this way, by moving from forest to trees, by announcing each result clearly in prose before wading into numbers and statistics, and by summarizing frequently, you permit the readers to decide just how much detail they want to pursue at each juncture and to skip ahead to the next main point whenever that seems desirable. After you have demonstrated that your quantitative results are statistically reliable, it is often useful to become more informal and to describe the behavior of particular individuals in your study. The point is not to prove something but to add richness to your findings, to share with the readers the "feel" of the behavior: "Indeed, two of the men used an entire box of tissues during the showing of the heart operation but yet would not pet the baby kitten owned by the secretary."

The following example is from the results section of the same sex-biased advertising study cited earlier.

RESULTS

Do sex-biased job advertisements discourage men and women from applying for "opposite-sex" jobs? As shown in Figure 20.1, our results clearly suggest this to be the case.

Consider first the results for women. When the jobs of lineman and frameman were advertised in a sex-biased format, no more than 5% of the women were interested. When these same jobs were advertised in a sex-unbiased format, 25% of the women were interested. And when the ads for lineman and frameman were specifically written to appeal to women, nearly half (45%) of the women in our sample were interested in applying for one or the other of these two jobs ($\chi^2 = 8.53$, $p < .01$, one-tailed). In other words, sex-biased advertisements do discourage women from applying for so-called male jobs; more women would be interested in applying for such jobs if the ads' sex biases were removed; and even more women would be interested if affirmative action ads were specifically written to recruit them.

The results for men show a similar, but not identical, pattern. As can be seen in Figure 20.1 men are generally more interested in the jobs of operator and service representative than women are in the jobs of lineman and frameman. (This difference may be due, in part, to the fact that Pacific Telephone does employ male operators in the Bay Area.) Despite this fact, the results clearly indicate that sex-biased job advertisements still tend to discourage men from applying for jobs as operator and service

FIGURE 20.1 PERCENTAGE OF MEN AND WOMEN WHO WERE INTERESTED IN APPLYING FOR EITHER OF THE "OPPOSITE-SEX" JOBS

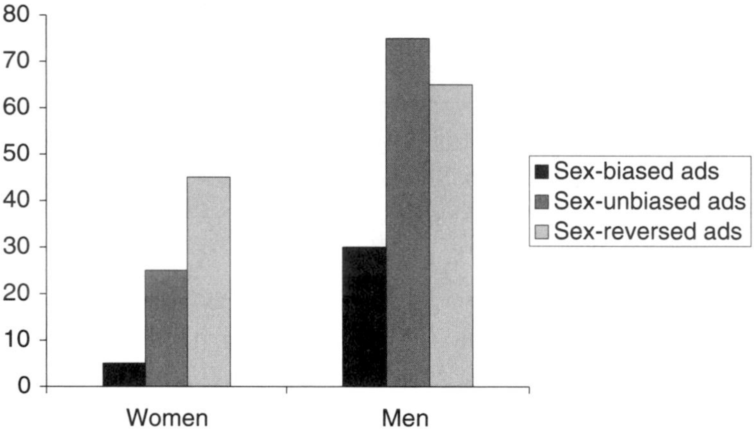

Note: Each data point represents 20 participants.

> representative ($\chi^2 = 9.09$, $p < .01$, one-tailed). For when the sex bias is removed, the percentage of men interested in applying for one or the other of these jobs jumps from 30% to 75%. Wording these ads in sex-reversed "affirmative action" format does not further increase the percentage of men who are interested. [Neither does it significantly reduce it, however ($\chi^2 < 1$, ns).] It may be that 75% is the maximum one can expect for any particular job and that a sex-reversed format would serve to further increase male interest for "female" jobs with lesser initial interest.
>
> The results thus indicate that sex bias in the content of a job advertisement does serve to aid and abet discrimination by discouraging both men and women from applying for "opposite-sex" jobs.

The data in Figure 20.1 can be displayed in many ways. For example, the x-axis could have been labeled with the three kinds of ads, with the bars representing women and men, respectively. This format would not have paralleled the discussion in the text as well because the investigators were less interested in a comparison of women and men than in the comparison of the ad types. The data also could have been displayed in a table with the exact percentages in the cells of the table. Tables are particularly useful if you have several categories or variables, which would make a figure too cluttered or visually confusing. You might have to try several different ways of displaying your own data until you find the one that conveys your findings most clearly.

Because the x-axis in Figure 20.1 represented discrete categories (women and men), the data were displayed as a bar graph. If the x-axis had represented a quantitative scale, however, it would have been more appropriate to display the data as a line graph. For example, Figure 20.2 shows how one might display participants' interest in opposite-sex ads as a function of their age and sex.

Discussion

As we noted earlier, the discussion section is often combined with the results section; for more complex studies or studies with more extended or abstract implications, it often appears separately. In either case, the discussion forms a cohesive narrative with the introduction, and you should expect to move materials back and forth between the introduction and discussion as you rewrite and reshape the report. Topics that are central to your argument will appear in the introduction and possibly again in the discussion. Points you have decided to subordinate might not be brought up at all until the discussion section. The closing discussion is also the "bottom" of the hour-glass-shaped format and thus proceeds from specific matters about your study to more general concerns (about methodological strategies, for example) to the broadest generalizations you wish to make.

Begin by telling us what you have learned from the study. Open with a clear statement on the support or nonsupport of the hypotheses or the answers to the questions you first raised in the introduction. Do not, however, simply reformulate

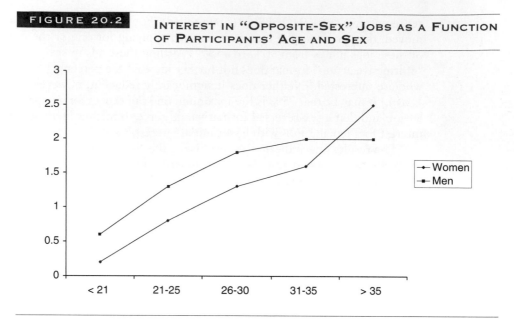

FIGURE 20.2 INTEREST IN "OPPOSITE-SEX" JOBS AS A FUNCTION OF PARTICIPANTS' AGE AND SEX

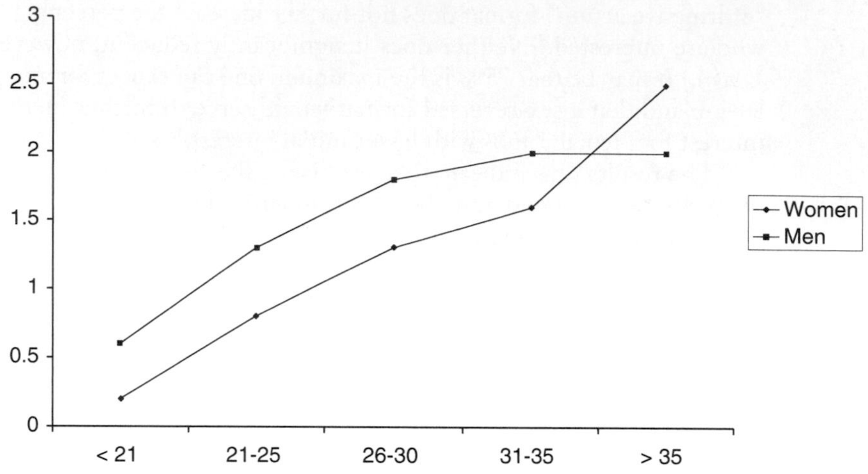

and repeat points already summarized in the results. Each new statement should contribute something new to the reader's understanding of the problem. What inferences can be drawn from the findings? These inferences could be at a level quite close to the data or could involve considerable abstraction, perhaps to the level of a larger theory regarding, say, emotion or sex differences. What are the theoretical and practical implications of the results?

It also is appropriate at this point to compare your results to those reported by other investigators and to discuss possible shortcomings of your study, conditions that might limit the extent of legitimate generalization or otherwise qualify your inferences. Remind the reader of the characteristics of your sample and the possibility that it might differ from other populations to which you might want to generalize, of specific characteristics of your methods that might have influenced the outcome, or of any other factors that might have operated to produce atypical results. But do not dwell compulsively on every flaw. In particular, be willing to accept negative or unexpected results without a tortured attempt to explain them away. Don't make up long, involved, pretzel-shaped theories to account for every hiccup in the data. There is probably a −.73 correlation between the clarity of an investigator's results and the length of his or her discussion section. Don't contribute to this shameful figure.

But suppose that on the contrary, your results have led you to a grand new theory that injects startling clarity into your data and revolutionizes your view of the problem. Doesn't that justify a long discussion section? No! In this case you should rewrite the entire report so that you begin with your new theory. As we noted earlier, your reporting task is to provide the most informative and compelling framework for your study from the opening sentence. If your new theory does that, do not wait until the discussion section to spring it on us. A research report is not necessarily a chronology of your thought processes.

The discussion section also includes a discussion of questions that remain unanswered or new questions that have been raised by the study along with suggestions for the kinds of research that would help to answer them. Indeed, suggesting further research is probably the most common way of ending a research report.

Common, but dull! If you are following the hour-glass-shaped format of the research report, the final statements should be broad general statements about human behavior, not precious details of interest only to social scientists. Consider: "Thus, further research will be needed before it is clear whether the androgyny scale should be scored as a single continuous dimension or partitioned into a four-way typology." No, no! Such a sentence might well be appropriate somewhere in the discussion, but please, not your final farewell. Why not "Perhaps, then, the concept of androgyny will come to define a new standard of mental health, a standard that will liberate men and women rather than incarcerate them"? Yes, yes! End with a bang, not a whimper!

Summary or Abstract

A research report often concludes with a brief summary that restates in barest outline the problem, the procedures, the major findings, and the major conclusions drawn. Most journals have now replaced the summary with an abstract, an even briefer summary that appears at the very beginning of the article rather than at the end.

An abstract is only about 125 words or less. It permits potential readers to get a quick overview of the study and to decide if they wish to read the report itself. It is very difficult to write because it is so condensed, and it will require slaving over every word to attain clarity. You cannot summarize everything in an abstract or even in a more extended summary at the end of your report if you choose that format. Instead, you must decide what you wish to highlight, and this implies that you should write the abstract or summary last, after you have a firm view of the structure and content of your complete report.

The title of your report itself serves to summarize your study; it, too, should convey the content of your study as accurately and as clearly as possible so that a potential reader can decide whether or not to go further. The most informative titles are those that manage to mention both the dependent and independent variables (e.g., "Emotional responses of men and women to visual stimuli as a function of self-esteem and being observed by parents"). Here is the title and abstract of the sex-biased advertising study:

DOES SEX-BIASED JOB ADVERTISING "AID AND ABET" SEX DISCRIMINATION?

Two studies are reported which indicate that both sex-biased wording in job advertisements and the placement of help-wanted ads in sex-segregated newspaper columns discourage men and women from applying for "opposite-sex" jobs for which they might well be qualified. Both studies were originally conducted and presented as part of legal testimony in actual sex discrimination cases.

References

All books and articles cited in the text of a research report are listed at the end of the report under the heading "References." They are arranged alphabetically according to the first author's last name, a format that parallels the way in which they are cited in the text. The following three references are to journal articles cited in this chapter. The italicized numbers are volume numbers; they are followed by the page numbers.

Bem, S. L., & Bem, D. J. (1973). Does sex-biased job advertising "aid and abet" sex discrimination? *Journal of Applied Social Psychology, 3,* 6–18.

Festinger, L., & Carlsmith, J. M. (1959). Cognitive consequences of forced compliance. *Journal of Abnormal and Social Psychology, 58,* 203–210.

Martyna, W. (1978). What does "He" mean? *Journal of Communication, 28,* 131–138.

The following references are to books cited in this chapter.

Festinger, L. A. (1957). *A theory of cognitive dissonance.* Stanford, CA: Stanford University Press.

Strunk, W., Jr., & White, E. B. (2000). *The elements of style* (4th ed.). Boston: Allyn and Bacon.

The following example illustrates how to list a chapter that appears in an edited book. The reference itself is to an extended version of the chapter you are now reading; it is written for those preparing articles for publication in professional journals.

Bem, D. J. (2002). Writing the empirical journal article. In J. M. Darley, M. P. Zanna, & H. L. Roediger III, (Eds.), *The compleat academic: A career guide* (2nd ed.). Washington, DC: American Psychological Association.

Appendix

The appendix to a research report contains copies of materials used in the research that would be too extensive to include in the report itself. These might include questionnaires, attitude scales, stimulus materials, or photographs and drawings of experimental apparatus or the research setting. These are materials that would help someone else duplicate your experiment in detail. A second appendix might contain tables of data or additional data analyses that are too extensive or too peripheral to include in the report itself. This is information that would enable an interested reader to explore your data in fine detail or to answer questions about your results that you omitted or that might not even have occurred to you.

Because journal space is at a premium, most journal articles do not have appendixes. Readers who have questions about the data or who wish to replicate the experiment themselves usually communicate directly with the original investigator. Doctoral dissertations, masters theses, and research reports for class assignments, however, usually do include such appendixes. In fact, it often is useful in research reports for class assignments to include an appendix containing the raw data themselves. Often an instructor will be able to spot findings in the data that might have been overlooked or to suggest alternative ways of organizing or analyzing them.

In short, whether or not an investigator includes appendixes in a report depends a lot on who the readers will be and the likelihood that they will find the supplementary materials useful. But as we noted earlier, the report itself should still be self-contained; a reader should not have to consult an appendix to understand the methods or results. For example, even if your entire survey questionnaire is contained in an appendix, you should still provide a few sample items from it in the method section.

Some Suggestions on Procedure and Style

Accuracy and Clarity

The overriding criteria for good scientific writing are *accuracy* and *clarity*. If your report is interesting and written with flair and style, fine. But this is still a subsidiary virtue. First strive for accuracy and clarity.

Work from an Outline

Even though the standardized format we have described here will go a long way toward organizing your report, you will be able to produce a more coherent report with a minimum of rewriting if you first organize the main points in outline form, examine the logic of the sequence, check to see if important points are omitted or misplaced, and so forth. As we suggested earlier, it sometimes is helpful to begin with the results section, and it also is useful to think of your introduction and final discussion as part of the same conceptual narrative.

Write Simply. Use Examples. Use Friends as Reviewers

As we noted earlier, it should be possible for nonprofessionals to read your report and comprehend what you did and why even if they know nothing about statistics, research design, or the substantive area of your research problem. This goal is achieved by writing simply, with a minimum of jargon, and using frequent examples to illustrate and introduce technical concepts. The more abstract the subject matter, the more you need examples to tie it to the reader's own experience and previous level of knowledge. Read over your own writing, trying to take the viewpoint of an intelligent but nonprofessional reader. Ask at each point, "Do I know yet what this concept means?" "Is this clear?" The ability to take the role of a "naive" reader or listener is the most important skill in writing or teaching. It is not easy. And because it is not easy, you should use your friends as reviewers, especially those who are unfamiliar with the subject matter. If they find something unclear, do not argue with them or attempt to clarify the problem verbally. If they have read carefully and conscientiously, they are always right: By definition, the writing is unclear. Their suggestions for correcting the unclarities might be wrong, even dumb. But as unclarity detectors, readers are never wrong.

Omit Needless Words

Virtually all experienced writers agree that any written expression that deserves to be called *vigorous writing*, whether it is a short story, an article for a professional journal, or a complete book, *is* characterized by the attribute of being succinct, *concise*, and to the point. *A sentence*—no matter where in the writing it occurs—*should contain no unnecessary* or superfluous *words*, words that stand in the way of the writer's direct expression of his or her meaning and purpose. In a very similar fashion, *a paragraph*—the basic unit of organization in English prose—should contain *no unnecessary* or superfluous *sentences*, sentences that introduce peripheral content into the writing or stray from its basic narrative line. It is in this sense that a writer is like an artist executing a drawing, and it is in this sense that a writer is like an engineer designing a machine. Good writing should be economical *for the same reason that a drawing should have no unnecessary lines*, *and* good writing should be streamlined in the same way that *a machine* is designed to have *no unnecessary parts*, parts that contribute little or nothing to its intended function.

This prescription to be succinct and concise is often misunderstood, and *requires* judicious application. It certainly does *not* imply *that the writer* must *make all* of his or her *sentences short* and choppy *or* leave out all adjectives, adverbs, and qualifiers. Nor does it mean that he or she must *avoid* or eliminate *all detail* from the writing *and treat* his or her *subjects only in* the barest skeleton or *outline* form. *But* the requirement does imply *that every word* committed to paper should *tell* something new to the reader and contribute in a significant and nonredundant way to the message that the writer is trying to convey.

You have just read a 303-word essay on brevity. It is not a terrible first draft, but a good writer or copy editor would take its message to heart and, by crossing out all the nonitalicized words, cut it by 81%. Savor the result:

> Vigorous writing is concise. A sentence should contain no unnecessary words, a paragraph no unnecessary sentences, for the same reason that a

> drawing should have no unnecessary lines and a machine no unnecessary parts. This requires not that the writer make all sentences short or avoid all detail and treat subjects only in outline, but that every word tell. [59 words]

This essay on brevity was written by Strunk and White (2000, p. 23) under the heading: "Omit Needless Words." Obey their injunction, for it is the most important piece of advice in this chapter. Research reports also should omit needless concepts, topics, anecdotes, asides, and footnotes. Clear any underbrush that clutters your narrative. If a point seems peripheral to your main theme, remove it. If you can't bring yourself to do this, put it in a footnote. Then when you revise your report, remove the footnote.

Avoid Metacomments on the Writing

Expository writing fails its mission if it diverts the reader's attention to itself and away from the topic; the process of writing should be transparent to the reader. In particular, the prose itself should direct the flow of the narrative without requiring you to play tour guide by commenting on it. Don't say: "Now that I have discussed the three theories of emotion, we can turn to the empirical work on each of them. I will begin with the psychoanalytic account of affect . . . ." Instead, move directly from your discussion of the theories into the literature review with a simple transition sentence like, "Each of these three theories has been tested empirically. Thus, the psychoanalytic account of affect has received support in studies that . . . ." Don't say: "Now that we have seen the results for negative affect, we are in a position to examine men's and women's emotional expression in the realm of positive affect. The relevant data are presented in Table 2 . . . ." Instead, use a transition sentence that simultaneously summarizes and moves the story along: "Men may thus be more expressive than women in the domain of negative emotion, but are they also more expressive in the domain of positive emotion? Table 2 shows that they are not . . . ." Any other guideposts needed can be supplied by using informative headings and by following the advice on repetition and parallel construction given in the next section.

If you feel the need to make metacomments to keep the reader on the narrative path, then your plot line is probably already too cluttered, the writing insufficiently linear. Metacomments will only oppress the prose further. Instead, copyedit. Omit needless words; don't add them!

Use Repetition and Parallel Construction

Inexperienced writers often substitute synonyms for recurring words and vary their sentence structure in the mistaken belief that this is more creative, stylish, or interesting. Instead of using repetition and parallel construction, as in "Men may be more expressive than women in the domain of negative emotion, but they are not more expressive in the domain of positive emotion," they attempt to be more creative: "Men may be more expressive than women in the domain of negative emotion, but it is not true that they are more willing and able than the opposite sex to display the more cheerful affects."

Such creativity is hardly more interesting, but it is certainly more confusing. In scientific communication, it can be deadly. When an author uses different words to refer to the same concept in a technical article—where accuracy is paramount—readers will justifiably wonder if different meanings are implied. This example is not disastrous, and most readers will be unaware that their understanding flickered momentarily when the prose hit a bump. But consider the cognitive burden carried by readers who must hack through this "creative" jungle:

> The high-dissonance participants were paid a small sum of money while being given a free choice of whether or not to participate, whereas the participants we randomly assigned to the large-incentive treatment (the low-dissonance condition) were not offered the opportunity to refuse.

This (fictitious) author should have written:

> High-dissonance participants were paid a small sum of money and were not required to participate; low-dissonance participants were paid a large sum of money and were required to participate.

The wording and grammatical structure of the two clauses are held rigidly parallel; only the variables vary. Repetition and parallel construction are among the most effective servants of clarity. Don't be creative; be clear.

Be Compulsive. Be Willing to Restructure

The best writers rewrite nearly every sentence in the course of polishing their successive drafts. The probability of writing a sentence perfectly the first time is vanishingly small, and good writing requires a high degree of compulsiveness and attention to detail. But whether or not to worry about writing style in the course of producing the first draft is to some extent a matter of individual taste. Some experienced writers spend a long time over each sentence, carefully choosing each word. But when the purpose is to convey information rather than to achieve a literary production, it probably is true for most people that time is saved in the long run by writing the first draft as quickly as possible. Once it is on paper, you can go back and rewrite sentences and paragraphs, fortified by the knowledge that at least a first draft of the report has already been produced. In writing and rewriting, it is important to remember that a badly built building cannot be salvaged by brightening up the wallpaper. Rewriting often means restructuring, not just tinkering with sentences or paragraphs. Sometimes it is necessary to restructure totally a research report, even to go back and do more data analysis, just to iron out a bump in the logic of the argument. Do not get so attached to your first draft that you are unwilling to tear it apart and rebuild it. Rewriting often means restructuring.

Person and Voice

In the past, scientific writing employed the third-person passive voice almost exclusively ("The experiment was designed by the authors to test the hypothesis that . . ."). This is dull and clumsy and is no longer the norm. It is now permissible to use the first person and desirable to use the active voice. Do not refer to yourself as "the author" or "the investigator." Do not refer to yourself as "we" unless there really are two or more authors or investigators involved. You may refer to yourself as "I" as long as you do it sparingly; constant use of the first person tends to distract the reader from the subject matter, and it is best to remain in the background. Leave the reader in the background, too. Do not say, "The reader will find it hard to believe that . . ." or "You will be surprised to learn . . . ." Perhaps you are wondering what you *can* do. You can let people and their behavior serve as the subjects of sentences: "Individuals appear to cling to their prejudices even when . . . ." "Racial prejudice, then, diminishes when persons interact . . . ." You may also refer to the reader indirectly from time to time: "Consider, first, the results for men . . . ." You may also refer to yourself and the reader as "we" in some contexts: "We can see in Table 1 that most of the tears are produced . . . ."

Tense

Use the past tense when reporting the previous research of others ("Bandura reported . . ."), how you conducted your study ("Observers were posted behind . . ."), and specific past behaviors of your participants ("Two of the group members talked . . ."). Use the present tense for results currently in front of the reader ("As Table 2 shows, the emotional film is more effective . . .") and for conclusions that are more general than the specific results ("Sex-biased advertising, then, leads qualified applicants to ignore . . .").

Avoid Language Bias

Like most publishers, the American Psychological Association now has extensive guidelines for language that refers to individuals or groups. Here is a summary of some of those guidelines.

Research Participants It is no longer considered appropriate to objectify those whom we study by calling them *subjects.* Instead use descriptive terms that either identify them more specifically or that acknowledge their roles as partners in the research process, such as *college students, children, individuals, participants, interviewees,* or *respondents.*

Sex and Gender The issue of language bias comes up most frequently with regard to sex or gender, and the most awkward problems arise from the use of masculine nouns and pronouns when the content refers to both sexes. The generic use of "man," "he," "his," and "him" to refer to both sexes is not only misleading in many instances, but research shows that readers think of male persons when these forms are used (Martyna, 1978). Sometimes the results are not only sexist but humorous in their naive androcentrism: "Man's vital needs include food, water, and access to females" (quoted in Martyna, 1978).

In most contexts, the simplest alternative is the use of the plural. Instead of writing, "The individual who displays prejudice in his personal relations is . . .," write, "Individuals who display prejudice in their personal relations are . . . ." Sometimes the pronoun can simply be dropped or replaced by a sex-neutral article (e.g., *the*, *a*, or *an*). Instead of writing, "The researcher must avoid letting his preconceptions bias his interpretation of results," you can write, "The researcher must avoid letting preconceptions bias the interpretation of results."

If it is stylistically important to focus on the single individual, the use of "he or she," "him or her," and so forth is acceptable but clumsy if used very often. Alternating *he* and *she* is both confusing and distracting. Similarly, alternatives like *he/she* or *s/he* are unpronounceable and grate on the eye. Don't use them.

Stylistic matters aside, however, you must be accurate in your use of pronouns when you describe your research or that of others. Readers must be explicitly told the sex of experimenters, observers, and participants. When referring to males, use male pronouns; when referring to females, use female pronouns. (See, for example, the earlier description of the Festinger-Carlsmith study, which used male participants.) Under no circumstances should you omit or hide sex identity in a misguided attempt to be unbiased.

The problems of gender reference become easier when we move away from pronouns. Words like *man* and *mankind* are easily replaced by terms like *people* and *humanity*. Instead of manning projects, we can staff them. The federal government has already desexed occupational titles so that we have letter carriers rather than mailmen; in private industry we have flight attendants rather than stewardesses. And in life, children need nurturing or parenting, not just mothering. In all these cases, you will find it easy to discover the appropriate sex-neutral term if you think of the activity rather than the person doing it.

Next, watch out for plain old stereotyping. The author who asserts that "research scientists often neglect their wives" fails to acknowledge that women as well as men are research scientists. If the author meant specifically male research scientists, he (she?) should have said so. Do not talk about ambitious men and aggressive women or cautious men and timid women if the use of different adjectives denotes not different behaviors on the part of men and women but your stereotyped interpretation of those behaviors. Don't make stereotyped assumptions about marital sex roles by saying that "The client's husband lets her teach part-time" if all you know is that the client teaches part-time. If the bias is not yours but someone else's, let the writing make that clear: "The client's husband 'lets' her teach part-time." "The husband says he 'lets' the client teach part-time." "The client says her husband lets her teach part-time." "The client says sarcastically that her husband 'lets' her teach part-time." The client and her husband are allowed to say such things. You are not.

And finally, select examples with care. Beware of your assumptions about the sex of doctors, homemakers, nurses, and so forth. Why not "The athlete who believes in her ability to succeed . . ."? Let our writing promote the view that women's vital needs are the same as men's: food, water, and access to equality.

Racial and Ethnic Identity Preferences for names referring to racial and ethnic groups change over time. For example, *African American* and *Black* are currently acceptable terms, whereas *Negro* and *Afro-American* are now obsolete. Similarly, *Asian* and *Asian American* are currently acceptable designations, whereas *Oriental* is not. As these examples illustrate, hyphens should not be used in multiword designations, and terms like *Black* and *White* are considered proper nouns and should be capitalized.

Depending on their historical countries of origin, individuals might prefer to be called *Hispanic*, *Latino*, or *Chicano* (*Latina* and *Chicana* for women). *American Indian* and *Native American* are both accepted terms for referring to indigenous people of North America; but, technically, only the latter category includes Hawaiians and Samoans. It often is relevant to be more specific in describing your participants. For example, it might be pertinent to know that they were *Cuban*, not just *Hispanic*; *Chinese*, *Vietnamese*, or *Korean*, not just *Asian*.

If you are uncertain about how to describe your research participants, ask them.

Sexual Orientation Like terms referring to racial and ethnic identity, terms referring to sexual orientation also change over time. For example, the term *sexual orientation* itself is now preferred to the older *sexual preference*—which implies a temporary free choice rather than an enduring disposition. Although terms like *homosexual* and *homosexuality* are still technically correct and may be used in phrases such as "a homosexual orientation" or "more Americans now accept homosexuality," they should be avoided when referring to individuals or groups. Instead of referring to *homosexuals* or *bisexuals*, use *lesbians*, *gay men*, or *bisexual men and women*. In some contexts, the word *gay* can be used to include both men and women (e. g., "the gay rights movement"), but when referring to individuals or groups, retain the distinction between gay men and lesbians.

Disabilities When referring to individuals with disabilities, maintain their integrity as individuals and human beings by avoiding language that equates them with their conditions. Don't use nouns such as *neurotics*, *schizophrenics*, *manic-depressives*, *the mentally retarded*, or even *the disabled*. Also avoid terms that imply victimization (e.g., "suffers from schizophrenia," "AIDS victim") or that can be interpreted as a slur (e.g., *cripple*). *Challenged* and *special* are often considered euphemistic and should be used only if preferred by those who participate in your study. In general the preferred forms of description are "person with ______" or "person living with ______" or "person who has________."

One exception is the Deaf (note the capitalized word). Many—but not all—individuals who are deaf or hearing impaired do not regard themselves as disabled but rather as members of a distinctive culture, a linguistic minority who communicate in a sign language. They take pride in referring to themselves as Deaf and their community as the Deaf. If your study involved deaf participants, your description of them should honor their preferences when possible.

Where to Find Additional Guidance

Two documents can provide additional information concerning the preparation of your research report. The *Publication Manual of the American Psychological Association* (5th ed., 2001) provides highly specific information about the exact format used in the professional journals and general advice on format and style. The style described in the *Publication Manual* differs from some of the examples in this chapter. If you are actually preparing a report for a journal, you should consult the *Manual*, look at articles in the journal itself, or read the extended version of the chapter you are now reading (Bem, 2002). There are many books on how to write expository prose, covering grammar, word usage, punctuation, and style. One of the best is *The Elements of Style* by Strunk and White (2000). It is brief, informative, and entertaining.

Enough advice. Go write your report.

Summary

The research report should reflect the results of a study, rather than any preconceived ideas that the investigator might have prior to conducting the study. The structure of the research report can be described as an "hourglass" format. The introduction constitutes the top portion of the hourglass in that it begins with a general statement, followed by a narrower discussion of theories and literature that are most pertinent to the phenomenon being researched. The subject of the investigation is then more specifically outlined beginning with the central question to be explored and an explanation of its significance. The introduction can end with a brief paragraph describing the study itself in general terms, leaving the details to the method section. The method and results sections form the neck of the hourglass. The method section describes in detail the participants, the way in which the study was conducted, and the methods employed to measure the behaviors under examination. The results section presents the findings, including any tables, figures, and statistical analyses of the data. The hourglass then widens again in the discussion. This section brings the research report to a conclusion, beginning with specific implications and ending with broad conclusions. The summary restates in a brief, concise format the problem, the procedures, the major findings, and the major conclusions drawn from the study. Current journals have now replaced the summary with the shorter abstract, which precedes rather than follows the research report. The title of the report also serves to describe the study and should reflect as much as possible the content of the report. The research report should be written in a clear, accurate style that can be understood by nonprofessionals.

The use of the first person and the active voice is now preferred over the third person and the passive voice. The past tense is used when reporting the past research of others and in describing your own procedures. The present tense is used to discuss results currently in front of the reader or conclusions that are more general than the specific results. Do not use generic masculine terms such as "he" or "man" when referring to both men and women. It is also important to avoid offensive language when discussing sex, gender, ethnicity, sexual orientation, and disability.

The *Publication Manual of the American Psychological Association* (2001) was mentioned as a reference for further questions of style in the formatting of social science reports.

On the Web

http://www.wooster.edu/psychology/apa-crib.html An on-line "crib sheet" for quick reference regarding APA style and format.

http://www.psych.cornell.edu/dbem/writing_article.html Read the extended version of this chapter for those preparing articles for professional journals.

Further Reading

Becker, H. S. (1986). *Writing for social scientists: How to start and finish your thesis, book, or article.* Chicago: University of Chicago Press.

Sternberg, R. J. (1993). *The psychologist's companion: A guide to scientific writing for students and researchers.* New York: Cambridge University Press.

Sternberg, R. J. (Ed.) (2000). *Guide to publishing in psychology journals.* New York: Cambridge: Cambridge University Press.

BIBLIOGRAPHY

Adair, J. G., & Epstein, J. S. (1968). Verbal cues in the mediation of experimenter bias. *Psychological Reports, 22*, 1045–1053.

Adler, F. (1947). Operational definitions in sociology. *American Journal of Sociology, 52*, 438–444.

Adorno, T. W., Frenkel-Brunswik, E., Levinson, D. J., & Sanford, R. N. (1950). *The authoritarian personality*. New York: Harper & Row.

Ambady, N., & Rosenthal, R. (1992). Thin slices of expressive behavior as predictors of interpersonal consequences: A meta-analysis. *Psychological Bulletin, 111*, 256–274.

American Psychological Association. (2001). *Publication manual of the American Psychological Association* (5th ed.). Washington, DC: Author.

Anderson, B. A., Silver, B. D., & Abramson, P. R. (1988). The effects of the race of the interviewer on race-related attitudes of Black respondents in SRC/CPS National Election Studies. *Public Opinion Quarterly, 52*, 289–324.

Anderson, C. A., & Anderson, K. B. (1996). Violent crime rate studies in philosophical context: A destructive testing approach to heat and southern culture of violence effects. *Journal of Personality and Social Psychology, 70*, 740–756.

Anderson, C. A., & Dill, K. E. (2000). Video games and aggressive thoughts, feelings, and behavior in the laboratory and in life. *Journal of Personality and Social Psychology, 78*, 772–790.

Anderson, J. E., & Dahlberg, L. L. (1992). High-risk sexual behavior in the general population: Results from a national survey. *Sexually Transmitted Diseases, 19*, 320–325.

Anderson, N. H. (1961). Scales and statistics: Parametric and nonparametric. *Psychological Bulletin, 58*, 305–316.

Aronson, E. (1966). Avoidance of inter-subject communication. *Psychological Reports, 19*, 238.

Aronson, E., Stephan, C., Sikes, J., Blaney, N., & Snapp, M. (1978). *The jigsaw classroom*. Thousand Oaks, CA: Sage Publications.

Aronson, E., Wilson, T. D., & Brewer, M. B. (1998). Experimentation in social psychology. In D. T. Gilbert, S. T. Fiske, & G. Lindzey (Eds.), *The handbook of social psychology* (4th ed., Vol. 1, pp. 99–142). New York: McGraw-Hill.

Arriaga, X. B. (2001). The ups and downs of dating: Fluctuations in satisfaction in newly formed romantic relationships. *Journal of Personality and Social Psychology, 80*, 754–765.

Arthur, J. A., & Case, C. E. (1994). Race, class, and support for police use of force. *Crime, Law, and Social Change, 21*, 167–182.

Astorino-Courtois, A. (1995). The cognitive structure of decision making and the course of Arab-Israeli relations, 1970–1978. *Journal of Conflict Resolution, 39*, 419–438.

Audia, P. G., Locke, E. A., & Smith, K. G. (2000). The paradox of success: An archival and a laboratory study of strategic persistence following radical environmental change. *Academy of Management Journal, 43*, 837–853.

Bakeman, R., & Gottman, J. M. (1997). *Observing interaction: An introduction to sequential analysis* (2nd ed.). New York: Cambridge University Press.

Balch, G. I. (1974). Multiple indicators in survey research: The concept "sense of political efficacy." *Political Methodology, 1*, 1–43.

Bales, R. F. (1970). *Personality and interpersonal behavior.* New York: Holt, Rinehart & Winston.

Barbarin, O. A., Richter, L., de Wet, T., & Wachtel, A. (1998). Ironic trends in the transition to peace: Criminal violence supplants political violence in terrorizing South African Blacks. *Peace and Conflict: Journal of Peace Psychology, 4*, 283–305.

Barker, R. G., & Schoggen, P. (1973). *Qualities of community life.* San Francisco: Jossey-Bass.

Baumrind, D. (1964). Some thoughts on the ethics of research: After reading Milgram's "Behavioral study of obedience." *American Psychologist, 19*, 421–423.

Beaman, A. L. (1991). An empirical comparison of meta-analytic and traditional reviews. *Personality and Social Psychology Bulletin, 17*, 252–257.

Becker, H. S. (1967). Whose side are we on? *Journal of Social Problems, 14*, 239–247.

Becker, L. J., & Seligman, C. (1978). Reducing air conditioning waste by signalling it is cool outside. *Personality and Social Psychology Bulletin, 4*, 412–415.

Becker, L. J., Seligman, C., & Darley, J. M. (1979, June). *Psychological strategies to reduce energy consumption.* Center for Energy and Environmental Studies, Report 90.

Bem, D. J. (2002). Writing the empirical journal article. In J. M. Darley, M. P. Zanna, & H. L. Roediger III (Eds.), *The compleat academic: A career guide* (2nd ed.). Washington, DC: American Psychological Association.

Bem, D. J., & Honorton, C. (1994). Does Psi exist? Replicable evidence for an anomalous process of information transfer. *Psychological Bulletin, 115*, 4–18.

Bem, S. L., & Bem, D. J. (1973). Does sex-biased job advertising "aid and abet" sex discrimination? *Journal of Applied Social Psychology, 3*, 6–18.

Berk, R. A., & Rossi, P. H. (1977). Doing good or worse: Evaluation research politically examined. In M. Guttentag & S. Saar (Eds.), *Evaluation studies review annual* (Vol. 2, pp. 77–90). Thousand Oaks, CA: Sage Publications.

Berkowitz, L., & Donnerstein, E. (1982). External validity is more than skin deep: Some answers to criticisms of laboratory experiments. *American Psychologist, 37*, 245–257.

Berry, D. S., & Hansen, J. S. (2000). Personality, nonverbal behavior, and interaction quality in female dyads. *Personality and Social Psychology Bulletin, 26*, 278–292.

Bertell, R., Jacobson, N., & Stogre, M. (1984). Environmental influence on survival of low birth weight infants in Wisconsin, 1963–1975. *International Perspectives in Public Health, 1*(2), 12–24.

Birnbaum, M. H. (Ed.). (2000). *Psychological experiments on the Internet.* New York: Academic Press.

Bishop, G. F., Oldendick, R. W., & Tuchfarber, A. J. (1983). Effects of filter questions in public opinion surveys. *Public Opinion Quarterly, 47*, 528–546.

Blaney, N. T., Stephan, C., Rosenfield, D., Aronson, E., & Sikes, J. (1977). Interdependence in the classroom: A field study. *Journal of Educational Psychology, 69,* 139–146.

Blascovich, J. (2000). Using physiological indexes of psychological processes in social psychological research. In H. T. Reis & C. M. Judd (Eds.), *Handbook of research methods in social and personality psychology* (pp. 117–137). New York: Cambridge University Press.

Blascovich, J., Mendes, W. B., Hunter, S. B., Lickel, B., & Kowai-Bell, N. (2001). Perceiver threat in social interactions with stigmatized others. *Journal of Personality and Social Psychology, 80,* 253–267.

Blurton-Jones, N. (Ed.). (1972). *Ethological studies of child behavior.* London: Cambridge University Press.

Bogardus, E. S. (1933). A social distance scale. *Sociology and Social Research, 17,* 265–271.

Bollmer, J. M., Harris, M. J., & Dotson, S. (2001). *We hurt most the ones we love: Differences in teasing across relationship type.* Unpublished manuscript, University of Kentucky.

Boruch, R. F. (1975). On common contentions about randomized field experiments. In R. F. Boruch & H. W. Riecken (Eds.), *Experimental tests of public policy* (pp.108–145). Boulder, CO: Westview Press.

Bradburn, N., & Sudman, S. (1979). *Improving interview method and questionnaire design.* San Francisco: Jossey-Bass.

Brannigan, G. G., & Merrens, M. R. (Eds.). (1993). *The undaunted psychologist: Adventures in research.* New York: McGraw-Hill.

Brickman, P., Folger, R., Goode, E., & Schul, Y. (1981). Micro and macro justice. In M. J. Lerner (Ed.), *The justice motive and social behavior.* New York: Plenum.

Brickman, P., & Stearns, A. (1978). Help that is not called help. *Personality and Social Psychology Bulletin, 4,* 314–317.

Brockner, J., Grover, S., Reed, T., DeWitt, R., & O'Malley, M. (1987). Survivors' reactions to layoffs: We get by with a little help for our friends. *Administrative Science Quarterly, 32,* 526–541.

Bromet, E. B., Parkinson, D. K., Schulberg, H. C., Dunn, L. O., & Gondek, P. C. (1982). Mental health of residents near the Three Mile Island reactor: A comparative study of selected groups. *Journal of Preventive Psychiatry, 1,* 225–276.

Bromet, E. B., Schulberg, H. C., & Dunn, L. O. (1982, August). *The TMI nuclear accident and patterns of psychopathology in mothers of infant children.* Paper presented at the 90th Annual Meeting of the American Psychological Association, Washington, DC.

Buckle, A., & Farrington, D. P. (1994). Measuring shoplifting by systematic observation: A replication study. *Psychology, Crime, and Law, 1,* 133–141.

Burnham, J. R. (1966). *Experimenter bias and lesion labeling.* Unpublished manuscript.

Bush, M., & Gordon, A. C. (1978). Client choice and bureaucratic accountability: Possibilities for responsiveness in a social welfare bureaucracy. *Journal of Social Issues, 34*(4), 22–43.

Buss, D. M., & Schmitt, D. P. (1993). Sexual strategies theory: An evolutionary perspective on human mating. *Psychological Review, 100,* 204–232.

Campbell, A., Converse, P. E., Miller, W. E., & Stokes, D. E. (1954). *The voter decides*. Evanston, IL: Row and Peterson.

Campbell, D. T. (1969a). Definitional versus multiple operationalism. *et al, 2*, 14–17.

Campbell, D. T. (1969b). Reforms as experiments. *American Psychologist, 24*, 409–429.

Campbell, D. T. (1979). Assessing the impact of planned social change. *Evaluation and Program Planning, 2*, 67–90.

Campbell, D. T., & Erlebacher, A. (1970). How regression artifacts in quasi-experimental evaluations can mistakenly make compensatory education look harmful. In J. Hellmuth (Ed.), *Compensatory education—a national debate: Vol. 3. The disadvantaged child* (pp. 597–617). New York: Brunner/Mazel.

Campbell, D. T., & Fiske, D. W. (1959). Convergent and discriminant validation by the multitrait–multimethod matrix. *Psychological Bulletin, 56*, 81–105.

Campbell, D. T., & Stanley, J. C. (1966). *Experimental and quasi-experimental designs for research*. Chicago: Rand McNally.

Cannell, C. F., Fisher, G., & Bakker, T. (1965). Reporting of hospitalization in the health service interview. *Vital and Health Statistics*, Series 2, Number 6. Washington: U.S. Public Health Service.

Carlsmith, J. M., Ellsworth, P. C., & Aronson, E. (1976). *Methods of research in social psychology*. Reading, MA: Addison-Wesley.

Carstensen, L. L., Pasupathi, M., Mayr, U., & Nesselroade, J. R. (2000). Emotional experience in everyday life across the adult life span. *Journal of Personality and Social Psychology, 79*, 644–655.

Carter, L. F. (1971). Inadvertent sociological theory. *Social Focus, 50*, 12–25.

Caspi, A., Begg, D., Dickson, N., Harrington, H., Langley, J., Moffitt, T. E., & Silva, P. A. (1997). Personality differences predict health-risk behaviors in young adulthood: Evidence from a longitudinal study. *Journal of Personality and Social Psychology, 73*, 1052–1063.

Chassin, L., Pitts, S. C., & DeLucia, C. (1999). The relation of adolescent substance use to young adult autonomy, positive activity involvement, and perceived competence. *Development and Psychopathology, 11*, 915–932.

Chein, I. (1956). Narcotics use among juveniles. *Social Work, 1*, 50–60.

Chen, H., & Nilan, M. (1998, November). *An exploration of Web user's internal experiences: Application of the experience sampling method to the Web environment*. Paper presented at the WebNet 98 World Conference, Orlando, FL.

Cherlin, A., & Walters, P. B. (1981). Trends in United States men's and women's sex-role attitudes: 1972 to 1978. *American Sociological Review, 46*, 453–460.

Christensen, L. (1988). Deception in psychological research: When is its use justified? *Personality and Social Psychology Bulletin, 48*, 252–253.

Christie, R., & Geis, F. L. (1970). *Studies in Machiavellianism*. New York: Academic Press.

Cialdini, R. B. (2001). *Influence: Science and practice*. Boston: Allyn & Bacon.

Cicirelli, V., & Granger, R. (1969, June) *The impact of Head Start: An evaluation of the effects of Head Start on children's cognitive and affective development*. A report presented to the Office of Economic Opportunity pursuant to Contract B89-4536. Westinghouse Learning Corporation, Ohio University. (Distributed by Clearinghouse for Federal Scientific and Technical Information, U.S. Department of Commerce, National Bureau of Standards, Institute for Applied Technology. PB 184-328.)

Cohen, J. (1960). A coefficient of agreement for nominal scales. *Educational and Psychological Measurement, 20*, 37–46.

Cohen, J. (1977). *Statistical power analysis for the behavioral sciences.* New York: Academic Press.

Cohen, J. (1994). The earth is round ($p < .05$). *American Psychologist, 49*, 997–1003.

Conger, R. D., Cui, M., Bryant, C. M., & Elder, G. H., Jr. (2000). Competence in early adult romantic relationships: A developmental perspective on family influences. *Journal of Personality and Social Psychology, 79*, 224–237.

Conti, R. (2001). Time flies: Investigating the connection between intrinsic motivation and the experience of time. *Journal of Personality, 69*, 1–26.

Cooper, H. M. (1984). *The integrative research review: A social science approach.* Thousand Oaks, CA: Sage Publications.

Cooper, H. M., & Rosenthal, R. (1980). Statistical versus traditional procedures for summarizing research findings. *Psychological Bulletin, 87*, 442–449.

Cooper, W. H. (1981). Ubiquitous halo. *Psychological Bulletin, 90*, 218–244.

Cressey, D. R. (1953). *Other people's money: A study in the social psychology of embezzlement.* New York: Free Press.

Cromer, A. H. (1993). *Uncommon sense: The heretical nature of science.* New York: Oxford University Press.

Cronbach, L. J. (1951). Coefficient alpha and the internal structure of tests. *Psychometrika, 16*, 297–334.

Csikszentmihalyi, M., & Csikszentmihalyi, I. (Eds.). (1988). *Optimal experience: Psychological studies of flow in consciousness.* New York: Cambridge University Press.

Csikszentmihalyi, M., Larson, R., & Prescott, S. (1977). The ecology of adolescent experience. *Journal of Youth and Adolescence, 6*, 281–294.

Davis, J. A. (1968). *Elementary survey analysis.* Upper Saddle River, NJ: Prentice Hall.

Davis, J. A., & Smith, T. W. (1992). *The NORC General Social Survey: A user's guide.* Thousand Oaks, CA: Sage Publications.

Dawes, R. M. (1972). *Fundamentals of attitude measurement.* New York: Wiley.

Dawes, R. M. (1977). Suppose we measured height with rating scales instead of rulers. *Applied Psychological Measurement, 1*, 267–273.

Dawes, R. M., & Moore, M. (1979). Guttman scaling orthodox and randomized responses. In F. Peterman (Ed.), *Attitude measurement* (pp. 117–133). Gottingen: Verlag fur psychologie.

Dawes, R. M., & Smith, T. L. (1985). Attitude and opinion measurement. In O. Lindzey & E. Aronson (Eds.), *Handbook of social psychology* (3rd ed., pp. 509–566). New York: Random House.

Dempster, F. N. (1988). The spacing effect: A case study in the failure to apply the results of psychological research. *American Psychologist, 43*, 627–634.

Dillman, D. A. (1972). Increasing mail questionnaire response in large samples of the general public. *Public Opinion Quarterly, 36,* 254–257.

Dillman, D. A. (1978). *Mail and telephone surveys: The total design method.* New York: Wiley.

Dillman, D. A. (2000). *Mail and Internet surveys: The tailored design method* (2nd ed.). New York: Wiley.

Dillman, D. A., Phelps, G., Tortora, R., Swift, K., Kohrell, J., & Berck, J. (2001). *Response rate and measurement differences in mixed mode surveys using mail, telephone, interactive voice response and the Internet.* Retrieved July 6, 2001, from http://survey.sesrc.wsu.edu/dillman/papers/Mixed%20Mode%20ppr%20_with%20Gallup_%20POQ.pdf

Dipboye, R. L., & Flanagan, M. F. (1979). Research settings in industrial and organizational psychology: Are findings in the field more generalizable than in the laboratory? *American Psychologist, 34,* 141–150.

Dollinger, S. J., Preston, L. A., O'Brien, S. P., & DiLalla, D. L. (1996). Individuality and relatedness of the self: An autophotographic study. *Journal of Personality and Social Psychology, 71,* 1268–1278.

Duncan, S., & Rosenthal, R. (1968). Vocal emphasis in experimenters' instruction reading as unintended determinant of subjects' responses. *Language and Speech, 11,* part 1, 20–26.

Durand, J. (1960). Mortality estimates from Roman tombstone inscriptions. *American Journal of Sociology, 65,* 365–373.

Durkheim, E. (1951). *Suicide.* (J. A. Spaulding & G. Simpson, Trans.). New York: Free Press. (Original work published 1897.)

Economic Report of the President. (1964, January). Annual Report of the Council of Economic Advisers, transmitted to the Congress. Washington, DC: U.S. Government Printing Office.

Endler, N. S., Macrodimitris, S. D., & Kocovski, N. L. (2000). Controllability in cognitive and interpersonal tasks: Is control good for you? *Personality and Individual Differences, 29,* 951–962.

Epley, N., & Huff, C. (1998). Suspicion, affective response, and educational benefit as a result of deception in psychology research. *Personality and Social Psychology Bulletin, 24,* 759–768.

Ericsson, K. A., & Simon, H. A. (1984). *Protocol analysis: Verbal reports as data.* Cambridge, MA: MIT Press.

Erikson, K. T. (1976). *Everything in its path.* New York: Simon & Schuster.

Eysenck, H. J. (1978). An exercise in mega-silliness. *American Psychologist, 33,* 5–17.

Farrar, E., & House, E. R. (1986). The evaluation of PUSH/Excel: A case study. In E. R. House (Ed.), *New directions in educational evaluations.* London: Palmer Press.

Farver, J. M., & Howes, C. (1993). Cultural differences in American and Mexican mother-child pretend play. *Merrill Palmer Quarterly, 39,* 344–358.

Fazio, R. H., Powell, M. C., & Herr, P. M. (1983). Toward a process model of the attitude-behavior relation: Accessing one's attitude upon mere observation of the attitude object. *Journal of Personality and Social Psychology, 44,* 723–735.

Fazio, R., & Williams, C. (1986). Attitude accessibility as a moderator of the attitude-perception and attitude-behavior relations: An investigation of the 1984 presidential election. *Journal of Personality and Social Psychology, 51*, 505–514.

Feldman Barrett, L., & Barrett, D. J. (2001). An introduction to computerized experience sampling. *Social Science Computer Review, 19*, 175–185.

Festinger, L. A. (1957). *A theory of cognitive dissonance.* Stanford, CA: Stanford University Press.

Festinger, L., & Carlsmith, J. N. (1959). Cognitive consequences of forced compliance. *Journal of Abnormal and Social Psychology, 58*, 203–210.

Festinger, L., Riecken, H. W., & Schachter, S. (1956). *When prophecy fails.* Minneapolis: University of Minnesota Press.

Flanders, N. A. (1970). *Analyzing teaching behavior.* Reading, MA: Addison Wesley.

Fogg, L. F., & Rose, R. M. (1999). Use of personal characteristics in the selection of astronauts. *Human Performance in Extreme Environments, 4*, 27–33.

Fosse, R., Stickgold, R., & Hobson, J. A. (2001). Brain-mind states: Reciprocal variation in thoughts and hallucinations. *Psychological Science, 12*, 30–36.

Frank, G., Johnston, M., Morrison, V., Pollard, B., & MacWalter, R. (2000). Perceived control and recovery from functional limitations: Preliminary evaluation of a workbook-based intervention for discharged stroke patients. *British Journal of Health Psychology, 5*, 413–420.

Frey, J. H. (1989). *Survey research by telephone* (2nd ed.). Thousand Oaks, CA: Sage Publications.

Frey, J. H., & Oishi, S. M. (1995). *How to conduct interviews by telephone and in person.* Thousand Oaks, CA: Sage Publications.

Fridlund, A. J. (1991). Sociality of solitary smiling: Potentiation by an implicit audience. *Journal of Personality and Social Psychology, 60*, 229–240.

Friedman, M., & Rosenman, R. H. (1974). *Type A behavior and your heart.* New York: Knopf.

Gable, S. L., Reis, H. T., & Elliot, A. J. (2000). Behavioral activation and inhibition in everyday life. *Journal of Personality and Social Psychology, 78*, 1135–1149.

Gable, S. L., & Shean, G. D. (2000). Perceived social competence and depression. *Journal of Social and Personal Relationships, 17*, 139–150.

Garfield, E. (1992, October 12). Psychology research 1986–1990: A citationist perspective on the highest impact papers, institutions and authors. *Current Contents*, pp. 5–15.

Gelsinger, P. (2000). *Jesse's intent.* Retrieved July 6, 2001, from http://www.primr.org/jessesintent.html

Gilovich, T. (1991). *How we know what isn't so: The fallibility of human reason in everyday life.* New York: Free Press.

Glass, D. C., & Singer, J. E. (1972). *Urban stress: Experiments on noise and social stressors.* New York: Academic Press.

Glass, G. V. (1978). In defense of generalization. *Behavioral and Brain Sciences, 3*, 394–395.

Glick, P., Fiske, S. T., Mladinic, A., Saiz, J. L., Abrams, D., Masser, B., Adetoun, B., Osagie, J. E., Akande, A., Alao, A., Brunner, A., Willemsen, T. M., Chipeta, K.,

Dardenne, B., Dijksterhuis, A., Wigboldus, D., Eckes, T., Six-Materna, I., Exposito, F., Moya, M., Foddy, M., Kim, H., Lameiras, M., Sotelo, M. J., Mucchi-Faina, A., Romani, M., Sakalli, N., Udegbe, B., Yamamoto, M., Ui, M., Ferreira, M. C., & Lopez, W. L. (2000). Beyond prejudice as simple antipathy: Hostile and benevolent sexism across cultures. *Journal of Personality and Social Psychology, 79,* 763–774.

Goffman, E. (1963). *Stigma.* Upper Saddle River, NJ: Prentice Hall.

Graber, D. (1971). The press as opinion resource during the 1968 presidential campaign. *Public Opinion Quarterly, 35,* 168–182.

Gray-Little, B., & Hafdahl, A. R. (2000). Factors influencing racial comparisons of self-esteem: A quantitative review. *Psychological Bulletin, 126,* 26–54.

Green, B. F. (1956). A method of scalogram analysis using summary statistics. *Psychometrika, 21,* 79–88.

Greenberg, B. S., & Brand, J. E. (1993). Cultural diversity on Saturday morning television. In G. L. Berry & J. K. Asamen (Eds.), *Children and television: Images in a changing sociocultural world* (pp. 132–142). Thousand Oaks, CA: Sage Publications.

Greeno, J. G. (1994). Gibson's affordances. *Psychological Review, 101,* 336–342.

Greeno, J. G. (1998). The situativity of knowing, learning, and research. *American Psychologist, 53,* 5–26.

Greenwald, A. G., & Farnham, S. D. (2000). Using the Implicit Association Test to measure self-esteem and self-concept. *Journal of Personality and Social Psychology, 79,* 1022–1038.

Greenwald, A. G., McGhee, D. E., & Schwartz, J. L. K. (1998). Measuring individual differences in implicit cognition: The Implicit Association Test. *Journal of Personality and Social Psychology, 74,* 1464–1480.

Groves, R. M. (1987). Research on survey data quality. *Public Opinion Quarterly, 51,* S156–S172.

Groves, R. M., & Kahn, R. L. (1979). *Surveys by telephone.* New York: Academic Press.

Gutek, B. A. (1978). Strategies for studying client satisfaction. *Journal of Social Issues, 34*(4), 44–56.

Guttman, L. (1944). A basis for scaling quantitative data. *American Sociological Review, 9,* 139–150.

Hall, J. A., Carter, J. D., & Horgan, T. G. (2000). Gender differences in nonverbal communication of emotion. In A. H. Fischer (Ed.), *Gender and emotion: Social psychological perspectives* (pp. 97–117). New York: Cambridge University Press.

Hall, S., & Oliver, C. (1997). A graphical method to aid in the sequential analysis of observational data. *Behavior Research Methods: Instruments and Computers, 29,* 563–573.

Hamilton, D. L. (1981). Cognitive representations of persons. In E. T. Higgins, C. P. Herman, & M. P. Zanna (Eds.). *Social cognition: The Ontario Symposium* (Vol. 1, pp. 135–160). Hillsdale, NJ: Erlbaum.

Harlow, H. F. (1958). The nature of love. *American Psychologist, 13,* 673–685.

Harmon-Jones, E., & Sigelman, J. (2001). State anger and prefrontal brain activity: Evidence that insult-related relative left-prefrontal activation is associated with experienced anger and aggression. *Journal of Personality and Social Psychology, 80*, 797–803.

Harris, M. J. (1991). Controversy and cumulation: Meta-analysis and research on interpersonal expectancy effects. *Personality and Social Psychology Bulletin, 17*, 316–322.

Harris, M. J., Milich, R., Corbitt, E. M., Hoover, D. W., & Brady, M. (1992). Self-fulfilling effects of stigmatizing information on children's social interactions. *Journal of Personality and Social Psychology, 63*, 41–50.

Hartsough, D. M., & Savitsky, J. C. (1984). Three Mile Island: Psychology and environmental policy at a crossroads. *American Psychologist, 39*, 1113–1122.

Hastie, R. (1988). A computer simulation model of person memory. *Journal of Experimental Social Psychology, 24*, 423–447.

Hastie, R., & Kumar, P. A. (1979). Person memory: Personality traits as organizing principles in memory for behaviors. *Journal of Personality and Social Psychology, 37*, 25–38.

Hedderman, C. (1994). Decision-making in court: Observing the sentencing of men and women. *Psychology, Crime, and Law, 1*, 165–173.

Hedges, L. V., & Olkin, I. (1985). *Statistical methods for meta-analysis.* Orlando, FL: Academic Press.

Himmelfarb, S., & Edgell, S. E. (1980). Additive constants model: A randomized response technique for eliminating evasiveness to quantitative response questions. *Psychological Bulletin, 87*, 525–530.

Hirt, E. R. (1990). Do I see only what I expect? Evidence for an expectancy-guided retrieval model. *Journal of Personality and Social Psychology, 58*, 937–951.

Holsti, O. R. (1969). *Content analysis for the social sciences and humanities.* Reading, MA: Addison-Wesley.

Houts, P. S. (1980a). *Health-related behavioral impact of the Three Mile Island nuclear incident: Part I.* Report to the TMI Advisory Panel on Health Research Studies, Pennsylvania Department of Health. Hershey: Pennsylvania State University.

Houts, P. S. (1980b). *Health-related behavioral impact of the Three Mile Island nuclear incident: Part II.* Report to the TMI Advisory Panel on Health Research Studies, Pennsylvania Department of Health. Hershey: Pennsylvania State University.

Hoyle, R. H. (1988). *Effects of basic features of social situations on four aspects of self-esteem: The social nature of self-appraisal.* Unpublished doctoral dissertation, University of North Carolina, Chapel Hill.

Hoyle, R. H. (1993). On the relation between data and theory [Comment]. *American Psychologist, 48*, 1094–1096.

Hughes, C., Rodi, M. S., Lorden, S. W., Pitkin, S. E., Derer, K. R., Hwang, B., & Cai, X. (1999). Social interactions of high school students with mental retardation and their general education peers. *American Journal on Mental Retardation, 104*, 533–544.

Humphreys, L. (1970). *Tearoom trade: Impersonal sex in public places.* Chicago: Aldine-Atherton.

Hunt, M. (1999). *The new Know-Nothings: The political foes of the scientific study of human nature.* New Brunswick, NJ: Transaction Publishers.

Hunter, J. E. (1997). Needed: A ban on the significance test. *Psychological Science, 8*, 3–7.

Isen, A. M. (1984). Toward understanding the role of affect in cognition. In R. S. Wyer & T. K. Srull (Eds.), *Handbook of social cognition* (Vol. 3, pp. 179–236). Hillsdale, NJ: Erlbaum.

Isen, A. M., & Levin, P. F. (1972). Effect of feeling good on helping: Cookies and kindness. *Journal of Personality and Social Psychology, 21*, 384–388.

Janis, I. L. (1997). Groupthink. In R. P. Vecchio (Ed.), *Leadership: Understanding the dynamics of power and influence in organizations* (pp. 163–176). Notre Dame, IN: University of Notre Dame Press.

Judd, C. M., & Kenny, D. A. (1981). *Estimating the effects of social interventions.* New York: Cambridge University Press.

Juvonen, J., & Graham, S. (2001). *Peer harassment in school: The plight of the vulnerable and victimized.* New York: Guilford Publications.

Kaplan, J. (1988). The use of animals in research. *Science, 242*, 839–840.

Kasarda, J. D. (1976). The use of census data in secondary analysis: The context of ecological discovery. In M. P. Golden (Ed.), *The research experience.* Itasca, IL: Peacock.

Kawakami, K., Dovidio, J. F., Moll, J., Hermsen, S., & Russin, A. (2000). Just say no (to stereotyping): Effects of training in the negation of stereotypic associations on stereotypic activation. *Journal of Personality and Social Psychology, 78*, 871–888.

Kelman, H. C. (1968). *A time to speak: On human values and social research.* San Francisco: Jossey-Bass.

Kenny, D. A., & Berman, J. S. (1980). Statistical approaches for the correction of correlational bias. *Psychological Bulletin, 88*, 288–295.

Kernis, M. H., Grannemann, B. D., & Barclay, L. C. (1989). Stability and level of self-esteem as predictors of anger arousal and hostility. *Journal of Personality and Social Psychology, 56*, 1013–1022.

Kidder, L. H., & Cohn, E. S. (1979). Public views of crime and crime prevention. In I. H. Frieze, D. Bar-Tal, & J. S. Carroll (Eds.), *New approaches to social problems: Applications of attribution theory.* San Francisco: Jossey-Bass.

Kidman, L., McKenzie, A., & McKenzie, B. (1999). The nature and target of parents' comments during youth sport competitions. *Journal of Sport Behavior, 22*, 54–68.

King, L. A., Scollon, C. K., Ramsey, C., & Williams, T. (2000). Stories of life transition: Subjective well-being and ego development in parents of children with Down Syndrome. *Journal of Research in Personality, 34*, 509–536.

Kline, P. (1994). *An easy guide to factor analysis.* London: Routledge.

Kluegel, J. R., & Smith, E. R. (1982). Whites' beliefs about Blacks' opportunity. *American Sociological Review, 47*, 518–532.

Koslowski, M., Pratt, G. L., & Wintrob, R. N. (1976). The application of Guttman scale analysis to physicians' attitudes regarding abortion. *Journal of Applied Psychology, 61*, 301–304.

Kraut, R. E., & Johnston, R. E. (1979). Social and emotional messages of smiling: An ethological approach. *Journal of Personality and Social Psychology, 37*, 1539–1553.

Krosnick, J. A., & Alwin, D. F. (1988). A test of the form-resistant correlation hypothesis: Ratings, rankings, and the measurement of values. *Public Opinion Quarterly, 52,* 526–538.

Kruglanski, A. W. (1975). The human subject in the psychology experiment: Fact and artifact. In L. Berkowitz (Ed.), *Advances in experimental social psychology* (Vol. 8, pp. 101–147). New York: Academic Press.

Langlois, J. H., Kalakanis, L., Rubenstein, A. J., Larson, A., Hallam, M., & Smoot, M. (2000). Maxims or myths of beauty? A meta-analytic and theoretical review. *Psychological Bulletin, 126,* 390–423.

Latané, B. (1990). From private attitude to public opinion: A dynamic theory of social impact. *Psychological Review, 97,* 362–376.

Latané, B., & Nida, S. (1981). Ten years of research on group size and helping. *Psychological Bulletin, 89,* 308–324.

Lavine, H., Borgida, E., & Sullivan, J. L. (2000). On the relationship between attitude involvement and attitude accessibility: Toward a cognitive-motivational model of political information processing. *Political Psychology, 21,* 81–106.

Lee, F., & Hallahan, M. (2001). Do situational expectations produce situational inferences? The role of future expectations in directing inferential goals. *Journal of Personality and Social Psychology, 80,* 545–556.

Lee, T. W., & Maurer, S. D. (1999). The effects of family structure on organizational commitment, intention to leave, and voluntary turnover. *Journal of Managerial Issues, 11,* 493–513.

Leventhal, T., & Brooks-Gunn, J. (2000). The neighborhoods they live in: The effects of neighborhood residence on child and adolescent outcomes. *Psychological Bulletin, 126,* 309–377.

Levin, H. M. (1978). A decade of policy developments in improving education and training for low-income populations. In T. D. Cook (Ed.), *Evaluation studies review annual* (pp. 521–570). Thousand Oaks, CA: Sage Publications.

Lewin, K. (1951). *Field theory in social science.* New York: Harper & Row.

Lewis, S. (1925). *Arrowsmith.* New York: Harcourt Brace.

Likert, R. (1932). A technique for the measurement of attitudes. *Archives of Psychology, 140,* 5–55.

Linville, P. W. (1987). Self-complexity as a cognitive buffer against stress-related illness and depression. *Journal of Personality and Social Psychology, 52,* 663–676.

Locke, E. A. (1996). Motivation through conscious goal setting. *Applied and Preventive Psychology, 5,* 117–124.

LoSciuto, L. A. (1971). A national inventory of television viewing behavior. In E. A. Rubenstein, G. A. Comstock, & J. P. Murray (Eds.), *Television and social behavior* (Vol. 4, pp. 33–86). Washington, DC: U.S. Government Printing Office.

Lucker, G. W., Rosenfield, D., Sikes, J., & Aronson, E. (1977). Performance in the interdependent classroom: A field study. *American Educational Research Journal, 13,* 115–123.

Lusk, B. (1999). Patients' images in nursing magazine advertisements. *Advances in Nursing Science, 21,* 66–75.

Lyman-Henley, L. P., & Henley, T. B. (2000). Some thoughts on the relationship between behaviorism, comparative psychology, and ethology. *Anthrozoos, 13*, 15–21.

Lynn, L. E., Jr. (1977). Policy relevant social research: What does it look like? In M. Guttentag & S. Saar (Eds.), *Evaluation studies review annual* (Vol. 1). Thousand Oaks, CA: Sage Publications.

Market Navigation, Inc. (2000). *Client guide to the focus group.* Retrieved July 6, 2001, from http://www.mnav.com/cligd.htm

Marsaglia, G. (1984). *A current view of random number generators.* Paper presented at the 16th Symposium on the Interface between Computer Science and Statistics, Atlanta.

Martyna, W. (1978). What does "he" mean? *Journal of Communication, 28*, 131–138.

Masters, J. R. (1974). The relationship between number of response categories and reliability of Likert-type questionnaires. *Journal of Educational Measurement, 11*, 49–53.

Matt, G. E. (1989). Decision rules for selecting effect sizes in meta-analysis: A review and reanalysis of psychotherapy outcome studies. *Psychological Bulletin, 105*, 106–115.

Mauldin, W. P., & Marks, E. S. (1950). Problems of response in enumerative surveys. *American Sociological Review, 15*, 5.

McCord, J. (1978). A thirty-year followup of treatment effects. *American Psychologist, 33*, 284–289.

McCord, J. (1979, September). *Treatment that did not help.* Paper presented at the Annual Meeting of the American Psychological Association, New York.

McDill, E. L., McDill, M. S., & Sprehe, J. T. (1969). *Strategies for success in compensatory education: An appraisal of evaluation research.* Baltimore: Johns Hopkins Press.

McGee, M. G., & Snyder, M. (1975). Attribution and behavior: Two field studies. *Journal of Personality and Social Psychology, 32*, 185–190.

McKenna, K. Y. A., & Bargh, J. A. (1998). Coming out in the age of the Internet: Identity "demarginalization" through virtual group participation. *Journal of Personality and Social Psychology, 75*, 681–694.

Meehl, P. E. (1978). Theoretical risks and tabular asterisks: Sir Karl, Sir Ronald, and the slow progress of soft psychology. *Journal of Consulting and Clinical Psychology, 46*, 806–834.

Michaels, M. L., Roosa, M. W., & Gensheimer, L. K. (1992). Family characteristics of children who self-select into a prevention program for children of alcoholics. *American Journal of Community Psychology, 20*, 663–672.

Milgram, S. (1974). *Obedience to authority: An experimental view.* New York: Harper & Row.

Miller, C. T., & Downey, K. T. (1999). A meta-analysis of heavyweight and self-esteem. *Personality and Social Psychology Review, 3*, 68–84.

Mohr, C. D., Armeli, S., Tennen, H., Carney, M. A., Affleck, G., & Hromi, A. (2001). Daily interpersonal experiences, context, and alcohol consumption: Crying in your beer and toasting good times. *Journal of Personality and Social Psychology, 80*, 489–500.

Monahan, J. L., Murphy, S. T., & Miller, L. C. (1999). When women imbibe: Alcohol and the illusory control of HIV risk. *Psychology of Women Quarterly, 23*, 643–651.

Mook, D. G. (1983). In defense of external invalidity. *American Psychologist, 38*, 379–387.

Moore, T. E., & Cadeau, L. (1985). The representation of women, the elderly, and minorities in Canadian television commercials. *Canadian Journal of Behavioural Science, 17*, 215–225.

Neuberg, S. L., Judice, T. N., Virdin, L. M., & Carrillo, M. A. (1993). Perceiver self-presentational goals as moderators of expectancy influences: Ingratiation and the disconfirmation of negative expectancies. *Journal of Personality and Social Psychology, 64*, 409–420.

Nisbett, R. E., & Wilson, T. D. (1977). Telling more than we can know: Verbal reports on mental processes. *Psychological Review, 84*, 231–259.

Nowak, A., Vallacher, R. R., Tesser, A., & Borkowski, W. (2000). Society of self: The emergence of collective properties in self-structure. *Psychological Review, 107*, 39–61.

Nunnally, J. C. (1978). *Psychometric theory* (2nd ed.). New York: McGraw-Hill.

Nunnally, J. C., & Bernstein, I. H. (1994). *Psychometric theory* (3rd ed.). New York: McGraw-Hill.

Oksenberg, L., Coleman, L., & Cannell, C. F. (1986). Interviewers' voices and refusal rates in telephone surveys. *Public Opinion Quarterly, 50*, 97–111.

Orne, M. (1962). On the social psychology of the psychological experiment. *American Psychologist, 17*, 776–783.

Orne, M. T. (1969). Demand characteristics and the concept of quasi-controls. In R. Rosenthal & R. L. Rosnow (Eds.), *Artifact in behavioral research* (pp. 143–179). New York: Academic Press.

Osgood, C. E., Suci, C. J., & Tannenbaum, P. H. (1957). *The measurement of meaning*. Urbana: University of Illinois Press.

Osgood, C. E., & Walker, E. G. (1959). Motivation and language behavior: A content analysis of suicide notes. *Journal of Abnormal and Social Psychology, 59*, 58–67.

Palmgreen, P., Donohew, L., Lorch, E. P., Hoyle, R. H., & Stephenson, M. T. (2001). Television campaigns and adolescent marijuana use: Tests of sensation seeking targeting. *American Journal of Public Health, 91*, 292–296.

PANE (People Against Nuclear Energy) v. United States Nuclear Regulatory Commission, 673 F. 2d 552 (D.C. Cir. 1982) (order vacating NRC decision); 678 F. 2d 222, 235 (D.C. Cir. Filed April 2, 1982) (amended interim order); 678 F. 2d 222, 228 (D.C. Cir. 1982) (Wilkey dissenting in part).

Park, B. (1986). A method for studying the development of impressions of real people. *Journal of Personality and Social Psychology, 51*, 907–917.

Parry, H. J., & Crossley, H. M. (1950). Validity of responses to survey questions. *Public Opinion Quarterly, 14*, 62–80.

Paulhus, D. L. (1991). Measurement and control of response bias. In J. P. Robinson, P. R. Shaver, & L. S. Wrightsman (Eds.), *Measures of personality and social psychological attitudes* (pp. 17–59). New York: Academic Press.

Payne, S. L. (1951). *The art of asking questions.* Princeton, NJ: Princeton University Press.

Pennebaker, J. W., & Francis, M. E. (1996). Cognitive, emotional, and language processes in disclosure: Physical health and adjustment. *Cognition and Emotion, 10,* 601–626.

Perrine, R. M., & Heather, S. (2000). Effects of a picture and even-a-penny-will-help appeals on anonymous donations to charity. *Psychological Reports, 86,* 551–559.

Pettigrew, T. F. (1998). Intergroup contact theory. *Annual Review of Psychology, 49,* 65–85.

Petty, R. E., Rennier, G. A., & Cacioppo, J. T. (1987). Assertion versus interrogation format in opinion surveys: Questions enhance thoughtful responding. *Public Opinion Quarterly, 51,* 481–494.

Petzel, T. P., Johnson, J. E., & McKillip, J. (1973). Response bias in drug surveys. *Journal of Consulting and Clinical Psychology, 40,* 437–439.

Phillips, C. J. C., & Morris, I. D. (2001). A novel operant conditioning test to determine whether dairy cows dislike passageways that are dark or covered with excreta. *Animal Welfare, 10,* 65–72.

Phillips, D. P., Carstensen, L. L., & Paight, D. J. (1989). Effects of mass media news stories on suicide, with new evidence on the role of story content. In D. R. Pfeffer (Ed.), *Suicide among youth: Perspectives on risk and prevention* (pp. 101–116). Washington, DC: American Psychiatric Association.

Price, D. (1966). Collaboration in an invisible college. *American Psychologist, 21,* 1011–1018.

Quinn, R. P., Gutek, B. A., & Walsh, J. T. (1980). Telephone interviewing: A reappraisal and a field experiment. *Basic and Applied Social Psychology, 1,* 127–153.

Rathje, W. L., & Hughes, W. W. (1975). The garbage project as a nonreactive approach: Garbage in . . . garbage out? In H. W. Sinaiko & L. A. Broedling (Eds.), *Perspectives on attitude assessment: Surveys and their alternatives.* Washington, DC: Smithsonian Institution.

Rice, S. A. (1929). Contagious bias in the interview: A methodological note. *American Journal of Sociology, 35,* 420–423.

Rind, B., Tromovitch, P., & Bauserman, R. (1998). A meta-analytic examination of assumed properties of child sexual abuse using college samples. *Psychological Bulletin, 124,* 22–53.

Rizzo, T. A., & Corsaro, W. A. (1995). Social support processes in early childhood friendship: A comparative study of ecological congruences in enacted support. *American Journal of Community Psychology, 23,* 389–417.

Robinson, J. P., Shaver, P. R., & Wrightsman, L. S. (Eds.). (1991). *Measures of personality and social psychological attitudes.* San Diego, CA: Academic Press.

Rogers, E. M., & Storey, J. D. (1987). Communication campaigns. In C. R. Berger & S. H. Chaffee (Eds.), *Handbook of communication science* (pp. 817–846). Thousand Oaks, CA: Sage Publications.

Rosch, E. (1988). Principles of categorization. In A. M. Collins & E. E. Smith (Eds.), *Readings in cognitive science: A perspective from psychology and artificial intelligence* (pp. 312–322). San Mateo, CA: Kaufmann.

Rosenberg, M. J. (1969). The conditions and consequences of evaluation apprehension. In R. Rosenthal & R. L. Rosnow (Eds.), *Artifact in behavioral research* (pp. 279–349). New York: Academic Press.

Rosenthal, R. (1968). Experimenter expectancy and the reassuring nature of the null hypothesis decision procedure. *Psychological Bulletin Monograph Supplement, 70* (6, Pt. 2), 30–47.

Rosenthal, R. (1969). Interpersonal expectations. In R. Rosenthal & R. L. Rosnow (Eds.). *Artifact in behavioral research* (pp. 181–275). New York: Academic Press.

Rosenthal, R. (1976). *Experimenter effects in behavioral research* (Enlarged ed.). New York: Wiley.

Rosenthal, R. (1991). *Meta-analytic procedures for social research* (Rev. ed.). Thousand Oaks, CA: Sage Publications.

Rosenthal, R. (1994). Science and ethics in conducting, analyzing, and reporting psychological research. *Psychological Science, 5*, 127–134.

Rosenthal, R., & Rosnow, R. L. (Eds.). (1969). *Artifact in behavioral research.* New York: Academic Press.

Rosenthal, R., & Rosnow, R. (1984). Applying Hamlet's question to the ethical conduct of research: A conceptual addendum. *American Psychologist, 39*, 561–563.

Rosenthal, R., & Rosnow, R. L. (1991). *Essentials of behavioral research: Methods and data analysis* (2nd ed.). New York: McGraw-Hill.

Rosenthal, R., & Rubin, D. B. (1978). Interpersonal expectancy effects: The first 345 studies. *Behavioral and Brain Sciences, 3*, 377–386.

Rosenthal, R., & Rubin, D. B. (1986). Meta-analytic procedures for combining studies with multiple effect sizes. *Psychological Bulletin, 99*, 400–406.

Rosnow, R. L., & Rosenthal, R. (1989). Statistical procedures and the justification of knowledge in psychological science. *American Psychologist, 44*, 1276–1284.

Rosnow, R. L., & Rosenthal, R. (1997). *People studying people: Artifacts and ethics in behavioral research.* New York: Freeman.

Ross, L., Lepper, M. R., & Hubbard, M. (1975). Perseverance in self-perception and social perception: Biased attributional processes in the debriefing paradigm. *Journal of Personality and Social Psychology, 32*, 880–892.

Rubinstein, S., & Caballero, B. (2000). Is Miss America an undernourished role model? *Journal of the American Medical Association, 283*, 1569.

Sackett, G. (1978). Measurement in observational research. In G. Sackett (Ed.), *Observing behavior (Vol. II): Data collection and analysis methods* (pp. 25–42). Baltimore: University Park Press.

Sampson, E. E. (1977). Psychology and the American ideal. *Journal of Personality and Social Psychology, 35*, 767–782.

Scambler, D. J., Harris, M. J., & Milich, R. (1998). Sticks and stones: Evaluations of responses to childhood teasing. *Social Development*, 7, 234–249.

Schmader, T., Major, B., & Gramzow, R. H. (2001). Coping with ethnic stereotypes in the academic domain: Perceived injustice and psychological disengagement. *Journal of Social Issues, 57*, 93–111.

Schuman, H., Bobo, L., & Steeh, C. (1985). *Racial attitudes in America: Trends and complexities.* Cambridge, MA: Harvard University Press.

Schuman, H., & Duncan, O. D. (1974). Questions about attitude survey questions. In H. L. Costner (Ed.), *Sociological methodology 1973–1974* (pp. 232–251). San Francisco: Jossey-Bass.

Schuman, H., & Presser, S. (1979). The open and closed question. *American Sociological Review, 44,* 692–712.

Schuman, H., & Presser, S. (1996). *Questions and answers in attitude surveys: Experiments on question form, wording, and context.* Thousand Oaks, CA: Sage Publications.

Sears, D. O. (1986). College sophomores in the laboratory: Influences of a narrow data base on social psychology's view of human nature. *Journal of Personality and Social Psychology, 51,* 1173–1182.

Seligman, C., & Hutton, R. B. (1981). Evaluating energy conservation programs. *Journal of Social Issues, 37*(2), 51–71.

Shadish, W. R., Cook, T. D., & Campbell, D. T. (2001). *Experimental and quasi-experimental designs for generalized causal inference.* Boston: Houghton-Mifflin.

Sharpe, D. (1997). Of apples and oranges, file drawers, and garbage: Why validity issues in meta-analysis will not go away. *Clinical Psychology Review, 17,* 881–901.

Sherif, M., & Hovland, C. I. (1961). *Social judgment: Assimilation and contrast effects in communication and attitude change.* New Haven, CT: Yale University Press.

Shrauger, J. S., & Osberg, T. M. (1981). The relative accuracy of self-predictions and judgments by others in psychological assessment. *Psychological Bulletin, 90,* 322–351.

Shweder, R. A., & D'Andrade, R. G. (1980). The systematic distortion hypothesis. In R. A. Shweder & D. W. Fiske (Eds.), *New directions for methodology of behavioral science: Fallible judgment in behavioral research* (pp. 37–58). San Francisco: Jossey-Bass.

Sieber, J. (1992). *Planning ethically responsible research.* Thousand Oaks, CA: Sage Publications.

Siminoff, L. A., Erlen, J. A., & Sereika, S. (1998). Do nurses avoid AIDS patients? Avoidance behaviours and the quality of care of hospitalized AIDS patients. *AIDS Care, 10,* 147–163.

Simon, B. L. (1987). *Never married women.* Philadelphia: Temple University Press.

Sinclair, L., & Kunda, Z. (2000). Motivated stereotyping of women: She's fine if she praised me but incompetent if she criticized me. *Personality and Social Psychology Bulletin, 26,* 1329–1342.

Smith, C. P. (2000). Content analysis and narrative analysis. In H. T. Reis & C. M. Judd (Eds.), *Handbook of research methods in social and personality psychology* (pp. 313–335). Cambridge: Cambridge University Press.

Smith, S. S., & Richardson, D. (1983). Amelioration of deception and harm in psychological research: The important role of debriefing. *Journal of Personality and Social Psychology, 44,* 1075–1082.

Smith, W. J., Chase, J., & Lieblich, A. K. T. (1974). Tongue showing: A facial display of humans and other primate species. *Semiotica, 11,* 201–246.

Snowdon, D. A., Kemper, S. J., Mortimer, J. A., Greiner, L. H., Wekstein, D. R., & Markesbery, W. R. (1996). Linguistic ability in early life and cognitive function and Alzheimer's disease in late life. *Journal of the American Medical Association, 275*, 528–532.

Sobel, S. B. (1978). Throwing the baby out with the bathwater: The hazards of followup research. *American Psychologist, 33*, 290–291.

Sommer, K. L., Horowitz, I. A., & Bourgeois, M. J. (2001). When juries fail to comply with the law: Biased evidence processing in individual and group decision making. *Personality and Social Psychology Bulletin, 27*, 309–320.

Spoth, R., Redmond, C., & Shin, C. (2000). Modeling factors influencing enrollment in family-focused prevention intervention research. *Prevention Science, 1*, 213–225.

Stack, C. B. (1975). *All our kin: Strategies for survival in a Black community.* New York: Harper Colophon.

Stamp, J. (1929). *Some economic factors in modern life.* London: King & Son.

Stevens, S. S. (1968). Measurement, statistics, and the schemapiric view. *Science, 161*, 849–856.

Stewart, D. W., & Shamdasani, P. N. (1990). *Focus groups: Theory and practice.* Thousand Oaks, CA: Sage Publications.

Stone, P. J., & Nicolson, N. A. (1987). Infrequently occurring activities and contexts in time use data. *Journal of Nervous and Mental Disease, 175*, 519–525.

Strayer, F. F., & Strayer, J. (1976). An ethological analysis of social agonism and dominance relations among preschool children. *Child Development, 47*, 980–989.

Strube, M. J. (1985). Combining and comparing significance levels from nonindependent hypothesis tests. *Psychological Bulletin, 97*, 334–341.

Strube, M. J., Gardner, W., & Hartmann, D. P. (1985). Limitations, liabilities, and obstacles in reviews of the literature: The current status of meta-analysis. *Clinical Psychology Review, 5*, 63–78.

Strunk, W., Jr., & White, E. B. (2000). *The elements of style* (4th ed.). Boston: Allyn and Bacon.

Sudman, S. (1976). *Applied sampling.* New York: Academic Press.

Szalai, A., Converse, P., Feldheim, P., Scheuch, E. K., & Stone, P. J. (Eds.). (1972). *The use of time: Daily activities of urban and suburban populations in twelve countries.* The Hague: Mouton.

Tajfel, H. (1982). Social psychology of intergroup relations. *Annual Review of Psychology, 33*, 1–39.

Taylor, H. (1998, May 4). Myth and reality in reporting sampling error: How the media confuse and mislead readers and viewers. *The Polling Report.* Retrieved July 6, 2001, from http://www.pollingreport.com/sampling.htm

Thomas, D. L., & Diener, E. (1990). Memory and accuracy in the recall of emotions. *Journal of Personality and Social Psychology, 59*, 291–297.

Thomas, W. I., & Znaniecki, F. (1918). *The Polish peasant in Europe and America: Monograph of an immigrant group.* Chicago: University of Chicago Press.

Thompson, C. P., Skowronski, J. J., & Lee, D. J. (1988). Telescoping in dating naturally occurring events. *Memory and Cognition, 16*, 461–468.

Thorndike, E. L. (1920). A constant error in psychological ratings. *Journal of Applied Psychology, 4*, 25–29.

Thornton, G. C. (1980). Psychometric properties of self-appraisals of job performance. *Personnel Psychology, 33*, 263–271.

Thurstone, L. L. (1929). Theory of attitude measurement. *Psychological Bulletin, 36*, 222–241.

Tourangeau, R., & Rasinski, K.A. (1988). Cognitive processes underlying context effects in attitude measurement. *Psychological Bulletin, 103*, 299–314.

Trope, Y., & Ferguson, M. J. (2000). How and when preference influence inferences: A motivated hypothesis-testing framework. In J. A. Bargh & A. K. Apsley (Eds.), *Unraveling the complexities of social life: A festschrift in honor of Robert B. Zajonc* (pp. 111–130). Washington, DC: American Psychological Association.

Tukey, J. W. (1969). Analyzing data: Sanctification or detective work? *American Psychologist, 24*, 83–91.

Tunnell, G. B. (1977). Three dimensions of naturalness: An expanded definition of field research. *Psychological Bulletin, 84*, 426–437.

Turkheimer, E., & Waldron, M. (2000). Nonshared environment: A theoretical, methodological, and quantitative review. *Psychological Bulletin, 126*, 78–108.

Turner, J. C. (1987). *Rediscovering the social group: A self-categorization theory*. Oxford: Blackwell Publishers.

Urbaniak, G. C., & Plous, S. (2001). Research Randomizer. Retrieved September 5, 2001, from http://www.randomizer.org/

Viney, L. L. (1983). The assessment of psychological states through content analysis of verbal communications. *Psychological Bulletin, 94*, 542–563.

Walker, S. G., Schafer, M., & Young, M. D. (1999). Presidential operational codes and foreign policy conflicts in the post-cold war world. *Journal of Conflict Resolution, 43*, 610–625.

Wang, M. C., & Ramp, E. A. (1987, November). *The national follow through program: Design, implementation, and effects*. Philadelphia: National Institute of Education.

Warner, S. L. (1965). Randomized response: A survey technique for eliminating evasive answer bias. *Journal of the American Statistical Association, 60*, 63–69.

Webb, E. J., Campbell, D. T., Schwartz, R. D., Sechrest, L., & Grove, J. B. (1981). *Non-reactive measures in the social sciences* (2nd ed.). Boston: Houghton Mifflin.

Wehby, J. H., Symons, F. J., & Shores, R. E. (1995). A descriptive analysis of aggressive behavior in classrooms for children with emotional and behavioral disorders. *Behavioral Disorders, 20*, 87–105.

Weick, K. E. (1985). Systematic observational methods. In G. Lindzey & E. Aronson (Eds.), *The handbook of social psychology* (Vol. 1, pp. 567–634). New York: Random House.

Weiss, C. H. (1972). *Evaluating action programs.* Boston: Allyn & Bacon.

Weiss, C. H. (1986). The stakeholder approach to evaluation: Origins and promise. In E. R. House (Ed.), *New directions in educational evaluation* (pp. 145–157). London: Palmer Press.

Wener, R. E., & Keys, C. (1988). The effects of changes in jail population densities on crowding, sick call, and spatial behavior. *Journal of Applied Social Psychology, 18,* 852–866.

Wheeler, L., & Nezlek, J. (1977). Sex differences in social participation. *Journal of Personality and Social Psychology, 35,* 742–754.

Wheeler, L., & Reis, H. T. (1991). Self-recording of everyday life events: Origins, types, and uses. *Journal of Personality, 59,* 339–354.

Wheeler, L., Reis, H. T., & Nezlek, J. (1983). Loneliness, social interaction, and sex roles. *Journal of Personality and Social Psychology, 45,* 943–953.

Whyte, W. F. (1943). *Street corner society.* Chicago: University of Chicago Press.

Willems, E. P. (1969). Planning a rationale for naturalistic research. In E. P. Willems & H. L. Raush (Eds.), *Naturalistic viewpoint in psychological research* (pp. 44–71). New York: Holt Rinehart & Winston.

Williams, B. (1978). *A sampler on sampling.* New York: Wiley.

Williams, K. D., Cheung, C. K. T., & Choi, W. (2000). Cyberostracism: Effects of being ignored over the Internet. *Journal of Personality and Social Psychology, 79,* 748–762.

Williams, W., & Evans, J. W. (1972). The politics of evaluation: The case of Head Start. In P. H. Rossi & W. Williams (Eds.), *Evaluating social programs: Theory, practice and politics* (pp. 247–264). New York: Seminar Press.

Wortman, C. B., & Rabinovitz, V. C. (1979). Random assignment: The fairest of them all. In L. Sechrest, S. G. West, M. Phillips, R. Redner, & W. Yeaton (Eds.), *Evaluation studies review annual* (Vol. 4, pp. 177–184). Thousand Oaks, CA: Sage Publications.

Zautra, A. J., Reich, J. W., Davis, M. C., Potter, P. T., & Nicolson, N. A. (2000). The role of stressful events in the relationship between positive and negative affects: Evidence from field and experimental studies. *Journal of Personality, 68,* 927–951.

Zuckerman, M. (1994). *Behavioral expression and biological bases of sensation seeking.* New York: Cambridge University Press.

Zuckerman, M., DePaulo, B. M., & Rosenthal, R. (1981). Verbal and nonverbal communication of deception. In L. Berkowitz (Ed.), *Advances in experimental social psychology* (Vol. 14, pp. 1–59). New York: Academic Press.

AUTHOR INDEX

SUBJECT INDEX

Stell and Maran's
Head and Neck Surgery